FLESH REBORN

MCGILL-QUEEN'S FRENCH ATLANTIC WORLDS SERIES
Series editors: Nicholas Dew and Jean-Pierre Le Glaunec

The French Atlantic world has emerged as a rich and dynamic field of historical research. This series will showcase a new generation of scholarship exploring the worlds of the French Atlantic – including West Africa, the greater Caribbean region, and the continental Americas – from the sixteenth century to the mid-nineteenth century. Books in the series will explore how the societies of the French Atlantic were shaped and connected by trans-oceanic networks of colonialism, how local and indigenous cultures and environments shaped colonial projects, and how the diverse peoples of the French Atlantic understood and experienced their worlds. Especially welcome are histories from the perspectives of the enslaved and dispossessed. Comparative studies are encouraged and the series will accept manuscript submissions in English and in French. Original works of scholarship are preferred, though translations of landmark books in the field will be considered.

Le monde atlantique français est devenu un domaine de recherche riche et dynamique au sein de la discipline historique. La présente collection a pour vocation d'accueillir une nouvelle génération d'ouvrages explorant les espaces de l'Atlantique français – y compris l'Afrique de l'Ouest, la grande région des Caraïbes et les Amériques continentales – du début du XVIe siècle jusqu'au milieu du XIXe siècle. Les œuvres qui y sont publiées explorent de quelles manières les sociétés de l'Atlantique français sont façonnées et reliées par les réseaux transocéaniques issus du colonialisme, de quelle manière les cultures locales et leurs environnements influencent les projets coloniaux, et comment les divers peuples de l'Atlantique français comprennent et expérimentent leurs mondes. Les ouvrages donnant la parole aux esclaves ou aux acteurs traditionnellement dominés sont particulièrement bienvenus, tout comme les recherches comparées. La collection est ouverte aux manuscrits rédigés en anglais ou en français, de préférence des monographies originales, ainsi qu'aux traductions de livres ayant marqué le domaine.

1 Architecture and Urbanism in the French Atlantic Empire
State, Church, and Society, 1604–1830
Gauvin Alexander Bailey

2 Flesh Reborn
The Saint Lawrence Valley Mission Settlements through the Seventeenth Century
Jean-François Lozier

FLESH REBORN

The Saint Lawrence Valley Mission Settlements through the Seventeenth Century

JEAN-FRANÇOIS LOZIER

McGill-Queen's University Press
Montreal & Kingston • London • Chicago

ISBN 978-0-7735-5344-6 (cloth)
ISBN 978-0-7735-5345-3 (paper)
ISBN 978-0-7735-5397-2 (ePDF)
ISBN 978-0-7735-5398-9 (ePUB)

Legal deposit third quarter 2018
Bibliothèque nationale du Québec

This book has been published with the help of a grant from the Canadian Federation for the Humanities and Social Sciences, through the Awards to Scholarly Publications Program, using funds provided by the Social Sciences and Humanities Research Council of Canada.

Funded by the Government of Canada | Financé par le gouvernement du Canada | Canada | Canada Council for the Arts | Conseil des arts du Canada

We acknowledge the support of the Canada Council for the Arts, which last year invested $153 million to bring the arts to Canadians throughout the country. Nous remercions le Conseil des arts du Canada de son soutien. L'an dernier, le Conseil a investi 153 millions de dollars pour mettre de l'art dans la vie des Canadiennes et des Canadiens de tout le pays.

Library and Archives Canada Cataloguing in Publication

Lozier, Jean-François, 1980–, author
Flesh reborn : the Saint Lawrence Valley mission settlements through the seventeenth century / Jean-François Lozier.

(McGill-Queen's French Atlantic worlds series ; 2)
Includes bibliographical references and index.
Issued in print and electronic formats.
ISBN 978-0-7735-5344-6 (hardcover). – ISBN 978-0-7735-5345-3 (softcover). – ISBN 978-0-7735-5397-2 (ePDF). – ISBN 978-0-7735-5398-9 (ePUB)

1. Indians of North America – Saint Lawrence River Valley – History – 17th century. 2. Indians of North America – Saint Lawrence River Valley – Government relations – History – 17th century. 3. Saint Lawrence River Valley – History – 17th century. 4. Canada – History – 17th century. I. Title.

E78.Q3L69 2018 971.4004'97 C2018-904492-6
C2018-904493-4

This book was typeset by True to Type in 10.5/13 Sabon

Contents

Figures

Acknowledgments

Among the many traits shared by the culturally diverse peoples at the center of this book was a habit of thanksgiving. The twenty-first-century world of academic book publishing knows its own ritual of acknowledgment, its core wisdom in many ways not so different from the *Te Deums* or *Ohenton Karihwatehkwen* that were heard in the churches and longhouses of the Saint Lawrence valley during the seventeenth century: before all else, give thanks. It makes it all the more meaningful and pleasurable to have this opportunity to express my deep gratitude to those without whom this book would not have been possible.

I am profoundly indebted to Allan Greer for his unfailing guidance and encouragement, as well as to Jan Grabowski, Kenneth Mills, Denys Delâge, and Roy Wright for providing me with essential advice at critical junctures over the years. Their enthusiasm for the past has been contagious, and they continue to inspire me as a teacher, researcher, and writer. Sadly, Roy passed away as I was finalizing this manuscript. He will be sorely missed. Beyond this core, a great number of colleagues, friends, and acquaintances have also enriched my knowledge and insights into the subject matter of this book – or otherwise supplied me with precious distractions and emotional support. I would like to extend a word of thanks to Emma Anderson, Alain Beaulieu, Damien-Claude Bélanger, Carl Benn, Matthew Betts, John Bishop, Darren Bonaparte, Kevin Brousseau, Marge Bruchac, Brian Carroll, Philippe Charland, Isabelle Charron, René Chartrand, Leslie Choquette, Muriel Clair, Paul Cohen, Peter Cook, Sébastien Côté, Edward Countryman, Wahsontiio Cross, Christian Crouch, Kerri Davis, Sylvie Dépatie, Catherine Desbarats, Dominique Deslandres, Anne

DeStecher, Guy Dondo, Alexandre Dubé, Matthew Dziennik, Robert Englebert, Timothy Foran, Joseph Gagné, Xavier Gélinas, Maxime Gohier, Suzanne Gousse, Benoît Grenier, Gilles Havard, Adrienne Hood, Christophe Horguelin, Frédéric Hottin, Martin Hubley, Ann Hunter, Cornelius Jaenen, Anik Laflèche, Jonathan Lainey, François Lalonde, Anne Marie Lane Jonah, Patrick Laurin, David Ledoyen, Peter MacLeod, Kathryn Magee Labelle, Alexandre Michaud, Cory Karhowane McComber, Françoise Moreau-Johnson, Michel Morin, Jan Noel, Alison Norman, Christopher Parsons, Forrest Pass, Thomas Peace, Joshua Piker, Jean-Luc Pilon, Lisa Poirier, Eric Pouliot Thisdale, Brian Rice, James Rice, Michael Rice, Daniel Richter, Léon Robichaud, Daniel Rück, Brett Rushforth, Karen Ryan, Laura Sanchini, Francis Scardera, Margaret Schotte, Renaud Séguin, John Steckley, Nicole St-Onge, Andrew Sturtevant, Guillaume Teasdale, Éric Thierry, James Trepanier, Roland Viau, and Thomas Wien. If I have left anyone out, it was not my intention.

Over the years I have also benefited from the support of several wonderful institutions, including the University of Toronto, where I first set out to write the dissertation that has grown into this book, and the Canadian Museum of History, where its underlying ideas had the opportunity to mature. A temporary professorship at the University of Ottawa, combined with a leave of absence from the museum, made it possible to bring the project to fruition – I am exceedingly grateful to Dean Oliver, Alan Elder, and Jean-Marc Blais, at the museum, as well as to Kevin Kee, Kouky Fianu, and Sylvie Perrier, at the University of Ottawa, for having allowed this accommodation.

The Social Sciences and Humanities Research Council contributed to the initial iteration of this project by means of a generous doctoral fellowship, and short-term research fellowships from the Newberry Library and American Philosophical Society provided me with profoundly stimulating experiences. I have likewise gained much from the opportunity to test some of my findings at conferences organized by the Canadian Historical Association, the Institut d'histoire de l'Amérique française, the Omohundro Institute of Early American History, the French Colonial Historical Society, the American Society for Ethnohistory, the Algonquian Research Conference, the Conference on Iroquois Research, and the Wendat and Wyandot Studies Conference. The book at hand would be very different, and far less interesting, were it not for the feedback received on such occasions.

Many thanks to the helpful staff of Library and Archives Canada,

Bibliothèque et Archives nationales du Québec, of the library and archives of the Canadian Museum of History and Canadian War Museum, of the American Philosophical Society, Newberry Library, New York Historical Society, New York State Archives, Bibliothèque nationale de France, Archives nationales de France, and of the libraries of the Universities of Toronto and Ottawa. A special note of appreciation goes out to Marc Lacasse and David Émond, of the Archives du Séminaire de Saint-Sulpice de Montréal; Theresa Rowat and Jacques Monet, of the Archive of the Jesuits in Canada; Peter Gagné, of the Centre de référence de l'Amérique française; Marlaine DesChamps, of Union College, Schenectady; Agnès Vatican, of the Archives départementales de la Gironde; as well as to Éric Chalifoux, of Recherches amérindiennes au Québec. Several other people fielded my email queries and cold calls in search of unpublished archaeological and urban planning reports: William Moss, Eric Dumas, and Dominique Lauzier, of the Ville de Québec; Martin Blais, of the municipality of L'Ancienne-Lorette; and Réginald Auger, of Université Laval.

I am indebted to McGill-Queen's University Press for seeing the merit of this project. Kyla Madden and Ryan Van Huijstee shepherded the process with an enthusiasm and patience for which I am ever grateful. Additional thanks go to Finn Purcell and the broader editorial team, as well as to the anonymous referees who reviewed the manuscript, to Colleen Gray for her thoughtful editing, and to Andrée Héroux for her cartographic skills.

Finally, I would like to thank the people closest to me, who have endured the most. I dedicate this book to Albert and Françoise Lozier, to Genevieve Bonenfant – and to Augustin and Étienne who, while I was plodding along on this manuscript, suddenly brought new perspective into my life.

FLESH REBORN

Introduction

On the last day of June 1665, ten or twelve men gathered to welcome Alexandre de Prouville de Tracy, Louis XIV's newly landed lieutenant general in America. They represented a community of perhaps a hundred Wendats – Hurons as the French knew them – who had spent the last fifteen years residing at the heart of the French colony, the last nine of them at the very core of its capital, the town of Quebec, almost a thousand kilometers from the land their people had occupied in far greater numbers a generation earlier. They had been forced from this homeland by the Haudenosaunee, or Iroquois Confederacy, who also jeopardized the existence of New France. Louis XIV, having taken over the colony two years prior from an apathetic charter company, now sent some thirteen hundred soldiers under Tracy's command to ensure the defeat of this common enemy.[1]

It is difficult to get a clear picture of this encounter. The French state had not yet developed its colonial office, and its governors were not yet in the habit of having their clerks record and send to court detailed minutes of their councils with Indigenous diplomats. Our only glimpse of them comes from the *Relation* prepared by the personnel of the Society of Jesus, or Jesuits, and published in Paris a year later. Characteristically, these missionary chroniclers leave us guessing about many features of the meeting. Tracy, having fallen ill at sea, "weak and reduced by fever," had asked the townspeople to dispense with the reception that had been prepared for him, and instead went to the church of Notre Dame de Québec to thank his God for the safe journey with a *Te Deum*, the standard hymn of praise. Whether out of personal curiosity, a sense of the occasion, or because the locals explained to him that it would be impolitic to dispense with it, the lieutenant general also agreed to hear the Wendats who were "determined" to welcome him "according to the customs of their country." These were not only precious allies, but also neighbours whose presence would have been impossible to overlook. The "Fort des Hurons," a palisaded enclosure which contained their longhouses, occupied the space between the town's church and Château Saint Louis, the governor's residence and seat of government itself. Where, exactly, the Wendats and Tracy met is unclear. Perhaps it was in the Château, in the absence of Governor Daniel de Rémy de Courcelle who would arrive only later that fall, or maybe it was in the building that until recently had served as a courthouse, where Tracy soon established his own household. It is also possible that the meeting took place within the Wendat enclosure, in the longhouse where these Indigenous people usually held their councils. Perhaps it occurred in the open air, outside any of these structures. Besides the Wendat headmen and Tracy himself, the assembly included some of Tracy's retinue of personal guards and pages, and very likely other officers and leading colonists. The bishop, François de Laval, who had presided over the church ceremony, may have been present as well. A few Jesuits were certainly there, acting as translators – probably their superior, Jérôme Lalemant, François-Joseph Le Mercier who would soon succeed him, and undoubtedly also Pierre-Joseph-Marie Chaumonot, all men who had spent years living among the Wendats.[2]

Le Mercier, who reported the event, did not think it useful to name the speaker for his readers, figuring that it was enough to simply tell them that he was one of the oldest and most distinguished of the Wendat leaders. The names of leaders mentioned elsewhere during these years allow us to speculate, if hopelessly, that it may have been Louis Taiaeronk, Louis Thaondechoren, or Joseph Sondouskon – or someone else altogether. We do not know whether this man and his peers had donned wool coats in the French style, as Indigenous leaders had taken up the habit of doing on diplomatic occasions, or whether they were dressed in more traditional fashion in a deerskin breechclout, wearing over their naked shoulders a mantle of beaver, moose, or bear skin ornamented with paint or dyed porcupine quills. These men probably wore necklaces and bracelets of wampum, white and deep purple shell beads of great value, but also glass beads, and quite likely crucifixes and devotional medals too. Le Mercier mentions that the speaker punctuated his speech with presents of dressed and painted moose skins, as was the custom, to ritually support his words.[3] These words, as far as the missionary was concerned, were what mattered most. The transcript of the encounter, although it was most certainly condensed, filled ten pages of the printed *Relation*. The Wendat elder spoke with facial expressions, gestures, and an eloquence that left a deep impression on the assembly, addressing the lieutenant general as Onontio, meaning "Great Mountain," the name that Indigenous allies had come to use to refer to successive French governors:

> You see at your feet the wreck of a great country, and the pitiful remnant of a whole world, that was formerly peopled by countless inhabitants. But now you are addressed by mere carcasses, only the bones of which have been left by the Iroquois, who have devoured the flesh after broiling it on their scaffolds. There was left in us nothing but the merest thread of life; and our limbs, most of which have passed through the boiling cauldrons of our foes, had no more strength – when, raising our eyes with extreme difficulty, we saw on the river the ships that were bringing you, and, with you, so many soldiers sent us by your Great Onnontio [*sic*] and ours.
>
> Thereupon the Sun seemed to shine upon us with brighter beams, and to illuminate our fatherland of old, which had been so many years overcast with clouds and darkness. Then our lakes and rivers appeared calm, and without storms or breakers; and, to tell you the truth, I seemed to hear a voice issuing from your vessel, and saying to us, from as far as we could discern you: 'Courage, O desolate people! Your bones are about to be knit together with muscles and tendons, your flesh is to be born again, your strength will be restored to you, and you shall live as you did live of old.'[4]

The imagery in this speech remains as powerful today as it was then. These words speak to the interplay of change and continuity that is at the heart of every historian's endeavour, including this book. They invite us to explore the ways in which the Saint Lawrence valley, even as it became the center of French colonial settlement, became a space of renewal and regeneration for a range of Indigenous peoples who were experiencing great upheavals. The Wendats who were living within the town of Quebec at the time of Tracy's arrival had previously spent half a decade settled on the Island of Orleans, and within a few years they would move not far from Notre Dame de Foy, before occupying a succession of two sites known as Lorette. Their experience was unique, but the evocations of social collapse, resiliency, and renewal, are emblematic of the collective experience of Indigenous peoples who, beginning in the late 1630s, established, under the auspices of Jesuit and later Sulpician missionaries, a string of settlements along the Saint Lawrence River – more accurately, the river that the French called Saint-Laurent, and that these peoples tended to conceptualize, in each of their languages, as the Great River or Big Waterway: Ladawanna in Wendat, Wepistukujaw Sipo in Innu, Kitcikanii sipi in Algonquin, Ktsitekw in Wabanaki, or Kaniatarowanenneh in Mohawk.[5]

By the end of the seventeenth century, there existed four or five mission communities in the Saint Lawrence valley, depending on how a community is defined: Lorette (today Wendake), Arsikantegouk (Saint François, today Odanak), Kahnawake (Sault Saint Louis), and the twinned sites of Kanehsatake (La Montagne) and Skawenati (Sault au Récollet), all of which persist to this day, albeit not in precisely the same locations and forms. They were inhabited on a more or less sedentary basis by a total of some two thousand persons. They were not merely French missions, but indeed Indigenous communities formed as a result of intersecting desires, needs, and priorities. Following an initial period of official and ecclesiastical optimism with regards to the assimilation of these communities' residents, clear boundaries took shape between the two groups. This population engaged with its French neighbours, but though by the final third of the century the latter came to represent a large demographic majority in the area, the former were never absorbed by them. In fact, during the seventeenth century rather few of either group ever learned to speak the language of the other, and cross-cultural marital unions were relatively rare. Through to the end of the French Regime and well beyond it, the inhabitants of the mission settlements maintained traditional kinship structures, languages, and subsistence patterns.

The story of the formation and development of the mission communities of the Saint Lawrence valley jars with the expected narrative of contact in early America: here, Indigenous populations did not simply withdraw or disperse before an advancing colonial frontier; rather, they drew closer to European settlement, carving out a place for themselves in its immediate vicinity. The questions at the heart of this book, then, center on why and how peoples were brought together to form new political and social entities, both on a localized scale at the level of individual mission settlements, and on the regional scale at the level of what might be called, for lack of a better term, the Franco-Indigenous alliance.

***

This book is thus preoccupied by the spaces and processes of settlement. At first glance, there is something disturbing in this perspective, considering the ways in which "Indigenous peoples" and "Settlers" tend to be understood as two distinct and conflicting groups. Yet thinking in terms of "settlement," which can both refer to places and processes, turns out to be a productive way of considering the subject matter. First, the process of sedentarization – of settling down – was a central feature of the encounter of Innu and Algonquin peoples with French missionaries and officials, to which the first portion of this book is devoted. These nomadic hunter-gatherers belonging to the great Algonquian linguistic and cultural family experimented with the establishment of a more permanent presence at specific points on the land. Secondly, while there is no question that the Innu and Algonquins occupied the Saint Lawrence valley when French settlers established themselves there in the first decade of the seventeenth century, the notion of settlement aptly describes the way in which other groups who came to reside in the missions later in the century came from afar. To be sure, the Wendats, Iroquois, and Wabanakis had deep ties to the Saint Lawrence: some of their ancestors had lived alongside it in the sixteenth century, and they continued to visit it periodically to hunt, fight, and trade. But the establishment of lasting communities there involved major population displacements away from more recent home territories. In the case of the Wendats, it was a migration of nearly a thousand kilometers by canoe and across portages, from the shores of Georgian Bay and Lake Simcoe in present-day Ontario. For the Iroquois of what is today upstate New York and the Wabanakis of Maine, New Hampshire, and Vermont, it was a journey that reached as much as half that distance. Seventeenth-century French observers on occasion spoke of Huron and Iroquois "colonies," in a way that jars with our modern-day conceptualizations but gives us an important historical insight.[6]

Thirdly, the notion of settlement is also useful to describe, beyond the processes involved, the diverse spaces of community under investigation – archaeologists, more so than historians, are used to this way of designating sites of habitation in all their dynamism and ambiguities. All mission communities underwent periodic relocations within the Saint Lawrence valley, in keeping with the pressures of the environment and tensions arising from the proximity of colonists, and their social composition fluctuated with the seasons and rhythms of war and peace. Their residents maintained longstanding seasonal subsistence patterns that hinged on the combination of agricultural activity with hunting and fishing expeditions which kept most away from their villages for the greater part of the fall and winter. They also shuttled to traditional homelands to visit family and friends, to find partners, to trade, and to take part in diplomatic and military activities, and as a result, residential groups were often reconfigured. Mission communities also exhibited a range of spatial arrangements. Some, namely those of the Wendats and the Iroquois, corresponded to houses clustered together within a palisade that clearly defined spaces which the French called tended to call *bourgs* (towns) or *villages*. But others, while having at their core a "fort" which corresponded to a missionary compound containing a chapel and residence, and perhaps a few dwellings for the leading Indigenous neophytes, tended to consist of houses spread beyond along the water and near fields; they functioned more as sites of summertime gathering and ritual, and as service centres rather than year-round population centers.

A fourth and final meaning of settlement also emerges as central to this story, namely the resolution of a dispute or conflict between parties. Indeed, the formation and development of the mission communities of the Saint Lawrence valley is intimately linked with armed conflict and its outcomes. The expressions of despair and hope voiced by the Wendat elder points to the ways in which the diverse peoples who came to form these communities were harrowed by disease, famine, and war – with the Iroquois representing the principal military threat through the century. No imagery could more strikingly communicate what had happened to them than that of the tortured, cannibalized, and decomposing victim of the Iroquois, the human body being here equated with the political and social body. Other Wendat speakers, besides the one alluded to above, similarly described their nation during these years as "devoured and gnawed to the very bones, by war and famine," and their people as "carcasses [...] able to stand only because you support them"; or as "fragments of a once flourishing nation," a "remnant of living carrion," "the skeleton of a great people, from which the Iroquois has gnawed off all the flesh, and which he is striving to suck out to the very marrow"; "the wreck of a great country, and the pitiful remnant of a whole world," now "mere carcasses, only the bones of which have been left by the Iroquois, who have devoured the flesh after broiling it on their scaffolds" and after passing it "through the boiling cauldrons." The Wendats were not alone in using this imagery. Some Loups, or Mahicans, are similarly recorded as having explained to French interlocutors that they had "become a small nation, the flesh taken from our bodies."[7]

War, long recognized as a fundamental process of historical change, played a critical role in shaping these communities. But we must not be deceived by the rhetoric and reality of violence into crafting narratives of victimhood, weakness, and passivity.[8] Indeed, these communities shaped their own circumstances, as well as the course of war and peace in the region. Conflict was at once a destructive process, and an integrative, incorporative, and creative one. Even as it tore populations apart and from their lands, it brought people together spatially, politically, and culturally. It challenged, reconfigured, and created personal and collective identities and solidarities, in ways often unexpected. *Flesh Reborn* accordingly explores the entanglement of community-building, identity formation, armed conflict, diplomacy, kinship, leadership, and migration. It is about how blood was at times spilled and at times mingled, and how bodies, individual and political, were destroyed and remade.

The power of the Wendat address to Tracy lies not only in its vivid evocation of violence and trauma, but also in its expression of renewal. Before being displaced from their homeland on the shores of Georgian Bay, the Wendats' mortuary customs had involved something known as the Feast of the Dead, a ritual by which the dead were periodically disinterred and reburied in communal ossuaries. These mass reburials were often triggered by settlement relocation, reflecting the desire to keep the dead in the neighbourhood of the living. The people would pull the remains of their relatives from the individual graves in which they had initially been interred, cleaning the remains of flesh and sinew as necessary. They then wrapped the dry bones in beaver robes and brought them into their homes for a feast, before transporting them to a new burial site and lowering them in a common pit. The Feast of the Dead was a time for public mourning, celebration, and the reaffirmation of ties. "By means of these ceremonies and gatherings,"

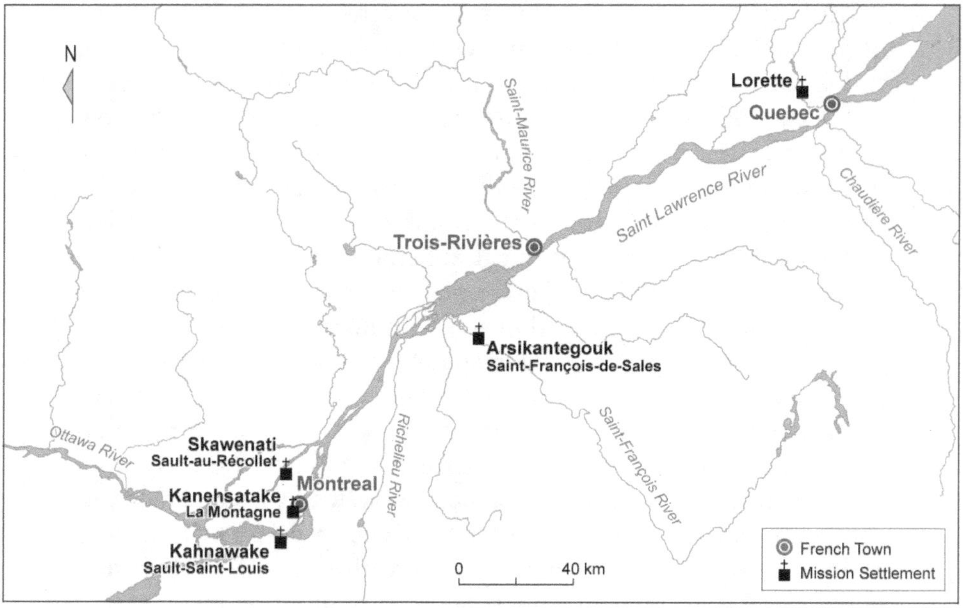

Figure 1.1 The Saint Lawrence valley, showing the location of mission communities by 1701. (Map by Andrée Héroux)

explained the French Recollet missionary Gabriel Sagard who witnessed such an event, "they contract new unions and friendships amongst themselves, saying that, just as the bones of their deceased relatives and friends are gathered together and united in one place, so also they themselves ought during their lives to live all together in the same unity and harmony, like good kinsmen and friends."[9]

The arrival of the French and the adoption of new beliefs and practices changed this. Not radically, at first: in 1636, another missionary, the Jesuit Jean de Brébeuf, noted the presence of fifteen to twenty baptized Wendats among the bodies reinterred during a Feast of the Dead ceremony.[10] But the Christianized Wendats, who when pushed out of their homeland by an Iroquois offensive sought refuge in the Saint Lawrence valley, chose to leave the bones of their ancestors behind and to align their mortuary practices with those of their French allies and neighbours. They developed a new vocabulary of alliance, new ways of affirming and reaffirming their ties, of creating relationships. It is, therefore, not surprising to find that the Wendat elder's address to Tracy echoes not only the rituals of Indigenous warfare and burial, but also the teachings of the missionaries that his people had been making their own. Indeed, the elder's words track unmistakably onto those of the Old Testament prophet Ezekiel, who describes a dream-like vision in which he is transported to a valley of death littered with dry bones. Commanded by God to prophesy, Ezekiel sees before him the bones reconnected with tendons, covered with flesh and skin, and resurrected. The remains are revealed to be those of the people of Israel in exile, to whom God asks Ezekiel to speak on his behalf: "My people, I am going to open your graves and bring you up from them; [...] I will put my Spirit in you and you will live, and I will settle you in your own land."[11]

To be clear, each of the diverse peoples who established themselves in the mission settlements of the Saint Lawrence valley in the seventeenth century had their own social and cultural baggage, and neither the Algonquins, Innu, Iroquois, or Wabanakis shared the custom of mass reburial with the Wendats. Yet, as with the violence of war, the rhetorical motifs and imagery evoked by their elder speak to their collective experience.

***

It follows from their centrality to the French colonial project, both as sites of religious indoctrination and of strategic importance, that the mission settlements came to occupy a choice position in the writings of the period and of modern historians. Beginning in the late nineteenth century, a few of the Roman Catholic missionaries assigned to the communities descended from seventeenth-century foundations developed a keen interest in local history which led them to compile notes on the subject and to publish a handful of brief articles and longer monographs. The preoccupations of these early ecclesiastical-avocational scholars were conspicuously rooted in their faith: they were above all captivated by their own predecessors, the Jesuit and Sulpician missionaries of the French Regime, heroic figures in their eyes, devout, dedicated, and tireless; the Indigenous populations to whom they had ministered were sketched out as the recipients of their teachings, faithful new Christians on the whole, though often fickle and occasionally seditious.[12]

With the exception of an isolated foray into the subject by the historian G.F.G. Stanley, who in a 1950 article, "The First Indian 'Reserves' in Canada," outlined the mission settlements of the Saint

Lawrence valley under the French Regime as benevolent precursors of modern-day reserves, it was not until the late 1970s that academic scholars began to pay attention to the subject. Working in the new perspective of ethnohistory, blending the sources, methods, and insights of both history and anthropology, pioneering studies by Gordon Day of the "complex peopling" of Odanak or by James Ronda of the Jesuit "experiment" at Sillery, among others, emphasized the diversity and complexity of motivations for relocation, pointing to the way in which economic and political motives, beyond religion, were central to the formation of these communities.[13] The mission settlements and their inhabitants also began to be featured in studies centered on the peoples from which they had detached themselves and with whom they retained intimate links, with, for example, scholars providing brief overviews of the Wendat settlement near Quebec as an epilogue to the story of the Wendats writ large, or of the formation and development of Kentake, Kahnawake, and Kanehsatake in the context of broader studies of the Iroquois Confederacy.[14]

This first wave of academic histories, pushing back against their ecclesiastical-avocational precursors, tended to argue that the inhabitants of the mission settlements engaged with Christian teachings only to the extent necessary to achieve peaceful coexistence with their missionaries and neighbours. James Ronda saw the "Sillery experiment" as a missionary failure, owing to its inhabitants' refusal of the cultural suicide that it represented. David Blanchard, working on Kentake and Kahnawake, concluded that Catholic practice was merely a "thin veneer calculated to enable traditional belief and practice and the pursuit of more secular interests."[15] More recent scholarship, however, drawing from a rich literature on religious encounters throughout the early modern world, has instead emphasized the way in which these communities constituted sites of vibrant religious negotiation and hybridization. Conversions were widespread, and though they were sometimes superficial, very often they were manifestly deep and sincere. Rather than a wholesale acceptance of Catholicism or rejection of Indigenous customs, a synthesis, by means of selective appropriations and adaptations, produced unique forms of syncretic Indigenous Catholicism. Missionaries exercised a form of leadership, but they were often themselves followers.[16] Thus, though it may be tempting, in light of its echo of Ezekiel's prophecy, to dismiss the Wendat elder's words as mere parroting of missionary speech or pandering to missionary sensitivities, the broader context instead invites us to see in it a genuine fusion of Iroquoian and Christian motifs, spiritualties, and aspirations, of a sort that was typical of the experience of the mission settlements' inhabitants.

Through the 1990s, the context of the Oka Crisis and of increased litigation, negotiation, and advocacy surrounding the rights of First Nations bands descended from the seventeenth- century's mission settlements, spurred further research and publication by Québécois and Canadian academic and public historians, most notably relating to Kahnawake, Kanehsatake, and Wendake/Lorette. The emerging consensus has been that while the members of these communities were subject to pressures from colonial officials, they received privileges and exemptions, notably in matters of criminal law, on account of their considerable economic and military significance.[17] Scholars working on the history of war have similarly demonstrated these communities' independence from the French and their ability to pursue their own political and military objectives – "parallel warfare," to use the expression of the historian Peter MacLeod. The French depended on the assistance of their Indigenous allies, but they could not dictate the terms of their participation in intercolonial conflicts.[18] Finally, scholars have recently begun pushing back against the persistent stereotype of French colonialism as gentle, a view famously encapsulated in Francis Parkman's old adage that "Spanish civilization crushed the Indian; English civilization scorned and neglected him; French civilization embraced and cherished him." Notwithstanding the realities of Indigenous autonomy and accommodation on the ground, as far as the mission settlements or any other contact zones are concerned, there should be no doubt that the French colonial project was one aimed at political domination. That the French generally lacked the means to impose themselves must not make us lose sight of this fact.[19]

Outside of a short but pithy book on the subject by Marc Jetten, drawn from a masters' thesis, attempts to approach the mission settlements of the Saint Lawrence valley as a whole have tended to miss their mark.[20] In the 1990s a few researchers honed in on the idea that these communities had been united in a "Confederacy of the Seven Fires" or of "Seven Nations." Initially they posited this entity's emergence in the late seventeenth century, but soon they came to understand that it was a much later development: the direct consequence of the fall of New France in 1760, and of an effort by Great Britain to give preeminence to the people of Kahnawake, whose friendship the

British had been cultivating since the turn of the century, by fostering the formalization of new political entity, with the familiar Six Nations Confederacy offering, if not a true model, at least a label. This rectification came a little late, however, for the notion of the "Seven Nations" has since entered academic and popular discourse as a persistent shorthand to designate the inhabitants of the mission settlements through the French Regime.[21] The seventeenth-century history of the mission communities was certainly entangled, as this book demonstrates, but this entanglement was of an altogether different, less straightforward nature.

***

In reconstructing the history of the mission settlements and their inhabitants from an ethnohistorical perspective, *Flesh Reborn* thus elaborates upon a scholarship that is rich but fragmented. It does its best to contend with the unevenness of the source material. The effort at reconstructing the encounter of the Wendat elder and Tracy with which this book opens gives an idea of the challenges at hand. Only in 1669 did Louis XIV establish the office of Secretary of State for the Navy, whose responsibility included the colonies, and which corresponded to an official government department with a permanent staff; and only in the decades that followed was the practice of maintaining and archiving a regular official correspondence instituted – and even then, allusions to the mission settlements within this correspondence were terse. The Recollet *frères*, the Jesuit *révérends pères*, and the Sulpician *messieurs* who ministered in the Saint Lawrence valley had different approaches not only to missionary work, but also to record keeping. The Jesuits are best known for their annual *Relations*, full of rich ethnographic and diplomatic detail, published for a metropolitan audience between 1632 and 1672. For this period, as well as for the years following, there exists in parallel a small hodgepodge of letters and reports. Neither the Recollets nor the Sulpicians produced a comparable body of writing – though in the case of the Sulpicians, the outgoing correspondence of their superior in Paris with missionaries in the colonies has survived. All of this is to say that not all mission settlements and not all periods were documented with the same care, and that it is therefore necessary to develop a high level of tolerance for archival silences and uncertainties.

Missionaries and colonial officials serve as valuable, and indeed unavoidable, relays of information, but it is important to not forget that they were biased observers and reporters. They often misunderstood the words and behaviours of the peoples with whom they engaged. Even a first-rate missionary such as the Jesuit Pierre Potier, who in the mid-eighteenth century spent some time among the Wendats of Lorette before pursuing his ministry among those of Detroit, might thus jot down in an enumeration of aphoristic thoughts that he picked up or came up with along the way that "the Native is a Paradox (he is impenetrable [and] incomprehensible, he does not act like he speaks, thinks, etc.)."[22] It must be further stressed that the nineteenth-century published transcriptions and translations of sources, on which scholars have relied heavily, add another layer of misunderstanding. The Thwaites edition of the *Jesuit Relations'* description, for example, of a tense council in 1684 has the League Iroquois jeering against those of the mission settlements and forcing them to "*perdre leur place*" (lose their place), which was imaginatively translated as "lose their places in the council" – while the original *Relation* merely indicates that this had forced them to "*perdre leur chasse*" (miss out on the hunt). Similarly, while the narrative of the Sulpician missionary François Vachon de Belmont published by the Quebec Literary and Historical Society indicates that the warriors of Kahnawake "*firent* échapper" (*allowed to* escape, or *made* them do so) a hundred of captive Mohawks in 1693, the original manuscript indicates that they simply "*virent échapper*" (*saw* escape).[23] While such errors are by no means plentiful, they have left an impact on our understanding of the subject matter.

Although the colonial record must not be taken at face value, it also must not be too easily dismissed either. When read between the lines and against the grain, to use two expressions beloved of historians, these sources serve as necessary points of entry into seventeenth-century realities. Triangulating the source material put to paper by as broad a range of observers as possible – French, English, and Dutch – makes it possible to draw closer to historical realities. Appraising and comparing observations emanating from different individuals, interest groups, and colonies provides remarkable opportunities to arrive at a fuller understanding of murky events. Conference and council minutes, transcriptions of judicial and quasi-judicial examinations, and more rarely of informal conversations, allow Indigenous voices to shine through and grant us precious insights into individual and collective perspectives.[24] In keeping with the principles of ethnohistory, I have also drawn from linguistic materials, including early Indigenous dictionaries, as well as archaeological research, and oral traditions – and gained a wealth of insights and inspiration from encounters with people descended from the inhabitants of these seventeenth-century mission settlements.

***

One of the effects of considering the mission settlements as Indigenous communities, rather than merely as locations for missionary activities, is to grant visibility to people who have been hidden from history, and to make it possible for us to begin to appreciate the historical agency of finer units of analysis than those that have tended to feature in the literature. Paying close attention to the nuances of identity, solidarity, and enmity is key to understanding patterns of conflict and migration. The French described the inhabitants of the mission settlements as *nos Sauvages* (our Natives) and as *Sauvages chrétiens* (Christian Natives). In the final decades of the seventeenth century the multiplication of missions and converts in the continent's interior gave rise to a more precise designation, that of *Sauvages domiciliés*. The adjective, translated most simply as "domiciled," or otherwise "resident" or "settled," had until then been occasionally used in reference to the Frenchmen who had established their residence in the colony, i.e. *Français domiciliés*. Afterwards it became a convenient way to distinguish the Indigenous populations which had established a fixed residence in the heartland of the colony from the more distant French-allied or nominally Christianized peoples. Anglo-American colonists meanwhile referred to the inhabitants of the mission settlements collectively and vaguely as "Canada Indians," "Canadian Indians," "Praying Indians," "French Indians," or "French Praying Indians," and spoke of the "French and *their* Indians." Terms such as this obscure the very real independence that the inhabitants of these communities enjoyed.[25]

Although one must rely on labels such as "Algonquin," "Huron," "Iroquois," or "Abenaki" in some contexts, it is important to recognize their inadequacy in others. Terms of convenience, they conceal an array of collective and personal identities. While the insufficiencies of the documentary record make it impossible to produce biographical scholarship that comes anywhere close to what has been written about Catherine or Kateri Tekakwitha – to this day the most famous resident of Kahnawake, or of all the mission settlements for that matter – they make it possible to catch glimpses of other significant life trajectories. Attentiveness to the personal names that appear in scattered sources, and a willingness to reconcile their garbled orthographies, has several benefits. It allows a clearer sense of the contingencies of these communities' history, and of the role of Indigenous agency in their formation. The leadership and networks of individuals – complex individuals, not pasteboard saints – influenced the formation, development, and political orientation of the mission communities. Settlement or resettlement in the vicinity of the French was a venture promoted or opposed by specific, charismatic persons who mobilized their kinship and communal relations and were empowered by them. Among Algonquians and Iroquoians alike, influence was more widely spread than an overly cursory reading of the sources might suggest. While male chiefs, also referred to as captains or sachems, and warriors loom largest in the record, their influence rested not only on personal ability and personality but on networks of relatives and friends among whom women occupied a crucial position. The latter's role is generally obscured in the seventeenth-century sources, both as a result of their authors' Eurocentric prejudices, and as a result of the gendered nature of interactions which meant that these male colonial observers rarely had the opportunity to sit in on the political discussions of women. There is no doubt, however, that women played a fundamental role when it came to migration and community relocation – especially so among Iroquoians, where women were responsible for the household and fields, but also among Algonquians.

Individuals are also important because they can serve as tracers which make it possible to detect the activity and relations of wider groups and networks that are otherwise gestured to only vaguely in the sources. They emerge as a key to understanding broader population movements and geopolitical developments. It is by following individuals and personal names that we can thus make sense of patterns of migration and conflict, and that we can get a sense of continuities through mobility, intermarriage, or adoption. Following individuals similarly forces us to revise old monoliths and binaries – French-Iroquois, for example, Iroquois-Huron, or Algonquian-Iroquoian. As mentioned above, without exception, the mission settlements came into being as heterogeneous, multiethnic, and multinational communities. Although French missionaries and officials failed in their initial ambition to turn the Indigenous residents of the mission settlements into perfect Frenchmen and Frenchwomen, these communities became dynamic sites of ethnic and linguistic assimilation, developing internal cohesions of their own. Diverse Algonquian peoples fused at Kamiskouaouangachit, and so did Wendats near Quebec, and later Wabanakis at Msakkikkan, Néssawakamighé, and Arsikantegouk; similarly, assimilative processes initiated in Iroquoia reached fruition in the mission settlements of the Saint Lawrence valley, with the Mohawk language and ethnic identity coming to dominate at both Kahnawake and Kanehsatake.

Retrieving the names which the inhabitants of the missions used to describe and distinguish *themselves* is much more problematic. Period dictionaries and ethnohistorical upstreaming make it possible to translate many colonial ethnic labels in a way that brings us closer to the historical actors and to their sense of self. In some cases, I have chosen to privilege, with a measure of confidence, Indigenous labels over colonial ones, and to speak of Innu (rather than Montagnais), Wendats (rather than Huron), and Wabanakis (rather than Abenakis), in keeping with a practice that is increasingly common among scholars. In other cases, however, owing to the silences and ambiguities of the sources, I have found it preferable to retain old colonial labels in an effort to avoid referring to seventeenth-century peoples by the ethnic designations that, though used to refer to their descendants today, they are uncertain to have used themselves. I have thus accordingly avoided translating the term "Algonquin" as Anishnabeg, and in light of the fluid boundary that existed between the Innu and Algonquins during the early seventeenth century, I have found it useful to adopt the neologism "Saint Lawrence Algonquians" for occasional use (see chapter 1). More hesitatingly, I have also deemed it safest to retain the term "Iroquois": while the notions of Haudenosaunee (or Rotinonhsionni in Mohawk, "People of the Longhouse," i.e. members of the Five Nations Confederacy) and Onkwehón:we ("Real Men," i.e. ethnic Iroquois) would become conflated in the nineteenth century and take on new meanings in more recent times (with the latter term now being used to refer to Indigenous peoples more broadly), the seventeenth-century sources suggest the distinction may have been a crucial one (see chapter 8).

I have been bolder when dealing with the names of mission communities, given their centrality in the book. Beyond familiar toponyms such as Kahnawake and Kanehsatake, readers will thus encounter less familiar ones such as Kamiskouaouangachit instead of

Sillery, and Msakkikkan and Néssawakamighé to designate the Wabanaki missions on the Chaudière River. In my attempt to come as close as possible to these distant senses of self and place, I use Wendake to refer to the old Wendat homeland, otherwise known as Huronia, located between Georgian Bay and Lake Simcoe, but not to refer to the settlement established near Quebec. Indeed, the evidence indicates that the inhabitants of the latter knew it as Lorette or, reflecting their own pronunciation, *Roreke*; only in the twentieth century, in the context of the community's self-affirmation, did it come to share the name of Wendake itself. In the same way, I use Arsikantegouk rather than the current name of Odanak to describe the Wabanaki community established on the Saint François River at the very end of the seventeenth century, as the current name, meaning "the village," only came into use in the nineteenth century. In transcribing Indigenous place and personal names, I have attempted a measure of spelling-standardization that offers a compromise between the seventeenth-century sources and current conventions (replacing, for example, the omicron-upsilon ligature, which appears as an open-topped 8, with the letters "ou" or "w," depending on the case). I hope that readers will forgive the apparent idiosyncrasy of this nomenclature, and appreciate that it reflects at once the unevenness of our historical knowledge and a purposeful effort to drive home the point that these mission settlements were, above all, Indigenous communities. In keeping with increasingly widespread usage in Canada, I have opted to use "Indigenous," rather than "Aboriginal," "Indian," or "Native" – with the exception of quotations translated from the French, where I rely on the latter term as the most satisfactory equivalent to the French "Sauvages."

My attempt at defining identities as precisely and faithfully as possible should not be taken to mean that all of these identities were rigidly defined, static, or exclusive. On the contrary, identities were often fluid, multiple, and nested.[26] A single individual, for example, might depending on the given circumstances feel a greater and more meaningful attachment to her or his identity as a Haudenosaunee, or an Onkwehonwe, or a Garihwioston, or a Kahnawakeronon, or a member of the Turtle Clan at Kahnawake, or an Oneida of Kahnawake, or a former Wendat – or to any combination of these identities. Social identity and community membership were constantly renegotiated and redefined. In the Saint Lawrence valley of the seventeenth century, individuals and groups can be thought of as being in a continual process of "becoming," as a result of migration, incorporation, amalgamation, coalescence, dissociation, dispersal, and resettlement.

***

What follows, then, takes the form of a narrative history of the mission settlements of the Saint Lawrence valley through the seventeenth century. The timeline of their formation makes it possible to cleave to a rough chronological order. The first two chapters, entitled "Sowing Seeds" and "Friends and Brothers," examine the Innu and Algonquin experimentation with settlement. While history books tend to begin the story of these unique social and political entities with Jesuit initiatives and the institutionalization of the mission community commonly known as Sillery in 1639, the seeds of these entities can be found deeper. And whereas scholars who have considered the formation of the earliest mission settlements during these years have tended to emphasize missionary action, here they are reimagined as a joint creation, the result of intersecting French and Indigenous desires, needs, and priorities. Old summer gathering places such as Kamiskouaouangachit (Sillery) and Metaberoutin (Trois Rivières) acquired a new importance. The trajectory of the missions established there corresponded closely with the intensification of the Iroquois offensive and the decline of the Algonquians of the Saint Lawrence as a military power.

Chapters 3 and 4 turn towards the Wendats. Rather than portraying the resettlement of Wendats near Quebec as the epilogue to the destruction of Huronia, or as a meagre prologue to the more recent history of the Wendats, these chapters seek to place their community's early history at the center of the analysis. In trying to gain a clearer understanding of the subject, "The Enemy's Arms" examines how over six hundred individuals sought safety in the Saint Lawrence valley. Exploring Wendat-Iroquois relations during this period reveals the extent to which force and persuasion were part and parcel of a broader socio-cultural pattern of incorporation. "Promised Lands" recounts how the refugee community was subjected to considerable pressures, as Iroquois warriors and ambassadors in turn negotiated with, cajoled, and threatened them in an effort to prompt their relocation. These chapters invite us to see that the tendency among colonial chroniclers and contemporary historians to generalize about "the Hurons" and "the Iroquois" (or "the Five Nations") has obscured the extent to which patterns of war and peace were shaped by more localized solidarities. They also allow us to see that what historians and the popular historical imagination conceive of as the "Franco-Iroquois" wars more often than not had as their principal protagonists not the French, but rather their allies of the mission settlements.

For the Wendat community that found an uncertain refuge near Quebec, an opportunity for regeneration came with the Franco-Iroquois peace settlement of 1667. After this date, large numbers of visitors and migrants streamed from Iroquoia towards the Saint Lawrence valley and its mission settlements. Picking up on the theme of warfare as an integrative process, chapter 5, entitled "Flesh Born Again," probes the range and limits of integration. Through the return of the Wendats from Iroquoia, a distinct Wendat community would persist near Quebec. Yet through the establishment of Kentake (La Prairie), and later Kahnawake (Sault Saint Louis) and Kanehsatake (La Montagne), many Wendats and other "New Iroquois" would complete a process of assimilation begun in the villages of Iroquoia. And by the early 1680s, the inhabitants of these communities had developed a vibrant religious and political identity distinct from those from which they had detached themselves. Chapter 6, "Against Their Own," centers on the falling-out of the mission and League Iroquois and again shows how patterns of kinship and migration played a significant role in shaping patterns of war and peace making. Through the 1680s, the inhabitants of the missions sided with the French in their campaigns against the distant and faintly related Senecas. Yet, with the outbreak of European war in 1689, they found themselves unhappily drawn into a war against their close relatives among the Mohawks, Oneidas, and Onondagas. While most Iroquoianists who have considered these two decades have tended to place the emphasis on the fundamental unity of the Iroquois through time and space, this book supports the view that for a time the divisiveness and violence were very real.[27]

Before picking up the story of the conflict among Iroquois through the final decade of the seventeenth century, however, chapter 7, "In Their Place," chronicles how hundreds of displaced Wabanakis from what is today northern New England sought temporary or long-term refuge in the colony, both within and outside of the mission settlements. Processes described in previous chapters – not merely the Indigenous search for refuge, but also alliance building, evangelization, migration, and military mobilization – mutually reinforced each other in the formation and transformation of nominally "Abenaki" mission settlements at Msakkikkan and Néssawa-kamighé (on the Chaudière River), as well as at Arsikantegouk (on the Saint François River).

Chapter 8, "The Tree of Peace" – an Iroquoian diplomatic metaphor for a solidly grounded coexistence – considers the intensification of warfare between the mission and League Iroquois during the century's last decade, and their ultimate reconciliation. The contours of the military and diplomatic activity that ensued corresponded closely to long-standing incorporative patterns of war. Out of this situation, the Christian Iroquois, and particularly the people of Kahnawake, emerged as a power to be reckoned with: while scholars have deemed the "Great Peace of Montreal" in 1701 to have been a triumph for either the French or the Five Nations, here it is argued that it was also a triumph for the mission communities.[28]

With the Great Peace of Montreal, the book ends at a well-known moment of Franco-Indigenous history. Ideally, the subject should be studied across the entire period of the French Regime, from the 1630s to 1760, even beyond into the late eighteenth and early nineteenth centuries. However, the practical constraints of publication make it necessary to begin by confining our attention to the seventeenth century alone. Eighteenth-century developments, including the further evolution and relocation of these communities as well as the formation of new missions at Aouanagassing (Île aux Tourtres) in the first decade of the eighteenth century, and Wowenak (or Wôlinak, Bécancour), Oswegatchie (La Présentation), and Akwesasne (Saint Régis) at midcentury, as well as the continued impact of the Saint Lawrence valley's mission settlements on the history of the region, are best left for a future volume.

***

A note on measurements: in the following pages distances are described in kilometers or in leagues, the latter referring to the *lieue* of the French sources, the length of which was not always consistent but which can be understood to correspond to roughly four or five kilometers (two or three miles). Following the land-surveying practices of the period, plots are meanwhile described in *arpents*, a measure that could be either lineal (58.5 meters or 192 feet) or areal (1 square arpent corresponding to about 3,400 square meters or 0.84 modern acres). The *livre* was the basic monetary unit of account.

1

Sowing Seeds

Patterns of Subsistence, Settlement, and Conflict among the Saint Lawrence Algonquians, 1600–1637

The Saint Lawrence is one of North America's most vital waterways. A deep gash in the earth's crust exposed as the glaciers receded some ten thousand years ago, this river forms together with the Great Lakes a hydrographic system that reaches far into the heart of the continent, and whose watershed spans about a million square kilometers. Like waterways of comparable proportions across the globe, it has unavoidably forged the social and cultural fabric of the peoples who have inhabited its vicinity. The Indigenous presence along this Great River dates to the melting of the ice shelf over nine thousand years ago. Time immemorial is another way to put it.[1]

The contours of the river and its surroundings are by and large the same today as they were in the seventeenth century. It begins as an extended arm of Lake Ontario flowing northeastward between a multitude of islands, tumbling over a succession of rapids that, since the mid-twentieth century, have been smoothed over by the digging of the Saint Lawrence Seaway. The Saint Lawrence's principal tributary, the Ottawa River, joins the main stream at a swelling called the Lake of Two Mountains, before dividing through a number of channels that trace the contours of the Montreal archipelago. Past the last of the rapids, the river continues its course downstream, occasionally divided by a number of long and narrow islands, to the mouth of another major tributary, the Richelieu River, which flows from the south. It broadens out, reaching a width of some fifteen kilometers, to form Lake Saint Pierre, narrowing again as it nears the place called Trois Rivières, the distinctive three mouths of the Saint Maurice River. As the Canadian Shield increasingly encroaches upon the river, its banks, gently sloping until this point, turn into steep cliffs. The freshwater flow begins to reverse with the tides. Upon reaching the mouth of yet another key tributary, the Chaudière River, it suddenly narrows at Quebec before opening again to encircle the Island of Orleans, widening from one kilometer to fifteen by the time it reaches the eastern end of the island. Between a rugged north shore and a more open south shore, the estuary keeps steadily widening. The water becomes brackish and the tides grow more pronounced. Near the mouth of the Saguenay River, the second largest tributary after the Ottawa, the riverbed drops dramatically and the freshwater flow mingles with cold arctic saltwater. The river keeps widening until it ends, by geographical convention, at the point where it becomes the Gulf of the Saint Lawrence.

The climate of the region is essentially a continental one, with generally reliable weather on a day-to-day basis. Paul Le Jeune, first superior of the Jesuit missions in Canada, gave his French readership a glimpse of the river at its most pleasant, describing an occasion when he was "sailing gently down the middle of the great river, in the beauty of a golden day [...]," belying the ways in which on windier days the river could become treacherous, or the fact that the rapids strewn along its path west of the Island of Montreal could prove deadly to even the most skilled of canoeists.[2] Over its long course, the river covers a wide range of natural environments. The vegetation, far denser then than today, gradually shifts from deciduous, to mixed, and to coniferous boreal forest; broad-leaved species, such as yellow birch and maple, intermingle with cedar, spruce, jack pine, aspen, and white birch before giving way to them. The river was bordered in many places by marshes, wet meadows, and swamps. Its waters were home to a multitude of fresh water species from the Great Lakes to the estuary, and to salt water species from the estuary to the gulf. Massive flocks of migratory birds used the riverbanks as seasonal breeding grounds, and the adjacent forests teemed with game. Mammals such as mink, muskrats, otters, and beaver could be found along the freshwater segments of the river, while larger sea mammals, such as the beluga and walrus, thrived in the upper estuary. Beginning around the eleventh century CE, some of the region's Indigenous inhabitants adopted the cultivation of maize from neighbours to the south.[3]

Owing to its vast dimensions, convenient orientation, and favourable environment, the Saint Lawrence came to play an essential role in the European colonization of North America. In the sixteenth century, its gulf became the site of yearly visits by fishermen, whalers, and eventually fur traders. By the turn of the seventeenth century, when the French established a permanent presence on the territory that they claimed as New France, it was becoming apparent that the river they took to calling the Grande Rivière de Saint Laurent or Fleuve Saint Laurent provided an exceptional riverine entrance to the heart of the continent. Whereas during their earliest mid-sixteenth-century explorations the French had briefly encountered an agricultural, village-dwelling population in this region whom archaeologists and historians have called the Saint Lawrence Iroquoians, it was by the early seventeenth century home to seminomadic Innu and Algonquin peoples who subsisted primarily on hunting, fishing, and gathering. Meanwhile, the French, whom these Algonquians called *Mistigoches*, meaning, "men who travel in wooden vessels" or who "work in wood," arrived with solidly entrenched notions that a settled, agricultural way of life was the very essence of civilization and the best sowing ground for religion.[4]

Projecting their best hopes onto more distant nations, particularly the Wendats, whose sedentary patterns of residence and subsistence agriculture suggested a greater potential for conversion and civilization, French officials and clergy, first the Recollets and then the Jesuits, nevertheless persisted in nursing an ambition for the settlement of the nomadic Algonquian bands who lived closer to the heart of their young colony. Algonquian words and actions in the early seventeenth century indicate a genuine willingness to experiment with this possibility. Engagement with the idea and practice of a sedentary, agricultural way of life was for them a means of responding to risk and uncertainty. Like tapping into the new sources of technological and spiritual power offered by the newcomers, or courting their friendship more generally, it offered ways of ensuring the security and wellbeing of relatives and friends. This engagement was not merely a response to French invitations and pressures, but very much the product of Algonquian experimentation, calculations, and initiatives.

Although the French were conditioned to perceive a dichotomy – which historians dependent on their writings and embedded in the same broad cultural universe have echoed in their scholarship – between their own sedentary lifestyle and their neighbours' nomadism, lived experience was not so rigidly polarized. On a tentative and occasional basis, Algonquians experimented with crop cultivation. Some entertained the possibility of coming together to form more permanent fortified settlements at places such as Quebec and Trois Rivières that, in addition to being now occupied by Frenchmen, had served as long-standing seasonal gathering sites. This did not represent as radical a shift in subsistence and residence patterns as we might assume, for Saint Lawrence Algonquians could recall a time when some of their ancestors had lived in this way. And even as they experimented anew with this way of life, they never fully abandoned their seasonal hunting and gathering activities. Flexibility characterized Algonquian societies, and patterns of subsistence and residence were negotiated from year to year, according to shifting circumstances, in response to changing needs.

While history books tend to begin the story of the mission settlements of the Saint Lawrence valley with Jesuit initiatives and the institutionalization of the mission community commonly known as Sillery in 1639, the seeds of this settlement are buried deeper.[5] In attempting to untangle the complex relation between patterns of subsistence and settlement, and to make sense of Franco-Algonquian experimentation in this domain, this first chapter hones in on war as a driving force. What would differentiate the late 1630s and 1640s from the previous decades would not only be the intensification of missionary efforts, but also the intensification of the Iroquois offensive against their Algonquian neighbours and long-standing enemies. As Father Le Jeune put it uncharitably, "fear is the forerunner of faith in these barbarous minds."[6] Fear, he might also have written, was also a forerunner of settlement, for the Saint Lawrence Algonquians' growing interest in Christianity and willingness to experiment with a way of life that was more solidly fixed in space corresponded tragically with their decline as a military power.

***

The Indigenous peoples found in the writings of the French explorer and pioneering colonizer, Samuel de Champlain, and in the Jesuits' *Relations* during these years are very often referred to as undifferentiated *Sauvages* (Natives), and it is only the specific context which allows us to grasp who they were. This ambiguity reflects a broader reality of the Saint Lawrence valley during the first half of the seventeenth century.[7] To untangle the complex relation between patterns of subsistence, settlement, and conflict first requires addressing the region's ethnolinguistic landscape. Taking a page from the archaeologists who decades ago began using the name "Saint Lawrence Iroquoians," as noted above, to label the peoples who inhabited the region in the sixteenth century, we might thus speak of "Saint Lawrence Algonquians" to conceptualize the unity and fluidity of those peoples who had come to occupy the region by the early seventeenth.

In attempting to define for the European readers of the *Relations* the peoples who occupied this area, the Jesuit Barthélemy Vimont wrote that they consisted of "two sorts of persons: one Montagnais, the other Algonquins. The Montagnais are those who reside nearer Kebec, and are thus called on account of our high mountains. The Algonquins are further upriver."[8] Such exonyms – names given by outsiders – derived from the makeshift language of European explorers and traders in their conversations about and with the people they encountered. Both names had entered the French lexicon less than half a century earlier: Montagnais, an apparent translation of the ethnonym applied by the Basques in the late sixteenth century, referring as noted by Vimont to the mountainous north shore of the lower Saint Lawrence; Algonquin appearing first as "Algoumequin" under Champlain's pen in 1603, most probably from the Etchemin or Maliseet word for "our relatives, our allies" and used in reference to a people allied to the Montagnais he encountered at Tadoussac that year.[9]

Unsurprisingly perhaps, the people to whom either of these two broad labels were affixed did not use them in reference to themselves. *Nêhiraw Iriniw* and its variants are the seventeenth-century endonyms which map most neatly onto the name Montagnais; today, their descendants privilege the term *Innu*. Today's Algonquins call themselves *Anishinaabe* and *Omàmiwinini* (with the former term used more globally to refer to Algonquian peoples across the Great Lakes and Ottawa River watersheds, and the latter to refer to Algonquins more specifically), but whether or how either of these terms were used by their seventeenth-century ancestors is less certain. The oldest known Algonquin dictionary, an anonymous manuscript dating to about 1661, provides two translations for "Algonquin": *Nehiroïsik* and *Ŏtichkŏagami*. It is likely that Nehiroïsik referred to the peoples of the Saint Lawrence and Ottawa River watersheds, and it is by its very form telling of the proximity of their language and identity to that of their neighbours further downriver. The Jesuit missionary Pierre-Michel Laure echoed this reality in his early eighteenth-century dictionary of Montagnais, inviting his readers to "note that the Algonquins of Trois-

Rivières appropriate the name that they [the Montagnais] give themselves[,] *nehiroiriniu.*" The term *Ŏtichkŏagami* and its variants, meaning "those facing the lake" or those "at the last stretch of water," appear for their part to have referred to Algonquian peoples who lived further west. "Under the name Outiskoüagami," explained the *Jesuit Relation* for 1671, "are included various Nations of which the principal one dwells in the country of the Nipissiriniens," that is, the Nipissings themselves and their neighbours along the Mattawa and French Rivers.[10]

While linguists today distinguish "Cree-Montagnais-Naskapi" and "Ojibwe" (or Anishinaabemowin, of which Algonquin proper is deemed a dialect) as two separate languages, it may be more useful to think of the early seventeenth-century reality as a linguistic and sociocultural continuum. Commenting on the mutual intelligibility that characterized this Saint Lawrence Algonquian world through the prism of his personal aesthetic, Paul Le Jeune observed: "It seems to me that they [the Montagnais or Innu] do not pronounce it well. The Algonquains [*sic*: Algonquins], who differ from the Montagnaits [*sic*] only as the Provençals from the Normans, have a pronunciation that is altogether charming and agreeable."[11]

Algonquins and Innu were united, beyond language, by a common form of social organization centered on atomistic, exogamous, bilineal, and highly mobile family hunting bands, which assembled in summer but otherwise dispersed and ranged widely through the rest of the year to hunt, fish, and gather their subsistence. Related families who habitually came together formed political units which the French used the terms *gens* (people) or *nation* to describe, and which anthropologists in the last century conceptualized as regional bands. The Montagnais thus included those whom the French on rarer occasions bothered to distinguish, in an entirely unsystematic fashion, as Tadoussaciens, Chicoutimiens, Kakouchaks (or *Porcs-Épics*, Porcupines), Piékouagamiens, Chomonchouanistes, Nekoubanistes, Petits-Mistassins, Outakamis, Bersiamites, Papinachois, Ouchestigoueks, Oumamioueks, Chisedecs, Petits-Esquimaux, Attik Irinouetchs (or *Gens du caribou*, "Cariboo People"), Nitchik Irinouetchs (or *Gens de la Loutre*, "Otter People"), Ouneskapis (Naskapis), and so forth.[12] This is also true of the Algonquins upriver, from Trois Rivières up the Saint Lawrence and the Ottawa Rivers. As one missionary explained, "under the name and language of the Algonquins we include many nations. Some are very small and others are very populous: [they include] the Wawiechkariniwek [Weskarini or Petite Nation], the Kichesipiriniwek or Natives of the Island [...] the Onontchataronon or the Iroquet nation, the Nipisiriniens, the Mataouchkairiniwek, the Sagachiganiriniwek, the Kinouchebiiriniwek and several others."[13]

Members of any given regional band tended to be related to each other by close bonds of kinship, to occupy and identify with specific places and territories, and to recognize leaders among their number. They also tended to speak in ways that made it possible to distinguish them from their neighbours: the meticulous linguistic study of two seventeenth-century French-Montagnais dictionaries betrays evidence of as many as a dozen different dialects. But linguistic, social, and political boundaries between regional bands were fluid. Culture and language united, rather than divided these peoples, both within and across the broad "Montagnais" and "Algonquin" categories.[14] Some Algonquins could thus be referred to in the early 1640s as "neighbours of the Montagnais, and as if mingled with them," a description that likely accounts for the ethnic ambiguity that surrounds many individuals and family bands that appear in the sources, and that anticipates Father Laure's observation, eighty years later, that the Algonquins of Trois Rivières and the Montagnais referred to themselves by the same name – Nehiro Iriniu.[15]

Innu and Algonquin social organization reflected the challenging environment of the boreal shield, where poor soil and long winters meant that agriculture could not be counted on as a reliable source of food. Abundant animal and vegetal sustenance could be found through the summer months, but in wintertime these resources became too scarce to allow the existence of large groups. Fall was accordingly a time of intensive and generalized hunting, fishing, and foraging for everything that might be stocked to complement the winter's hunt and provide a measure of insurance against the attendant seasonal threats: the unusual vigor of the cold weather; the unexpected rarity of game; the death, injury, or illness of a hunter. Access to resources through the fall and winter was facilitated by the distribution of families over a large territory, thus minimizing competition. Accordingly, each of these family hunting bands spent nine or ten months out of the year in relative isolation.[16]

Men directed movements and selected sites of encampment. Usually the most skilled and experienced hunter was recognized as head of a hunting band, though his power and status was informal. A man, his wife, and their dependents, young children and elderly parents, commonly joined with one, two, or three grown sons and their families, or perhaps with a more distant relative and his own family. The same few families tended to join their efforts from one year to the next, and to return to specific territories to which the head of the band claimed an exclusive right to hunt. Over time the composition of every hunting band evolved: a son might break away and join another band, for example, often that of his wife's family, or form one of his own. Marriage was exogamous in a way that led to the perpetual recombination of hunting bands and integration of individuals from more distant groups. The flexibility of the kinship system, whereby belonging could be transmitted bilaterally, either in reference to the father or mother, further facilitated geographical and social mobility in times of scarcity. The same environment which imposed restrictions on group size thus fostered the existence of expansive links between families, regional bands, and neighbouring groups. To have relatives in communities spread over a great distance was the norm.[17]

Seasonal abundance made it possible for large numbers to assemble. Towards the month of May, the hunting bands began to get ready for the trip to summer gathering places often contiguous with the territories where they had spent the winter. Algonquian speakers called these great seasonal agglomerations *outenau* or *otenaw*, the same word which was used to describe a village.[18] Through the months of June, July, and August, family bands reconnected with relatives and friends, shared news and stories of winter adventures, and contracted marriages. These gatherings often corresponded to the regional band unit – the *nation* or people – and tended to foster a localized sense of belonging, though it was not uncommon either for members from more than one regional band to come together for a season, or to visit briefly another regional band's gathering site to reinforce alliance networks and coordinate military expeditions. If times of dispersal and cold weather called for smaller, more temporary huts or wigwams, conical in shape and assembled from a dozen poles covered with four or five rolls of birch bark or animal skins, gathering season occasioned the construction of larger and more solid structures. Some were also conically shaped but framed with twenty or thirty poles. Others were shaped like an elongated rectangle, reminiscent of the longhouses of the Iroquoians and more southerly Algonquians, albeit not as large. These larger dwellings could accommodate fifteen to twenty people each, though Champlain reported seeing an uncommonly spacious one at Tadoussac where some eighty to a hundred people were seated for a feast. When the time came to disperse once again, houses large or small were dismantled, with the choicest pieces of bark that had gone into their covering being rolled or folded to be reused at the next encampment.[19]

Structural suppleness characterized this social organization, as did the sharing of a common world view and environment, the existence of an extended relative network, and the primacy of individual autonomy and freedom of movement. A gathering site might be temporarily abandoned in response to ecological, demographic, or strategic pressures, and a new gathering site designated, at which point individual families affiliated with it had the option of satisfying themselves with the new location or of affiliating themselves with a different regional band. Marriage and other personal motives also led individuals and families to voluntarily abandon one regional band and habitual gathering place for another. These multiple movements did not necessarily entail the abandonment of hunting territories, but they did foster a perpetual redefinition of networks of belonging.[20] This too explains why an individual described as an "Algonquin" in one issue of the annual *Relations* might thus be described confusingly as a "Montagnais" in another.[21]

***

The point at which the Saint Lawrence River narrowed most dramatically – variously called *Uepishtikueiau* or *Wabistigouiak* in Innu dialects, *Wabitikweiang* or *Kipwatikweiang* in Algonquin ones, and *Gepeg* in Mi'kmaq, all of which meant "narrowing of the water" – occupied an important place in this Algonquian landscape. Several related bands of Innu and Algonquins periodically returned there. For a handful of family bands which returned in wintertime to hunt large game, these surroundings appear to have been a preferred or reserved hunting territory. In the summertime, however, the area drew large numbers owing to its numerous natural advantages. The narrowing of the river made this a prime fishing location. Migratory birds flew through and could be caught in what to the French seemed infinite numbers. Innu oral tradition also reveals that in this area the bark of birch trees attained a thickness particularly suited to the crafting of canoes.[22] So too did the French recognize Quebec – a francization of *Gepeg* – as an advantageous site, though more for strategic purposes than for reasons having to do with the bounty of nature. The narrowing of the river made this the best site from which to control the access of commercial competitors' ships to points upriver. Moreover, the height of land afforded an unusually long range of observation, and its cliffside had much defensive potential. It was here that the French established, in 1608, the *habitation* or fur-trading compound that would eventually become the colony's capital. For a decade after its foundation, Quebec remained little more than a trading post, staffed by a few dozen men. Nevertheless, from the outset there was a marked contrast between French and Algonquian modes of occupation. The colonial settlement featured permanent architectural structures, both residential and defensive, and was a site of agricultural activity. As early as 1608, the initial post's first residents cleared a garden and began dabbling in the culture of rye, wheat, maize, and a great variety of local and imported garden vegetables. Farming operations expanded with the arrival of the Recollets in 1615, and the following year with the landing of a first family of settlers.[23]

This is not to say that the sedentary, agricultural life was entirely novel and intrinsically foreign to the Algonquians of the Saint Lawrence and its tributary rivers. Maize was for both Algonquins and Montagnais an appreciated resource. Quantities of it, in the form of dried kernels and meal, were regularly obtained by exchange with neighbouring intensive agriculturalists. Some Algonquin bands from the Ottawa valley, like their Nipissing neighbours, were known to habitually encamp for the winter near Wendat villages in the area of Georgian Bay to avail themselves of this food source.[24] In addition to this trade, Algonquins also produced their own crops on a small scale. During his first journey up the Ottawa River in 1613, the French explorer Champlain came across a summer encampment of Kinouchepirini at Muskrat Lake (near present-day Cobden, Ontario) and saw "their gardens and fields, where there was some maize." He learnt that they prepared land for cultivation by cutting and burning the trees, then stirring up the ground a little and planting kernels one by one. Further upriver, among the Kichesipirini at Alumette Island, Champlain saw not only corn, but also squash, beans, and peas – the latter was not a native species, and had been obtained through trade with the Europeans on the Saint Lawrence.[25]

Algonquian agricultural – or horticultural – endeavours represented an extension of the knowledge base and skill used in the harvesting of seemingly wild resources such as fruits, nuts, leaves, and roots. The gathering of such foods and medicines was indeed not a random and happenstance search, but rather a process that involved a cyclical return to familiar locations and often a degree of management in the form of weeding and sheltering.[26] The scale of maize cultivation in the Saint Lawrence valley and its tributaries at the time of contact is impossible to quantify with any precision, but fleeting references in the earliest exploration accounts make it clear enough that it was quite modest. It was real enough, however, to give lie to the persistent dichotomy in the historical and anthropological literature between Algonquian foragers and Iroquoian farmers. A less simplistic conceptualization of modes of subsistence in the region might – as with language – present itself as a gradation, rather than as a rigid contrast, ranging from the intensive agriculture of the Iroquoians and southerly Algonquians, to the less intensive agriculture of the Algonquins of the Ottawa River and upper Saint Lawrence to Trois Rivières, and to its absence among the Innu further north and downstream. Thus Champlain could observe that the Algonquins of the Ottawa River were "more given to hunting than to tilling the soil, contrary to the practice of the Ochataiguins [Wendats]," and that, though the soil near Quebec was very good and suitable for cultivation, the locals did not "take the trouble to sow Indian corn, as do all their neighbours, the Algonquins, Ochastaguins [Wendats], and Iroquois."[27] It is telling that the Innu words for maize (*mentamin*) and seed (*mentaminikan*), as recorded half a century later by the Jesuit missionary Antoine Silvy, were of Algonquin origin.[28]

Agriculture of a more intensive sort was also, for Saint Lawrence Algonquians, a feature of a not-too-distant ancestral past. Algonquins still referred to the Island of Montreal as *Minitik outen entagougiban*, "the Island where there was a village."[29] This was, most certainly, an echo of the community known as Hochelaga in Jacques Cartier's writings of the previous century, or of another less well-known successor village. The Saint Lawrence Iroquoians who had at that time occupied the Saint Lawrence valley did not form a discrete political unit, but they shared key cultural traits, including palisaded villages comprised of longhouses, intensive agriculture, and a rich ceramic tradition. Their disappearance from the region by the turn of the century has long been the subject of debate. The current scholarly consensus, grounded in historical and archaeological evidence and supported by oral traditions, points not to a complete disappearance, but instead to a wide dispersal and relocation, as war captives or refugees, among neighbouring groups. Population growth, coupled with continued climatic cooling, seems to have provoked social and political strife.

Many of the Saint Lawrence Iroquoians were incorporated within Wendat and Iroquois societies, as they shared very similar patterns of residence and modes of subsistence, but many also merged with Saint Lawrence Algonquian bands.[30]

The intergenerational memory of ancestors' village life and reliance on intensive agriculture was sometimes very concrete: "My grandfather," explained one elderly Algonquin when touring the Island of Montreal with a Jesuit, "tilled the soil on this spot. Maize grew very well on it, for the sun is very strong there." Taking in his hands some earth, he added: "See the richness of the soil; it is excellent."[31] At other times, this recollection was expressed – or recorded – as a more abstract collective claim. The Onontchataronon, or Iroquet Nation, whose very name suggests a filiation with the Saint Lawrence Iroquoians, for example, told the French that their "ancestors formerly inhabited the Island of Montreal," while the Kichesipirini and other Algonquin nations similarly explained that they had "in earlier times cleared the land, and had a settlement" near Mount Royal, on the island, but that they had been forced to abandon it "as they were too often molested by their enemies."[32] Here and there in the Saint Lawrence valley, reminders of this not-too-distant past could still be observed during the early decades of the seventeenth century. At the juncture of the Saint Maurice and the Saint Lawrence Rivers, where the French would eventually establish the town of Trois Rivières, "the ends of [...] blackened stakes" could still be seen, "remains of a good palisade, which formerly surrounded a village," near which there were cleared fields where corn had been cultivated.[33] The Algonquian world had roots reaching back to the Iroquoian world.

The Iroquois were often singled out in Algonquian collective memory for destroying these older villages, and the military threat they continued to pose was cited to explain why people had "lost the habit" of agriculture.[34] Asked by Champlain, during his 1613 visit, why they continued to inhabit a location as barren as the upper Ottawa valley, the Kichesipirini explained that "they were forced to do so, in order to be safe, and that the roughness of the region served as a bulwark against their enemies." But, they proposed, should the French build an outpost at the rapids on the Island of Montreal, as Champlain had suggested that he intended to do, "they [the Algonquins] would leave their abode to come and live near us [the French], feeling assured that their enemies would do them no harm while we were with them."[35]

This was a seminal moment, or at the very least the earliest recorded iteration of mutual pledges that may very well have been voiced in other undocumented settings. From his base at Quebec, Champlain had quickly grasped the centrality of the Island of Montreal as a crossroads of the Saint Lawrence, Ottawa, and Richelieu Rivers, and concluded that an advance post there would greatly benefit the fur trade and his western explorations. In 1611, he had surveyed a site on the south side of the island, at the foot of the Sault Saint Louis (Lachine) rapids, and ordered the trees there to be cut and the ground to be levelled to prepare for building what he named "Place Royale" or Royal Square. As he waited for his allies, Champlain had his men prepare two test gardens, one in a meadow and the other in a wooded area that they cleared. The seeds that they sowed, he observed, "all came up quickly and in perfect condition, which shows the good quality of the soil."[36]

Champlain, having sailed back to France in the fall of 1611 and returned to the colony in the spring of 1613, now announced to the Kichesipirini that his people would collect building materials within the year, with the aim of constructing a fort and cultivating land at the Island of Montreal during the next. "When they heard this," reported the Frenchman, "they gave a great shout of approval."[37] The prospect of having French allies reclaim for them the Island of Montreal and its vicinity as a site of summer gathering and trade was an appealing one. But Algonquin willingness to settle down would not be tested so soon, as Champlain was in no better position to construct an outpost than he had been three years before, obliged as he was to periodically return to the metropole to defend the colony's interests and his own. Having spent the summer of 1613 in the Saint Lawrence valley, he again left for France, where he stayed another year and a half. Only three decades later would the French succeed in establishing a permanent settlement on the Island of Montreal.

***

From the outset, New France's administration was entrusted by the Crown to a succession of financiers and merchant partnerships which promised to settle and develop the territory in return for exclusive rights to its furs. Seen through the commercial prism, Indigenous peoples were understood as partners or, more callously, mere suppliers. Champlain's declarations to the Kichesipirini in 1613 must be understood in this context. He was enthusiastic at the idea of extending the reach of the fur trade, and the establishment of a paired Franco-Algonquin settlement on the Island of Montreal was a means to achieve this aim. His approach was likewise informed by preconceived notions of the merits of the agricultural and sedentary lifestyle. In accordance with biblical and classical influences, early modern Europeans, including the French, conceptualized civilization as synonymous with these traits.

To be sure, a double standard was at work, insofar as the early modern French were themselves a highly mobile people. Proverbial French attachment to native soil notwithstanding, much of the workforce was in constant flow within the home kingdom, even across its borders; refugees of war sought to escape armies, both enemy and friendly; itinerant preachers roamed the land with zeal; and, until Louis XIV fixed his abode at Versailles late in the century, the monarch himself moved from palace to palace with his court at a dizzying rhythm. Officials, traders, and varied personnel who served at Quebec and in the other posts of the embryonic colony were no less mobile, coming and going across the Atlantic, often staying put for only a season – Champlain himself would make the journey twenty-nine times. Blind to the paradox, French observers placed the Indigenous peoples they encountered into one of two categories: there were those who "live assembled in villages" and who "cultivate the fields," producing enough to sustain themselves year round, and having "some sort of political and civic life"; and then there were others, like the Montagnais and Algonquins, whose peripatetic way of life barely raised them beyond the "condition of beasts."[38] Although commercial profit remained the fundamental impulse of colonization in these early decades, the civilizing mission gradually came to occupy an important place in French thinking about Indigenous peoples.

It is in the writings of Marc Lescarbot, who reported in 1612 on his experience in Acadia, that we find the earliest call to sedentarize the Algonquian hunter-gatherers of the vast expanses claimed as New France. Whereas good missionaries would be sure to reap great fruits as soon as they reached more sedentary agriculturalists such as the Armouchiquois (Wabanakis) and Iroquois, he wrote, the "vagabond and divided" Mi'kmaq and Wolastoqiyik or Maliseet who lived in the immediate vicinity of the French posts in Acadia needed "to be assembled by the culture of the soil and forced in this way to reside in one place. For whoever has made the effort to cultivate a piece of land does not leave it easily. He fights to preserve it with all his courage." In

Lescarbot's thinking, agricultural bounty would ensure sedentism, and a solid colonial settlement would be a precondition to this shift. Only by harvesting wheat and raising cattle and fowl themselves would the French be in a position to offer inspiration to their Algonquian neighbours and sustenance to tide them over during their gradual transition from nomadism to the sedentary life. All of this, he concluded, would not be possible without the strong financial backing of the king of France or some other great prince.[39]

Champlain had been a companion of Lescarbot in Acadia, and this line of reasoning may very well have informed his exchanges with the Algonquins. The Christianizing and civilizing mission, which do not appear to have greatly preoccupied him during his first decade in New France, came to occupy an increasingly important place in Champlain's thinking – his personal religious awakening conveniently coinciding with the growing influence at court of the *dévots*, the Catholic party. When he returned to Quebec in 1615, it was in the company of four Recollets, men belonging to a French branch of the Order of Friars Minor or Franciscans. Other missionaries had served in Acadia, but these four, at Champlain's invitation, were the first to reach the Saint Lawrence valley to attend to the spiritual needs of the colonists and to convert the Natives. The Recollets had apparently not given much prior thought to the forms that their activity might take, but it was not long before they realized that nomadism posed considerable challenges to evangelization: the seasonal dispersal of unaccompanied bands during the hunting season unavoidably encouraged religious backsliding; there were far too few missionaries to accompany each family band as they scattered; and, besides, having to keep up with any one of them entailed considerable physical and mental hardships. Faced with such challenges, the Recollets sketched the contours of a missionary and colonial program reminiscent of that of Lescarbot. Indigenous peoples were to live among the French, and to achieve this required two interdependent conditions: the sedentarization of the former, and the development of a settler colony. "The surest means" to convert the Natives, wrote Brother Denis Jamet, head of the Recollet contingent in the colony, in the summer of 1615, "[...] is French settlement." The Algonquians would, "little by little become accustomed [to this lifestyle] by seeing the fruits of labor," they would receive religious instruction alongside the colonists, and be bound to adopt the latter's ways of life. As another Recollet later expressed it, "by cultivating the land, we will find ways of cultivating souls."[40]

This remained the Recollets' core policy until the departure of their order from the Saint Lawrence valley in 1629. Yet it was more easily sketched out than carried out. Owing to their order's strict vow of poverty, they were not well equipped to provide to Algonquian bands the sort of material enticements and transitional assistance for which their ambitions called. They remained wholly dependent on compatriots most of whom, given the centrality of the fur trade to the colonial endeavour, were in no hurry to act on preconceived notions of the inherent superiority of the settled, agricultural life. Although the French at Quebec began to till and sow the soil as early as 1608, as noted previously, farming operations remained small – not for another nineteen years did the first plow arrive in the colony. Colonists remained dependent on foodstuffs brought by ship.[41] What is more, though Champlain himself and a few of his companions and patrons shared the missionaries' vision of a thriving settler colony, most traders saw it as a threat to their profits. Each new Frenchman on the ground represented a potential competitor, and the promise of stationary Montagnais and Algonquins was equally unappealing. Mindful that business depended on the latter's wide-ranging hunt, some fur traders went as far as to warn the Recollets that they would drive away any local family they attempted to settle near Quebec.[42] French efforts to impose a commercial monopoly and restrict Indigenous freedom of trade compounded these difficulties, fostering an intercultural relationship that was in these early decades occasionally strained and punctuated by interpersonal violence.[43]

Nonetheless, Quebec remained a vibrant site of engagement. Through these years, some Algonquian family bands and individuals encamped in the vicinity. The extent to which they were altering their subsistence and residential pattern in so doing is difficult to ascertain, but it appears to have been minimal. They exploited the area's natural bounty, traded with colonists, and drew on the material assistance of the missionaries and officials.[44] In 1622, an Innu by the name of Miristou allowed Champlain and the Recollets to hope for more. He had spent the fall, winter, and spring in the vicinity of Quebec with thirty followers, apparently in an attempt to cultivate the French alliance and to gain the newcomers' support in a bid for leadership among his people. It so happened that the colonial trading monopoly was being turned over from one merchant consortium to another, and that Champlain was eager in this uncertain context to demonstrate his worth and secure his own position of authority. When, come June,

Miristou approached him for his support, Champlain asked him to first set about cultivating maize near Quebec with his thirty followers, and to "tak[e] up their fixed residence there." In this way, they would become self-sufficient. If they complied, promised Champlain, the French would regard his people as "as brothers."[45]

Reporting on this encounter, Champlain confided to his readers that he hoped that his request would encourage others to henceforth seek out the consent of the French before electing a chief. In this way, he reasoned, "we should begin to assume a certain control over them, and be able the better to instruct them in our faith." Miristou declared himself willing to go along with Champlain's proposal, but was clearly not inclined to submit to his control. He and his followers began to clear a plot of land at half a league's distance from the habitation. They sowed a portion of it, covering about seven arpents, limited we are told only by the lack of seed corn. Judging this to be "enough for a beginning," Champlain was satisfied. Indeed, it was respectable work at a time when the colonists themselves had at the most eighteen or twenty arpents under cultivation.[46] Yet it was not long before Miristou, who took up the name of Mahigan Aticq Ouche (Wolf Stag), upon being named as chief, drifted back with his followers towards Tadoussac, having satisfied their immediate needs. His fields are not mentioned again in the colonial record, and the Jesuits who arrived at Quebec in 1625 observed that little progress had been made in terms of either evangelization or sedentarization.[47]

Adopting casual agriculture in the vicinity of Quebec increased the economic security of family bands, but it did not fundamentally disrupt their hunting, fishing, and gathering activities. Crops represented a dietary supplement rather than a staple, and their production in this particular context, rather than a measure aimed at complete self-sufficiency, may very well have been undertaken above all as a symbolic gesture calculated to elicit the generosity of the French. This production did not lead to a year-round, permanent occupation of the area, either. Agricultural work, the building of permanent dwelling structures, and coalescence within a fortified village were discrete variables, however strongly related they may have been in the minds of the French officials and missionaries. In these early years Algonquians were visibly willing to experiment with one or the other at different times, to satisfy immediate needs of sustenance or security, in a way that did not entail rapid or extreme cultural change. The pattern displayed by Miristou persisted, with various Algonquian bands preferring different sites: some encamped near the habitation, on the river and at the foot of the cliffside, where the Lower Town of Quebec would spread; others gathered near the Recollet convent, which, because the habitation's surroundings were crowded, had been built about a kilometer west on the Saint Charles River; and yet others stayed near the Jesuit residence, constructed on the Saint Charles's opposite bank.[48] To the rare ones who did show an inclination to work the land and settle down, missionaries of both orders were quick to offer whatever support they could, designating plots of land for them that hired hands cleared for the sowing of maize or wheat. Rather few of the individuals who orbited around Quebec in this way are named in the colonial record, and those who are tend to disappear from view as soon as they enter it, in a way that suggests the fleeting nature of their engagement with the settled life. A few names stand out, however – individuals who would continue in the coming years to play a central role in Algonquian experimentation with sedentism. Prominent among them were a certain Chomina and his brother Negabamat, as well as a man named Manitougache, whom the French had nicknamed La Nasse (The Hoop Net). The latter, an Innu, spent the summer of 1626 assembled with his twenty followers near the Jesuit residence. Of that number, three or four individuals took the time to clear two or three arpents of land and sow them with maize.[49]

The Jesuits were much better organized and better funded than the Recollets, but they too ran headlong into the bulwark of Algonquian nomadism. They experimented with what they called flying missions, following hunting bands as they dispersed during the cooler months, and with the establishment of an elementary school. Projecting their evangelical hopes onto more distant nations, primarily the Wendats, whose semisedentary, agricultural lifestyle suggested a greater potential for conversion and civilization, they nevertheless continued to entertain an ambition for the settlement of Algonquian bands closer to the heart of the colony. "[W]e shall work a great deal and advance very little," wrote Father Le Jeune, "if we do not make these barbarians stationary." Elsewhere, he reiterated the belief that it would be a great blessing for the bodies and souls of the Innu "if those nations were stationary, and if they became docile to our direction, which they will do, I hope, in the course of time. If they are sedentary, and if they cultivate the land, they will not die of hunger, as often happens to them in their wanderings; we shall be able to instruct them easily."[50]

***

Hunger – both of the literal and of the perceived spiritual kind – was one argument in favour of the settled, agricultural life. Fear was another. Conflict would have considerable influence on these early experiments with alliance, agriculture, and village aggregation. In 1627, war was declared between France and England, leading to a brief maritime sideshow to the Thirty Years' War. New France represented a vulnerable target. Although it drew on a vast and profitable trading network, presence on the ground remained light, amounting to a handful of *habitations*, simple trading posts strung along the Saint Lawrence valley and Acadia, occupied by barely a hundred individuals, most of whom resided at Quebec. Relatively few were established on a permanent basis, and their number included only a dozen women and girls.[51] The capture of Tadoussac and of the supply fleet by English privateers made it impossible for the Recollets to furnish provisions to a few Innu who had asked to be assisted for a year or two, to allow them time to prepare enough fields to sustain themselves. When Quebec itself capitulated to these privateers in 1629, the rare Algonquian families who had begun to grow crops in the vicinity decamped.[52]

The year 1627 was also significant for another event, the foundation of the Compagnie de la Nouvelle-France or Company of New France, also known as Compagnie des Cent-Associés or Company of One Hundred Associates. Frustrated by the merchants' failure to do more for the settlement and development of the colony, King Louis XIII and his chief minister, Armand Jean Du Plessis, Cardinal de Richelieu, chartered this new joint stock company and entrusted it with exclusive trading privileges, considerable power, and a more sharply defined mandate. The company was expected to settle four thousand colonists in the decade and a half to come. The stipulation that they should be Catholics, and that Protestants would henceforth not be welcomed in New France, reflected a hardening attitude towards the relationship between colonization and religion. The company's charter formalized the assimilationist approach to Indigenous peoples sketched out by Champlain and the Recollets. "[T]he only means of leading these peoples to knowledge of the true God is to settle the said lands with natural French Catholics so as to, by their example, prepare these nations to the Christian religion, to a civil way of life." It was further stated that "the *Sauvages* who will be led to the faith and to profess it will be considered natural Frenchmen."[53] Thus, when the French took back possession of Quebec, in the summer of 1632, following a peace treaty with England, it was with the understanding that, in theory at least, neophytes would be granted the status of French subjects.

The Algonquians of the Saint Lawrence valley who orbited around Quebec during this period revealed themselves less preoccupied by the English interloping in the valley than by the increasing intrusion of their long-standing enemy, the Iroquois. The previous decade had been a relatively quiet one on this front, largely because conflict with another Algonquian group far to the south, the Mahicans, had occupied the Mohawks.[54] The French returned to a changing landscape of war. In November of 1632, a sense of pressing danger brought Manitougache alias La Nasse and his band to encamp near the Jesuits' new residence, relocated from the east bank of the Saint Charles River to the heights of what would become Quebec's Upper Town. They had orbited around Quebec before the English intrusion, and immediately upon the return of the French, Manitougache had made a display of goodwill by declaring his intention to rebuild his cabin nearby and to resume his experiment with agriculture. Safety, rather than sustenance, now prompted his action. He had decided to interrupt his band's hunt because of reports that two or three families had been "devoured by large unknown animals, which they believed were Devils" and which had been spotted downriver in the vicinity of Cap Tourmente and Tadoussac.[55]

The basis for these fears became clearer in the following days, when Manitougache once again appeared with his family before the Jesuits at their residence. Now, however, he reported that a large number of Iroquois had been spotted near Quebec, and that this was causing great alarm among his people. Wishing to put his loved ones in a safe place, Manitougache asked the missionaries "if his wife and children could not come and lodge with us." Alas, priestly scruples made for a less than welcoming reception, as the Jesuits responded that while the boys would be welcome, the women and girls would not be allowed to stay. Even in France women were prohibited from spending the night in Jesuit residences, they explained, adding quite rudely that "just as soon as we could close our doors" they "would not again be opened" to Manitougache's female relatives. As an alternative, the missionaries suggested that he and his family might find strength in numbers by linking with one of the several Innu family encampments in the area, promising that some arquebusiers would be sent there to protect them. With no other alternative, Manitougache complied and was welcomed by an unnamed captain who invited him and his people to stay with his own "until the fright should have passed away." As soon as he had placed his followers in safety, Manitougache returned to the Jesuits' residence, displaying his intent to maintain a relationship based on reciprocity and making a show of his willingness to participate in their mutual defence against the Iroquois. "If he had to die," he declared to the missionaries, "he wanted to die near us." A week later he set out to erect a cabin near the missionaries' residence, built with boards and nails, in an effort to emulate the newcomers' building style. Though no Iroquois warriors materialized in the region of Quebec that winter, the persistent threat of enemy raids meant that defensive cooperation was on everyone's mind.[56]

***

Towards the end of May 1633, a band of Algonquians travelling in eighteen canoes arrived at Quebec from upriver. Their leader was a man known to the French as Capitanal, a name or title that seems derived from a trading pidgin word for "captain" or chief, rather than rooted in his own people's idiom. He was considered to be the "principal captain of the Three Rivers," the place called Metaberoutin by Algonquian speakers and Trois Rivières by the French, where the waters of the Saint Maurice River flow by three channels into the Saint Lawrence. Capitanal is otherwise an elusive figure, seldom mentioned in the sources. A later allusion refers to his people as Montagnais, but indications that their country lay towards Trois Rivières, rather than downriver near Quebec or Tadoussac, has led some historians to describe them instead as Algonquins – they were no doubt among those peoples in-between.[57] Though the French had reoccupied Quebec and begun to rebuild the previous year, Champlain had just now returned to take command. Fearing that Capitanal's canoes would continue downstream to Tadoussac to offer their furs to several English vessels still anchored there, Champlain visited his encampment on 24 May. Both men shared a desire to reestablish the longstanding relationship between their peoples, and to expand on its foundations.[58]

Addressing Capitanal through his interpreter, Champlain tried his utmost to dissuade him from travelling onwards to trade with his enemies. He invoked the old alliance, arguing forcefully "that the French had always loved and defended" Capitanal's people and "that he had assisted them in person in their wars."[59] Aged about sixty, the Frenchman was the older of the two; his counterpart was, it is likely, just over half this age, about as old as the alliance itself. At a great *tabagie* or feast held at Tadoussac in 1603, five years before the establishment of the trading post at Quebec, Champlain and his commander at the time, François Gravé du Pont, had extended on behalf of their king, Henri IV, an offer of diplomatic and military assistance to the Innu-Algonquin-Maliseet coalition, to assist them in making peace with their enemy, the Iroquois, or otherwise in defeating them. From the perspective of the Algonquians of the Saint Lawrence valley, the incorporation of the French newcomers into their preexisting alliance network, which stretched into the interior to the Wendats and beyond, had represented an opportunity to secure a privileged access to trade goods and assistance against a long-standing enemy. French entry into this alliance had meanwhile served the purposes of merchants, for whom it was a means of expanding the fur trade and excluding rival traders. It had also advanced the Crown's ambition of forming a permanent colony in the Americas.[60]

In 1609, 1610, and again in 1615, Champlain demonstrated his commitment to the alliance by joining his new Innu, Algonquin, and Wendat allies in campaigns against the Mohawks and Onondagas. Glossing over the fact that these early experiences had disenchanted him of the military dimension of the intercultural alliance, and that he had not picked up his arquebus in eighteen years, Champlain reminisced how during his last campaign he had fought and bled alongside Capitanal's own father, taking an arrow on the battlefield where the other man had died. He professed that if he now returned to the colony, it was to see his allies again and to fulfill the desire that they had expressed in years past that a French habitation or post should be made in their country to defend them "against the incursions of their enemies." Champlain announced his readiness to comply with their wish, pledging that "he would not fail to satisfy them all as soon as he attended to the more urgent affairs."[61]

Capitanal listened attentively to the Frenchman, and responded with disarming eloquence and modesty. He and his people cherished dearly the old alliance with the French, and he protested that he did not intend to meet with the English downriver. He had sent some moose skins in that direction, it was true, but they were destined for other Algonquian nations, and meant to strengthen the alliance that united them against the Iroquois. As far as the claim that his people had asked for the establishment of a French post at Metaberoutin or Trois Rivières was concerned, he declared emphatically that he could not recall it. "I do not know that I have asked for it," he said, adding that he could not remember his elders speaking of it either. He saw through Champlain's benevolent rhetoric and understood that French inroads upriver were not purely altruistic. Still, Capitanal and his people welcomed the project, seeing that it could be mutually advantageous. "You will make, to begin with, a house like this to live in," he responded, designating a small space with his hand, "that is to say, you will make a fortress" – an impressive word perhaps, but referring here merely to a fortified trading compound like those the French had already built at Tadoussac and Quebec. "Then you will make another house like that," he went on, gesturing at a larger space, "and then we shall no longer be dogs who sleep outside, we shall go into that house." The missionary chronicler who reported on this meeting observed that this second house was metaphorical, and that the speaker meant by it a "*bourg fermé*" (enclosed village). "You will sow wheat," added Capitanal, having noted that the land was better upriver, in his country, than at Quebec. "We shall do as you do, and we shall no longer go to seek our living in the woods; we shall no longer be wanderers and vagabonds." Responding to Champlain's assertion that Jesuit missionaries would gladly live and minister among them, the Algonquin leader expressed the caveat that "this good fortune will be for our children; we, who are already old, shall die ignorant. This blessing will not come as soon as we should like to have it." After Champlain's concluding words, to the effect that "when that great house shall be built, then our young men will marry your daughters, and we shall be one people," the Algonquians laughed heartily and went away.[62]

Capitanal's words thus pandered to his interlocutors and mirrored, with diplomatic dexterity, their aspirations and prejudices. He flattered them with hyperbolic self-abasement, disavowing his people's "wandering, vagabond" way of life, declaring, for example, that he was "only a poor little animal, crawling about on the ground," while the French were "the great of the earth, who make all tremble." The Algonquian laughter which concluded the meeting was understood by the French as joyful agreement with all that had been said, but with hindsight we might also interpret it as a giddy response to the fanciful character of French ambitions.[63] Surely, the two parties did not have quite the same thing in mind when they spoke of villages and fields. Yet though the French sense of permanence mapped imperfectly on the relative, flexible sort of arrangement that Capitanal and his people no doubt envisaged, the evolving context made the latter willing to experiment with the idea of settlement.

***

The Jesuit *Relations* of the 1630s and 1640s make a great deal of "the fear that the Algonquins [and Innu, for that matter] have of their enemies, the Iroquois."[64] The missionaries' pastoral predisposition to view the Algonquians as lambs for the slaughter, in desperate need of salvation, both spiritual and temporal, goes a long way towards explaining why. The pervasiveness of terror, not unlike the perils of nomadism, became a recurrent trope: upon rumours that enemy warriors were prowling in the vicinity, the Innu all "trembled with fear"; the news of men killed or captured in war, even of a single loss, "frightened" them tremendously. Even victories, which might otherwise have been cause for rejoicing, brought panicked apprehension: the reprisal that was expected after the killing, on one occasion, of a prominent Iroquois man, made "these poor wretches live in fear."[65]

Missionary paternalism aside, such expressions of anxious vulnerability did rest on a basis of truth, for family bands who spent much of the year dispersed in search of game did present an attractive target for hostile war parties. Although ranging through great wooded expanses provided a band with a measure of security, its small size and prolonged isolation from related and allied groups meant that if caught up by determined enemy warriors it was in no state to defend itself. Encampments were not fortified. In this context, attentiveness to the slightest signs of a possible enemy presence in the area – suspicious tracks, the circulation of vague reports, or dreams and shamanic visions – was a key to survival. Even as they delighted in dismissively pointing out that the Innu and Algonquins were inclined to exaggeration and quick to give "a thousand false alarms," and that dreams and visions of lurking Iroquois war parties most often "passed away in smoke," the Jesuits were glad for the fact that fear seemed to incline these vulnerable populations to value the newcomers as allies and spiritual guides. "Fear is the forerunner of faith in these barbarous minds," and "calamities attract the Natives," judged Paul Le Jeune.[66]

The menace was no illusion. In this early contact period, wars were fought by Iroquoians and Algonquians in part to improve material circumstances with the manufactured goods introduced to the region by the Europeans. By securing access to hunting territories, trading routes, and posts, trade goods and tradable pelts became new forms of plunder, an additional material reward for war.[67] But the impact of waves of disruptive and traumatic epidemics was arguably greater still. While it is not impossible that European diseases spread to the Saint Lawrence valley as early as the sixteenth century and contributed to the dispersion of the Iroquoians there, recent archaeological studies have cast doubts on this. Only in the first decades of the seventeenth century, after sustained colonization began, did various pathogens, including smallpox and measles, begin to shake Indigenous societies. Documentary evidence suggests that the first epidemic in the Northeast occurred in New England in 1616–18, but that it did not spread far. The first major epidemic to strike Iroquoian populations and their neighbours in the interior occurred in 1634–35. Other waves followed, including, in 1639, another smallpox epidemic which this time spread from Quebec to the Innu and Algonquins, and from there westward. The impact was decimating: among the Wendats and Mohawks, the mortality rate has been estimated at approximately 60 percent.[68] Demographic decline led to societal destabilization. For Iroquoian peoples, pressures to incorporate outsiders in keeping with mourning war patterns, aimed at replenishing the human and moral strength of the community, acquired a new importance as a means of making up for these unprecedented population losses.[69]

The Five Nations of the Iroquois League, in particular, became an increasingly menacing foe to their neighbours through the 1630s and 1640s. In this context of intensified warfare they had a marked advantage over the Algonquians of the Saint Lawrence and Ottawa valleys, due to their densely populated agricultural, palisaded village communities which facilitated both defence and offence. The abundance of men and food stores made it easier to mobilize large forces and undertake long-distance expeditions. The Iroquois had yet another notable advantage, this one over their Iroquoian neighbours too, in the form of firearms which they began to acquire from the Dutch in 1637; it would be some time before the French would agree to furnish their own trading partners and notional allies with the same. Though scholars have debated the effectiveness of muskets compared to bows in this context, the former provided two signal advantages: penetrating power and shock value.[70] This initial edge was multiplied over time, as victories raised Iroquois confidence and demoralized their opponents, and as the taking of captives strengthened them while weakening others – a central theme of several subsequent chapters.

***

Although during these years Algonquian hunting bands occasionally sought refuge at Quebec, Trois Rivières – or Metaberoutin – remained the centre of their experimentation with sedentism. In 1634, within a year of Champlain's meeting with Capitanal, the French constructed an outpost there. The juncture of the Saint Lawrence and Saint Maurice Rivers was a site which Algonquins and Innu, as well as Attikameks from the upper Saint Maurice drainage and others, seemed to "like [...] better" than Quebec, stopping there more often, for longer periods, and in greater numbers. With the French post's establishment, and the creation of a Jesuit residence within its walls, the missionaries hoped that an important seasonal gathering site might evolve into a permanent Indigenous settlement. But though the missionaries posted at La Conception, as the new residence was named, began to instruct and baptize more people than at Quebec, and though they announced their readiness to have a patch of land cleared, sowed with maize, and cultivated by hired hands for the first family which could be persuaded to give up its nomadic lifestyle, the offer elicited little immediate interest. That year the project lost its principal promoter when Capitanal was beset by illness and died unexpectedly. Significantly, he was buried near the settlement of Trois Rivières, according to his wishes, and Champlain "had a little enclosure placed around his grave, to distinguish it" – a metaphorical palisade that must have reminded onlookers of the one for which the late chief had asked.[71] The elderly Champlain himself passed away a little over a year later.

In the face of a new wave of violence and a decisive shift in the balance of power between the Iroquois and their neighbours, the appeal of the project – finding strength in numbers and in alliance by coalescing into an enclosed village in the shadow of a colonial settlement – did not die with the two men. A peace treaty between the Algonquins and their Mohawk adversaries in the fall of 1634 proved short-lasting, and bands of Weskarini and Kichesipirini Algonquins from the Ottawa River, and others from Trois Rivières, clashed sporadically with

Iroquois warriors from the summer of 1635 onwards.[72] Other leaders picked up where Capitanal and Champlain had left off. On 27 April 1637, an Innu named Makheabichtichiou, with another unnamed headman from Tadoussac, asked to speak with Champlain's successor, Governor Charles Huault de Montmagny, at Quebec. Though not officially recognized as a principal chief of his nation, Makheabichtichiou "played the captain" to a band of Innu and Algonquins owing to his great skill as a warrior and an orator. He had spent the winter encamped with his followers near the Jesuit residence. His request for a meeting was very likely the outcome of councils held with other band leaders. People were coming in after the winter hunt, and just a few days earlier another Innu captain from Tadoussac had passed through on his way to meet up with Algonquins around Trois Rivières to mount a joint raid against Mohawk Country.[73]

Makheabichtichiou opened his meeting with Governor Montmagny by declaring that they had learned from their deceased leader – Capitanal, perhaps – that some years ago Champlain "had promised to help them enclose a village at the Three Rivers, to clear the land, and to build some houses." They "had often thought about it," he explained, and now some of them had at last resolved "to locate there, and to live in peace with the French." He went on to give some context: "We have two powerful enemies who are destroying us. One is ignorance of God, which is killing our souls. The other is the Iroquois, who are slaughtering our bodies. They force us to be wanderers. We are like seeds which are sown in diverse places, or rather like grains of dust scattered by the wind: some are buried in one place, some in another." Pointing out that game had become scarce in the vicinity, he went on to plead that "unless we reap something from the earth, we are going to ruin." He asked for assistance in this settlement, in keeping with the promise made by Champlain.[74]

Father Le Jeune, who responded alongside Montmagny, reminded the two Innu that assistance was entirely dependent on their willingness to become sedentary and have their children instructed in the Christian faith. He announced that a school would be built for that purpose at Trois Rivières, but that in the meantime they should leave their children at Quebec, a proposal which elicited Makheabichtichiou's resistance. We catch a glimpse here of some of the reluctance that had gone unstated or unrecorded during earlier discussions. While Makheabichtichiou took the opportunity to publicly declare his "wish to believe in God," he indicated that his people were not all of the same mind. Indeed, many resented the Jesuits' efforts to regulate their way of life; some, far from believing that the French were valuable allies, had come to believe that those who united with them only died. Makheabichtichiou countered to these naysayers that "we ourselves are being ruined, that no more harm could happen to us than is happening every day, for we are dying every moment." Though reluctance was again voiced when the two men returned to their people to report on their meeting with the governor, the "old men all decided that they ought to begin to clear the land and avail themselves of the help of the French," with the stipulation that they should first await the arrival and approval of one of their chiefs who was absent and remains unnamed in the record.[75]

The return in the following weeks of Innu and Algonquin warriors who had left for Mohawk country around the time of the meeting caused great alarm. They had been flatly defeated, and their respective captains had been killed. In contrast with the orderly return of warriors during the previous year's expedition, survivors straggled back with reports that the enemy was fast approaching.[76] Apprehension of the Iroquois caused a "panic" to spread among the Algonquins and others then assembled at Trois Rivières. On 14 May they "begged that their wives and children might be taken into the [French] fort, to be in a place of safety." In an effort to further the settlement project, the French replied that if they returned on the following morning some stakes would be lent to them "with which to enclose a sort of village under the shelter of the fort." At the crack of dawn the next day they all showed up to carry off the stakes, and within a matter of hours of hurried work they had prepared a site where they now "found themselves barricaded."[77]

In the apprehensive weeks that followed, the Algonquians at Trois Rivières strengthened their defences by erecting a second palisade, distant about a foot and one half from the first one, intending to fill in the space with branches and mud. "It seems that they wish to fortify themselves for good," reported the enthusiastic Jesuit Father Jacques Buteux to his superior. Once the alarm had passed, however, it became apparent that only two families were taking steps to clear land for cultivation nearby: that of a man named Etinechkawat, described as a "Montagnais Captain" but who is elsewhere portrayed as being "from the country of the Atticamege," that is, an Attikamek from north of Trois Rivières; and that of a man named Nenaskoumat, who had already sown more than half an arpent and now declared that next year he would "make a great field [...] if he can get some help." Buteux gladly gave the two men a present of some corn seed, which they promptly planted, and promised them "every assistance, in proportion to our limited means."[78]

Time and again, what the Jesuits hoped would be the foundation of a lasting settled Algonquian community at Trois Rivières revealed itself to merely be a variation on the traditional pattern of the seasonal encampment. Bands, having benefited from the immediate assistance they desired, showed little interest in radically altering their subsistence and residence patterns. The "sort of village" put up in May of 1634 turned out to be of the temporary kind, lasting only the season. In 1639, following a show of force undertaken by Governor Montmagny at the head of a well-armed flotilla in response to renewed Iroquois movements in the region, the bands that orbited around Trois Rivières held once again a series of councils during which many of them "decided to embrace the Christian faith and to dwell near the French." Once again they erected "good and long cabins" close to the town, and allowed the missionaries to entertain the hope that they were settling down permanently. They did not.[79] The following year, a woman who had arrived at Trois Rivières as part of a famished band seeking assistance gave the missionaries cause to hope that she would "stimulate her compatriots to clear the land" when, with five children that she had taken in, she began to prepare a "fine, large" field of corn. The fact that she had been captured as a child by the Iroquois, and that she had spent most of her life living an agricultural village life among them before being recaptured by Algonquins, explains her atypicality.[80]

In an effort to urge the coalescence of a sedentary community at Trois Rivières, the Jesuits formalized the status of their residence there, which they began calling La Conception in honour of the Immaculate Conception of the Virgin Mary. But the peak of eighty neophytes encamped in the vicinity of the town and associated with the mission, attained during its first years, was never again reached.[81] A half dozen years later, in 1647 and 1648, the Algonquins, who periodically returned to the area, held a council in response to renewed pressures from the Iroquois, at which they publicly professed their interest in the Christian faith and raised, once more, the possibility of establishing a more sedentary presence.[82] But still, nothing would come of it. The French outpost at Trois Rivières itself remained unsubstantial in these years, and the area remained very much exposed to enemy harassment. To missionary minds, the "diversity of nations which assembled at Trois Rivières occasioned, all these years, an indescribable confusion."[83]

The effect of the Iroquois menace was far from straightforward, for as much as it might represent for the Algonquians a powerful argument for settlement, it could represent an equally strong argument against it. In spite of the arrival of French newcomers, the Saint Lawrence valley was no safer now than it had been generations before, when ancestors had withdrawn from it under pressure from their enemies. A group of Attikameks, from up the Saint Maurice River, explained it well to the missionaries in later years. Having promised that they would draw closer to Trois Rivières, and settle about a day's journey from there "as much in order to learn the way to heaven as to cultivate the land," they had been dissuaded from it by the threat of Iroquois incursions. "We are not men of war," their chief explained, "we handle the paddle better than the javelin. We love peace. That is why we keep as far as possible from occasions for fighting. If we could overcome these people who wish to massacre us, we would very soon be near you."[84] Other Algonquian bands and individuals were considerably more bellicose in their rhetoric and actions, but they too continued to prefer an approach to subsistence and defence which rested on mobility and flexibility rather than coalescence. Dividing into small bands and family groups had long been favoured as a means of evading detection by the enemy, and it would long continue to be so.

The intercultural dialogue and experimentation of these early years did nonetheless sow the seeds of a mission settlement community, this one closer to Quebec, at the site known as Kamiskouaouangachit to the Algonquians and Saint Joseph or Sillery to the French. Its emergence, a focus of the next chapter, was among the factors that discouraged the formation of a comparable community at Trois Rivières. Figuring that the mingling of neophytes with the droves of unconverted who passed through the one site and periodically assembled there would not be conducive to the development of a Christian community, the Jesuits concentrated their limited resources on the other. Thus it was at Kamiskouaouangachit that the most enthusiastic neophytes and allies of the French coalesced.[85]

2

Friends and Brothers

Leadership, Alliance, and Settlement at Kamiskouaouangachit and Beyond, 1637–1650

In the spring of 1638, a man named Negabamat approached the Jesuits at Quebec. Like Capitanal before him, he is one of those individuals whom the sources at times describe as a "Montagnais" and at times as an "Algonquin," hinting at the fluid boundary between the two groups. A decade earlier, he and his late brother Chomina had been known to conduct their winter hunt in the vicinity of the French settlement. It may be that the pair had special rights over this area as a family hunting ground. Manifestly, they were also establishing special claims to the friendship of the French. Chomina had never accepted baptism, but he had adopted the Recollet Joseph Le Caron as a brother and a faithful ally, and it was said that he and Negabamat were the only two Algonquians who offered to take up arms with the French against the English before the surrender of 1629. "We had not known one who was a more faithful and serviceable friend," French explorer Champlain said of Chomina, on finding him to have passed away in the interval before the French returned to Quebec.[1] Since then, the surviving brother Negabamat had tended to orbit around Trois Rivières. Now he returned with Nenaskoumat – a man, alluded to in the previous chapter, who had been noticed by the missionaries for his unusual interest in engaging in agriculture – and their respective families, amounting to some twenty persons, to take up residence in the house that the Jesuits had prepared on a sandy cove, about a league and one half upriver from Quebec. This was a site long favoured by the Saint Lawrence Algonquians, who occupied it on a seasonal basis for its abundant fisheries, and who knew this stretch of shoreline as Kamiskouaouangachit – a name which has in recent times been mistakenly believed to mean "place where we come to fish," "where we spear salmon," or "eel point," but which was in reality a reference to "red sand," the dark reddish schist that characterized the area.[2]

On this site of Kamiskouaouangachit, which the French came to call Saint Joseph and Sillery, would coalesce the first mission settlement of the Saint Lawrence valley. This development was not merely or even principally the product of missionary initiative, as it has often been portrayed, but indeed was fully a joint creation, the intersection of Indigenous and French desires, needs, and priorities. It represented the continuation and materialization of the intercultural dialogue and experimentation that had occurred in previous decades around religion, sedentism, agriculture, and collective defence. This dialogue and experimentation, moreover, was very much shaped by the leadership of charismatic Algonquian figures – like Capitanal or Makheabichtichiou might have turned out in earlier years – who sought, in these difficult times, an innovative way to ensure the perennity of their family bands and wider networks. "We have some influence among those of our nation," Negabamat declared to the Jesuit superior Father Le Jeune in 1638, suggesting that he and his friend Nenaskoumat would in time attract many more followers. Sure enough, the pair quickly emerged as the "two chief pillars" of the nascent mission community, drawing, during the summer, many other families to cluster around the Jesuit residence.[3] By 1642, the presence of some 35 to 40 neophyte families established on a more or less year-round basis was observed there, "in addition to an unspecified number of unconverted ones." The following year, the mission was said to be nearing 150 inhabitants; by 1645, they reportedly numbered 167. Hundreds more visited the mission on a less regular basis.[4]

Though missionary sources foster an impression of permanence, Kamiskouaouangachit was a sedentary community only in a relative sense. The outstanding majority of the people who came to orbit around the mission continued to reproduce a traditional seasonal subsistence pattern, encamping in the vicinity of the mission during the warm months to fish and forage; even most of those who could be considered residents of the mission tended to spend the winters away, hunting.[5] Still, the mission settlement of Kamiskouaouangachit was not merely a missionary delusion or a rhetorical construction. It was something new. A significant infrastructure distinguished this site from other seasonal gathering sites and from the intercultural experiments at sedentarization previously undertaken at Trois Rivières. It became a service centre, where both spiritual and material assistance could be obtained from the Jesuits and, for a time, the Augustinian sisters. It also boasted permanent constructions. Besides the bark cabins that were put up and dismantled on a yearly basis, the people of Kamiskouaouangachit acquired over a dozen houses built in the French style, a chapel, a hospital, a wooden palisade, and eventually a stone fort. In addition to their fishing weirs, they had gardens and fields – tended, albeit, more by the missionaries' hired help than by the neophytes themselves.

Kamiskouaouangachit was a site of considerable investment for the French, but it was also a site in which Algonquian peoples invested themselves heavily. A new community emerged there – people came to share a sense of collective belonging, associated with a place and with a way of life that blended tradition and innovation. Public dedication to Christianity and to the French alliance marked the distinctive identity that emerged there. The people of Kamiskouaouangachit, also known as "Christians of Saint Joseph" or "Christians of Sillery," adopted a rhetoric and a practice of inclusion and exclusion based around their interpretation of missionary teachings. As privileged interlocutors of the French, they acquired for a time ascendancy within the long-standing alliance that opposed the Saint Lawrence Algonquians and their Wendat allies against the Iroquois. A handful of especially assertive leaders articulated and promoted this collective orientation. The names that Negabamat, most notably, would go on to accrue in the few years following the mission's foundation – Noel and Tekouerimat – are emblematic of his vision and influence. Noel, his baptismal name, was a reference to the mission's chief financial backer across the Atlantic, Nöel Brûlart de Sillery. Tekouerimat, the chiefly title given to him by his own people, was for its part related to the root *tak8erimau*, which an early missionary dictionary glosses as "*je le tiens, je le refrène, je l'arrête*" (I hold, I restrain, I stop). As the French verb *arrêter* (stop) also carried the meaning of sedentarization, it is tempting to see in this name – plausibly connoting "He who settles him/her/them" – an expression of this man's vocation as one of the chief proponents of a village community where nomads were called upon to change their way of life.[6]

***

Negabamat and Nenaskoumat's expressions of interest in the settled life in 1637 and 1638 came at just the right time. The Jesuits' calls for financial assistance from across the Atlantic were answered by Noël Brûlart de Sillery, a wealthy and influential shareholder of the Company of New France, and a pious former ambassador who was ordained as a priest in his later years. His family had a long-established interest in France's colonial project. As foreign minister and long-serving lord chancellor of France, his older brother, Nicolas Brûlart de Sillery, had been among the more powerful supporters of Champlain. In 1618, colonial chronicler Marc Lescarbot had dedicated one of his publications to the chancellor, expressing his hopes that "vagabond peoples" of New France might by his "favour, assistance and support, [...] be one day settled [*arrêtés*]."[7] Though the family had lost some of its influence at court with the advent of Louis XIII, they retained their interest in the colonies. In 1634, as he prepared himself to join the priesthood and divested himself of much of his fortune, Noël first explored the possibility of funding the construction of a school at Quebec for the instruction of Indigenous and French girls. By 1637, however, he had been persuaded by Le Jeune to fund the Jesuits' enterprise of conversion and sedentarization instead.[8] Recognizing the Algonquian predilection for the site of Kamiskouaouangachit, Le Jeune orchestrated a series of land transactions. He made arrangements to secure rights to the site through another pious benefactor, François Déré de Gand, commissary of the Company of New France's storehouse at Quebec. That June, de Gand obtained seigneurial title to the land from Governor Montmagny. Almost immediately he authorized the Jesuits to establish their mission there, for by July of 1637 they had begun the construction of a first small house, a new *résidence*. This missionary residence, the adjoining mission, and the nearby cove took the name of Saint Joseph, under whose patronage the enterprise was placed, as well as of Sillery, in honour of Noël Brûlart, the enterprise's main earthly benefactor.[9]

Kamiskouaouangachit had not been the Jesuits' first choice. The observation that the Algonquins, Innu, and Attikameks "like the Three Rivers better than Quebec, [...] stop there more often, and in greater numbers," had made Metaberoutin the most obvious choice of a site where a mission settlement might be further encouraged. Yet the Jesuits feared that the mingling of neophytes with the droves of unconverted who passed through the area and periodically assembled there would not prove conducive to the development of a Christian community. Moreover, as the westernmost colonial outpost, Trois Rivières was too exposed to Iroquois harassment.[10] The Island of

Montreal, although the subject of the earliest discussions of settlement a quarter century before, between Champlain and the Kichesipirini, remained even more vulnerable, and the French had not yet dared to establish a post there. Kamiskouaouangachit offered the relative advantage of distance from the war front and of proximity to the main colonial settlement.

More than anything, however, it was the fisheries that lent appeal to Kamiskouaouangachit. While the Jesuits would never acknowledge as much in their published *Relations*, they noted in private memoranda arising from subsequent disputes over the exploitation of these rich aquatic resources that "the design and expectation of this fishing has been the only, or at least the principal reason why these poor *Sauvages* have chosen the land at Sillery to establish a residence and accustom themselves to stay there." They had "not been willing to accept any other place to cultivate, though more advantageous for grain, with the sole design that the Sillery cove was most advantageous for the eel fisheries, which forced [us] to make their church and houses on this site which are there to fix them even more." In the context of intensifying warfare, eels, which when smoked and dried or rendered into grease could provide sustenance throughout the winter, had become an especially precious resource. These fisheries, it was explained, were "more necessary to them now than ever because of the great dangers involved in going far to seek their subsistence owing to the frequent hostilities of the Iroquois."[11]

It was in this context that Le Jeune had been driven to make arrangements to secure title to the land. In July of 1637, he began directing the construction of a first small house, a new residence for the missionaries to be named after Saint Joseph. The cove in which this house was built was, as a matter of fact, but a subsection of Kamiskouaouangachit as it was originally understood by the Saint Lawrence Algonquians. This "place of the red sand" most certainly corresponded to a much lengthier stretch of shoreline, extending between the point of land the French themselves called Cap Rouge, in reference to the red hues of the exposed stone cape, and the narrows of Quebec a dozen kilometers further downstream.[12] People gathered to form an *outenau*. The French translated this word as "village," but it referred to a distinctly flexible arrangement. The cabins of family bands were not assembled tightly in a single spot, but strung along the shore in a way that was continuously adapted to the dynamics of water. Every year, they reassessed the landscape, the ways in which the ice floes had nudged the contours of the shore and kneaded tidal flats, to find the best place to install their weirs and most convenient locations for their dwellings. That said, the cove which came to be associated most specifically with the mission had distinct advantages. Besides the consistent abundance of the eel harvest, it was nestled below a wooded bluff and thus offered shelter from the winds that elsewhere raked the river's shores. It also featured several freshwater sources. Archaeological research attests to an Indigenous presence there going back as far as six thousand years.[13]

Negabamat and Nenaskoumat, as with the site itself, had not been the missionaries' first choice. In having a second small house in the French style built at Kamiskouaouangachit during the winter of 1637–38, the Jesuits instead intended to offer it to a man named Etinechkawat whom they destined "to be the foundation and base of the reduction of Saint Joseph." An unimpressive orator according to his contemporaries, Etinechkawat was nevertheless held in high esteem and exerted considerable moral authority as "a Captain by descent" and as "a man of good sense, and courageous." There was good reason to hope that his conversion and settlement would attract a much larger Innu and Algonquin population. However, even though Etinechkawat had shown a tentative interest in clearing a field at Trois Rivières in the spring of 1637, he persisted in disappointing the missionaries by resisting conversion and settlement. Thinking back on this time, he later explained to Le Jeune: "I was afraid my people would look upon me as a Frenchman, hence I did not wish to give up the customs of my nation to embrace those of yours."[14] Negabamat and Nenaskoumat were quicker to appreciate the opportunity presented by the missionaries. Thus it was that the two men, with their respective families, amounting to some twenty persons, arrived at Kamiskouaouangachit at the end of the winter hunt of 1638 to take up residence in the house that had been prepared with Etinechkawat in mind.[15]

***

Historians have often repeated that the mission at Sillery or Kamiskouaouangachit, and the other mission settlements that would later appear in the Saint Lawrence valley, were modeled on *reducciones de Indios* established by Jesuits among the the Guaraní of Paraguay.[16] Indeed, the annual reports produced by the South American missionaries circulated widely, and fed the imagination of those who came to the Saint Lawrence valley. In the *Relation* of 1632, Paul Le Jeune compared the Wendats to the Guaraní; in 1637, he wrote to a fellow missionary that to read the reports of what was occurring in Paraguay was to catch a glimpse of what would someday be accomplished in New France. In 1638, in a letter to his superior general in Rome, Le Jeune used *reduximus*, the Latin equivalent of the Spanish *reducción* to refer to the settlement of Kamiskouaouangachit; in the *Relation* of 1639, he referred to "Sillery, where the *Réduction* of Sauvages was made."[17] In the sacramental register of the mission, the term "reduction" was also used: regularly from Le Jeune's first act in April 1638 to June 1640; twice in January and October 1641; and sixteen times in 1649–50. Otherwise the terms "*residentia*" (residence), "*sacello*" (chapel), "*ecclesia*" (church), or "*oppidum*" (fort) were preferred.[18] This unsystematic use of the term reduction and its disappearance from the *Relations* as early as 1639 and from the registers after 1650, indicate the limits of the concept. If Jesuit efforts in South America offered a model, it was only in the loosest sense. A superficial understanding of what was happening in the missions of Paraguay, and a quick realization that the human realities of the Saint Lawrence valley were of a different sort altogether, made a close emulation impossible. Abandoning the expectation that Indigenous peoples could be assimilated to colonial society in the short term, from the 1630s onwards the Jesuits of New France adopted an approach that privileged Christianization above francization.[19]

Arguably, it was Indigenous leadership, much more so than missionary vision, that made Kamiskouaouangachit. The emergence of leaders in this location was in keeping with Algonquian traditions surrounding chiefs or "captains," as the French translated the word *Ukimau* (in Innu) or *Okima* (in Anishnabemowin).[20] Among the Innu and Algonquins, leadership of regional bands derived from a combination of achievement, heredity, and election. There existed "two kinds of captains," as one Jesuit explained: "those by right of birth," prominent chiefs whose nomination rested on genealogical considerations and who were ritually installed for life, and "those by election," task-oriented leaders who emerged for more limited diplomatic, commercial, or military purposes.[21] Etinechkawat was clearly of the former type; Negabamat may very well have begun as one of the latter, though his adoption of the name Tekouerimat, noted for the first time in 1639 and passed on to a

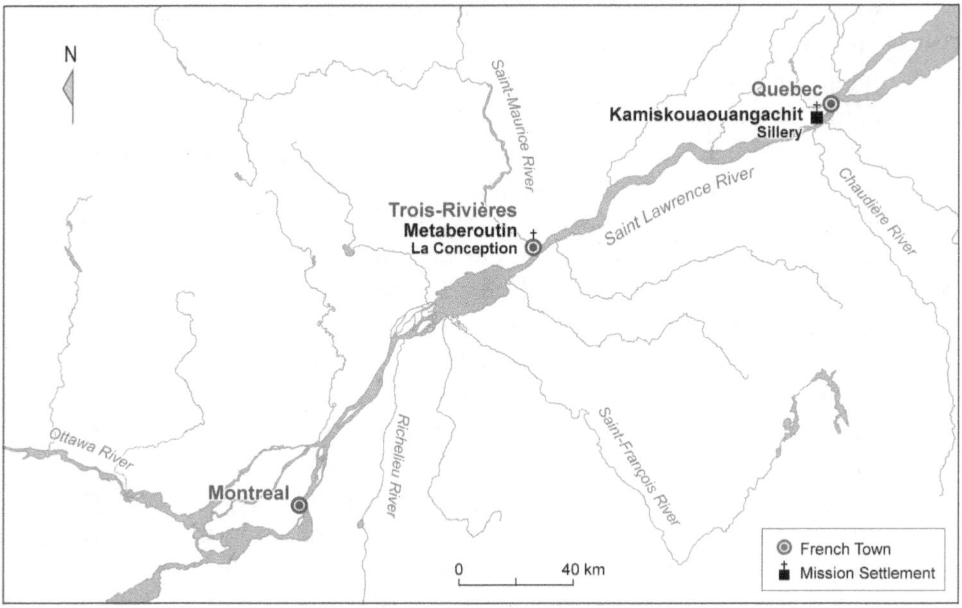

Figure 2.1 Saint Lawrence Algonquian settlements, 1639–50. (Map by Andrée Héroux)

series of male relatives after his death, suggests that he transitioned from one category to the other.[22]

The authority of both type of leaders did not rest on an institutional or coercive power, but rather on the ongoing approval of the group. It flowed from personal character, skill as hunter and shaman, and wisdom. By experience and instinct such men understood the territory well, knew the places where, for example, eels abounded, where beavers dwelled, where moose travelled. Hence each year they were able to guide people to areas where they could conveniently meet their needs. There are indications that leaders of groups were considered to have special rights over hunting territories and could redistribute them. It was by ensuring at the same time the management of resources and the satisfaction of the needs of all families that such men were able to assert themselves and maintain their influence. Leaders were expected to give generously, to motivate others to reach consensus and follow a given course of action through example and persuasive oratory, to display proficiency in hunting and in warfare, as well as a capacity to ensure the well-being of their followers through their knowledge of the land and their relationships with its human and nonhuman occupants.[23] By tapping into Christian beliefs and rituals as new sources of spiritual power, and by cultivating an alliance with the French, neophyte leaders were innovating within well-established structures. Accepting baptism, Negabamat alias Tekouerimat took on the Christian name of Noël in honour of his community's material benefactor and in an apparent confirmation of his personal standing. Nenaskoumat for his part assumed the name François-Xavier, in honour of the great Jesuit missionary Saint Francis Xavier as well as of the other benefactor of the mission, François Derré de Gand, who was present at the ceremony.[24]

Disease posed challenges to the community and its leadership, but it also offered opportunities. Within a year of its founding, the "*bourgade encommencée*" or "incipient village" of Kamiskouaouangachit was temporarily evacuated at the missionaries' own insistence to prevent its ruin by a smallpox epidemic.[25] One of the missions' first two "pillars," Nenaskoumat, did not survive long after his baptism in December of 1638. Its other pillar, Negabamat alias Tekouerimat, was himself brought to the brink of death. At this juncture he demonstrated his investment in the community by selecting his eventual successors, declaring to the missionaries that "when I am dead," a given family, regrettably unidentified in the record, "will take my place."[26] But Tekouerimat would not die just yet. The epidemic scare had the effect – paradoxically in light of the ways in which such scares could also push people away from the missions – of increasing the appeal of missionary teachings and strengthening neophyte leadership. As survivors, Tekouerimat and others achieved a degree of acquired immunity which afforded them a greater resistance and more solid health in the face of subsequent epidemic waves. This invariably reinforced their aura of spiritual power and moral authority within their own bands and in their relations with others. The establishment of a cemetery near the mission, where the less fortunate might be buried, also contributed to the coalescence of a community, insofar as Kamiskouaouangachit emerged as a funerary site, where genealogical memory and relationships with the world beyond could be perpetuated.[27]

The spread of the sickness throughout the Saint Lawrence valley in 1638 and within Etinechkawat's own family appears to have played a key role in convincing the reluctant "captain by descent" to at last convert and relocate with his own followers at Kamiskouaouangachit.[28] As noted earlier, most newcomers to the missions were reproducing a traditional seasonal subsistence pattern, encamping on the site and its vicinity during the warm months to fish and forage, with few if any intending to remain year-round. But missionary liberality did have an impact on the traditional movements of the Saint Lawrence Algonquians, and did make a contribution to the emergence and consolidation of population. It also encouraged the reinforcement of links that had until then been more distended. The arrival of visitors from afar who were tempted to settle there on a somewhat more permanent basis, notably some Kichesipirini Algonquins from the Ottawa valley, prompted the leaders, during the summer of 1641, to formalize the bases of the community and to reinforce their claims to authority.[29]

Without consulting the missionaries, Etinechkawat, Tekouerimat, and another leading neophyte, the Algonquin Étienne Pigarouich, convened other bands in the region to "offer them strong inducements to believe. If anyone showed himself an open enemy to the faith, they resolved to drive him away from the village that they are beginning." During the council, the three men spoke in turn, with Etinechkawat speaking last. "I believe that the only means of restoring your nation," he urged the visitors, "which is going to destruction, is for you all to assemble and to believe in God." The handful of men who voiced their objections to these pressures included Makheabichtichiou, the renowned warrior and orator who just three years earlier had himself expressed the desire to embrace Christianity and settle down near Quebec. However, on account of his determined polygamous ways, he was now marginalized. Having failed to produce a consensus during the meeting, Etinechkawat, Tekouerimat, and Pigarouich asked the missionaries to act in secret with the governor so that he might "prompt them to appoint some captains to lead them in their small affairs." Accordingly, the governor convened the principal men of the mission and advised them that they should elect chiefs.[30]

Etinechkawat's own name was not put forward for election, for "being a Captain by descent, everyone gave him the first rank" by default. The Christian men whose names had been elicited, certainly including Tekouerimat and plausibly Pigarouich, won a sweeping victory which was ratified by the community in the missionaries' absence. Besides the three captains elected to lead in collaboration with Etinechkawat, the assembly selected three other persons unnamed in the record: a "Captain of prayers" who would be responsible for communicating the missionary teachings to the rest of the community, and two others who would "keep the young men to their duty." During the council, those assembled "confirmed the resolution they had made to cultivate the land" with the governor's assistance.[31]

***

Kamiskouaouangachit did promise a "means of restoring [the] nation," to borrow Etinechkawat's phrase. Beyond the natural bounty of the eel fishery, it became a privileged service centre where French assistance both material and spiritual was apportioned. Importantly, though the Jesuits gave themselves the starring role in the *Relations*, they were not alone in providing for the neophytes. Several servants assisted them with physical labour, and nuns brought their own considerable resources and zeal to the mission in its early years.

In August of 1639 a ship brought to Quebec six young women from two religious orders: three Augustines de la Miséricorde de Jésus from Dieppe and three Ursulines from Tours. The latter were teachers, and they intended to build a school in the colony; the former were nursing sisters, intent on founding a *hôtel-Dieu*, as hospitals were called. Upon their arrival, the three Augustinian sisters rushed to Kamiskouaouangachit where the locals were astonished to learn that these white-gowned women were virgins. The sisters had expected to serve the Indigenous people from their residence in the town, as had the Ursulines, but mortality there was so high during their first winter that their would-be patients dubbed it "the House of Death" and stayed away. Seeing that illness and death followed them and touched other nations, the Algonquians changed their mind and began sending their sick from Kamiskouaouangachit to the nuns' hospital in town, which also began to feed the healthy with provisions given or lent from its stores. The inconvenience was such that they asked the nuns to come to Sillery, "because they did not like it at Quebec."[32]

While the Ursulines chose to remain at Quebec, the marked Algonquian preference for Kamiskouaouangachit determined the Augustinians to relocate their operation there. The small cove of Saint Joseph being occupied, they selected as a site in the next cove upriver, separated from the Jesuits' mission by a small hill that jutted from the bluff out to the water; this second cove became known as "Anse du Couvent" or Convent Cove. About 150 meters separated the Jesuits' residence from the site where, with great ceremony, they laid the first stone for their own dwelling, on 9 July 1640. At first, the nuns lodged with the Jesuits and then in the nearby house of the colonist Pierre de

Puiseaux, before occupying their half-built house in December. Completed the following year, this large stone house featured a north-facing gable and two chimneys, windows, wood floors, interior partitions, and a space that served as chapel. A fence surrounded the compound, which variously was called the convent or the hospital.[33]

While the Jesuits sought to inspire confidence with their *Relations*, the Augustinians' own annals reveal that the first winter spent at the convent-hospital was a harrowing one. "Cold and misery" reigned. The three sisters fell gravely ill: Marie Guenet, Mère de Saint Ignace, the superior, "spit up blood," and one of her sisters died early in the year.[34] Still, they could count on some eight or ten servants who assisted them and their clientele, and their presence confirmed the mission's function as a site where the most vulnerable could receive special attention. With the arrival of moose-hunting season, Innu and Algonquin bands departed, leaving the children, elderly, and infirm in the care of the nuns and missionaries, being "very happy to be unburdened from them and to not be forced to kill those who could not follow them in their travels, as they formerly did."[35] Once it became clear that the scattering of small bands offered little protection from the ravages of epidemic disease, it also became a place where the sick sought out medical attention and the sustenance that they were too weakened to find on their own – food in the form of flour and biscuit, but also kettles, blankets, and firewood, the cutting of which kept the missions' servants busy. In illness and death, the spiritual expertise and the teachings of the missionaries and nuns offered a measure of comfort. Due to one such epidemic wave in 1642, the Augustinians witnessed a great augmentation of the number of people to whom they provided attention at Kamiskouaouangachit, some three hundred in all. On account of the dirt, grease, and smoke, the nuns reluctantly decided that year to dye their white garments brown with walnut bark and logwood extract from their dispensary.[36]

To the people of Kamiskouaouangachit, the French acted the part of providers. In the first years, it was not only the missionaries and nuns who distributed foodstuffs and supplies, but also Governor de Montmagny and the Company of New France's storekeepers.[37] As one neophyte put it, in a letter dictated for a benefactor of the mission back in France, and published in the *Relation* of 1642–43, "ouwatch endrakiwatch. Nisasikis ka mininita arokesi kat peiik wemichtigouch witchihitch itchi Kitikeian," meaning, "I am old. I can no more work; would to God that a Frenchman would aid me to cultivate the land."[38]

As another stated a few years later to the Augustinians, "take courage, my Mothers, God will give you what is necessary to help us. He who has made everything has made us very happy by bringing you here. You will save our lives by lodging and feeding us; we will pray God that he will give you always the means of assisting us."[39] But the arrangement was reciprocal, and the neophytes were quick to offer gifts of eels and game, furs and skins. Some of these gifts elicited squeamishness: the Augustinian sisters' annalist confided that the nuns gratefully accepted the abundance of smoked meat that the Algonquians brought them after one winter hunt but could not come around to eating it themselves, and, out of disgust, instead passed it along to their workmen whom they plied with wine for the occasion. Gifts of eel were more welcome, as were beaver pelts and moose skins. Given the reluctance to sully the purity of the missionary project by associating it with commerce, the sources make it possible to only catch but the faintest glimpses of this economic activity. However, they do hint at its scale: the Jesuits' unpublished journal for 1646 notes that the neophytes harvested some forty thousand eels that year, "most of which were sold" to colonists at a rate of a hundred for a half-écu, for a total of two hundred écus or over six hundred livres.[40]

Besides solace in times of disease and penury, Kamiskouaouangachit promised a measure of protection in times of war. Yet the site, low-lying and nestled below a wooded bluff, was not a well protected one. One of the nuns complained that the plot on which their house had been built "was configured in a way that made it possible for two hundred men to easily hide very near us without being spotted," a situation that was equally true of the Jesuits' residence.[41] In the spring of 1641, fear spread that the Iroquois would attack. Having discussed peace with Governor Montmagny but failed to reach an agreement, "they withdrew and threatened to come to Sillery." The missions' residents relocated their cabins close to the nuns' house, which as it was larger and entirely built of stone, "seemed stronger to them than that of the Jesuit Fathers." For additional protection, a "large enclosure of stakes" was built just beyond the nuns' gardens.[42] The Jesuits' compound appears to have been similarly enclosed by a palisade sometime before December 1642, as suggested by the Latin reference to the "*oppidum Sancti Josephi vulgo Silleri*" ("*Fort* of Saint Joseph, commonly called Sillery") in the sacramental registers.[43]

In 1643, the "fear of the Iroquois" drew many natives to Kamiskouaouangachit, asking to have some "houses in the French style" built near the Augustinians' dwelling so that they might find safety there. The Jesuits had had a series of such houses built near their own residence, a few with stone walls, but most of them likely timber-framed or half-timbered, and topped with gabled roofs: the one first intended for Etinechkawat but taken up by Negabamat and Nenaskoumat (1637–38), followed by four others (1640), and then two more (1643). In response to the demands of the neophytes, the nuns had three more houses built at great expense near their own and distributed blankets and kettles to the families who came to occupy them. They balanced their expenses by retaining only four of their ten servants. Governor Montmagny sent soldiers to guard the hospital compound, six at a time. Still, the mission's staff could not go about its business except at great risk.[44]

Quebec offered a fallback position. Already in 1642, the Augustinian nuns, amidst renewed alarms of war, were considering returning to the town. On that occasion, the neophytes asked the sisters to ensure a retreat for them where they might at least place their most vulnerable relatives out of harm's way if the war did intensify.[45] In the spring of 1644, the Iroquois captured some Algonquins, Wendats, and Frenchmen on the Saint Lawrence. Montmagny explained that he had no soldiers to spare, and asked the Augustinian sisters to withdraw to the safety of Quebec. The people of Kamiskouaouangachit expressed their desire to do the same, as "they did not wish to remain in this mission anymore." Indeed, the neophytes did not wait for the nuns' departure, "and were the first to leave the village." Having made a polite show of reluctance, the Augustinians left the mission on 29 May 1644 with a few remaining families. At Quebec, the Algonquians built their cabins in the courtyard of the Augustinians' new hospital, which was completed that summer in the Upper Town, but "not feeling themselves in safety in their bark cabins, [...] because the enemy could easily set them on fire," they asked for French-style houses similar to those that had been built for them at the mission. The nuns agreed to have a small house constructed, and it was presented to them in December. On that occasion, one of the neophytes expressed his people's gratitude: "This is very well, the Iroquois will never think that we are here; here we are safe." Most of the Algonquians who might otherwise have orbited around Kamiskouaouangachit spent the winter with the Augustinians, except those who resolved to go hunting when it was learnt that the Iroquois had withdrawn a little.[46]

Though the Augustinian sisters never returned to Kamiskouaouangachit after 1644, the Algonquians resumed their orbit around the mission which continued to function as a hospital and hospice, and to serve their material, spiritual, residential, and defensive needs. That same year, the Jesuits had a more substantial chapel built of stone in their compound, which three years later was dedicated to Saint Michel, the archangel Michael. At least seven little houses in the French style were clustered around the Jesuit residence, and three around the former Augustinian residence which likely continued to be used by the neophytes until the end of the decade. As the war intensified, the missionaries would invest further in the site's defensive structures, rebuilding a palisade around their compound, erecting a stone windmill overlooking it, and eventually a bastioned stone fort.[47]

***

The link between leadership, kinship, political alliance, and conversion was a strong one. In their effort to communicate the meaning of their religion to their audience, missionaries employed indigenous terms for "leader" to designate the Christian God. In prayers composed by Le Jeune in the 1630s, he used the word "*utkimau*" (or *utchimau, oukhiman, oukhimame*), meaning "captain," as the term of address for the divinity.[48] The parallel conceptualization of God as a father, beyond expressing his divine primacy, pointed to the bonds of kinship which united all Christians. "Is it not true," asked Le Jeune, rhetorically, to an Innu leader before the mission's establishment, "that you cherish those of your own nation more than [you cherish] the Algonquins who are your allies? Monsieur the Governor does the same. All those who believe in God are of his nation; he holds and loves them as such."[49] Neophytes concurred. Their conception of the new religion built upon traditional senses of identity based on kinship. For individuals uprooted from different kin groups and nations as a result of the waves of epidemics and warfare of the late 1630s and 1640s, the new Christian beliefs and behaviours offered a basis for the preservation of old support networks and the construction of new ones, and furnished a vocabulary for the expression of feelings of unity, solidarity, and alliance.[50]

In their relations with their relatives, friends, and acquaintances in places such as Trois Rivières and Tadoussac, the people of Kamiskouaouangachit quickly took on the role of enthusiastic promoters of

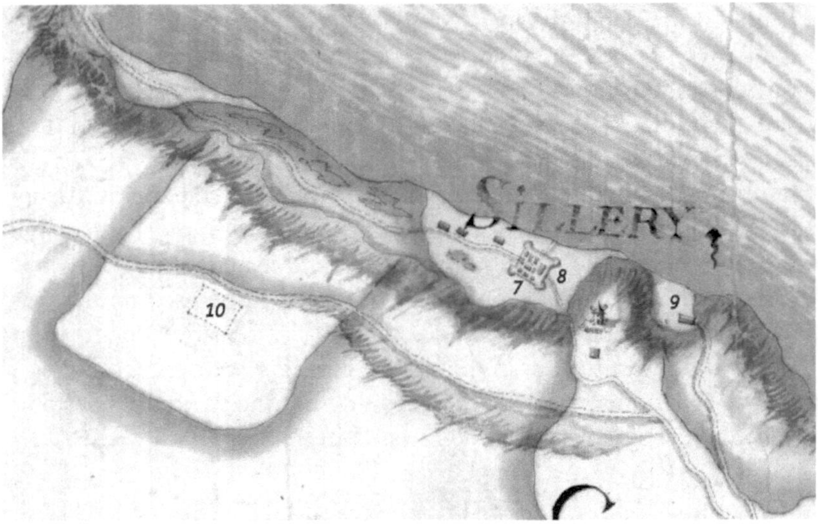

Figure 2.2 Kamiskouaouangachit (Sillery) as depicted by the engineer Robert de Villeneuve, ca. 1685–86. The fort and chapel (7, 8) are visible, as is the former Augustinian hospital (9), and the windmill. The structures persisted but the mission community itself was by this late date located on a site above the bluff (10). (BNF, Département des cartes et plans, GE SH 18 PF 127 DIV 7 P 4, "Carte des Environs de Québec," 1685–1686)

their new faith and of their new community. As soon as the mission's residents had planted their fields in the spring of 1640, their leaders informed the missionaries that they were going to trade with the people of the Saguenay and to invite the "Captain of Tadoussac" and his people to embrace the faith and, they said, to resettle near them. The missionaries expressed astonishment at this, not having themselves suggested or heard any other colonists suggesting such proselytism.[51] So as to make their invitation more persuasive, the neophytes amassed a large quantity of wampum – white and purple shell beads of great worth, either woven into symbolic belts or threaded on loose strings – to which the missionaries contributed a share. If the people of Tadoussac reacted positively to their invitation, they expected that they would go on to invite even more distant nations to do the same. "In order," they declared, "that we may all have only one God, and one way of doing things."[52] Though the people of Kamiskouaouangachit may very well have hoped to convince others to reside among them, given the pressures that this would have placed on the local resources it seems more plausible that their intention was to further their community's standing as a diplomatic and ritual center. The hereditary chief of the Innu of Tadoussac, Neapmat alias Etouet, responded by requesting that a priest be sent to them. Consequently, Le Jeune carried out the first baptisms there in 1641.[53] In an effort to encourage resettlement, the Augustinians donated some buildings near theirs for the express purpose of housing the Innu of Tadoussac.[54] While it is unclear whether or not this measure prompted the relocation of any of the latter, it is apparent that in the decade that followed the Innu came to recognize the mission's residents' privileged access to the French and to the Christian God. During the winter of 1647–48, in a move that illustrated the bonds between the two communities, it is said that Etouet "gave the district most abounding in game" in his parts to Tekouerimat.[55]

While some neophytes from Kamiskouaouangachit travelled to Tadoussac that summer of 1640, others went to Trois Rivières. They included Etinechkawat, who preached along the same lines: "We shall be very soon relatives indeed," he declared to the Attikameks at Trois Rivières, with whom he happened to be related, exhorting them to conversion. "My true relatives are those who believe in God, and who are baptized, for I shall be eternally with them. We have only one Father, who is God; since you desire to know him, you will very soon be among my relations. The kinship that we have according to the flesh, is a trifling matter: you must be baptized, to be my true relative."[56] Two years later Etinechkawat again preached to Attikameks at Trois Rivières, inviting their captain, with gifts, to come and see Kamiskouaouangachit and the clearings that had been prepared for them. At Etinechkawat's urging, they spent the winter there, provisioned with maize and eels by the neophyte community, acquiring religious instruction from the missionaries.[57]

The Saint Lawrence valley Algonquians' network of allies stretched even farther to the west and south. Arriving in the early years of the century, the French had witnessed first-hand the long-standing alignment of the Innu, Algonquins, and Wendats against their common foe, the Iroquois. The French settlement at Quebec furthered the bonds of friendship and alliance between these groups, as an increasing number of Wendats canoed down the Ottawa River and the Saint Lawrence to trade.[58] For Wendats interested in strengthening their ties to the French and neophytes, Kamiskouaouangachit became, in the 1640s, an obvious site of instruction and fraternization. A Wendat presence can be observed in the mission's registers as early as June

1641, when Jesuit Father Barthélemy Vimont baptized a man named Charles Tsondatsaa, with Governor Montmagny himself serving as godfather; two other Wendats who spent the following winter at the mission also were baptized there in the following spring. A handful of others were baptized that year and the next, including one identified as being from the Attignehongneac village of Taenhatentaron and another from the Attignawantan village of Arente. Though the Jesuits, for want of means to support them, were not as of yet inclined to encourage these visitors to remain at the mission for good, they hoped to form a cadre of young Wendat men who could assist their missionary endeavours in Huronia.[59]

This strengthening of ties had an undeniable strategic dimension. Charles Tsondatsaa became the first Wendat to receive a gun, presented to him by Governor Montmagny upon his baptism with the explicit advice that he should use it to protect himself against the Iroquois. On this occasion, the governor proclaimed his willingness to extend his protection to those Wendats who were willing to declare themselves Christians, implying thereby that he would not be extending it to non-Christians. The captain of the "Christians of Saint-Joseph," most likely Jean-Baptiste Etinechkawat, or perhaps Tekouerimat, made a declaration of his own to the newly baptized Tsondatsa: "You cannot imagine the joy of our hearts in seeing that you have adopted our belief, and have chosen this little church in which to be made our brother. [...] we have henceforth but one Father, who is God, and but one common Mother, which is the Church; [...] your friends are their [our] friends, and [...] your enemies are their [our] enemies." As Montmagny had given the convert an arquebus, the people of Kamiskouaouangachit presented him with gunpowder to use with it.[60]

The Innu and Algonquins of the Saint Lawrence also cultivated a relationship with the Algonquians who inhabited the lands to the south and east, most notably with the Wabanakis of the Kennebec and Penobscot Rivers, in what the French then called Acadia and what is today New England. Algonquians all, they shared a similar set of social structures, subsistence and residence patterns, beliefs and customs; they spoke languages that, though not mutually intelligible, were sufficiently related that individuals from one group could achieve with relative ease some degree of understanding of the other's tongue. The range of their hunting grounds overlapped in the woodlands of the south shore of the Saint Lawrence, and it was not uncommon for bands from the two regions to hunt together and intermarry. It is likely that these interactions became more frequent as hunting patterns shifted to accommodate trade with the Europeans on the Atlantic coast, with Wabanakis ranging increasingly far to the north in search of coveted beaver pelts. The Saint Lawrence Algonquians were also united with the peoples of Acadia by a common enmity towards the Iroquois. Periodically, small groups of men from the Kennebec came down the Chaudière and Saint Lawrence Rivers towards the vicinity of Trois Rivières "to help their allies in their wars."[61]

Interaction among the peoples who orbited around Kamiskouaouangachit, including occasional intermarriage, allowed the Jesuits to hope that the mission would in no time be "inhabited by Abnaquiois."[62] For the leading neophytes there, religion joined trade goods as part of a new symbolic vocabulary by which intertribal relations could be negotiated. The murder of Makheabichtichiou, that onetime promoter of settlement who had abandoned the mission community for Wabanaki country as a result of his opposition to the enforcement of Christian monogamy, paradoxically contributed to the consolidation of bonds between this distant population and the neophytes. When two Wabanaki ambassadors came to Kamiskouaouangachit to make amends for the murder committed by one of their inebriated countrymen, Etinechkawat and Tekouerimat intervened as mediators to mollify the angry relatives of the deceased who lived at Trois Rivières, taking the opportunity to renew the peace between their people and the visitors. One of the principal neophytes, plausibly Tekouerimat, stated the conditions under which this peace might be further strengthened: "If you wish to bind our two nations by a perfect friendship, it is necessary that we should all believe the same: have yourself baptized, and cause your people to do likewise; that bond will be stronger than any gifts. We pray to God, and know no other friends or brothers than those who pray like us."[63] Etinechkawat, pressed by a Wabanaki captain who wished to marry one of his young relatives, refused to allow the union until the man had received instruction and been baptized. On many occasions like this one, the prospect of matrimonial unions with outsiders provided leading neophytes with opportunities to extend their network and to police its boundaries.[64]

The complaints of the French Capuchin missionaries in Acadia, who worried about the effects that Jesuit competition might have on their own endeavors, coupled with the misgivings of Governor Montmagny, who saw Wabanaki visitors as commercial interlopers who would drain valuable furs away from the Saint Lawrence valley, proved to be major hindrances to the rapprochement. Still, a handful of Innu, Algonquin, and Wabanaki leaders, notably Tekouerimat, persisted in their efforts to cultivate an alliance between their peoples by visiting each other's villages through the 1640s and early 1650s.[65] Making friends and brothers had always been of importance, but in the context of the Iroquois's intensifying offensive it took on an even more vital character.

***

The fluidity of movement of Algonquian populations, and the significance of leadership and war among the contingencies of settlement, are well illustrated by the case of Tessouat and his people. Over the years, the French became acquainted with a succession of men who under that name succeeded each other as hereditary chiefs of the Kichesipirini or "Captain of the Island" (Allumette Island, on the Ottawa River). Champlain met the first Tessouat at the great *tabagie*, or feast, held at Tadoussac in 1603, and saw him again on several occasions over the next decade. As chief of the Kichesipirinis and main spokesman for them, he may very well have been the person who in 1613 explained to the French explorer that his people had been forced to withdraw up the Ottawa River because "the roughness of the region served as a bulwark against their enemies," and who declared that they would gladly come live near the French if they followed through with their plan of building an outpost on the Island of Montreal, "feeling assured that their enemies would do them no harm."[66] The evidence makes it impossible to say whether the Tessouat who died within months of Champlain's death in 1636 was this same man or a successor; by the early 1640s, another man had succeeded to the name and leadership of the Kichesipirini. The Tessouat dynasty was known to restrict passage up the Ottawa River, across their territory, and thereby access to Huronia. But while Champlain had nonetheless regarded the first bearer of the name as an unusually wise and kind man, subsequent individuals with this name acquired among the French and their allies a reputation as arrogant and mean-spirited troublemakers.[67]

At least two groups of Kichesipirini had been attracted to Kamiskouaouangachit after the foundation of a mission there: some thirty persons who arrived in the spring of 1640, and an unknown number who arrived in the fall of 1641. The first group confessed to the missionaries that while they were relatives of the latest Tessouat, they were not very fond of him. Yet this Tessouat was himself among the second group of Kichesipirini who travelled to Kamikouaouangachit. He and his followers had come to explore the possibility of wintering at the mission where some of their relatives had been spending time. They were well received by the neophytes, in keeping with Indigenous traditions of hospitality, but before long Tessouat began to pick at the emergent community's foundations.[68]

Though he proclaimed that he and his people desired to "bring about a closer union" between themselves and the Christians of Kamiskouaouangachit, and agreed that it was fitting "that they should all live together," Tessouat made a case for settling somewhere far from Quebec.[69] This was a signal challenge to the leadership of Etinechkawat and Tekouerimat. Discovering that his idea failed to find much appeal among the followers of the two men, who were both invested in the embryonic mission settlement, Tessouat and his people fell back on Trois Rivières for the winter. When, in the spring of 1642, these Kichesipirini relayed a new invitation to the people of Kamiskouaouangachit, this time to accompany them on an expedition against the Iroquois, most of the neophyte warriors refused. Tessouat's people were officially rebuffed by Etinechkawat who, responding on behalf of the community, declared that, "your argument is not properly stated; you have inverted your words. You say 'Let us go to war, and then we will be baptized.' Reverse your language, and say 'Let us be baptized, and then let us all go together to war.'"[70]

Now orbiting around Trois Rivières and the Jesuit residence of La Conception, Tessouat and his nephew Oumastikouei (The Toad) confirmed their reputation as troublemakers, in constant conflict not only with the local missionaries but also with Pieskaret, another Kichesipirini who had by this time emerged as the leader of the local Christian community.[71] The foundation of Ville Marie (later to be known as Montreal) that same year, in 1642, provided Tessouat with an opportunity to consolidate his dwindling sphere of influence. The Island of Montreal, which occupied a key position within the world of the Algonquins of the Ottawa River, was closer than Kamiskouaouangachit to what Tessouat and his followers had in mind as a proper village site. As indicated in the previous chapter, the Kichesipirini believed that they had "in earlier times cleared the land, and had a settlement near this mountain [Mont-Royal]" which they had been forced to abandon "as they were too often molested by their enemies." The Onontchataronon's ancestors were similarly said to have inhabited the island in former times. Algonquins still referred to the Island of Montreal as *Minitik outen entagougiban*, "the Island where there was a village." Some of the elderly recalled that their grandparents' generation had grown corn there and had passed down a knowledge of the spots on the island where the good exposure to sunlight and rich soil had made horticulture most viable.[72]

Discovering this interest, the Jesuit missionaries did not hesitate to urge them to "return to their country," that is, the Island of Montreal, informing them of the plans of the French to send people to succor them and promising to give them assistance to build their houses and till the soil.[73] The missionaries' ambition was validated by Algonquins who passed through the region to exploit its abundant game or on their way to war, and who, in keeping with what Champlain's Kichesipirini interlocutors had intimated several decades earlier, suggested that "they would have settled there, long ago and in great number, if they had had there, as at present, a place of refuge against the Iroquois."[74] There was no doubt in the minds of the Jesuits, nor of the devout secular administrators of Ville Marie, who hoped to recreate through evangelization the purity of the primitive church, that the island and its vicinity would in time be home to a diversity of "Algonquins, as much those of the Island as of the Petite Nation, the Onontchataronon, and many others who are in those quarters, some Hurons, and even also some Iroquois."[75] However, it seemed likely that there would never be a large number, "until either the Iroquois are subjugated, or we make peace with them," as these foes had caused for the time being "too much terror" to the potential neophytes and villagers.[76]

Unlike Quebec and Trois Rivières, which had both evolved from commercial outposts into towns, Ville Marie owed its origins to evangelical zeal. At about the same time as Noël Brûlart de Sillery was agreeing to fund the Jesuit misson at Kamiskouaouangachit, another set of wealthy and pious patrons back in France had banded together as the lay Société de Notre Dame de Montréal. With the utopian purpose of establishing on the Island of Montreal a town devoted to the conversion of Indigenous peoples and the edification of colonists, they secured the title to it. Two members of the society, Paul de Chomedey, Sieur de Maisonneuve, and Jeanne Mance, would direct the effort on site. In 1641, the pair arrived at Quebec with settlers and supplies and, notwithstanding the opposition of Governor Montmagny and the reservations of Jesuits who thought them foolhardy to make themselves so vulnerable to the Iroquois, the following year they built their outpost of Ville Marie on the Island of Montreal.[77]

Although this new colonial settlement in these early years amounted to little more than a fort, it quickly became a site of occasional refuge for the Algonquin family bands that came and went through the region, as well as a convenient rallying point for war parties on their way to or from Mohawk country. Towards the end of February 1643, Tessouat's nephew, Oumastikouei, arrived at Ville Marie after having spent part of the winter along the Richelieu River. The Jesuits François du Perron and Joseph-Antoine Poncet, who had wintered at the new outpost, found him more receptive to missionary entreaties than he had been in recent years. He displayed "a special liking for that place" and, upon promises that a field of his own choosing would be given to him and that two French field hands would be placed at his disposal for a year, he declared his interest in receiving religious instruction and settling down. Arriving from Trois Rivières shortly thereafter and informed of the liberal terms that had been offered to his nephew, Tessouat in turn promised to settle there with his people and finally embrace the faith – yet threatening that if he was not welcomed here he would go to Wendat country, where missionaries would surely instruct him as he pleased. Thrilled at the prospect of converting and sedentarizing a prominent leader who had until then seemed so opposed to their work, the Jesuits hastily instructed and baptized him, and solemnized his marriage. That Tessouat received after the latter ceremony a "fine arquebus" from de Maisonneuve, "with the articles necessary for its use," is a reminder of the military stakes of conversion.[78]

In March of 1643, within weeks of Tessouat's baptism, a dozen warriors showed up at Ville Marie to report the death of Pieskaret – the Kichesipirini who in these years had emerged as the leader of the neophyte community at Trois Rivières, and who had led these men and eight others on the warpath against the Iroquois. Included among these individuals in the skirmish were some of Tessouat's relatives. No doubt preoccupied with their immediate security, these warriors stated their desire to settle near the French town and asked for baptism. The French at Ville Marie, however, could only offer security of a relative sort. The area's great vulnerability and consequent inadequacy as a potential site of settlement was made apparent when both Tessouat and Pieskaret – for reports of the latter's death had been premature – informed de Maisonneuve that their people had now resolved to instead spend the summer at Trois Rivières with other bands to mourn together the loss of their men, deliberate on the course of action, and seek assistance against the common enemy.[79] Notwithstanding his expressions of interest in Ville Marie in the spring, Tessouat was still at Trois Rivières in mid-December; the next year, his presence was noted at Quebec.[80] As long as the Montreal region remained an exposed frontier in the war against the Iroquois, the formation of a stable Algonquian mission community there would be impossible.

***

An encounter which occurred on 18 May 1645, when Pieskaret brought two Mohawk captives to Governor Montmagny "and to the Christian *Sauvages*, his friends," at Kamiskouaouangachit, is revealing of the distinctive status and identity of the young community. Etinechkawat greeted the arriving canoes by proclaiming that the prisoners would not be mistreated: "You know well that we now proceed in a different fashion than we formerly did. We have overturned all our old customs. That is why we receive you quietly, without harming the prisoners, without striking or injuring them in any way." During the discussions that ensued, Pieskaret highlighted the extent to which the neophyte community seemed to have aligned its interests with those of the French: "It is to you that I address my words," Pieskaret began, "you who are but one and the same thing, you who have but one secret, you who whisper into each other's ears. It is to the Captain of the French, and to you who in the past three years have become French, – to you, Negabamat; to you, Etinechkaouat – to whom I address my voice; you are but one council. Listen to me."[81] Of course, profound differences persisted between the Algonquian residents of Kamiskouaouangachit and their French neighbours, which would have made clear to all that neither of the two men had lost their distinctive identities. Nevertheless, Pieskaret's language points to the extent to which the community which had coalesced around the mission settlement under the leadership of Negabamat alias Tekouerimat and Etinechkawat was recognized by other Algonquians as distinct and intimately aligned with the French. It is also an indication that no such coalescence had occurred among the neophytes of La Conception.

In an attempt to open a dialogue with the Mohawks, with the aim of freeing the flow of pelts towards the colony, Montmagny allowed the two captives a measure of freedom. Shortly thereafter, he released a third captive who had been taken the previous year so that he might carry an offer of "universal peace" to the enemy. [82] The Mohawks, who were around this time on tense terms with their Dutch neighbours and trading partners, responded positively to the overture by sending an embassy to Trois Rivières. Algonquins, Innu, Attikameks, and Wendats were present during the peace conference. Before the official Franco-Mohawk proceedings began in the courtyard of the French fort at Trois Rivières on 12 July 1645, Algonquins and Innu invited the Iroquois visitors "to their feasts, and they gradually accustomed themselves to converse together." During the closing council which occurred two days later, following Montmagny's remarks, Pieskaret and Tekouerimat in turn addressed the Mohawks, offering pelts and elk skins to condole the deaths of the enemies killed in battle and to allay the grief of their relatives and friends. Tekouerimat declared on that occasion that, "as he and his people at Sillery had the same heart as their elder brother Monsieur the Governor, they offered but one present with his." At the conference convened for the ratification of the peace agreement that September, the "principal captains of three or four Algonquin nations" (including the Kichesipirini and Onontchataronon, the others unspecified in the published account), who had been absent at the earlier meeting, confirmed the peace.[83]

Though it seemed that the French were willing to stand as mediators and guarantors of a universal peace, the public proceedings were paralleled by secret negotiations tending towards a more limited arrangement. During his stay at Trois Rivières in July, the Mohawk ambassador had two private meetings with Governor Montmagny at which he revealed, contrary to what he had stated during the public proceedings, that his people had no intention of making peace with the Algonquins. Offering a substantial present to the governor, he advised him that, "if he desired peace for both himself and the Hurons, he should abandon the Algonquins without shelter." Reportedly, the governor initially refused to accept the gift and to relinquish his support for his allies. However, during the second meeting he qualified his objections, declaring "that there were two kinds of Algonquins: one like ourselves, recognized as Christians; the other, unlike us. Without the former, it is certain, we do not make a peace; as for the latter, they themselves are the masters of their own actions, nor are they united with us like the others."[84] The broader context suggests that by *Christians* the governor actually meant *settled*, excluding those who, like Tessouat (and perhaps also Pieskaret), had accepted baptism but failed to redefine themselves as Christians and fully align their interests with those of the French. Unbeknownst to them, the governor was willing to abandon some of his allies.

That fall of 1645 the Algonquians of the Saint Lawrence were given cause to think that the peace would be short-lived. A hunting band composed of Algonquins and Innu from Kamiskouaouangachit was attacked: three persons from the community were killed, and three others were wounded (including a son of the late François-Xavier Nenaskoumat, that early pillar of the mission community, whose wound proved fatal). Though the Mohawks were initially suspected, the survivors revealed that the attackers spoke a different tongue. It was eventually learned that they were Sokokis, Western Wabanaki-speaking inhabitants of the upper Connecticut valley; during the winter that followed, these Sokokis presented the scalps of their victims to the Mohawks in a bid to reignite the war.[85] In January 1646, the peace was further jeopardized when the Saint Lawrence Algonquians learnt with astonishment, from a visiting Wendat, that the Mohawks were plotting to exclude them from the peace agreement. The French were forced to deny the rumour that the governor had agreed to this. Angered, the residents of Kamiskouaouangachit considered striking first by falling upon the Mohawk hostages whom Montmagny was about to release. Upon hearing that they were planning to "play an evil trick" on those men during their return, the governor thought best to delay the hostages' departure.[86]

It was most likely due to fear of enemy raiders that towards the beginning of April the approximately twenty-two persons who had stayed behind at the mission while the rest of their people had gone out hunting decided to abandon their cabins and encamp closer to Quebec. Only when the rest of the community returned from the hunt, shortly after Easter, did this group feel comfortable returning home.[87] Still, the Mohawks persisted in their outward signs of goodwill. During a third Franco-Mohawk conference held at Trois Rivières on 7 May, the visiting ambassador offered condolence presents to the relatives and friends of the persons killed the previous fall, assuring them that the attack had been carried out by isolated warriors, and that "they had had no knowledge of it until after the act was done, and that all the captains of the country had condemned this outrage." The people of Kamiskouaouangachit's reaction to these assurances that the Algonquins would not be excluded from the peace agreement was not recorded. Tessouat was for his part adamant, proclaiming that though he remained exceedingly distrustful of the Mohawks, neither he nor his followers would be the ones to first breach the peace, reminding the governor that "he should not walk all alone in safety within the roads which he had levelled and broken, but that this happiness should also be common to the Algonquins and to the Hurons."[88]

As the peace was short-lived, the French willingness to exclude unconverted Algonquins from their negotiations would not be tested. The Mohawks had not succeeded in convincing the other nations of the Iroquois Confederacy to accept the conditions of this universal peace, and the killing in October of 1645 of Isaac Jogues, the Jesuit who was attempting to extend the mission field to Mohawk country, extinguished what remained of French goodwill.[89] Tessouat and his Kichesipirini followers, who had once again displayed an intention of wintering near Ville Marie and of planting corn there in the spring, were persuaded by the rumours of Mohawk disingenuousness to instead remain in the vicinity of Trois Rivières. The Onontchataronon leader Tawiskaron and the Matoueskarini leader Makatewanakisitch, expressing their resolve to "recover […] as their country" the Island of Montreal which their "ancestors [had] formerly inhabited," held out a little longer through an anxious season.[90] The threat of enemy raids was becoming tangible, not only here but downriver as far as Quebec. In the early days of March 1647, Mohawk war parties ambushed several Algonquin bands in the vicinity of Trois Rivières, killing among others Pieskaret and Tawiskaron. That April, Tekouerimat and Etinechkawat returned to Kamiskouaouangachit from their hunt earlier than expected, having been pressed by "the fear of the Iroquois."[91]

***

The choice, in 1647, of the archangel Saint Michael as patron of the stone church at Kamiskouaouangachit is telling. Whereas the mission had initially been dedicated to the fatherly Saint Joseph, growing danger called for the consecration of the ritual centre at its core to the heavenly figure who led God's armies against those of Satan – conveniently, it was also the name of Michel de Marillac, a royal counsellor whose heirs had offered funds for the construction of the church.[92] Indeed, that year marked the beginning of an intensive, decade-and-a-half-long Iroquois offensive against the inhabitants – Algonquian, French, and soon Wendat – of the Saint Lawrence valley. Iroquois aggression had serious ramifications for the people of Kamiskouaouangachit who, besides arming themselves spiritually, took part in defensive operations with their allies, rebuilt their wooden palisade that lay in a state of disrepair, and asked Governor Montmagny to erect a stone fort. In 1648, a stone windmill was built on the bluff nearby which could not only mill the grain produced at the mission but also serve as an observation tower and a stronghold in case of attack.[93] As fortifications could only go so far in protecting the neophyte community, the state of war heightened the already considerable fluidity of movement. Jesuit Father Jérôme Lalemant, writing in the year's *Relation*, accordingly made no effort to distinguish the neophytes of Kamiskouaouangachit from those of Trois Rivières. In one passage, he explained that "their enemies pursue them so closely that, like frightened pigeons, they fly to the first and safest dovecote that they find."[94] Passing through Kamiskouaouangachit once more in an effort to find refuge and coordinate a broader Algonquian response to the threat posed by the enemy, Tessouat was exhorted by Tekouerimat, as on many occasions before, to embrace the faith. "I will have no one near me who does not firmly believe in God," he warned.[95] It was in response to such explicit and implicit pressures that the Algonquins who had continued to orbit around Trois Rivières held a council, in late 1648, at which they publicly professed their interest in the Christian faith, raised once again the possibility of establishing a more sedentary settlement there, and resolved that apostates or hardened traditionalists "shall not find shelter within the French fort." They named Charles Pachirini, an Algonquin chief of Weskarini origin who over the previous decade had periodically returned to Trois Rivières and Kamiskouaouangachit, and who was judged to be one of the most fervent Christians among them, to coordinate the settlement. By granting a small lot within the town's walls to Pachirini, Governor Montmagny formalized the arrangement by which some families sought safety there.[96]

At Kamiskouaouangachit, work on the stone enclosure planned two years earlier was begun in 1649. By 1651, the community finally found itself with a "good and strong wall, which is flanked at the four corners and can withstand the assaults of the Iroquois." As a result, people apparently regrouped themselves at Kamiskouaouangachit "all the more willingly." Tekouerimat, who remained at the head of the

Figure 2.3 Archaeological fieldwork on the site of the mission at Kamiskouaouangachit (Sillery) has revealed an abundance of artefacts, and animal and human remains. Devotional objects – crosses and rings – such as those presented above were distributed widely to neophytes.
(Photo: Ville de Québec)

community in Etinechkawat's old age, gave these newcomers "clearly to understand that the walls which had been built there were not for the purpose of sheltering vice, but of preventing it from entering."[97] In a parallel effort to bolster the defences of the Saint Lawrence's inhabitants, Tekouerimat and the Jesuit Gabriel Druillettes travelled up the Chaudière and down the Kennebec Rivers to ask both the Wabanaki residents of the region and, less successfully, the authorities of northern New England for "assistance against the Iroquois." At the same time, the pair undertook efforts to broaden the alliance from the familiar Eastern Wabanakis of the Kennebec to the more distant and less familiar Western Wabanakis, including the Sokokis who in previous years had caused trouble.[98]

Tekouerimat also begged for assistance from the French. "We see ourselves dying and being exterminated every day," he lamented in a letter dictated, in 1651, for his good friend Father Le Jeune who had gone back to France. "The Iroquois are weak, but you are strong; the Iroquois are few in number, but you are very numerous. If you wish to destroy our enemy utterly, you will do it, and give us life once more." In a subsequent letter he was equally insistent: "Make haste to come, and to bring us many sword-bearers, in order to drive away the Iroquois from our heads. We shall soon be departed souls; do not wait until we are in the grave before coming to see us. [...] Speak to the great Captain of France, and tell him that the Dutch of these coasts are causing our destruction, by furnishing firearms in abundance, and at a low price, to the Iroquois, our enemies. Tell him to give aid to those who are baptized. That is all I have to say."[99]

Tekouerimat's rhetoric of despair reflected a new, dire state of affairs. The phase during which Algonquians regrouped themselves "all the more willingly" at Kamiskouaouangachit to benefit from its heavily fortified state proved rather short-lived. Quebec and nearby Kamiskouaouangachit, the heart of the French colony, had been sufficiently distant from Iroquoia and was well buffered by Trois Rivières so as to remain protected through the intermittent warfare of the 1640s. As the Iroquois demonstrated, by the end of the decade and through the 1650s, their ability to strike with impunity at this very heart, the mission settlement and its vicinity began to lose the appeal that it had possessed as a site of safety and subsistence. Algonquians increasingly turned away from the mission settlement, recentering their lives around hunting territories and gathering sites further north including along the Saguenay River, Lake Saint Jean, the upper Saint Maurice River, and their innumerable tributaries. While colonial observers blamed this shift on the ravages of epidemic diseases and brandy, and while some historians have in more recent years added that it may have been prompted by a desire to resist the sort of cultural change that missionaries expected, it becomes more tempting to view the intensification of the Iroquois offensive as its root cause.[100]

For one, the agriculture which the neophytes of Kamiskouaouangachit practiced on a modest scale took on an increasingly precarious dimension, as field workers made attractive targets to enemy marauders. Algonquian neophytes soon abandoned their experimentation with this new activity. As late as 1651 the Jesuits reported that "not a few" of the neophytes were cultivating fields, but references largely disappear thereafter.[101] Fishing, hunting, and foraging in the vicinity also became increasingly risky in these years. The fact that Etouet, the captain of Tadoussac, "gave the district most abounding in game" in his parts to Tekouerimat during the winter of 1647–48 points not only to the strong ties between the two men and their relatives but also to the people of Kamiskouaouangachit's need to secure access to more distant, safer hunting grounds.[102] A 1650 memorandum from the Jesuits for its part indicates that in the last "year or two that their Iroquois enemies have become more fearsome, and [because] they feared more their incursions," the neophytes had not dared to set up fishing encampments as was their custom at Pointe à Puiseaux, the easternmost extremity of the cove of Kamiskouaouangachit.[103]

The invasion of the Wendat homeland by the Iroquois and the arrival beginning that year of hundreds of refugees in the Saint Lawrence valley also had far reaching consequences for the Algonquians who had coalesced at Kamiskouaouangachit. The presence of these newcomers applied pressure on limited environmental and missionary resources, making it all the more necessary to seek subsistence further afield. The Wendat presence, moreover, brought to the region unprecedented numbers of Iroquois warriors, buoyed by their success and bent on pursuing the people who had escaped. By 1655, the Jesuits observed of Kamiskouaouangachit that the Iroquois were "incessantly prowling about this village," intent on "the destruction of the Christian Algonquins and Hurons, whose shattered remnant we preserved in the fort of Sillery."[104] The fact that these people were housed in the fort itself at this time, rather than up and down the cove as they had been in the past, is indicative not only of the danger to which they were exposed but also of the fact that their numbers were fewer than in previous years. An accidental fire, which in June of 1657 destroyed the Jesuits' residence, church, and most of the houses in the compound, was an additional blow to the community. It took three years for the residence to be rebuilt, and three more for the reconstruction of the chapel.[105]

As Algonquian neophytes developed a more distended relationship with the mission settlement, missionaries responded by seeking opportunities in the growth of the French population, ceding the lands surrounding Kamiskouaouangachit to settlers, which further fuelled the Algonquian withdrawal. In November 1649, the Augustinian sisters became the first to sell off their property – the stone house and plot that they had abandoned five years earlier. It was purchased by the widow Anne Gasnier, and soon thereafter transferred to her son-in-law, Denis-Joseph Ruette d'Auteuil, who made it into a manor house and began exercising his right to the eel fisheries along the shore. Around this time the new governor, Louis d'Ailleboust de Coulonge, and his employees also began to contest the fishing rights that the neophytes had until then enjoyed at various points along the shores.[106] The Jesuits began ceding grants of land to colonists at Sillery, enclosing the Indigenous community's land base: ten concessions in 1652 and a further block of forty-one concessions in 1663.[107]

A similar process occurred at Trois Rivières, which Algonquians had continued to visit to trade, hold diplomatic conferences, and receive religious instruction without ever coalescing into a political entity comparable to Kamiskouaouangachit. They found safety there in times of danger, encamping within the town's palisade, albeit in smaller numbers and for smaller periods of time than in the 1630s and 1640s. From its mixed origins, the mission of La Conception evolved decisively into a parish for settlers: in 1661, the Jesuits who had been posted there relocated to the seigneury of Cap de la Madeleine, just east of the mouth of the Saint Maurice River; within a few years, the title to the sole town lot that had been reserved for the use of neophytes, namely for Charles Pachirini and his relatives, had been transferred to a Frenchman. Algonquian families that had orbited around Trois Rivières adjusted their movements, occasionally trading in town but otherwise seeking infrequent missionary assistance at Cap de la Madeleine where the Jesuits shared an enclosure with French settlers. It was not long before that site too evolved into a parish for the latter. By the early 1670s, the two Jesuits stationed there had withdrawn, with Governor Frontenac explaining that it was "because too few Natives come there presently."[108]

***

As late as 1669, the Jesuits remarked in their *Relation* that "Sillery [is] where the leading Captain is appointed, and where he is accustomed to dwell." The occasion for this precious observation was a great gathering of Algonquins, Montagnais, Mi'kmaq, Wabanakis, Maliseet, Attikameks, Nipissings, and Wendats who had assembled at Kamiskouaouaganchit to witness the naming of a new Tekouerimat. The former bearer of the name, Noël Negabamat alias Tekouerimat, had died three years earlier, and his relatives had chosen a war chief named Negaskaouat to take on his title and responsibilities – to "resurrect" him, as was the customary phrase. However, the nature of the mission at Kamiskouaouaganchit had changed since its heyday in the 1640s. Although it retained some importance as an occasional ritual and diplomatic centre, it had long ceased to be a site of Indigenous experimentation with the settled life. That the mission continued to serve as the "accustomed dwelling place" of the old Tekouerimat until his death is perhaps best explained by the fact that the site had, since the very beginning, been valued as a hospice for the elderly and infirm. Throughout the 1650s and 1660s most of the bands who continued to recognize his leadership had turned to Tadoussac, the Saguenay River, Lake Saint Jean, and the upper Saint Maurice River. In his final years the first Tekouerimat was described more broadly as "the Christian of longest standing," and "chief of the Algonquins of Quebec." It is revealing of the shift that, in succeeding him as the new Tekouerimat, Negaskaouat was himself described as a war chief "from Tadoussac." Although the latter would return periodically to the old mission, he does not appear to have attached himself to it in the same way as his predecessor.[109]

The distinct community of Innu and Algonquins that for a time had coalesced as people *of* Kamiskouaouangachit – "Christians *of St. Joseph,*" "Christians *of Sillery*" – was relatively short-lived. Mobility, as a preferred strategy of defence and subsistence, and dispersal as a means of dealing with external pressures, thus prevailed among the Saint Lawrence Algonquians. While the experiment of Kamiskouaouangachit might have been deemed a failure both by French observers and historians after them, it is not so clear that Algonquians perceived it in this way. The mission had served its purpose, for a time, in the context of a way of life where migration, gatherings, and scatterings were norms rather than exceptions. Yet the site itself would in subsequent decades be given a new life – resurrected, so to speak, not unlike Tekouerimat. In 1669, the Wendats established their community at Notre Dame de Foy, within the Jesuit seigneury of Sillery, but some 3.5 kilometers inland. Then, in the early 1670s, a new wave of Algonquians – Wabanakis from the south this time – would come to occupy Kamiskouaouangachit.

3

The Enemy's Arms

Iroquoian Lifeways, Warfare, and Wendat Migration to the Saint Lawrence Valley, 1649–1651

In the early decades of the seventeenth century, the Wendat homeland – Wendake, or Huronia, between Georgian Bay and Lake Simcoe in present-day Ontario – had boasted a population of about twenty to thirty thousand, divided into up to thirty communities belonging to four or perhaps five confederated nations: the Attignawantan, Attigneenongnahac, Arendarhonon, Tahontaenrat, and Ataronchronon.[1] The devastation wreaked by the epidemics of the 1630s and early 1640s reduced that population by about a third. Weakened by disease and death, by the concomitant disruption of subsistence activities and political structures, and further destabilized by divisions generated by the dissemination of Christianity by French missionaries and Indigenous proselytes, the Wendats were poorly equipped to repulse their enemies' incursions. Gaining in intensity in these years, the campaigns of the rival Iroquois Confederacy culminated in an all-out offensive against the Wendat homeland between 1649 and 1651. One by one, its villages fell to the invaders.[2]

The enemy's aim was not to destroy, but rather to absorb. "The design of the Iroquois, as far as I can see," observed the Jesuit missionary Isaac Jogues in June of 1643, "is to take, if they can, all the Hurons and, having put to death the most considerable ones and a good part of the others, to make of them but one people and only one land." A century later, another colonial commentator, the New Yorker Cadwallader Colden, elaborated along the same lines: "It has been a constant maxim with the Five Nations [Iroquois], to save children and young men of the people they conquer, to adopt them into their own Nation, and to educate them as their own children, without distinction; These young people soon forget their own country and nation and by this policy the Five Nations make up the losses which their nation suffers by the people they lose in war."[3] These were perceptive observations, though a closer inspection reveals that, beyond captivity and tormented executions, force and persuasion were part and parcel of the broader socio-cultural pattern of incorporation. Iroquois warriors and ambassadors in turn negotiated with, cajoled, and threatened their opponents, interweaving generous pledges of unity and renewal with reminders that noncompliance would be met with ruthless violence. As another French commentator put it, "they exert their industry to engage the other nation to give themselves up to them; they send them gifts and the most skilled people of their nation to harangue them, and to let them know that if they do not give themselves up they will not be able to avoid destruction [...]; yet on the contrary, if they were willing to surrender and disperse in their longhouses, they would become the masters of the other men."[4]

The motif of using speech rather than violence to eliminate and integrate outsiders featured prominently in the traditional accounts of the Iroquois League's founding: in times immemorial, the Great Peacemaker Deganawida had used words to transform Hiawatha from a cannibal warrior to a messenger of peace; later, the pair had gone on to use reason to straighten the twisted mind and body of the tyrannical shaman Thadodaho, converting him to the ways of peace. The League's founding epic, the Great Law of Peace, contained provisions according to which any person of any nation who showed a desire to obey its laws would be welcomed to join the Five Nations. Deganawida had furthermore given the Iroquois a mandate to be proactive in bringing foreigners into the fold and establishing universal peace. In the Seneca version of the Great Law recorded by the anthropologist Arthur C. Parker in the early twentieth century, it was stipulated that first the foreign nation was "to be persuaded by reason and urged to come into the Great Peace." If these advances were rejected, the Five Nations were to "end the peaceful methods of persuasion," and declare a war which would "continue until won by the Five Nations."[5] The rhetoric used by Iroquois diplomats and warriors through the 1640s and 1650s was thus conciliatory. As Iroquois military supremacy grew increasingly indisputable, a mounting number of Wendats gave serious thought, in the words of two of their captains, to "throwing themselves into the arms of the enemy."[6] But many, intent on maintaining their distinct identity, sought other solutions.

It is in this context that over six hundred individuals travelled to the Saint Lawrence valley, founding there what colonial observers called a "Huron Colony," and carved a place for themselves at the heart of the Franco-Indigenous political sphere. Like the Innu and Algonquins on whom the previous two chapters have focused, these Wendats sought safety. Yet settlement in mission communities represented something quite different for the Wendats than it did for these Algonquian neighbours, for village life and agriculture were at the very core of their Iroquoian world. The French settlements in whose shadow the Wendats now sought safety paled in comparison to the village world of Huronia. Quebec had grown in half a century from a bare outpost to a proper town, but its proportions remained modest. The patch of land at the foot of the cliffside, near the river, where Champlain had built the first *habitation*, was cramped, and the town necessarily grew on the heights above. There, the Fort or Château Saint Louis became, in 1646, the governor's official residence and seat of government; it was also in the Upper Town that the Jesuits, Augustinians, and Ursulines had built their abodes. French colonists had begun to spread out, slowly turning the adjacent woodland into a countryside. Trois Rivières, established in 1634, and Montreal, in 1642, remained little more than fortified compounds, each home to about fifty inhabitants. In all, the French population of the Saint Lawrence valley at midcentury amounted to less than fifteen hundred.[7]

In examining the circumstances that led the Wendats to the Saint Lawrence valley, this chapter makes the case that this relocation represented both a dramatic upheaval and a continuation of well-established patterns of Iroquoian mobility. It also probes the meaning and conduct of war among the Indigenous populations of the Northeastern Woodlands, in an effort to understand the nature of the pressure that Wendats and Saint Lawrence Algonquians alike began to face from the Iroquois in the 1640s, and to appreciate the appeal of cultivating the French alliance and establishing new villages near colonial settlements. War destroyed, but war also created. In the Saint Lawrence valley, fragments from different Wendat villages and, significantly, different constituent nations of the Wendat Confederacy, came together. To the Iroquois, and particularly the Mohawks and Onondagas, they continued to represent a tantalizing target – a great human prize to be incorporated through diplomacy and violence.

***

The creation of a Wendat community in the Saint Lawrence valley – and, as we shall see in chapter 4, later Iroquois communities – represented the transplantation of a well-established way of life. With modes of residence and subsistence patterns similar to those of the Saint Lawrence Iroquoians who had occupied this territory in the sixteenth century, the Wendats and Iroquois, who at the time of contact were established in what is now Ontario and New York, were settled agriculturalists of a sort that the French considered more civilized than their Algonquin and Innu neighbours. In the closely related Iroquoian languages, villages were called "*gannata*" or "*kanata*" among the Iroquois, and "*andata*" or "*carhata*" in Wendat.[8] They corresponded to clusters of longhouses, and ranged in size from hamlets of fifty individuals or less to large towns occupied by as many as two thousand people. The longhouse, the characteristic dwelling of Iroquoian peoples, was built as an elongated rectangle averaging seven by twenty-five meters, but it could also stretch to sixty. It was framed by a structure of sapling poles and rafters that arched at the top to form a vaulted roof some five to nine meters above the ground, and was entirely covered in sheets of bark. An entrance was located at each end of the longhouse, and an aisle about four meters wide ran down its centre. Platforms ran along both sides of that aisle for people to sit and sleep, and along its centre was placed a series of open hearths, each of which was shared by two nuclear families who occupied the adjacent living space. On the basis of three or four hearths per longhouse, two families per hearth, and five to six members per family, the average longhouse lodged thirty to fifty persons. Its length depended on the size of the extended family group that occupied it. Additional families could be accommodated by building an extension on one end of the structure. Among the Iroquois, the phrase "extending the rafters" took on the meaning of both the addition of new individuals to a longhouse and, in a metaphorical sense, of the incorporation and adoption of new groups into the society as a whole.[9]

The perimeter of the clustered longhouses was typically protected by a palisade four to ten meters high, formed with tree trunks planted in single or multiple rows and intertwined with branches and sheets of bark. The French referred to Iroquoian villages as "*bourgs*" (towns) or "*bourgs fermés*" (enclosed towns), while the English, reflecting the impressive sight that these fortified settlements made, took to calling them "castles." Such palisades served as windbreaks and snow fences, but their primary function was to offer protection from enemy attacks and a deterrent against them. Frequently, villages were also built on easily defensible terrain such as hilltops, and in some cases further secured by ditches and earthworks. One or two gateways, which could without difficulty be closed off in case of danger, controlled access in and out of the village. Platforms running along the palisade's top allowed the defenders to observe the approach of enemies, dart them with arrows and pelt them with stones, and put out the fires with which they might try to make a breach. Like the longhouses themselves, palisades represented a great investment in labour and were built and regularly maintained to last through many years. But the village, as a built environment, reflected a community's dynamism and changing composition. Over time it underwent episodes of expansion and contraction as needed to accommodate the arrival and departure of families and groups.[10]

Around the village lay the clearing. Iroquoian agriculture was of the slash-and-burn or swidden variety – anthropologists and historians have tended to use the term horticulture, to distinguish it from farming that makes use of the plow, but this term tends to underestimate its scale and productivity. Controlled fire was used in combination with axes to open space for cultivation and simultaneously increase the fertility of the soil through the addition of ash. An expanse of fields was prepared immediately adjacent to the village, but it was also common for other plots to be worked in convenient sites at a short distance in the woods. In the ash-enriched soil, Iroquoian women grew the distinctive triad they knew as the "three sisters": maize, beans, and squash. Maize grew first, allowing beans to twine themselves up its stalks, while squash thrived about its base, with its broad leaves choking out competing weeds and reducing evaporation, and with its prickly vines dissuading vermin. The bean plants returned to the soil some of the nitrogen leached out by the maize. In addition to growing well together, these three staple crops complemented each other nutritionally to form the core of a balanced diet. Sunflower too was grown for its seeds and oil, and tobacco for its ceremonial and social roles. But maize, because of its high yield and caloric density, was the foundation of Wendat and Iroquois subsistence. Pounded into flour or soaked to make hominy, it was made into soups, mush, and bread. Dried, shelled, and placed in large bark containers in the longhouses' storage areas and in underground storage pits, it could provide sustenance from one harvest to the next, and serve as insurance against the droughts, frosts, and insects that occasionally spoilt a year's crop. Maize was, as European observers put it, the "sole staff of life" and the "the chief of their riches."[11]

Subsistence activities followed an annual cycle that divided the work of women and men, and reconciled agriculture with hunting, fishing, and gathering. As soon as the snow melted in early spring, men, having already killed many of the trees by girdling them, laboured to turn forests into fields, removing vegetation with fire and blades. Towards the end of May, women took over, preparing the ash-enriched soil with digging sticks and hoes in order to seed it. Women continued to tend the crops throughout the summer before gathering them in late August or early September. In addition to planting, maintaining, and harvesting the fields, women made forays beyond the village to gather berries, roots, and other edibles, and to collect firewood. Tending the fires of the longhouse and cooking the meals was also their responsibility. Men typically left the village during the warm season to hunt and fish, and to undertake military, commercial, and diplomatic expeditions. Hunting and fishing occurred year-round, but the most productive seasons for both were fall and early winter (October to December) and late winter to early spring (February to March). While the great majority of women and children remained in the village from spring to the early fall, it was not unusual for them to accompany men to hunting and fishing camps in the late fall and early spring, with the effect that villages were at times nearly emptied. During periods away from the longhouse, Iroquoian hunting and fishing bands lived in temporary bark shelters similar to the wigwams of their northern Algonquian neighbours. But the longhouses offered a welcomed comfort in the cold of winter – and whereas wintertime was for the Innu and Algonquins an essential hunting season, the Wendats and Iroquois were less reliant on it, and could subsist on the agricultural reserves accumulated during the warm season. With spring, the basic cycle of agriculture and excursions began anew.[12]

These generalizations considered, seventeenth-century European references to the rhythm of the Iroquoian subsistence cycle are not always consistent. As one Jesuit missionary working among the Senecas during the late 1660s observed, with some exasperation and perhaps exaggeration, "the greater part of the people who belong to the villages […] are at war, or out hunting, during *nine* months of the year."[13] Such observations suggest that the timing and intensity at which particular activities were carried out varied somewhat from community to community and, in response to the failure of a crop or the scale of a war, from year to year. As the century wore on, the European fur trade may also have had an impact on traditional subsistence patterns, inducing the winter hunt – the time of year when beaver is easiest to catch, and when its pelt is thickest – to take on greater importance for Iroquoians than previously.

While the "forest" – the space of hunting, warfare, and diplomacy – was considered in Iroquoian thought to be a male symbolic domain, the "clearing" – the space of residence and agriculture – was considered to be a female one. The central economic role of Iroquoian women as agricultural producers vested them with a singular social standing. "Nothing is more real [...] than the women's superiority," observed Joseph-François Lafitau, the Jesuit missionary and protoethnographer, in his description of the Iroquois. All of this could have been said of Wendat women too. "It is they who really maintain the tribe, the nobility of the blood, the genealogical tree, the order of generations and conservation of the families. In them resides all the real authority: the lands, fields and all their harvest belong to them; they are the souls of the councils, the arbiters of peace and war; they hold the axes and the public treasure; it's to them that the slaves are entrusted; they arranged the marriages; the children are under their authority; and the order of succession is founded on their blood." Men cleared fields and built longhouses, but these spaces belonged to women.[14]

An individual's role within the community was shaped by gender, age, and kinship relations. In Iroquoian society an individual was at once a member of a nuclear family, a lineage, and a clan, and belonged to a village, a nation, and a confederacy. The lineage was the basic unit of society. Made up of one or more senior women and her progeny, it was, more precisely, a matrilineage: descent was matrilineal, meaning that an individual was considered to belong to the same kin group as her or his mother; residential patterns were matrilocal, meaning that brothers and sons usually left their mothers' houses for those of their wives, even though they continued to belong to the lineage and clan of their birth. Households, and villages by extension, consisted in essence of related women living out their lives beside each other, together with a fringe of spouses from other lineages and their common children. Those women who stood out most by a combination of seniority and competence headed the lineage – within each house the senior woman was the authority – and, as clan matrons, presided over yet another key unit of Iroquoian socio-political organization. Clans drew groups of lineages together, forming an extended matrilineal family. Every nation was made up of three to nine clans, each of which had in each community its separate leaders and council of elders. While clan cohesion was strongest within the village community and the nation, the sense of kinship that it fostered stretched beyond them. The Bear, Deer, and Turtle Clans, most notably, could be found in all of the Iroquois and Wendat nations.[15]

Men conducted the political and diplomatic affairs of the village, nation, and confederacy. Iroquoian women's authority is comparatively discrete in the historical record, notwithstanding the observations of Lafitau and other attentive colonial chroniclers. Missionaries and colonial officials, as men, were rarely privy to the councils and exchanges in which women shaped the destinies of their communities. Moreover, coming from a world where political power was the prerogative of men, they were not well conditioned to appreciate the ways in which female and male leadership complemented and supported each other.

Much of what has been noted in the previous chapter regarding the character of leaders in Algonquian societies can also be taken to apply to their Iroquoian counterparts. Wendat and Iroquois chiefs commanded the respect of their people from a combination of achievement, heredity, and election. They exercised their authority only insofar as they acted upon consensus within their community, or succeeded in facilitating it. Villages often had more than one civil headman or peace chief, often referred to in English writings by the Algonquian loan-word *sachem*. These individuals were ritually installed for life and their nomination rested on genealogical considerations. They were selected within specific lineages, which for this reason were especially honoured, and upon their death a successor was typically chosen by leading matrons in consultation with other women from among his sister's sons. The chief's house – or, more properly, that of his matrilineage – tended to be larger than the others in the village, so as to serve as a meeting place for councils, for ceremonies, and entertainment. Another category of chief, whose standing was not hereditary, derived its status from skill at council oratory and achievement on the warpath – yet these men too depended on the support of leading women, who presided over both their recognition and censure. It would appear that throughout the seventeenth century, population losses due to epidemic diseases had the effect of eroding traditional power structures by allowing young war chiefs to take on some of the roles of civil chiefs, and to exercise an unprecedented importance in their peoples' political and external affairs.[16]

In grappling with the political structure of the Wendats upon his arrival in their homeland in 1638, Jesuit superior Jérôme Lalemant spoke of "four nations, or rather four different collections or assemblages of grouped family stocks – all of whom, having a community of language, of enemies, and of other interests, are hardly distinguishable except by their different progenitors, grandfathers, and great-grandfathers, whose names and memories they cherish tenderly. They increase or diminish their numbers, however, by the adoption of other families, who join themselves now to some, now to others, and who also sometimes withdraw to form a band and a nation by themselves."[17] Apart from the readily apparent inaccuracy – the progenitors that mattered were grandmothers and great-grandmothers, not their husbands – the statement captures the organic character of the nation and confederacy among Wendats and Iroquois alike. The Iroquoian nation – peoples who shared a common culture, language, and extended kinship bonds – occupied a cluster of neighbouring villages. There was a good deal of porosity between communities of the same nation, encouraged by the cross-cutting ties of family. Matrilocal residence patterns meant that men might find a wife and a new home in a village different from that of their birth, but that they maintained obligations to members of their matrilineage, that is, to their mothers, sisters, and sisters' children. Clan membership meant that individuals had extended kin in other villages, both within their own nation and beyond.

By the time of contact with Europeans in the early seventeenth century, the Iroquoian nations who occupied what is today Ontario and New York were also united at a higher level of political organization, that of the league or confederacy. As noted earlier, the Wendat Confederacy was composed of four nations, or perhaps five: the Attignawantan (People of the Bear), Attigneenongnahac (People of the Cord), Arendarhonon (People of the Rock), Tahontaenrat (People of the Deer), and Ataronchronon (People of the Marshes, who may have been a division of the Attignawantan rather than a distinct constitutive nation). The first two were accorded senior status as founding members and largest nations of the confederacy; the Attignawatan alone occupied half the seats on the confederacy council. This council of the Wendats is less well understood than that of the Iroquois, but it appears to have brought together most of the civil headmen of each nation.[18]

The fact that the term "Wendats," as *Hoüandate*, *8endat*, or *Ouendat*, appears more rarely in the early *Relations* than do the names of individual nations is indicative of the way in which localized identities mattered most.[19] The same was true of the Five Nations who had been united into a confederacy through the mythical action of the Great Peacemaker Deganawida and the prophet Hiawatha: Mohawk (*Kanien'kehá:ka*, "People of the Flint"), Oneida (*Onyota'a:ka*, "People of the Standing Stone"), Onondaga (*Onöñda'gega'* "People of the Hills"), Cayuga (*Gayogohó:no'* "People of the Great Swamp"), and Seneca (Onöndowága, "People of the Hills," like the Onondaga). A sixth, the Tuscarora, would join them in the early eighteenth century. Together, these Iroquois nations were called the *Rotinonsionni* or *Haudenosaunee*, in reference to the symbolic longhouse that gathered the nations. The confederacy council of the Iroquois usually met at Onondaga, the principal village of the central nation, and was made up of hereditary chiefs from each of the constituent nations.[20]

Iroquois and Wendat confederacy-wide councils each gathered periodically for feasts and discussions, bringing together leading men of different nations and giving them an opportunity to reaffirm old friendships and to discuss subjects of mutual interest. These confederacies provided their constituent nations with mechanisms to prevent disputes from erupting between them and for settling grievances without resorting to bloodshed. But they remained loosely knit formations. It was at the level of the lineage and the village, and secondarily at the level of the nation, that leadership manifested itself and that political and military support could be mustered and coordinated. By the mid-seventeenth century the Iroquois and the Wendats were each united in a way that allowed them to maintain internal peace and turn violence outward, but neither confederacy possessed the means of elaborating and carrying out a unified foreign policy.[21]

The fact that local communities – not the Wendats or the Iroquois as ethnic wholes – were the basic unit of political action is a key to understanding the patterns of conflict and migration outlined in this and subsequent chapters. Iroquoian mobility is a second key. Although village dwellers, the Wendats and the Iroquois were sedentary only in a relative sense. As noted above, the rhythm of the seasons drew community members away from their villages, whether to hunt, fish, and gather their subsistence, or to trade, wage war, and make peace with neighbours. Moreover, families and individuals occasionally relocated from one community to another, and communities themselves shifted their location on a regular basis. It was the norm for individuals to live at a succession of two or three sites during the course of their lifetime, perhaps even more. Alluding to the social and cultural centrality of this pattern, one seventeenth-century Mohawk dictionary transcribed the word *tekanatakwa*, as "lift the camp, transport the village, move, emigrate."[22]

Owing to a variety of factors, such relocations usually occurred every ten to twenty years, though some villages stayed in place for as long as half a century. Chief among these factors was the exhaustion of local resources. Swidden agriculture enriched the soil in the short and medium term, but in the long run it had a detrimental effect. The need to travel increasingly further from the village to find firewood and trees and bark suitable for house and palisade maintenance was another issue. In a way that emphasized continuity, the name of a village was sometimes transferred from the old site to the new one, just as the names of individuals were reused within the lineage. Village relocation was typically a gradual process. Time was allowed to make advance preparations at the new site: to clear new fields and build new structures, before the old ones were entirely abandoned; and perhaps to move the poles of houses and palisades, as well as bark sheeting, from one site to the other. Communities often retained a strong sense of affiliation with their former residence location. It was not uncommon for a village site and associated fields to be reoccupied several generations after they had been abandoned, once soil fertility and suitable firewood had been sufficiently replenished to support a community.[23]

Socio-political circumstances, not just soil exhaustion and resource depletion, led to the relocation and reconfiguration of communities. Insofar as Iroquoian communities depended on consensus, and as disagreements were more frequent in large villages, it was not uncommon for a segment of the community, usually one or several lineages, to splinter and join another village or form a new one. Crop shortages and epidemics may have contributed to encouraging large communities to divide into smaller ones; the wartime influx of refugees or captives, after swelling a community's population, often resulted in its division in the longer term. Unsurprisingly, the migrations, fusions, and fission of communities prompted by war were the most dramatic. Champlain observed that in normal circumstances a village relocated only one to three leagues away, but that "when forced by their enemies to decamp [they] move to a greater distance," citing a nation that had moved some forty to fifty leagues, or over two hundred kilometers.[24]

Village relocations and reconfigurations were often prompted by the dream of an influential community member, but such dreams can be assumed to have occurred or to have been acted upon in response to the sort of pressures described above. In reality, resettlement occurred only after serious deliberation within a community. In normal circumstances a new village site was prepared long before the old was abandoned, although the perils of wartime brought about departures that were more rushed. At such times, male chiefs, responsible as they were for military affairs and better equipped to gauge an enemy threat, may have had a particular influence on the decision-making process. A Jesuit observed how, as the Iroquois warriors and diplomats were closing in on Huronia, a council was held after which "the Captains went through the streets, urging the women to begin pounding their Indian corn, and collecting their provisions – to be ready to start in three days," and that the "the women set to work to do what they were commanded."[25] As a rule, however, the will of women was paramount. As stressed earlier, the household, the village, and the fields around them were spaces over which women's authority prevailed, and it follows that the decision to abandon one site in favour of another would have been of utmost concern to them. As keepers of the lineage, women had the principal stake in the relocation or reconfiguration of the household. And while men may have been best equipped to identify a new village site on the basis of its defensible qualities and of the ease with which longhouses and a palisade might be built there, these were secondary factors. Women were best prepared to judge a site's agricultural potential – its very ability to sustain a village.

Women's crucial leadership in the formation and relocation of communities is captured in the creation stories of the Wendats and Iroquois, according to which the first woman – variously called Awenhai, Ataensic, Otsitsa, Iagnetci, or Sky Woman – fell from the heavens onto the back of a giant turtle, in effect bringing her descendants from the Sky World to Earth. More concretely, this leadership was illustrated in a story that, in the early eighteenth century, some Mohawks told the Jesuit Pierre-Joseph Lafitau about the origin of their nation. Their ancestors, they explained, "wandered a long time under the leadership of a woman named Gaihonariosk. This woman led them all through the north of America. [...] she stopped at last at Agnié [Mohawk] where the climate seemed to her more temperate and the lands more suitable for cultivation. She then divided the lands for cultivation and thus founded a colony which has maintained itself ever since."[26]

***

War was an integral and cyclical part of life, among Iroquoians and Algonquians alike, as it was for early modern Europeans. Modern ethnography, and its underlying evolutionary typologies, has tended to have a distorting effect by presenting some social and cultural features and patterns as quintessentially Iroquois or, somewhat more broadly, Iroquoian. Yet Iroquoians and Algonquians of the Northeastern Woodlands had more in common than is often assumed, and a measure of generalization is possible.[27] War's deepest roots could be found in a people's will to survive and prosper, to achieve balance in their environment, to maintain group unity and autonomy, to protect and improve material circumstances in changing conditions. Though the need to secure access to limited resources and maintain freedom of movement along trade routes tended to translate into hostile intergroup relations, the parties involved did not tend to think about violent conflict in this way. Instead, it was the real or imagined transgressions of outsiders – ranging from the killing, wounding, or capture of a relative, to suspicions of sorcery, thievery or trespassing, and to a variety of breaches of protocol and public insults – that provided the proximate causes of war. Where a high degree of mutual understanding, positive reciprocity, and regular intermarriage characterized intergroup relations, minor affronts might be tolerated and more serious grievances could be resolved peacefully through symbolic and material compensations. Where there existed a long history of strained relations, of mutual contempt, suspicion, or fear, communities easily tipped into a cycle of violence.[28]

The noncoercive structures of Iroquoian and Algonquian societies, coupled with the dynamic relation that existed between personal autonomy and collective responsibility, made for particularly volatile intergroup relations. Individual warriors could raid without the sanction of their chiefs and elders, who had no power beyond persuasion to prevent from taking violent action those who nursed vengeful feelings or who thirsted for the prestige that feats of arms imparted. As such, there existed two interrelated and often blurred levels of intergroup aggression: one characterized by the sporadic, back and forth raids of small war parties; the other, by the involvement of entire communities, often of a broader network of allies, and by the fielding of veritable armies. Large-scale mobilization of the latter type was preceded by long periods of public discussion and argument, during which speakers tried to achieve consensus by shaping perceptions and invoking common values in a way that focused negative opinion on the enemy, assigned blame on them for recent transgressions, and recalled more distant ones, making war a moral duty for community members.[29]

Kinship structures, beyond serving as the basic organizing principle of daily life and a context for biological and social reproduction, provided the basis for the cooperative effort required to carry out war. Although speakers at war councils, like warriors, were invariably male, Algonquian and Iroquoian women played an important role in the waging of war and the cultivation of peace. Women could instigate a raid by urging their men on, challenging their honour, and requesting that they prove their masculinity by protecting their dependents or by humiliating the enemy. Beyond that, divergent means of reckoning kinship and subsistence patterns translated into differences as to how war was conducted. Among Iroquoians, the concentration of population in village communities as well as the cross-cutting ties of matrilineality and matrilocality facilitated extensive cooperation among men, making possible the mobilization of larger forces and long-distance warfare more feasible.[30] Iroquoian women, moreover, as clan leaders and agricultural labourers, played a more decisive role in the making of war and peace than their Algonquian counterparts. Though Iroquois or Wendat warriors could set out with hostile intent on their own initiative, it was the prerogative of clan matrons to request action in response to the death of a clan member. Conversely, when they judged a given warlike project to be foolhardy or otherwise detrimental to the community, women could hinder the activity of warriors by restricting their access to the supplies of corn meal required to carry out any campaign.[31]

Despite the rhetoric of killing which permeated speeches and stories, wars in the Indigenous northeast were fundamentally wars of capture. A warrior's greatest prize was to return with a living enemy. Whatever scalps could be brought back were valued as war trophies, tangible proof of military accomplishment and spiritually charged objects of power. They were, however, of only secondary value, as a stand-in for human beings.[32] Captives, on the other hand, could serve an array of purposes. They could be used to mediate intergroup relations: one might be sent back as an envoy to convey a message designed to appease the enemy or to humiliate him; be released as a sign of goodwill and an invitation to peace; be offered as a diplomatic gift to draw a third party into the war; or be retained as a hostage. Equally significantly, captives provided a means of dealing with the emotional distress of death among the captors' people. Torture, often leading up to execution, was very often the culmination of the war party's effort. It was an occasion that allowed noncombatants – the elderly, children, adolescent men, and most significantly women – to partake in the defeat and humiliation of their foes. An entire society was given the opportunity to demonstrate its superiority over its adversaries and signal its ferocity to potential enemies. Individuals who had lost a loved one to the enemy were meanwhile afforded the opportunity of purging their grief. The tormenting of captives, observed Lafitau, was "a thing which each one does with more or less fury according as he is more or less aroused by the losses caused him by the war."[33]

Captives who represented less of a threat, women and children in the main, would most often be allowed to live and be given the opportunity to join their captors' community. Here again, the range of possibilities reflected the distinctive social organizations and subsistence patterns of Algonquians and Iroquoians. For Innu, Algonquins, and northern Wabanaki peoples, whose basic social unit was the highly mobile, atomistic family band, and whose reliance on hunting required a great deal of flexibility and meant that they periodically lived on the edge of starvation, captives represented something of a liability. Accordingly, these societies tended to be selective about who they kept alive and sought to assimilate. More often than not, captive adults appear to have been treated as slaves, as liminal individuals devoid of kinship relations, who had no basis for claiming reciprocal obligations and whom no one would avenge. If the captive's labour proved unsatisfactory, he or she could be killed by his or her master without fear of repercussion. But captives might otherwise be well treated. Those who demonstrated a willingness to reject their former lives and identities and to develop affective ties to their captors would be incorporated into the group as kin through either marriage or adoption as the child or sibling of a household head.[34]

For Iroquoians more than for Algonquians, then, warfare was a distinctly incorporative endeavour. Agricultural abundance made it less of a luxury to maintain captives alive, and semisedentary village life pro-

Figure 3.1 Two victorious Iroquois (Seneca) warriors returning with a captive and two scalps, drawn by the Jesuit missionary Pierre-Joseph-Marie Chaumonot. (Detail from ANOM, Fonds des Colonies, C11A 2: 263, "Mémoire au sujet des neuf familles qui composent la nation," ca. 1666)

vided a more conducive context for their management and assimilation. Matrilineal clans structured the experience of captivity. As noted earlier, it was a clan matron's prerogative to request action when a member of her clan had been killed by outsiders. It was to the grieving matrilineages that captives were distributed, and up to them to determine their fate through internal consultation. A captive who seemed an improper candidate for adoption would be tortured to death, or alternatively maintained in a precarious state of slavery. A captive who showed more promise would meanwhile be adopted as a new member of the lineage and given the opportunity to assimilate into his or her new family's society, replacing symbolically and literally a dead relative.[35] From a functionalist perspective, the extent to which intergroup conflict provided northern Iroquoian societies with a means of dealing with death on both a psychological and demographic level has prompted ethnohistorians after Daniel Richter to label this broad pattern of behaviour and belief a "mourning war complex."[36]

Among Iroquoians, both ritual execution and adoption served an emotional need to alleviate grief and demonstrated a will to incorporate outsiders into the community. Both Iroquois and Wendats, even as they tormented a captive to the point of death, would address the victim using kinship terms such as "uncle" or "nephew." The cannibalism with which such executions culminated offered an opportunity to absorb the enemy's spiritual power, in an extension of cultural values associated with the incorporation of others (the Iroquois's Algonquian neighbours to the east and north, it should be noted, did not practise cannibalism and feared their enemy all the more for it). The rhetoric that surrounded the attack and destruction of enemy nations was itself replete with metaphors of incorporation through mutilation and consumption. Among the usual figures of speech for making war or peace among the Iroquois was the setting up or breaking of the war kettle, the vessel in which captives were cooked, literally and metaphorically. To destroy an enemy settlement translated as *gannatagarien* in Mohawk: "to eat a village." Another expression, *we-hait-wat-sha*, used by the Onondagas in relation to their seventeenth-century captives, as recalled by one nineteenth-century informant of the ethnologist Henry Rowe Schoolcraft, meant "a body cut into parts and scattered around. In this manner, they figuratively scattered their prisoners, and sunk and destroyed their nationality, and built up their own."[37]

***

It is convenient, but often misleading, to think of the midcentury wars merely as wars between "the Iroquois" and "the Hurons," not only because they involved other peoples, but because war was a fundamentally local matter, and patterns of conflict and incorporation were shaped by specific solidarities. As the Jesuit Paul Le Jeune observed, the Iroquois certainly did have a tendency to "lend a hand to one another in their wars."[38] Yet as this chapter and the next demonstrate, throughout this period, effectively concerted military or diplomatic action involving more than a few constituent nations was the exception rather than the norm.

Divergences were readily apparent in the Iroquois offensive. The thrust of the 1640s against the Wendats was spearheaded by the Senecas, Cayugas, and Onondagas. It was not until the fall of 1646 that the Mohawks and Oneidas, who had until then had focused their own energies on the Algonquians of the Saint Lawrence valley and east of the Hudson River, joined in the offensive against Huronia. Then, by late 1647, tensions surfaced between the Onondagas, who with Caygua and Oneida support were willing to make peace with their enemy, and the Mohawks, who with Seneca support were set against it. During the winter that followed, a group of Mohawks scuttled the possibility of accommodation by ambushing a Wendat embassy on its way to Onondaga country. Through 1648 and 1649, the Onondagas, Cayugas, and Oneidas persisted in seeking peace, whereas the Mohawks and Senecas carried out a massive and critical assault on Huronia. It was only towards the end of 1649, with the total defeat of the Wendat Confederacy in sight, that the Onondagas returned to the fray.[39] Competition between the League's western and eastern nations over the privilege of incorporating the survivors would persist for at least a decade.

In the same way, the paths of the constituent nations of the Wendat Confederacy – the Attignawantan, Attigneenongnahac, Arendarhonon, Tahontaenrat, and Ataronchronon – diverged and converged under pressure from the Iroquois. In 1647, while the Attignawantan were willing to put up armed resistance and for that purpose sought the alliance of the Susquehannocks of what is now southern New York, Pennsylvania, and Maryland, it was the Arendarhonon under the leadership of their principal headman Jean-Baptiste Atironta who entered into peace negotiations with the Onondagas.[40] It may be that the Attignawantan, as the oldest and largest segment of the Wendat Confederacy, of which until recently they had represented a good half numerically, and whose political affairs they still tended to dominate, were more confident in their ability to match arms with the enemy. Conversely, the Arendarhonon had a smaller population and occupied the exposed eastern frontier of Huronia, towards Lake Simcoe, making them less able to sustain a drawn-out conflict and more inclined to parley.[41]

The wave of Mohawk and Seneca attacks in 1647 left no doubt that the Arendarhonon were especially vulnerable. Before the year was over they were compelled to abandon their villages and seek refuge in other Wendat communities, primarily those of the Attigneenongnahac, the second oldest and second most important nation of the confederacy. The following year, however, the latter were in turn beset by Mohawk and Seneca warriors. In 1649, the Attigneenongnahac villages that had held out were overrun, as were those of the Ataronchronon. Droves sought refuge at the Jesuit mission of Sainte Marie, but were forced to seek it elsewhere when it too was assaulted.[42]

The palisaded compound of Sainte Marie, on the Wye River (today Midland, Ontario), had been the base of Jesuit operations in Huronia since 1639, and the missionaries and their lay personnel numbered a little over sixty men. They could offer little material and defensive assistance during the invasion, and what they did offer was intimately tied to the spiritual aid that they dispensed. While the number of baptisms administered should by no means be interpreted as a measure of the thoroughness with which beliefs and practices were accepted by the Wendats, it does leave a clear impression of the pace at which the latter increasingly turned to the French for assistance during this period of crisis. By the spring of 1646, it is estimated that about five hundred Wendats considered themselves to be Christians; from the spring of 1646 to the end of winter 1647, another five hundred were baptized; another eight hundred in 1647–48; over seventeen hundred more in 1648–49, and again as many as that through the summer and fall of 1649.[43] The reluctance, calculation, and impulsivity that factored into the decision of turning to the missionaries after having rebuffed their advances for so many years varied from one individual to the next. It was an act of self-preservation, filled with desperation and hope.

At the same time, men, women, and children crossed over to the Iroquois by the thousands, individually and in groups of various sizes. This too was an act of self-preservation. To accept the enemy's invitations was the surest way to survive, an ultimate resort to avoid certain death on the battlefield or at the stake. No doubt many of the people who crossed over thought of it as a temporary solution, insofar as they may have hoped to make an escape as soon as favourable circumstances presented themselves, or expected that within a few years their Iroquois hosts would allow them to leave on their own terms. All were not equally reluctant, however, for there was among the "enemy" an ever-growing number of friends and relatives.

Already before the campaigns of the 1640s, as a result of earlier conflicts and peacetime encounters, individuals of Wendat origin could be found residing among the Iroquois and, to a lesser extent, vice versa.[44] We can speculate that the spiritual kinship of clan structures played a role in the social integration of these voluntary migrants. Wendat men and women belonging to the Turtle, Wolf, Bear, Beaver, Deer, and Hawk Clans would presumably have recognized a special affinity to the Iroquois who belonged to the clans of the same name, and vice versa.[45] For Wendats staunchly opposed to the growing influence of Jesuit missionaries and to their countrymen's appropriation of the newcomer's religion, relocation to Iroquoia offered a means of holding on to a traditional way of life and the stability that they associated with it. Many of the Wendats in Iroquoia whom colonial chroniclers were quick to label "slaves," "captives," or "renegades" might more accurately be thought of as refugees. Among their Iroquois hosts they proclaimed that it was the Christian faith and prayer which "had attracted all sorts of misfortunes on their nation, which had infected it with contagious diseases, which had made their hunting and fishing less productive than when they lived following their ancient customs."[46]

The ever-growing presence of Wendats in Iroquoia, ranging from enthusiastic refugees to unwilling captives, had a snowball effect. As two chiefs explained to their missionaries in the spring of 1650, many of their people had among the Iroquois "a great number of relatives who wish for them, and counsel them to make their escape as soon as possible from a desolated country if they do not wish to perish beneath its ruins." Similarly, a few years later, a Mohawk orator argued to a group of Wendats that they would find in his villages "their kinsfolk who had been formerly carried away captive, and who bore their absence only with regret and inconsolable sadness. He said they were waiting for them with love, and would receive them with joy."[47]

Most dramatically, the Tahontaenrats and a large number of Arendarhonon, after failing to find safety among the Neutrals, a neighbouring Iroquoian people, would give themselves over freely to the Senecas and collectively resettle among them in 1651. Describing the results of this migration, the Jesuit superior Paul Ragueneau noted that these Wendats "now live as peacefully" with the Senecas "as if they had never been at war." Instead of joining preexisting communities these migrants formed a satellite village apart from those of the Senecas where they lived, according to Paul Le Jeune, "satisfied to be united with them in good feeling and friendship."[48] One of the advantages of collective, voluntary resettlement, thus, was the possibility of retaining a distinctive cultural identity, and no doubt a measure of political autonomy. Perhaps these Wendat migrants hoped or expected, in time, to be formally recognized and integrated within the Iroquois League on equal footing with its other five constituent nations – to associate with them, rather than be assimilated by them.

***

As the villages of Huronia fell one by one, their harried inhabitants evaluated their options. Famine, and the vulnerability to disease that malnutrition entailed, compounded the woes of war. While many Wendat men and women chose to "to throw themselves into the arms of the enemy" individually or in groups during the assault on their desolated homeland, others remained intent on avoiding incorporation among the Iroquois. Some scattered in small groups in the forests north of Lake Huron or west towards Lake Michigan and Lake Superior, while others sought refuge in vain among neighbouring Iroquoian groups, the Tionnontaté (Petuns), Neutrals, and Eries. A few even contemplated finding refuge among their distant Susquehannock allies to the south, in what is today Pennsylvania.[49] It is in this diasporic context that many resolved to cast their lot with the French, relocating first within Huronia, and eventually to the Saint Lawrence valley and the vicinity of Quebec.

For a people to seek temporary or permanent refuge in the arms of a friendly nation, even a distant one, was not an uncommon occurrence in the Great Lakes region, or for that matter throughout Indigenous North America. This pattern represented an extension of the notions of hospitality and of the mutual obligations that undergirded alliance, friendship, and trade. Missionaries had witnessed the prevalence of this firsthand. In 1639, in a bid to avoid defeat at the hands of the Iroquois, six hundred Wenros from the south shore of Lake Ontario negotiated their move to Huronia. As Paul Ragueneau would explain:

> It is customary among these peoples, even with the unbelievers, that, when a nation seeks refuge in any foreign country, those who receive them immediately distribute them over different households, where they not only give them lodging, but also the necessities of life [...]. I have very often seen this hospitality practiced among the Hurons: as many times as we have seen nations devastated, or villages destroyed, or some fugitive people, seven or eight hundred persons would find, as soon as they arrived, benevolent hosts, who stretched out to them their arms, and assisted them with joy, who would even divide among them a share in lands already sown, in order that they might be able to live, although in a foreign country, as in their motherland.[50]

The idea of living in the Saint Lawrence valley was not entirely new either. Towards the end of the sixteenth century, the Wendats had absorbed some of the Saint Lawrence Iroquoians. As with the Algonquins of the Ottawa River discussed in the previous chapters, it is certain that some of them maintained intergenerational memories of village life along the Saint Lawrence River. Though the seventeenth-century sources make no suggestion that the refugees harboured a sense that they were returning to ancestral territories, statements recorded in later years hint that this may have been the case. In 1773, one of the leaders of the Wendats of Lorette, near Quebec, one of the several communities descended from the Wendat diaspora, declared to a British deputy superintendent of Indian Affairs that they were regarded by all other Indigenous nations as the "original proprietors of this country." Three years later, a German visitor to the same community elicited from its members the explanation that their people had "by many and bloody wars with the neighboring Indian nations and with Europeans, lost all their land [...] Formerly, their land extended from the Island of Orleans, on the St. Lawrence, to Montreal." In the nineteenth century, the members of another community descended from this diaspora, the Wyandots of Anderdon, Ontario, held that their ancestors had in distant times inhabited "a country north-eastward from the mouth of the St. Lawrence, somewhere along the gulf coast," and that subsequently they had villages in the vicinity of where Montreal and Quebec were later established. As a result of war, they had migrated westward, from "their ancient homes" to the Great Lakes.[51]

Through the early decades of the seventeenth century, Wendats paddled down the Saint Lawrence on a regular basis to trade with their Algonquian and French allies, and to take part in military operations alongside them. It was not uncommon for them to remain for several months at a time at Quebec, Trois Rivières, or Kamiskouaouangachit, particularly when the onset of winter or enemy blockades delayed their return journey.[52] As early as 1637, the Jesuits dreamt that the handful of Wendats who were receiving religious instruction at Quebec would form the core of a permanent community there, and that within a few years "there would be here a village of Christian Hurons, who would help in no slight degree to bring their compatriots to the faith, through commerce with each other." In these years it was hoped that their sedentary way of life would incite the nomadic Innu and Algonquins to settle down and adopt a more disciplined lifestyle.[53] After the founding of Ville Marie on the Island of Montreal in 1642, some Wendats, like the Ottawa River Algonquins discussed in the previous chapters, showed an interest in resettling there as long as the French were willing and able to provide them with assistance against their Iroquois enemy.[54] Nothing came of it until the Iroquois invasion of Huronia pressed the issue.

***

The journey to the Saint Lawrence valley was by all accounts a Wendat initiative. In early 1649, the Wendats displaced by war assembled at the fortified but increasingly vulnerable mission of Sainte Marie and dispatched one of their captains – the Christianized Arendarhonon chief Jean-Baptiste Atironta, it is almost certain – to Quebec to see if the French might give their assent to their resettlement there and to ask for material assistance to undertake the move.[55] As they awaited a response, most of the community fell back with its missionaries to the nearby island of Gahoendoe or Saint Joseph (today Christian Island, in Georgian Bay), where other Wendats had already taken refuge and where more soon flocked. The hastily fortified mission at Gahoendoe, dubbed Sainte Marie (II), was crowded; Ragueneau, overestimating by perhaps a few thousands, claimed that its population reached a hundred cabins, each of which contained sixty to eighty persons, or between six and eight thousand in all. After enduring a winter of great famine and unrelenting enemy depredations during which many perished, the majority intended to disperse in small groups through the forest, among distant nations, or, with resignation, cross over to the enemy. Some leaders, however, fearing that "the greater number will meet their death where they hope to find life," and wishing to maintain a measure of social cohesion among their people, were intent on preventing this dispersion.[56]

In May or June 1650, before Atironta had even returned from Quebec with an answer as to the French stance on his people's migration, the refugees of Gahoendoe convened a major council to discuss the situation. As a result, two of the eldest captains, said to represent about six hundred persons, approached Father Ragueneau. "My brother, take courage," the unnamed men pleaded. "You alone can bestow upon us life, if you will strike a daring blow. Choose a place where you may be able to reassemble us, and prevent this dispersion. Cast your eyes toward Quebec, and transport thither the remnants of this ruined nation. Do not wait until famine and war have slain the last of us. [...] If you listen to our wishes, we will build a Church under shelter of the fort at Quebec. There, our faith will not die out; and the examples of the Algonquins and of the French will hold us to our duty. Their charity will alleviate, in part, our miseries."[57]

Whether or not this speech was an accurate reflection of the speakers' religious conviction, the request was couched in terms that were bound to appeal to the Jesuit missionaries at Gahoendoe. After much consultation and prayer for divine guidance, the latter concluded that "God had spoken to us by the lips of these captains," and that the time had come to undertake a speedy retreat towards the Saint Lawrence valley. Approximately three hundred Wendats, described as "almost all [...] Christians," left in the company of their missionaries on 10 June 1650. Betraying some doubt that this hasty eastward journey was the wisest course of action, the other three hundred who had also expressed an interest promised to follow after the harvest.[58]

The route up Lake Huron to the French River, up to Lake Nipissing, down the Mattawa and Ottawa Rivers, to the Saint Lawrence and then on to Quebec, took roughly fifty days. Passing along the Island of Montreal and contemplating the area's advantages, this first group of refugees gave some thought to establishing themselves there but decided against it owing to its exposure to the enemy. They reached Quebec on 28 July.[59]

***

Having reached Quebec, most of the Wendat refugees erected their longhouses in the Upper Town between the Ursulines' monastery and the Augustinians' hospital, a short distance from the Jesuits' residence and the governor's seat at Château Saint Louis. About a third of the refugees was taken in by the Augustinians, the Ursulines, and their secular foundress and benefactress Marie-Madeleine de la Peltrie, who had a house nearby, as well as three or four other prominent townspeople. The others established encampments close to the Hôtel Dieu or on the Jesuit estates of Notre Dame des Anges, east of Quebec, and Sillery, at or near the mission of Kamiskouaouangachit.[60] It was with mixed feelings that the French must have welcomed them, for the colony was in the midst of a financial crisis. In addition to years of mismanagement by the Company of New France, that held exclusive rights to the fur trade and ultimate responsibility for the settlement, the Iroquois offensive now shattered the commercial network that until then stretched into the continent's interior. Still, French and Algonquians alike welcomed the refugees. Most certainly the people of Kamiskouaouangachit held a council to welcome the newcomers, whom they recognized as "their Ancestors' allies" and who had become brothers in the Christian faith. "Since I was baptized," explained one of the mission's leaders on another occasion, "it seems to me that I have gained a great many relatives. When I enter the Frenchmen's Church, I am told that the French are my relatives. When I see a baptized Huron, I look upon him as my relative."[61]

Unable to see to their own subsistence for the first several months after their arrival, the Wendats relied heavily on the daily distributions of corn and pea soup by the missionaries and nuns.[62] On 30 December 1650, the refugees who had found some relief at Quebec endured a new and unexpected ordeal when fire broke out at the Ursuline monastery. Spreading from the bakery a few hours after midnight, by morning it left little of the building standing. The nuns and their boarders escaped in their nightclothes, managing to save but a few things. The Wendats shared in the Ursulines' suffering. Over the past year, the nuns had shouldered part of the task of providing for the refugees. Since their arrival a little over a decade ago, they had developed intimate connections with some Wendat families whose girls spent time in their school. Several Wendats had been in the building when the fire started. The father of one girl, who was at first thought to have perished in the flames before being located alive, found solace in religion and in the strength of his relationship to the French. "God sends us a severe trial," he declared, "but it is enough for us that he has had mercy on us and has called us to the faith. My daughter is now in Heaven, since she has been baptized; and we will follow her, because we wish to die good Christians."[63]

The Wendat refugee community as a whole echoed these sentiments, meeting with the Ursulines at the Augustinian convent where they had found shelter after the fire. On behalf of his people, a captain by the name of Louis Taiaeronk addressed the "Holy Virgins." He described their sorry state, their destruction by war and famine: "These carcasses are able to stand only because you support them." "Alas!" he went on, "this sad accident that has happened to you increases our woes and renews our tears." The sight of a house of prayer and charity reduced to ashes in an instant, explained Taiaeronk, had been a bitter reminder of the desolation of their ancestral homeland. It had "brought back to our minds the universal destruction by fire of all our houses, of all our villages, and of the whole of our country. Must fire follow us everywhere? Let us weep, let us weep, my beloved countrymen; yes, let us weep for our misfortunes which were solely ours before, but which we now share in common with these innocent maids." The Ursulines had now been "reduced to the same state of misery as your poor Hurons [...] You are now without a country, without a house, without provisions, and without succor except from Heaven, of which you never lose sight."[64]

It was an opportunity for the Wendat refugees to express their collective grief and gratitude to the Ursulines, and to reciprocate the compassion and charity that they had received from them. They presented the nuns with two large wampum belts, of twelve hundred beads each, which were believed to amount to all of the wampum they had taken with them from their homeland. This gift, even as it was meant to express condolences, was also calculated to prevent the loss of a precious ally. "We fear but one thing which would be a misfortune for us," declared Taiaeronk. "We fear that, when the news of the accident that has happened to you reaches France, it will affect your relatives more than it does yourselves. We fear that they will recall you and that you will be moved by their tears." The reflexes of Iroquoian matrilineality shine through these words. Thinking of the grief that the news would cause the mothers of the nuns back in France, the refugees worried that, "the first thought that nature will inspire in those disconsolate mothers will be to recall you to them, and to procure for themselves the greatest consolation that they can have in the world, thereby procuring also your good. A brother would do the same for his sister, an uncle and an aunt for their niece. And afterward we would be in danger of losing you, and of losing in your persons the assistance for which we had hoped." Taiaeronk and his people urged the nuns to be steadfast: "Do not allow yourselves to be persuaded by love of kindred; and show now that the charity that you have for us is stronger than the ties of nature." Taiaeronk offered the first wampum belt, to "root your feet so deeply in the soil of this country that no love for your kindred or for your own country can withdraw them from it." With the second belt, he asked the nuns to lay the foundation of a new building, a house of prayer, where schooling could resume – as well as the dispensation of both spiritual and material assistance. The echo of the Wendats' own experience is palpable. They had faced this very predicament, not only the destruction of their homes, but also the pressures of kin. In relocating to Quebec, they had resisted the calls, from enemies and kin alike, to withdraw in other directions or to relocate to Iroquoia. "Such are our desires," concluded Taiaeronk, "they are likewise yours, for doubtless you could not die happy if, when dying, this reproach could be cast at you that, through too tender a love for your relatives, you had not contributed to the salvation of so many souls which you have loved for the sake of God, and which will be your crown in Heaven."[65]

The encounter of the Wendats and the Ursulines points to the importance of reciprocity in this story, but also to the underlying significance of women. Although men appear to dominate the discussions and decisions that led a large number of Wendats to the Saint Lawrence valley, this gendered bias is above all a result of the male-generated nature of the colonial record. As stressed earlier in this chapter, women exerted considerable influence in matters of policy and collective decision making, particularly so in matters of dispersal and resettlement, which were intimately linked to their gender's traditional areas of responsibility. The decision to abandon a village site – households, fields, lands – in favour of another one was a central concern for women.[66] It is most certain that behind the actions of such male figures as Jean-Baptiste Atironta or Louis Taiaeronk lay the will of a key number of senior women who believed or at least hoped that their clans would find a safer haven near the French in the Saint Lawrence valley than anywhere else. Though the French chroniclers of this upheaval are singularly inattentive to this fact in their writings, it is fair to suspect that this resettlement involved specific matrilineages and clan segments rather than a mere collection of individuals and nuclear families.[67]

***

Wendat and Jesuit plans in the medium and long term are unclear. The idea of integrating the refugee community with the Algonquians at Kamiskouaouangachit may have been entertained briefly, but in light of the differences between the two neophyte communities this was never attempted. In the spring of 1650, the missionaries considered installing the Wendats on their domain at Notre Dame des Anges, about five kilometers downriver from Quebec. But the governor, the missionaries, and the Wendats themselves instead set their sights on the western tip of the still wooded and thinly populated Island of Orleans in the Saint Lawrence River. Amidst rocky outcrops they selected a sandy cove which, in addition to offering a convenient embarkation point, was well supplied with fresh water by means of a

Figure 3.2 France, in the guise of its regent Queen Anne, brings the Christian faith to the Wendats. While the representation of intercultural relationships, material culture, and Saint Lawrence valley landscape are fanciful, this allegorical painting is indicative of how the French conceptualized their missionary project. (Attributed to Frère Luc, *La France apportant la foi aux Hurons de Nouvelle France*, ca. 1666. Musée des Ursulines de Québec)

small creek. In later years, the site would take on the name of "Anse du Fort" (Fort Cove) in memory of this establishment. In the final week of March 1651, the Wendats, who had been scattered throughout the region, gathered there. A few months later they were joined by the approximately three hundred individuals who initially had remained behind at Gahoendoe, but who after fleeing north to Manitoulin Island now resolved to join their countrymen near Quebec.[68]

To secure the use of the site, the Jesuits had to negotiate with the seigneurs, François de Chavigny de la Chevrotière and Éléonore de Grandmaison. Following their arrival in the colony a decade earlier, the couple had lived for a time in a homestead at Sillery where they were neighbours of the Algonquians of Kamiskouaouangachit. Well connected and in high standing with the colonists, Chavigny then received a seigneury some distance upstream from Quebec and the mission, but in the face of the growing Iroquois threat the couple instead chose to relocate downstream, to the Island of Orleans, in 1648. The following year, they received a second seigneurial grant corresponding to the western tip of the island. Only a few colonists had begun to clear the land here and there around the island, and Grandmaison became the first woman to take up residence among them. Discussions between the Jesuits and the couple must have begun during the winter of 1651 if not earlier, but Chavigny's unexpected death that year left his young widow, Grandmaison, to finalize the arrangement. She agreed to cede to the missionaries and their wards the use of a plot measuring six arpents by ten, but only for the duration of eight years following the initial seeding. Some of this land had already been cleared, but most was still wooded. While compassion towards the refugees may have played a role in the decision, plainly this was a savvy business deal. After her time near Kamiskouaouangachit, Grandmaison well understood the impact of a mission settlement on the landscape. The construction of buildings by the Jesuits' employees, and the clearing of fields by the Wendats would greatly improve the value of her land; their presence also would offer a measure of protection against the enemy. It was not unheard of for a Frenchwoman – and more specifically a widow – to do business in this way, but it was not the norm; yet for the Wendats, it would have seemed only natural for a woman to have a say in the allocation of land. In a spirit of reciprocity, they agreed to assist Grandmaison with her various household chores.[69]

The refugee community that the French took to referring to as the "Huron Colony" quickly made the site on the Island of Orleans its own. In the distance across the water they could see Quebec. They spent the spring and summer of 1651 clearing fields and erecting longhouses, and, though rumours of an impending Iroquois offensive that fall brought them to seek greater safety by encamping in front of Quebec's parish church, they soon returned to the island.[70] The Jesuits had "a redoubt or a sort of fort" constructed there, a wooden enclosure of dimensions comparable to the fort abandoned on

Gahoendoe. Alongside the longhouses therein, they built what they described as a "rather nice" chapel and a small residence, staffed that first year by two missionaries and four domestics.[71] All around, the refugees began working the preexisting fields and clearing new ones. In mid-April 1651, the lands that had already been cleared on behalf of Grandmaison and her late husband were allotted into thirty portions and distributed among them. "All were satisfied," reported the Jesuits, "and sowing was immediately begun." The first year on the island was not easy. Plagued by famine during their last winter in Huronia, the Wendats had brought little to no seed supply to their new location, and must have obtained some from the Jesuits, from French settlers, perhaps even from the people of Kamiskouaouangachit. The missionaries went through great expenses to feed the refugees; the latter nonetheless succeeded in harvesting "a tolerably good quantity" of maize that fall. They expanded their fields, clearing woods by controlled fire and working the ash-enriched soil. Already by the next year, they had begun "to reap as much Indian corn there as they were accustomed to reaping in their own country" – enough of a surplus, in fact, to now supply the Jesuits at Quebec and to trade cornmeal for furs with the Innu at Tadoussac. By 1656, if not earlier, the full sixty arpents set aside for their use on the island had been cleared.[72]

In parallel with their agricultural work, the Wendats continued to hunt, fish, and forage on a seasonal basis. This was made possible by the hospitality of the people of Kamiskouaouangachit and their neighbours, who allowed their insertion within their own territories. In 1824 the grand chief of the Wendats of Lorette, Nicholas Vincent Tsawenhohi, reported that according to the traditions of his elders, almost two hundred years earlier, their people had made "an alliance together to live in peace and in common" with neighbouring Indigenous nations, by which they "should eat with the same spoon in the same plate," meaning that they "should hunt together on the same lands to avoid all squabbles between them."[73] The refugees' claiming of surrounding hunting territories and reclaiming of a key position in the fur trade was as swift as their return to agriculture. Not only did this allow them to improve their material condition, it also enabled them to reciprocate the assistance that they were receiving from the French. One of the missionaries' detractors later wrote that around these years they had managed to earn revenue of as much as ten thousand livres annually from beaver skins – representing up to two thousand pelts – obtained from the Wendats at the Island of Orleans. The Jesuits complained of their "excessive" expenses in their *Relations*: they had anticipated that they would need to spend three thousand livres a year to establish the Wendats near Quebec, but the first year alone it cost them about eight thousand livres to feed them and supply them with hatchets, kettles, clothing, and the other necessities of life. But in reality, such expenses were largely compensated by the neophytes.[74]

***

As the Tionnontatés, Neutrals, and Eries in turn dispersed in the face of the Iroquois offensive through the lower Great Lakes, a number of Wendats who had initially sought refuge among these nations reoriented their hopes towards the Saint Lawrence valley. They continued to trickle into the region, some settling on the Island of Orleans, others instead remaining for a time in the vicinity of Trois Rivières and Montreal to hunt and fish, and plant a little corn. Arrivals were announced that sometimes proved premature, as when, in May 1651, messengers reached Trois Rivières reporting that some of the Tahontaenrat and Arendarhonon, who had been living with the Neutrals, were on their way – there is no evidence that they ever did reach the Saint Lawrence, the bulk relocating instead among the Senecas. By 1653, the total number of these refugees was generously estimated to be between five and six hundred individuals, a population comparable to that of a small- to medium-sized village in Old Wendake, at a time when, to reiterate, the French settlers of the Laurentian colony themselves numbered only some fifteen hundred.[75]

Notwithstanding the tendency of French chroniclers to lump people together under the "Huron" label, this refugee population was necessarily a heterogeneous one. It seems safe to assume that members of lineages and clan segments undertook the journey together, rather than as isolated individuals or nuclear families, but it is difficult to say what clans were more abundantly represented than others. Eight to twelve clans had existed in Old Wendake, of which the Deer, Turtle, Wolf, Bear, Beaver, Snake, Porcupine, and Hawk were the most prominent, but strikingly the clans which moved to the Saint Lawrence valley failed to capture the attention of commentators. Sometime between the middle of the seventeenth century and the end of the eighteenth, the Wendats of Lorette abandoned traditional modes of reckoning kinship in favour of the patrilineal, nuclear family. In the middle of the eighteenth century, one Jesuit missionary, based on his time at Lorette, noted that "there are among the Natives different *bandes* [i.e. clans]," citing as example the Beaver, Bear, Wolf, Deer, Partridge, and Turtle. A military officer visiting a little later wrote that the community was itself divided into three "families," those of the Turtle, the Vulture, and the Wolf. It is unclear whether the Vulture (or more accurately, Hawk) here refers to a clan proper, or if it is the result of a case of mistaken identity following from the title borne by the community's principal chief at the time, who was called Tsaouenhohoui in reference to a bird of prey. By the nineteenth century, members of the community instead recalled affinity to the Bear, Deer, Turtle, and Wolf Clans.[76] We may thus speculate that the bulk of the mid-seventeenth-century migrants belonged to these four clans, and that in the middle- to long-term they absorbed lineages from the clan segments among them that were not so strongly represented. As Wendat society underwent a dramatic scaling down, traditional modes of reckoning kin were adapted to avoid strictures against marrying within one's clan and make it possible to find mates within a small community.

The presence among the mid-seventeenth-century migrants of elements from each of the constituent nations of the Wendat Confederacy is more safely discerned, though in impressionistic rather than numerical terms. The Attignawantan appear to have predominated, as they had been the most numerous nation of the confederacy and the one which included the largest number of Christian converts. Oral tradition recorded among the Wyandots of Anderdon, Ontario, in the late nineteenth century seems to support the idea that the Attignawantan were numerous, for it held that the "portion of them [the Wendats] belonging to the Bear Clan [*sic*: nation]" had left the shores of Lake Huron to relocate near Quebec in the second quarter of the seventeenth century, returning to "their ancient homes" there. The Attigneenongnahac and Arendarhonon were also well represented among the refugee community, even if most of the Arendarhonon had apparently joined the Senecas at the same time as the Tahontaenrat.[77] Though the affiliation of someone like Louis Taiaeronk, who addressed the afflicted Ursulines on behalf of his people, is unknown, the identity of a few other prominent figures is somewhat better documented: Jean-Baptiste Atironta, who travelled to Quebec in 1649–50 to ask for permission to join the French near Quebec, was Arendarhonon; Atsena, who a few years later begins to loom large among the migrants, was a principal chief of the Attignawantan.[78] A handful of individuals also had roots in neighbouring nations: at least one of the leading members of the refugee community, Louis Thaondechoren was described as being "de la nation des Tionontateronons," that is, of Tionnontaté or Petun origins.[79]

As Mohawk and Onondaga warriors and diplomats persisted in their efforts to pursue the fragments of the once powerful Wendat Confederacy into the Saint Lawrence valley, the significance of the old divisions between Attignawantan, Attigneenongnahac, and Arendarhonon would come to the foreground, before fading abruptly thereafter.

4

Promised Lands

Wendat Endurance in the Saint Lawrence Valley, 1651–1666

Addressing the Ursulines after the destruction of their house by fire in 1650, Louis Taiaeronk alluded to "the remnant of a country that once was flourishing and that is no more, the country of the Hurons," and grieved that his people were now "without a country." The same issue of the *Jesuit Relations* that recounted these words reported that, by the summer of the following year, the Wendats installed at the Island of Orleans already "claim[ed] to have found there their second country." They had cleared fields, and erected their longhouses, clustered in a village within what the Jesuits described as a "sort of fort" with a "rather nice" chapel. In the distance, across a stretch of the Saint Lawrence, they could see the town of Quebec.[1]

How, exactly, the Wendats conceptualized this second country is difficult to say. It is possible that they understood this latest relocation as a traumatic continuity, rather than a clean break, within their social and cultural experience. Settling on the Island of Orleans may have felt particularly fitting, given that the literal meaning of their name, Wendats, was "Islanders." In more recent times, the Wendats have known the island as *Lawendawinen Tiatontarehi*, "the island sliding by [*sic*] where the river narrows [i.e. Quebec]," or simply *Ah8endoe*, "the Island," but at the time they took to calling it "the Island of Saint Mary."[2] In so doing, they emphasized the link between this latest home and the defunct missions – Sainte Marie I and II – in their ancestral homeland. The name echoed the importance of matrilineality and matrilocality within Iroquoian society, with the Virgin Mary standing in as mother to the battered Christian community. In 1653, the mission's chapel was formally designated Visitation de Marie in her honour and the missionaries formed a sodality in order to inspire great zeal and emulation, the Congregation of Our Lady. Consisting of ten to twelve members at first, this "elite of the Christians" who deemed themselves "worthy children of the Virgin" swelled rapidly.[3]

The Wendat migrants may very well have considered this region to be ancestral ground, in keeping with the traditions recounted in later centuries. The homecoming, if so, was by no means a joyous one. Distant intergenerational recollections offered little solace compared to the far more vivid and painful memories of the homeland that they had occupied during their lifetime, and where more recent ancestors had lived and were buried. The uprooting had been traumatic. As Taiaeronk explained to the Ursulines, he and his people had had the misfortune of witnessing "the universal destruction by fire of all our houses, of all our villages, and of the whole of our country."[4] No doubt many entertained the idea that their displacement was a temporary circumstance, and that they could in short time return to the shores of Georgian Bay and Lake Simcoe. It soon became clear, however, that a return to the old homeland – which eventually took on the name of Wendake Ehen, translated by missionaries as "La Défunte Huronie," or the "Late Land of the Wendats" – was not an option.[5]

Among the Five Nations, and in particular the Mohawks and Onondagas, the ambition to incorporate the dispersed remnants of the once powerful confederacy – to "remove them [...] either with their consent or by force" – was as strong as ever, and neither the palisade erected on the Island of Orleans nor the small garrison nearby at Quebec guaranteed their safety.[6] The 1650s and early 1660s represented for the Wendat refugees a nadir. The Onondagas and the Mohawks turned to a formal peace with the French and the Wendats as the means by which to compel the latter's migration, but their forceful and often secretive diplomatic overtures came to a head, giving way to a new cycle of violence and coercion. The distinction between enemies and friends was not always an easy one to make in these years. The Wendats, invariably interested in receiving news of their relatives in Iroquoia, parleyed with enemy war parties which often included some of their former countrymen. In keeping with the patterns described in the previous chapter, warriors negotiated with their adversaries as often as they attacked them, and diplomats waged a parallel campaign of seduction and intimidation. As one Mohawk deputy explained to a gathering of Wendats: "Fear not, I no longer look upon you as an enemy, but as my relative. You shall be cherished in my country, which shall also be yours." On another occasion, an Onondaga explained to a Wendat assembly that his country "would be to them a promised land."[7]

The crucial question of the decade following the dispersal would be whether the Wendats would find their land of peace and promise in the Saint Lawrence valley, as they had hoped, or rather in Iroquoia. This question was central not only to the relations of the Wendats and Iroquois, but to the whole geopolitics of the region insofar as the relationship between the French and the Iroquois through these years was largely shaped by the Wendat question.[8] Colonial officials and missionaries proved incapable of offering the security that the Wendats sought, first on the Island of Orleans and, when pressured away from it, in the town of Quebec itself. The Wendats saw their numbers shrink from killings, captures, and reluctant acceptance of Iroquois invitations: the initial three hundred migrants, having swelled to five or six hundred in the decade's first years, were whittled down to perhaps a hundred before its end. For the outstanding majority of the refugees from the shores of Georgian Bay, migration to the Saint Lawrence valley had merely delayed an inevitable exodus to Iroquoia; yet for a minority the Saint Lawrence valley indeed proved to be a land of endurance and regeneration. Under pressure from the Iroquois, families and individuals from different Wendat villages and, significantly, different constituent nations of the Wendat Confederacy, converged to form a new community and remake a new Wendake.

***

After their arrival in the Saint Lawrence valley, Wendat men and women did not hide in their new village on the Island of Orleans. They could not afford to. Many of them continued to travel up and down the Saint Lawrence valley to hunt, fish, and reach out to friends and relatives. Some did not integrate into the village community immediately, preferring instead to orbit around Trois Rivières and Montreal. Collectively, they remained extremely vulnerable to attacks and overtures. The Iroquois sent raiding parties to the Saint Lawrence valley with increasing frequency between 1650 and 1653, striking against Algonquians, Wendats, and Frenchmen alike. During these three years, a minimum of forty Wendats were captured or killed in the region, most of them in the vicinity of Montreal and Trois Rivières, representing between 5 and 10 percent of the men and women who were seeking refuge among the French. Although some of these captives managed a subsequent escape, this population loss was substantial and demoralizing.[9] The Wendats responded to violence in kind when possible, tormenting and killing enemies who occasionally fell into their hands. Contrary to the Iroquois, their precarious position in the decade that followed the dispersion, coupled with the fact that their defensive operations only netted male captives, meant that adopting enemies in accordance with tradition was unfeasible.[10] The distinct advantages of the Iroquois were clear on this front, and the presence of what French chroniclers variously described as "Renegade and Iroquoiscized Hurons" among the warriors who prowled about was unnerving. A note left by the Jesuit Joseph-Antoine Poncet, who in August of 1653 was seized with his lay assistant at Cap Rouge, just seven kilometers upriver from Kamiskouaouaganchit and twenty from the mission on the Island of Orleans, indicated that the war party that captured him was made up of four Mohawks and "six Hurons, turned Iroquois."[11]

That summer and fall of 1653 marked a critical shift in the tactics of the Mohawks and Onondagas. The warriors who struck at Cap Rouge had detached themselves from an army of six hundred Mohawks that proceeded to surround Trois Rivières during the last week of August. While the French garrison used its cannons to keep the attackers at bay, the latter burnt houses, sacked crops, and slaughtered livestock in the outlying countryside. Soon, however, the French were perplexed to see their Wendat allies venture out of the town's stockade to approach the enemy, "eager to learn news of their relatives and friends who had formerly been taken in wars, and had become Iroquois." Before long "there was nothing to be seen but conferences and interviews between Iroquois and Hurons"; this continued for several days, "so that one would have said there had never been any war between them." During the course of this mingling, the Mohawks were troubled to discover that they had lost the initiative to the Onondagas. A little over a month before, sixty of the latter had arrived at Montreal and made peace overtures to officials there "on behalf of their whole nation"; a small Oneida delegation had followed shortly thereafter, asking to be party to the Onondagas' peace. Responding to the evolving circumstances, the leaders of the Mohawk army – among whom a man named Teharihogen appears to have been the most influential – decided that they too would turn to diplomacy. They approached the officials at Trois Rivières to express their desire to enter into peace talks, promising to free Father Poncet as proof of their sincerity. The Mohawks did not merely intend to be party to the Onondagas' peace, however. As the latter's ambassadors passed through on route from Montreal to Quebec, Teharihogen's warriors intercepted them. Only after relieving the Onondagas of most of the presents of wampum and furs with which they intended to further their peace talks, and imposing on them a handful of observers, did the Mohawks let them proceed on their way.[12]

At Quebec, the Onondagas met with Governor Jean de Lauzon, who had arrived in the colony with his commission two years earlier, just a few months following the establishment of the Wendat village on the Island of Orleans. It was there, on 4 September, that the first conference occurred, in the presence of the Wendats and Algonquian delegates from Kamiskouaouangachit. The Onondaga ambassador made a series of conciliatory speeches, mourning the dead and clearing the way for peace, supported with presents of beaver skins and wampum. His final words were, more pointedly, "to exhort the Hurons to accept whatever decision Onontio the great Captain of the French, should choose to make concerning peace." Three days later, when Lauzon reciprocated with gifts of his own to confirm his desire for peace, he left that clause unanswered. Nonetheless, the Onondagas left contented on the next day, promising to return during the winter to report on the happy effect that news of this peace would have on their nation.[13]

The Mohawk delegation that had been forced upon the Onondagas, headed by a certain Andioura, made its speeches in the following days. Andioura's pledges of peace and friendship elicited an impatient response from Tekouerimat, principal chief of Kamiskouaouangachit, who chided him and his people for their past duplicity, and who advised them that if they were truly interested in peace they ought to send back the Algonquin women whom they were holding captive so that they might come back to dwell in their country. The unnamed Wendat captain who spoke last was more conciliatory. Turning to Tekouerimat, he declared that "the old disputes must now be forgotten" and that the Algonquins should not abuse the blessings of Heaven in such a time of triumph. A second Wendat captain closed the proceedings by telling the Mohawks that to achieve peace they should deliver on their promise to bring back Father Poncet, and that this would "seal it more firmly [...] than if you brought back to us a whole world of Hurons."[14] An odd assertion at first glance, but one that makes sense in a context where the Wendats had no hope that the Mohawks would release any of their relatives.

To absorb the very last of the Wendats – to add *them* to their relatives – was the primary objective of the Iroquois, and peace with the French was a novel means to this end. Onondagas and Mohawks both vied for the same objective, to reinvigorate themselves by the influx of adoptees, and both had cause to worry that the persistence of a Wendat community in the Saint Lawrence valley, by continuing to represent a hope of freedom and an invitation to escape, would pose a challenge to the smooth assimilation of captives and reluctant migrants already living in their villages. The available evidence makes it clear that this aim was a divisive one, with Onondagas and Mohawks undertaking efforts that were not merely parallel but conflicting. Challenged as to the sincerity of his people when they first approached the French at Montreal that summer, the Onondaga ambassador had explained to his French audience "that a careful distinction must be made between nation and nation; that the Onnontaëronnons [Onondaga] were not faithless, like the Anniehronnon [Mohawk] Iroquois, who cherish, deep in their breast, their rancor and bitterness of heart, while their tongues are uttering fair words."[15] The Mohawks persisted in considering it their prerogative, as the easternmost nation of the confederacy – the metaphorical eastern door of the longhouse – to lead Iroquois's dealings with the inhabitants of the Saint Lawrence valley. On more than one occasion, the tensions between the two nations threatened to boil over into open violence. "I declare war on you," an outraged Onondaga would announce to Mohawk warriors who intercepted a Franco-Wendat delegation under his escort the following year. Nothing came of this declaration, but the harshness of feeling that it exemplified remained lively through the decade.[16]

In early November of 1653, Teharihogen returned from Mohawk country to Quebec with a small delegation, bringing back Father Poncet and announcing that his elders would come in the spring to ratify a general peace. On 6 November, during the night that followed his meeting with Governor de Lauzon, Teharihogen visited the Wendats in secret, presenting them with wampum belts "of rare beauty" and "told them plainly that the purpose of his journey was to sever their connection" with the French "and to transfer their Huron colony to his own country." The negotiation with the governor, he revealed, "was only meant to conceal their game" and to give his delegation "more means of speaking with us [the Wendats] without suspicion, and of conducting this whole affair smoothly and effectively." The Wendat leaders responded to the Mohawks with wampum and gifts of their own which the Iroquois recipients interpreted as tokens of their willingness to comply.[17]

A few days after the departure of the Mohawk ambassadors, who returned to their country just as winter was setting in, the senior captains of the Wendats revealed to the missionaries and governor what had transpired. Displaying the wampum belts that the ambassadors had offered in secret, they explained in dramatic terms that they were presents "from the depths of hell, from a demon who spoke to us in the awful stillness of a dark night – a demon who inspires us with fear, since he loves only darkness and dreads the light." The captains explained that their people "dared not reject these presents [...] for that would have been to break with them and refuse the peace, which we must try to keep, since we are powerless to carry on war." Yet they harboured great misgivings about the Mohawks' true intentions: "Perhaps, too, they are treating with the French in sincerity, and, while pretending to wish to deceive you [the French], really wish to deceive us [the Wendats], after removing us from under your protection; for he who commits one treachery is capable of committing more than one." In revealing this and inviting the advice and support of the officials and missionaries, the captains declared that they were "resolved to live and die" with them.[18]

Lauzon instructed envoys to catch up with Teharihogen's delegation, as they passed through Trois Rivières on their way back home, to reveal that he knew of their secret diplomacy. In the wake of this failed effort, Mohawk thoughts again turned to force as a means of severing the Wendats' connection with the French and of obtaining their relocation. In late December, a Mohawk delegation approached Dutch officials at Fort Orange (soon to become Albany, New York) asking them to send a letter on their behalf to Lauzon: "[I]f they, the Maquas, should become involved in any war or trouble with your honor's Indians," the officials wrote, "they request that your honor and your honor's nation would not interfere."[19]

The Onondagas too tried their hand at covert diplomacy. It soon came to light that at some point in the fall, the Wendats had communicated to them a message, secretly and "of their own accord," with two supporting presents. However, a crucial misunderstanding arose as to the precise meaning of this message: the Wendats strictly meant to lay a metaphorical mat at Onondaga to ensure that their captive relatives living there would not come to harm should hostilities ever resume, or at least this is what they later claimed; the Onondagas meanwhile understood it as a pledge that the Wendats finally agreed to join them in their country. Following up on this expectation, an Onondaga delegation reached Quebec on 30 January and proceeded immediately the next day across the ice to the settlement on the Island of Orleans. Again the discussions were kept from the French. In a secret nightly council held with a handful of Wendat captains and elders, its head Tsiraenie explained that a band of five hundred Onondaga men and women were on their way to "carry away the village from the Island" in the spring. During the discussions that followed, the Wendat leaders protested that their "speech and thought had been altered," and that their people did not intend to relocate. Tsiarenie, unsatisfied, opted for a ruse. He proposed that, in light of the state of peace that now prevailed, the Wendat leaders convince their people to resettle at Montreal in the following spring. The five hundred Onondagas would meet them there to escort them to their country. Urging them to bypass traditional decision-making processes, Tsiraenie advised them to keep this plan secret from all but three or four of their people, even from their wives – implying not merely that the women were likely to reveal the scheme to others, but also that they were among the most committed to their community's independence. As heads of households in a matrilineal society, they had more to lose than their men from their people's incorporation into foreign clans and lineages.[20]

While a few of the leaders approached by Tsiraenie were willing to go along with this plan, others hesitated. One of them revealed the nature of the discussions to the Jesuits, who in turn, brought the issue to the attention of Governor Lauzon. A frantic series of councils occurred during which the Wendats and the French leadership sought solutions to what they understood to be a common predicament. The Wendats were highly sensitive to the precariousness of their situation. "It is now your turn to speak, Onontio, and not ours," the oldest of the captains pleaded with Lauzon. "We have been dead for four years, ever since our country was laid waste. Death follows us everywhere, and is always before our eyes. We live only in you, we see only through your eyes, we breathe only in your person; and our reasoning is without reason, except in so far as you give it to us. It is then for you, Onontio, to draw us out from these perils by telling us what we must do."[21] To refuse the advances of either the Onondagas or the Mohawks would mean to rekindle a war which neither the Wendats nor the French were capable of sustaining. The only available course of action was to delay the migration as much as possible. They agreed that the elders should force the Onondagas to bring the discussion out into the open and to involve the governor. At stake for the French was the relative strength of their position in the geopolitics of the region, the opportunity to be allowed to intervene in a diplomatic development from which they had been sidelined. For the Wendats, the hope was that the tangle of multilateralism would stall the demanded migration and avert the threat of renewed violence. The Onondagas would be required to ask Onontio "to relax his arms a little, and to give liberty to the Hurons whom he held under his protection." Queried as to what the governor should reply – proof that, against appearances to the contrary, the Wendats had not fully relinquished their fate to the French – the elders declared, "let him answer that it will be possible in two years."[22]

Tsiraenie, persuaded by the Wendat elders, brought the matter to the attention of the French. During a public council, he presented the wampum he had brought and an "invitation was extended to the Huron colony to make itself a new country in lands formerly hostile, which, they were assured, would be to them a Promised land."[23] His Wendat counterpart responded as planned, agreeing that they would go through with the resettlement, but on two conditions: that they postpone it for at least one year, and that in the meantime the Onondagas prepare by welcoming the Jesuits among them. "Wherever our Fathers should decide to go," their speaker made it known, "the [Wendat] colony would follow them." Lauzon supported this proposal with presents of his own, exhorting the Onondagas to give a cordial reception to the Wendats, and beseeching them not to pressure those families which were not yet ready to make the journey or otherwise disinclined to undertake it. The Wendats should be allowed freedom to go where they wished, he asserted, "even though some should feel disposed to seek the country of the Anniehronnon Iroquois [Mohawks], and others Sonnontwanne [Senecas]; and even though still others should long for their former country, or choose to continue their abode with the French."[24]

***

A French missionary later disparaged the seemingly conflicting promises made to the Mohawks and Onondagas as the "imprudence of the Huron in giving himself to two masters."[25] There was more to it than mere carelessness. Indeed, the Wendats' conflicting promises are partly explained by the divisions that existed among them. Although their captains tend to be anonymous in the sources – to say nothing of the women who exercised a great influence behind the scenes – occasional exceptions to this rule hint at the ways in which, even in exile, the constituent nations of the Wendat Confederacy, as in previous years, continued to diverge in response to the advances of the Iroquois. It was the Attignawantan chief Atsena who had responded with gifts to Mohawk invitations in the fall of 1653, seemingly giving an indication of his people's willingness to resettle among them; a few years later, the Onondagas were directing their wampum belts to Arendarhonon leaders.[26]

Subsequent events would make it clear that the Attignawantan, Attigneenongnahac, and Arendarhonon were not all of the same mind as to the most hopeful, safest course of action as a last recourse. But for the time being this population responded to Iroquois pressures by converging. Taken as a whole, the Wendats who had found refuge in the Saint Lawrence valley preferred "to continue their abode with the French," as Governor Lauzon had put it. Tsiraenie's devious suggestion that the task of leading the community to Montreal should be left to a mere three or four individuals, who would need to keep the secret even from wives, demonstrates plainly enough the broad consensus that prevailed. Thus, contradictory promises also appear as a concerted, purposeful policy. Fostering divisions among the Iroquois was a way for the Wendats of delaying migration, perhaps even indefinitely, and leaving, as the *Relation* phrased it, "each of the Iroquois Nations hopeful of winning to its own side the Hurons, whom they so eagerly desired," and the surest means of averting a renewed war.[27]

Most of the Wendats who had in the last few years of diaspora orbited around Trois Rivières to escape mounting Iroquois pressure – and who appear to have included Atsena and thus perhaps a core of Attignawantan – joined the village on the Island of Orleans in April of 1654.[28] Just as they sought strength in numbers, the Wendats also sought strength in religion and the bonds that it fostered in their effort to resist, as best as they could, Iroquois overtures and threats. Wampum and the pledges that accompanied it were the means by which the Iroquois sought to appeal to the Wendats, and it was a way for the Wendats to strengthen their own bonds with the French. In 1654, the Congregation of Our Lady undertook to make a special wampum belt destined to the congregation of the Jesuits' Professed House – one of the order's residences in Paris – which had numbered among the mission's benefactors and which shared a common Marian devotion with them. The gesture was calculated to reciprocate past gifts and elicit further spiritual and financial assistance. The women of the Congregation of Our Lady had taken up the habit of pooling beads of wampum, both to constitute a "public treasury" with which to help the less fortunate members of the refugee community, and to honour and propitiate the Virgin Mary whose likeness in the chapel they adorned with a beaded crown and belts. With missionary encouragement they innovated by incorporating roman characters in their design, writing in dark beads upon a background of white the words *Ave Maria gratia plena* – "Hail Mary, full of grace" – the opening words of the rosary, the traditional prayer for the intercession of the mother of Christ. The accompanying speech, formulated by Jacques Oachonk, Louis Taiaeronk, and Joseph Sondouskon, chiefs of the community who held the formal offices of the congregation, and written down on their behalf by Jesuit Father Pierre-Joseph-Marie Chaumonot, expressed plainly the way in which the Wendats of the Island of Orleans conceptualized their bond with the French. "We are brothers," they declared to their audience across the ocean, "since the mother of Jesus is our mother as well as yours."[29] Whereas the Algonquian neophtyes encountered in the previous chapter were inclined to conceive of themselves as sharing a divine father with the French, the Wendats, in true Iroquoian fashion, drew their sense of alliance and kinship from the understanding that what mattered was their common divine mother.

But bonds of religion and metaphorical kinship at the same time pulled the Wendats in the opposite direction. The Onondagas responded with enthusiasm to the proposal that the refugees of the Island of Orleans would be more inclined to relocate among them if they first welcomed a Jesuit mission. In September of 1655, an Onondaga embassy came to confirm their peace with the French, the Algonquins, and the Wendats. The link between the extension of the mission field and the relocation of the refugee community was patent as the chief ambassador reiterated their invitation for the French "to build a new Sainte-Marie, like that whose prosperity we formerly witnessed in the heart of the Huron country."[30] On this occasion, the Onondagas wielded kinship metaphors in an effort to position themselves as brothers of the French and a parent to their allies. The Onondaga ambassador described Governor Lauzon as both someone who had "cherished the Algonquins and Hurons in his bosom, with all the love of a *mother* holding her child in her arms," and who "had sustained life in all the Nations that became your allies and took refuge in your arms," as well as someone who had "extended to them also a *father*'s care and love." The Onondaga offered a gift to the governor to symbolically strengthen his arms, urging him to hold these allies even "more firmly" and "not tire of embracing them; let them live within your bosom, for you are the father of the country."[31]

The earliest recorded formulation of the idea that some of Onontio's allies were his children, rather than his brothers, had occurred in September 1645 when a French embassy in Mohawk country was asked to thank Onontio for restoring the good sense of his Algonquin children. Yet it was in the context of the 1650s that the idea became more prevalent, at a moment in time where the rhetorical infantilization of the Wendats suited the purposes of both the Iroquois and French. The mixed parental metaphors wielded during the Onondaga embassy of September 1655, like the apparently contradictory call for the governor to release and hold on to his children, conveyed a case for resettlement in a shared Iroquoian idiom: while, up to this point, Onontio had acted as a mother to the Wendats, he was now becoming their father, that is, someone bound to allow them to go reside elsewhere – namely, at Onondaga. Urging Onontio to hold on to his allies even more firmly and at this juncture let them live within his bosom also meant, more concretely, preventing the Wendats from moving to Mohawk country in the interval.[32]

During the meeting with the Onondagas, the case for migration was further strengthened by the speech of a "Huron Captain, formerly a captive of the Iroquois [e.g. Onondagas], and now a Captain among them" who had accompanied the embassy. "My brothers," said this unnamed man, addressing the Wendats in the audience, "I have not changed my soul, despite my change of country; nor has my blood become Iroquois, although I dwell among them. My heart is all Huron, as well as my tongue. I would keep silence, were there any deceit in these negotiations for peace. Our proposals are honest; embrace them without distrust."[33] What the Wendat listeners thought of this is not clear. What is obvious is that the French had weighed their options and had come to see the Onondaga threat to the Wendats as an opportunity for themselves. The Jesuits had grown convinced that the benefits of establishing a mission in Onondaga country outweighed its risks. From this perspective, the careful injection of the Wendat neophytes among the heathen Iroquois promised to solidify the peace and radically advance the spread of Christianity.[34]

Two months later, Fathers Pierre-Joseph-Marie Chaumonot and Claude Dablon travelled to Onondaga to make a formal reply and to establish the footings of a new mission on Lake Gannentaha (as they called Onondaga Lake), accompanied by as many as eighteen Wendat ambassadors. On the very day of their arrival, Chaumonot publicly assured the local elders that the "Huron question" had been resolved, and that the Wendats would soon "plant their village" nearby. The Wendat ambassadors who accompanied the two missionaries may possibly have taken part in private meetings, from which the missionaries were excluded, with the Onondaga leadership or with the numerous Wendat "prisoners and renegades" who lived there, but during the public councils that occurred over a week-long conference they allowed Chaumonot and Dablon to speak on their behalf. At one point during the declarations of mutual goodwill, an Onondaga spokesman declared that he and Onontio "were now but one," and "since the Hurons and Algonquins were Onnontio's [*sic*] children, they must be his also." With two presents, cast at the missionary's feet, the Onondaga proceeded to adopt them. No one objected.[35]

Yet subsequent events revealed that the "Huron question" was far from resolved. The degree of autonomy – indeed, the very safety – that the Wendats could expect among their Onondaga hosts was called into question. In the months that followed these optimistic encounters, a Wendat captive who had escaped from Onondaga reached the Island of Orleans where he assured his countrymen and the missionaries that his former captors' "sole design was to attract to their country as many French and Hurons as possible, and then to kill them in a general massacre." He was so persuasive that the Wendats who had promised the Onondagas that they would relocate to their country decided against carrying through with their plan and attempted to convince the Jesuits to do the same. The missionaries' zeal for the faith would cause their death, they argued, begging them not to "cast [themselves] into so manifest a danger" by proceeding.[36]

It seems improbable that the Onondagas intended to massacre the Wendats who willingly joined them. Still, the Onondaga delegation that came to Quebec and the Island of Orleans with a small number of Senecas in the spring of 1656 to escort missionaries and migrants had a difficult time countering these claims. The Mohawks represented an even more manifest danger. Diplomatically outmaneuvered by the Onondagas, in April they sent a force of three hundred warriors to the Saint Lawrence valley with the intention, if necessary, of resorting to violence to compel the Wendats to come and live among them, rather than anywhere else in Iroquoia. At Trois Rivières, the district governor Pierre Boucher attempted with presents to dissuade the warriors from pursuing their journey downriver. The Mohawk captains countered with wampum belts of their own, reiterating the solidity of their peace with the French and promising to return home as long as Onontio was willing to "close the doors of his houses and of his forts against the Onnontageronnon [Onondagas], who wishes to be my enemy." Following the intervention of Jesuit Father Simon Le Moyne, the Mohawk force dispersed in search of wild game, allowing the French to believe that a crisis had been averted.[37]

If the Mohawks had any intention of hunting peacefully and returning home, however, it vanished with the news that French and Wendat doors remained open to the Onondagas. A violent incident heated tempers even further. Two Mohawk warriors, having detached themselves from the main force around Trois Rivières to maraud in the vicinity of the Island of Orleans, had ambushed and killed a young Wendat man. One of the warriors had managed to escape, but the other was captured, brought back to the mission settlement, and condemned to burn. The victim happened to be the only son of one of the community's most prominent couples, a man of good qualities who was "destined for the office of captain," and his death caused much grief. The missionaries attempted to dissuade his relatives from carrying out the execution, hoping that the prisoner might be used to negotiate with the advancing Mohawk army, but in vain.[38]

On 17 May, the Onondaga ambassadors set out from Quebec back towards Onondaga with a large contingent of missionaries, lay brothers, and soldiers, who intended to establish a mission settlement on the shores of Onondaga Lake. They were accompanied by a few Wendat migrants or emissaries.[39] The Onondagas seemed on the cusp of a diplomatic victory. By welcoming missionaries, not only were they strengthening their relationship with the French, they were fulfilling the condition set out by the Wendats themselves two years earlier, which promised to usher their massive resettlement. Yet the convoy travelled no further than ten to twelve leagues from Quebec when its tail was ambushed by the secretly reassembled Mohawk army. Gaining the upper hand with no difficulty, the Mohawks mistreated the Onondagas and bound the Wendats. After some discussions, the assailants relented and freed their captives for "fear of becoming involved in a war" with the Onondagas, offering the unconvincing explanation that they thought the canoes carried only Wendats – with whom they were still at war.[40]

Three days later, on 20 May, the Mohawk force converged on the Island of Orleans before news of the skirmish had time to reach the Wendats or the French. Bypassing Quebec under the cover of darkness and landing on the island before dawn, the raiders scattered in ambush near the fields. They caught the villagers by surprise as they went out to work that morning. While some of the Wendats managed to find refuge in the mission's fort, a large number were seized and forced to embark in the waiting canoes. The *Relation* for that year reported that seventy-one persons were captured or killed; the account of the Ursuline superior, Marie de l'Incarnation, reported eighty-five captives and six killed outright.[41]

In an effort to maintain the Franco-Mohawk peace, the raiders were careful not to harm the few colonists encountered in the area during the attack. By noon, the triumphant warriors departed. They paddled past Quebec in broad daylight, forcing their captives to sing, mocking both their Wendat victims and the French who stood by passively as their allies were carried off. The scene elicited the pity of the townspeople, who were appalled to discover that Governor Lauzon categorically refused to intervene for fear that it would jeopardize the peace which the colonists enjoyed, or that it might endanger the safety of the missionaries who had left for Onondaga country three days earlier. When the Mohawk army reached the vicinity of Trois Rivières, a Jesuit stationed there could do no more than visit their camp to console the unfortunate captives.[42]

Following Marie de l'Incarnation's numbers, the fact that only six persons were killed during the raid on the Island of Orleans reminds us that the Mohawks' intention was not so much the physical destruction of the Wendat community as the incorporation of its members. The captives included "a large number of young women who were the flower of that [Wendat] colony." But they also included men like Jacques Oachonk, the prefect or head of the mission's lay confraternity, the Congregation of Our Lady, and according to the missionaries "the most fervent of all our Christians," as well as Joachim Ondakont, one of the community's most celebrated and skilled warriors. In Mohawk country, the captors granted their lives to all of the captives except six of the "principal Christians" whom they promptly put to death – in other words, the leaders who had been the fiercest opponents of relocation, among whom was Oachonk.[43]

In the wake of the attack, the village on the Island of Orleans was abandoned. Some families appear to have gone to live temporarily at Kamiskouaouangachit, but most found refuge in a fortified encampment laid out for them on the orders of Governor d'Ailleboust in the Upper Town of Quebec, between Château Saint Louis and the parish church. There they were joined by a handful of individuals who found a way to escape their captors after the raid, including a severely mutilated Ondakont. This ultimate refuge, nestled at the very heart of the colony, quickly became known as the "Fort des Hurons" or "Fort des Sauvages."[44]

***

The withdrawal from the Island of Orleans to Quebec did not entail a complete desertion of the fields there. Although seigneurial title to the land was transferred back to Éléonore de Grandmaison and her new husband, Jacques Gourdeau de Beaulieu, the Jesuits made sure that the Wendats continued to be allowed to cultivate their fields there until 1660, as per the earlier agreement for an eight-year term of occupation, and that they be permitted to encamp within the old fort when they worked. In addition, the missionaries secured title to another plot of land at the Pointe de Lévis on the south shore of the Saint Lawrence, opposite Quebec, where they had forty-four arpents cleared for the use of Wendat families. A few French settlers, taking pity, offered additional plots here and there to Wendat acquaintances, who in turn reallocated them within the community in accordance with individual needs. Fear of additional Iroquois depredations severely curtailed their labour, however, and it was often under armed escort that the Wendats continued to work these scattered fields.[45]

French forts and palisades could only do so much to protect a people who needed to work their fields, to hunt, fish, and gather plants to survive. Seeing that so many of their loved ones had been taken by force and no doubt fearing, with good reason, that the same would unavoidably happen to them, the Wendats remaining in the area sued

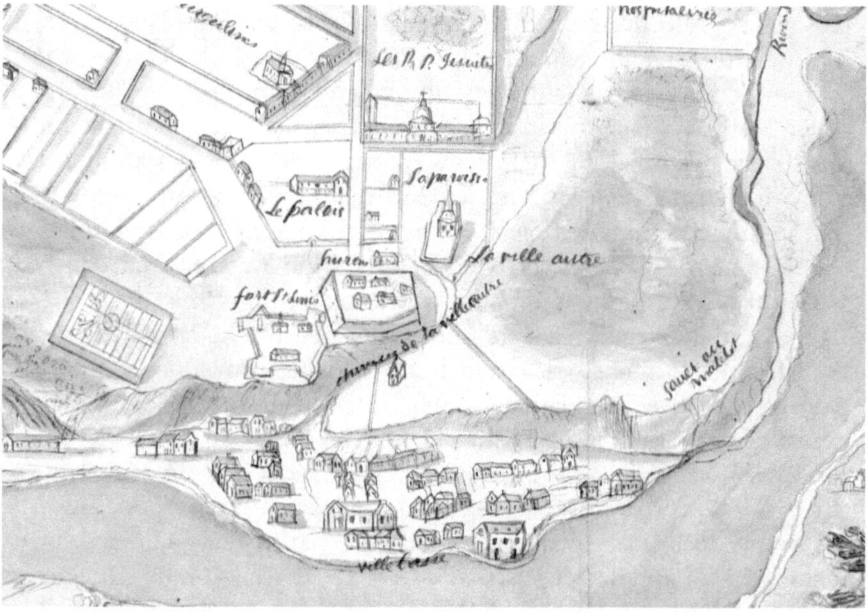

Figure 4.1 Map of Quebec showing the Wendat compound (labelled "Hurons") in the Upper Town, between Fort Saint Louis, the parish church, and the Ursulines' visiting quarters. (Detail from Jean Bourdon, "Le Véritable plan de Québec fait en 1663," BNF, Département des cartes et plans, GE SH 18 PF 127 DIV 7 P 3)

for peace with the Mohawks. In the fall of 1656, three Wendat emissaries travelled to Mohawk country to conclude an accord which hinged on the refugee community's resettlement there in the following spring. Two Mohawk ambassadors spent the winter at the Island of Orleans, as guests in the house of Atsena the Attignawantan.[46] That spring, a body of about one hundred Mohawk warriors entered the Saint Lawrence valley to make sure that the Wendats complied with their promise of the previous fall. On 1 April, two Mohawks arrived at Quebec from Montreal with presents for the Wendats. Meanwhile, the Onondagas responded to these unwelcome developments with a show of force of their own, breaking with the steadfastly diplomatic approach that in recent years had distinguished them from the Mohawks. In the first days of May 1657, some fifty to one hundred Onondaga warriors arrived in the vicinity of Quebec, threatening war against the Wendats and harassing French colonists. During a first council, in the presence of representatives of the Wendats, Algonquins, Innu, and French, as well as of a few Mohawk deputies, the Onondagas excused themselves "for having come for the Hurons, their brothers, with arms in their hands." They had been compelled to do so, they claimed, by the discovery that under Mohawk influence the Wendats had reneged on their earlier promises to join them. All parties present reiterated their willingness to maintain peace and harmony, and the issue of the Wendat migration was negotiated in a series of private councils aimed at achieving a compromise.[47]

Again, the Onondagas were outmaneuvered by the Mohawks. On 15 May, the former's delegation headed home from Quebec in the company of three Wendat envoys who intended to further discuss the resettlement. The hundred Mohawk warriors who lay in the vicinity of Trois Rivières and Montreal intercepted them and dissuaded the three Wendats from proceeding to Onondaga country. A delegation of twenty to thirty Mohawks headed by Teharihogen, the man who had initiated the secret discussions in 1653, went on to Quebec. Reaching the town on 28 May, he met with the Wendats in council. "Four years ago," he declared, "you begged me to take you by the arm, to raise you and bring you to my country. You did sometimes withdraw it when I wished to comply with your request; that is why I struck you on the head with my hatchet. Withdraw it no more, for I tell you in earnest to get up. It is time for you to come." Teharihogen asked the interim governor, Charles de Lauzon de Charny, the son of Jean de Lauzon, to let the Wendats go and to allow Father Simon Le Moyne to accompany them to Mohawk country. During the night-long internal consultations that ensued, divisions within the refugee community manifested themselves. While the Attignawantan (or Bear Nation) agreed to join the Mohawks, the Arendarhonon (Rock Nation) reaffirmed their pledge to join the Onondagas, and the Attigneenongnahac (Cord Nation) opted to remain at Quebec.[48]

In reporting the events of the summer of 1657, the *Relation* allows us to catch a rare and final glimpse of the relations between the constituent nations that had made up the former Wendat Confederacy. The insight is rare because since the invasion of Huronia, colonial chroniclers had ceased to refer to the constitutive Indigenous national segments, favouring instead the convenient collective label of "Huron"; final, because no mention would ever again be made of these national segments in colonial writings after 1657. This shift in terminology reflects a lack of interest in Indigenous identity politics on the part of the French, but it also mirrored the very real process of cultural and political convergence that occurred in the Saint Lawrence valley during the 1650s and 1660s. While the sources do not hint at how the Wendat refugees defined themselves in this period, it seems clear that under the pressures of invasion and forced migration, the distinct cultures and identities of the refugees who shared a common fate gradually merged. The cultivation of a common Christian identity among the Wendat refugees contributed to this process of convergence, as surely did the increasing tendency of missionaries and officials to think of and approach them as "Hurons" rather than Attignawantan, Arendarhonon, or Attigneenongnahac.

In the summer of 1657, these cultural and political cleavages still mattered. A decade earlier, in 1647, as indicated in the previous chapter, it was the Arendarhonon who attempted peace negotiations with the Onondagas, while the Attignawantan were strongly opposed to them.[49] In the fall of 1653, it was the Attignawantan leader Atsena who had responded with gifts to Mohawk invitations. Conversely, in May of 1657, it was to the Arendarhonon that the Onondagas had directed their secret wampum belts.[50] Presumably, the refugees' leanings were influenced by these longstanding relationships and by the presence of a critical mass of Attignawantan captives and migrants living among the Mohawks, and conversely of Arendarhonon living among the Onondagas.

An element of explanation for the Attigneenongnahac desire to remain with the French can also be teased from the activities of their most prominent leader, Étienne Annaotaha. In the previous decade, he had emerged as one of the staunchest and most flamboyant opponents of the Iroquois. Already recognized in 1649 as "the most esteemed in the country for his courage and his exploits over the enemy," he was captured the following year but managed a prompt escape. At Gahoendoe Island, after the departure of the first Wendat contingent for the Saint Lawrence valley, he brought about the death of thirty Onondaga ambassadors by cunning – or from the Onondaga perspective, treachery. In July 1652, in the vicinity of Trois Rivières, he seized another ambassador, a Mohawk this time, who was executed soon thereafter. Both the Onondagas and Mohawks thus had good reasons to wish ill of Annaotaha – in fact, the French believed that the Iroquois's desire to avenge these acts had been a cause of their hostility in recent years.[51] Without doubt, Annaotaha's Attigneenongnahac relatives and friends were party to his exploits. His actions can be interpreted as an expression of a suspicion, a hatred even, of the Iroquois that was more pronounced among them than among other segments of the Wendat population. Recent occurrences had done little to ease tensions. On 12 May 1657, less than two weeks before the council at which the three nations that made up the refugee communities agreed to part ways, an Onondaga warrior had killed a nephew of Annaotaha near Quebec. Though the head of the Onondaga delegation had dissociated himself from the killing and done his best to atone for it with customary presents, it takes no stretch of the imagination to understand that hard feelings persisted.[52] Annaotaha and his Attigneenongnahac relatives and followers had strong personal reasons to resent both the Onondagas and the Mohawks, and to fear that in spite of assurances to the contrary, their reception among either nation would be tricky at best, or at worse fatal.

The maneuvering of the Mohawks and Onondagas had left the French in an uncomfortable position. Officials and missionaries were torn between, on the one hand, the desire to maintain a fragile Franco-Iroquois peace and to make missionary inroads among the Five Nations, and, on the other, the fear that recent displays of Iroquois hostility augured poorly for the safety of the Wendats. A corollary to the Jesuits' willingness to sanction the relocation of the refugees among the Onondagas, where they might spiritually reinforce the embryonic mission of Sainte Marie de Gannentaha, was their great distrust of the Mohawks. Reiterating the position of diplomatic detachment adopted by his father since 1654, interim governor Lauzon de Charny chose to wash his hands of the affair, declaring that, "Onontio loves the Hurons. They are no longer children in swaddling-clothes, but are old enough to be out of tutelage. They can go where they wish, without being hindered in any way by Onontio. He opens his arms to let them go." Lauzon de Charny could hope that a compromise, by which the Arendarhonon would relocate among the Onondagas and the Attignawantan among Mohawks, would satisfy everyone and ease the tensions that were endangering the fragile peace. Nevertheless, he attempted to delay the migration, denying the Mohawks the boats that they had requested to transport the Wendats and beseeching the Wendats to wait until they had a chance to meet the next governor before departing.[53]

Annaotaha and the Attigneenongnahac were not alone in harbouring some reservations about resettlement away from the Saint Lawrence valley. Notwithstanding Iroquois assurances of goodwill and the existence of privileged relationships between the Attignawantan and the Mohawks, and between the Arendarhonon and the Onondagas, after a decade of resistance there was much risk involved in yielding to pressures from either nation. When the Attignawantan headman Atsena announced his people's decision to the Mohawk ambassador Teharihogen, it was with a heavy heart: "I am at your service. I cast myself, with my eyes shut, into your canoe, without knowing what I am doing. But, whatever may betide, I am resolved to die. Even if you should break my head as soon as we are out of range of the cannon here, it matters not; I am quite resolved."[54] Attignawantan reluctance to proceed with this resettlement was made plain on the expected day of departure, 2 June, at which time only fourteen women and children embarked for Mohawk country.[55] It took the intervention of a second Mohawk delegation in early August of that year, once again backed by a strong military force of about one hundred warriors, to put a stop to these delaying tactics. On 21 August, "some" Wendats left Quebec in the company of Mohawks, followed five days later by another group of unspecified size, accompanied by Father Le Moyne.[56] Whether these represented the last of the Attignawantan at Quebec, or merely another handful of families, it is impossible to say.

The Arendarhonon who had resolved to join the Onondaga, by this point numbering a little over fifty, of which four-fifths were women and children, had meanwhile left Quebec on 16 June. Beyond Montreal they travelled westward with Jesuit Father Ragueneau and a few other Frenchmen, escorted by about thirty Onondagas and fifteen Senecas. Though it was the likelihood of encountering a large force of Mohawks intent on laying claim to these Arendarhonon that caused the most apprehension, harm soon came from an unexpected direction. Within days of having left Montreal, on the way up the Saint Lawrence, one of the Wendat migrants was killed for murky reasons by an Onondaga captain of the escort; the incident snowballed into a melee during which all the Wendat men were killed and the women and children were seized – a massacre of the sort that had been feared. Heavily outnumbered and devoid of authority, the French members of the party were unable to intervene. When Ragueneau attempted to calm tempers and to secure concessions in favour of the survivors, the Onondaga captain defiantly retorted that by releasing the Wendats the French had empowered him to treat them as he pleased.[57]

In early September, another group of Onondagas approached the Wendats at Quebec. According to one count, as a result of recent outmigration to Iroquoia, those who remained at Quebec now numbered approximately 130, a fraction of the 500 or 600 tallied on the Island of Orleans four years earlier. It seems safe to assume that they were primarily Attigneenongnahac.[58] Having spent the summer along the Saint Lawrence and apparently unaware as of yet of the massacre perpetrated by their compatriots, these Onondagas, in a continued effort to persuade them to relocate to their country, presented new belts and strings of wampum to the community's leaders, "giving them a thousand assurances that they would be very welcome." The Wendats showed some inclination to comply, but convinced their interlocutors to postpone the journey until the following spring. News of the massacre, reaching town in the early days of October, unsurprisingly spelled the end of the plan.[59]

***

Onondaga elders promptly conveyed their assurances that they had nothing to do with the massacre of the Arendarhonon migrants in the summer of 1657, and that they did not approve of the behaviour of the rash young men who had committed it. It was of little reassurance. Onondaga, Oneida, and Mohawk bands were now reported to be prowling between Trois Rivières and Quebec, intent on doing mischief to Wendats, Algonquins, and Frenchmen alike. In concert with the principal colonists, the new interim governor, Louis d'Ailleboust, resolved that the hostilities and pillaging of the Iroquois would be tolerated no more. The half-decade during which French governors had taken great care to avoid jeopardizing the peace that their people enjoyed had proven illusory for their Indigenous allies. During a council with the Wendats and Algonquins on 24 October 1657, Governor d'Ailleboust declared that they were free to conduct offensive and defensive operations as they pleased. The French would not be the first to strike or break the peace, but they would henceforth defend their allies if they were ever attacked in the vicinity of the colonial settlements. This was a noteworthy shift in French colonial policy.[60]

With the intensification of raids in the Saint Lawrence valley, the forceful diplomatic overtures of the Mohawks and Onondagas that had characterized the period from 1653 to 1657 came to a halt. The issue of Wendat resettlement disappeared from the Franco-Iroquois negotiations that continued to occur sporadically thereafter, and it becomes impossible to discern in the sources any further evidence of Mohawk-Onondaga competition over the fate of the small refugee community at Quebec. This is not to say that the Iroquois did not continue to entertain for a time a hope of drawing this community to them by force, as suggested by the rumour which reached the ears of Marie de l'Incarnation in 1659, to the effect that a large Iroquois army was amassing to "carry away our new Christians, and as I believe, as many Frenchmen as they can."[61]

The Algonquins did not wait for d'Ailleboust's invitation in the fall of 1657 to respond to Iroquois aggression, sending a war party of their own to the Richelieu River in the days preceding their meeting with the governor. The Wendats were a little slower to take the field. Perhaps it was for fear of what might happen to their numerous relatives living among the enemy. Perhaps they were also discouraged from taking arms by the Jesuits, who were understandably worried about what open war might mean for their mission of Sainte Marie de Gannentaha on the shore of Onondaga Lake. That preoccupation dissipated before long, however, with the news that the fledgling mission had been abandoned amidst rumours that it would soon be attacked by the Mohawks. Its evacuated personnel reached the safety of the colony in the first days of April 1658, and a first Wendat war party, twenty-three warriors in three canoes, left Quebec on 15 June.[62]

During his welcoming reception in early August of 1659, the latest governor, Pierre de Voyer d'Argenson, gave a clear indication of the new French willingness to encourage war by distributing arms to the representatives of the allied nations. With guns, gunpowder, lead, swords, hatchets, and iron arrowheads, he metaphorically wiped away the tears shed for the death of their peoples and restored their voice so that they might exhort their young men to battle.[63] Indeed, in that summer, in June and August, Wendats took part in defensive operations alongside Algonquins and Frenchmen.[64] Then, in April of 1660, the great war chief Étienne Annaotaha mobilized the largest Wendat war party in a decade, numbering forty warriors who left Quebec with him and were joined on the way by four Algonquins from the vicinity of Trois Rivières. Near Montreal they were reinforced by an additional seventeen Frenchmen, led by a certain Adam Dollard des Ormeaux. While French-Canadian historiography and collective memory has long focused on the latter, inflating his importance in this historical event, it is all but certain that the older and more experienced war chief Annaotaha acted as the party's leader.[65]

One of the forty warriors, Ignace Tsaouenhohoui, would explain after the fact that they had been motivated by "the desire to repress the furor of the Iroquois, to prevent him from carrying away the rest of our women and children, for fear that by carrying them away they make them lose the Faith, and after paradise."[66] The religious sentiment was no doubt genuine, but the core consideration was probably the threat of seeing a small community further dislocated in this world rather than the next. And in reality, it is most plausible that Annaotaha and his warriors aimed to surprise isolated hunting bands and war parties along the Ottawa River. By striking blows in this way, they could raise the morale of their people and capture men and women who might serve a diplomatic purpose as hostages.

The expedition would prove disastrous for the Wendats of Quebec. At the foot of the Long Sault rapids on the Ottawa River (today Chute à Blondeau, Ontario), the party was beset by a force of some two to three hundred warriors from the League's western nations, primarily Onondagas but including some Senecas and perhaps Cayugas. The greatly outnumbered Wendats and Frenchmen took refuge in a makeshift fort only to find the besiegers reinforced within a few days by an additional five hundred Mohawks, Onondagas, and Oneidas. On Annaotaha's prompting, a "Huronised" Oneida from his party – that is, an adopted Wendat of Oneida origin – went out with two of the leading Wendats to obtain "some good terms." Given the Iroquois's incorporative efforts and successes over the preceding decade and a half, the enemy force itself included a number of "Iroquoiscised" Wendats. During the tense truce that followed the parley, a number of the latter summoned their compatriots in the defenders' camp to abandon the uneven fight. As a result, most of the Wendat defenders, twenty-four or thirty men, chose to defect. This was a typical response to such situations in a cultural context where the violence of battle and the more delicate pressures of diplomacy were never far from each other. Fighting to the death might be praised and admired in the early modern European way of war, but such self-sacrifice did not have the same gloss in the small-scale societies of North America. The value of warriors' lives surpassed that of strategic gains.[67]

Annaotaha was among the few who remained with the French and Algonquins. His impressive and controversial war record made it unlikely that, even in the case of voluntary surrender, he would be spared from torture and death.[68] After a siege of seven to ten days, the Onondagas and Mohawks stormed the makeshift fort, killing Annaotaha in the process. The five French captives were tortured to death, as were some of the captured Wendats and Algonquins. The men who had voluntarily defected were at first treated like captives, but most were eventually spared. Of the forty Wendat warriors, the *Relation* reports that only seven were burnt, a number that may very well refer to both those killed in battle and the few who were put to death afterwards.[69] After the destruction of Huronia a decade before, and the assault on the Island of Orleans four years earlier, the loss of some forty men was a terrible blow to the Wendat community at Quebec. One commentator described them as "the flower of all those of importance that remained here with us." Another spoke even more dramatically of "the forty *remaining* Hurons."[70]

The community thus remained vulnerable. Its bark-covered longhouses nestled at the heart of the colonial capital were well protected, but venturing out to carry on necessary subsistence activities continued to involve considerable risks. During fall of 1662, the Iroquois captured another five Wendats who were harvesting fields that they had retained on the Island of Orleans and in the seigneury of Lauzon, along the south shore of the river.[71] In May of the following year, officials at Montreal imprudently lodged four Mohawk would-be deputies with a small band of Wendats who had established a hunting camp nearby. Surprising their hosts after an evening of good cheer, the guests killed three of them and captured another three. A few weeks later, the enraged relatives of the victims retaliated by indiscriminately killing an Onondaga visitor to the town.[72] The murders of May 1663 became the last-documented Iroquois attack against a group consisting solely of Wendats in the Saint Lawrence valley. By the fall of that year, both the French and their allies began enjoying a lull in the enemy offensive – this was less a result of successful defensive operations on their part than of the fact that the Five Nations were distracted by other wars.[73]

***

One Jesuit observed, with a mixture of compassion and pride that, for the shattered community which mourned the loss of Annaotaha and his men in 1660, "prayer took the place of lamentation."[74] Such a remark might be qualified by pointing out that a decade later, one of the community's highly esteemed members, Joachim Annieouton, admitted that, though he had accepted baptism and shown himself assiduous in attending mass and prayers, his conversion had been feigned. "Ah, my Father, I have been deceiving you hitherto," he confessed. "You urged me very often to become converted; and I, to gratify you and rid myself, as I then used to say, of such importunity, granted you in appearance what you wished of me."[75] Still, the complexities of personal belief notwithstanding, it is clear that the political community defined itself as Christian and that its members, as a whole, sought and found a good measure of solace in Christian beliefs and practices.

That this was the case should not surprise, for the subset of the Wendat population that had chosen to seek its safety in the Saint Lawrence valley, and to hold firm through a decade of diplomatic and military pressure, corresponded to those who had most enthusiastically embraced the new faith. During the difficult years that followed the destruction of Huronia, missionary teachings offered ready meaning to traumatic experiences and a dynamic basis for the construction of new social bonds and support networks – as they had for the Algonquians of Kamiskouaouangachit. Most significantly perhaps, these teachings offered ways of channeling grief at a time when traditional beliefs and practices were proving difficult to adapt to the new context. Indeed, the Wendats of Quebec's ever-diminishing number of warriors made it difficult to carry out traditional mourning mechanisms that hinged on the capture or killing of enemies. By contrast, the stoic resignation in the face of adversity that was advocated by the missionaries offered ways of grieving that were more practicable at this juncture, as did the belief that death represented a transition to a better life and an opportunity to be reunited with loved ones.

The Jesuit's remark might also be qualified by noting that prayer, in reality, did not entirely replace lamentation, which continued to feature prominently in the rhetoric of Wendat leaders in these years. It is difficult to fathom the extent to which the experience of the Wendat refugees clustered near Quebec was shaped by personal and collective loss and bewilderment in the decade and a half that followed their departure from their ancestral homeland. In offering condolences to the Ursulines for the loss of their convent by fire in 1650, Louis Taiaeronk described his nation as "devoured and gnawed to the very bones, by war and famine" and his people as "carcasses [...] able to stand only because you support them." In the welcome addresses that they gave upon the arrival of Bishop François de Laval in 1659 and of

Lieutenant General Alexandre de Prouville de Tracy in 1665, Wendat spokesmen similarly emphasized social collapse and dependency. No imagery could more strikingly express what had happened to their people than that of the tortured, cannibalized, and decomposing victim of the Iroquois, the human body being here equated with the political and social body. Addressing Laval, an unnamed speaker described his people as "fragments of a once flourishing nation," "remnant of living carrion," "the skeleton of a great people, from which the Iroquois has gnawed off all the flesh, and which he is striving to suck out to the very marrow." The elder who welcomed Tracy likewise declared that he spoke on behalf of "the wreck of a great country, and the pitiful remnant of a whole world," now "mere carcasses, only the bones of which have been left by the Iroquois, who have devoured the flesh after broiling it on their scaffolds" and passing it "through the boiling cauldrons."[76]

The sense of loss was very real, and the appraisal of diminished political and military capacity was lucid. Yet beyond expressing Wendat despair, such plaintive performances were intended to instill compassion in the French audience and to stir the Crown out of its lethargy. The orator who welcomed Bishop Laval in 1659 clarified the stakes: "If you would have a Christian people," he declared, "the infidel must be destroyed." "If you can obtain from France armed forces to humble the Iroquois," it would be possible by destroying even just two or three of their villages to open a path to vast lands and many nations who yearned only for "the light of the Faith." This line of argument made the most of the audience's sensibilities and priorities. But it also staked the Wendats of Quebec's claim to the centre of the Christian alliance, at a time when the Algonquians were distancing themselves from the mission settlement at Kamiskouaouangachit. "On our life depends that of countless peoples; but our life depends on the death of the Iroquois," concluded the speaker, drawing a parallel between the life of the soul and the body. "Give life to your poor children."[77]

Louis XIV's new interest in the colony promised to breathe new life into the refugee community – in a more concrete, practical fashion than the solace of religion. The young king began his personal rule in 1661, and two years later rescinded the monopoly that the Company of New France had held since 1627. The chartered company had failed, both as a commercial and colonizing enterprise. The king and his energetic chief minister, Jean-Baptiste Colbert, set about reorganizing colonial institutions. While it is unclear whether the pleas of the neophytes reached the ears of the king, the latter was certainly prompted to act by officials, missionaries, and leading colonists, who argued that the Iroquois were to blame for the sluggishness of the colonial venture. The king responded by dispatching reinforcements: Alexandre de Prouville de Tracy, whom he appointed lieutenant general in the Americas, and thirteen hundred soldiers.[78] The Wendats' address to Tracy, quoted at the outset of this book, communicates abundantly well the optimism these troops generated. "Courage, O desolate people!" proclaimed the speaker, as if speaking to his people, "your bones are about to be knit together with muscles and tendons, your flesh is to be born again, your strength will be restored to you, and you shall live as you did live of old."[79]

There was more to the Wendats' welcoming address to Tracy than hybrid Iroquoian and Christian expressions of death and rebirth, however. After having expressed loss and a sense of social collapse, the speaker made a case for the continued strategic value of his people. However diminished and battered, the Wendats of Quebec retained a crucial expertise. They could not contribute very many warriors to a forthcoming campaign, but they were in a position to offer indispensable advice to the officers and soldiers who lacked essential experience in Indigenous ways of war – an understanding of Iroquoian warfare, of the environmental conditions in which it took place, and of the social and cultural centrality of incorporation. Marching against the Iroquois was not something that could be attempted lightly.

Mixing symbolic language with practical considerations, the Wendat speaker offered war paint with which Tracy might inspire fear among his enemies. Turning to the soldiers, he advised them to load their muskets so well that, upon reaching the enemy's country, the noise made by their discharge would not only spread panic among the Iroquois, but would resound as far as Quebec. "His meaning," as the Jesuits who acted as linguistic and cultural interpreters during the meeting understood, "was that the Iroquois, Savages although they were, were not so contemptible as to render it unnecessary to provide good arms and equipment for their conquest." Along similar lines, the speaker raised concerns about the soldiers' uniforms. While they corresponded to the height of European military fashion, they were visibly inappropriate for the task at hand. The Iroquois, who fought entirely naked so as to minimize the impediments to their agility in dense woodlands, would represent an elusive target. "When you have defeated him, you will not have captured him – especially as you are embarrassed with clothing ill-adapted for running through thickets and underbrush." He said this as he offered a girdle – perhaps an actual girdle, though more likely a wampum belt designed to get the point across – which might hold up the long skirts of their coats.[80] Beyond practical sartorial advice, the speaker was drawing attention to capture as the fundamental objective of Iroquoian warfare.

On that note, the elder's final and most important point was that "the element of greatest strength" among the enemy consisted of captives of Wendat, Algonquin, French, and various other origins, who he claimed made up almost two-thirds of their numbers and were compelled to bear arms by their captors. The surest means of defeating the Iroquois was to turn this strength into a weakness. It would not be very difficult, he declared, to entice these captives away "from the service of those cruel masters, for whom they had only fear and hatred in their hearts, and not love." It would suffice for the army to announce to the enemy, as it neared their villages, that they could either hand over their captives or suffer the consequences. "If they delivered them up, they themselves would be defenceless; if they refused, we could compel them by force, while the captives would voluntarily take our side, seeing that their own safety lay with us." Thus it would be possible to "defeat that haughty Iroquois without striking a blow."[81]

***

Algonquians who had been out hunting at the time of Tracy's arrival reassembled at Quebec some weeks thereafter to welcome him. The *Jesuit Relations* mentions "Algonquins," specifically, but it is likely that they represented a mix of peoples whom in other contexts might have been labelled both Algonquins and Montagnais, for it was the elderly Noël Tekouerimat who, as "the Christian of longest standing," spoke in their name. Pledging allegiance to the French alliance, he exhorted Tracy to act in concert with his people to ensure "the destruction of the Iroquois and the publication of the Gospel." With his last present, he prompted the Algonquin chiefs who stood around him to step forward, and he offered them to Tracy, "to march with him and attend him on the expedition that he was about to undertake."[82]

Preparations for the campaign soon got under way. Although Lieutenant General Tracy had tactfully listened to the Wendat recommendations during his ceremonial welcome, he and his staff proceeded to disregard them altogether. Surely it was with astonishment that the Wendats of Quebec learned that their allies intended to carry out their expedition in winter, even though the French officers and men had spent less than six months in the colony and were woefully ignorant of what the cold season entailed. It was worrying, moreover, to see that Tracy, Governor Daniel Rémy de Courcelle, and Intendant Jean Talon, had not taken the precaution to furnish the men with sufficient provisions or the necessary equipment – crucial snowshoes, axes, and blankets were missing.[83]

It is likely that the Wendats of Quebec voiced objections to this ill-conceived enterprise. After the successive blows of the 1650s, their warriors were in short supply. Iroquois peace overtures may also have dissuaded them. In recent years, the four westernmost Iroquois nations had shown themselves accommodating. In fact, the Onondagas had agreed to a truce with the French in 1661, and news of the French soldiers' arrival brought them back. An Onondaga delegation of six ambassadors reached Quebec in the first days of December in 1665, and concluded on the thirteenth a formal treaty with Tracy on behalf of their nation as well as of the Seneca, Cayuga, and Oneida. There is no evidence that these ambassadors spoke directly with the Wendats, but it is not impossible.[84]

Addressing Tracy on behalf of the four western nations, the chief ambassador Garakontié declared that they regretted having taken up arms against the French, stressing that "they intended only to destroy the Algonquins and Hurons their mortal enemies, protected by the French arms." Furthermore, he pledged that "the Hurons and Algonquins dwelling to the north of the River Saint Lawrence [...] shall not be henceforth disturbed in the hunt by the four Iroquois nations or troubled in their commerce going down to trade at Montreal, Three Rivers, Quebec or anywhere else, either by land in the woods, or by water in their canoes, on any pretext whatsoever." On the contrary, because the Algonquins and Hurons were subjects of the king and had been taken under his protection, the Iroquois "shall be obliged to assist them in all their wants, whether in hunting, in peace or in war; and that the differences and enmities which have existed between the said Algonquins and Hurons and between the Iroquois ceasing by the present treaty, there shall be a mutual friendship and assistance between all the said nations who shall live fraternally for their mutual defence under the common protection of the said Lord the King." Garakontié asked for the release of an Iroquois woman, a captive of the Algonquins who resided at Trois Rivières, as well as of "a Huron woman belonging to a refugee family at Seneca, currently a captive in the Huron fort at Quebec." The convoluted nature of this description speaks to the complexity of the personal identities and collective solidarities that had been shaped by the mid-century wars.[85]

Mohawk reluctance to be party to the negotiations determined the colonial authorities to go forward with their campaign. Colonial authorities had expected that both their Wendat and Algonquian allies would be persuaded to contribute warriors to the expedition, but by the time the campaign got under way in January of 1666, only some thirty "Algonquins" were expected to take part. They were slow to reach the agreed-upon meeting point, and, in his haste, Governor Courcelle decided to leave without them, so that, in the end, not a single allied warrior accompanied the five to six hundred soldiers and militiamen who proceeded along the Richelieu River, Lake Champlain, and Hudson River during what turned out to be one of the harshest and longest winters in thirty years. Instead of reaching the country of the Mohawks, as planned, the army, after a harrowing journey, stumbled upon the Dutch outpost of Schenectady. Courcelle decided that to return home was now the wisest course of action. He tried to pass the blame for his expedition's dismal failure onto the Algonquins. It was the first in a long line of complaints, voiced by colonial officers distressed by the apparent unreliability of their Indigenous allies, that would stretch until the very end of the French Regime. Yet, significantly, the feeling was not universal. Other officers recognized the crucial assistance that the allies ultimately provided. As Lieutenant René Gaultier de Varennes believed, "if they had not encountered the Algonquins during their return they would not have brought back a single soldier; they would all have died of hunger."[86]

Seneca ambassadors reached Quebec in May to ratify the peace, followed by Oneidas in early July. The Oneida ambassadors promised to "restore all the Frenchmen, Algonquins, and Hurons whom they hold prisoners among them of what condition and quality they may be." They demanded "reciprocally among all other things the restoration to them in good faith, of all those of their nation who are prisoners at Quebec, Montreal, and Three Rivers."[87] While the Oneidas claimed that the Mohawks had asked them to subscribe to the peace on their own behalf, the latter persisted in their attacks. The French pursued with equal vehemence their efforts to destroy the Mohawks, more careful this time to elicit the assistance of their allies. Eighty to a hundred warriors, mainly Algonquins, given that Wendat men were in short supply, joined Captain Pierre de Saurel when, in the final days of July, he responded to Mohawk raids by leading an impromptu force of two hundred soldiers and militiamen up the Richelieu River. The fact that this was a summertime operation surely made it a more inspiring undertaking. Nevertheless, Saurel found ways of frustrating his allies. When, within a few days' march of the enemy villages, his small army was approached by a Mohawk embassy, the officer decided to order an about-face to escort the ambassadors to Quebec. Believing that these enemies should have been handed over to them, the allied warriors were greatly offended.[88]

It was with some relief, no doubt, that the allies learnt that Tracy, Courcelle, and Talon, anticipating their duplicity, rejected the Mohawks' conciliatory overtures, and resolved to launch a third campaign.[89] The authorities' appreciation of local climactic and human conditions had evolved over the last year. They reached the conclusion that fall would be the best time to carry out the campaign, and they were careful to amass the required supplies. For a time they worried that their allies, vexed by the previous operations, might not agree to take part in this one. But, as Talon remarked in a letter to minister Colbert, they concluded that it would surely be possible to secure their participation "by means of arguments and by presents."[90]

At thirteen hundred men, including one hundred Algonquins and Wendats, Tracy and Courcelle's army in October of 1666 was the largest ever fielded in the colony. The Indigenous allies played a critical role as guides, hunters, and porters. On several occasions, through the most difficult passages between Lake Champlain and the Mohawk valley, warriors took on the thankless task of carrying inept Frenchmen on their backs. At one point, Tracy was himself saved from drowning by a "strong and brave" Wendat warrior. This time, the army did not fail to reach the Mohawk villages. When, after three of them had been sacked, Courcelle hesitated to move on to the final and largest one, it was an Algonquin woman – an indication that the "warriors" were not only men – who had spent part of her youth in captivity among the Mohawks before returning to her homeland, who, seizing a pistol in one hand and grabbing the commander with the other, urged him on. "Come," she said, "I will lead you straight to it."[91]

While the French and their Indigenous allies hoped to surprise the Mohawks, and expected to meet with some resistance, they found all four villages forewarned and abandoned. Only a few old men, women, and children were discovered in the furthest and largest of the four, Tionnontoguen. The army spent a few days destroying the fields and food stores, laying waste and setting fire to magnificently decorated longhouses, and plundering tools, kettles, "and rest of their riches." Having intoned the *Te Deum*, the emblematic hymn of divine praise and thanks, planted crosses bearing the arms of France, and solemnly taken possession of Mohawk country in the name of Louis XIV on 11 October, the army began its journey home.[92]

***

The sources do not hint at how the Wendats, or the Algonquians for that matter, reacted to the sacking of the Mohawk villages. Having seen their own villages reduced to ashes almost twenty years earlier, the former must have been glad for the opportunity to reciprocate at last. Yet there is cause to suspect that it was not with straightforward joy. Indeed, evaluated from a perspective where captive taking was the primary objective of war, the destruction of the Mohawk villages in the fall of 1666 had been a failure. "When you have defeated him, you will not have captured him," the elder had warned Tracy. The expectation that the "captives" of Wendat, Algonquin, and French origin would find the opportunity to leave their "cruel masters" during the enemy's withdrawal had proven overly optimistic. As the French, Algonquin, and Wendat force neared the enemy's villages, no opportunity had presented itself to compel the Mohawks, either by threats or force, to deliver up the foreigners in their midst. Nor is there evidence that any of the latter seized the opportunity to escape from "the service of those cruel masters." Indeed, the risks involved in such an undertaking were great; in one of the abandoned villages the invaders discovered "the mutilated bodies of two or three Natives of another nation, [...] half burned over a slow fire," plausibly individuals who had attempted to escape or were suspected of planning the same.[93]

Still, the sacking of the Mohawk villages did represent a belated vindication of the decision to side with the French and their God. The Wendats who had sought safety at the heart of the French colony a decade and a half earlier had found very little of it until then. Their number had been whittled down, with their consent and by force, from a height of approximately six hundred to a core of less than a hundred. At last, after so many years on the defensive, and two expeditions characterized by ineptitude and failure, the Franco-Indigenous alliance had struck a signal blow against its long-time foe. In the spring of 1667, Mohawk emissaries returned to the negotiating table more committed to peace than ever. That July, their delegates accepted to be party to the peace to which the other Iroquois nations had already agreed, creating a context conductive to new forms of regeneration.[94]

5

Flesh Born Again

New and Old Iroquois in the Mission Settlements, 1667–1680

The peace of 1667, and the royal takeover that had preceded it, became a transformational moment in the history of the New France. It ushered a phase of colonial expansion, as fur traders, missionaries, and would-be discoverers streamed beyond the Saint Lawrence valley. Within it, settlers established homesteads in areas that until then had been too exposed, particularly in the vicinity of Montreal and along the lower Richelieu River. Hundreds of discharged soldiers and officers of the Carignan-Salières regiment joined them on the land. So too did the Wendats leave the safety of the fortified encampment in the Upper Town of Quebec, where they had spent a decade, for fertile lands on nearby Jesuit estates. Having planned their relocation during the winter of 1667–68, they spent a year on the Jesuit seigneury of Notre Dame des Anges, a short distance to the north of the town, before installing themselves to its west on the seigneury of Sillery in the spring of 1669. They did not settle at the old mission of Kamiskouaouangachit on the cove itself, but rather a short distance inland, in a place called the *côte* Saint Michel. This new mission settlement, which soon became known as Notre Dame de Foy, was occupied until 1674, at which time it relocated to a point further west, to a site that took on the name of Lorette.[1]

That neither of these villages was surrounded by a palisade is indicative of the newfound security that the Wendat community enjoyed. The peace settlement of 1667, obtained on favourable terms, brought about an opportunity for regeneration, not merely because the community ceased to fear enemy war parties from Iroquoia, but because large numbers of Wendats and peoples of diverse origins

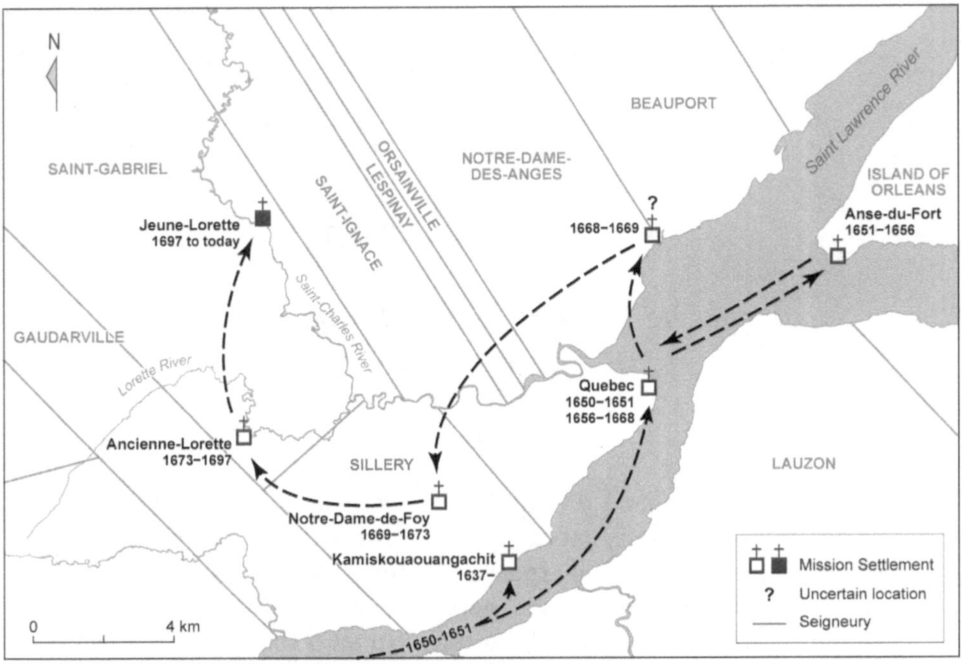

Figure 5.1 Relocations of the Wendat community near Quebec, 1650–1700. (Map by Andrée Héroux)

began streaming from there towards the Saint Lawrence valley and its mission settlements. This, then, was something along the lines of what the Wendat elder who had welcomed Lieutenant General Tracy had presaged. The military and diplomatic success of the Five Nations through the 1640s and 1650s had allowed their villages to maintain relatively high population levels in spite of the steep mortality rates brought about by warfare and epidemics. However, the resultant societies were fragile. As the elder had implied, the absorption of thousands of refugees and captives, in the swift span of some three decades, entailed a loss of social cohesion among the victors. His claim that these elements represented more than two-thirds of the population of Iroquoia echoes other estimates from the period. By 1657, the Jesuit Father Le Jeune observed that the villages of the Senecas "contain more foreigners than natives of that country." Certain communities comprised more foreigners than others. Most dramatically, the village of Gandougarae in Seneca country was said to be composed entirely of Wendats, namely those who had resettled en masse from the missions of Saint Michel (the name of the former mission to the Tahontaenrats, of no relation to the location of the same name in the seigneury of Sillery) and Saint Jean Baptiste (that of the former mission to the Arendarhonon) seven years earlier, as well as of Attiwendaronk (Neutrals) and Onnontiogas (Wenros or Eries, perhaps, or western Algonquians).[2] The Jesuit missionaries who, after the conclusion of the peace, hurried to resume their work in Iroquoia, observed the same demographic trend. In 1667, Wendats and Algonquins were reported to make up two-thirds of the population of the village of Oneida, where they had "become Iroquois in temper and inclination," and a similar proportion of the Mohawk village of Gandaouagué.[3] At around the same time, the three Cayuga villages were described as composed partly of Cayugas, partly of Wendats, and partly of Susquehannocks.[4] This population movement is reflected not only in the historical sources, but also in the archaeological record, as recognizably Wendat and Neutral material culture traits become visible on Iroquois sites at midcentury.[5] While Wendats appear to have been the most numerous among the refugees and captives of Iroquoia, the presence of seven different nations was attested among the Onondagas, and of as many as eleven among the Senecas.[6] The Iroquois, wrote the Jesuit superior Jérôme Lalemant in 1660, had become "for the most, only aggregations of different peoples whom they have conquered."[7]

Among the missionary chroniclers who pointed to the processes of incorporation and ethnic realignment, the most insightful described it as one of naturalization, distinguishing the old stock "*francs Iroquois*" from the foreign-born "*Iroquois naturalisés.*" Alternatively, we might speak of "Old Iroquois" and "New Iroquois," with the crucial caveat that in the Iroquoian context biological descent did not strictly determine personal identities.[8] With peace, large numbers of these "New Iroquois" streamed towards the Saint Lawrence valley and its mission settlements – an unanticipated consequence of the mourning wars. Picking up on the theme of warfare as an integrative process, this chapter probes the limits of integration in Iroquoia as well as the fusion of diverse social fragments in the mission settlements of the Saint Lawrence valley. As the elder had predicted, through the return of Wendats, the refugee community would see its bones "knit together with muscles and tendons," its "flesh […] born again," and its "strength […] restored." Yet his nation would not be remade precisely as it had been "of old," for though a distinct community would persist near Quebec, many of the Wendats and other "New Iroquois" newcomers would instead choose to relocate in the Montreal region, forming a new mission settlement at Kentake (La Prairie), which would in turn subdivide to form two others, Kahnawake (Sault Saint-Louis) and Kanehsatake (La Montagne). Unsurprisingly, the Christian religion and the activity of its French and Indigenous promoters played a key role in the expansion of the mission settlements. So too did the policies of Louis XIV and Jean-Baptiste Colbert, the king's chief minister and soon to be secretary of state for the Navy and colonies, who developed an enthusiasm for the francization of Indigenous peoples. At the same time, however, this expansion also followed from well-established Iroquoian patterns of migration and community formation, of village relocation, fusion and fission, in a way that reflected the fault lines created by previous decades of war.

***

The integration of foreigners into midcentury Iroquois society could take many forms, as outlined in the previous chapters. Through ritual adoption and marriage, newcomers could be enfranchized to become full-fledged members of their adoptive society, assuming all of the rights and obligations that followed. This was easiest to achieve for those who had crossed over willingly. Among coerced war captives, women and children stood the highest chance of being allowed this opportunity, as they were less likely than men to escape or resort to violent resistance, and perceived to be more apt to assimilate. As one Jesuit noted, "many a young man will not hesitate to even marry a prisoner, if she is very industrious; and thereafter she will pass as a woman of his country."[9] It was not uncommon for such naturalized women, children, or even for men, to attain positions of considerable trust and authority within their adoptive community. Such was the case, apparently, of the unnamed "Huron captain, formerly a captive of the Iroquois, and now a captain among them," who had accompanied the Onondaga embassy to Quebec in 1655.[10]

Yet for all the remarkable elasticity of Iroquoian incorporative practices, not all newcomers were so thoroughly assimilated. It was not uncommon for captives to be maintained in a state of precarious servitude. The French used the word *esclave* (slave) to refer to the unnaturalized war captives of the Iroquois, reflecting the fact that they were often subjected to abusive treatment and to the constant threat of death if their behaviour proved unacceptable to others. A parallel distinction was made within Iroquoian languages, where a common set of words ordinarily referred to both captives and domestic animals (*enaskwa*, in one Mohawk word list), to their respective taking or taming (*kenaskonnis*), and to the act of driving either along (*kenaskwenhawis*).[11] An individual whose adoption and assimilation was indefinitely delayed remained as an outsider to the community, little more than a beast. "Among the Iroquois," concluded one missionary, "the life of a captive is valued no more than that of a dog, and it needs only a slight disobedience on his part to merit a hatchet-stroke."[12]

More subtly but no less crucially, many of the New Iroquois – the well-integrated adoptees, women and men who had married into their adoptive communities, who had given themselves over freely or who, captured as children, had spent the better part of their lives there – retained a distinct identity, more or less pronounced from one individual to the next, that overlapped with their new ethnic alignment. For former captives, the psychological shock of violent capture and uprooting, something that we would recognize today as akin to post-traumatic stress disorder, must have continued to disrupt their lives and to foster feelings of alienation. Even for the willing, "happy" migrants, assimilation was far from immediate. The Wendat-Onondaga captain alluded to earlier could thus explain to his kinsmen: "I have not changed my soul, despite my change of country; nor has my blood become Iroquois, although I dwell among them. My heart is all Huron, as well as my tongue."[13] Attachment to an old network of relatives and friends, to a language and a culture, and to the memory of a shared experience, could only fade gradually at a rate that varied from one individual to the next. Personal identities were contextual, and often multiple and layered, experienced and articulated according to the contingencies of circumstance. New and Old Iroquois did not form two strictly divided groups, but rather two ever-evolving modes of belonging.

Beyond the persistence of ancient beliefs and practices, the endurance of comparatively new ones also contributed to the ongoing split between community members and outsiders. Many Wendats clung to elements of Christianity. Some of them had been initiated by French missionaries and Wendat proselytes before or during the ruin of their homeland. Others had since then been initiated by fellow captives, adoptees, and after 1667, by the swelling number of converts among the Old Iroquois themselves.[14] Especially for captives, who had particularly good reasons to accept the promise of a better life after death, there was solace to be found in these beliefs and practices, as well as in the distinctive identity and group solidarity that they fostered. The resistance or inability of many the New Iroquois to swiftly merge into the mass of the Old made them the object of resentment. In a vicious cycle of social tension, this resentment played its part in reinforcing the persistence of divisions. If in 1656, within five years of their mass resettlement to the country of the Senecas, the Tahontaenrats and Arendarhonon might appear to an outside observer to be "united" with their hosts "in good feeling and friendship," by 1672–73 they were described as "miserable" and "abandoned." The Neutrals, who in a similar fashion had "given themselves voluntarily" to the Onondagas, were also by this time "treated like slaves by them."[15] Throughout Iroquoia, fault lines persisted between New and Old Iroquois.

***

The reversal of Iroquois success in war and diplomacy through the release of captives had been a recurrent discussion point during peace negotiations. The Wendats, painfully aware that their reduced military strength gave them little leverage, do not appear to have been so bold as to raise the issue themselves. But the Saint Lawrence Algonquians typically felt no such reserve. During one encounter in 1646, Tessouat the Kichesipirini challenged the Mohawks to show their good faith by granting freedom to the "children of the Algonquins, or even the adult persons who should still be in their country." In 1653, Tekouerimat of Kamiskouaouangachit likewise advised Mohawk deputies that if they were truly interested in peace they should send back the women whom they were holding in captivity so that they might come back to dwell in "the country of the Algonquins."[16]

Beside the stipulation that past hostilities should be forgotten and that cordial relations should ensue, the Franco-Iroquois peace talks carried out between 1665 and 1667 also hinged on the movement of people between Iroquoia and the Saint Lawrence valley. The delegation that came to Quebec in December of 1665 to negotiate a peace on behalf of the four westernmost Iroquois nations was headed by the Onondaga chief Garakontié, who had been one of the most consistent promoters of peace through the previous decade. He had been among those who welcomed the establishment of Sainte Marie de Gannentaha in 1656, and was credited for having given warning of the impending attack on that mission two years later, thus allowing for its safe evacuation. In 1661, he had brought about a truce between his people and the French, and brokered the release of nine Frenchmen.[17] Now, in 1665, on behalf of all four western nations, Garakontié extended an invitation to missionaries and, acknowledging "the advantages they have derived from the union with the French and from the communication they had with them, when they had them in their habitations," in reference to the short-lived mission of Sainte Marie de Gannentaha, he asked that some French families settle among the Onondagas, Cayugas, and Senecas. These nations offered to aid them in their establishment "and to sustain them with their power against those nations that would wish to oppose or retard it." Tracy committed himself on behalf of the French king to sending along some families and missionaries the next spring after the ratification of the treaty, on condition that in each of these countries "fields shall be granted suitable for the erection of cabins to shelter said families and to plant some Indian corn, to be furnished for seed, in exchange for such their provisions as shall be transported for that purpose by the French." He in turn asked that there be sent from each of the four upper nations to Montreal, Trois Rivières, and Quebec, "two of the principal Iroquois families to whom fields, grain and Indian corn shall be furnished, besides the privilege of hunting and fishing in common, which shall be granted them." Garakontié's delegation brought back two Frenchmen, in consideration of which Lieutenant General Tracy arranged for the release of an Iroquois woman, captive of the Algonquins who resided at Trois Rivières, as well as of "a Huron woman belonging to a refugee family at Seneca, currently a captive in the Huron fort at Quebec." As noted earlier, the convoluted quality of the latter description speaks to the complexity of personal identity and collective solidarity, and reflects how the distinction between restored captives, visitors, hostages, and migrants was not always clear-cut.[18]

Seneca ambassadors who came to ratify the peace treaty in May of 1666 likewise expressed their willingness to send some of their families to reside near the French, while demanding that some missionaries and French families be sent to live among them. The Senecas would "not only prepare cabins in which to lodge them, but [...] they would moreover aid to construct forts to shelter them against the incursions of their common enemies, the Andastaëronnons [Susquehannocks] and others." In July, Oneida ambassadors who came next to ratify the treaty on their own behalf and on that of the Mohawks in turn promised to "restore all the Frenchmen, Algonquins, and Hurons whom they hold prisoners among them of what condition and quality they may be," and to send families "to serve, like those of other nations, as the most strict hostages for their persons and dispositions." They demanded "reciprocally among all other things the restoration to them in good faith, of all those of their nation who are prisoners at Quebec, Montreal, and Three Rivers," and that French families and missionaries be sent to them.[19] So too did Tracy remind the emissaries who, in the wake of the destruction of the Mohawk villages, were sent back to their villages that November, of this crucial condition. When these emissaries reappeared in the colony with no prisoners in tow in April of 1667, they were rebuked and given two additional months to comply under threat of a new invasion. When, that July, the Mohawks finally agreed to be party to a definitive peace, it was yet again stipulated that they would bring back all of their captives, and that both sides would offer families as hostages.[20]

Eager to expand the mission field, the Jesuits responded with enthusiasm. Fathers Jacques Frémin and Jean Pierron rushed to Mohawk country, while Father Jacques Bruyas journeyed on to the Oneidas; Fathers Julien Garnier and Pierre Millet followed suit to the Onondagas.[21] A manuscript speech drafted in Wendat with a Mohawk and Oneida audience in mind, penned by one of these missionaries or possibly for one of them by someone like Father Chaumonot, speaks of reconciliation, forgiveness, and unity among all peoples. "Quit your cruelty," asked the missionary, visibly addressing an Old Iroquois core, "[…] the humans that were Huron, Petun, Neutral, Trakwae, Erie, Nipissing, and Algonquin […] You caused them all to perish completely." The missionary explained that the French invasion of Mohawk country had not been meant to kill anyone, but rather to "capture those who believe, so they would believe again, and do good again" – an allusion to the Mohawks who had welcomed the ministry of the Jesuit Isaac Jogues two decades earlier, and quite possibly to the Wendat neophytes who had come by force or consent to Iroquoia. The missionary also drew on the idiom of family. Those who had not yet accepted the Christian faith were urged to do so, and if they did, the missionary assured them that they would thereby become as founders of new lineages within an enlarged family extended on earth and in heaven. That many members of the audience had Wendat friends and relatives living near Quebec went unstated, but the thought of renewing relations with them cannot have been far from their minds.[22]

***

From the *Relations* and other chronicles of this period we can catch glimpses of the parameters and contingencies of migration and settlement. There was, for example, the elderly Pierre Atironta. He was probably of Arendarhonon origin, for his name had been borne by two of that nation's leaders, including Jean-Baptiste Atironta, who had played a key role in the migration of his people to the Saint Lawrence valley in 1650. Jean-Baptiste had been killed by the Iroquois that same year, and Pierre had received his name some time thereafter. The circumstances of Pierre Atironta's capture are unknown, but it was said that he "suffered greatly during his captivity," and it appears that he was among the first few Wendats to return to Quebec and to reintegrate the community, as it relocated from the town to Notre Dame des Anges, and then Notre Dame de Foy. Atironta rapidly learned his prayers and rose to the rank of *dogique* or prayer captain in his longhouse, quickly becoming a pillar of the community. At the time of his death in December 1672, he was described as the "Captain of the Hurons."[23]

Then there is the case of an Algonquin woman, one of several French and Indigenous women and girls whom the Iroquois relinquished at this time and who were handed over to the Ursulines to be reeducated, whose case reveals how bonds created in Iroquoia might draw individuals of Old Iroquois stock to the Saint Lawrence valley. Her Iroquois husband "had such a passion for her," in Marie de l'Incarnation's telling, that he had followed her to Quebec. As the Ursuline superior explained it, "he was continually in our visiting room, for fear that the Algonquins would take her away." He was seen "moaning, losing his speech, stomping around, and coming and going like a madman." His young wife apparently found his insecurity terribly amusing. At length the Ursulines felt compelled to release the woman to her husband on condition that he convert to Christianity.[24] It is not clear what became of the pair afterwards, whether they remained in the Saint Lawrence valley or returned to Iroquoia.

The renewal of relations did not come easily to all, particularly for young men of distant Wendat origins who had reached adulthood in Iroquoia. Two men who had come to Notre Dame de Foy from the country of the Iroquois, "where they had been prisoners of war," decided to return there "on finding themselves persecuted for their evil ways." But to ensure their welcome, they thought it necessary to take a captive or carry off a scalp. They targeted a Wabanaki man, got him drunk, and bound him. The Wendats, having heard of the affair, notified the intendant Jean Talon, who sent out soldiers to stop them.[25] In a similar vein, another young man who arrived from Iroquoia sang, in a fit of drunkenness, "that he was bent on going back thither, but did not intend to make his appearance there empty-handed," by which he meant that he intended to kill someone and carry off his scalp. This prompted the rebuke of one of the community members, Joachim Annieouton. "My cousin," he said to him, "are you not ashamed to talk like that? Is it possible that you are so unnatural as to wish to rejoice our enemies by murdering one of your kinsfolk? Have you not still a brother, a sister, and other relatives here? Will you, then, forsake them to go and give yourself up again as a slave to barbarians, who have brought ruin upon our country?" Two of the young man's comrades responded to the scolding by throwing Annieouton on the ground and stabbing him several times. Fifty days later, Anneiouton died from his wounds after forgiving his assailants and dissuading relatives from exacting revenge on them.[26] Presumably these young men did not remain in the community.

The case of François-Xavier Tonsahoten and his wife Catherine Ganneaktena further illustrates the contexts and contingencies of migration and highlights the importance of persistent ethnocultural fault lines. Like many of those who trickled into the Saint Lawrence valley after the conclusion of the peace, the pair were New Iroquois: Tonsahoten was a Wendat who had been captured and adopted by the Oneida during the invasion of his homeland; Ganneaktena was born to the "nation des Chats" or Eries, and was probably adopted by the Oneidas in the mid-1650s at the time of her people's demise. Both appear to have integrated well within their adoptive community, having entered it at a young age. When Father Jacques Bruyas arrived at Oneida in September of 1667, he quickly befriended Ganneaktena and came to depend on her. During the winter of 1667–68, both she and Tonsahoten accompanied Charles Boquet, one of the Jesuits' ablest lay assistants, back to Montreal. The northward journey was undertaken for a variety of reasons. As a courtesy, the couple had volunteered to escort Boquet back home, for which they could expect the reciprocal advantage of being introduced by him to the missionaries, officials, and traders of the colony. Ganneaktena's blossoming interest in Christian teachings reportedly represented a motivation for the journey. While Tonsahoten is said to have hoped to receive medical treatment among the French for an ailing leg, it is very likely that he also saw it as an opportunity for reconnecting with Wendat relatives from which he had long been separated. Finally, their Oneida community may have sanctioned the journey as a means of strengthening the peace with the French, in the spirit of the negotiations.[27]

Having reached the vicinity of Montreal, Tonsahoten and Ganneaktena's seven-person band set up camp for the winter on the south shore of the Saint Lawrence River facing the town, just below the rapids. This site corresponded to one end of a portage, the other end of which connected to the Richelieu River, and was thus a key position on the route between the Montreal archipelago and the Mohawk River. A wealth of archaeological material points to the fact that this was a site of occasional encampments well before European contact. Fish were abundant here, and the water had the advantage of freezing and thawing out earlier in the season than at other nearby points. And importantly, the small promontory on which the settlement would grow was surrounded by a prominent natural plain, a feature that attracted deer and that made it possible to work the land without needing to clear it first. To the Iroquois, the site was known as Kentake, meaning "at the meadow." The French called it La Prairie de la Madeleine.[28] Towards the end of the season the band was joined there by another one to which belonged Ganneaktena's aunt. In mid-April – at which time the group had swelled to some thirty individuals, all from Oneida – Tonsahoten went on ahead to Quebec with Father Boquet. Having some Wendat relatives at Notre Dame des Anges, he naturally fell in with the community where he was eventually joined by his wife and eight or ten other relatives. There they stayed for a time, receiving religious instruction before being baptized with others in great pomp by Bishop François de Laval.[29]

Though Tonsahoten was pressured by his Wendat relatives to remain with them, and though it is said that Ganneaktena would have gladly stayed there owing to her blossoming interest in Christianity, he was "determined to return to his country" – Oneida country, that is. Ganneaktena's aunt and other relatives must have been equally impatient, for they themselves "had no acquaintances at Quebec," and it had been only with great difficulty that Ganneaktena had convinced them to accompany her there.[30] These details remind us that the possibility of reconnecting with family and friends was the most powerful enticement to visit or join the Wendats at Notre Dame des Anges or, later, Notre Dame de Foy. In the absence of such bonds of kinship (as in the case of the aunt), or when such bonds had been weakened by time (as it must have been for Tonsahoten), there were few reasons to remain with that community. Between those who wished to stay in the Saint Lawrence valley and those who instead wanted to return home, a compromise was reached. As a result, ten to twelve Oneidas decided in the fall of 1668 to spend another winter at Kentake.[31]

Of the approximately two hundred individuals who travelled from Iroquoia to Quebec and spent time among the Wendat community during the peace negotiations and their immediate aftermath, only a fraction elected to remain. In 1668, the community numbered only 150 persons. In other words, it was barely more populous than it had been three years earlier.[32]

***

Tonsahoten and Ganneaktena's band was one of many moving beyond the Iroquois homelands to the north shore of Lake Ontario and to the upper Saint Lawrence in the years that followed the peace of 1667. The temporary establishments of Seneca, Cayuga, and Oneida hunting bands along the northern shore of Lake Ontario would result, by the end of the decade, in the formation of a number of stable settlements, the inhabitants of which the French would collectively describe as "Iroquois du Nord" or North Iroquois. By the mid-1670s, there existed six or seven such Iroquois villages on the north shore of Lake Ontario: Ganneious, an Oneida community on the Bay of Quinte; Kenté, a Cayuga community near the isthmus of the Quinte peninsula; Ganaraské, another Cayuga community at the mouth of the river of the same name; Quintio, on Rice Lake; Ganestiquiagon, a Seneca village near the mouth of the Rouge River; Teyaiagon, a Seneca community near the mouth of the Humber River; and Quinaouatoua, on the portage between the western end of Lake Ontario and the Grand River, likely another Seneca community. In parallel, Mohawk and Oneida hunters and traders journeyed on a regular basis into Algonquin and French territories on the Ottawa and Saint Lawrence Rivers.[33]

The Montreal region was a familiar country to these easternmost Iroquois. Just as it was for the Algonquins and Hurons, it was an ancestral territory. Potsherds found in the Mohawk River valley indicate that a century earlier its people, like the Algonquins and the Wendats, had absorbed some Saint Lawrence Iroquoians refugees or captives. Like the Wendats, the Iroquois called the Island of Montreal "Tiotiake." The meaning of this name remains obscure, but the leading interpretation is that it refers to something "breaking up," conceivably in reference to the dispersion of the Iroquoian peoples who had lived there until the late sixteenth century. Mohawk oral tradition holds that this was the northern edge of their nation's traditional territory.[34]

Like the region which stretched along the north shore of Lake Ontario, the Island of Montreal and its vicinity was a point of passage to lands further north, not to mention a conveniently situated hunting ground. Evidence of the area's persistent appeal as a settlement site has been outlined in previous chapters. Shortly after the founding of Ville Marie, Algonquins and Wendats had shown an interest in resettling there as long as the French were willing and able to provide them with assistance against their Iroquois enemy; passing through a little less than a decade later during their exodus from Huronia to Quebec, the first contingent of refugees had given some thought to establishing themselves there, but decided against it owing to the region's exposed situation. Another reminder of the region's attractiveness can be perceived in the ruse that an Onondaga diplomat tried to employ in 1655: in an effort to effect the migration of the Wendats of the Island of Orleans, he secretly proposed to the leaders of the refugee community that they "allege that they were attracted by the beauty of Montreal and wished to make their home there" (the idea being that, come spring, they would undertake the journey there with their people, only to be met by several hundred warriors and spirited away to Onondaga Country).[35]

The region was also plentiful in game, as wildlife had the opportunity to thrive there during decades of intermittent war. With the conclusion of the peace, the French observed that many bands now came from Iroquoia "to hunt in the region of Montreal and settle aimlessly in various areas on the island."[36] A century later, one resident of Kahnawake recalled that "our forefathers going to hunt chiefly in this neighbourhood was one of the principal reasons for our setting upon the River St. Lawrence near Montreal."[37] The region's enticing commercial possibilities was another principal cause of this population movement. Montreal, by this time, was a town of almost seven hundred inhabitants. From its pious origins as Ville Marie, it had evolved into a hub of the fur trade. Meanwhile, the 1664 surrender of New Netherland to the English upset existing networks. As Father Bruyas noted, the price of cloth had become so dear at Fort Orange (Albany) that the Iroquois were now determined to obtain it in Montreal.[38]

***

The northward movement from Iroquoia to the Saint Lawrence valley coincided with a crucial shift in the French Crown's attitude toward Indigenous peoples. The suppression of the Company of New France paradoxically marked a return to its charter principles as far as this population was concerned. The act establishing the Compagnie des Indes Occidentales, or French West India Company, created by Louis XIV and Colbert in 1664 to take over the colony's commerce, echoed Louis XIII and Richelieu's earlier charter in its specification that "those who shall be born [...] to Natives converted to the Catholic, Apostolic, and Roman faith, [shall be] deemed French subjects [*régnicoles*] and naturals."[39] The instructions issued to colonial officials by the king and his chief minister during these years elaborated on this point. In 1665, Governor Courcelle was told that the king had two principal aims with regards to the "*Indiens naturels.*" The use of the term, a borrowing of the Spanish "*Indios naturales,*" rather than the habitual "*Sauvages,*" betrays Louis XIV's imperialistic frame of reference. At the same time as he drew inspiration from his Iberian counterparts, he was defining himself against them and the accusations of exploitation and usurpation of land that were commonly levelled their way. The first of these aims was "to procure their conversion to the Christian and Catholic faith as soon as it will be possible," and the second was that "subsequently, these Indians be made his subjects, contributing usefully to the growth of trade." However, the king requested that religion and subjecthood not be forced upon anyone. Officials and colonists were to treat Indigenous peoples "with gentleness, justice, and equity, without ever doing them wrong or violence," and the land on which they lived was not to be appropriated under pretext that settlers would make better use of it. The king's intention was that Indigenous peoples would embrace subjecthood willingly, recognizing it to be in their own interest.[40]

"Francization" became policy. Viewed from court it seemed like a sensible way of addressing the chronic shortage of immigrants. "To increase the colony," Colbert wrote Intendant Talon in 1666, "[...] it seems to me that, instead of waiting to benefit from the new settlers who could be sent from France, the most useful way to achieve it would be to try to civilize the Algonquins, the Hurons, and the other Natives who have embraced Christianity; and to persuade them to come to settle in a community with the French, to live with them, and educate their children in our ways and our customs."[41] This assimilation would, like the immigration policy undertaken to send hundreds of marriageable *Filles du Roi* from the metropole to the colony, have the specific benefit of remedying the marked imbalance of the sexes still persisting among settlers. Writing with further instructions shortly after the previous, Colbert instructed Talon that he should "try to attract these peoples, especially those who embraced Christianity, in the vicinity of our habitations, and if possible to have them live there so that after some time, having one law and one master, they may form one people and one blood [*un mesme peuple et un mesme sang*]."[42] Louis XIV and his chief minister, in essence, were rekindling the assimilative aspirations that Champlain and the Recollets had entertained half a century earlier.

A first step towards fusing Indigenous and French peoples was to place the two groups under the same juridical regime. Propelled by the Crown's directives, the colony's Sovereign Council – a body composed of the intendant, governor, bishop, and several leading inhabitants, just recently established at Quebec as part of the Crown's administrative reforms – adopted measures to remove some of the distinctions that had until then been made. In April of 1664, the council decreed that France's Indigenous allies would henceforth be submitted to French criminal laws.[43] In November of 1668, the council lifted the state's longstanding ban against the sale of intoxicating beverages to Indigenous people. The king's officials, Governor Courcelle and Intendant Talon, thus prevailed over Bishop Laval and the missionary lobby which remained staunchly opposed to this trade. The council's decree explained that by sanctioning this trade, Indigenous peoples would be "introduced [...] to the company and commerce of the most honest people," instead of being encouraged to keep on "living in the woods" where colonists of a lesser sort were free to take advantage of them.[44]

Laval and the community's religious orders acknowledged the king's intentions and went through the motions of complying with them. The Jesuits assured Talon that they would "work hard to change the ways of the Natives."[45] However, by this time, having laboured in the colony for a half century, they understood the Crown's expectations to be unrealistic. "It is a very difficult thing," Marie de l'Incarnation expressed the feeling, "not to say impossible, to francisize or civilize them."[46] Louis XIV and Colbert, urged on by Talon, asked the religious orders to contribute to the objective of assimilation by focusing on young Indigenous children, teaching them the French language and ways of life. It had been many years since the Jesuit college at Quebec had welcomed any Indigenous boys, and while the Ursulines had taken in a few girls as pensioners in recent decades, few had stayed long. Bishop Laval responded to royal pressure by expanding the mission of the seminary he had founded at Quebec, creating a primary school, the "Petit Séminaire," where half a dozen Wendat students were mixed in with French ones. However, the results were not encouraging. Indigenous children showed little enthusiasm for the substance and style of teaching, and their parents were reluctant to turn them over. The last Wendat pupil left the Petit Séminaire in March of 1673.[47]

At the core of this shift in policy and practice was a struggle over the division of State and Church. The Society of Jesus, in particular, had stirred the envy and resentment of key figures in the colony and at court. In light of complaints that the Jesuits had appropriated in the colony "an authority that surpasses the boundaries of their true profession," Louis XIV instructed Talon to look into their affairs. Other intendants and governors would thereafter be instructed along similar lines. Frontenac was asked to "be very considerate with regard to them" in light of their contribution to the development of the colony, but told that if they overstepped their authority, he should "make known to them with courtesy [*avec douceur*] the line of conduct they are expected to follow, and, in case they do not yield, he will diplomatically oppose their designs without appearance of rupture or partiality, and he will advise His Majesty of all so that he may be in position to apply the proper remedy."[48] The near monopoly that the Jesuits seemed to hold over Indigenous affairs was among the bones of contention. So too was the abundance of land that their order had been granted over the years. The Crown's regularization of the seigneurial system, though it was not specifically targeted at the Jesuits, left them scrambling to justify and protect their extensive holdings, several of which remained unsettled and unimproved.[49]

These years also saw a new set of actors step onto the missionary stage. In 1663, the heavily indebted Société de Notre Dame relinquished its title to the seigneury of the whole island of Montreal in favour of the Société de Saint Sulpice, which six years earlier had established a parish and a seminary at Ville Marie. Headquartered in Paris, the latter society was a free association of secular priests, meaning that it did not demand of its members the vows of poverty and obedience typical of regular orders like the Society of Jesus. Also in contrast with the Jesuits, the Sulpicians were Gallican in ideology, meaning that its members tended to value the authority of the monarch and the state as much as that of the pope and the Church – and indeed Louis XIV and Colbert came to view them as a valuable counterweight to Jesuit power in the colony.[50] Although they too entertained missionary ambitions, the Sulpicians attached to the newly formed Seminary of Montreal lacked the collective expertise to launch themselves in the wider missionary field, and instead concentrated on serving the area's settler population: during the decade stretching between their arrival in 1657 and 1667, the sacramental registers of the town's parish, Notre Dame, recorded the baptism of only eleven Indigenous individuals.[51] The Iroquois peace, however, and the Crown's assimilative fervor, created new opportunities. In October of 1668 two Sulpician priests, François de Salignac de la Mothe-Fénelon and Claude Trouvé, travelled to Lake Ontario and founded a mission at the Cayuga village of Kenté on its north shore. At around the same time, a few other Sulpician priests, including René de Bréhant de Galinée, began to minister on an irregular basis to the Algonquin and Wendat families that now encamped at various points on the upper Island of Montreal, above the Lachine rapids, for the purpose of hunting and trading.[52]

While the Jesuits were not about to establish a new mission on the Island of Montreal, as it was the Sulpicians' prerogative, they aimed to do so on one of their neighbouring seigneuries. In 1636, they had been granted Île Jésus, a large island of about half the size of Montreal, from which it was separated by the Rivière des Prairies. In 1647, they were granted the seigneury of La Prairie on the south shore of the Saint Lawrence (not to be confused with the aforementioned river), and in 1657 they were gifted that of L'Assomption, on its north shore just upriver from the Montreal archipelago. Though these grants were made with the understanding that as seigneurs the Jesuits could settle there "such persons as they shall please," they had not occupied them on account of the war.[53] With the conclusion of a solid peace in 1667, and in the context of the Crown's tightened regulation of the seigneurial system, the Jesuits were eager to develop at least one of these seigneuries and establish a missionary presence there. The sites to the north of the Island of Montreal were briefly considered. In the summer of 1667, Father Dablon and Louis Thaondechoren, one of the leading figures among the Wendats of Quebec, toured the Rivière des Prairies and L'Assomption rivers, returning "with great satisfaction." But for whatever reason – the inclinations of Ganneaktena and Tonsahoten's band, quite possibly – the Jesuits decided to instead invest their human and material resources at La Prairie.[54]

Louis XIV and Colbert's exhortations during these years explain why, in the Saint Lawrence valley, Iroquoian mission communities were paired off with French *habitants*, the two groups living next to each other and sharing religious spaces and services. The Wendat community that had spent a decade ensconced at the "Fort des Hurons" within the town of Quebec left it in the spring of 1668 for the Jesuit seigneury of Notre Dame des Anges, to the north, before resettling, the following year, in the seigneury of Sillery, to the west. Notre Dame des Anges and neighbouring Beauport were fertile and familiar ground – in 1650, some Wendat families had encamped there, and the Jesuits had considered it as a site for their mission before settling on the Island of Orleans. However, the area was by this time too densely settled by colonists to properly accommodate the mission community.[55] The vast hinterland of Sillery offered a better balance. In describing the Wendats' installation at the place called côte Saint Michel within that seigneury in the spring of 1669, Father Claude Dablon stressed in the annual *Relation* that the area was "thickly settled by the French, to profit by the latter's good example, and, in turn, to edify the French by their own piety and devotion," and that they had built their chapel there "in union with the settlers of the place."[56] At La Prairie the Jesuits would similarly settle rent-paying habitants side by side with neophytes, the initial handful of newcomers from both groups spending their first winter "living under the same roof [in a] simple shed of boards, upright and leaning one against the other in a ridge like an ass's back."[57] Within a few short years the missionaries would return to favouring a stricter segregation between the two groups, convinced that the French influence on Indigenous peoples tended to be more corrupting than salutary, but for now the ideal of proximity endorsed by the Crown prevailed.

***

The Jesuit missionary Father Pierre Raffeix, who was posted at La Prairie, made it clear to Tonsahoten, Ganneaktena, and their half dozen followers during the winter of 1667–68 that their settlement on that site would enjoy missionary assistance. It was some time, however, before this seasonal encampment of a family hunting band grew into a proper village. As noted previously, of the approximately thirty Oneidas reportedly encamped in the vicinity of Montreal in April of 1668, only ten or twelve returned to Kentake in the fall of that year. During the winter that followed, even this dozen scattered in the neighbouring woods for the habitual winter hunt, returning only periodically to La Prairie's makeshift chapel to attend the Christian feasts. In an effort to fix these families there for good, Raffeix had a plot of land cleared and sowed for them by hired hands as he awaited their return in the early spring of 1669. It was only then that Ganneaktena and Tonsahoten made a commitment to settle by building a true longhouse for the two families who lived there, to replace the smaller makeshift cabins that they had occupied until then. In keeping with well-established patterns of settlement, the decision to remain there was Ganneaktena's more than that of her husband. In the missionaries' retelling of the settlement's origins it was she who "forced her husband to take La Prairie as his abode," and it was again she who "did not fail to win over" the hunting bands that passed through. Her house was open to all, and the generosity for which she was renowned reinforced her authority and strengthened the growing mission community. "She fed the French and the Natives with the fruit of her husband's hunt," explained Chauchetière several years after her death, "she was liberal to excess [and] this liberality made her beloved of everyone." Elsewhere he described her as "the foundation stone of the mission."[58]

In spite of the site's manifest advantages, this decision to stay at Kentake could not have been an easy one, as the late winter and spring of 1669 were marked by a troubling series of violent incidents. After long years of war, the ways of peace did not come easily to everyone. A few soldiers from the Montreal garrison intent on stealing furs murdered "one of the most prominent" Senecas, who was on his way to town to trade after a winter hunting along the Ottawa River. An Oneida family, composed of three men, two women, and two children, encamped on the banks of the Mascouche River, north of the Island of Montreal, was massacred by a fur trader and his two employees. It came to light during the latter's trial that they had committed this act with the aim of stealing fifty-three moose hides, twenty-three beaver skins, and sundry belongings, but it is tempting to see, behind this act of criminal violence, antagonisms shaped by decades of conflict: one of the guilty men had been in the service of the missionaries in Huronia between 1641 and 1646, when the Iroquois offensive began; another had himself been captured by the Oneidas in 1652 and seems to have spent over a decade among them.[59]

The news of the killings soon reached Oneida country and made "all this nation very angry." The Senecas were similarly incensed by the death of one of their own. "It is beyond a doubt that an affair of this nature is very unfavourable," wrote Father Jacques Frémin anxiously from Onondaga, "and capable of rekindling the war between the Iroquois and the French."[60] Colonial authorities were consequently quick to identify and punish the guilty who had "exposed, by the means of their avarice and concupiscence, the whole country to a total destruction" and whose great crimes consisted not only in murder and theft, but in having "hindered the Natives from coming in peace to settlements and having here a favourable retreat." The guilty soldiers were executed in front of Seneca delegates, while the three who had killed the Oneidas, having fled into the interior, were condemned to death in absentia. Governor Daniel de Rémy de Courcelle was careful to send wampum belts to the Senecas and to the Oneidas to express his regrets and disown the guilty parties.[61]

Tonsahoten, Ganneaktena, and their followers must have been greatly troubled by the murders – the six Oneidas would have been acquaintances of theirs, perhaps even relatives or close friends. Yet, no doubt owing to official efforts to disavow the killings, they were not dissuaded from returning to Kentake after the hunt. If anything, it is possible that these violent incidents contributed to the attraction of that site, where a missionary presence offered a measure of protection against potentially murderous colonists. The embryonic settlement attracted the attention of the Iroquois hunting bands dispersed around the Island of Montreal and along the upper Saint Lawrence towards Lake Ontario. Between 1669 and 1673, visitors came by the hundreds. "Curiosity," observed Father Chauchetière, "attracted them to La Prairie." Traditional subsistence patterns played a key role in the settlement's growth. The people of Kentake who dispersed for the winter hunt unavoidably encountered in the process the hunting bands of relatives and acquaintances. On these occasions, they vaunted the advantages of their new settlement, both material and spiritual, and extended invitations to join them there, at least for a visit if not the long term. "[H]unting," Chauchetière explained, "was the pretext which they then adopted in order to come to live at La Prairie. The Christians who left La Prairie, in going to hunt beasts, went also to hunt men."[62]

While many of the curious who were drawn to Kentake left uninspired by the fledgling community and its close ties to the French, others were inclined to stay on a more permanent basis for the very same reasons that had motivated Tonsahoten and Ganneaktena. The Jesuits' willingness to hire colonists to do the initial agricultural work of clearing and sowing fields for the newcomers, was an attractive feature – just as it had been for the Algonquians of Kamiskouaouangachit decades earlier. "These visitors, seeing the corn very fine, resolved to remain there and build their cabins," as Chauchetière put it.[63] By the end of 1669, the settlement at Kentake numbered five such longhouses, sheltering perhaps 50 persons. By the fall of 1671, it was said to number 18 or 20 families, an estimated 100 to 120 individuals in perhaps a dozen longhouses.[64]

By 1671, the encampment at Kentake had grown into a respectable village community. An important council was held that summer during which its inhabitants decided to remain there indefinitely.[65] In the *Relation* of 1670–71, the formal name of the new mission appeared in print for the first time: Saint François Xavier des Prés. Hence, a tentative Indigenous and missionary experiment had evolved into a more consequential affair. The choice of name reflected missionary devotion to Saint Francis Xavier, the pioneering Jesuit apostle to the Indies. More significantly, however, this choice stood as a testament to the prominence among the founders of the community of emigrants from Oneida, where Father Bruyas had named his mission Saint François Xavier.[66] It was perhaps also indicative of the personal influence of Tonsahoten within that community, for he had himself taken on the baptismal name of François-Xavier.[67] The steady arrival of newcomers now made it necessary to formalize and legitimize the political structure of the village. In the summer of 1671, two chiefs, following what the missionaries took to be Iroquoian custom, were chosen by common accord, one to oversee general administration and war, and the other to supervise the exercise of Christianity.[68] The first of the two was plausibly Tonsahoten, who

Figure 5.2 Claude Chauchetière drew this image of Tonsahoten and Ganneaktena's family arriving at Kentake from Oneida almost two decades after the fact. It is an allegorical, rather than a faithful depiction, evoking the built environment of La Prairie in a more finished and idealized state than it would have been at the time. Some buildings erected by the French workers may have had a gabled roof and timber walls, but the newcomers built for themselves longhouses in the traditional Iroquoian style. ("Les six [*sic*] premiers sauvages de la Prairie viennent d'Onneiout sur les neiges et les glaces," ca. 1686, Archives départementales de la Gironde, Série H, Bordeaux)

at the time of his wife's death two years later would be described as the community's "first captain."[69]

***

The New Iroquois, adoptees and captives of Wendat and various other origins, featured prominently among the newcomers to the Saint Lawrence valley during the late 1660s and through the 1670s. Kentake, in particular, was in its early years characterized by a great ethnic diversity, and by the range of hyphenated identities of its residents. Describing the first settlers, Chauchetière noted that "one was from the *nation des Chats* [Eries], another from the Hurons, a few *francs Iroquois* [Old Iroquois], others Gandastogues [Susquehannocks]."[70] Soon the mission was said to be home to individuals from as many as twenty-two nations, "many of which have completely different languages," including "Outouagannah" (a generic name for Algonquians of the western Great Lakes), "Gentagega" (a subdivision of the Eries), Algonquins, Innu, Nipissings, "Loups" or Mahicans, and Sokokis.[71] Many of these newcomers were, like the Wendat-Oneida Tonsahoten and Erie-Oneida Ganneaktena, relatively well-integrated adoptees who, for various reasons, chose to cast their fate with the French. Others were escaping a state of virtual slavery. As Chauchetière remarked, "many who were not naturalized Iroquois resolved to steal away and come to La Prairie. Many thus slipped away during all the following years."[72] The attraction of the mission settlements was such, however, that they appealed not only to the New Iroquois. Old-stock Iroquois came too, this to the great joy of the missionaries who saw in the willingness of former captors and captives to come together as the portent of a Christian utopia. "*Habitabit lupus cum agno,*" the *Relation* for 1672–73 quoted from the Book of Isaiah: "The wolf shall dwell with the lamb."[73]

For New and Old Iroquois alike, kinship ties and family networks acted as a catalyst to migration. Individuals attracted to life at Notre Dame de Foy or Kentake most often brought their spouses, children, and relatives. When an unnamed Mohawk neophyte returned from the mission settlement at Notre Dame de Foy to his country to bring back his entire family, a resident named Marie Tsaouenté took the opportunity to address a wampum belt to her father, who still lived among the Mohawks, to convince him to "join her here to find his salvation."[74] Women were generally observed to be the most enthusiastic promoters of the mission settlements. The Jesuits were quick to chalk this is up to the fact that theirs was "the pious sex," resorting to Catholic constructions of femininity and oversimplifying the way in which gender was at play. In Wendat and Iroquois societies, female lineages and leadership formed the very basis of kinship solidarities and community cohesion. It was only natural for women such as Catherine Ganneaktena and Marie Tsaouenté to endeavor to reconstitute extended families.[75]

To strengthen their heterogeneous communities, such women drew on the array of traditional and innovative means at their disposal. The figure of the Virgin Mary, as in years past, continued to offer a pole of attraction as Iroquoian women explored the merits of various religious devotions. The new mission church at Sillery's côte Saint Michel was upon its establishment in 1669 dedicated to l'Annonciation de Notre Dame, in honour of the archangel Gabriel's announcement to the Virgin Mary that she would become the mother of Jesus. However, the community's enthusiasm at the arrival of a wooden statuette of the Virgin from the shrine of Notre Dame de Foy in Dinant, Belgium, was such that the mission was promptly renamed.[76] A few years later, the women of the community inquired to know more about the "Saint Esclavage de Marie" (Holy Bondage of Mary). This devotion, newly popularized in France and in fashion at the Ursuline convent at Quebec, exalted the faithful's total surrender to the Virgin and must have spoken to the painful experiences of Iroquoia. But devotion to the Holy Family, which instead insisted on the theme of kinship, and particularly on the maternal bond between Mary and the Infant Jesus, proved more appealing. In 1671, responding to the interest of the women, the Jesuit missionary Chaumonot instituted there a chapter of the Congrégation de la Sainte Famille. The devotion caught on at Kentake too, where another chapter was soon formalized.[77] This lay confraternity, much like that of Our Lady founded at the Island of Orleans in a time of comparable upheaval two decades earlier, was a means by which peoples sought to bridge differences and achieve a more solid union.

In 1670 or 1671, the Wendats who after the dispersal of midcentury had merged with the Tionnontatés and remained in the Great Lakes area instead of seeking refuge in the Saint Lawrence valley sent some of their chief men to Quebec to ask for the protection of the French against the Dakota who had recently declared war on them. Their embassy was well received and given presents as an invitation to

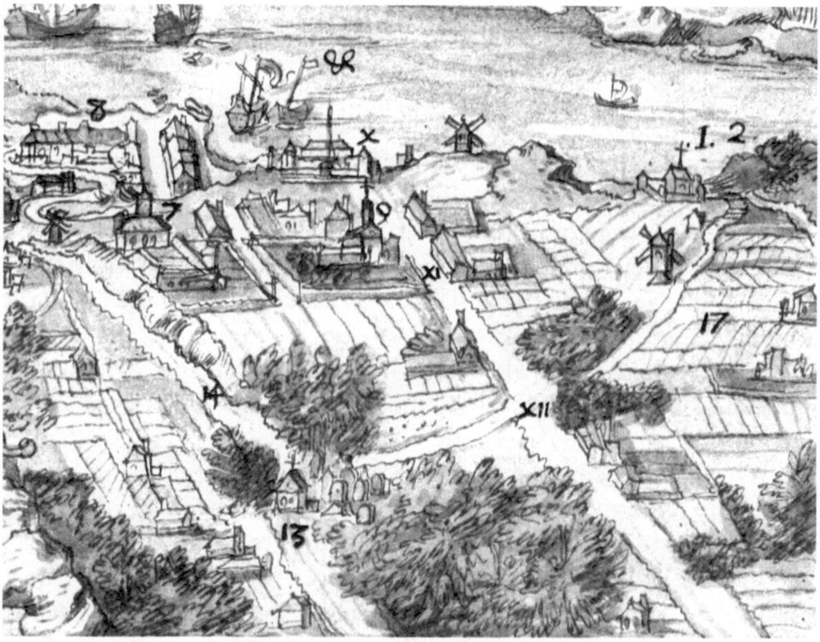

Figure 5.3 Bird's eye view of Quebec (in the top left corner) and its vicinity showing the Wendat village with its domed longhouses at Notre Dame de Foy (13) as well as the old mission compound at Kamiskouaouangachit or Sillery (I). (Detail from Jean-Baptiste Franquelin's "L'entrée de la Rivière du St-Laurent, et la ville de Québec dans le Canada," ca. 1671–73, BNF, Département des cartes et plans, GE SH 18 PF 127 DIV 6 P I D)

become Christians and to join the community at Notre Dame de Foy. The ambassadors seemed pleased, and left the Jesuits expecting that their people, totaling about five hundred, would relocate there in the spring. But there is no evidence that any did come. Rather, they established their village in the place called Michilimackinac, at the straits of Mackinac, between Lakes Huron and Michigan, where the Jesuits established a mission for them in the summer of 1671.[78] People kept coming from Iroquoia, however, to both Notre Dame de Foy and Kentake. Through the early 1670s, an ever-increasing number of them travelled from the villages of the Mohawks, and especially from the one called Gandaouagué – as the Jesuits rendered a name, meaning "at the rapids," later rendered by others as Caughnawaga and Kahnawake. As the easternmost village of the Mohawk valley, Gandaouagué in recent years had been acutely exposed to spiritual and military offensives.

Though during the 1640s Father Isaac Jogues's early effort in this community had fared poorly, it was here that Fathers Frémin, Bruyas, and Pierron had built their first chapel when they returned in earnest to Iroquoia in 1667. They found a particularly receptive audience, especially among the women and men of Wendat origin who by this time represented an estimated two-thirds of the population of this village.[79] They also found a community that was in the process of rebuilding itself, having been razed to the ground during the French invasion of the previous year. Although the solid Franco-Iroquois peace made it unlikely that this disaster would soon be repeated, the village remained vulnerable to the raids of the now well-armed Mahicans from east of the Hudson River, with whom the Mohawks were still at war. In August of 1669, it endured a particularly trying siege. Three to seven hundred enemy warriors were repelled *in extremis* thanks to the leadership of a man named Togouirout (likely meaning "His Tree Stands Upright"), more commonly known to the Dutch and English as Kryn or Cryn, and to the French as *le Grand Agnier* or The Great Mohawk – a figure who would come to play a central role in the unfolding story of the mission settlements of the Saint Lawrence.[80]

As the continuing activity of Jesuit missionaries and Indigenous proselytes through the 1670s exacerbated the rift between Christians and traditionalists in Mohawk country, waves of epidemics, combined with the socially disruptive inroads of the New York liquor trade, further contributed to making life there intolerable for New and Old Iroquois alike.[81] At some point in 1672 or 1673, a Wendat captain named Jacques Onnhatetaionk and his family left the Mohawk village where they had spent the previous fifteen years for Notre Dame de Foy. Arriving there with the intention of joining the community, he explained that he had grown disturbed by the drunkenness that reigned among the Mohawks and fearful that his children would adopt these disorderly habits.[82]

Onnhatetaionk and his followers may have belonged to a group of fifty persons known to have travelled at about this time from an unnamed Mohawk village to Notre Dame de Foy, or otherwise been incited by this group's departure.[83] By this time, even Togouirout the Great Mohawk, a war chief of high stature and by all accounts of Old Iroquois stock, had apparently grown disenchanted with life at Gandaouagué. Having visited Kentake during the winter hunt and been favourably impressed by what he had seen, he rounded up forty of his people in secret and led them there in June of 1673. Here as elsewhere, it is tempting to sense the discrete influence of women beyond the conspicuous leadership of men. It is all but certain that most of these latter migrants belonged to the Turtle Clan, as that clan dominated at Gandaouagué and as Togouirout himself was one of its members.[84]

The mix of spiritual and strategic motives that incited these men and women to abandon Gandaouagué was captured by Father Bruyas when he explained to the recently arrived governor Louis de Buade de Frontenac that they sought to "take refuge in your arms as in an asylum, where they hope to preserve their faith and be secure from their enemies."[85] A shift in missionary strategy also factored into this latest wave of resettlement. For the past twenty years the Jesuits had tended to view their mission settlements of the Saint Lawrence valley as secondary to whatever missions could be established among the Iroquois. Louis XIV's new-found assimilative ambitions had not produced an immediate sea change in their missionary policy. But the challenges encountered in Iroquoia, coupled with the discovery that so many neophytes were eager to leave it, now led Father Lamberville to reason that "to make them good Christians in their own country is a difficult thing, and one that will take a long time to accomplish, but if we could gradually detach them from their dwelling-place, and attract them to our Wendat colonies, it would be very easy to make worthy Christians of them in a short time."[86]

It is likely that it was in an effort to capitalize on the recent wave of migrants, or perhaps as a response to the fact that newcomers increasingly favoured the village of Kentake over Notre Dame de Foy as their destination, that a "squadron of Hurons" decided to accompany Frontenac during his expedition to Cataraqui (current-day Kingston, Ontario) in late June and July of 1673. It was headed by Louis Thaondechoren, a Wendat of Tionnontaté birth who had found himself among the refugees to the Saint Lawrence valley in the 1650s, and who, after managing an escape from Annaotaha's disastrous expedition, had emerged as one of the most zealous members of the community in the exercise of Christian piety. When the Wendats settled at Notre Dame de Foy, Chaumonot appointed him to lead them in prayer during his occasional absences. The Jesuit account of Thaondechoren's errand in 1673 states that his intention was to use the governor's conference with the Iroquois as an opportunity to "carry the Gospel and publish the name of Jesus-Christ." An official's account paints a more complex and compelling picture. During his conference with the Iroquois, Frontenac voiced his allies' concern, blaming the "cruelty" that the Iroquois exercised against their "Huron brothers" who lived among them by "preventing them from coming to visit their parents" in the Saint Lawrence valley and "calling them slaves and threatening to break their heads." Thaondechoren took the floor next. Describing the advantages of Christianity, his speech nevertheless centered on the migration of his countrymen. He offered a wampum belt to his Iroquois counterparts in the hope that they would not refuse his people's request that they "allow the return of their relatives among them." The celebrated Onondaga chief Garakontié, responding on behalf of the League nations, apparently agreed in principle.[87]

While Frontenac was overseeing the foundation of the fort which would bear his name at Cataraqui, Thaondechoren proceeded to Onondaga in the company of Garakontié and two other Wendats. He encountered there a particularly receptive audience of Wendats and Neutrals. Even as he is said to have "sowed in the mind of many infidel Iroquois the seeds of the Faith," he "excited in the hearts of the Christian Hurons a great desire to travel to Quebec to fulfill in peace the duties of Christianity, with more liberty than they have in the country of their captivity." The Neutrals, who had willingly given themselves over to the Onondagas only to find themselves treated no better than slaves, took the opportunity to convene Thaondechoren to a secret council and asked him to convince Onontio to send soldiers who might cover their escape to the colony. Knowing that the governor would be loath to threaten the Franco-Iroquois peace by going along with such schemes, Thaondechoren could make no commitment. He nonetheless suggested that the Neutrals could withdraw to the newly built Fort Frontenac at Cataraqui, on the pretext of carrying out their regular hunt, where the French would receive them kindly and from whence they would ensure their safe passage to Quebec.[88] It was, in essence, the same ruse that two decades earlier an Onondaga diplomat had proposed to the Wendats of the Island of Orleans. But Thaondechoren's discussions with the Neutrals were never followed through.

***

Frontenac, who served two mandates as governor of New France in 1672–82 and 1689–98, was quick to develop an adversarial relationship with the Jesuits. Encouraged in this thinking by Louis XIV and Colbert, he felt that the missionaries had not lived up to their responsibility of francization. The way in which the Jesuits went about ministering to the neophytes without teaching them the colonists' language or customs annoyed him greatly, as did their periodic requests for the expansion of their seigneurial holdings to accommodate the mission settlements. He also consistently opposed their efforts to extend their missions beyond the Saint Lawrence valley, countering that they should focus their efforts on those that had already begun. In an – ultimately unsuccessful – attempt to demonstrate that assimilation was feasible and that anyone could be better at it than the Jesuits, Frontenac went as far as to take a couple of Iroquois boys into his household. Although he was more sympathetic to the Sulpicians, soon they too attracted his displeasure with their strict morality and their resistance to the imperious way in which he exercised his authority.[89]

Within a few years of Frontenac's arrival, the Jesuits began to push back against the policy of integration. During the fall of 1673, less than five years after its installation at Notre Dame de Foy, the Wendat community moved to a new site, further west from Quebec and deeper in the woods. The lack of arable land and of firewood was cited by Father Chaumonot as the reason why the relocation had become necessary. The fact that the mission "was increasing every day" owing to arrivals from Iroquoia made these needs even more pressing.[90] It is also likely that the missionaries meant to isolate the Indigenous community from its French neighbours, many of whom were only too eager to offer brandy to the neophytes in exchange for their pelts. The specific site proposed by the Jesuits, on their seigneury of Saint Gabriel, beyond that of Sillery, had the additional advantage of advancing their order's property interests in two ways. The redistribution to colonists of the acreage already cleared at the former site promised to increase seigneurial revenues, while the removal of the neophyte community from the seigneury of Sillery also neutralized eventual challenges to the order's title over this grant, which had ambiguously been made two decades before to the "*Sauvages*," in trust to the Jesuits.[91]

Whereas some of the mission settlement relocations during the seventeenth century were driven by Indigenous communities themselves, the degree to which the Wendats partook in this particular initiative is debatable. "After much searching, and still more prayers," explained one missionary account, the Wendats "have not themselves found a place more suitable than that which we have granted them." The annual *Relation* hints that while the move was accepted by the community, and appreciated by many, the feeling was not universal. At least one woman demonstrated sadness at the thought of leaving Notre Dame de Foy on account of her great attachment to her fields there.[92]

Work at the new site began in January 1673. Under the Jesuits' direction, French workmen cleared an initial site on a promontory, and then, finding that access to the first was too impractical, prepared a second site by hastily erecting a dozen houses which in turn proved too small and close to each other and had to be replaced during the summer of the following year by longhouses built by the Wendats themselves. The missionaries imposed an unusual village layout upon the settlement, quite different from those of Iroquoian tradition, by arranging the houses around a square centred on the mission's chapel. The new community took on the name of Lorette – in reference to Loreto, Italy, a renowned site of Marian pilgrimage centred on a house, the *Santa Casa*, in which the Holy Family was believed to have lived and which was believed to have been flown over from Palestine by angels. The Virgin of Loreto held a special personal meaning for Chaumonot, who as a wayward youth had found his calling during a pilgrimage there. The Wendat community, given their collective attachment to the avocation of Mary as a mother and to the notion of the Christian family, proved eminently receptive to this figure. A chapel designed by the missionary to serve as centerpiece for the village, made of brick like the Santa Casa and following the same dimensions, was constructed over the summer and fall of 1674. For its inauguration, on 4 November, Chaumonot and the other Jesuits gave a feast for the community, distributing presents in the way of blankets, cloth, and hatchets, and obtaining from its members a pledge that they would not drink liquor in excess, and that whomever would henceforth become intoxicated would be driven away from the village.[93]

Migrations from Iroquoia brought the total population of Lorette to about 300 in 1675.[94] The population of Kentake probably reached about the same level that year, having numbered, with daily arrivals, 280 in 1674.[95] While in 1673 Father Lamberville might still describe both communities as "Huron colonies," the influx of Old Iroquois heralded a new phase in the evolution of the mission settlements and in the formation of local identities. The migration of Togouirout and his followers to Kentake, in particular, would have a multiplying effect – Chauchetière hailed it in hindsight as the "first shock given to infidelity." If the first to settle at Kentake had been Oneidas by adoption

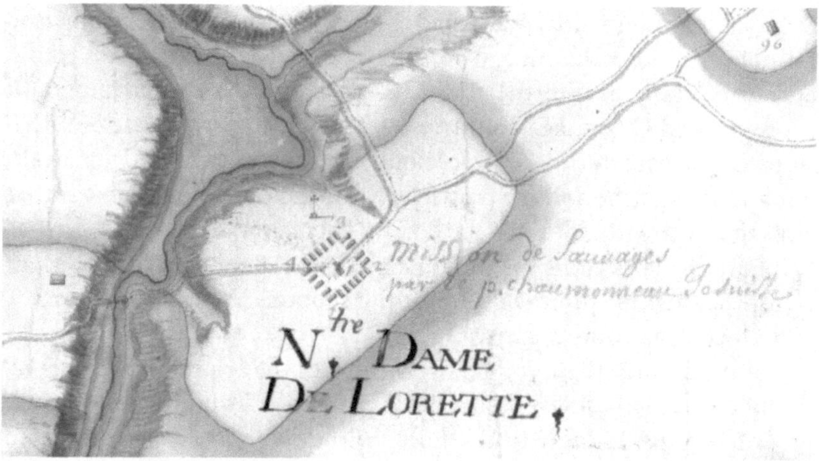

Figure 5.4 The mission settlement at Lorette (today Ancienne Lorette), occupied between 1673 and 1697, as it appears on Robert de Villeneuve's map (Detail from "Carte des Environs de Quebec," 1685–1686, BNF, Département Cartes et plans, GE SH 18 PF 127 DIV 7 P 4)

or birth, the newcomers from the Mohawk villages, and from Gandaouagué in particular, now "took the first rank."[96]

The political structure adopted in 1671 to respond to the growth of the community, according to which one chief oversaw civil and military affairs and a second oversaw religious matters, was found to be maladapted to the changing face of the community. In 1673 it was deemed necessary to name a chief for each of the three most numerous nations in the village, namely the Mohawks, Wendats, and Onondagas. When a council was assembled for this purpose, the Mohawks and Onondagas quickly named their respective leaders, but the deliberations dragged on among the Wendats.[97] Tonsahoten appears to have been disputing the nomination with another, if not several, Wendat men. In the absence of indications of the time of year in which it occurred, it is tempting to link the timing of this reorganization with the illness of Ganneaktena, which began when she was working the fields in the late summer of that year and carried on until her death in early November.[98] It is likely that the disagreement over the choice of chief was not rooted merely in the personalities and abilities of the men involved, but rather in the divergent experiences of the last two decades. The passage of time had frayed the old solidarities of Huronia, allowing a variety of new local solidarities and leaders to emerge.

Wendats from Oneida, who had figured prominently among the founders of Kentake and who still retained a measure of moral authority, clashed with the more recent Wendat arrivals from both Mohawk and Onondaga countries. It is not impossible that old divisions of the sort outlined in previous chapters, between Attignawantan and Arendarhonon for example, flared-up. The outcome was that Tonsahoten maintained his authority. Thereafter he is alluded to as "captain of the Hurons" of the mission, someone "deferred [to] in all things, as the first and the senior of the captains" by his two Mohawk and Onondaga counterparts.[99]

Compounding these matters was the fact that the site of Kentake, though occupied for less than a decade, was, like its political structure, proving poorly adapted to the influx of newcomers. The yield of the corn fields had been impressive in the first few years, but had since become insufficient to satisfy the needs of the community. At the same time as traditional agricultural methods were slowly depleting the soil of the first fields, the fact that much of the area's acreage was too humid to cultivate maize discouraged the preparation of new ones. Missionary stores, which supplemented the growing community's needs, were stretched to the maximum. "Poverty," according to Chauchetière, now characterized life at the mission.[100] While the people of Kentake appear to have had a greater say in their move than those of Notre Dame de Foy at around the same time, similar factors contributed to both relocations. At Kentake even more so than at Notre Dame de Foy, the proximity of French habitants and the expansion of their numbers caused growing worry, as the Indigenous community became increasingly exposed to the peddling of liquor that many of its founders, in leaving Iroquoia, had specifically sought to evade. For the Jesuits the silver lining of the situation was the same: an opportunity to expand their seigneurial holdings and, by ceding the mission community's fields to rent-paying habitants, their revenues. Thus by late 1674 if not earlier, the Jesuits were thinking about relocation and considering potential sites. They briefly considered the area to the north of the Island of Montreal, sending Father Antoine Dalmas to tour around Île Jésus to evaluate the area's potential for "some project" involving "a settlement of Natives" – but they did not pursue the matter.[101] Instead, the Jesuits applied to Governor Frontenac and then to the newly arrived intendant, Jacques Duchesneau de la Doussinière et d'Ambault, for an additional land grant beyond the western boundary of the seigneury of La Prairie. While Frontenac, ever resentful of the Jesuits, dismissed this request out of hand, Duchesneau proved much more amenable, allowing, in January of 1676, the people of Kentake to clear and sow fields along two leagues of river frontage. Owing to the governor's persistent opposition, the grant was not officialized by Louis XIV until 1680, but by then the Jesuits and the people of Kentake had long since transplanted their mission settlement there.[102]

In this context, a number of Wendat families marginalized by political divisions at Kentake opted to detach themselves from the village and set their sights on the Island of Montreal. It seems safe to assume that these corresponded to the families who had failed to get their preferred candidate recognized as chief in 1673.[103] In 1675, a delegation of Wendats from Kentake headed by a certain Achindwanes and accompanied by Father Frémin petitioned the Sulpician seigneurs of Montreal, in the presence of the district governor François-Marie Perrot, for a plot of land there. In his address to Gabriel Souart, the acting superior of the seminary, Achindwanes glossed over the existence of social tensions at Kentake, instead complaining about the smallness and barrenness of their fields. He asked Souart for help in forming a new village, for a priest, and for the religious and civil authorities to provide them with assistance in times of famine and during the hunting season.[104]

The success of Achindwanes and his followers speaks to the strength of the discontent at Kentake, of their leeway of action within the community, as well as of their ability to pressure unenthusiastic missionaries into allowing the move. Frémin and the other Jesuit missionaries at Kentake had, most likely, tried their best to convince Achindwanes and his followers to remain in the community, assuring them that it would soon be relocated to a more amenable site. Perhaps they proposed as an alternative a move to Lorette, hoping to counter Sulpician competition in the mission and the dangers of drunkenness and dispossession that a relocation closer to the town of Montreal seemed to foreshadow for these breakaway Wendats.[105]

The Sulpicians had reasons of their own to be reluctant in the face of this request. Their missionary ventures over the previous decade, both on the north shore of Lake Ontario and on the upper Island of Montreal, had yielded disappointing results. Around 1672, the seminary's most able missionary, François de Salignac de La Mothe-Fénelon, was recalled from Kenté in an effort to establish an Algonquin mission on a solid footing at a site called Gentilly and on the adjacent Courcelle Islands (today the suburb and island of Dorval). But in 1674, both Fénélon and his would-be successor, his colleague and cousin François-Saturnin Lascaris d'Urfé, were embroiled in a quarrel with Frontenac over the governor's imperious involvement in the fur trade and were subsequently recalled to France. Initial efforts at Gentilly were not followed through. Over the next few years, Kenté was allowed to dwindle, having lost the governor's confidence and becoming increasingly expensive, before being abandoned in 1680.[106] Souart's answer to Achindwanes was thus measured. He suggested that his people needed to consider the move very carefully, and that it might not be in their best interest to abandon the care of the Jesuits who, as they spoke their language (the Sulpicians as of yet did not), were best equipped to minister to them.

Faced with Achindwanes's insistence, Souart agreed to offer a tract of land and two missionaries. Perrot, as district governor, gave his approval. The site that was chosen was called La Montagne by the French and Kanehsatake by its inhabitants, meaning "at the foot of the hill," in reference to Mount Royal. A few Wendat families had already moved there before the second week of December of 1675, when four arpents were surveyed and marked off for the mission. One source hints that the founding core consisted of eight warriors with their wives and families. Within a few months a Sulpician missionary, Guillaume Bailly, took up his post.[107] The ground was fertile and sloped in a way that provided ideal drainage and exposure to the sun, allowing Kanehsatake, within a decade, to produce surpluses that reportedly fed the people of the other mission across the Saint Lawrence River through a quarter of the year. The proximity of the French town of Ville Marie, moreover, offered attractive commercial possibilities. As Bailly's successor, François Vachon de Belmont, would boast, this was "a location that much charms and attracts the Natives."[108]

The split created much bitterness. "This separation was painful," explained Chauchetière in his chronicle, "and did not fail to keep their minds at variance for some time."[109] Tonsahoten was himself torn in his loyalties. In the late spring and early summer of 1676, as the people of Kentake prepared to move their village to a new site, at the foot of the rapids about six kilometers upstream, within view of the old, he instead began planning to move to Kanehsatake. In the process, he "spoke very harshly" of his village, offending several people including its two other captains, Togouriout and his Onondaga counterpart, who were shocked to discover his discourse upon their return from the winter hunt. These two, who had until this time deferred to Tonsahoten as the "first and most senior of the captains," became resentful and for a time ceased to hold him in high regard. Soon, however, the parties made an effort to reestablish harmony. Tonsahoten followed the community as it relocated to the new site at the rapids in July, and there he gave up the land that was allotted to him to cultivate for the construction of the mission chapel. Jesuit Father Cholenec explained that it was "to show his affection for the faith," but it was also to demonstrate his attachment to the community and regain some of the prestige that he had lost. Togouirout and the Onondaga captain, recognizing the need to avoid division and urged on by Frémin or Cholenec who counselled that "for the glory of God and the welfare of the mission they should become reconciled with him," made conciliatory gestures of their own. Returning from the small game hunt in the fall or early winter of 1676 they each in turn "gave feasts" to Tonsahoten, "thereby putting him on a footing with them – or, rather, putting him above their own heads, to be thereafter the master of the others."[110] The crisis of leadership passed. As of January 1677, the Jesuits of Kahnawake could breathe a sigh of relief that Tonsahoten had resolved to remain in the mission, and indeed he stayed there until his death in 1688. For having been the founding member of the community, Chauchetière tells us, he was until the end called "the father of the believers."[111]

The new site to which the people of Kentake relocated, a short distance upriver from the old, took on the French name of Saint François Xavier du Sault, or more simply *le Sault*, meaning "the Rapids," and was called by its inhabitants Kahnawake, "at the foot of the rapids," both to describe the landscape and in recollection of the village of the same name in the Mohawk valley (Gandaouagué), from which a critical mass of migrants were arriving.[112] Its inhabitants thereafter became known as Kahnawakeronon or *gens du Sault*: People of the Rapids. In 1677, the mission on the slope of the mountain was meanwhile dedicated to the Virgin Mary, under the name of Notre Dame des Neiges (Our Lady of the Snows). Its residents, the Kanehsatakeronon, came to be known by the French as *gens de la Montagne* or People of the Mountain, though the Indigenous name could be more accurately translated as People of the Foot of the Hill.[113]

***

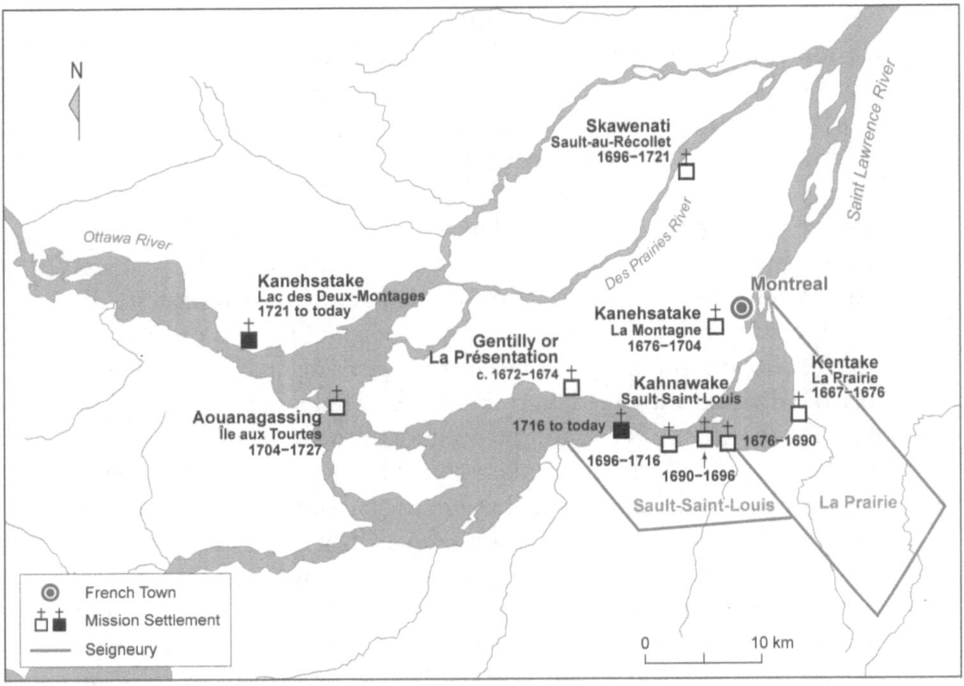

Figure 5.5 Mission communities of the Montreal region, including early eighteenth-century foundations and relocations. (Map by Andrée Héroux)

In an attempt to strengthen their ranks, the small core of Wendats who had forsaken Kentake for Kanehsatake sent a delegation to Lorette, around the time of their relocation in 1675–76, for the purpose of inviting some of that community's inhabitants to join them. In the *Relations*, the Jesuits, careful not to expose the ways in which their missions were undermined by those of the Sulpicians, tiptoed around the issue. A few years later they allude obliquely to the fact that frost and rain had prevented the crops from ripening for a couple of years in succession at Lorette, and that its residents "had been invited to move elsewhere where they might find foodstuffs in abundance."[114] Some seventy years later, a headman from Lorette would recall that the people of Kanehsatake had complained to his own that they were only young men and that they thus lacked a council. Responding to their appeal, the people of Lorette "gave a chief" to the new village and established a constitution for the community which was embodied in twelve wampum belts.[115] It is safe to assume that not only a chief, but several families took this opportunity to migrate from one mission to the other. This resettlement would have been particularly alluring to those Wendats who were unhappy with the outcome of the relocation from Notre Dame de Foy to Lorette a few years earlier. It would also have been especially appealing to those who wished to retain links with Iroquoia, or for that matter with the Wendat community that had merged with the Tionnontatés (also known as Petuns) and found a different refuge in the western Great Lakes after the great dispersal. Perhaps the chief in question was none other than the elderly Louis Thaondechoren. Although Father Chaumonot tells us that the latter was one of the more fervent promoters of the relocation of the village from Notre Dame de Foy to Lorette, it is well documented that in previous years he had explored the possibility of a mission settlement near Montreal. In the summer of 1667, just before the Jesuits decided to commit themselves to the mission at Kentake, he was the one who in the company of a missionary had toured the order's seigneurial holdings to the north of the island.[116] Crucially, at the very moment that Achindwanes and his people were settling at Kanehsatake, in the spring of 1676, Thaondechoren is said to have made a journey from Lorette "to go to see his countrymen, who had come to Montreal to trade, in order to exhort them to become Christians."[117] The countrymen referred to here were perhaps Wendats-Tionnontatés visiting from the Great Lakes, for he was himself of Tionnontaté origin, but this may very also be a muddled allusion to the Wendats of Kentake who had come to the island to settle. Certainly the fact that Thaondechoren does not appear thereafter in the *Relations* relating to Lorette, or for that matter in any of the writings of the Jesuits, would support the theory that he relocated to the Sulpician mission.

In 1677, according to Chauchetière, the Wendats of Lorette sent an "exhortative wampum belt" to Kahnawake. On a background of dark purple shell beads, white ones outlined a series of squares in a way that recalls the famous "Hiawatha belt" which embodies the union of the Five Nations – except that these elements converge on large cross instead of a pine tree of peace. The missionary chronicler summed up the belt's meaning by observing that, through it, the Wendats were inviting the people of Kahnawake to take up the Christian faith for good, to build a chapel as soon as possible, and to "combat the various demons who conspired for the ruin of both missions."[118] The context of the foundation of Kanehsatake hints at its fuller meaning as an expression of goodwill and a call to reconciliation, internal and external: reconciliation at Kahnawake, plausibly, between the Wendat captain and his Mohawk and Oneida counterparts; reconciliation between the people of Kahnawake and Kanehsatake; and quite possibly reconciliation between those of Kahnawake and Lorette, for in supporting the secessionists the latter had no doubt incurred the disapproval of the former. Implied in this gift of wampum was the people of Lorette's understanding that they held primacy within the French alliance and the Christian family, of which they had been early adopters and adoptees.[119]

Father Chauchetière writes that the wampum belt was well received. It was hung up in the church at Kahnawake, just above the altar, to stand as a testament to the common faith and goodwill that united the two communities.[120] In reality, the community of Lorette continued to feel the disruptive pull of the upriver missions for a few years more at least. In an address to the canons of Chartres Cathedral dictated to Chaumonot in 1680, Lorette's leaders alluded to the ongoing danger. "[O]ur houses united as a village are incessantly surrounded by nations issued from the depths of the earth to lead us there and treat us as slaves, in horrible hollows where fire is never extinguished." They thanked the canons of Chartres for having sent them, in return for a votive wampum belt, a silver reliquary filled with the fragments of several saints' bones. "This nation, exited from the bowels of the earth, will not be able to suffer the presence of these bones which shall serve as a palisade to our village against their attacks." Beyond the metaphorical language, we are made to understand that a core population was adamant in its desire to remain independent from the new, increasingly Iroquoiscised mission communities. The thought of their alliance with the clerics of the cathedral across the sea, they hoped, would help them resist further invitations.[121]

Most of the community's population gains in the years immediately following the peace treaty were undone in the decade that followed by the strong gravitational pull of Kanehsatake and, perhaps to a lesser extent, Kahnawake. The community numbered 150 persons in 1668; by 1675, it had swelled to approximately 300 individuals. By the time of the 1685 census, however, Lorette once again numbered only 146 persons; and when another was taken three years later, the village was said to contain 131 individuals. Disease contributed in a small way to this depopulation, but outmigration was most certainly its main cause.[122]

Figure 5.6 Wampum belt given by the people of Lorette to those of Kahnawake in 1677. It continued to adorn the church there until its theft in 1974. (Reproduced from Devine, *Historic Caughnawaga* [1922])

***

All of this was probably not the outcome hoped for by the elder who, on welcoming Lieutenant General Tracy in 1665, described his wish to see Wendat bones knit together with muscles and tendons, and Wendat flesh born again. Yet in these years his community had been reinvigorated, gaining if not the power and prosperity that it had once enjoyed, at least solid foundations which would allow it to persist in its distinct identity. Having welcomed New and Old Iroquois alike in the few years that immediately followed the peace accord, Lorette now reemerged as an unambiguously Wendat community. Many of its members, including its leaders, had experienced captivity. For some, it had been brief. Louis Thaondechoren had been captured by the Iroquois in the debacle at Long Sault in 1660, but had managed an escape and return to the community shortly thereafter. So had Ignace Tsaouenhohoui – a name, referring to an eagle or osprey – who belonged to a prominent lineage, quite possibly of the Deer Clan, and was considered "captain of his nation" until his death in 1670. Others had spent decades among the Iroquois, returning from captivity only after the peace. Pierre Atironta, already elderly when he returned from Iroquoia, soon emerged as a pillar of the community; he too was described as "captain of the Hurons" at the time of his passing in 1672. Jacques Onnhatetaionk, who arrived from Mohawk country in 1672–73, was in turn installed as a leading captain by the clan mothers immediately upon his arrival. Pierre Andahiacon, who died in 1676, in a similar fashion was recognized as one of the community's "worthy captains" soon after his return from Iroquoia.[123] Many of these men derived their authority from their female relatives or spouses. Andahiacon's wife, Jeanne Assenragenhaon, for example, had migrated to the Saint Lawrence valley with him, and was a renowned and long-standing Christian. In Old Wendake she had been the hostess of Fathers Le Mercier, Ragueneau, and Chastelain. While she had lost her first husband during the Iroquois invasion, she had maintained her faith during two decades in Iroquoia, and converted two successive husbands there, of whom Andahiacon was the last. The missionaries described her as "the chief of all our Christian women in intelligence, fervor, and constancy."[124]

Significantly, the movement of Wendat individuals and families from Iroquoia after years of captivity altered the ethnic makeup of the community, insofar as the Attigneenongnahac (or Cord) character that appears to have for a time predominated after 1657 became less marked. The identity of leaders and the parts of Iroquoia from whence they returned allow us to glimpse this shift. Pierre Atironta was likely of Ahrendarrhonon (Rock) origin, as his name had been borne by two of that nation's leaders before the destruction of Huronia. Meanwhile, the number of families said to be returning from Mohawk country suggests an increased presence of Attignawantans (Bear). Additional evidence for this shift comes from the fact that variations of the name formerly used for the Attignawantan appear in eighteenth-century Wendat-Tionnontaté dictionaries as referring to the inhabitants of Lorette: one dictionary gives Attinnia8enten, Hatindia8Ointen, Hatingia8Ointen, Hatindia8Ointen, Hatingia8Ointen, and another Hatendia8enten.[125] In defining themselves to others in their diplomatic discourse, the community for its part appears to have preferred the label of "Wendat Loretronon" (or, reflecting their pronunciation, *Rorekronon*): Hurons of Lorette.[126] Meanwhile, the Kahnawakeronon and Kanehsatakeronon – People of the Rapids and People of the Mountain – who from diverse origins had found new homes in the Saint Lawrence valley would, in decades marked by the renewal of war, increasingly come to define themselves as Iroquois.

6

Against Their Own

War between the Christian and League Iroquois, 1684–1690

Whereas Lorette was fated to remain a small but decidedly Wendat community, Kahnawake and Kahnesatake were emerging as increasingly populous and Iroquois ones. By 1685, the two villages had attained a respective population of 682 and 222.[1] To place this in perspective, population estimates for the whole of Iroquoia during the second half of the century hover around 8,000 or 9,000. Of that total, the population of the Mohawk villages numbered about 1,500, that of the Onondagas at a little over that number, and the Oneidas about 600 to 800.[2] Due to the arrival of waves of Old Iroquois who had come in from these villages, and to the need for a common identity and mutually intelligible language among New Iroquois of diverse origins, the process of assimilation that had begun in Iroquoia was completed on the shores of the Saint Lawrence.

This process was quicker at Kahnawake, which had become the favoured destination for newcomers. The departure of the most discontented Wendat elements from Kentake circa 1675 allowed harmony to return to the community which relocated to the rapids. Allusions to "Huron" chiefs, or to a distinct Wendat presence at the mission for that matter, disappear in the years thereafter. Writing in January of 1677, Jesuit Father Pierre Cholenec explained that the mission was governed by four captains, "2 Hurons and 2 Iroquois," but that he expected that "we shall shortly have there 4 captains of the principal Iroquois nations," with changing structures of leadership reflecting the evolving self-definition of the broader population.[3] Oneidas, who had numbered among the first founders of the community, were joined by another noticeable wave led by Ogenheratarihiens, a captain of their nation who, having quarrelled with a fellow captain on the occasion of a village relocation, and undergone the distress of his brother's death around the same time, moved to Kahnawake. Baptized Louis, his relocation to the mission and that of his wife, Marie Garhi, attracted others from Oneida country and from the north shore of Lake Ontario, many of whom accepted religious instruction and some of whom chose to relocate there for the longer term. He became the mission's "fourth captain," and was judged to be the most eloquent.[4] It was the newcomers from Mohawk country, however, who came to predominate at Kahnawake – a name which itself reflected that ascendancy. When he penned, in 1686, his chronicle of the mission's early years, the Jesuit Chauchetière observed with exaggeration but tellingly, that the "warriors of Anié [i.e. Mohawks] have become more numerous at Montreal than they are in their own country," and indicated that though ten or twelve nations were represented at Kahnawake (not the twenty-two reported in the early years, it will be noted), all of them were Iroquois speaking.[5]

Kanehsatake's founding Wendat core was slower to be submerged, though it too in time evolved to adopt an Iroquois identity. Of the fifteen individuals from the village who were cited in judicial proceedings of the seigneurial court of the island of Montreal during the period from 1677 to 1686, a full seven were identified as Wendats. More impressionistically but no less tellingly, Bishop Saint-Vallier and Governor Denonville, writing in 1688 and 1690 respectively, both described the mission as being composed of "Iroquois *and* Hurons." But the trend was nonetheless for the mission to evolve, much like Kahnawake, in the minds of colonial administrators into the "*Iroquois* mission of La Montagne."[6]

Both missions were in many ways extensions of Iroquoia. Their residents retained traditional matrilineal kinship structures and subsistence patterns that hinged on the combination of agricultural activity with hunting and fishing expeditions that drew most of the population away from its village for much of the year. They used Iroquois dialects to communicate – Mohawk increasingly. Men and women shuttled to and from the Saint Lawrence and Iroquoia to visit family and friends, to find partners, to trade, and to take part in ritual obligations. Yet, despite such high mobility and overlapping identities, Christianity and the French alliance were nevertheless emerging as fundamental components of individual and collective identity for the people of the two mission settlements, crucial means of understanding and negotiating internal and external belonging. It is tantalizing to hypothesize that while they continued to view themselves and be viewed by other Iroquois as Onkwehón:we ("Real Humans," i.e. *ethnic* Iroquois), many residents of the missions ceased to consider themselves Haudenosaunee (or Rotinonhsionni, "People of the Longhouse," i.e. members of the League). While the distinction between these two terms would become conflated in the nineteenth century, and come to take on a different meaning in more recent times, there is good reason to think that the difference did matter during the decades under examination. From the available evidence, those whom the French called "*Iroquois chrétiens*" or Christian Iroquois appear to have conceived of themselves as "Garihwioston" (in period sources Karikwists, Karigouistes, Caraguists, Garih8ioston). The term translates as "Believers," "Those who Pray," or "Christians," but is rooted in the notion of Karihwiio, or Kariwiio, which has a noteworthy pedigree in Iroquois culture. Combining the words for "good" and for "thing, business, affair, word, message, news," this idea of the "Good Word" appears in retellings of the Great Law offered by Deganawida, the Peacemaker, as one of the cardinal principles of the Iroquois League. With the arrival of the French missionaries, the word came to be used as a natural translation of "Gospel." In more recent times, from the beginning of the nineteenth century onward, the same term would come to be used to refer to yet another set of spiritual teachings, those of the Seneca prophet Handsome Lake, which to this day forms the core of the Longhouse Religion.[7]

This particular identity came to matter because of the way in which war came to divide the allies of the French and the Five Nations. At the same time that the peace settlement of 1667 initiated an important population movement from Iroquoia to the mission settlements of the Saint Lawrence River, it also ushered in a wave of French expansion to the *pays d'en haut* (upcountry, literally) of the Great Lakes and beyond. Colonial outposts multiplied in the interior under the governorship of Frontenac, as traders, officers, and missionaries strengthened old commercial partnerships and political alliances with the Tionnontaté Wendats, Odawas, and Ojibwas, and extended new ones to the Potawatomies, Menominies, Miamis, Mascoutens, Kickapoos, Illinois, and others. In the spring, Odawa canoes laden with furs sometimes stopped at Kahnawake before pursuing on to Montreal.[8] The Odawa's neighbours, the Tionnontaté Wendats who had remained in the Great Lakes through the years of dispersal, and now settled at

Michilimackinac and accepted among them a Jesuit missionary, also created opportunities for diplomacy and trade for the inhabitants of the missions of the Saint Lawrence valley. As mentioned in the previous chapter, some of these Tionnontaté Wendats visited Quebec (and presumably Notre Dame de Foy) in 1670 or 1671, and some Wendats from Notre Dame de Foy visited Michilimackinac in 1672. Reference to Louis Thaondechoren's journey from Lorette to the Island of Montreal in 1676 to meet with "his countrymen, who had come to Montreal to trade," also seems to imply such intercourse.[9] The colony's judicial archives further document the case of three Wendats from Kanehsatake, Louis Ouacouts alias Le Boiteux (the Lame One), Jean Gatessa, and Denis Oukwouté, who in 1682 accepted goods and cash worth 3304 livres from a Montreal merchant to buy beaver pelts at Michilimackinac, partnering for the occasion with Marie-Félix Arontio, one of the few Wendats of Lorette to marry a Frenchman, whom the Jesuits asked to serve as a courier for them.[10] The relative rarity of such references to residents of the missions in the abundant records of French expansion across the pays d'en haut, however, demonstrates that on the whole they played only a minor part in this westward thrust. Yet they could not help but being embroiled in the conflict that this push westward brought about as, through the late 1670s and early 1680s, the willingness of French traders to supply the nations of the interior with firearms and promote their coalition became cause for alarm among their traditional western Iroquois enemies – the Senecas, in particular, who began to threaten and strike, prompting French campaigns of retaliation.[11]

The people of Kahnawake and Kanehsatake would confront the Iroquois of the League, both as diplomats and as warriors. In 1684 and 1687, they set out against the Senecas; in 1693, they struck in Mohawk country, and in 1696 against the villages of the Onondagas and Oneidas. "Who would have ever believed," marvelled the Jesuit Claude Chauchetière, "that faith and religion would have united them so thoroughly with the French as to make them take up arms against the Iroquois [...,] their own nation"?[12] Turning the question on its head, modern scholars have tended to minimize the involvement of the mission villagers in this conflict, arguing that they resisted French calls to arms, taking part only reluctantly in joint military efforts and going out of their way to avoid actual combat.[13] The evidence does not comfortably support this interpretation: during the final two decades of the seventeenth century, Iroquois did fight, kill, and capture other Iroquois. To be sure, some of mission villagers did resist – a number of warriors chose to sit out campaigns, and some families returned to Iroquoia – and in matters of strategy and tactics their war chiefs often deviated from the governor's will. However, collectively they stood out as staunch allies of the French. The why lies not merely in the strength of their religious commitment, as Chauchetière and other missionary chroniclers may have liked to think, but in the specificity of their identities and relationships. The first phase of the war did pit *Iroquois* against *Iroquois* on some level, but not on the level that mattered most. As with the Wendat-Iroquois conflict described in previous chapters, patterns of migration and kinship played a fundamental role in shaping patterns of war and peace making: the fact that Kahnawake and Kanehsatake were populated mainly by migrants from Mohawk, Oneida, and Onondaga villages made war against the Senecas possible during the 1680s; only at the turn of the 1690s, as the war evolved into an altogether new phase, would they feel compelled to take up arms against people whom they deemed to be friends and relatives.

***

The fact that the inhabitants of Kahnawake and Kanehsatake retained strong cultural ties and kinship bonds with the "Infidel Iroquois" of the Five Nations, even as they cultivated a distinct religious and political identity which drew them closer to the French, made them a target of suspicion in this increasingly tense period. Governor Frontenac and his clique, whose dislike of the Jesuits extended to their missions and residents, were characteristically captious. The Kahnawakes were alarmed, circa 1679, by rumours that officials wished to hold their captain – Togouirout, it is most likely, or perhaps Tonsahoten – accountable for the insolence of the League Iroquois and to imprison him for his role in "complicating affairs."[14] Although the Jesuits shared many of the governor's reservations about the Iroquois of the League, they could not disagree more when it came to their wards in the mission settlements. In these increasingly troubled times they grew convinced that their missions played a crucial strategic role. "Those barbarians," Father Thierry Beschefer, superior of the Jesuit mission at Quebec, wrote of the Five Nations, "have often resolved to wage war against the French, but they have always been checked by those whose kindred were at the Sault." The Mohawks, in particular, had continually refused to give their consent to such a war because their "nephews and children" lived among the French.[15] The view appears to have been shared by the principal officers and merchants of the colony, and Governor Joseph-Antoine Le Febvre de La Barre, who succeeded Frontenac in the fall of 1682, was quick to espouse it. Writing to the Secretary of State for the Navy within a little over a month after his arrival, he explained that Kahnawake in particular was "one of the things that will most engage the Iroquois to make peace with us." He knew rather little about this mission as of yet – as betrayed by the fact that he mistakenly referred to it as the "*mission iroquoise du saut de Sainte Marie*" – but he had absorbed the belief that its development had all but depopulated Mohawk country and that, because all four eastern nations of the League had relatives there, they could be easily "adjusted" and isolated from the westernmost Senecas.[16]

In response to the disappointments of francization and to the arguments that the Jesuits and their supporter Intendant Duchesneau had been mustering in their effort to obtain a royal confirmation of the allotment of land for the mission at the rapids, the court's optics on the mission settlements had been shifting. The wording of Louis XIV's grant for the land of Sault Saint Louis, when it was at last issued in 1680, indeed echoed the belief that it was necessary "to retain the Iroquois, even to increase their number and extend by this means the lights of faith and the gospel."[17] In 1681, Duchesneau asked the king's minister Colbert that funds be allocated to provide presents to the inhabitants of the mission settlements to attract an even greater number of people there. He made a strong case for the economic importance of the missions, beyond whatever merits they might have in terms of religion. The Iroquois needed to be maintained in the colony's orbit because they served as crucial suppliers of furs. They also needed to be allowed to retain their traditional clothes and diet, he went as far as to argue, "so that they would not become effeminate and they would be fitter and less constrained for the hunt, which makes their wealth and ours."[18]

To be sure, officials did not completely disavow the ideal of francization. Although Duchesneau and others were willing to give Indigenous men some leeway as hunters and warriors, they continued to believe that women could and should be integrated into colonial society, at least on a small scale – overlooking the way in which it was female work that transformed dead animals into commodified pelts. In that same letter to Colbert, the intendant asked for funds for the girls who left the care of the Ursulines upon reaching adulthood, a suggestion which led Louis XIV to establish the following year the "king's gift," an endowment with which to furnish a dowry of fifty livres to every Indigenous girl who married a Frenchman. This measure failed to make any impact. Pointing out that "there is hardly one or two who marry each year," Duchesneau's successor, Jacques De Meulles, proposed that it might be more appropriate to give these girls a pig, some wheat, and hemp seeds as dowry instead of money; La Barre, for his part, advised that the funds should simply be repurposed to provide dowries to French girls. De Meulles, visibly unimpressed by the fact that those few girls taken in by the Ursulines over the years learnt only to pray and speak French, also proposed the creation of a "manufacture for Native girls" where they might instead acquire skills like spinning, sewing and knitting, caring for cattle, and milking cows. Such practical skills, he reasoned, would make a greater contribution to the colonial economy and eventually rub off on the girls' Indigenous husbands. But the idea was fleeting, and nothing came of it.[19]

Among those who held on the longest to the ideal of francization were the Sulpicians, and particularly François de Vachon de Belmont, who succeeded Guillaume Bailly as director of the missions at Kanehsatake (La Montagne) in 1680. He believed that the Jesuits were far too indulgent in their approach to the missions – that they sought to maintain the neophytes "in Native coarseness" ("*grossièreté sauvage*") – and they conversely thought of him as a bothersome dilettante. His administration of the mission on the mountain slope was idiosyncratic, in keeping with the relative independence which governed the relationship of Sulpician priests to the seminaries of Montreal and of Paris, and he drew on his considerable family fortune in an effort to carry out his vision there. Forming its children into two classes, Belmont endeavoured to teach them not only the fundamentals of religion, but to sing mass in Latin, and to speak, read, and write in French; while the boys received additional training in the rudiments of drawing, woodturning, tailoring, and shoemaking, the girls, under the care of two sisters of the Congrégation de Notre Dame (a religious community of French women based in Montreal, not to be confused with the lay confraternity of the same name that had been established among the Wendats), were taught sewing and other skills deemed proper for their sex. Exceptionally, two young women joined the Congrégation de Notre Dame, Marie-Barbe Atontinon in 1679 and Marie-Thérèse Gannensagouas shortly thereafter. Although they served as teachers at the mission, Belmont's ambitious educational program appears to have held little appeal for Kanehsatake's residents or, indeed, made little lasting impact on them.[20]

Exasperated by the disruptions that liquor was causing at Kanehsatake in spite of his best efforts, even Vachon de Belmont ultimately grew adamant and began advocating that, while the people of his mission might yet be civilized in time through the schooling of their youth, a safe segregation should be maintained between neophytes and settlers.[21] "For a long time, it was believed that settling the Natives near our dwellings was a good means of accustoming them to living like us and learning our religion," wrote Governor Jacques-René de Brisay de Denonville to Colbert de Seignelay in 1685, upon arriving in the colony to replace La Barre. "I realize, Monseigneur, that the very opposite has happened for, instead of growing accustomed to our laws, [...] they have communicated to us everything that is wicked about them, and [...] they have likewise taken on only what is most wicked and vicious in us." In light of the Saint Lawrence valley's mission settlements' political and military value in a context of renewed war, he nonetheless announced himself eager to support them and to further the eventual formation of new ones.[22]

***

Colonial officials' beliefs were not unwarranted for, as "Iroquois" aligned with the French, the people of Kahnawake and Kanehsatake were indeed perfectly placed to mediate relations. When an expected Seneca embassy failed to show up at Montreal in December of 1682, four of Kahnawake's principal chiefs and Kanehsatake's head chief journeyed with the fur trader and interpreter Charles Le Moyne (known among the Iroquois as Akouessan, the Partridge) to insist that they send a delegation so that the newly arrived La Barre might resume the discussions initiated by his predecessor. Threatened upon their arrival in Seneca country, these emissaries nevertheless proved persuasive, for a Seneca embassy reached Montreal in July, followed by delegates from the other four nations that August. During the Franco-Iroquois councils that ensued, the deputies from Kahnawake and Kanehsatake continued to lend their support to the French position. From the governor's perspective, they had "done their duty very well."[23] Visiting Kahnawake for the first time in the summer of 1683, he found "much goodwill" among its inhabitants. The chiefs enthusiastically pledged that their village would supply 150 warriors in case of war, even against the Iroquois of the League if the latter were so bold as to break their peace with the French.[24]

Reports that the Senecas had resumed their raids against the Illinois and Miamis, and, in early 1684, the news that they had dared to attack the French outpost of Fort Saint Louis in the Illinois country, determined the governor to go to war against the offending nation.[25] Sometime in late spring or early summer of 1684, La Barre's decision was announced at Kahnawake. Three courses of action, presented by the missionaries and digested by the community's leaders, were discussed in council: the villagers could return to Iroquoia from whence they had come; they could remain in the mission settlement without taking any action; or they could accompany the French to war. The Kahnawakes are reported to have found the first two alternatives unsatisfactory: to leave their village would mean abandoning the Christian faith (and, if we push beyond the missionary's reporting biases, abandoning expanded hunting grounds and networks of trade and alliance); and to remain there without taking part in operations would, by provoking French mistrust, similarly undermine the community's relations with its colonial neighbours. The people of Kahnawake instead concluded that "having but one and the same faith with the French, they should also to run the same risks together."[26]

For Chauchetière, there was no doubt that it was "Faith and religion" that "had so thoroughly united them with the French as to cause them to take arms against the Iroquois and their own nation."[27] Indeed, the inhabitants of the two mission settlements had developed over the previous decade and a half a vibrant religious and political identity distinct from that of the Five Nations – they viewed themselves as Christians and allies of the French. To be sure, the boundary between traditional and missionary teachings was fluid; notwithstanding the tendency of Jesuit and Sulpician chroniclers to portray the Christian Iroquois as having thoroughly rejected ancient practices to embrace the new religion, a great religious eclecticism characterized life in the mission. Though baptism served as a crucial initiation ceremony, an apparent requirement for full membership in the community, not everyone living in the villages was baptized. And even among the baptized, some of whom were long-term inhabitants of the villages, a number of traditional shamanic practices persisted – offerings to the sun and dream divination, for example – and were adapted to the new context. Christianity had nevertheless emerged as a fundamental constituent of individual and collective identity for the people of the two mission settlements, a crucial means of understanding and negotiating internal and external relationships.[28]

The Garihwioston of Kahnawake and Kanehsatake, like the inhabitants of other mission settlements, valued the rituals and symbols of the new religion for their sacred qualities, as ways of accessing the divine, as a means of sharing in the source of French power, and of counteracting some of the divisive trends that now seemed to characterize society in Iroquoia. Crucially, the vocabulary of the new religion provided the social and cultural cement which generated a sense of shared belonging within the mission settlements and allowed the formation of cohesive communities out of culturally heterogeneous fragments. Through salient gestures and symbols, the Kahnawakes and Kanehsatakes set themselves apart from – and above, some of them believed – the people of Iroquoia. Common observances gave rhythm to the day and to the year, as men and women came together for the recitation of prayers, for mass – attended by almost all on Sunday and feast days, and by a substantial number on other days of the week – and for the celebration of baptisms, weddings, and funerals. Rituals of collective and individual penance, both public and private, were observed. Crucifixes and rosaries were worn as a means of accessing the sacred and as markers of affiliation. Even though the absolute temperance that had characterized Kentake's first decade was breaking down by the early 1680s as a result of colonists dabbling in the brandy trade, a formal prohibition persisted and its ideal remained very much alive. Traditional religious customs and liberal sexual practices, categorized as sinful by French missionaries and Indigenous proselytes, were similarly rejected.[29]

Invested most heavily in this distinct Christian identity and privileged bond to the French were the leading figures of the mission communities. It was in no small part due to their ability to promote the new religion and attract droves of migrants that leaders such as Togouirout the Great Mohawk and the Oneida Ogenheratarihiens – and the influential women behind them – achieved prominence at Kahnawake. Such figures exercised what we might recognize as a form of patronage over the local church. Ganneaktena and Tonsahoten made the foundational donations of wampum to the chapel at Kentake, including by offering the wampum belt that the latter used to wear when he went to war; as noted earlier they also supplied the land for the construction of the new chapel at the time of the move to Kah-

was beteekent met het merk van Cryn
Cryn een Schillepatt
Accordeert met syn Principale
Quod attestor

Figure 6.1 Mark of Togouirout, here referred to by his Dutch name of Kryn or Cryn (in the above right corner). Individuals typically signed deeds and treaties with a clan symbol, here a turtle. (Detail from a deposition in favour of Jacques Cornelius Van Slyck, 12 September 1683, Schaffer Library, Union College, Schenectady)

nawake. When that second building was destroyed in a storm in the fall of 1683, Togouirout offered his family's newly built longhouse to replace it; the following year, as he was preparing to go to war, he presented as "a monument to his piety" an impressive eight-branched bronze candelabrum very similar to the one which then adorned the Dutch Reformed church in Albany, where he purchased his gift for the exorbitant amount of twenty-four beaver pelts.[30] As Chauchetière noted, it was in no small part due to the fact that the captains of Kahnawake "gave such a skillful spin to the affair" that the entire community expressed the desire "to perish rather than lose their faith" upon being invited by La Barre to wage war against the Senecas.[31]

To "lose" the Christian faith, beyond losing access to potent spiritual forces, entailed a weakening of bonds to an ever-expanding network of French and Indigenous actors, brothers, and sisters through baptism, who shared overlapping beliefs and practices.[32] Moreover, to ignore La Barre's plea for assistance would run counter to the dynamics that lay at the center of the relationship between Onontio – the French king (Great Onontio or Onontio Goa) and his representative in the colony, the governor general (Onontio proper) – and his allied "children." Paralleling the metaphor of brotherhood, that of fatherhood was first tentatively introduced in the 1640s, extending first to the Algonquins and Wendats, before being institutionalized beginning in the early 1670s. By 1690s if not well before that, orators from the Kahnawake and Kanehsatake spoke publicly of the governor, Onontio, as their "Father" and of their people as numbering among the "Children" who owed him obedience. Beyond the realm of rhetoric, this relationship can more accurately be understood as one not of obedience, but of mutual obligation. In this respect, Iroquoian traditions presented a model: although clan affiliation was matrilineal, kinship retained a bilateral dimension insofar as a sense of pronounced reciprocity governed the relationship of a son to his father's lineage. Significantly, this reciprocity manifested itself in times of war, when a family lost one of its members: "The children become obligated to their fathers' lodge, to which they are strangers," observed Jesuit missionary Joseph-François Lafitau, "and contract the obligation of replacing them [the deceased]."[33]

A response to Onontio's call to arms would have been made all the more necessary by his willingness to embrace, in this context of reciprocity and mutual obligation, the role of provider. Indeed, in anticipation of war, La Barre initiated a generous policy of gift giving that in effect grafted itself onto both the missionary practice of supplying material assistance in times of need, and onto the exchange of presents that traditionally accompanied diplomatic rituals. Within weeks of his arrival, even though he had not yet visited Kahnawake, the governor was writing to the king in support of the maintenance of the annual grant of 500 livres to the missionaries there. The following summer, he gave special gifts to the four ambassadors who travelled to Iroquoia, and during the distribution of presents that followed the conference held at Montreal that August he took particular care to give a generous share to the Christian Iroquois. A few months later, in recognition of the community's good will, La Barre was again petitioning the king for funds to assist in rebuilding the village's destroyed chapel.[34] Thereafter, his successors at the head of the colony would continue to view – albeit with varying degrees of enthusiasm (Denonville) or repugnance (Frontenac) – the distribution of presents as crucial to maintaining the cooperation of the warriors and diplomats of the mission settlements.[35]

To maintain the cooperation of the inhabitants of the mission settlements during these years, French officials also agreed to juridical compromises that in effect nullified the Sovereign Council's decree of 1664, which had held that Indigenous offenders would be subjected to the same penalties as the French in criminal cases. The traditional punishment of offenders – "murderers, thieves, traitors and sorcerers," as enumerated by the Jesuits in an early *Relation* – among Iroquoians and Algonquians alike had little in common with that prescribed by European law. Murder was atoned for with presents, and only if the accused or his relatives refused to offer any were the relatives of the victims entitled to seek violent retribution.[36] This understanding of conflict resolution persisted in the mission settlements, and colonial authorities now proved willing to accommodate it. In January of 1684, the Sulpician Joseph Mariet, who served as Vachon de Belmont's assistant at Kanehsatake, was accosted by a drunken twenty-three-year-old Wendat named Nicolas Tonaktouan, who lifted a hatchet about the priest's head saying that he was "a dog that had to die" before other community members arrived to restrain him. Although Tonaktouan was a newcomer there, who had been born and raised at Lorette but had spent the six previous years living among the Tionnontaté-Wendats in the west, the local mission communities rose to his defence, arguing that in light of his drunkenness he could not be held responsible for his action. Two chiefs from Kahnawake intervened in his favour before governor La Barre, as did the Jesuit missionaries (no doubt to the great displeasure of the Sulpicians) who stressed that the punishment of the accused would result in "very dangerous consequences for the country." The court, sensitive to these pressures, released Tonaktouan from prison, merely banishing him and imposing a fine of a hundred livres – in essence allowing him to atone with presents in keeping with the custom of his people.[37] The precedent was followed, with colonial officials showing residents of the mission settlements and their visiting relatives a type of leniency for which no colonist could hope. In 1686, Governor Denonville and Intendant Jean Bochart de Champigny, acknowledging to the Secretary of State for the Navy that they "needed the Natives," chose not to seek the prosecution of another intoxicated warrior who had killed a Frenchman, on account of his having kin at Kahnawake. The decision proved wise, for that warrior distinguished himself during the following year's campaign, impressing everyone by slaying a Seneca with a single stroke of his sword.[38] In the same way, Denonville and Champigny showed great leniency toward a young man from Kahnawake accused of raping and murdering a French girl in the summer of 1689. As the trial got under way and the accused, Étienne Tehagaraweron, lingered in jail, the chiefs of the village and his relatives there applied stern pressure to the governor and intendant, going as far as to threaten to leave the mission. In ordering the discontinuation of the trial and the release of Tehagaraweron, Denonville and Champigny cited the fact that such action was "absolutely essential to avoid it [this departure], given the unfortunate consequences that could ensue" and stressed that the matter was "of an extreme importance to the service of the King and to the authority of the Colony."[39]

***

While spiritual and metaphorical kinship, enacted through shared beliefs and rituals, as well as through mutual obligations, induced the inhabitants of the mission settlements to assist their French "brothers" and "fathers" in their war, an equally crucial factor was the absence of ties to the Senecas. Though Chauchetière and other commentators might marvel at the fact that the Christian Iroquois had agreed to wage war against "their own nation," this constituted a gross oversimplification of identity and overstatement of solidarity among the Five Nations. As observed in the previous chapter, the men and women who settled in the mission settlements from the late 1660s onward came overwhelmingly from the eastern Iroquois nations: Oneidas formed an initial core at Kentake, but they were soon submerged by waves of Mohawk newcomers. Impressionistic nineteenth-century abstracts from the sacramental registers of Kanehsatake, the originals of which were subsequently destroyed in a fire, indicate that the mission did welcome some Senecas between 1680 and 1683. Still, Mohawks were coming to dominate at Kanehsatake too, alongside a substantial Onondaga minority and the original Wendat core.[40]

Notwithstanding occasional tensions, ties between the residents of the mission settlements and their villages of origin remained strong. Conversely, the Senecas' demographic contribution to the mission settlements had been negligible. The few people observed to have moved from those villages to Kanehsatake between 1680 and 1683 appear to form the exception that proves the rule: people moving precisely because they were making the purposeful choice to align themselves with the French and their allies in a context of looming war. Overall, the tenuous nature of solidarity across the League's constituent nations, and the geographical, biological, and conceptual distance that separated the Christian Iroquois from the Senecas provides the key to understanding their actions through the 1680s. As the Albany fur trader Anthony Lespinard would observe just a few years later after encountering Togouirout, he and the rest of his people "were no ways inclined to engage in the war if the Maquas [Mohawks], Oneydes [Oneidas] and Onnondages [Onondagas] were concerned, because their brethren, sisters, uncles, aunts, etc. were there," but they were willing to "immediately join" the French against the Senecas.[41]

The challenge, as recognized by both La Barre and the leading men at Kahnawake and Kanehsatake, was to obstruct the League's potential political and military unity. In preparation for the campaign against the Senecas, two of their number (including Togouirout), were dispatched with wampum belts to the Mohawks, two others to the Oneidas (including Ogenheratarihiens), and three to the Onondagas. These emissaries were to make it clear that the French wished only to avenge the misdeeds of the Senecas, who by their recent aggression had breached the peace accord made at Montreal the previous year; the French and their allies had no quarrel with the other four nations, and intended to live with them as friends.[42] In many ways, this diplomatic gambit was in keeping with the proselytizing habit of the mission communities' leaders over the past decade and a half. In fact, it was now reported with apprehension at Albany that Togouirout and two other men who arrived at the Mohawk villages had among their aims that of inciting their inhabitants "to move to Canada."[43]

To be sure, consensus was not total at Kahnawake. Many warriors, following their personal dispositions or bending to those of their families' leading women and men, chose to remain home at the risk of disappointing their French father and brothers. These included one of the village's four chiefs, the Oneida Ogenheratarihiens, who took part in the diplomatic offensive but was unwilling to join the military operations that followed, leading some to believe that he would abandon the village.[44] Some nine or ten households – a roughly estimated one hundred individuals – sure enough registered their discontent or alarm by leaving the village the year of the campaign. Vincent Bigot, Jesuit missionary among the Wabanakis recently settled at the village of Saint François de Sales near Quebec, attributed this departure to the ravages of brandy. Those who left Kahnawake, he claimed, "said that they had withdrawn there solely to live in peace, far from the disorders caused by intemperance; but that they found themselves as greatly annoyed by drunkards as they were in their own country."[45] But while liquor may very well have contributed to driving men and women away from the mission, the timing makes it likely that a key factor was the looming war against the Senecas, another major complication for those who wished only to "live in peace."

Enthusiasm ran highest at Kanehsatake and at Lorette: during the muster at Cataraqui, the warriors of each village respectively numbered 60 and 40, representing a remarkably high rate of mobilization for a community whose total population would be reported the following year as being of 222 and 146 (a rate of 1 warrior fielded for each 3.7 individuals in the community). The small size of these communities likely contributed to the feasibility of reaching such a consensus and a thorough mobilization. At Lorette, where memories of the Senecas' role in the destruction of Huronia remained vivid, even men who were well past their prime and older boys who had not yet been initiated to the art of war responded to the call to arms: French officers described that contingent as consisting of "mediocre" men, in comparison to the "good men" of Kahnawake and Kanehsatake. Kahnawake's contingent of 101 warriors (a rate of 1 warrior per 6.8 persons), though representing a third less than the numbers pledged by the community the previous year, was nevertheless the single largest besides that of the French, and alone it represented almost a quarter of the total 410 Indigenous warriors present at Cataraqui on 18 August 1684.[46]

With these warriors advancing towards Cataraqui as part of La Barre's army, Christian Iroquois delegations came and went to Onondaga where "a general assembly of all the Iroquois" was being held to discuss the situation. Their urging that the Senecas "give satisfaction" to Onontio was reciprocated by the Onondagas' resolve to mediate a peace.[47] With his forces poorly provisioned, decimated by malaria, and in no state to carry out the offensive, La Barre was compelled to accept humiliating terms at a peace conference at La Famine, on the south shore of Lake Ontario. Accounts of the proceedings on 5 September 1684 allow us to catch a glimpse of what the campaign meant for the people of Kahnawake and Kanehsatake. Indeed, the final point made by the Onondaga speaker, Otreouti, during the discussions – which were otherwise devoted to the affairs of the French, their allies in the Upper Country, and the Senecas – concerned the missions' inhabitants specifically. He requested that the governor "prevent the Christians of Sault-Saint Louis and la Montagne from coming among us to attract our people to Montreal; make them cease to dismember our land as they do every year."[48] Chauchetière's summary of these proceedings suggests an even more divisive encounter, during which the Iroquois of the Five Nations spoke harshly to the Christian Iroquois, jeering at them, "renouncing," and threatening them.[49]

The willingness of the Onondagas, Cayugas, and Oneidas to lend their diplomatic support to the Senecas at this critical juncture ushered in unprecedented tensions between the inhabitants of the missions and those of Iroquoia.[50] The people of Kahnawake took the threats uttered at La Famine seriously enough that they decided to cut short their fall hunt in order to devote themselves to fortifying their village. A bastioned pentagonal wooden palisade was completed with haste during the beginning of the following year and crowned shortly thereafter by the addition of a single iron cannon delivered on the orders of the new governor of Montreal, Louis-Hector de Callière.[51] At Kanehsatake, Vachon de Belmont did his best to improve the mission complex, enclosing its chapel and administrative buildings within a rectangular stone masonry wall – of which two corner turrets have survived to this day, along Sherbrooke Street in downtown Montreal – and the adjacent longhouses within a rectangular wooden carpentry palisade erected, in the missionary's words, "for the security of the Natives in their extreme danger."[52]

The Iroquois offensive turned out to be diplomatic, rather than military. In the months that followed La Barre's campaign, the Oneidas made an appeal to Ogenheratarihiens, whose unwillingness to join in the expedition seemed to signal dissatisfaction with the French alliance and life at Kahnawake. Their chief captain had just passed away, they explained, offering him the opportunity to take on his position if he was willing to return among them. Ogenheratarihiens rejected the offer, countering that they should instead become Christians and join him in the Saint Lawrence valley – but his demeanor was such that throughout the year following the campaign the missionaries continued to fear that he might choose to leave the mission.[53] Mohawk overtures proved more consequential. Arriving in 1683, Governor Thomas Dongan of New York took the opportunity presented by the Onondagas, Cayugas, and Senecas' request for assistance to extend English claims over the Five Nations and to undermine the standing of the French among them. In 1686, he encouraged the Mohawks to advocate the return-migration of their relatives in Canada, promising that the latter would be provided with "as much land as they needed" at Saratoga on the lower Hudson, as well as a Catholic priest who might "instruct them in religion."[54] While a segment of the

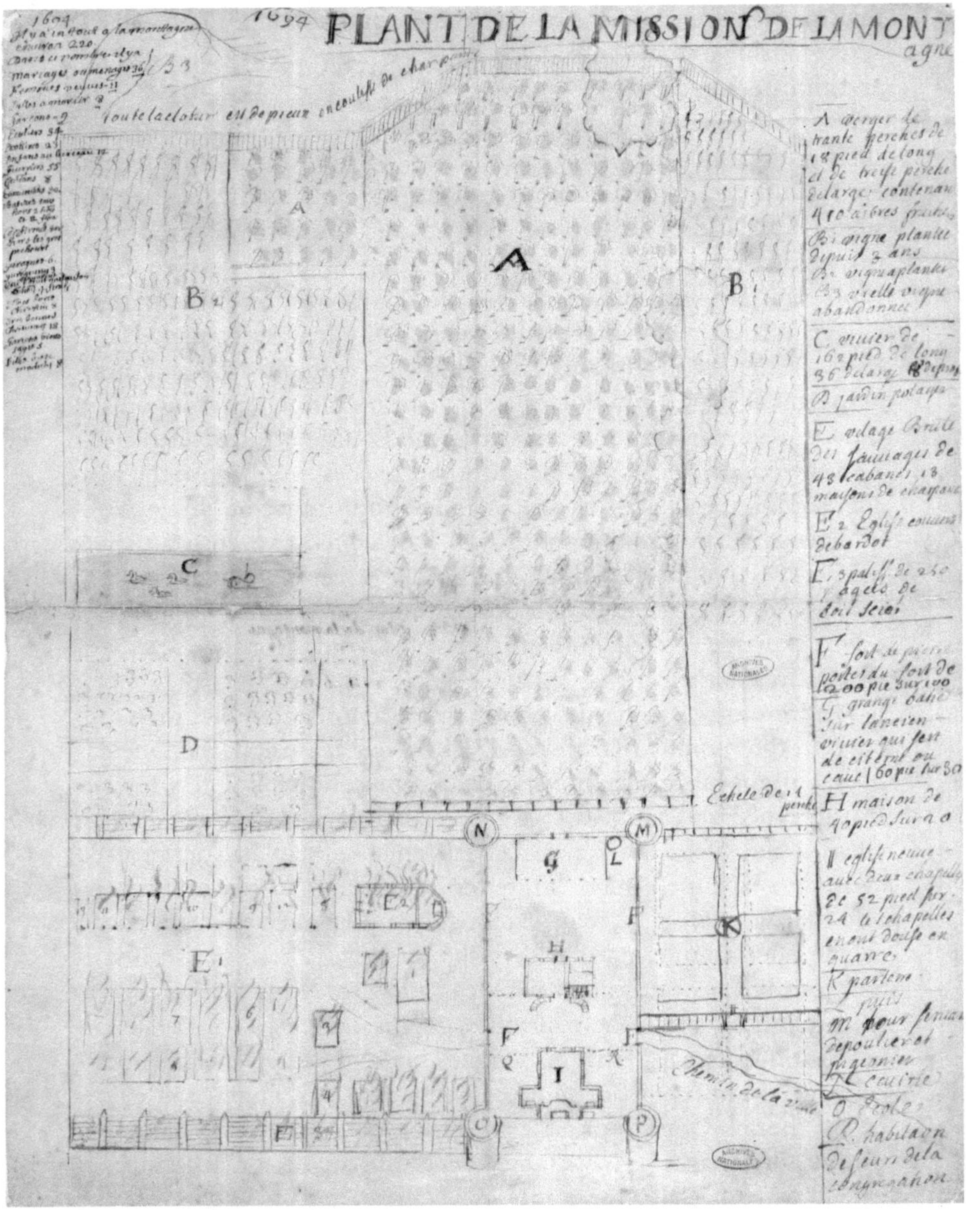

Figure 6.2 This plan of Kanehsatake, drawn by François Vachon de Belmont to illustrate the ravages of the fire in 1694, shows the missionary compound with its stone wall (F) and towers (M, N, O, P), church (I), residence (H), and the palisaded village with visible flames (E). Gardens and orchards were laid out to the north (A, B, D). ("Plant de la mission de la Montagne," 1694, ANF, N/III/Canada/12)

Mohawk leadership was likely inclined to let their relatives in the mission settlements be, another needed no convincing that their return-migration should be induced. In the late summer of 1686, a man named Onnonragewas (confusingly known to the Dutch at Albany as Janetje but to the English there as Lawrence), who had spent some time at Kahnawake and been baptized there before resettling in Mohawk country, journeyed back to the mission to convey the invitation to its people. Back in Albany, Onnonragewas gave a misleading report to the effect that all the Christian Iroquois had answered that "they would be very willing to come to live at Sarachtoge [Saratoga]," and that Onontio would not object to this relocation. The number of families that showed interest in returning to Mohawk country was in fact more limited: eight, reports one source, including those of a certain Garistasi (or Le Fer, "The Iron") and his brother Kakare.[55] Along with Onnonragewas, these two men would emerge as the staunchest promoters of a return-migration in the following years.

***

The campaign solidified the reputation of the mission settlements in the eyes of colonial officials. Governor La Barre was satisfied with the performance of the missions' warriors – even those of Kanehsatake, of whom the governor had had low expectations beforehand, probably owing to his tendency to favour the Jesuits over Sulpicians, in the end impressed him as "very good soldiers and faithful subjects of the king."[56] But La Barre's lackluster leadership, and the "shameful peace" that he had negotiated at La Famine, upset many and led to his prompt recall by Louis XIV. The new governor, Jacques-René de Brisay de Denonville, instructed to intimidate the League with French military might, began plotting another offensive against the Senecas as soon as he landed in the colony in the fall of 1685. He allowed two years of careful preparation.[57] In early 1687, Denonville sent word to the Christian Iroquois to remind them "that it is necessary to destroy the Iroquois in order to establish religion; to destroy the Iroquois, it is necessary to attack them."[58] The actual message was no doubt couched in more nuanced terms, for although Denonville secretly hoped to conduct operations against all of the Five Nations, the target of his initial efforts would again be the Senecas, whose persistent depredations against allies and traders in the interior constituted a strong *casus belli*. By all accounts the leadership of the mission settlements again responded with commitment. Togouirout, but this time also Ogenheratarihiens, and a third captain, respectively representing the Mohawks, Oneidas, and Onondagas, headed Kahnawake's contingent. It was at about this period that the Albany trader Anthony Lespinard, upon encountering Togouirout "the Indian General" at Chambly along the Richelieu River, observed him to be "very true to the French" and heard him explain that his community "would immediately join with the French in the war against the Śniekes [Senecas]" as long as their Mohawk, Oneida, and Onondaga relatives remained uninvolved.[59]

Estimates of the Saint Lawrence mission warriors involved in the expedition range from about 250 to 350. Kanehsatake and Lorette provided about the same number of men, 50 to 60 and 40 respectively; Kamiskouaouangachit fielded 60 to 100 Wabanakis; as well as Algonquins from the bands that orbited around Trois Rivières in numbers ranging from 10 to 60. As Ogenheratarihiens's participation indicates, willingness to engage against the Senecas was more generalized at Kahnawake than it had been three years earlier. Though the community fielded about the same number of men on this occasion, around 100 or 120, in light of recent outmigration this represented a much more complete mobilization of the community's warriors (1: 4.5/5, as opposed to 1: 6.5/7).[60] A handful of members of the Kahnawake contingent felt strong-armed into taking part in the campaign, among whom were Garistasi and Kakare, who had returned to the village after the winter hunt with the intention of soon relocating to Mohawk country. The testimony subsequently given at Albany by one Adandidaghko, a Mohawk from the village of Tionnontoguen who had come to Canada to see relatives and obtain beaver skins to trade among the Dutch and English, only to be caught up in the preparations for war, allows a glimpse into the nature of the coercion. When he meant to return home, his "relations would not suffer it because the French had given contrary orders." When these Christian relatives inquired whether he intended to "go and fight with the French against the Sinnakes or not," he answered no. His relatives reportedly replied that "you shall be forced to go, and the French will put you in prison till the war is done and the army returns."[61]

Denonville was indeed intent on surprising the enemy and ready to imprison those persons who threatened to jeopardize his campaign. Before the army's departure from Montreal, he sent a detachment of fifteen Frenchmen to seize an Onondaga and three other Iroquois who were in the vicinity of the Châteauguay River, on the south shore of the Saint Lawrence river west of Kahnawake, purportedly "to spy on what was going on, and [who] said a thousand impertinences about the governor." They were promptly placed in the prison at Montreal.[62] However, beyond such a pointed intervention, neither Denonville nor any of the French had any coercive authority over the inhabitants of Kahnawake and Kanehsatake. Instead, it was the pressure of relatives invested in the French alliance, rather than largely unenforceable threats of imprisonment by colonial authorities themselves, that "forced" a small minority of men, such as Garistasi, Kakare, and Adandidaghko, to take a reluctant part in the expedition.

Denonville's resolve to ensure the secrecy and security of his army by seizing every Iroquois encountered along the route of the upper Saint Lawrence and throughout the north shore of Lake Ontario did, however, clash with the natural tendency of the Christian Iroquois to make distinctions between elements of the Five Nations. When the scouts of the advancing army spotted a band fishing on the island of Toniata, a party of Christian Iroquois was immediately deployed in cooperation with a corps of Algonquins and Wabanakis, under the supervision of Jacques Le Moyne de Sainte-Hélène, to encircle them. According to Louis Henri de Baugy, the officer who served as Denonville's aide-de-camp during the campaign, the deployment of the Christian Iroquois on this occasion had been intended as a test, "to arouse their honor and see if they would do what they had promised." Baugy's misgivings were in a sense borne out when, upon learning that their intended targets had withdrawn to Cataraqui, these warriors expressed relief to Sainte-Hélène and made it known that it would have saddened them to carry out the capture. Relief was short lived, though, for upon arriving at Cataraqui on 3 July, the warriors discovered there some two hundred Cayugas, Onondagas, and Oneidas who had been seized by a ruse after having been invited to a great feast on Denonville's orders.[63]

Though contemporary French observers might lump these prisoners together under the rubric of "Iroquois," the missions' warriors would have recognized them plainly as Cayugas, Onondagas, and Oneidas, and as relatives and friends. This must have been particularly true for the men of Kanehsatake, given that many of the people who currently found themselves in custody had orbited around the now defunct Sulpician missions of the north shore of Lake Ontario, and that over the years these missions had constituted something of a recruiting ground for their own community near Montreal.[64] Disgusted and alarmed by the behaviour of their French allies, who had not respected their desire not to take part in the war if their relatives were involved, about a hundred Christian Iroquois warriors took advantage of the confusion of the army's departure from Cataraqui on the morning of 4 July to return to their villages. Meanwhile, Garistasi and a second man chose to slip away towards Seneca country to warn its inhabitants of the impending attack.[65]

A solid core of some 120 Christian Iroquois, no doubt predominantly consisting of those warriors who had no kinship ties to the prisoners or otherwise felt little affinity with them, remained with the army as it made its way across Lake Ontario and towards the Seneca villages. When three or four Seneca scouts appeared at a distance and asked what the intentions of the French were, it was a Christian Mohawk who, interpreting for his French brothers-in-arms, shouted out defiantly from the lines: "You blockheads, I'll tell you what I have come to do: to war upon you; and tomorrow I will march up with my army to your castles."[66] At a half league from the main Seneca village of Ganondagan, the army engaged in battle with an opposing force of approximately 450 Seneca warriors. While commentators noted that the Odawa warriors posted on the right flank faltered, and that confusion and disorder momentarily set in among the soldiers and militiamen, the conduct of the warriors of the mission settlements was universally praised. In retelling the episode, even Baugy deviated from his habitually mistrustful tone: "Our Christian Natives [...] performed deeds of valour, our Iroquois outdid themselves and showed that they surpassed by far the Senecas and that we could henceforth trust them."[67] That the Christian Iroquois had not shirked the action was further confirmed by the fact that 3 or 4 of their number lay among the army's dozen dead, including a chief from Kanehsatake named Tegaretouan (The Sun), recognized as that community's "first Christian," as well as Kahnawake's celebrated Ogenheratarihiens.[68]

The days that followed the advancing army found the four Seneca villages abandoned and smoldering. The divergent priorities of the allies became readily apparent when Denonville ordered the destruction of the adjoining corn fields and the abundant stores. The warriors of the missions understood that to starve out the Senecas would turn them into a burden for the other four nations, and could only serve to unite the League and harden its attitude towards the French. The Christian Iroquois accordingly refused to destroy the Seneca's corn or, when they separated themselves from the main force to scout and loot the surroundings, to facilitate the Frenchmen's job by pointing out outfields.[69] Divergences again manifested themselves when Denonville made it known that his intention was to proceed to Niagara to build a fort there. Victorious in battle, weary after a long campaign, and eager to get started on the fall hunt, the mission warriors were reluctant to press on. Togouirout and his men momentarily ceded to the governor's arguments, but when the time came to embark – and in an echo of what another group of warriors had done three weeks earlier – the warriors set out eastwards in the direction of Cataraqui. Only after Denonville's insistence and one warrior's impassioned speech did all but two of the Christian Iroquois canoes resolve to accompany the army until the end of the campaign (the reluctant Kakare being aboard one of the two that did not remain with the governor).[70]

No sooner had their warriors returned from the campaign – the governor and the bulk of his army having spent only five days at Niagara – than the Christian Iroquois sent emissaries southward to probe the intentions of the League's eastern nations and to ensure that they remained neutral. Togouirout and seven other men, including Kakare and Adandidaghko, journeyed towards the Mohawk villages. About halfway there, they encountered a party of sixty warriors from the Mohawk village of Tionnontoguen intent, in solidarity with the Senecas, on raiding Canada in retaliation for the recent invasion. After calling out from a distance to make sure that the party itself included no Senecas, Togouirout approached them, delivered his message, and dissuaded the warriors from going any further. While Kakare and Adandidaghko journeyed on towards the Mohawk villages, four of the would-be raiders accompanied Togouirout back to Kahnawake.[71] Meanwhile five Christian Onondagas from the mission had been dispatched to Onondaga with wampum belts and presents to "persuade them not to war" and to offer, on Denonville and Bruyas's instruction, the release of the prisoners taken on the way to Cataraqui.[72] This would have been a persuasive argument. In June of 1688, an Onondaga, Cayuga, and Oneida delegation headed by Otreouti arrived at Montreal to declare the neutrality of their peoples. In response, the people of Kahnawake and Kanehsatake handed over ninety-one prisoners whom the colonial officials had entrusted to them.[73]

Freed captives were not alone in streaming back to Iroquoia around this time. As in 1684, the realization that to remain in Canada meant being drawn into a large-scale conflict, now coupled with English promises that lands and a priest would be made available, led a wave of individuals and families to abandon the mission settlements. Kakare and his brother Garistatsi, who had been contemplating this move for some time, and who had turned out to form the most reluctant element during the recent campaign, returned to Kahnawake by the winter of 1688. The first of the two explained to the missionaries that he had come back "for his religion['s] sake," but in reality the pair had journeyed to fetch their close relatives and to encourage others to undertake the return migration to Mohawk country. According to Vachon de Belmont, some thirty men and twenty women left the community as a result of these and other visitors' entreaties.[74] The extant census records confirm that Kahnawake experienced a significant dip in population between 1685 and 1688, from 682 individuals to 485, and that Kanehsatake's population similarly fell from 222 to 181.[75]

Back in Mohawk country, Garistasi and Kakare settled in the village of Tionnontoguen, which was quickly emerging as a center of Anglophile sentiment and Mohawk Protestantism. It should not be surprising that many of the men and women who had been disappointed by life in the Canadian missions did not reject Christianity altogether. They found that Protestantism offered a promising alternative to Roman Catholicism: insofar as the Frenchmen's religion had torn Iroquoia apart, draining its population and power northward, the religion of the New Yorkers, they reasoned, might provide the means of reversing the trend. Mohawk leaders' oft reiterated requests for English missionaries were partly answered by the intervention of the Dutch Reformed minister Domine Godfredius Dellius who, having taken the pulpit at Albany in 1683, began to cultivate an Indigenous constituency in the fall of 1689; by the following year, he was taking an active part in Indigenous affairs as a close collaborator of the town's officials.[76] Garistatsi, who within a few years would emerge as Tionnontoguen's "chief sachem," as well as Kakare and Onnonragewas, were among those who developed and nurtured the strongest ties to the minister and the magistrates.[77] Over the next few years they would continue to act as the most persistent promoters of a return-migration from Canada to Mohawk country, alternating between diplomatic and military means to achieve it.

***

The offensives of 1684 and 1687 – the fumbling effort of one Onontio and the treacherous behaviour of another – pushed the Five Nations

League to its greatest unity and fullest elaboration yet. Events unfolding on both sides of the Atlantic would complicate relations between the Christian and League Iroquois even further. During the summer of 1688, a party of Tionnontaté Wendats from Michilimackinac attacked an Iroquois delegation en route to Montreal to ratify the terms discussed by the Onondaga Otreouti earlier that summer. Amidst false reports that Denonville had ordered the attack, the projected peace settlement fell through.[78] During the winter that followed, across the ocean, Louis XIV invaded the German Palatinate, and William of Orange deposed James II of England in a "Glorious Revolution." In the spring, England and the Dutch Republic declared war against France, joining the Holy Roman Empire, Spain, and Sweden in what soon would become formalized as the Grand Alliance or League of Augsburg. Governor Dongan, along with the mayor of Albany and fur trader Peter Schuyler, and Domine Dellius, redoubled their efforts to incite the Five Nations to wage an open war against the French.[79]

The Five Nations' response to this new context was very much in keeping with the traditional patterns of incorporative warfare and diplomacy. As one Mohawk chief explained it to Dongan in early August of 1687, "we are much inclined to get our Christian Indians back again from Canida, but know no way to effect it except by taking one or more of their prisoners and send[ing] them into the castle to tell the rest that they may come freely, and to know why they fight against their brethren."[80] Through the summer of 1689, rumours of an impending major offensive against the colony by the Five Nations reached the ears of the Christian Iroquois. When a certain Jean-Baptiste Honnentarionni from Kanehsatake encountered a party of Iroquois on the Island of Montreal, they stole his shirt and wampum bracelet and told him that they would give them back only if he persuaded the people of his village to return to Iroquoia. The French, they explained, "were lost." Despite the fact that a Kanehsatake chief vouched for the validity of this report, neither missionaries nor officials believed it. Louis Ateriata, an early Onondaga resident of Kentake who had visited France and received Louis XIV as godfather but had since been banished from the mission on account of his loose morals, now returned to Kahnawake with alarming reports. Owing to his dubious reputation, they were similarly dismissed.[81]

French mistrust would have grave consequences. On 5 August, a combined Five Nations force estimated at fifteen hundred warriors fell in a surprise attack on the parish of Lachine, located across the river and just a few kilometers upstream from Kahnawake. Over eighty colonists were captured or killed in the raid. The next day some thirty to fifty warriors from the two nearby mission settlements responded by joining the French troops in a poorly orchestrated and disastrous defensive maneuver. Although word circulated that the raiders aimed only at the French, and not at the Christian Iroquois, at least seven men from Kahnawake were killed in the affair, and a few more from both villages were taken prisoners.[82]

The "Lachine Massacre," as it became known, understandably caused much alarm among both the French and their allies. The Kahnawakes and Kanehstakes who had been willing to go to war only against the distant and unrelated Senecas now clearly faced the hostility of united elements of the Five Nations. In late August or early September, five "Praying Canada Indians" were captured by Mohawks on Lake Champlain.[83] It was rumoured that Kahnawake, whose fortifications were already in an advanced state of disrepair, would be the next target of the Five Nations and of the English. According to Jesuit chronicler Pierre-François-Xavier de Charlevoix and to Vachon de Belmont, "fear overtook the Natives" who henceforth ceased to "consider themselves safe in their village." At Denonville's urging, the people of the mission sought refuge in a makeshift encampment within the recently fortified town of Montreal, even though a substantial segment of the community believed this measure to be excessive.[84]

***

The French were convinced that the raid on Lachine had been incited by the English. Frontenac, who returned to the colony two months after the event to replace Denonville, began plotting a series of major strikes against the neighbouring colonies.[85] In parallel, various parties made tentative steps towards reconciliation with the Five Nations. During the general council of eighty chiefs of the Five Nations that opened at Onondaga on 1 February 1690, Ateriata – who was described in the reports that reached Albany as "chief Sachem of the praying Indians," misleadingly so in light of his tricky relationship to the missions – presented a wampum belt and advised his interlocutors "to meet the Governor of Canada as he desires. Agree to this if you would live." Ateriata presented two other belts, one on behalf of one prominent Iroquois who remained captive in the colony, and the other on behalf of the Jesuit missionary Jean de Lamberville and officers and fur traders Jacques Le Moyne de Sainte-Hélène and Joseph-François Hertel de la Fresnière, all of whom also advised the Five Nations that "it will be for your advantage" to send delegates to Cataraqui in the spring. Unconvinced, the council resolved to send no one to meet with Onontio and declared that it would not consider peace until the all prisoners remaining in French custody had been released.[86]

During these discussions, a three-pronged winter attack was under way, in which war parties departing from Montreal, Trois Rivières, and Quebec aimed to carry out raids along the frontiers of New York and New England. At Montreal, 80 Christian Iroquois warriors (mainly from Kahnawake) under Togouirout's leadership joined 16 Algonquins and about 110 soldiers and militiamen under the command of Lieutenants Nicolas d'Ailleboust de Manthet and Jacques Le Moyne de Sainte-Hélène.[87] Almost invariably, period accounts of such intercultural military endeavours depict colonial officers as commanding French and Indigenous men alike. Yet their position was not so much that of commanders as that of negotiators. Men like Manthet and Sainte-Hélène enjoyed no coercive authority over the warriors whom they accompanied; at the most, they could hope to earn the respect and deference given to war chiefs through demonstrations of bravery, ability, and generosity. Only through inspiration, persuasion, and negotiation could they shape the course of an expedition and ensure that the parallel objectives of the people of the mission settlements and of the colonial authorities continued to overlap.[88]

The party set out from Montreal in late January 1690 with orders to proceed opportunistically down the Hudson and to strike against whatever enemy position could be destroyed with minimal risk. While the campaign had been one of Frontenac's initiatives, the course of the expedition leaves no doubt as to where the leadership resided. During a war council held towards the southern end of Lake George, the warriors "rejected heartily" Manthet and Sainte-Hélène's proposal that they attack Albany. Much more familiar than the French with the region, the Christian Iroquois understood the difficulty of attacking such a populous, well-garrisoned, and fortified town. Instead they proposed an offensive against the hamlet of Schenectady. Hoping to sway their allies, the officers proposed to defer the decision until the party reached a fork in the path. By that time, however, it was Manthet and Sainte-Hélène who had made up their minds and abandoned the hope of changing that of their allies.[89]

As the raiders neared Schenectady in the afternoon of 8 February, it was Togouirout who "urged on all to perform their duty, and to forget their past fatigue, in the hope of taking ample revenge for the injuries they had received from the Iroquois at the solicitation of the English, and of washing them out in the blood of those traitors."[90] Pleased to discover that Schenectady's stockades were unmanned, the raiders launched a surprise assault around midnight. Over the course of about two hours, sixty colonists were killed and twenty-seven more were taken prisoner. Meanwhile, to make the point that the French and their allies held the English responsible for the attack on Lachine, some thirty Mohawks who had been in the village were spared (even if Manthet and Saint-Hélène had wished to harm them, it is unlikely that Togouirout and his men would have allowed it).[91] Consequently, it was only with great difficulty that the officials at Albany finally persuaded the warriors of the two easternmost Mohawk villages – led by the familiar Onnonragewas, as it happens – to join a force of militiamen and allied Mahicans in vain pursuit of the raiders.[92]

The resounding success of the raid on Schenectady, coupled with that of the attacks against Salmon Falls by Frenchmen and Algonquins who had left Trois Rivières, and against Casco by soldiers and Wabanakis who had left Quebec, sent shock waves through the English colonies.[93] For the Christian Iroquois, who had grown convinced that the New Yorkers were ultimately responsible for jeopardizing their relationship with their relatives and friends in Iroquoia, the triumph was tempered by tragedy. Buoyed by the success of the raid on Schenectady, Togouirout raised a party of Kahnawakes and Kanehsatakes, who were joined by a handful of Frenchmen, to venture towards the Hudson in May of 1690. Somewhere to the south of Lake Champlain they surprised two bands of unidentified enemy hunters, Mahicans it is likely, taking forty-two prisoners in all. Tragically, the triumphant party was attacked during the return journey by French-allied Algonquins and Wabanakis from the vicinity of Trois Rivières, who mistook them for League Iroquois and Englishmen. Several were killed and wounded on both sides – Togouirout numbering among the former – before the misunderstanding could be cleared up. The Great Mohawk was mourned by Kahnawakes and French alike, the latter of whom generally acknowledged this to be an "irreparable" loss.[94]

Togouirout's death coincided with the end of a first phase in the conflict which, during the last two decades of the seventeenth century, pitted Iroquois against Iroquois. By now, Mohawks were taking up arms against Mohawks, Oneidas against Oneidas, and Onondagas against Onondagas. To wage war against the Senecas or the English was one thing for the people of Kahnawake and Kanehsatake, but to do so against relatives was quite another. As Jesuit missionary Bruyas observed during the months following the death of the man who had most defined his community's politics during the previous decade and half, the "most reasonable men at the Sault" had as a result grown disgusted with the war.[95] Yet the conflict would reach new levels of intensity before it could be resolved. In the meanwhile, another evolving reality of settlement and alliance in the Saint Lawrence valley was that old Mohawk and Wabanaki foes were increasingly drawn into coexistence with each other – something which the circumstances surrounding Togouirout's death brings into view.

7

In Their Place

Wabanaki Alliances and Migrations, 1675–1700

During the final quarter of the eighteenth century, the Wendats and Iroquois who had established a lasting presence in the mission settlements of the Saint Lawrence valley were joined by yet another population, this one coming from Wabanaki – the Dawn Land, or the Sunrise Country – corresponding to what is today northern New England. The French invariably placed these Peoples of the Dawn Land under the headings of "Abenakis" and "Sokokis," and recognized their kinship with those whom they called "Loups." Yet such labels hid a great diversity of identities and relationships, as had those of "Montagnais" and "Algonquins" earlier in the century. These peoples belonged to the Eastern Algonquian cultural continuum, among which anthropologists distinguish Eastern Wabanàkis/Abenakis and Western Wabanakis/Abenakis, principally on the basis of linguistic difference. Broadly, Eastern Wabanaki dialects were spoken in what is today Maine, an area to which the French referred, along with what is today New Brunswick and Nova Scotia, as *Acadie* or Acadia. Western Wabanaki dialects were meanwhile spoken in New Hampshire, Vermont, and northern Massachusetts. Further dialectal subdivisions paralleled political subdivisions, which often corresponded to specific river watersheds.

The distinction between "Abenakis" and "Sokokis," as the French used the terms, broadly mapped onto these Eastern and Western divisions, with the first of these two names being the most capacious. The Western Wabanakis who reached the Saint Lawrence valley included Sokokis proper from the Connecticut River, but also Pocumtucks from further down that river, Pennacooks from the Merrimac River, and Pigwackets from the Saco and Pisquataqua Rivers. Mixed in among them were a small number from other Algonquians from further south – the presence of Nipmucks and at least one Narragansett is attested. The French referred to these diverse Algonquians as "Loups" (Wolves), the same name which they normally used for the Mahicans, who inhabited the upper Hudson valley immediately to the west of Wabanaki country. From the headwaters of the Connecticut it was possible to follow Lake Champlain and the Richelieu or Saint François Rivers, or smaller tributaries, to reach the Saint Lawrence. Eastern Wabanakis meanwhile followed the Kennebec, Penobscot, and Androscoggin Rivers to reach, by way of portages, the Chaudière River whose mouth merged with the Saint Lawrence just a few kilometers upstream from Quebec, almost facing Kamiskouaouangachit.[1] The French occasionally used the term "Canibas" (Kennebecs) to refer to the people whom the English distinguished more finely as Kennebecs and Penobscots, but more often than not they were merely folded under the generic "Abénaquis."[2]

Through the middle decades of the seventeenth century, the Wabanakis cultivated their alliance with the inhabitants of the Saint Lawrence valley, both Algonquian and French, by trading and mounting joint military efforts. They occasionally intermarried with the Innu and Algonquins. Then, in 1675, there occurred an event that sparked a process of large-scale migration. Over the summer and fall of that year, Indigenous resistance against English encroachments sparked by the Wampanoags of Plymouth Colony spread, first to neighbouring groups such as the Nipmucks of central Massachusetts and the Pocumtucks of the Connecticut valley, and then further on to the Wabanaki inhabitants of the Merrimac, Saco, Androscoggin, and Kennebec Rivers. The ensuing conflict, most familiarly known as King Philip's or Metacomet's War, but which in its northern theatre might more accurately be conceptualized as the First Anglo-Wabanaki War, brought about the beginning of what scholars have variously described as an "Algonquian diaspora" or "Abenaki diaspora."[3] During the first winter of the war, Indigenous populations deserted their vulnerable villages on the coast and along major waterways. They scattered in small hunting bands throughout their home territories, in keeping with traditional subsistence patterns and in a way that made it harder for the enemy to find them. However, some bands drifted farther into the interior than usual as an additional precaution. Of the latter, a number journeyed westward, towards the Hudson, the Mohawk River, and the villages of Iroquoia. Others travelled northward, to the headwaters of the rivers they knew well, and in some cases on to Canada where they formed the core of new mission communities. The two major river networks which linked Wabanaki country to the Saint Lawrence valley dictated patterns of movement and settlement: Eastern Wabanakis gravitated towards Kamiskouaouangachit, while Western Wabanakis were instead drawn to the region between Montreal and Trois Rivières where in the short term they largely escaped missionary attention.[4] A first band of some thirty refugees reached Kamiskouaouangachit in about the month of May 1676, "after suffering during the winter from so unusual a famine that many of them died." By October of that year, the Jesuit missionary Jean Enjalran could report that 150 Wabanakis had reached the mission, and that an uncounted number of primarily Sokoki refugees had assembled near Trois Rivières.[5]

In the decades that followed, the continual advance of English settlement up the coast and into the interior of Massachusetts, New Hampshire, Maine, Connecticut, and Vermont, and the intertwining of local and imperial conflicts forced the abandonment of villages, agricultural zones, fishing sites, and hunting territories. Hundreds of displaced Wabanakis and neighbouring Algonquians sought temporary or long-term refuge in the Saint Lawrence valley, both within and outside of the mission settlements. To accommodate the influx of newcomers, "Abenaki" mission settlements were formed and transformed: the mission at Kamiskouaouangachit was given a second life. Whereas it was "the country of the Algonquins that had previously made a very flourishing mission" there, as Bishop Saint-Vallier explained to a French readership in the mid-1680s, "God has substituted a few years since the Abnakis in their place."[6] During this decade, the mission located on the Chaudière River, on the south shore of the Saint Lawrence not far from Kamiskouaouangachit, took on the name of Saint François de Sales, while among its inhabitants it became known as Msakkikkan and subsequently Néssawakamighé. The mutually reinforcing processes outlined in previous chapters – alliance building, evangelization, patterns of kinship and migration, defence – were central to the emergence and development of this new community.

***

The broad application of the names "Abenaki" and "Sokoki" in seventeenth-century sources to Indigenous peoples from northern New

England, while obscuring more precise identifications and betraying the inadequacy of colonial observations, is nonetheless a powerful reflection of the common characteristics of these populations and the flexibility of relations among them. Indeed, in addition to related languages and dialects, the Wabanakis shared broadly similar social, cultural, and political patterns. The basic unit of subsistence was the band, consisting of several nuclear families linked by blood or marriage, amounting to ten to thirty individuals. Although leadership was male and kinship was patrilineal, residence patterns were not strictly patrilocal. Through the spring and summer, and often in the coldest days of midwinter, bands related through common experience, contiguity of territory, and intermarriage gathered together as village communities. Hunting, fishing, and gathering were the primary means of subsistence, but Wabanaki communities living in the milder climates to the west of what is today Maine engaged in intensive corn agriculture, of a sort reminiscent of their Iroquoian neighbours. This allowed them to achieve a greater density and degree of stability than other Algonquian peoples to the north of the Saint Lawrence. Such villages shifted location every decade or so to accommodate the clearing of new fields. Those tribal entities differentiated by English observers and upon which historians have since relied – the Penobscots, Kennebecs, Amariscoggins, Pigwackets, Pennacooks, Cowasucks, and Sokokis being the most prominent – tended to be centered on one such village community or to correspond to a few related ones. Many of these villages were palisaded, though houses were often spread out along the water and near fields, rather than packed into the core. The prevailing form of dwelling was the conical bark wigwam, but in the denser agricultural villages to the south and west long rectangular structures with arched roofs and lodging one to four related nuclear families were also common.[7]

As noted in chapter 2, the Wabanakis' network of allies extended to the Algonquians of the Saint Lawrence valley. Some scholars, following Frank Speck's early twentieth-century forays into the subject, have spoken of a "Wabanaki Confederacy" to describe the relationship that existed among the Wabanakis and their Wolastoqiyik (Maliseet) and Mi'kmaq neighbours to the east, but the term is a misnomer when used in reference to the seventeenth century, suggesting as it does the existence of relatively rigid structures at a time when alliances of a far more fluid sort prevailed. There is no question, however, that owing to their shared social structures and cultures, closely related languages, intermarriage, and trade, there existed a general feeling of unity among the Wabanakis – and this even though tensions and violence occasionally erupted, particularly between the Sokokis and other nations. Common antagonism against the Mahicans further west, against the Iroquois, and increasingly against the English, tended to strengthen these bonds, as did the way in which war forced people to move, divide, and recombine.[8]

The waterways and portages linking Wabanaki country to the Saint Lawrence valley were already well trodden by the time the French arrived in the area, with the Chaudière River offering an entry into the region for the Eastern Wabanakis, and the Saint François and Richelieu Rivers presenting others to the Western Wabanakis. These populations had affinities with the region's Algonquin and Innu inhabitants. Algonquians all, they shared similar beliefs and customs, and spoke languages that, though not mutually intelligible, were sufficiently related that individuals from one group could achieve with relative ease some degree of understanding of the other's tongue. The range of their hunting grounds overlapped in the woodlands of the south shore of the Saint Lawrence, and it was not uncommon for bands from the two regions to hunt together for a season and for some of their members to intermarry. It is likely that these interactions became more frequent through the early decades of the seventeenth century as hunting patterns shifted to accommodate trade with the Europeans on the Atlantic coast, and with Wabanakis ranging increasingly further than before to the north in search of coveted beaver pelts. Other commodities followed this path to reach the Saint Lawrence valley, including not only manufactured goods from across the ocean but also wampum, which was fashioned from clam and whelk shells from the waters off what is today New York, Connecticut, and Massachusetts, and perhaps corn, which was more abundantly cultivated in these more southerly regions. A common enmity towards the Iroquois also united the Algonquians of the Saint Lawrence and the Wabanakis. Periodically during the 1630 and 1640s, small groups of men from the Kennebec came down the Chaudière and up the Saint Lawrence Rivers towards the vicinity of Trois Rivières "to help their allies in their wars."[9]

As observed in chapter 2, visits and the occasional marriages at Kamiskouaouangachit had allowed the Jesuits to hope that the village would soon be "inhabited by Abnaquiois."[10] Two Wabanaki ambassadors who had visited there in 1640 to make amends for the murder of an Algonquin man in their country took the opportunity to renew the peace between their people and the people of Kamiskouaouangachit. One of that community's principal men, Noël Tekouerimat it is likely, had on this occasion explained the importance of the new faith: "If you wish to bind our two nations by a perfect friendship, it is necessary that we should all believe the same: have yourself baptized, and cause your people to do likewise; that bond will be stronger than any gifts. We pray to God, and know no other friends or brothers than those who pray like us."[11] Through the 1640s, a handful of Algonquins, Innu, and Wabanakis leaders persisted in their efforts to cultivate an alliance between their peoples by occasionally visiting each other's villages. One Wabanaki captain, having been catechized by one of the mission's residents during a winter hunt spent together, was insistent that he receive baptism, saying that "he should not be refused on account of his being a stranger, because Paradise is as much for those of his Nation as for the others." He went as far as to proclaim that "he wished to remain always with the Christians of Sillery, in order to maintain his Faith," as soon as he had a chance to return to his country to settle his personal affairs. Though this man, having been baptized as Jean-Baptiste, was killed by an Iroquois war party on the journey back to his home country and thus prevented from having to either follow through or renege on his pledge, a small handful of other Wabanakis did assimilate into the community over the years.[12]

Between 1650 and 1653, Noël Tekouerimat and the Jesuit Gabriel Druillettes undertook efforts to broaden the alliance from the familiar Eastern Wabanakis of the Kennebec to the less familiar Western Wabanakis. It was not uncommon for Algonquins, and sometimes Innu, to encounter bands of Sokokis and Loups in the woods that lay east of the Richelieu River and Lake Champlain, where their hunting ranges overlapped. Although some of their respective elders could recollect an "ancient friendship" between them, the language barrier and the apprehensive climate fostered by the Five Nations' aggression meant that encounters now tended to be characterized by violence. Hunting parties frequently mistook each other for the dreaded Iroquois and came to blows; the dead, even when mistakes were elucidated, cried for vengeance.[13] Tekouerimat and Druillettes's efforts to extend the Franco-Indigenous alliance to the Sokokis, "to tie the knot of the ancient friendship that had once been maintained between them," as well as to the Sokokis' own Pocumtuck, Pennacook, Mahican, and Minisink allies, began to yield results in 1653.[14] The renewal of this peace cleared the way for Sokokis and these "Loups" to hunt to the south of the Saint Lawrence valley and trade in its French establishments. The destruction by the Iroquois of the main Sokoki village of Squakheag in 1663, and the conclusion of the Franco-Iroquois peace of 1667, both appear to have contributed to this northward movement.[15]

These Sokokis and Loups reached the Saint Lawrence valley in small and highly mobile numbers, and tended to roam its south shore between the mouth of the Richelieu River and Trois Rivières. Among the areas that held a particular attraction was the delta of the Saint François River, which, by a chain of streams and portages, reached far into the Western Wabanaki homelands in what is today Vermont and New Hampshire. The point at which the Saint François merged into the Saint Lawrence, at the westernmost extremity of a swelling known as Lake Saint Pierre, was described by the chronicler Claude-Charles Le Roy Bacqueville de La Potherie at the turn of the century as "one of the most pleasurable and most delightful areas on earth." It featured both mature woods and prairies, and game abounded there: migratory birds "in profusion" in the spring and fall, and wood ducks all year long; Lake Saint Pierre and the Saint François River's channels abounded with fish. "This area is therefore like the center of the best of all that we could dream of in Canada," La Potherie concluded, regretting that its only disadvantage was its vulnerability in times of war.[16]

Jean Crevier, one of the more prominent fur traders at Cap de la Madeleine near the town Trois Rivières, took up residence at the mouth of the Saint François River in 1668 or 1669, having secured a seigneurial claim to it which was confirmed a few years later. In parallel to his activity as an enterprising seigneur, which entailed running a manorial farm of modest scale and seeing to the gradual settlement of the area by French habitants, Crevier remained thoroughly involved in the trade with Indigenous peoples – as were, indeed, several of the colonists who joined him there. His wife, Marguerite Hertel, was herself the daughter of a prominent interpreter and trader, and she appears to have been as much involved in the business as her husband; their son Joseph took an active role in it too, as did relatives on the Hertel side, including her brother, the officer and interpreter Joseph-François Hertel de la Fresnière. From time to time, the Crevier-Hertel seigneurial couple served as godparents to Indigenous children baptized at the parish church of Sorel. At seventeen kilometers' distance, it was the closest church until the inauguration of one within their own seigneury in 1687. Yet the pair was noted as being among those who, in spite of the condemnation of the church, engaged briskly in the liquor trade. One of twenty prominent colonists convened by Frontenac in 1678 to opine on the subject, Jean Crevier expressed a view that reflected his experience on the Saint François River: "[I]f the trading of spirits is not permitted, it would do considerable harm to the country, insofar as the large number of Sokoki Natives who have established themselves there and who are brought up with liquor amongst the English, would return to them and deprive the *habitants* of the great profit that they bring them."[17] Through the last quarter of the century, the Jesuits would focus their attention on those Wabanakis willing to settle at Kamiskouaouangachit and along the Chaudière River, while those who remained along the Saint François River would continue to live beyond the bounds of the mission community – and earn a reputation for being people of a particularly unruly sort.

***

Kamiskouaouangachit had long since been in decline by the time war in New England began pushing unprecedented numbers of Wabanakis towards the Saint Lawrence valley. Reporting on the state of the Jesuit residence there in 1676, Father Jean Enjalran described it as "a solitary house" staffed by four priests and a lay brother. The bastioned stone fort still stood. Within it, the chapel of Saint Michel, reconstructed in 1663 on the ruins of the one that had been destroyed by fire six years earlier, could be described as "handsome" but it now served primarily as a parish church for the area's French habitants. The place had come to be valued less as a mission per se than as a linguistic training ground for missionaries preparing for journeys into the Great Lakes or Saguenay hinterlands. "[W]e have only a few Algonkin families, who come here at certain times," explained Enjarlan. Kamiskouaouangachit nevertheless continued to retain its importance as a ritual and diplomatic center for the Algonquins and Innu, and male descendants of the mission's influential first leaders, Tekouerimat and Etinechkawat, continued to be recognized as its heads. It so happened that Charles Negaskaouat, alias Tekouerimat, had just died in 1675.[18]

The several hundred Wabanakis who reached the mission beginning in the late spring of 1676 "were gladly received [and] adopted" by the few people who continued to orbit around it.[19] Like their Iroquoian neighbours, though on a much more limited scale, the Innu, Algonquins, and Wabanakis all used formalized adoption as a means of incorporating outsiders into the community.[20] In this context it would have been conceived of, at least in part, in religious terms, as described in earlier chapters: through baptism, neophytes were adopted into the family of the Christian God. Perhaps the refrain intoned thirty-six years earlier – "we know no other friends or brothers than those who pray like us" – was again repeated. In any case, it would have been apparent to the Wabanaki newcomers to Kamiskouaouangachit, and particularly to the leaders who had guided their followers there, that conversion to the new religion was a key to solidifying the alliance with the local community, with the missionaries, and with the neighbouring colonists.[21]

A captain named Pirouakki, who arrived at Kamiskouaouangachit in the spring or summer of 1676 and who enjoyed considerable prominence among the refugees, was quick to appropriate the spiritual power and seize the practical advantages that Christianity represented. Like Togouirout at Kentake only a few years earlier, he may have perceived in the missionary teachings an antidote to the epidemics, drunkenness, and wide-ranging cultural disruptions that his people were facing in these times of upheaval and exile. More cynically, he may have realized that conversion was a prerequisite to securing whatever material assistance the missionaries were willing to offer. Following an initial meeting with the Jesuit missionary, Father Jacques Vaultier, Pirouakki displayed an "incredible ardor to become a Christian, and to incite the others to procure the same happiness for themselves." He responded to Vaultier's invitation to come to church, brought with him "those over whom he had more special authority, because they were his nearest relatives," and took the habit of exhorting on a daily basis the others to do the same and of denouncing drunkenness. In November both he and his wife were baptized. While she took on the name of Françoise, he assumed that of Michel – a badge of his importance in light of the fact that Sillery's parish church was consecrated to Saint Michael. What is more, he appears to have gone on to be acknowledged as the new Tekouerimat, succeeding Charles Negaskaouat alias Tekouerimat as the mission community's "first captain." The evidence for this is circumstantial but convincing:

five years later the mission's chief was indeed named *Michel* Tekouerimat and was married to a *Françoise*; no other couple bearing the same two baptismal names appear in Sillery's sacramental registers.[22]

Though a small number of Western Wabanakis reached Kamiskouaouangachit as a result of the First Anglo-Wabanaki War, these tended, as in past decades, to gravitate towards Trois Rivières and Montreal and to set up small encampments in the vicinity of Sorel and Lake Saint Pierre.[23] Most of these refugees, like those who arrived at Kamiskouaouangachit, came in search of a safe place where they might weather the storm. It was because "they did not wish to get mixed up in the war that most of the Natives of New England had with the English, [that] they had left their country to live among the French," claimed a Jesuit petition for funding submitted to the Crown a few years later.[24] A small number may have intended to use Canada as a base of operations, and its traders as a source for the lead shot and gunpowder necessary to continue hostilities – certainly this is what New Englanders believed that they sought.[25]

In fact, French colonial authorities offered little material or moral support to the visiting warriors. The imperial contest on North American soil was simmering, and Frontenac was intent on preventing the arrival of Wabanakis from drawing the colony into another ruinous conflict against the Five Nations (even as he sponsored an aggressive westward expansion of the fur trade that would do just that). Meeting with some of the refugees, he "received them on condition that they would not return to make war on the English" and informed them that they were not to fight the Iroquois "on the territories of the French."[26] As one resentful Wabanaki warrior would put it to one of his captives during the final stretch of the war, "the French love the English better than the Indians."[27]

Lack of official sympathy was but one of many causes of concern for the refugees. The Jesuits of Kamiskouaouangachit were not as proficient in the Wabanaki language as they were in Innu and Algonquin, and accordingly had some difficulty communicating with the newcomers. More significantly, the missionaries lacked the means to adequately supply them with provisions, even though fields were available around the mission. The food shortages which plagued Kamiskouaouangachit through much of 1676 were compounded during the summer by a "serious illness."[28] A few years later, the western explorer René-Robert Cavelier de La Salle would encounter in current-day Michigan a diverse group of "Sauvages de la Nouvelle-

Angleterre" who as a result of the war had set out in search of a new country. "They did not choose it amongst our habitations," they explained to him, "because of the rarity of beaver as well as the difficulty of making clearings, because they [these habitations, i.e. the Saint Lawrence valley] consist only of forests." Instead, these wandering refugees now hoped to establish themselves either with the Iroquois or "in some other good country similar to that which they had left."[29] From his vantage point at Kamiskouaouangachit, the Jesuit missionary Jacques Bigot was forced to concur that "the country in which they lived is much better than this one with regard to food, to hunting, and to fishing."[30]

Indeed, the Saint Lawrence valley could seem like a pale substitute for Wabanaki country. At Kamiskouaouangachit all but the most zealous catechumens – Pirouakki was identified as one of these stalwarts – left on a regular basis, and in keeping with traditional subsistence patterns nearly all of them scattered for the winter hunt.[31] Discovering that the bulk of Metacomet's supporters had capitulated, and that the head rebel's own death in August of 1676 had largely ended the conflict in the south, these bands attempted to return to the lands from which they had been driven away. Many were dismayed to discover that settlers and garrisons had taken their place. Frustrated, one party of Pocumtucks and Norrwottucks, who had found what they hoped would be only a temporary refuge in Canada, launched a devastating raid on both the towns of Hatfield and Deerfield on the Connecticut River in September of 1677. Another band of Pennacooks and Nipmucks returned to the Merrimack valley, but quickly made up their minds not to remain and did their best to convince relatives who had spent the last two years around the headwaters of the Connecticut to accompany them back to Canada.[32]

***

Hostilities between New England and the Wabanakis came to an end in April of 1678, when Governor Edmund Andros negotiated a treaty with the last of the hostile bands. But the persistent threat posed by real and rumoured Mohawk raiding parties, who had been invited by the English to assist in the repression of the uprising, continued for a few years to serve as a spur to migration to Canada.[33] Though hostilities abated, the relocation of families from the Kennebec to Kamiskouaouangachit had a snowballing effect. As with Kentake, the importance played by subsistence patterns and bonds of kinship in drawing Wabanakis to the Saint Lawrence valley, and to Kamiskouaouangachit in particular, was considerable. One missionary noted of the newcomers who arrived there in the late 1670s: "Several returned to Acadia: some to bring hither their fathers and mothers; some their brethren; others their best friends, and even all their countrymen, if they could, and with such eagerness for their salvation that, on their arrival, the missionary found them already instructed in most of our mysteries."[34]

Father Jacques Bigot, who with his brother Vincent had recently taken over the mission, chronicled in a haphazard fashion this influx of Wabanakis: during the first six months of 1681, it received sixty newcomers, of whom forty received baptism; on 13 September, twenty arrived (including the purportedly "most noted of all the captains"); during the spring and summer of the following year, more than one hundred persons reached the mission. These numbers, claimed Bigot, did not include those "who stay here only a month or two."[35] Owing to the rapid expansion of the mission's population and the fact that over the half century since its foundation its site had grown increasingly hemmed in by the plots of French habitants, it became necessary to relocate. The newcomers themselves pressed Bigot on this matter, claiming that "if there had been sufficient space for them to be received there and grow their Indian corn for their subsistence," they would more readily have settled near the French and embraced their religion.[36]

The most appealing sites were located along the lower stretch of the Chaudière River, which flowed from the south into the Saint Lawrence almost opposite Kamiskouaouangachit. This river's most distinctive feature was the way in which, a short distance before reaching the larger stream, its waters plunged dramatically from a height of about thirty-five meters – it was to this "Sault de la Chaudière," meaning Kettle Falls, in reference to the resulting mist and bubbling of water, that the tributary owed its name. From there the Chaudière reached far inland to the watersheds of the Kennebec and Penobscot Rivers, making this a crucial canoe route. Its lower stretch was as yet sparsely settled by colonists, and fell within the expansive seigneury of Lauzon, which happened to belong to Charles de Lauzon de Charny, who since serving as interim governor at the height of the Iroquois assault on the Wendat refugees had joined the priesthood and retired to France. The Jesuits appear to have acquired a first plot of land along the river from his representatives before 1679, but it was small, thickly wooded, and pleas for an allocation of royal funds to pay for its clearing remained unanswered.[37] At last, in July of 1683, Governor La Barre and Intendant De Meulles granted the Jesuits a serviceable tract of land for the use of the Wabanakis, beyond the seigneury of Lauzon, some fifteen leagues or fifty kilometers up the Chaudière River (about where Sainte Marie de Beauce stands today). The Wabanakis knew this site as Msakkikkan, meaning "Many Fields" – pointing to the presence there of clearings that could be sown with minor effort, and that must have drawn deer as well. It is very likely that this location was a regular site of encampment. "As that place is on the road that leads to their country," reasoned the missionaries, "it will induce many who are still in Acadia to come to settle among us."[38]

In December of 1683, Father Jacques Bigot inaugurated a small chapel built of bark along the Chaudière, placing it and his mission under the patronage of Saint François de Sales. Some uncertainty persists as to its exact location: while the use of the name Msakkikkan in the mission's sacramental registers suggests that it was initially established about fifty kilometers up the river, the village core could by the decade's end instead be found closer to the river's mouth, next to the falls themselves.[39] Such ambiguity notwithstanding, the foundation of the new mission was accompanied by a symbolic gesture: at the suggestion of their missionary, and in emulation of what the Wendats had done shortly after their arrival at the Island of Orleans three decades earlier and on a few occasions since, the neophyte community pooled wampum beads to prepare a token of devotion and alliance to be sent across the sea. Destined for the tomb of their new patron saint in Annecy, in the southeast of France, it was assembled by a neophyte named "Tall Jeanne" (*la Grande*) and had its extremities embroidered in porcupine quills by another woman named Colette. Like the wampum sent from Lorette to Chartres, it was large and bore a Latin inscription "S. Franc. Salesio Abnaq. D." (an abbreviation of "*Sancto Francisco Salisio Abnaquiis Donatum*," "Presented to St. Francis de Sales by the Abnaquis"). Before being sent off, it was first deposited in offering under the painting of the saint which adorned the mission's chapel. As with other such transatlantic exchanges of wampum, this present was an affirmation of collective identity designed to muster interest in the new settlement, and no doubt to elicit assistance in the form of funding or a reciprocal gift of relics which might sanctify and protect the community.[40]

The fact that women made the belt and, indeed, appear to have pooled from among themselves the beads to make it, points to their gender's importance in the coalescence of the new community. Though they lacked the institutionalized political power that Wendat and Iroquois women and clan mothers enjoyed in their matrilineal and matrilocal societies, Wabanaki women too played a powerful role in sustaining Catholicism among their people and attracting them to the mission settlements. A large number of persons belonging to the "cabin of a woman named Marguerite" (possibly Marguerite Weramihiwe or Weranmiwe) arrived at Kamiskouaouangachit beginning around 1680. By 1682, her "kindred" at the mission were said to number forty-five persons who "all lead a very exemplary life." By its sheer size and its energetic embrace of missionary teachings, this family soon gained prominence within the community. Elsewhere, in a similar fashion, Bigot again alludes to "the Cabin of a devout Christian woman," pointing to the authority of women over the household. Indeed, at various times of the year, women appear to have represented the majority of the mission's residents, along with the very young and the elderly, while men went off hunting on their own.[41] Bigot's complaints about the way women quarrelled with each other hints that the process by which family groups, who did not all belong to the same subdivisions of the Wabanakis, came together was not an easy one. Many of them "on their arrival here, manifested the keenest jealousy, and indulged in slander of all kinds," he reported, concluding that "these vices of envy and slander are not common among the men." Although he does not go on to explain the subjects of these quarrels, it is tempting to believe that he was referring to the dynamics of people who in coming together were searching for ways to best coexist: issues were being worked out, such as where individuals and families stood with respect to Christian beliefs and rituals, and no doubt who would be allotted the best fields and house sites.[42] The choice of Saint François de Sales as "father and patron" of the Wabanaki mission may have itself been a response to the perceived need for unity. Indeed, this bishop of Geneva and popular theologian, canonized less than twenty years earlier, had been especially noted for his conviction that love and gentleness were central to the relationship between God and humans, and to mending those social relationships that here on earth had been riven by the Reformation – a useful inspiration for an embryonic community in search of cohesion.[43]

Though the ritual and social center of the mission shifted to the new location, both sites welcomed a stream of migrants throughout the winter of 1684.[44] Unhappy at having to shuttle around, Jacques Bigot complained that "it has been impossible to assemble the people here," speaking of the mission along the Chaudière river, noting that they "are all quite far from one another, for they are mostly in the cabins in the country; some were at Coste de St. Ignace [in the seigneury of Gaudarville, immediately upstream from that of Sillery], others at St. Michel [in the seigneury of Sillery], others at the fort very near me."[45] The relocation of the heart of the mission on the Chaudière River, from fifty kilometers upriver to just below the falls at the river's mouth, may have occurred around this time in an effort to assemble this population, though it may also have taken place a few years later. In either case, the first palisaded enclosure of the fort to which Bigot was alluding was completed in the spring of 1685, and some families proceeded to build substantial lodges ("*grandes cabanes*") there. The bark chapel was destroyed in the spring floods, and that summer Bigot oversaw the construction of a new one in the fort's centre as well as of a residence for his use and for that of his assistant and lay servant. But that this second chapel was built "in a fortnight" suggests it was not much more elaborate than the first one. The census that year reported the presence of seventeen dwellings at the mission.[46] Arriving in October of 1689, Jesuit missionary Sébastien Rasle described a mission settlement located just three leagues or fifteen kilometers from Quebec, thus close to the falls, "in a forest" with cornfields nearby, with conical bark wigwams arranged "more or less like houses in cities" within a palisade of "tall and tight stakes." Significantly, in a dictionary of the Wabanaki language that Rasle compiled over the course of his career, he seems to indicate that the name of the mission at some point shifted from Msakkikkan to Néssawakamighé, with its inhabitants coming to be known as Ounessawakamighéwiak. The new name appears to have meant "double place" or "second place," a logical reference to this site's relationship to the principal mission at Kamiskouaouangachit.[47]

***

War with the Iroquois loomed large in the minds of the Wabanakis who came to the Saint Lawrence valley. Given the longstanding antagonism between the two groups, Governor Frontenac's demand that the refugees arriving in 1675–76 were not to fight the Iroquois "on the territories of the French" reflected both the need for avoiding the reopening of hostilities with the Five Nations and the necessity of preventing within the French alliance violence of the sort that might involve the people of Kahnawake and Kanehsatake.[48] As the relationship of the French and the Five Nations began to sour, rumours started to spread among the Wabanakis of Kamiskouaouangachit and Msakkikkan. In the summer of 1682, it was heard that "some Iroquois were to make a raid upon our cabins while our men were away hunting," wrote Father Bigot who felt it necessary to "get up at night, to soothe the minds of the women, and to dispel the fear that they felt on seeing an Iroquois or two in the woods."[49]

The prospect of war became more concrete in the fall of the following year when, at the request of Intendant De Meulles, the people of Kamiskouaouangachit and those of Lorette were asked to start building as many birchbark canoes as possible.[50] La Barre's expedition against the Senecas provided officials and missionaries with an unparalleled opportunity to capitalize on the recent wave of newcomers, both to expand the colony's military strength and to enlarge the mission community. With the assistance of Father Bigot, the governor made an appeal to the men of Kamiskouaouangachit and its newly formed satellite settlement of Msakkikkan, tugging at their pride by urging only the most courageous and loyal among them to join his campaign. What is more, he called on them to reach beyond the Saint Lawrence valley and secure the active participation of their relatives and friends in Acadia. Etienne Nekoutneant, the second son of the Marguerite alluded to earlier, was tasked with carrying presents and at least one wampum belt, inviting "all the Abnaquis who remain in Acadia" to join the residents of the twinned mission settlements and "march to war with the French against the Iroquois."[51] Nekoutneant's staunch opposition to drunkenness and his strict observance of missionary teachings had earned him, with the approval of the mission's two captains, the appointment of *dogique* in 1682. In this capacity, he presided over public prayers and was responsible for religious indoctrination at Kamiskouaouangachit. It is also likely that he undertook regular proselytizing journeys to Acadia. That he was one of the most sought-after godfathers among catechumens of Kamiskouaouangachit during the 1680s is an indication of his importance as a key intermediary between Christians and non-Christians, between the mission's regulars and its newcomers.[52]

Whereas La Barre's call to arms represented for the Christian Iroquois of Kahnawake and Kanehstakake a reconfiguration of traditional alliances, for the Wabanakis it was merely a new expression of longstanding animosities. It may very well have come at the perfect moment: rumours, beyond those that had circulated at the mission two years earlier, had just a few months before spread among the settlers of northern New England to the effect that the Penobscots and Kennebecs were preparing to attack them, and that Governor Dongan of New York had responded by promising to incite the Mohawks to crush them.[53] Whereas the Christian Iroquois made distinctions between each of the Five Nations, the Wabanakis do not appear to have made much if any differentiation between the Mohawks and the more distant Senecas. It is plausible that news of these developments reached Wabanaki ears, and that this steeled their resolve to strike first against the Iroquois or at the very least to strengthen their defensive alliance with the French. Several Eastern Wabanaki warriors and their families responded positively to La Barre and Nekoutneant's call. The influential Jean-Vincent d'Abbadie, Baron de Saint-Castin, a former officer of the Carignan-Salières regiment who had taken up the trading post at the Penobscot River in the mid-1670s, ingratiated himself with the locals and married a chief's daughter, certainly placed his own weight behind the French invitation, though he was unable to personally accompany the warriors because English interlopers had recently summoned him to abandon his trading post.[54] Mobilization would follow a similar pattern in the spring of 1687, when Governor Denonville would lead another army against the Senecas: once again, an invitation was sent to Acadia, though this time Jacques Bigot accompanied the community's emissaries to muster support; and once again, rumours that the English were inciting the Iroquois to war against the region's inhabitants likely contributed to the appeal of the joint expedition.[55]

In the summer of 1684, Father Bigot estimated that it was a total of eighty or a hundred Wabanaki, Algonquin, and Sokoki warriors (but certainly including a few Innu and perhaps even some Mi'kmaq) who went to war from or through Msakkikkan and Kamiskouaouangachit.[56] The fact that the campaign ended with a humiliating truce no doubt aggravated these warriors, much as it did those from the nations of the Great Lakes, given their displays of anti-Iroquois fervor and the fact that many had travelled a great distance to take part in the expedition.[57] A mysterious illness, characterized by intermittent fevers and imputed to a variety of outlandish causes by French observers, proved to be an ever-greater source of grief. While an outburst of smallpox may have compounded its effects, it is likely that the culprit was malaria, which until the nineteenth century was endemic in the wetlands of the upper Saint Lawrence and Lake Ontario. There are no indications that the Christian Iroquois were affected, doubtless because their population was more frequently exposed to malaria parasites in this area and had as a result a degree of immunity to them, but French soldiers and militiamen were plagued by these fevers. The warriors who had come from the east, too, were particularly hit. Several of the Sokokis who had established their encampments on the Saint François River, a short distance from its mouth, died during the winter as a result of the fever. From Kamiskouaouangachit and Msakkikkan, Jacques Bigot wrote that only one or two of all those who had gone to war "escaped the attack of a malignant fever," all the rest having fallen "dangerously sick."[58]

Bigot found that this ordeal had awakened in the Wabanakis an interest in Christian teachings but was left to worry about the effect that news of the sickness would produce in their homeland, "whether that will not prevent those from coming who already have some design of leaving Acadia to come here." It was in vain that he tried to convince those who showed inclinations to return there to instead remain, or to otherwise come back in the spring with friends and family. "[T]he rumour went around Acadia that all the Natives [of the missions] were dead," and as a result few came.[59] Among those who did die was Michel Tekouerimat – the man who under the name Pirouakki had arrived in 1676 and had inherited the title and legacy of Noël and Charles Tekouerimat as first captain of the mission. Falling ill in January of 1685 while he was away hunting around Beaupré, he died within a few days – it may have been a recrudescence of malaria contracted during the previous years' expedition, an unrelated infection of smallpox, or something else altogether. Father Jacques Bigot rushed to the scene, but the time of year made it unfeasible to bring his body back to Kamiskouaouangachit and lay him to rest among the other "captains of Sillery." The memorial service held in the French parish of Château Richer was nevertheless, by Bigot's reckoning, the most solemn that he had yet witnessed during his years in the colony, a testament to the fact that the deceased was deemed an exceptionally fervent and indeed model Christian by his countrymen and colonists alike.[60]

***

In 1686, the Jesuits purchased a small and as of yet unimproved lot of land at the falls of the Chaudière River, with fifteen arpents of frontage on the Saint Lawrence River and forty arpents deep stretching across a bend in the Chaudière River – this may correspond to the heavily wooded lot which the Jesuits seemed to have acquired, or attempted to acquire, as early as 1679. Presumably this was a more convenient site of encampment for the mission's inhabitants.[61] The years 1683–87 marked for the mission of Kamiskouaouangachit a final peak: during this period more baptisms were recorded in the combined registers there than during any other five-year period in the mission's fifty-year history, reflecting both the zeal of the brothers Jacques and Vincent Bigot and the dynamism of Wabanaki migration. However, early census records for the twinned missions of Sillery and Saint François on the Chaudière River point to what the missionaries were not quick to spell out: that though several hundreds passed through, the core community remained relatively small. The 1685 census tallied 488 residents but only seventeen houses, and the one which was conducted three years later reported 512 individuals and twenty-seven houses – numbers which, in light of average Wabanaki house capacities, suggest a semipermanent population perhaps closer to 85 and 135 individuals respectively.[62]

Not all of the newcomers embraced the Christian faith either. In keeping with their dedication to the gentle ways of Saint François de Sales, the Bigot brothers were unusually tolerant, allowing the unconverted newcomers to take part in religious ceremonies with the neophytes.[63] But the missionaries were more guarded with respect to the Western Wabanaki bands who roamed between the mouth of the Richelieu River and Trois Rivières, and for whom the Crevier seigneury appears to have constituted a pole of attraction. Citing the Sokokis's "inconstant nature" and their reputation for being "much inclined to drunkenness," Jacques Bigot thought it wise not to admit any to his mission without careful selection. "[O]ur mission is not yet sufficiently established in Christian piety," he declared, "to admit that sort of mixture." He entertained the idea of easing them into civility by means of an occasional "flying" (itinerant) mission, but he was kept too busy to undertake such trips himself and his superiors do not appear to have deemed this population sufficiently important to assign anyone else.[64] This small and nomadic population, while cher-

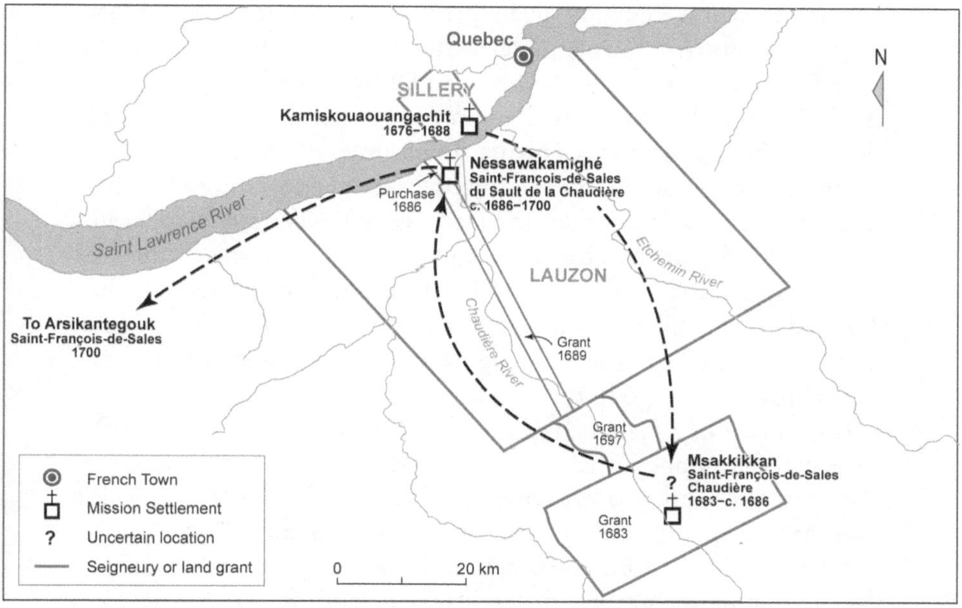

Figure 7.1 Mission settlements occupied by the Wabanakis, and lands acquired for their use by the Jesuits. Some uncertainty persists as to the precise location of the mission during the 1680s. (Map by Andrée Héroux)

ished by the local fur traders with whom it developed a close relationship, failed to capture the interest of the missionaries or colonial authorities. The census of 1692 was the first to allude to an Indigenous presence near the mouth of the Saint François River, and it tallied only twenty-five individuals.[65]

The authorities in New York, to the contrary, began during these years to actively court this very population. Anxieties about the northward flow of Indigenous peoples away from the English orbit and into that of the French were not generated only by the Iroquois, as outlined in the previous chapter, but also by those Algonquians whose ancestral territories lay to the east of the Hudson-Richelieu axis, namely Mahicans, Sokokis, Pocumtucks, and others, whom the English tended to vaguely lump together under the rubrics of "River Indians" (those who lived closer to the Hudson) and "North Indians" (the more distant ones to the north and west). Already in 1678, officials in Albany thought that the French were trying to attract not only the Mohawks, but also these "North Indians with the River Indians," who it was said were being given "great encouragement" in the form of "land and forts."[66] In 1684, a delegation of "north Indians [...] come from Canada" conferred with Governor Dongan at Albany, at the conclusion of which encounter they promised that they would resettle closer to the English town. During the summer of 1685, fifty-six men accompanied by about one hundred women and children indeed returned from Canada under the leadership of a certain Sadochquis. They revealed that they had gone to Canada "to live there" and had been embraced "as children" by its governor. Now, however, they declared to the Albany magistrates that "our thoughts and inclinations when we rose in the morning were always to come hither and to live at *Skachkook*" among their relatives.[67]

This village of Schaghticoke, on the Hoosick River near its confluence with the upper reaches of the Hudson River, forty kilometers northeast of Albany, had in a sense been New York's answer to Canada's mission settlements. During the First Anglo-Wabanaki War, the people of Albany and New York's provincial officials had grown worried about the Algonquians' northward exodus and sensitive to the need to strengthen their frontier. In August of 1678, Governor Andros ordered that these refugees should be directed to a convenient site and took the Albany magistrates' suggestion that the mouth of the Hoosick River, on the east bank of the Hudson, offered such a site. The village welcomed two hundred persons in its first year. It is likely that the area's Mahicans formed a substratum to the village's population, but they were soon joined by a variety of Sokokis, Pocumtucks, Norrwotucks, Woronokes, Agawams, Pennacooks, Narragansetts, Nipmucks, Wampanoags, and others. They retained close connections with their Wabanaki relatives. These identities are generally confused in period sources, reflecting a melding process: the community's inhabitants became known among the English as "Schaghticokes" or "River Indians," but the French continued to describe them as "Loups."[68]

Some of the Western Wabanaki bands which came to the Saint Lawrence valley were no doubt among the same who frequented the village on the Hudson. Several factors explain why, in the summer of 1685, a certain number of these people chose to return there. Schaghticoke was located much closer to the traditional homelands and hunting territories of this heterogeneous population. French willingness to go to war against the Senecas and by extension the Five Nations may also have worried – instead of thrilled – these Western Wabanakis who, as the Mohawks' closest and most vulnerable neighbours to the east, had much more to lose in a renewed war than their more distant Eastern Wabanaki counterparts. The fact that, like the people of Kamiskouaouangachit and Msakkikkan, the Western Wabanakis living near the Saint Lawrence valley had recently "been sick even to death," would have been viewed by them as yet another indication that alliance with the French and residence near them were not auspicious.[69]

At this juncture, the Schaghticokes' head sachem, Wamsachko, had proven a charismatic champion of rapprochement with Albany and New York. "[W]e are now come and are one body with him," explained the newcomers' speaker, "[...] we are fully resolved to live and die at Skachkook and there to be buried." They would "not be North Indians any longer but all River Indians [...] and behave our selves like River Indians." The speaker asked that colonial officials not worry if any of their people should absent themselves temporarily from the village. At the same time, he requested that "the path be shut" between there and Canada, for fear that the French governor "will maybe come here to look for us."[70]

The Albany magistrates welcomed these North Indians and requested that they send a belt of wampum to the rest of their nation still in Canada so that they too might come. A month later it was learnt that the people for whom this wampum was intended had themselves gone to Pennacook, on the Merrimack River, to be with their "brethren and friends." Though the invitation was redirected there, its appeal was lost amidst new rumours of impending Mohawk aggression against the Wabanakis.[71]

***

Of the approximately 350 Indigenous warriors who took part in Denonville's offensive in the summer of 1687, alongside 1647 soldiers and militiamen, 76 were reported to be from "Sillery" but likely consisted mainly of Eastern Wabanakis from Saint François de Sales and Acadia, and another 57 were said to belong to "Hertel's band" – these were Algonquins and Sokokis from the Trois Rivières government among whom the trader and officer Joseph-François Hertel de La Fresnière, the brother-in-law of Jean Crevier, had a credit comparable to that of fur trader and interpreter Charles Le Moyne and his family among the Christian Iroquois.[72] We can be sure that many of the Wabanakis, especially those who had journeyed all the way from Acadia, rejoiced at the destruction of the Seneca villages. For others, especially among the Western Wabanakis who in recent decades had ranged along the Lake Champlain axis, the campaign instead gave cause to reconsider their alignment with the French.

Indeed, in the months preceding the campaign, the interception and seizure of a convoy of Albany traders headed for Odawa country had exposed the heightened state of intercolonial tensions.[73] Several men described by the English as "River Indians" and the French as "Loups," possibly from Schaghticoke, were among the interlopers arrested. In recognition of cultural affinities and perhaps of bonds of kinship, they were handed over to the expedition's Wabanakis who treated them with "a great deal of kindness" and who at the campaign's end granted them their freedom and enough provisions for the journey to a short-lived "Castle [i.e. village] of Pennekook Indians," apparently located somewhere between Montreal and Albany, possibly along Lake Champlain, from which they returned home. At Albany these River Indians reported that the Wabanakis to whom they had been given had "declared their great dislike of the French warring with the Sinnekes" and for the French's mistreatment of the traders. These Wabanakis, they claimed, had also let them know that "it would be no hard matter to persuade them to come here."[74]

Thrilled by such assurances, Albany mayor Peter Schuyler and the town's commissioners of Indian Affairs resolved at once to send some of those they called "our Indians" with belts of wampum to that Penacook village, so that its inhabitants might in turn send some of their people as messengers to the Wabanakis in Canada. However, upon further reflection they decided to give a full report of the affair to Governor Dongan in New York, and await his instructions.[75] Though there is no evidence that Dongan acted on this report, it is likely that the River Indians pursued their attempts to win over their acquaintances and relatives in Canada. In early 1688 some of the Loups who had been spending time in the vicinity of Trois Rivières (quite possibly near the mouth of the Saint François River) packed up and left to resettle near Albany (probably at Schaghticoke). According to French accounts they were motivated by the desire to escape the debts they had incurred in town. In July they returned for a brief period in the company of other Loups, likely with the intent of convincing others to follow them. Out of frustration with the Canadian traders and colonists, or with the relatives and acquaintances who proved unwilling to accompany them back south, they caused havoc in the parish-es of Sorel and Boucherville, looting and setting fire to homesteads, going as far as to cause the death of one colonist.[76]

French officials and missionaries made remarkably little fuss about this incident, which they appear to have understood merely as a result of the colony's brandy trade and the volatility of intoxicated Indigenous people.[77] More preoccupying was the activity of eleven warriors led by a Penacook named Wampolack. Early that summer, he had approached Governor Denonville to request the permission to raid Schaghticoke. His party of eleven warriors consisted mainly of Penacooks, but also included one Nashua, one Pocumtuck, one Wappinger, and two probable Nipmucks; several of them had formerly lived at Half Moon, a seasonal encampment site at the junction of the Hudson and Mohawk Rivers, just north of Albany (now Waterford, New York). One of their aims, it is likely, was to contribute to the reunion of elements of a scattered community – through persuasion or if necessary capture. Denonville, wary of rupturing the peace between the colonies, denied the warriors the permission to set out on the warpath but allowed them to go on a reconnaissance mission. Suspicious of the party's true intentions, he cautioned two visitors from Albany who happened to be in Montreal at the time that Wampolack's party had left the colony. "[W]hen they are in the woods," he explained of the Wabanakis and Algonquian neighbours, washing his hands of the matter, "they do what they will."[78]

Denonville's misgivings had been justified. Near the Connecticut River, Wampolack's party encountered a band of Schaghticoke hunters and claimed to them that they were "going to fight by order of the Governor of Canada" against Native or English alike in response to recent Mohawk depredations. At a place called Spectacle Pond they killed five Algonquian allies of the English before moving on to Northfield, the uppermost settlement on the Connecticut River, where they killed six settlers. They may have gone on to Penacook to visit their relatives before returning to the Saint Lawrence valley with seven scalps and an Algonquian woman captive. When an angry Denonville confiscated these prizes, the warriors are said to have fled Canada.[79]

***

Everywhere the tenuous peace that existed between Wabanakis and New Englanders was cracking. The Penobscots were alarmed by Massachusetts' repeated raids on Saint-Castin's post at Pentagouet. To

Massachusetts' requests for a pledge of submission, they opposed refusal. The Pigwackets were in the meantime frustrated by a decade of encroaching English settlement, fisheries, and ranging livestock along the mouth of the Saco River. Attacks on cattle during the summer devolved into interpersonal violence, with casualties on both sides. The seizure of prominent Pigwacket leaders suspected of having caused the unrest was reciprocated by the capture of several colonists during a raid on New Dartmouth in September. When a group of settlers began building a fort at Casco, they were attacked by a party of Wabanakis. Having killed several, the warriors moved on to attack at Merrymeeting Bay and Sheepscot. Meanwhile, although several Pennacook leaders approached New England officials with pledges of continued friendship, most of their people were choosing to resist colonial intrusions.[80] Soon the Second Anglo-Wabanaki War would weave itself into the broader conflict that is remembered in history books as the War of the League of Augsburg or King William's War. With it, the Wabanakis would acquire an unprecedented strategic importance in the eyes of the French.

During the final year of his mandate, Denonville had grown particularly sensitive to the place of the Wabanakis of Kamiskouaouangachit and Msakkikkan in the grand scheme of colonial defence. While he appears to have been either unaware or unmoved by New York's recent efforts to attract the Loups away from the Saint Lawrence valley, New England's attempts to lure the Eastern Wabanaki of Acadia away from the French alliance were more difficult to ignore. Informed that Governor Edmund Andros of the Dominion of New England had made great presents to the Penobscots to conciliate them and retain them on lands claimed by the English, Denonville dispatched Father Jacques Bigot on his behalf to incite the Penobscots "to make new villages on the lands of the King" and warned the Secretary of State for the Navy that it would be necessary to offer them presents for that purpose.[81]

Though French officials in Acadia feared that this relocation would undermine their trade and defences and made their reservations known, Denonville was adamant. In October of 1688, to focus their efforts at Saint François de Sales on the Chaudière River, the Jesuits closed the sacramental registers of their Sillery mission, bringing it to an end fifty years after its foundation.[82] But the tract of land at Msakkikkan was not located conveniently enough, and the plot of land acquired near the falls in 1686 near the mouth and falls had not turned out to be as ideal as it first seemed. Responding in October of

1689 to Bigot's pleas that the people of his mission "would not be able to subsist at that site for long if they did not have a greater expanse of land," Denonville and Intendant Champigny granted an addition to it, narrow but stretching far inland, cutting through the seigneury of Lauzon and roughly following the winding course of the Chaudière River, almost linking with the tract further upriver at Msakkikkan.[83] Later that fall, the pair advised the Crown of the need to draw the Wabanakis who inhabited New England and were "disposed to make themselves Christians" to the mission on the Chaudière River, from where they might shield Quebec, and stressed the advantages of "sustaining them" with provisions and gifts of clothing, powder, and lead.[84]

The Pennacooks who had moved to Canada in recent years – "all" of the Pennacooks, claimed one report – had by the summer of 1689 returned to their ancestral lands on the Merrimack.[85] It is likely that some of these return migrants were among the Wabanakis who carried out the attack on Dover that June, in what became the first major incident of the Second Anglo-Wabanaki War. In describing the assault on the English settlement at Pemaquid in early August of that year, Intendant Champigny reported that the attackers were "for the most part of the mission of Sillery" (a misnomer, as the mission had by this time completed its relocation to Néssawakamighé at the falls of the Chaudière).[86] Wabanaki warriors also played a crucial role in Frontenac's three-pronged offensive during the following winter. The party that departed from Trois Rivières on 28 January was led by none other than Joseph-François Hertel de la Frenière, Jean Crevier's brother-in-law, and included the latter's son, Louis, as well as one of the seigneury's more prominent inhabitants, Jacques Maugras. The twenty French soldiers and volunteers were accompanied by five Algonquins and some twenty to twenty-five Sokokis. That the warriors who acted as the party's "principal pilots" had links to the Pennacooks is suggested by the fact that its initial target was Dunstable on the Merrimack. It was only after "often vary[ing] in their opinions about what place to fall upon," and being joined along the way by another party of ten warriors that they instead made up their minds to attack the New Hampshire frontier settlement of Salmon Falls on the Piscataqua River – closer to where that second group, led by a certain Wohawa or Wayhamoo, whom the English knew as Hope Hood, had their own roots. Striking there on the morning of 18 May, they achieved a resounding success. Taking minimal casualties of their own – Louis Crevier being among the few to lose his life – they carried away fifty-four persons and killed thirty-four more.[87]

Hertel and the bulk of his party joined up with a larger force which, leaving Quebec had in the meantime travelled up the Chaudière River to the Kennebec. Consisting initially of fifty Frenchmen led by the officer René Robinau de Portneuf and sixty Wabanaki warriors from Néssawakamighé, it was also reinforced by warriors from the area and by others brought from the Penobscot by Saint-Castin. This small army took the fort at Casco on 29 May before going on to destroy Pemaquid and Falmouth, achieving successes as resounding as those of Schenectady and Salmon Falls.[88] Some of the men who had accompanied Hertel had in the meantime been heading back to the Saint Lawrence valley to carry news of the first victory. It was with them that, on 4 June, Togouirout had his fatal run in. The confusion and violence of the incident is readily understandable. When asked why even women and children numbered among those killed at Salmon Falls, a French soldier captured shortly after the battle provided an explanation that evoked at once injuries that were recent and ancient: the warriors had killed them "to be revenged of the Mohacks, who had rosted & eaten off the fingers of theyr relations and had confessed to them that the English sett them on."[89] Puzzlingly, it was reported in Boston that Wohawa alias Hope Hood too died "by a strange mistake," after being ambushed and killed by a group of "French Indians" who mistook him for an enemy. While it is possible that the New Englanders mistook echoes of one feared fighter's demise as referring to the other, the coincidence is not impossible, and it is certainly tempting to imagine that both deaths occurred during the same incident.[90]

The discovery that there had been a great misunderstanding did little to soothe tempers. The event had reopened old wounds. It had after all been while fighting against Algonquians from New England that Togouirout had achieved initial fame as the "Great Mohawk" twenty years earlier. The conflict between the Iroquois of the missions and those of the League was, after all, a relatively new and uncertain development compared to the conflict which for over a century had pitted the Algonquians against the Iroquois. Even though traditional enemies now found themselves united by their alliance with the French and their joint occupation of the Saint Lawrence valley, mutual misunderstanding and distrust persisted. The joint participation of Christian Iroquois and a variety of Wabanakis and Sokokis in the expeditions of 1684 and 1687 had evidently not resulted in a perfect union. New relationships did not supplant old ones so quickly. Incensed by the death of their famous leader, the Kahnawake warriors refused categorically to free those whom they had captured in the scuffle. The Wabanakis in turn remained unwilling to free the few whom they had seized, and both groups parted ways.[91]

The crisis within the alliance dragged on until the fall of that year when, with the help of their missionary Jacques Bigot, the Wabanakis of Saint François submitted a written petition and a wampum belt to Frontenac asking that he use his influence to obtain the liberation of their people who were still being kept against their will at Kahnawake. At the same time, the Wabanakis sent a second wampum belt directly to their "Brother Praying Iroquois." The event, which was chronicled by Frontenac's secretary, is of particular interest because it is the earliest documented exchange between the inhabitants of the Saint Lawrence valley's Iroquois and Wabanaki missions. The tone of the Wabanaki overture was conciliatory. Had the incident, after all, not been a tragic misunderstanding? Was the accidental killing of a friend not merely one "of the misfortunes attendant on war, and which it is impossible to avoid"? While the Wabanakis assured their Christian Iroquois brothers that they bore them no ill will for the death of two of their own men, they reasoned that "you would have an ill-disposed heart, if after having mistaken my relatives, your allies, for enemies, after having carried them prisoners to your village, you would persist in detaining them when you are aware of your error." Though the Wabanakis partook in the Kahnawakes' grief over the death of Togouirout, they begged them to move on. "Let us weep for the brave who are dead, without allowing their deaths to upset our minds and estrange our hearts which prayer and friendship so long unite."[92]

The Kahnawakes offered only a partial response to these entreaties, releasing the principal chiefs of the Wabanakis and a few women. They promised to send the others over once they saw the Wabanakis of Acadia "all disposed to join their brethren who are settled here at the Sault de la Chaudière."[93] Perhaps this was a bluff, a pretext to retain prisoners whose incorporation in the community would compensate the recently departed in accordance with time-honoured traditions. But it is likely that at the same time the Kahnawakes sought to use this opportunity as leverage to strengthen the growing Franco-Indigenous family and to assert their community's preeminence within it. The missionaries, who hoped to strengthen their missions in the Saint Lawrence valley, may very well have encouraged them to adopt this stance.

***

Governor Frontenac, who had returned to the colony to replace Denonville in the fall of 1689, concurred with his predecessor that "of all the Natives," the Wabanakis "are the bravest and most formidable to the English." Yet, typically loathing of the Jesuits and all of their endeavours, he did not share Denonville's esteem for the missions of Sillery and Saint François. He dismissed, not unreasonably, his predecessor's argument that a strong Wabanaki settlement on the Chaudière would defend Quebec from English or Iroquois insults, reasoning that it was in Acadia that the Wabanakis could be of most use to the colony. "It is believed to be much more important to leave them in their old abodes, much more within range of waging war against the English," explained a memorandum on the state of affairs in Canada penned within a month of Frontenac's return to the colony, "than to attract them to Quebec to domesticate [*sic*] them there."[94]

Officials in Acadia, including the acting governor Joseph Robinau de Villebon, had long been of the same mind. In response to Villebon's lobbying and to Frontenac's apathy, in 1691 the Crown ordered that the annual presents to the Wabanakis henceforth be shipped directly to Acadia, rather than Quebec.[95] Jesuit petitions, supported by Champigny, that the funding allocated by the Crown to the allies be extended to the "Christian Abenakis" of Sillery (*sic*: Néssawakamighé, as the old mission was closed by this time) appear to have had no effect.[96] In this uncertain context, Jacques Bigot travelled to France to support the mission and find patrons, leaving his brother Vincent on site. Sailing in the fall of 1691, he brought with him an address written in Wabanaki intended for the chapter of Chartres Cathedral. This document, carried inside a tin box inscribed "Votum Abnaquiorum," curiously does not appear to have been accompanied by a wampum belt. At any rate, in reaching out to the canons of Chartres, Bigot certainly hoped to elicit attention and assistance of a sort that Saint François de Sales's shrine at Annecy had failed to offer in response to the wampum the community had sent it in 1684. Chartres certainly had a strong track record in its dealings with the people of Lorette. Sure enough, its canons responded by a letter in 1692, which announced the gift to the Wabanakis of a silver reliquary similar to the one which had been sent to the Wendats. The gift arrived with Jacques Bigot when he returned to the colony in 1694, with the "holy union" that had been thus contracted, "charming" the community. It bears noting that the cult of the Virgin Mary was not nearly as meaningful to the Wabanakis as it was to matrilineal Wendats and Iroquois. Nonetheless, subsequent correspondence between the mission and the canons of Chartres speak of a "union of adoption," by which the canons were acknowledged by the Wabanakis as "our lords and our fathers" and, more obliquely but perhaps more meaningfully, as "brothers." In 1699, Jacques's brother Vincent, who was by that time responsible for the mission, followed up by overseeing the preparation of a wampum belt for these patrons, inscribed "Matri Virgini Abnaquaei D.D" (Gift of the Abenaquis to the Virgin Mother), which was again reciprocated with an impressive silver reproduction of Chartres's famous statue of the Virgin.[97]

More abundantly supplied in Acadia than along the Saint Lawrence through the decade, Eastern Wabanakis tended to return or remain there. By 1692, when officials took the next census of the colony, the mission of Néssawakamighé on the Chaudière was home to 336 persons.[98] Upon his return from France in 1694, Jacques Bigot reported with enthusiasm that the community seemed to be growing. Most of the newcomers came from Acadia, where his brother Vincent had begun ministering. Others came from an area some forty leagues away, where Jacques had journeyed on three or four occasions in past years – in the vicinity of Trois Rivières and further upriver to the south shore of the Saint Lawrence near the Saint François River. Some of the newcomers Bigot encountered at Néssawakamighé had indeed come from this direction. Among them was a man whom Bigot described as one of the "principals of that nation," who had declared that, whereas Frenchmen made liquor so readily available in the place that he had left, the place to which he had come, i.e. the mission, "had made him wise." Though Bigot does not spell it out, the timing of the interest is also suggestive of another cause. The Iroquois had struck at the mouth of the Saint François River regularly since the outbreak of war: in the fall of 1689 they had burnt down the chapel that had been built for the colonists two years before, and during the most recent attack, in August of 1693, they had taken Jean Crevier, the seigneur himself, who had died shortly thereafter from the wounds he had sustained during his captivity. Though his widow Marguerite Hertel had taken over the duties of seigneuresse and the fur trade business, the death of this key interlocutor, in addition to the persistent danger posed by the Iroquois, may have pushed the Sokoki and Western Wabanaki family bands which orbited around the area to search elsewhere for safety and subsistence.[99]

The man who had come from that vicinity to Néssawakamighé and met with Bigot had told the traders who sought to retain him that "he would do everything in his power to engage the rest of the nation to withdraw with him and benefit from the [religious] instruction that he was receiving." That prospect had alarmed the French traders so much that they had lodged a complaint to their district governor at Trois Rivières, Claude de Ramezay, begging that he find ways of halting this migration and of forcing those who had already undertaken it to return. The identity of the complainants is not revealed, but it is quite probable that they included members of the Crevier and Hertel families. As a result of these deliberations, it was proposed to the families that usually orbited around that vicinity that a fort be built for them and staffed with a missionary. Two wampum belts were sent to the mission at Néssawakamighé in the fall of 1694 to invite those who had moved there to return to their former abodes nearer to Trois Rivières. Upon their reception, on 7 October, the neophytes resolved to refuse on the grounds that liquor was too abundant in that region and that its disorders made it unlikely that a missionary would stay there for long. None of the few who had visited them in the past had been able to stay, noted their chief, no doubt in allusion to Jacques Bigot himself, but also to Louis André, another Jesuit who in-between postings in the Great Lakes and the Saguenay had briefly, from November 1689 to March 1691, handled "parish duties for the French and the Natives" at Saint François. Although Bigot told the neophytes that he left them "complete freedom" on this matter, he was privately optimistic that this minor crisis would force the officials to pay more attention to the instruction of the Indigenous peoples in the Trois Rivières government who had until that point been "almost abandoned."[100]

***

The fifty to seventy warriors of Néssawakamighé, and those who in uncertain numbers habitually resided between the mouth of the Richelieu River and Trois Rivières, were active throughout the decade.

References to them are rare in the official French accounts of the intermittent raiding on the New England frontier, but this is easily explained by the fact that they acted in concert with relatives and friends who remained in the borderlands of Wabanaki country, in a way that made it impractical for colonial observers to distinguish one from the other. Indeed, on the year of his return to the colony, Jacques Bigot reported that the warriors of his mission on the Penobscot River, "joining those of the mission of which my brother has the care," (meaning Néssawakamighé on the Chaudière) were continually on the warpath against the English. Between that spring and fall of 1694 they had formed three or four war parties that appear to have been involved in the resounding victories against the settlements at Oyster River, New Hampshire, and Groton, Massachusetts.[101] In parallel, the Wabanakis from Néssawakamighé and the Algonquins and Sokokis from the vicinity of Trois Rivières also campaigned against the Five Nations. They were cited as taking part in the defence of the Montreal region against enemy raids, as well as in the campaigns against the Mohawks in 1693 and Onondagas in 1696; in 1695, men from Néssawakamighé were also among those who accompanied Frontenac when he travelled to Cataraqui with a small army to rebuild the fort that had been abandoned there a few years earlier.[102]

The Sokoki, Loup, and Algonquin bands who occupied the Lake Champlain and Richelieu axis had the most to fear from the Iroquois, as the region was exposed to the latter's raiding parties through the 1690s.[103] Franco-Iroquois accommodation towards the end of the decade consequently represented an opportunity for growth. Towards July 1697, "Joseph, Chief of the Soquokis residing among us [i.e. the French]," was returning from a raid during which his party had killed an Englishman when on the way he encountered a party of "Loups."[104] Whether or not this Joseph was the same man whose intention to move to the Chaudière had been noted in 1694 cannot be ascertained. For their part, the Loups may very well have been from Schaghticoke, which had borne the brunt of New York's war effort and suffered considerable demographic decline as a result of disease, military losses, and outmigration. As one of them explained to their neighbours, using the common idiom of war in the seventeenth-century northeast, they had "become a small nation, the flesh taken from our bodies".[105]

The Schaghticokes' alienation from their English neighbours had recently been heightened by the killing and imprisonment of some of their number, falsely accused of murder, at Hatfield in January of

1697. According to a Schaghticoke complaint, this had occurred for no other reason "than the hatred and malice that the English of that colony has against us."[106] The fact that a resolution to the Franco-Iroquois conflict, and with it of the war between the Wabanakis and the Iroquois, was in sight, also must have contributed to the appeal of alignment with the French and migration to the Saint Lawrence valley. Indeed, during the final ratifications of the Franco-Iroquois peace of 1701, the orator of the Wabanakis of Saint François, a certain Haouatchouath, declared that his people had been at peace with the Five Nations since 1697, at which time Frontenac had apparently removed the metaphorical hatchet from their hand.[107]

At any rate, in July of 1697, Joseph spent two days in discussions with the Loups. As a result, they authorized him to inform Frontenac "that they would return to settle among us [the French], as in former times, were they not apprehensive of his displeasure and merited to be chastised for the blow they struck on us at Saint François" – an apparent reference to an attack on the French homesteads at the mouth of that river seven years earlier. Upon reporting this to the governor, Joseph was permitted to tell them "that they would be willingly received, on condition that they should behave themselves and bring in their wives and children."[108]

***

When news of the Peace of Ryswick reached Canada towards the close of January 1698, the colonial war effort ground to a halt. Frontenac purportedly took measures to prevent the inhabitants of the mission settlements from continuing hostilities against New England, but mischievously approved that the Wabanakis of Acadia pursue the war until they could reach a peace settlement of their own with their English neighbours. The fact that the two groups had tended to fight alongside each other during the past decade makes it plausible that some of the warriors from the missions were among those relatives and friends from Acadia who struck at Andover, Haverhill, and Spruce Creek in Massachusetts through the late winter and spring of 1698. Only in January of 1699 did Penboscot, Kennebec, Androscoggin, and Saco leaders manage to negotiate with New England an end to the Second Anglo-Wabanaki War.[109]

These new circumstances – the imperial, Anglo-Wabanaki, and Franco-Iroquois peace settlements – coupled with the death of Frontenac, that adversary of the Jesuits and their missions, prepared the ground for a major shift in the importance and location of the Wabanaki missions in Canada. The Jesuit lands along the Chaudière, reserved for the use of the Wabanakis, had been expanded considerably over the past two decades, but they still proved inadequate. In 1697, the Jesuits petitioned Governor Frontenac and Intendant Champigny for yet another extension, again on the grounds that "the said Natives cannot subsist there any longer if they do not have a greater stretch of land." They were granted an additional piece of land along the Chaudière that March, which completed the link between the concession received in 1689 and that received in 1683 at Msakkikkan.[110] Still, the setting of the mission settlement continued to prove inadequate, and it was decided that it would be relocated up the Saint Lawrence to a site a short distance from the mouth of the Saint François River. The embryonic community established there had, under the leadership of two unbaptized captains, one of whom may have been the aforementioned Joseph, and possibly owing to the arrival of some of the Loups who in the summer of 1697 had shown an inclination to come, reached proportions that made it impossible for the missionaries to keep ignoring.[111]

Enumerating the Jesuit missions in a letter to the Secretary of State for the Navy in the fall of 1699, Intendant Champigny alludes not only to the Wabanaki mission on the Chaudière, but also another "at Saint-François above Trois-Rivières of Socokis" that was in the process of becoming reality.[112] It was only in August 1700, however, that the seigneuresse Marguerite Hertel, in her own name and as trustee of their minor children, as well as her eldest son, Joseph Crevier de Saint-François, an ensign of the colonial troops, officially gave the land to the "*Sauvages* Abenakis and Socokis and the Reverend Father Jacques Bigot of the Comp[any] of Jesus, [their] missionary." That the notarial contract which sealed the agreement was signed in the presence of Governor Callière and Intendant Champigny, at the former's residence in Montreal, suggest the way in which the transaction was expedited by the intervention of the highest authorities. The land in question consisted of a half league frontage at the end of their seigneury of Saint François, on both sides of the river and to the back of the seigneury, including the islands therein. It was granted free of the usual rents and obligations that linked seigneurs to their habitant tenants throughout the Saint Lawrence valley. That for the widow Crevier and her son the advantage of this arrangement lay in the business opportunities that it guaranteed them is borne out by the presence in the contract of a series of clauses by which they reserved certain rights: the right to build a house near the Wabanakis' "fort" where they could bake and sell bread and other foodstuffs (and certainly trade); to mow hay "for their profit" on portions of the land unused by the Wabanakis; and to appropriate any field cleared by them if it was ever abandoned. All of this to the exclusion of other colonists, the missionaries being the only others allowed to build a house on this stretch of land.[113] That this relocation was also a sound financial decision for the Jesuits, who could go on to sell the missions' cleared lands along the Chaudière to colonists, may also have factored in their decision – as it appears to have done in the relocation of other mission settlements evoked in previous chapters.

The governor's and the intendant's belief that the relocation of the mission was needed "for the service of the King and the advantage of the Colony" was stated at the outset of the contract. Viewed as burdensome interlopers in the Saint Lawrence valley through the 1640s, then helpless refugees in the late 1670s, the Wabanakis had thus come to be understood as crucial military allies during the 1680s and even more so during the intercolonial war of the century's final decade. The new location promised to dissuade Iroquois or Loups from undertaking any raids in the immediate area, as they had been prone to occasionally carry out in years past.[114] The relocation was also strategic because it promised to consolidate the mission community at a time when peace with the English and soon with the Iroquois was making it tempting for its members to return to their ancestral homelands. As of yet, only about one hundred French settlers in fifteen households lived on the seigneury of Saint François, while that of Lauzon was already populated by over four times that number.[115]

Like the old one, the new mission was placed under the patronage of Saint François de Sales, whose name conveniently matched that which the French had given the river half a century before. The name Néssawakamighé was meanwhile supplanted by the local appellation of Arsikantegouk ("empty cabin river" or "empty camp river," thought by some to be a reference to the area's reduced population as a result of disease and Iroquois attacks in the 1690s), though the renderings San Plassowa (Saint François) or Plaswa Ksal (Saint François de Sales) were also occasionally used by Wabanaki speakers – the current name of Odanak, meaning simply "the village," only dates to the nineteenth century.[116] While the transfer of the missionary infrastructure appears to have been straightforward, the merging of the people of Néssawakamighé with those already living at Arsikantegouk was by no means spontaneous. While a portion of the people of the former mission, including "some Loups and some Sokokis" accompanied Bigot to the Saint François River in the fall of 1700, those Wabanakis who maintained stronger ties to the Kennebec and Penobscot basin chose instead to withdraw fifteen leagues or fifty kilometers up the Chaudière, to the lands which corresponded to Msakkikkan, and from there many returned to Acadia, to be reabsorbed into their parent populations.[117] At the new mission settlement on the Saint François River, the two captains who already occupied the site responded differently to the arrival of the newcomers who did their best to convince them to embrace their religion. One rejected Christianity, provoking a crisis in leadership. Within a year or so of the mission's foundation all of its Christians "were on the verge of ceasing to recognize him as chief, unless he adopted better thoughts at the earliest." On the contrary, the other captain and his wife gave some of their fields to the newcomers and displayed much fervor in preparing themselves for baptism, which both received on Christmas day of 1701.[118] Several other "Sokoki" and "Abenaki" heads of bands, including many deemed to be reprobates, followed suit by paying a newfound attention to the missionary's preaching, publicly renounced drinking, and declaring that they "wished absolutely to remain here." By attracting surrounding bands of Sokokis and other Wabanakis – as well as a small number of Algonquins – who had until then travelled the woods and farms between Trois Rivières and Montreal, the mission rapidly swelled, increasing within a year the founding core of maybe 100 to 150 migrants from the Chaudière to perhaps three hundred.[119]

8

The Tree of Peace

The Escalation and Resolution of the Iroquois War, 1690–1701

The accommodation between the Five Nations, the French, and their allies that occurred in the final years of the seventeenth century and that culminated with the Great Peace of Montreal of 1701 marked a momentous shift. Togouirout's death in 1690 coincided with the end of a first phase in the conflict which, during the last two decades of the seventeenth century, pitted Iroquois against Iroquois. The Franco-Indigenous policy of isolating the Senecas, and trying to wage war against them alone, had unravelled. One of Togouirout's nephews, known by the French as La Plaque and plausibly named Onondaquiro in his own language, became particularly conspicuous on the warpath following his uncle's death. He must have felt the loss dearly. Unlike his uncle, he was considered to be a "rather bad Christian," but, like him, he nonetheless acquired a great renown for bravery and for being "strongly attached to the French."[1] In a particularly poignant episode reported by the chronicler Bacqueville de la Potherie, La Plaque recognized his father in the heat of combat against a Mohawk war party. "You have given me life, [and so] I give it to you today"; he told him, "but do not find yourself under my hand [again], for I will not spare you."[2] Even as it speaks of continued restraint, the substance of this altercation points to the less compromising tone of the early 1690s.

The warriors from Kahnawake and Kanehsatake who had died during the attack on Lachine in August of 1689 counted among the early victims of this intensified war. Hunting bands soon became targets. Étienne Ganonakoa or Tegananokoa of Kahnawake became another early victim. Having set out with his wife and another man for the fall hunt in August of 1690, he was captured a few weeks later by a party of fourteen Cayuga warriors and brought to Onondaga. There, Tegananokoa was tortured and executed. "My brother," one of his captors told him at the beginning of his ordeal, "you are dead. It is not we who kill you, it is you who are killing yourself, as you have left us to live among these dogs of Christians of the Sault." Or, at least, this is what the Jesuits related, based on what his wife told them following her escape. Fathers Cholenec and Charlevoix after him reported this, along with three other instances of Iroquois men and women captured and killed by other Iroquois, highlighting them as a cases of Indigenous martyrdom. Tegananokoa had been an exceptionally fervent neophyte, the missionaries reported, and he remained steadfast in his faith in the midst of the most painful torments. "I gladly give my life for a God who spilled all of his blood for me," he is reported to have told his captors. That his baptismal name of Étienne conveniently was the same as that of the figure revered as the first martyr of Christianity, called Saint Stephen in English, made him an ideal candidate for missionary promotion, and the ghastly violence of his death seemed like striking evidence of the fact that, as Charlevoix phrased it, the Five Nations in their entirety had now "declared all Christian Iroquois enemies of the homeland [*patrie*]."[3]

Of course, the Jesuit account of this death greatly oversimplifies the dynamics at play. It does not make explicit the fact that Tegananokoa's unyielding expressions of faith in the face of agonizing torment were a Christian variation of a tradition whereby captives were expected to respond to their tormentors with assertions of pride and defiance. Nor does it make it clear that Tegananokoa's fate might have been different if he had found himself not among Cayugas and Onondagas, but among Mohawks who would have included some of his relatives – though to be sure, Cholenec followed up this account with another of the death of two Onondaga women from Kahnawake, Françoise Gonannhatenha and Marguerite Garongoüas, put to death by their own Onondaga kin. Nor does the missionary account of Tegananokoa's tormented death make clear that captors and captives generally proved more accommodating than this with each other, something which the fate of the two people captured alongside him allows us to better appreciate. His wife was spared and eventually allowed to return to her native Mohawk country, where she remained until her son came from Kahnawake to fetch her. The other man was tortured and mutilated – losing a few fingers and having his leg slashed – but was then brought to the Caygua village and given a chance to integrate among his captors; taken along with a party of warriors heading towards Montreal, he seized the opportunity to flee and return to the mission.[4]

There is no question, however, that these years marked a shift in the meaning of war for the Iroquois of the mission settlements and their relatives of the League. The former were targeted, and they fought back. By one count, between the beginning of 1690 and the end of 1692, the Christian Iroquois were involved in the killing of upwards of sixty-six League Iroquois, mainly warriors, and in the capture of an additional forty-six. Meanwhile they saw at least twelve of their own killed, and a minimum of sixteen others captured. Not all of these deaths occurred on the war path. Though missionaries attempted to put an end to the ritual violence of war, colonial officials gladly encouraged it. In late 1689, an Iroquois woman was burnt at Kanehsatake – to Belmont's great chagrin but with Frontenac's shrugging acceptance, if not relish; in 1696, four men were burnt in Montreal before the assembled French townspeople, after having been summarily baptized.[5] This escalation of the conflict was marked by a return to familiar patterns of warfare, whereby a mixture of diplomacy and force were used to attempt a reunion with relatives. On both sides of the colonial divide, Iroquois now conceptualized peace and resettlement as inseparable: just as the Confederacy Iroquois insisted that the Christian Iroquois return to their ancestral communities in Iroquoia, the Christian Iroquois demanded that the Confederacy Iroquois join their ranks in the Saint Lawrence valley. To be clear, the wholesale relocation of the latter was ultimately neither desirable nor feasible, insofar as the arrival of thousands of newcomers to the region would have placed unbearable strains on the natural resources of the area and created tensions with settler neighbours. Yet the migration of certain individuals and family lineages did hold a key to reconciliation. The Great Peace of Montreal of 1701 can be thought of as a triumph of either French or Five Nations diplomacy, as scholars have tended to interpret it, but it was also in many respects a product of Christian Iroquois intervention.[6]

***

At some point during the summer or fall of 1690, within months of Togouirout's death, the Kahnawakes rebuilt their village on a new site on the south shore of the Saint Lawrence River, a few leagues west of where the old village had stood. It had become apparent that the social costs of the community's encampment within the confines of Montreal, which entailed unprecedented access to liquor and the attendant disturbances, greatly outweighed the arrangement's defensive benefits. Residents of the two mission communities now drawn in closer proximity had a few run-ins: a man called Sonawenton, presumably from Kanehsatake, killed another from Kahnawake named Kentaratyron; a certain Sonnawches from the latter village was also killed by a knife thrust into the armpit. Frontenac was extremely critical of his predecessor's decision.[7] Yet life beyond the town was dangerous too. Through the summer, the Iroquois raided French homesteads at various points between Trois Rivières and Montreal. On 4 September, a force of about 125 of their warriors accompanied by 42 Dutch and English men from Albany struck a quarter league from La Prairie – a little over ten kilometers east of Kahnawake.[8]

The following winter, most of the inhabitants of Kahnawake and Kanehsatake scattered for their hunt as usual, expecting that peace would prevail – Étienne Tegananokoa had been taken by a Cayuga war party specifically, after all, and this did not necessarily signal the hostility of the whole Five Nations against the people of the missions. Towards the very end of the hunting season, though, a band of hunters from the two villages was surprised in the vicinity of Chambly by a party of Mohawk warriors. A few of the hunters were killed in the clash, but the remaining 10 or 12 were taken prisoner. This presented the victorious warriors with an occasion to reciprocate the benevolence of those who had spared the Mohawks at Schenectady in February 1690, and to renew the diplomatic dialogue. Continuing their journey northwestward with their captives, the force of about 150 men encamped about two leagues from Kahnawake and sent 3 deputies onward to the village where they were admitted "without arms and as friends." They were headed by none other than Onnonragewas alias Lawrence, who, as noted in chapter 6, had in recent years been one of the most active promoters of a return-migration from the mission settlements to Iroquoia, and who had led the counterattack after the Schenectady raid. Releasing the captive hunters, he explained that while he had not been delegated by his community, he and the warriors genuinely desired to put an end to the war. They had hastened to Kahnawake to warn the people that a combined Five Nations force of 800 men was fast approaching, with the aim of "carry[ing] them off" and of wreaking as much destruction as possible on the colony. The only way of avoiding the violence of capture, he proposed, was for the village's inhabitants to relocate to Mohawk country.[9]

This approach was precisely in keeping with the pattern of military and diplomatic activity described in previous chapters, whereby demonstrations of goodwill and negotiations alternated with shows of force and violence, all aimed at persuading an opponent to migrate willingly, or if the occasion presented itself, of capturing them and forcing their migration. At midcentury the opponents targeted for absorption had been neighbouring nations (Wendats, Eries, Neutrals, Susquehannocks, etc.). Now they were stubborn relatives and acquaintances who had aligned themselves with an antagonistic French colonial power. Though they welcomed heartily Onnonragewas's attempt at reconciliation, the Kahnawakes rejected his suggestion that they abandon the village. In fact, fearing that they might be forcibly detained, the three visitors felt it necessary to give the impression that they and their relatives were themselves entertaining the possibility of relocating there. The Kahnawakes warned Onnonragewas that he should not go back on this pledge, and asked that in the meanwhile he exhort his people to suspend hostilities and to pressure their Mahican allies to do the same. Onnonragewas responded that he would make the other Iroquois nations and the governor of New York concur in his desire for peace, and that if they did not agree, he would abandon them "and [...] watch their defeat while smoking quietly on his mat."[10]

As Onnonragewas had warned, it was not long before a large contingent of warriors from the western and central Iroquois nations appeared in the vicinity of Montreal and dispersed to raid farmsteads throughout the region. About twenty of these warriors left their encampments to "surrender" and "risk themselves" among the Kahnawakes, leading the Jesuit missionary Bruyas to believe that more would soon follow.[11] The Kanehsatakes, who believed that in keeping with Onnonragewas' recent overtures their community "was not supposed to be subject to insult," were not so fortunate. An enemy party composed mainly of Onondagas struck there on 17 May, capturing thirty to thirty-five women and children who were out preparing the fields, and killing six or seven other persons in the process.[12]

Characteristically, in the weeks that followed, the Onondagas released two of the women, entrusting them with two secret wampum belts addressed to Louis Ateriata at Kahnawake and to a certain

Tamouratoüa at Kanehsatake. These two chiefs were thereby exhorted to return to their country and to bring along as many of their relatives and friends as possible. Failure to comply, they threatened, would bring about their "inevitable destruction." But the Onondagas had misjudged the commitment or impressionability of the pair (and of the clan matrons working behind the scene), for upon receiving the wampum belts they promptly presented them to the governor of Montreal, Louis-Hector de Callière, and reiterated their allegiance to the French.[13] Informed of Onnonragewas' overture and given the opportunity to discuss the matter with the two other deputies, Callière thought it best to leave the entire matter in the hands of the Kahnawakes.[14]

***

The complicated, apparently contradictory nature of the relations between the Christian and League Iroquois was a source of great frustration to the French. While the latter found it easier to wage their war against the Five Nations as a whole, the inhabitants of the missions persisted in approaching the conflict with a more nuanced perspective. Although warriors from all of the League's nations had collaborated in the attack against La Prairie, there was reason to believe as a result of Onnonragewas's overture that the easternmost nations were inclined to peace. When a party of Christian Iroquois and Frenchmen who had set out along the upper Saint Lawrence in response to the raid on Kanehsatake came upon a smaller party whom they recognized as Mohawks (and Oneidas), they heard them out for fear "of breaking off all accommodation between them and that canton [i.e. nation]," and allowed the bulk to return home unharmed on the agreement that a few would accompany the Christian Iroquois to meet with Callière and that they would send a formal embassy to meet with governor Frontenac.[15]

When reports reached the colony that a force of New Yorkers, Mohawks, and Mahicans, nominally led by the trader and Albany mayor Peter Schuyler, and including the ubiquitous Garistatsi and Onnonragewas, was advancing along the Richelieu River, the Christian Iroquois responded hesitatingly. Only "a few" of their warriors, under the leadership of the dogique Paul Honoguenhag from Kahnawake and cheered on by the Sulpician priest Gay of La Montagne, joined the reconnaissance force sent to meet it. During the fighting that followed the enemy's strike at La Prairie on the morning of 11 August, the small number of Christian Iroquois present fought bravely – with Honoguenhag being killed in the process. But it was the Wendats of Lorette, led on this occasion not by one of their own but by a Cayuga captive turned great friend of Frontenac, Ouréhouaré who earned the highest praise. A reinforcement of 120 warriors from Kahnawake who arrived an hour after battle could not be persuaded by the French commander to pursue the harried enemy. When gunshots were heard resounding from La Prairie, these warriors rushed back in that direction. It was soon discovered that these shots had merely been fired in honour of the officers who had died that morning.[16]

Whether these warriors genuinely believed that they were urgently needed at La Prairie (as they and their missionaries would protest), no doubt fearing that an enemy force had positioned itself between them and their village, or whether they had merely found a pretext to avoid fighting against Mohawks (as Frontenac would persist in believing), it is impossible to say.[17] Whatever the case may be, it is clear is that the conflict was continuing its escalation into a new, radicalized phase. A Mohawk and Oneida war party, led by Garistasi and motivated by the desire to avenge the death of Onnonragewas and others who had perished during the attack on La Prairie, surprised between Sorel and Chambly, along the Richelieu River, one of the many Christian Iroquois bands that had by necessity again scattered for the winter hunt, killing 4 and capturing 16. Instead of releasing these captives, as their countrymen had done in June of the previous year, they headed home with them. When a woman who had escaped the attacked reached Kahnawake, a party of 40 or 50 warriors launched an immediate pursuit. They caught up with the enemy along Lake Champlain, annihilating them and recovering their captives. Garistatsi, his son, Kakare, as well as a brother of Onnonragewas – "all the principal Captains" and "the best Indians," from the New Yorkers' perspective – were among the dead. After this defeat, the Mohawks and Oneidas complained to the New Yorkers that they had lost 90 men in two years' time, and that the three Mohawk villages could now only muster 130 men – less than half of what could be mustered a decade earlier.[18]

The French and their Indigenous allies were emboldened by the outcome of this latest encounter. When some of the warriors who had taken part in it journeyed to Quebec to inform Frontenac of the victory and to request that a new party be supplied to venture against the western Iroquois, the governor was only too happy to oblige. In February of 1692, about 120 warriors from Kahnawake, 40 from Kanehsatake, and 20 from Lorette set out along the upper Saint Lawrence River with another 120 Frenchmen. At the island of Toniata they surprised an encampment of 50 to 60 Senecas and Onondagas, killing 24 and taking 16 captives.[19] His enthusiasm boosted by a voyage to France from whence he had just returned, La Plaque followed up that September by mobilizing another war party of 160 Christian Iroquois warriors with the intention of striking against Mohawk country.[20] This party did not go far, however, turning back upon reports that a coordinated enemy offensive was afoot.

In response to recent setbacks, and to the encouragement of Peter Schuyler who pressed them to "lay their principal design against" the French Praying Indians, two contingents representing the League's western and eastern nations mounted a major offensive against Kahnawake. As the Mohawk chief Rode put it to Schuyler, they intended by persuasion or force to "put the Praying Indians out of a capacity of ever doing you or us any more harm."[21] Forewarned and reinforced by French troops, the people of Kahnawake were, however, exceedingly well equipped to repel the enemy's words and arms. In late October or early November of 1692, the western contingent, composed of up to 400 Onondagas, Cayugas, and Senecas, was the first to appear in sight of the village. Discovering that their arrival was expected and observing that the fortified mission village was strong enough to resist an assault, the besiegers remained at the edge of the woods and exchanged sporadic fire over the course of two days (or three or four, according to another account) as smaller parties turned to raiding French farmsteads throughout the region. Upon realizing that its intentions had been uncovered, the eastern contingent of 350 Mohawks and Oneidas, journeyed no further north than Lake Champlain.[22]

***

While the intimate relationship between the Kahnawakes and the Mohawks continued to worry Frontenac, Intendant Champigny reported at this time that "one cannot see more faithfulness and bravery than our Natives are showing on all occasions." The French had "a very great interest in treating them well."[23] The Christian Iroquois had until now demonstrated a willingness to take part in military operations against the distant and unrelated Senecas, to strike at the people of New York and New England, and to assist in defensive operations in the Montreal region, mounting pursuits in response to threats or attacks on outlying settlements, and on a few occasions escorting fur trading convoys past the most dangerous stretch of the Ottawa River. Throughout this period, their isolated hunters and fishermen had periodically fallen victim to enemy war parties.[24] Just as the acquaintances, friends, and relatives of the League had resolved to "lay their principal design against" them, the inhabitants of the missions began to resort to more drastic means to ensure their own security and to resolve the conflict in a way that would strengthen their community. During the showdown against the Onondaga, Cayuga, and Seneca warriors in 1692, an emerging Kahnawake leader named Tatakwiséré, "chief of the Oneidas of this mission," dragged out of the palisade the captive wife of the dreaded Onondaga war chief Black Kettle – at least one source suggests that she also happened to be Tatakwiséré's daughter. Because she had revealed an inclination to attempt to escape, and in a pointed gesture of defiance to the besiegers, he clubbed her to death. Proclaiming that he would show no mercy to defectors, he exhorted the people of Kahnawake to do the same.[25]

Having attempted "by all acts of kindness to persuade" their relatives "to come and join them and to unite with them in prayer," and having experienced the increasingly aggressive and intractable approach of their eastern Iroquois kinsfolk over the previous year, the Kahnawakes reached the conclusion that an attack against their villages was in order. Meeting with Frontenac and Callière, they "demanded permission to organize this expedition," requesting the assistance of regular troops and militiamen, and going so far as to specify which officers should accompany them (Nicolas d'Ailleboust de Manthet, a veteran of the raid on Schenectady, Augustin Le Gardeur de Courtemanche, and Zacharie Robutel de Lanoue, the three of whom had been at Kahnawake during the recent siege). Together the chiefs and governors agreed that the campaign's objective would be the complete destruction of the Mohawk villages, and that all women and children were to be captured "to populate the two Christian villages of their nation." The Christian Iroquois's initiative, firmly grounded in traditional patterns of war, meshed conveniently with Frontenac's own determination to launch a campaign against the Five Nations.[26]

The small army raised as a result of these discussions numbered some 600 men, including between 100 and 200 warriors from Kahnawake and Kanehsatake, led by Tatakwiséré among others, joined by a few Wendats of Lorette, Wabanakis from Néssawakamighé on the Chaudière, as well as Algonquins and Sokokis from the vicinity of Trois Rivières. Reaching the three Mohawk villages in mid-February, at a time when most of their inhabitants had dispersed for the winter hunt, the forces rapidly overcame those who had remained behind: between 220 and 350 Mohawk captives were taken. The Christian Iroquois were satisfied when these captives asked for clemency by volunteering to emigrate to the missions, claiming that they had been for some time intending to do so. While the French officers expressed their desire to press on to Albany, the Christian Iroquois war chiefs flatly refused and compelled the army's return to Montreal.[27]

During the attack and the return journey, the warriors of Kahnawake and Kanehsatake made it clear that "they alone were masters" of the prisoners. Well aware that the escorting of over two hundred captives from Mohawk country to Canada would slow down the force and facilitate an enemy pursuit, these masters released some of their captives with warnings that they would kill all those who remained in their custody should they find themselves pursued, and allowed many to flee. There happened to be among the captives a prominent Oneida man, a brother of Tatakwiséré. This man protested that his people were "very tired of the war" and that they would have proposed peace to the French if they had thought that they would be well received. In light of this, Tatakwiséré urged the French officers to agree to open negotiations. The latter declined, explaining that the governor had instructed them to make war and not peace, but nonetheless encouraged Tatakwiséré to respond on his own behalf. He immediately dispatched a message reinforced with a wampum belt to the Oneidas. "The natural affection that I have for my homeland [*patrie*] is not yet extinguished," his message declared, going on to blame its people for having responded with "treason and perfidy" to the affection that the Christian Iroquois had displayed towards them on numerous occasions, and to invite them to send a formal embassy to discuss the peace.[28]

Other prisoners, burdened with their children and provisions, feeling that they could not go on anymore, begged to be freed and promised that they would come to Kahnawake by themselves in the spring. The Christian Iroquois warriors, needing to hunt because they were running short on food, accepted. In the end only 64 or 70 prisoners out of the initial 220 to 350 reached Montreal, almost all women and children. Colonial commentators who had not taken part in the expedition were quick to cast aspersions on the loyalty of their allies for having failed to bring back more than that – conveniently forgetting that it was the Christian Iroquois who had initiated the campaign in the first place. From the latter's perspective, it had been a resounding success: they had taken many captives, and could expect that many would follow willingly.[29]

***

Sure enough, as in 1666, the destruction of the Mohawk villages initiated a significant northward migration. During that summer of 1693, many Mohawks voluntarily relocated to the mission settlements.[30] The show of force proved an equally powerful motivator for the Mohawks' closest neighbours. The Oneidas followed up on Tatakwiséré's invitation. That June one of their headmen named Taréha led a delegation of seven of his people to Canada, with the intention of obtaining the release of two boys belonging to his family who were captives at Kahnawake, and more ambitiously of meeting with Frontenac to explore the possibility of negotiating a solid peace. Offering to act as a mediator, Taréha allowed some ambiguity to persist about whom, exactly, he was representing. In one account, he was described as speaking on behalf of "the three principal families [clans] of Oneida," but in another it was said that "he came on behalf of his family and a portion of his village." An escaped captive who reached the colony shortly thereafter alternatively revealed to the governor that Taréha "was acting in good faith, but his adherents were not considerable." In any case, Taréha declared to Frontenac that if he was fortunate enough to reconcile his own nation with the French, his design was "to come among them and spend the rest of his days with his brothers of Sault S. Louis." Over the next few years, he carried out several more diplomatic journeys between Iroquoia and Canada.[31]

There existed powerful bonds of biological and spiritual kinship between the Oneidas and the residents of the mission settlements, Kahnawake in particular. As outlined in chapter 5, the founding core of that community had come from the village of Oneida, and although Mohawks now predominated, a regular influx from there had continued through the late 1670s. Tatakwiséré, who emerged as one of the most influential men at Kahnawake in the decade following the death of Togouirout, was of Oneida origin, and it is not impossible that he was a clan relative of Taréha.[32] The continued presence and influence at Oneida of the Jesuit Pierre Millet further contributed to this privileged relationship between the two communities. In charge of the mission at Oneida between 1672 and 1684, Millet had returned there as a war captive in 1689 only to be invited to take on the name of Otaseté and made into a hereditary chief of the Wolf Clan. Until his release in 1694, he continued to wield considerable moral authority at Oneida. His adoptive relatives of the Wolf Clan played a central role in the negotiation of a Franco-Iroquois settlement, and numbered among those most willing to contemplate the possibility of relocating to Canada. Behind the scenes, we can sense the influence of Suzanne Gouentagrandi, the clan mother who had adopted Millet and subsequently accepted baptism from him. She had shown herself to be one of the best friends of the French in all of Iroquoia. A sister of Taréḥa, it is all but certain that the latter's diplomatic activity during these years was an expression of policy that she, as clan mother, had a large role in shaping. Her name itself, meaning "they put things down before her" or perhaps more freely "they prostrate themselves before her," seems indicative of the high regard in which she was held.[33]

As Frontenac sent Taréha to Onondaga to mobilize a peace delegation that would be more representative of all Five Nations, the Christian Iroquois pressed the advantage. Having asserted themselves as a military power to be reckoned with by humbling the Mohawks, they returned to diplomacy as a means of establishing peace on their own terms. In the fall, Tatakwiséré dispatched a messenger to warn the Five Nations "to come speedily before the French destroyed them." The Onondagas took this threat sufficiently seriously to call back their dispersed hunting bands and to promise that a League delegation would meet with Onontio in the spring. But in February of 1694 two Mohawk elders arrived at Kahnawake to explain that no delegation would be coming, and that "if the Karigouistes [i.e. Garihwioston or Christian Iroquois] or the French have something to propose to the Five Nations" they would be welcome at an upcoming conference in Albany. The Christian Iroquois made their displeasure manifest. Before the two emissaries and Callière, in whose presence the Kahnawake headmen insisted on speaking, the Kahnawakes rejected these overtures and placed their full diplomatic weight behind the French. "We will have no correspondence with the Five Nations, but by order of the Governor of Canada our Father," went their ultimatum, and unless the League's deputies came before the Feast of Saint John on 24 June, "the way will be shut up for ever after, and our Father's ears will be stopped. We however assure you, that if the deputies come in that time the path shall be safe both coming and going."[34]

That a delegation headed by Teganissorens, one of the more prominent Onondaga chiefs and diplomats, did reach Kahnawake and then Quebec in early May must be interpreted not only as an indication of the Five Nations' willingness to entertain peace with the French in spite of English interference, but also of the Kahnawakes' considerable diplomatic weight. Further evidence of this was given during the conference held at Quebec, which was attended by all the leading men of Kahnawake and of Kanehsatake. At one point, Teganissorens addressed the Kahnawakes, "whom in former times I called Iroquois" (no doubt here a translation of *Haudenosaunee*, i.e. People of the Longhouse) but whom he now recognized as the children of Onontio and Christians, to act as mediators. Explaining that "you know us and know our ways of doing things," he prayed that they would foster thoughts of peace among both the French and the Iroquois, and that they would stifle all occasions for quarrelling. He said as much to the Kanehsatakes before addressing the people of the two mission settlements: "We have killed one another. Forget what has passed, as we intend to do on our side."[35]

The conference yielded constructive results, with Frontenac promising a temporary cessation of raids and guaranteeing the safety of any emissaries who would travel to the colony. In the weeks that followed, a second council was held at Montreal during which the headmen of Kahnawake and Kanehsatake answered the speeches addressed to them at Quebec. Reiterating their attachment to the French, they reproached Teganissorens for the fact that Mohawk war parties were still reported to be on the move. When the Onondaga diplomat attempted to transmit a secret wampum belt to two of the main chiefs of Kahnawake, as further encouragement to work towards peace and to keep the people of Iroquoia informed of the governor's dispositions, they refused to accept and promptly informed Callière of it – just as their predecessors had done three years earlier. By way of response to Teganissorens, they merely reiterated that the Five Nations should trust and conform to what their representatives had pledged at Quebec.[36]

Though at times they acted as colonial agents, relaying messages between the French and the Five Nations, and generally reinforcing the authority of Onontio, it is clear that the Christian Iroquois strove to mediate a peace on their own terms. When, in September 1694,

Frontenac declared to Cayuga and Seneca delegates that he had placed "the hatchet in their [his allies'] hands again" until representatives of all Five Nations sued for peace, many of the Christian Iroquois in attendance expressed reluctance. While they had made unqualified declarations of compliance with the governor's will in May, when the issue at hand was peace, they now showed themselves unwilling to take up arms at his whim. Instead, they reportedly challenged Frontenac, drawing his attention to the fact that the imperial conflict between France and England was the persistent stumbling block to peace: "If we take up the hatchet again, let us go and kill Cayenquiragoe [Governor Fletcher, and by extension the New Yorkers], for the sooner the better then there is an end."[37]

A modest party of warriors from Kahnawake ventured south towards Albany in March of 1695, but in the absence of substantial French support there was to be no major expedition against Cayenquiragoe and his people. The Christian Iroquois's diplomatic activity in the meantime continued unabated. Attending a council at Onondaga in February of 1695, a Mohawk from Kahnawake called Thioratarion and an Oneida from Kanehsatake named Ononsista ritually condoled the losses of the League and insisted that they comply with Frontenac's desire to receive their ambassadors. The Onondaga speaker Aqueendera reciprocated the condolence rituals, but he and his people were unwilling to entertain the proposals of Onontio. Instead he asked Thioratarion and Ononsista, and the people of their respective villages, to use their influence to persuade the governor to begin by releasing his prisoners. Aqueendera entrusted a wampum belt to Thioratarion, addressed to himself and Tatakwiséré, which was to symbolically remain hidden underground (i.e. secret) for three years. With it, the League Iroquois exhorted the two men to "think much of the union that ought to exist between us, and not forget that here [in Iroquoia] is your ancient country; that you ought to advise us of the designs of Onontio without letting him know it. Fear not visiting us: you will be always welcome."[38]

Throughout this period, the leading men and women in the Canadian Iroquois villages continued to privilege their relationship with the French, and their warriors continued to take part in Franco-Indigenous operations.[39] In judging Tatakwiséré to be "our friend and the most influential at the Sault" and accordingly expecting him to be secretive, Aqueendera and the League chiefs were only half right, for he resolved, in conjunction with the other leading men at Kahnawake, to reveal the nature of the secret communication to Callière and to expose Thioratarion, who favoured continued diplomatic secrecy.[40] Once again, League Iroquois efforts to short-circuit the relationship of the French and the Christian Iroquois were thwarted.

***

Wampum belts and mutual declarations of goodwill were circulating with unprecedented frequency between Iroquoia and the mission settlements of the Saint Lawrence valley, but reconciliation remained elusive. In response to the news of negotiations towards a separate peace settlement between the nations of the Great Lakes and the Five Nations, and fearing the English penetration in the interior that would unavoidably result from such an arrangement, colonial authorities proposed a new campaign for 1696. This time the Onondagas would be the target.[41] Though rather little is known as to how allied warriors were mobilized on this occasion, there is no evidence that the Christian Iroquois played the same leading role as during the campaign three years prior – but there is no evidence either of any reluctance to take part. Some 500 Kahnawake, Kanehsatake, Wendat, Wabanaki, Sokoki, Algonquin, Nipissing, and Odawa warriors numbered among the approximately 2,150 men who left the staging point of Lachine under the nominal command of the elderly Frontenac on 4 July. Undisturbed in its progress, the army found the main Onondaga village abandoned and already smoldering a month later.[42]

As Frontenac's army proceeded to loot and spoil the stores and crops of the villages, the governor sent a strong detachment under the command of Philippe de Rigaud de Vaudreuil towards the Oneida villages; at the same time, the worried Oneidas dispatched a delegation of their own. Vaudreuil's force reached the fields of the main Oneida village where they were met by Suzanne Gouentagrandi, the Wolf Clan mother, whom the French recognized as "the famous Christian woman of Onneiout who had saved Father Millet's life." Meeting with Vaudreuil, she offered to come with eighty of her people to join the Christian Iroquois near Montreal. Although accepting her terms, the French commander nevertheless saw fit to cruelly destroy the village and fields, explaining that "it was useless to think of preserving their grain [...] as they should want for nothing when settled among us," and likewise "that their fort and cabins would not be spared, either, as some were quite ready for their reception."[43]

The Kahnawakes had good reason to desire and expect that this latest demonstration of Franco-Indigenous military superiority would precipitate their reconciliation with the Oneidas on terms that strengthened their mission community both politically and demographically. Eager to ensure that the latter followed up on their pledge to join the fold in the Saint Lawrence valley, the Kahnawakes advised Frontenac to maintain a strong presence in Iroquoia through the winter of 1696–97 and made their displeasure manifest when he instead ordered the army to return to Montreal. A few months after the campaign, Tatakwiséré travelled to Oneida to ensure that its inhabitants complied with their promises of resettlement. Returning to Montreal in January of 1697, he was glad to announce that two bands totalling sixty persons were now on the way.[44]

The first of these bands, numbering from thirty to forty individuals, reached Montreal on 5 February. Its leader, a certain Otacheté who like Taréha belonged to Millet's adoptive Wolf Clan, explained to Callière that they had come to keep the promise made to "their Father" to join the ranks of his children and settle on his land. Asserting his followers' desire to maintain a distinctive identity and a good measure of autonomy, he requested that they be provided with land and assistance in the preparation of a site for a new village, "so that the name of Oneida may be preserved," and asked that Millet be assigned as their missionary. The remainder of the Oneidas expected to follow, he claimed, and had been prevented from doing so only by the Mohawks and the Onondagas who had retained them "each by an arm."[45]

By mid-1697, it was becoming abundantly clear that in spite of diplomatic maneuvering and shows of force of recent years only a minority of Oneidas and Mohawks were in reality ready to join their relatives and acquaintances near Montreal. Contrary to Otacheté's hopes and efforts, at Oneida it was resolved by the "general vote of old and young men and women" that none of their village "should again go to live at Canada."[46] A momentarily entertained hope of large-scale Mohawk resettlement was similarly dashed. In June, the Kahnawakes received an underground wampum belt by which the headmen of the Mohawk villages informed "their Brothers of the Sault that they were weary of fighting and had resolved to come and reside with them." But when a Kahnawake delegate reached the Mohawk villages to pursue the discussion, he was informed that there had been a miscommunication: the Mohawks had not implied a "willingness to come and settle among us," but merely desired to discuss peace; once peace was achieved, then "they would see what they should do."[47] When Oneida and Onondaga delegates appeared before Frontenac in the company of Otacheté in November of 1697, they discussed peace and went so far as to show an interest in adopting the Christian faith, but significantly made no allusion to the question of migration.[48]

***

No wholesale relocation from Mohawk or Oneida country occurred in these years, but through the incorporation of migrants and war captives the mission settlements compensated the losses from emigration and war that they had sustained during the previous decade, and grew beyond them. Between 1692 and 1698, the two years during which a census of the colony was taken, the population of Kahnawake increased by a full third, from 509 individuals to 790.[49] After its brief stay within the walls of Montreal, the community had established its village on a new site situated a short distance west of the previous one. By the nineteenth century, tradition held that it had been situated along a tumultuous stretch of river and was accordingly known as "Kahnawakon," meaning "in the rapids" (as opposed to Kahnawake, which meant "*at the foot of* the rapids"). However, this view is challenged by Governor Callière and Intendant Champigny's report to the minister of the Navy that the village was inland, "very far" from the river itself. In the eyes of these colonial officials, this location was proving inconvenient and, most worryingly, too exposed to enemy attacks. In 1694, the palisade that had been built there three years earlier was rebuilt and expanded upon at the Crown's expense, but by the following spring it was still in a ramshackle state. Callière, called upon to remedy the situation, travelled in person to inspect the fortifications and judged that, in spite of the recent work, they were "no longer worth anything." Rather than rebuild on the same site, a new "more convenient and advantageous" one was selected, a short distance west and this time directly on the Saint Lawrence River, at the juncture of a small creek and on a slight elevation. The building of a fort, church, and cabins took up the remainder of the year, and the mission's residents moved there in 1696.[50]

The separate village requested by Otachété for the newcomers from Oneida was never established. They joined the people of Kahnawake, where Father Millet was himself posted in 1698, no doubt in an effort to accommodate them. While the French records dwell on the interventions of men like Otacheté and Taréha, they also allow us to gain a glimpse of the ongoing influence of Suzanne Gouentagrandi, the Wolf Clan mother. She had shown herself the most receptive to the French alliance at Oneida, and it is likely that the male figures who loom large in the sources were merely carrying out policies that she was instrumental in shaping. She was among those who moved to Kahnawake with her extended family, following up on the pledge that she had made during the invasion of 1696. She lived out the rest of her life there, passing away there circa 1740 "in a happy old age," wrote Father Charlevoix who saw her in her final years, "after long edifying that town by the constant practice of all Christian virtues." The creek flowing into the Saint Lawrence next to the new village became known as "La Susanne" or the Suzanne River – a testament to her importance within her new community.[51]

Kanehsatake too was evolving as a result of the interplay of conflict, subsistence, and missionary politics. That mission did not attract nearly as many newcomers as did Kahnawake during these years, likely owing to its smaller core population, its lesser military and diplomatic importance, and the heterogeneity of its origins. By the decade's end, the population of the village on the slope of Mount Royal had diminished, from 212 in 1692 to 160 at the time of the 1698 census. However, this was due to a partial relocation of the community to a second site, that of Sault au Récollet, on the Rivière des Prairies, which ran along the north of the Island of Montreal – by 1698, that second site was home to 113 persons.[52] This outcome was the result of a much different process than the one which, some fifteen years before, had resulted in the split of Kentake into two distinct communities, Kanehsatake and Kahnawake. As Bacqueville de La Potherie phrased it, it was a single "mission […] divided in two," rather than two fully distinct communities.[53]

The new mission settlement at Sault au Récollet had been a long time in the planning. Upon assuming the direction of the mission at Kanehsatake, Sulpician priest François Vachon de Belmont had been prompt to arrive at the conclusion that relocation away from La Montagne was necessary. Its proximity to Kahnawake – ten kilometers to the south in a straight line – preoccupied him. The people of that mission, he complained, undermined the cohesion of his own by periodically trying to induce its residents to join them. More specifically, he noted that young men came to seduce women away – an interesting detail, in light of what we know about Iroquoian matrilineality and matrilocality, suggesting that the lineages at Kanehsatake may have been less solid than those that existed at Kahnawake. Most problematic, however, was the proximity of the French. While the presence of Montreal, less than two kilometers away, was one of the features that, in Belmont's phrase, "much charm[ed] and attract[ed] the Natives," along with the richness of the soil, it also made intoxicating beverages readily available.[54]

Since 1668, by decree of the Sovereign Council of New France, it had been legal to sell and trade liquor to Indigenous persons within certain restrictions: it was prohibited to incite their drunkenness, for example, or to peddle liquor to them in the woods or in their villages. But such regulations, as well as the clergy's insistence that engaging in this commerce remained a mortal sin, were commonly flaunted by tavern keepers, traders, and ordinary habitants eager to turn a profit. Owing to the mission's proximity to the town of Montreal and to Lachine, the latter of which served as the launching point for all traders' voyages into the interior, abusive drinking indeed appears to have become somewhat more prevalent at Kanehsatake than in other mission settlements, with the mission's "drunkards" causing regular disturbances and grief to Vachon de Belmont and his fellow missionaries. The Jesuit Bruyas, visiting that mission, declared that "no one could be saved there." Belmont was nevertheless shrewd in grasping the opportunity that, in spite of its great dangers, the neighbourhood of the French offered. As settlement spread through the Island of Montreal, the demand for good agricultural land was rapidly rising, and as seigneurs of the island, the Sulpicians stood to make a profit. Reallocation to colonists of the acreage cleared for the Indigenous community had the potential of making a valuable contribution to the Montreal seminary's coffers, and to help ensure the mission's long-term financial autonomy from its Parisian parent and from the Crown. Vachon de Belmont was thus intentionally careful not to recognize by contract the neophytes' ownership of their fields, lest this title complicate the eventual business of relocation.[55]

Vachon de Belmont's superiors only slowly came around to his views. Louis Tronson, superior of the Sulpician Seminary in Paris, reasoned that the mission had obtained the Crown's favour and financial support in large part because it served as a defensive bulwark for Montreal. To transfer it to a more remote location, he feared, would diminish its strategic significance and undermine future lobbying efforts. Then, there would be the expense of relocation and the risk of alienating the mission's residents.[56] The context of war made relocation impractical. Belmont himself appears to have realized all of this, for even as he continued to periodically advocate the idea of transferring the people of Kanehsatake away from the slopes of Mount Royal, he threw himself into the improvement of its structures and landscape. Combining his great personal wealth with the Crown's more modest grants, he built an impressive missionary compound – the "Fort de la Montagne" – consisting of a stone residence enclosed within a rectangular masonry wall, of one hundred by two hundred feet, cornered with round towers topped with elegant conical roofs. Unsatisfied with the wooden chapel that existed in the adjoining village, he oversaw the construction of a new stone chapel within this compound, a palisade of sawed timber around the village, and over the years had houses in the French style to add to its residents' Iroquoian longhouses: by 1694, the village contained 43 of the latter and 13 of the former. To the north of the fort and village he laid out large orchards, vineyards, and gardens, and even a regularly landscaped yard to its east – all with the view, it seems, of making Kanehsatake into a model mission and of eventually repurposing it as comfortable country estate for the Sulpicians.[57]

As the seminary grew more receptive to the possibility of relocating the mission, Vachon de Belmont's sights turned to the Rivière des Prairies, running along the north of the Island of Montreal, and honed in on the previously mentioned site of Sault au Récollet, which took its name from the adjacent rapids, themselves named after the drowning of a Recollet priest there sixty years earlier. The idea of a mission settlement along the Rivière des Prairies was not new. The Jesuits, who had been seigneurs of Île Jésus just across from it, had considered the area before deciding to establish themselves at Kentake. Father Claude Dablon, who had visited the area with the Wendat Louis Thaondechoren in July 1667, had reported on it "with great satisfaction." Though the Jesuits were forced to relinquish their title to Île Jésus five years later, having failed to exploit it, in 1674 another one of their own, Antoine Dalmas, was asked to investigate the potential of the area for "some project" involving "a settlement of Natives" – a site for the relocation of Kentake, it is likely. Nothing came of it, though from time to time during the late 1680s a Sulpician priest, Michel Barthélémy, ministered to the Algonquin family bands who hunted through the area.[58] In July of 1689, Vachon de Belmont put his plan for the Sault au Récollet in motion by leasing a plot of 180 arpents there in his personal name. Over the next few years, he hired

French workers to clear the site and build several structures, including in 1691 a stone fort of dimensions comparable to the one at La Montagne.[59] However, the moment was not yet convenient for a migration, for, in light of the threat posed by the escalation of the conflict with the Iroquois, it was difficult to make a case for depriving Montreal of one of its outlying defences. Then, on 11 September 1694, a great fire spread through Kanehsatake, destroying all of its forty-three cabins, its thirteen timber houses, its chapel, and its palisade – leaving intact Belmont's fort and the buildings within it, as they were made of stone. The culprit had not been enemy raiders, but rather a man from the community who, inebriated, had shot at the house of another man with whom he had been quarelling. The shot had sparked a fire which, on account of it being a windy day, engulfed the village in the span of three hours. The role that alcohol had played in this disaster provided Vachon de Belmont with his strongest argument yet in support of the relocation, furthering its idea in both the minds of the community and in those of his superiors.[60]

The Sulpicians finally agreed amongst themselves that the wisest way forward for the immediate future was to divide the community between the old and new sites, and drawing from the imagery of the gospel, to "separate the goats from the sheep." In light of the fact that a solid core of the mission's residents were reluctant to abandon it, such a division, rather than a full-scale relocation, was safest. A segment of Kanehsatake's population appears to have agreed with this course of action, as suggested by Bacqueville de La Potherie's claim that "the chiefs having noticed that debauchery [*libertinage*] had begun to corrupt the manners of the young warriors," and that it was these chiefs who asked Belmont "to make a second one at the Sault-au-Récollet."[61] A division of the mission had several other advantages. Maintaining a Sulpician missionary foothold at La Montagne averted the potential danger of being forced by the Crown to turn the site over to their Jesuit competitors. Dividing the mission was also advantageous for the Sulpicians in terms of personnel management: it meant that Robert Gay, who had grown unhappy as an assistant to Vachon de Belmont at La Montagne, could be entrusted with his own site and thus dissuaded from returning to France as he had been threatening to do. In the spring of 1696, Tronson at last gave his approval to the project. That September, upon their warriors' return from the summer campaign against the Onondagas, a first group of people relocated to the new site, accompanied by Gay.[62]

The Rivière des Prairies was called Skawenati by the Iroquois, meaning "on the other side of the Island," and the name came to designate the mission at Sault au Récollet. Belmont initially referred to it as "fort Nazareth," but it was soon renamed "Nouvelle-Lorette," or "Notre-Dame-de-Lorette," or "Petite [small] Lorette" to distinguish it from the other mission of that name. This evocation of the Holy Family and of the devotion to Our Lady of Loreto in particular, rather than a mere personal penchant on the part of the missionary, may very well have been designed to make the site more attractive to the Wendats and former Wendats of the community who, having moved from that other Lorette to Kanehsatake two decades earlier, had maintained old devotions – even though by this time they had by and large disappeared from the record as a distinct ethnic component of the mission's population.[63] La Potherie observed that Sault au Récollet was, of the two sites, "where the most debauched [*libertins*] reside." This implies that the Sulpicians, and perhaps the community's leadership itself, pushed towards that site certain members of the community – particularly young men – deemed too unruly and given to drink. The fact that responsibility for the second site was entrusted specifically to Gay is also suggestive of the way age dynamics were at play: he had earned a reputation for being an uncommonly daring chaplain on the warpath, and at the time of the relocation was, at the age of thirty-three, himself still a young man.[64] All of this said, there was not a sharp division between the residents of the two missions: for example, a certain Theonogarra, of Onondaga origin, could thus be described in court records as a "Native residing at La Montagne *and* at Sault des Recollets."[65]

The community leaders' lack of enthusiasm for a complete relocation to Skawenati is evidenced by the fact that the process would stretch out for almost a decade, with a second wave of villagers relocating in 1699, and the last of them only in 1704–5. Almost a century later, a chief recalled to a British official: "The Priest settled amongst us, and other clergy of this island [...] exhorted us strenuously to remove farther off from the Town where we would be more quiet and happy, and pointed out to us Sault au Recollet."[66] Indeed, Belmont, Gay, and a third Sulpician priest, Joseph Mariet, held several great feasts and distributed presents to influential members of the community in an effort to convince them to move to the new site. Tronson and the Sulpician superior in the colony, François Dollier de Casson, both advised caution to the missionairies, lest the people feel vexed.

"The best of all means to fix them at Lorette [Sault au Récollet] and to attract them there," advised the former, was not to constrain or chase them, but "to ensure that they can find more conveniences there than elsewhere." The sisters of the Congregation de Notre Dame relocated their school from the first site to the second, and contributed funds to the building of the chapel there. Though his superiors did their best to discourage Belmont from investing too much at La Montagne, lest those who had left would feel compelled to return, the missionary continued to pour his heart and money there. By the time Bacqueville de La Potherie visited La Montagne at the decade's end, he described its chapel has having lavish "walls [...] covered in panelling on which there are some ornaments, such as urns, niches, pilasters and pedestals, finished to look like red marble veined with white."[67]

In 1696, perhaps upon learning that the people of Kahnawake and Kanehsatake had established new villages, the Wendat leaders of Lorette approached Governor Frontenac and Intendant Champigny with the support of their missionaries to ask for a site of their own. Few if any of migrants from Iroquoia had joined the community during the previous two decades – the community remained small, numbering 152 persons in 1695 – but the fact that it had occupied the same site meant that fields had become less productive and more tightly hemmed-in by settlers. They asked for permission to settle in an area that they had identified themselves, between the seigneuries of Neuville and Gaudarville, on a stretch of land that had not yet been granted as a seigneury. Frontenac was not in a position to refuse, having been in the past chastized by the Crown for unreasonably opposing missionary endeavours – and indeed, he and Champigny agreed to grant land to the Jesuits at the Sault de la Chaudière for the use of the Wabanakis in March 1697, extending the grant made eight years earlier. But as far as the Wendat project was concerned Frontenac found a way to sideline the missionaries by offering the title to the Indigenous community itself. The terms that he offered were not particularly favourable, stipulating among other things that the latter would have to begin paying rents like any colonists after twelve years of occupation. Frontenac appears to have seen this as an opportunity to impose the model of settlement which he had always held dear, by which Indigenous peoples would be forced to integrate more thoroughly into colonial society. In light of these onerous terms, the Wendats never availed themselves of the grant. Instead, the Jesuits made arrangements for the community to relocate within the same seigneury of

Saint Gabriel to a site further north along the Saint Charles River, purchasing back for that purpose a lot that they had previously granted to a French habitant. This new site, to which the Wendat community moved in 1697, became known as Jeune Lorette – the abandoned one henceforth acquiring the name of Ancienne (Old) Lorette.[68]

***

The migrations from Iroquoia to the mission settlements that occurred as a result of recent diplomatic and military offensives provided the key to Christian and League Iroquois reconciliation. Waves of newcomers to these settlements brought communities on either side of the divide closer to each other than they had been in recent years, with the newest Christian Iroquois softening the attitudes of long-time, more zealous community members. The conclusion of the Peace of Ryswick between the France and England in September of 1697 also did much to ease relations.[69] Though Franco-Iroquois peace negotiations would remain inconclusive for a few years still, owing to Frontenac's insistence that his Great Lakes allies be included in any treaty and to his unwillingness to accept anything less than full submission from the Five Nations, the state of intercolonial peace gave a new vitality to the dialogue between the French, the Christian Iroquois, and those of the League – and particularly the Mohawks, whose ties to the New Yorkers had been the strongest. Until this point, those who had travelled to the missions from Iroquoia or vice versa had generally done so alone or in small official delegations. Now they could travel in larger groups. Early in the summer of 1698, several Kahnawakes, motivated by "curiosity, or a desire to see their relatives" reached the Mohawk villages.[70] Conversely, the French observed that during the fall "some Mohawk families came on a visit to their relatives at the Saut, and possibly some will settle there. They are left at perfect liberty, and walk daily in the streets of Montreal with as much confidence as if Peace were perfectly ratified. We do not wish to alarm them, and possibly their example will serve to bring the others to their duty."[71]

Benefitting from a greater freedom of movement than at any time during the previous decade, the Christian Iroquois continued to act as diplomatic emissaries between Montreal and Onondaga. Otacheté, though discredited among both the French and his people for having entertained fanciful ambitions of full-scale migration, continued to relay messages to Oneida and Onondaga. A young man from Kahnawake named Tegayesté, who had accompanied him on one occasion to Onondaga, was himself entrusted with a wampum belt at the time of his return in the fall of 1698, with which the Onondagas asked the Canadian Iroquois to intercede with the governor to obtain peace. Similar overtures had been made in the past, but this one appears to have represented something of a turning point. During the ratification of the Great Peace in the summer of 1701, the Kahnawakes' orator would remind the League delegates that "you sent us a belt *three years ago* to invite us to procure you peace," as he presented them with another "to tell you that we have worked at it."[72]

And work at it they did. When an intransigent Frontenac refused to receive the message and belt brought by the young Tegayesté, he exposed himself to the reproaches of the Christian Iroquois. According to the account of the meeting that reached the ears of the authorities in Albany, they expressed their amazement to Onontio that he was declining "those fair offers of peace, it is as if bereaved of your senses or drunk," and compared him unfavourably with the New Yorkers and Mohawks who, they claimed, were now all doing their part to promote "the public good, peace and tranquility of us all."[73] An Onondaga resident of Kanehsatake named Tsihenne, known among the French as Massias, intervened at this juncture and convinced Frontenac to send Tegayesté back in his (Tsihenne's) name to exchange conciliatory courtesies and to request that the Onondagas assemble all the Five Nations' and deliver them to Montreal in forty or fifty days. If the Five Nations complied, promised Tsihenne, a "firm peace" would result. But "if you hear not my word," his message to them went, "I will be the first to wage war against you."[74]

The significance of migration patterns and kinship bonds as both the motivation and means for reconciliation is manifest. Tsihenne and his wife, a Frenchwoman named Anne Mouflet who had been captured during the attack on Lachine in 1689, had relocated to Kanehsatake with an infant son only circa 1697 – indeed, Tsihenne appears to have inherited his nickname Massias or "Mathias" from the name of her first husband, Mathias Chatouteau, who had not survived captivity. Tsihenne's links to the people and leaders of Onondaga remained strong in spite of his withdrawal to the Saint Lawrence valley. Though he was recognized to be "entirely attached to the French nation," he often spoke on behalf of Five Nation deputies during their meetings with the French. The fact that a grown son of his from a previous marriage remained among the Onondagas and was recognized there as "one of the principal chiefs" expedited affairs even further. In January of 1699, this Ohonsiowanne or Great Earth ("La Grande Terre") reached the colony professing an inclination to visit his father.[75]

By this time the inhabitants of the mission settlements were exceedingly frustrated by the fact that the League Iroquois's leaders seemed uncommitted to peace and reconciliation. Ohonsiowanne was challenged on several occasions by the people of Kahnawake and Kanehsatake to account for the fact that the Five Nations had not sent a formal delegation to discuss peace with the French. They entrusted him with belts of wampum to warn the four western nations that this was the last time they would be asked to come and negotiate with Onontio. They would warn them no more, they said, scolding them for being "worse than beasts."[76] During subsequent councils held in Montreal in July and September of 1700, as the peace negotiations dragged on owing in part to English interference, the Christian Iroquois again "made great reproaches, and spoke with much haughtiness to the deputies" of the Oneidas and Onondagas.[77]

Notwithstanding such forceful language, the bottom line was conciliatory. The Kahnawakes and Kanehsatakes assured their interlocutors that if the Five Nations came to discuss peace, the French would listen to them and "consider it done."[78] The confidence of the Christian Iroquois in this respect may have derived from the recent death of Frontenac, in November of 1698, and the belief that the new governor would not be as obdurate as the previous one. Sure enough, in the spring of 1699, the inhabitants of the missions warmly welcomed the news that Callière had been named to the post. Over the previous decade and a half, as governor of Montreal, he had collaborated closely with the inhabitants of the mission settlements and developed with them a relation of mutual trust and understanding. A Kanehsatake orator called Paul Tsiheoui by Bacqueville de La Potherie, but who may in fact have been the aforementioned Tsiehenne (whose baptismal name seems to have been René), declared that the king had been wise to choose Callière. "[W]e have no doubt that we will be forever happy under your conduct," he told him publicly.[79] Hyperbole aside, there is good reason to believe that what might in other circumstances have been an empty courtesy was, in fact, an expression of real relief among the Christian Iroquois. Nowhere in the record can we find them addressing the late Governor Frontenac in such a laudatory fashion.

***

In March of 1699, two Christian Iroquois brought four prisoners to Onondaga to keep the flames of peace alive at a time when officials in Albany were doing their utmost to scuttle Franco-Iroquois accommodation.[80] If the presence in the mission settlements of men and women who, like Tsihenne, had willingly migrated, could hardly be debated, the existence there of persons kept against their will continued to trouble the Five Nations. This concern was far from new. At Quebec in the spring of 1694, Teganissorens had asked Frontenac to allow those who showed an inclination to return home to do so freely, but had made no claims on the other "prisoners" who might prefer to stay in the colony. Recognizing that the Christian Iroquois had parallel preoccupations, as a token of goodwill, Teganissorens released an Iroquois woman from Kanehsatake, and pledged that all of the prisoners of the Five Nations who wished to return home would eventually be released.[81] At Onondaga during the following winter, Thioratarion and Ononsista had in turn been asked to convince the people of their villages to deliver to Onontio all of the Iroquois and English held captive among them so that they might then be brought to Onondaga.[82] In 1698, it had been Tegayesté's turn to be entrusted by the Onondagas with a wampum belt for the people of Kahnawake, asking them to intercede with the governor of Canada for the release of the prisoners.[83]

The Kahnawakes and Kanehsatakes responded to these entreaties by periodically releasing some of their prisoners. However, they continued to retain a significant number of men and women against their will. In September 1700, a Seneca orator again insisted on behalf of the Five Nations that Callière intervene to free all prisoners not only held by the nations of the Great Lakes but also those of the missions.[84] At Onondaga in June of the following year, during an embassy headed by the officer Paul Le Moyne de Maricourt, one of Charles Le Moyne's sons, and by Father Bruyas, for the purpose of obtaining the release of the French captives of the Five Nations, Teganissorens yet again asked for the liberation of Iroquois captives in Canada. "I do not speak of the prisoners that are among the Dowaganhaes [Odawas], but those that are under your roof in Caghnuage [Kahnawake]," he declared, pointing to Bruyas, "and if they do not come it will be your fault. You will stir them up, but we expect that all those that are unwilling [i.e. to leave the mission], you will bind them and throw in our canoes."[85] This frustrated appeal for the return not only of those held captive against their will, but now also of those who had found a happy home in the mission settlements, was a far cry from the position voiced in 1694.

***

As noted previously, the Great Peace of Montreal has been described by some scholars as a triumph of French diplomacy and by others as a triumph of Iroquois diplomacy.[86] Without taking away from the value of those interpretations, the evidence suggests that it should also be recognized as a triumph for the Christian Iroquois. The Kahnawakes, in particular, had emerged as a military and diplomatic force to be reckoned with – the most powerful of Onontio's children east of the Great Lakes, and arguably of all his children on the continent. Warfare had confronted them with a challenge, but also provided them with an opportunity to assert in a powerful way their political and cultural independence from the Five Nations. They had demonstrated their ability to achieve results both as warriors and as diplomats. Much more than mere messengers relaying the communications of the French and the Five Nations, they had played a key role in bringing both parties to the negotiation table.

It is of much significance that when the delegates of the Five Nations and Great Lakes finally travelled to Montreal to take part in a great peace ratification conference in the summer of 1701, they first stopped and spent a day at Kahnawake. Bacqueville de La Potherie, who witnessed the proceedings, described in detail the arrival of the Onondaga, Cayuga, and Oneida ambassadors on 21 July, and of the peoples of the Great Lakes and the Senecas on the following day. The approaching canoes were greeted with joyous musket and canon salutes, and the village's streets were cleared of weeds and swept clean for this special occasion. The event had airs of a great family reunion. As the Kahnawake orator Ontonnionk (The Eagle) explained, his people were always eager to greet "a father, a brother, an uncle or a cousin" and were distressed when ambassadors of the Five Nations neglected to stop at Kahnawake, as they had unfortunately done during the peace negotiations of the previous year.[87]

The three-day halt at Kahnawake played a crucial diplomatic function. For the Iroquois hosts and guests, it corresponded to what is known as the "wood's edge" protocol, a key stage of the condolence ceremony when guests are ritually welcomed and the process of reconciliation begun. After disembarking, the Onondaga, Cayuga, and Oneida ambassadors headed straight for Tatakwiséré's longhouse. It was there that Ontonnionk greeted the ambassadors. Thanking them at length for having made the difficult journey, he set up the relationship between Kahnawake as "a small fire of dried brambles to get one's breath back," and Montreal "where the mat has been properly laid." He proceeded to go through the condolence ritual to ease their grief and clear their minds in preparation for the conference to come. The "true fire being at Montreal," added Ontonnionk, "they should not be surprised if they did not enter into any of the details of affairs." Still, even as he explained that Kahnawake was not the site of the council, he stressed that the Five Nations should henceforth always pass through here.[88]

A parallel ritual of reconciliation took place the next day after the arrival of the ambassadors of the Great Lakes and their entourage, who amounted to seven or eight hundred persons. Received with great excitement, their deputies and leading men entered the cabin of Haronhiateka (Burning Sky or Burning Cloud). "Chief of the Calumet," in other words keeper of a ceremonial pipe of the type used among the Algonquians of the Great Lakes and Mississippi valley to seal alliances and to declare peace or war, Haronhiateka led the visitors through the ritual dance associated with the pipe, each man rhythmically miming and singing his exploits before making conciliatory statements. Feasting and dancing ensued into the night.[89] Though universal in the western Great Lakes and Mississippi valley, calumet ritualism was only rarely practiced among the Iroquois: its deployment at Kahnawake is evidence of the community's complex links to the French-allied nations of the interior, and of their great adaptability as diplomats. The importance of Haronhiateka during these proceedings is also meaningful for another reason: he too was a relative newcomer to the community, having settled there only circa 1699.[90]

The role of the Christian Iroquois during the peace conference at the "true fire" of Montreal between 23 July and 7 August was muted in comparison. This should not come as a surprise, given that they had already made their peace with the Five Nations. The issue of the prisoners, if it had not been perfectly resolved during the preceding year, may have been further discussed and closed. Another issue brought to the table, the progressive disappearance of fur-bearing animals and the sharing out of hunting grounds, was apparently resolved by an agreement according to which the hunting territories of new and old allies would be pooled; the territories were metaphorically represented as a great dish, and a ladle and a knife were distributed to everyone so that they might serve themselves from it.[91] What part the Kahnawakes played in this arrangement was not recorded, though it is clear that over the next century they developed a strong conviction that they had on this occasion been given preeminence. In 1791, one of the village's chiefs gave a speech to the British authorities in which he claimed that the French king had assembled all the nations of the continent and laid his "dish" at the "great fire" of Kahnawake. Though this late eighteenth-century memory of preeminence had much to do with eighteenth-century developments, there was nevertheless a kernel of truth to it insofar as the prominence of Kahnawake among France's Indigenous allies would have been clear to the people assembled in 1701.[92]

During the closing speeches of the conference on 4 August 1701, Ontonnionk again asserted Kahnawake's preeminence. "For us [the Kahnawakes] who have the advantage of knowing more intimately and from a closer distance than they the true feelings of your heart," he declared to the French governor, referring to the other nations assembled, "we readily throw down the hatchet on your word, which we had only taken up at your command, and give the Tree of Peace that you have erected such strong, deep roots, that neither winds nor storms, nor other misfortune will be able to uproot it." When he was done, an orator named Tsahouanhos (plausibly the aforementioned Tsihenne alias Massias) spoke with equal fervor on behalf of the Kanehsatakes, declaring that he had no hatchet "other than that of my Father. As he carries us in his bosom, I return mine to him, and at the same time withdraw my hand, for he throws away his [own] hatchet."[93] It was Haronhiateka who, in spite of his status as a newcomer or perhaps precisely because of it, affixed his mark to the final peace treaty in 1701 on behalf of his new community.[94]

***

Unsurprisingly, the flowery rhetoric of devotion and obedience to Onontio made by Ontonnionk and Tsahouanhos during the proceedings of 1701 offer only an imperfect reflection of the course of war and peace during the previous two decades. The Christian Iro-

Figure 8.1 Marks of "Haronhiateka chef du Sault" and "Mechayon chef de la Montagne" on the manuscript ratifying the Great Peace of Montreal of 1701. These clan marks appear to represent deer, though it has been suggested by some scholars that Haronhiateka's might instead be a bear, based on external evidence that his name belonged to this particular clan. (Detail from ANOM, Fonds des Colonies, C11A: 19, 43v)

quois, undeniably, had had "the advantage of knowing more intimately and from a closer distance than they the true feelings" of Onontio's heart. But in their eyes Onontio's views had not always been "so just and so reasonable," and they had had as much of a hand as him in carrying the war hatchet against the enemy and laying it down. Under the leadership of men – and women, beyond the surface of the written record – whose influence was intertwined with the new religion, the inhabitants of the missions had decisively sided with the French in their campaigns against the distant and tenuously related Senecas. Drawn into a war against the English, and more reluctantly against their close relatives the Mohawks, Oneidas, and Onondagas, they had exchanged with the Iroquois of the League hatchet blows and wampum belts with disconcerting regularity – following a rhythm of violence and diplomacy that was very much their own, not merely dictated by the French.

From these years of conflict and dialogue, a new geopolitical landscape had emerged. It was something more than a return to the status quo of before 1684, at which time the old communities of Iroquoia had coexisted in peace with the new communities of Kahnawake and

Kanehsatake. The Five Nations were more united now than they had previously been: henceforth there could be no thought of going to war against the distant Senecas with the expectation that Mohawk, Oneida, and Onondaga relatives would not be "concerned," to borrow the term that Anthony Lespinard, the Albany trader, had used. More importantly perhaps, the Christian and League communities had each demonstrated their endurance: henceforth neither group would make any serious attempt to persuade the other to migrate "by […] acts of kindness" or to force it to do so by violence. France's 1701 peace with the Five Nations, and the latter's willingness to henceforth cleave to a policy of neutrality in times of intercolonial conflicts, would allow cordial relations to resume between the inhabitants of the missions and their relations and acquaintances in Iroquoia. There would yet be moments of tension and incidents of violence, but never on the scale seen in the final decades of the seventeenth century.[95]

Conclusion

During the winter of 1705, seventy to a hundred Wabanakis and a small number of Wendats from Lorette ventured for the seasonal hunt to the north of Trois Rivières, up the Saint Maurice River towards the watershed of Lake Saint Jean and the Saguenay. The circumstances which allowed the details of the event to enter the historical record were not happy ones. The Innu who occupied these lands regarded it as their exclusive hunting territory. Some of them, who had been mistreated and had their furs taken by the Wabanakis, lodged a complaint with French officials. Asked by the latter to account for their actions, the Wabanakis countered that they too had rights to the area. They had been led there by the "chief of the Abenaquis of the mission of St. François" (i.e. Arsikantegouk), a man named Outakamachiwenon alias Tekouerimat. As his son Louis testified, the contested hunting grounds had been "given" to his father by his grandfather, who he pointed out had been chief of the Algonquins of Tadoussac (*sic*).[1]

This moment is at once enigmatic and emblematic. Enigmatic because the late seventeenth-century sources do not provide a clear idea of the internal relationships and structures of leadership among the groups concerned. Though the French chroniclers failed to make any mention of it, the title of Tekouerimat had visibly lived on after the death of Michel Tekouerimat in 1685. It is a powerful reminder that the colonial record is fragmentary, and sorely wanting in its reporting of Indigenous realities. In this way, this moment is emblematic of the challenges that we face in trying to reconstruct the history of the mission settlements of the Saint Lawrence valley. It is also emblematic because it points to the frictions that accompanied the settlement of diverse peoples in the region, and most importantly it speaks to the interplay of continuity and change that characterized the formation and early evolution of its mission communities. The Wabanaki missions, though the most recent of the settlements, had roots that stretched back to the Innu and Algonquin communities of Kamiskouaouangachit. The figure of Noël Negabamat Tekouerimat, who had played such a key role in the early conceptualization of the mission settlement, persisted long after the title – "He Who Settles Them" – was adopted by its first bearer. Subsequent bearers of the name do not loom as large in the records of the eighteenth century as the first had in the seventeenth, but one is mentioned as late as 1749. That year the Wabanakis of Arsikantegouk and their missionary sent a letter to the canons of the cathedral of Chartres to "refresh [...] as if it were made anew" the union that their forebearers had contracted some sixty years earlier. The first of the five chiefs whose name was affixed to the document was called Michel *Terrouëmant*.[2]

The human landscape of the Saint Lawrence valley at the end of the seventeenth century was profoundly different from the one that had existed at its outset. A French population had established roots there, in growing towns and on multiplying farms, and alongside them had coalesced a string of Indigenous communities. Almost from the time of their inception, the latter's position in the region was marked by demographic disparity. All in all, those who were coming to be known as "*Sauvages domiciliés*" numbered about 2,000 compared to their 15,000 French neighbours – in other words, they represented a little less than a tenth of the Saint Lawrence valley's population. Their presence was nonetheless not negligible, and concentrated in a way that made it stand out. Kahnawake alone, with a population of 790 according to the 1698 census, or between 950 and 1,000 according to slightly later estimates, formed the third largest town in the colony, following Quebec (which numbered 1,988 in 1698) and Montreal (1,185). The size of the Wabanaki mission of Ariskantegouk was in flux, but it too was substantial: the mission on the Chaudière River had numbered 355 shortly before its relocation to the Saint François River, and within a decade its population at the new site would itself rise to about 1,250. Even the relatively small communities of Kanehsatake and Skawenati on the Island of Montreal, which numbered 160 and 113, respectively, in 1698, and Lorette, with 122, compare favourably with Trois Rivières, the third largest French agglomeration, which was home to a mere 358 colonists.[3] To give a sense of perspective, numbers also allow us to grasp the slightness of the missionary presence on the ground: in 1701, of their order's 48 members, only 4 Jesuits were stationed at Kahnawake, 2 at Ariskantegouk, and 1 at Lorette; the Sulpicians had 1 of their own at Kanehsatake, and 1 or 2 more at Skawenati.[4] These villages were not mere appendages of the French Catholic Church, they were in all respects Indigenous communities.

Although these communities continued to evolve – to fluctuate in size, to experience a few more relocations, and beginning in the nineteenth century to undergo massive social, cultural, and economic changes – by the end of the seventeenth century they had achieved an essential degree of stability. That they persist to this day is indicative of the unique foundational character of the period. The Wendats had journeyed from ancestral homelands in what is today Ontario, to the Saint Lawrence valley, to the Island of Orleans, to the center of the town of Quebec, before moving on, with influxes from Iroquoia, to Notre Dame de Foy, to the initial Lorette, and finally settling in 1697 at Jeune Lorette. Renamed Wendake – the place of the Wendats – in the 1980s, it remains to this day the home of the Huron-Wendat Nation.[5] The Wabanaki community of Arsikantegouk or Saint François lives on too, under the name of Odanak, meaning simply "The Village." That name, used only since the nineteenth century, evokes a context much changed from that of the late seventeenth century, at which point village communities – in the plural – remained very conspicuous across Wabanaki country.[6]

Kahnawake continues to thrive along the rapids, a short distance upriver from where it was located in 1696, following a final relocation in 1716. So too does Kanehsatake persist, though it underwent more substantial reconfigurations than any other mission settlement in the first decades of the eighteenth century. In the fall of 1704, the sacramental registers of the mission of La Montagne were officially closed, its inhabitants having completed their relocation to Skawenati, along the Rivière des Prairies. The following year, the bones from the cemetery were transported to the second site – an event which, while corresponding to a standard Catholic practice, may for some of the mission's inhabitants have recalled the old Feast of the Dead.[7] In 1721, the community again moved, this time to the north shore of the Lac des Deux Montagnes or Lake of Two Mountains, at the confluence of the Saint Lawrence and Ottawa Rivers, just opposite the westernmost point of the Island of Montreal and across from the mouth of the Rivière des Prairies.[8]

The names used to describe this mission community indicate the intricacies of continuity. The names of Kanehsatake and La Montagne continued to be associated in a haphazard fashion with the mission community during its occupation of Skawenati, even though it had abandoned that earlier site. The change of landscape in 1721 offered an opportunity to revive more fully and coherently the name of Kanehsatake – "at the foot of the hill" now referencing the elevation of the Two Mountains, which are today familiarly known as the Oka Hills. But the name of Skawenati too retained some currency after that date, as the mission still found itself on the "other side of the island." In their dealings with the Five Nations and with officials in Albany, as late as the 1730s and 1740s the Iroquois inhabitants of the mission at Lake of Two Mountains were indeed still referred to as "Skawenatis."[9]

Relocation to this new Kanehsatake was also the occasion for an amalgamation with the Algonquin and Nipissing population that orbited around a short-lived mission settlement, established by the Sulpicians in 1704, at Île aux Tourtes, or Aouanagassing, an island on the southern edge of this same Lake of Two Mountains, facing the westernmost point of the Island of Montreal.[10] In addition to these communities, three more would emerge in the eighteenth century as outgrowths of preexisting ones: a second Wabanaki community, that of Wôlinak (originally Wowenok), founded along the Bécancour River in 1704; Oswegatchie, a community occupied mainly by Onondagas on the upper Saint Lawrence River between 1749 and the mid-1760s; and finally the Mohawk community of Akwesasne, also established on the upper Saint Lawrence in 1754.[11]

While these communities have continued to loom large in the consciousness of their non-Indigenous neighbours, their occupation of earlier sites has meanwhile grown faint in memory. In the nineteenth century, the penultimate site of Kahnawake and Skawenati were each still remembered as Kanatakwenke, meaning "where the village was taken from."[12] French-Canadian farmers periodically came across reminders of Indigenous presence. In the late nineteenth century, the elderly living near the Chaudière Falls could recall that their plows had in earlier years brought up in their furrows human "bones or worm-eaten coffin planks." Meanwhile, the outcropping next to the former mission site at Sillery was, owing to the occasional discovery of human and material remains, remembered until recently as the "*Butte aux Sauvages*" (Native Hill). But suburban sprawl has further contributed to the erasure of these memories of settlement.[13] The name of Sillery persists, recalling to a certain extent the old mission, but those of Kamiskouaouangachit, Msakkikkan, and Néssawakamighé have long gone out of use. And while the name of the recently canonized Catherine Tekakwitha has continued to loom large in popular consciousness, one would be hard-pressed to find more than a handful of specialists who today recognize the names of the likes of Tekouerimat, Atironta, Ganneaktena, Tonsahoten, Togouirout, or Tatakwiséré, and who have a sense of the crucial role that these figures played in shaping the settlement – both Indigenous and French, given their broader impact on the geopolitics of the region – of the Saint Lawrence valley.

Although the experience of each mission settlement was distinct, they all shared certain commonalities. The men and women who formed and joined these communities had in common a readiness to experiment with cooperation and cohabitation, among each other and alongside French neighbours, and a willingness to adapt their personal and collective identities accordingly. They coalesced in search of regeneration in difficult times and sought out security and opportunities – political, cultural, material, and spiritual. In this context, a community such as that of the Wendats succeeded in rebounding from a position of extreme vulnerability to one of relative strength. By the end of the seventeenth century, the anxieties of mid-century had passed, and the sort of lamentation that had been common in the diplomatic rhetoric through the 1650s and 1660s ceased completely. These processes of regeneration brought together a range of peoples, including former enemies. Without exception, the mission settlements came into being as heterogeneous, multiethnic communities before more focused and lasting collective identities emerged. By the end of the seventeenth century, each of these communities had come to be recognized by the French as a crucial ally, deserving of attention and political accommodation. All things considered, their existence in the Saint Lawrence valley defined French colonial policy just as much as it was defined by it.

While the notion of "mission settlement" is insightful when it comes to describing the initial establishment of these communities through much of the seventeenth century, it comes across as a less accurate descriptor by the period's end. Given their size and the degree of stability that they had achieved, by this time they can be more usefully thought of collectively as "mission villages." They were a far cry from what the French had imagined early on. There is little doubt that these communities functioned as sites of religious conversion and perpetuation. Nineteenth- and twentieth-century shifts in culture and identity, namely the revalorization of traditional Indigenous spiritualties, has made it too easy to understate the importance of religion in the establishment of the communities. Yet the balance of the evidence shows that, during their foundational period, taking up residence there meant taking up the Catholic faith and its rituals – in a syncretic fashion, to be sure. As sites of assimilation to French culture and ways of life, however, the mission settlements meanwhile fell short. In the absence of coercive capabilities, Indigenous indifference forced missionaries and officials to adjust their expectations. The Jesuits were the quickest to understand this, already doing so by the 1640s, but before the end of the century the Sulpicians too reached the same conclusion.

Ways of life in the mission settlements did adapt to their surroundings over time. Lorette, as the oldest and smallest mission settlement, was at the forefront of this trend. The small scale of the community forced change in old family structures, including the abandonment of former restrictions against marrying within one's clan. Intermarriage with French and later English neighbours, relatively rare in the seventeenth century, became gradually more common. Whereas multifamily longhouses remained the predominant form of dwelling in the community at the end of the seventeenth century, these appear to have been wholly replaced by houses in the French style during the 1710s. And whereas it was reported in 1674 that just a few of the Wendats "knew French," by the middle of the eighteenth century most spoke it. Such transitions occurred at a slower pace at Kahnawake and Kanehsatake. There, with a few exceptions, multifamily longhouses persisted as the principal form of dwelling until the second half of the eighteenth century, and well into the nineteenth a majority of people still did not speak the language of their French or English neighbours.[14]

At the beginning of the eighteenth century, then, most of these key social and cultural shifts had yet to occur. Likewise, modes of subsistence in the mission settlements remained essentially those of Old Huronia, Iroquoia, and Wabanaki country. A little wheat was produced, and a small number of domestic animals were raised. But the culture of corn continued to dominate, diminishing only through the eighteenth and nineteenth centuries to be replaced by a greater reliance on hunting and fishing, for the communities' own subsistence and for sale, along with foraged plants and crafts, to the nearby townspeople. At Kahnawake and Kanehsatake, wage labour as canoe paddlers for the fur trading companies would take on a crucial economic importance beginning in the late eighteenth century, as it did for some of their French neighbours.[15]

One major shift that did occur around the turn of the seventeenth century, visible in hindsight, was the end of the traditional pattern of village relocation – and in this respect, it becomes clear that, though the mission settlements were not merely products of colonial policy, their existence was indeed shaped by it. Whereas the availability of land during the middle portion of the seventeenth century made it possible for Indigenous groups to choose land in the Saint Lawrence valley themselves, the ever-growing density of French settlement made this increasingly difficult. Settlement relocations beginning in the final quarter of the seventeenth century were more tightly constrained by the interplay of missionary and royal priorities. Lorette became the first of the mission settlements to achieve the sort of fixed place on the landscape that the French had initially envisioned for them. That the community remained in place after 1697, rupturing with ancient patterns of village relocation, had more to do with the priorities of the Jesuits than those of the neophytes themselves. Jesuit chronicler Pierre-François-Xavier de Charlevoix, observing the generally poor quality of the soil at Lorette, remarked a few decades later that his order had "good reasons for not allowing [the Wendats] to abandon it."[16]

Indeed, the customary need to secure new fields and firewood became fused with the Jesuits and Sulpicians' concern with achieving a compromise between proximity and distance between the mission communities, urban centers, such as Quebec and Montreal, and countryside cleared by the habitants. The missionaries rapidly grew attentive to the financial implications of Indigenous settlement and resettlement in the seigneurial zone. They took care to retain title to lands, and saw no qualms in using village relocation as an opportunity to sell off cleared and improved lands to French colonists. Paternalism was at the core of these dealings, insofar as Jesuits and Sulpicians genuinely believed that the future of the missions depended on their societies' own financial security. They assumed that they were better caretakers of the mission residents' interests than the latter could ever be themselves, and were blind to the possibility that their land transactions might have deleterious long-term effects on the communities whose well-being they had at heart.[17]

The interplay of missionary and court politics, well beyond the reach of the people of these communities, also came to bear on patterns of resettlement. This is well illustrated by the way in which the Jesuits petitioned the Crown in 1699 for a concession which would grant them full title to the seigneury of Sillery and resolve any ambiguity as to its status. In moving to a new Lorette two years earlier, the Wendat community had vacated this seigneury for that of Saint Gabriel. Yet Sillery had been granted by the Crown in 1651 to the "*néophytes sauvages chrétiens,*" under trusteeship of the Jesuits. As it was now devoid of such neophytes, the Jesuits thought best to argue that full seigneurial ownership was only a fair compensation for all that they had invested and continued to invest in their missions. Frontenac had recently died, and Governor Callière and Intendant Champigny supported the request. Louis XIV ratified it in May of 1702. But on that occasion the king made it clear that such magnanimity should not be expected in the future. This ratification, he declared, was made "although it is against the rule that [His Majesty] has made for himself to grant no more lands in Canada to religious communities," the latter being "already far too powerful in that country."[18] Louis XIV's death in 1715 opened the door for exceptions – a westward extension of the seigneury of Sault Saint Louis to the Jesuits for the final relocation of Kahnawake, and the seigneury of Lac des Deux Montagnes to the Sulpicians for that of Skawenati. Otherwise this policy would stand.[19]

***

Movement characterized the formational phase of these settlements not only in the way in which they periodically relocated, before ceasing to do so, but also in the way in which individuals and families continued to circulate between the villages of the Saint Lawrence valley and traditional territories. It was not uncommon for an individual's senses of identity and belonging to shift over his or her lifetime. To name but a few examples, this pattern is epitomized by individuals such as Haronhiateka and Tsihenne alias Massias, who during the negotiations of the Great Peace of 1701 acted as prominent representatives of Kahnawake and Kanehsatake, respectively, in spite of the fact that they had joined these communities a mere few years earlier. It is also exemplified by someone like La Plaque, the nephew of Togouirout the Great Mohawk. Through the 1690s he showed himself to be one of the staunchest allies of the French, but by 1705 Intendant Raudot reported that he had returned to Mohawk country, citing as an explanation his vices, the principal of which were apparently his "passionate love of women" and his habit of seducing other men's wives. Then, in 1709, La Plaque's name again crops up in the correspondence of French officials, where he is described as leading a party of scouts against the English in a way that implies that he had once more relocated to Kahnawake.[20]

Though it may be counterintuitive to think so, this porosity does not appear to have undermined the cohesion of the mission villages. Each of them came into being as a heterogeneous, multiethnic, and multinational community, but by the late seventeenth century long-lasting collective identities were in place. These identities were at once old and new. That which emerged at Lorette, even as it was solidly rooted in a prior Wendat sense of self, was at the same time fundamentally innovative in the way it melded together fragments of the Attignawantan, Attigneenongnahac, Arendarhonon, and to a lesser extent Tahontaenrat and Ataronchronon. What had been a broad ethnolinguistic category supplanted a range of distinct identities and dialects. Among the people of Ariskantegouk too, recognizably different groups began to merge together under the heading of "Abénaquis" or Wabanakis. While that village continued to attract Western Wabanakis, the new settlement of Wôlinak on the Bécancour River began to draw Eastern Wabanakis, but in the centuries that followed, even that broad ethnocultural division would fade.[21]

In places like Kahnawake and Kanehsatake, Old and New Iroquois merged. The weight of immigration from Mohawk country was such that, while the French took to referring to the inhabitants of both of these communities generically as "Iroquois," it was the Mohawk language and culture that came to predominate. And yet divergent roots persisted. In both of these communities, the Wendat language continued to be used well into the eighteenth century as the idiom of religious instruction. In 1735, one missionary posted at Kahnawake commented that "all our Natives understand Huron, and prefer it to Iroquois although the pronunciation is not so pleasing to the ear. Hence it is that they do not care to recite their prayers in their own tongue."[22] This usage was, to a large extent, the result of missionary practice – the fact that the Jesuits had developed a collective linguistic expertise among the Wendats before moving on to the Iroquois – but it may also have been a remote consequence of the fact that, in the middle decades of the seventeenth century, the New Iroquois of Wendat origin had loomed the largest among the proponents of Christianity.[23]

Ethnic heterogeneity remained most apparent at Kanehsatake. With the exception of Lorette of course, the Wendat component endured the longest there – the community having been founded as a result of the alienation of Wendats at Kentake. From time to time in the eighteenth century, Iroquois warriors from Kanehsatake joined up with the Tionnontaté-Wendats of Detroit, keeping alive old relationships.[24] At Kanehsatake, Algonquian families, primarily Algonquins and Nippissings from the Ottawa River watershed, also lived alongside the Iroquois. Periodically, since the early 1670s, the Sulpicians had attempted to minister to this population at various points on the Island of Montreal, and in 1704, around the time of the closing of the mission at La Montagne, the Sulpician René-Charles de Breslay and Governor Vaudreuil acted together to establish a new mission settlement for this nomadic population at Île aux Tourtes, or Aouanagassing, an island in the Lake of Two Mountains. As noted above, when the Sulpicians relocated their mission from Rivière des Prairies to the north shore of that lake, they redirected there the Algonquians who orbited around Aouanagassing, closing the latter mission in 1727.[25]

In terms of community, the mission settlement of Kanehsatake at the Lake of Two Mountains after that amalgamation thus had the particularity of being at once unitary and plural. A Sulpician missionary could thus describe it as consisting of "two villages," one of Iroquois and one of Algonquins and Nipissings, "which are separated one from the other only by the church which is common to both," while a visiting officer understood it as being "inhabited by three different nations: Nipissings, Algonquins, and Iroquois; they form three distinct houses [*cabanes*], although united in the same village." The Iroquois element dominated politically, owing to three equally powerful reasons: their more substantial numbers; the fact that their way of life rooted them more firmly in the village than their Algonquian neighbours, for whom the site served as something more akin to a gathering place; and their links to the Five Nations which ensured their strategic importance.[26] This intercultural division held until the middle of the nineteenth century, at which point the Algonquian population of the village left it for Kitigan Zibi (River Desert), a tributary of the Gatineau River, and other points in the Ottawa River watershed, which had long been part of their winter hunting grounds.[27]

These Algonquians who orbited around Skawenati, Aouanagassing, and later Kanehsatake at the Lake of Two Mountains, bring us back to the earliest days of the mission settlements. Most certainly, this population included descendants of individuals who in the middle of the seventeenth century had orbited around the short-lived mission settlements of Kamiskouaouangachit and Metaberoutin. For these families the mission settlements had not provided sites of permanence so much as a brief interlude. In light of the pressures of the Iroquois and the arrival of Wendats in the Saint Lawrence valley, resources rapidly grew scarce. These Algonquians found their sites of refuge and renewal elsewhere, opting to maintain old patterns of land occupation: a seasonal nomadism that brought them closer to the French settlements in the summer, but that led them to the hinterland of the Saint Lawrence's north in the fall and winter. While the Innu recentered their existence on the Saguenay and Lake Saint Jean watershed, a small number of Algonquins continued to return to various points along the Saint Lawrence through the eighteenth century. Dismissively described as "vagabonds" by officials, just as their forebearers had been during the first decades of the seventeenth, they nonetheless kept on supplying fur traders, taking part in military expeditions, and occasionally seeking out missionary instruction and ministry.[28]

***

Each of these mission communities could make legitimate claims to preeminence in the Saint Lawrence valley, recalling roots that stretched back deep in time and key moments of their histories. In 1756, a speaker on behalf of the Algonquins and Nipissings of Kanehsatake proclaimed his people's precedence on the territory during a meeting with delegates of the Iroquois Confederacy: "We are the first who had inhabited this land; we saw a white man (it was a Frenchman), we ran to him, he embraced us and we adopted him as Father. You, other Five Nations, came later."[29] As outlined above, some Wabanakis at Ariskantegouk could similarly trace their roots, through their relationship to Noël Negabamat alias Tekouerimat, back to a distant period. So too might the Wendats of Lorette take pride as the oldest mission community, given Kamiskouaouangachit's demise.[30]

Lorette indeed enjoyed within the Franco-Indigenous alliance a position that was well beyond its slight demographic proportions. Beyond the intergenerational memories of its distant roots in the world of the sixteenth-century Saint Lawrence Iroquoians, the community was invariably described by observers as the most pious and orderly of them all. "Their modesty is remarkable," one delighted missionary reported of its residents, "to the point where the French who pass through the village are astonished by it and blush when they compare themselves and their lifestyle with the Natives." This reputation earned them the moniker of "*Saints Sauvages*" or Holy Natives.[31] The mission's physical proximity to Quebec, the seat of the colonial administration, also made it possible for the people of Lorette to cultivate a privileged access to successive governors and intendants. This entailed, in some respects, a disadvantage, as suggested by the puzzling absence of the speeches or signatures of the community's representatives from the proceedings of the Great Peace of 1701. While some scholars have interpreted this absence to mean that Kondiaronk, the famous Tionnontaté Wendat leader from Michilimackinac, represented their community in addition to his own, the more plausible answer is that their proximity to the French governor was such that they relinquished their representation to him. Notwithstanding, Charlevoix described the Wendats in his writings as "the soul of every council." They were not shy in asserting their moral authority. In 1740, one of Roreke's most prominent eighteenth-century leaders, Vincent Onehatetaionk, was bold enough to travel to Kanehsatake and seize a dozen of the community's wampum belts, asserting his own people's "rights" over that community, evoking the part that they had played in its foundation sixty years earlier. Five years later, the same Onehatetaionk displayed a sense of self visibly unblemished by the hardships that in earlier times had led his people to the Saint Lawrence valley. He "boasted verey much of their libertyes and previledges above any other Nation," wrote a captive taken in New England, "and told me they was in subjection to no king nor prince in the Universe."[32]

Such confidence was widely shared among the inhabitants of the mission villages. The people of Kahnawake too could consider themselves to be above all others, forming by far the most populous of these communities, and having demonstrated during the final two decades of the seventeenth century that they had the military and diplomatic weight to match. They maintained this power through the end of the French Regime, and saw it institutionalized thereafter when their community became, under the influence of the British, the center of a new formation loosely uniting the mission settlements of the Saint Lawrence valley – the Seven Nations or Seven Fires Confederation.

This context of political achievement, combined with intergenerational memories of Iroquoian ancestors who had inhabited this space in distant times, came to define the community's evolving sense of self. One of the village's chiefs, meeting with the superintendent of Indian Affairs in 1791, recalled how ninety years earlier the French king had assembled all the nations of the continent (*sic*) – "Kanawageronon [i.e. Kahnawakes], Huron, Algonkin, Nipissing" – and, pointing to their common brotherhood and religion, asked them to remain at peace forever as he placed their "great fire" at Kahnawake.[33]

The way in which war had brought very diverse peoples to live alongside each other in the Saint Lawrence valley, and the mutual obligations of the military alliance, were from time to time recalled. During a council held at Kanehsatake on the shore of the Lake of Two Mountains in August 1741, the officer Jean-Baptiste-Nicolas-Roch de Ramezay spoke on behalf of the governor, Charles de la Boische de Beauharnois, alluding to the fact that at the time of its initial establishment at La Montagne, the community had "placed yourself under my wings [those of Onontio], and added that all those who would bite me would bite you too."[34] This was not a perfectly accurate summation of the interplay between war and the formation of the mission settlements. The ideal of mutual defence – and its tragic limits – had certainly been central to the relationship of the French with the Saint Lawrence Algonquians and the Wendats. But the people who arrived from Iroquoia through the late 1660s to the early 1680s came in a time of peace, with no expectation that they should need to take up arms alongside the French – indeed, the idea that to bite one was to bite the other is, in reality, to be found nowhere in the detailed proceedings of the meeting which occurred at the time of Kanehsatake's founding in 1675.[35] Nor did the French initially think of protecting the first waves of Wabanakis who came to the region in the late 1670s, or of being protected by them, though it was war that brought them there. It was only with the renewal of hostilities against the Iroquois and the outbreak of an imperial conflict against Britain and its colonies during the final two decades of the eighteenth century that New France came to depend on the residents of the mission villages for its defence. The bites to which Ramezay was alluding, projecting a recent reality onto a distant past, were British.

If, with the caveat that centuries are arbitrary units of time, a broad distinction might be made between the seventeenth century and the eighteenth as far as the history of the French and Indigenous inhabitants of the Saint Lawrence valley is concerned, it might be that whereas the threat represented by the Iroquois and the opportunities presented by them loom as the dominant theme of the first period, during the second they were replaced by British colonists. The Great Peace of 1701 marked the emergence of this new geopolitical landscape. Indeed, if the Iroquois wars and politics of integration had been central to the foundation of the mission settlements, war against Great Britain and the politics of imperial trade henceforth would be integral to their story. As the War of the League of Augsburg gave way to that of Spanish Succession, initiating a cycle of war and armed peace, Louis XIV opted for a new colonial strategy whereby New France's primary function would be to serve as a bastion of empire. In this perspective, the mission villages came to be understood by colonial officials above all as strategic bulwarks, rather than sites of religious and cultural change.[36] This increased appreciation for the crucial role of these communities in colonial defence did not put an end to French paternalism, however, and indeed contributed to amplifying colonial expectations of subservience – expectations which predictably clashed with the patterns of Indigenous self-determination firmly maintained during the foundational years of the seventeenth century.

Notes

ABBREVIATIONS

AJC Archive of the Jesuits in Canada, Montreal
ANF Archives nationales de France, Paris
ANOM Centre des archives d'outre-mer, Aix-en-Provence
ASQ Archives du Séminaire de Québec, Musée de la civilisation, Quebec City
ASSM Archives of the Sulpician Seminary, Montreal
ASSP Archives of the Sulpician Seminary, Paris
BANQ-M Bibliothèque et Archives nationales du Québec, Montreal
BANQ-Q Bibliothèque et Archives nationales du Québec, Quebec City
BNF Bibliothèque nationale de France, Paris
CMHS *Collections of the Massachusetts Historical Society*
CMNF *Collection de manuscrits contenant lettres, mémoires, et autres documents historiques relatifs à la Nouvelle-France, recueillis aux archives de la province de Québec, ou copiés à l'étranger*, Jean Gervais Protais Blanchet, Faucher de Saint-Maurice, and Narcisse Henri Edouard, eds.
CSPC *Calendar of State Papers, Colonial,* W. Noel Sainsbury, J.W. Fortescue, Cecil Headlam et al., eds.
DCB *Dictionary of Canadian Biography*, George W. Brown, Marcel Trudel, André Vachon, and David Hayne, eds.
DHSM *The Documentary History of the State Of Maine, containing the Baxter Manuscripts*, James Phinney Baxter, ed.
DHSNY *The Documentary History of the State of New-York,* E.B. O'Callaghan, ed.

HNF Marcel Trudel, *Histoire de la Nouvelle-France*
JRAD *The Jesuit Relations and Allied Documents*, Reuben Gold Thwaites, ed.
LAC Library and Archives Canada, Ottawa
LIR *The Livingston Indian Records*, Lawrence R. Leder, ed.
MNF *Monumenta Novae Franciae*, Lucien Campeau, ed.
NYCD *Documents relative to the colonial history of the state of New-York: procured in Holland, England, and France.* John Romeyn Brodhead, Berthold Fernow, and E.B. O'Callaghan, eds.
NYSA New York State Archives, Albany
PRDH Programme de recherche en démographie historique
RAPQ *Rapport de l'archiviste de la Province de Québec*

INTRODUCTION

1 Thwaites, ed., *JRAD* 49: 224–30.
2 Ibid.
3 *JRAD* 15:154; 17: 38; Tooker, *Ethnography of Huron Indians*, 20–2; Laberge, *Affiquets, matachias et vermillon*.
4 *JRAD* 49: 226–8.
5 [2] For "Wepìstùkwiyaht Sīpu," see McNulty, *Petite grammaire*. For "Kitcikanii sipi" ("*la rivière du grand liquide*"), see Cuoq, *Lexique de la langue algonquine*, 371. Wabanaki names include "Kchitegw/Ktsitekw/Gicitegw" (Great River), but also "Oss8genaizibo/Ws8genaisibo/Wsogenaisibo" (River of the Algonquins), and "Moliantegok/Moliantekw" (Montreal River). See Charland, "Définition et reconstitution," 232 and appendix E; Day, *Western Abenaki Dictionary*, 2: 380. For "Lada8anna," "Laooendaooena," see Poirier, *La toponymie des Hurons-Wendats*, 28–9. And for Kaniatarowanenneh, see Haudenosaunee Environmental Task Force, *Words That Come Before All Else*, 18.
6 For descriptions of the mission settlements as "colonies," see *JRAD* 35: 214; 36: 202; 41: 60; 56: 18; 57: 68, 76; ANOM, C11A 12: 137–137v, "Requeste à Monseigneur de Pontchartrain […]," 1692.
7 *JRAD* 36: 214; 45: 38–40; 49: 226–34; 35: 190; Leder, ed., *LIR*, 189–90; Wraxall, *Abridgement*, 60, 91; Brodhead et al., *NYCD* 4: 337, 575–7, 648–52, 743–5, 983–5, 990–2. On the symbolism of the body, see Carpenter, *Renewed, Destroyed, Remade*.
8 Cf. Labelle, "'Like Wolves from the Woods,'" and *Dispersed but not Destroyed*, 4–5, 27.
9 Sagard, *Grand Voyage*, 284–6; Seeman, *Feast of the Dead*.

10 Seeman, *Feast of the Dead.*

11 Book of Ezekiel 37: 1–14; Le Maistre de Sacy, *Ezechiel*, 550–63; Block, *Book of Ezekiel*, 364–91. On the deployment of this same biblical passage in the context of New England missionary work, see also Bross, *Dry Bones.*

12 On the Wendat mission, see Lindsay, *Notre-Dame de la Jeune-Lorette*. For the Wabanaki missions, see Maurault, *Histoire des Abénaquis*; Charland, *Histoire de Saint-François-du-Lac*, and *Histoire des Abenakis*. On Kahnawake, see Saint-François-Xavier parish archives, Kahnawake, Quebec, Burtin, "Histoire des Iroquois du Sault Saint-Louis avec Documents et pièces justificatives," 1881; Forbes, "Saint-François-Xavier de Caughnawaga," 131–6; Devine, *Historic Caughnawaga*; Béchard, *Original Caughnawaga Indians.*

13 Day, *Identity of Saint Francis Indians*; Ronda, "Sillery Experiment"; Blanchard, *Kahnawake*, "Patterns of Tradition and Change, and "Other Side of Sky"; Tremblay, "Politique missionnaire"; Green, "New People." For more recent studies, see Savard, "'Réduction' de Sillery"; Beaulieu, Béreau, and Tanguay, *Wendats*; Clair, "Du décor rêvé."

14 Trigger, *Children of Aataentsic*; Labelle, *Dispersed But Not Destroyed*; Sévigny, *Abénaquis*; Richter, *Ordeal*; Calloway, *Western Abenakis*; Parmenter, "At Woods' Edge," and *Edge of Woods*; Preston, *Texture of Contact*, 23–60; Beaulieu, *Convertir les fils.*

15 Ronda, "Sillery Experiment," 15; Blanchard, "Tradition and Change," esp. 134–78. See also Blanchard, "Other Side of Sky," 77–102.

16 Greer, *Mohawk Saint*, and "Conversion and Identity"; Bonaparte, *Lily Among Thorns*; Clair, "Du décor rêvé," "'Seeing These Good Souls,'" and "Corps et décor."

17 Delâge, "Les Iroquois chrétiens" (parts I and II), and "Les Hurons de Lorette"; Grabowski, "Common Ground." See also Trudel, "Hurons et Murray"; Jaenen, "Rapport historique"; Beaulieu, "Hurons de Lorette"; Vaugeois, *Fin des alliances*. Of interest are also the following reports, copies of which can be found in the Departmental Library of Indian and Northern Affairs in Ottawa: MacLeod, "Huron of Lorette"; Graves, "Huron of Lorette"; Stone, "Assessment of Murray Treaty," and "Report on Murray Treaty."

18 MacLeod, *Canadian Iroquois*; Haefeli and Sweeney, *Captors and Captives.*

19 Parkman, *Jesuits*, 2: 44. Cf., for example, Havard, *Empire et métissage*; Gohier, *Onontio*; Beaulieu, Béreau, and Tanguay, *Wendats*; Morin, "Fraternité"; Peace, "Two Conquests," 224–368.

20 Jetten, *Enclaves amérindiennes.*

21 For early allusions to the Seven Nations during the late eighteenth century,

see Boiteau, "Chasseurs hurons de Lorette"; Blanchard, *Seven Generations*, 275–82, and "Seven Nations of Canada; Ostola, "Seven Nations of Canada"; Delâge, "Iroquois chrétiens," part 2: 46–9; Calloway, *Western Abenakis*, 194–5, and *American Revolution*, 26–84. For claims of their roots in the seventeenth century, see Sawaya "Sept-Nations du Canada," and *Fédération des Sept Feux;* For the critique of this stance, see John A. Dickinson's review of Sawaya's *Fédération des Sept Feux* in the *American Historical Review* and Normand Clermont's in *Revue d'histoire de l'Amérique française*. For the revised interpretation, see Sawaya and Beaulieu, "Qui sont les Sept Nations?"; Sawaya and Delâge, "Les origines de la Fédération des Sept-Feux," and *Les Traités des Sept-Feux;* Sawaya, "Sept-Nations du Canada," and *Alliance et dépendance*; Lozier, "History, Historiography, and the Courts." For examples of the persistence of the error, see: Jaenen, "Christian *réductions*," 130; Bruchac, "Abenaki Connections," 271; Johnson, *Tribes of the Iroquois Confederacy*, 7; Sheppard, *Empires Collide*, 53.

22 Toupin, ed., *Écrits de Pierre Potier*, 278. On the production, reception, and limits of Jesuit writings in particular, see Greer, *Jesuit Relations*, 1–19; Berthiaume, "Fleurs de rhétorique"; True, *Masters and Students*.

23 Chauchetière, *Narration annuelle*; *JRAD* 63: 244; BNF, 13516, f.43v, Belmont, "Recueil de pièces sur l'histoire du Canada," and *Histoire du Canada*, 35.

24 On the sources, methods, challenges, and rewards of ethnohistory, see Havard, *Empire et métissage*, 21–30; Delâge, "Premières nations," 521–7; Fixico, *Rethinking American Indian History*; Krech, "State of Ethnohistory"; Axtell, "Ethnohistory"; Carmack, "Ethnohistory"; Barber and Berdan, *Emperor's Mirror*.

25 In the final decades of the French Regime the term *domicilié* was on rare occasion also applied to some groups in the interior, such as the Illinois or Tamarois. See, for example, ANOM, C11A 75: 214–214v, Jean-Paul Mercier to Beauharnois (?), 27 May 1741.

26 Ferris, *Archaeology*; Alfred, *Heeding Voices*, 18–19.

27 Cf. Green, "New People"; Richter, *Ordeal*; Blanchard, "Patterns of Tradition and Change," esp. 134–78; Parmenter, *Edge of Woods*.

28 See Havard, *Great Peace*; Brandão and Starna, "Treaties of 1701," 209–44.

CHAPTER ONE

1 Lothrop et al., "Early Human Settlement."

2 Thwaites, ed., *JRAD* 12:134.

3 Boyd, "Northernmost Precontact Maize."

4 The name Mistigoches and its variants, given as a result of their initial contacts, stuck well through the French Regime. On its use, see Champlain, *Works*, 2: 121; Campeau, ed., *MNF* 2: 421; Sagard, *Grand Voyage*, 148; Silvy, *Dictionnaire montagnais-français*, 104; Laure, *Apparat français-montagnais*, 419; Vincent, "Les sources orales innues," 5; Daviault, *L'Algonquin*, 198.

5 See for example Jetten, *Enclaves amérindiennes*; Ronda, "Sillery Experiment."

6 [2] *JRAD* 11: 88. Along similar lines, see ibid., 16: 110; 24: 254; 25: 110.

7 Scholars have generally failed to acknowledge the fluidity of the categories "Algonquin" and "Montagnais" in the early seventeenth century. Hubert and Savard are among the few to do so, in *Algonquins*, 23.

8 *JRAD* 23: 302–4. See also ibid., 54: 126.

9 Day, "Name 'Algonquin,'" 226–31.

10 Seventeenth- and eighteenth-century Jesuit sources consistently translate the term "Montagnais" with variations of Nehiraw-iriniw (lit. Nehiraw people), including Iriniou or irini8, and designate their language Nehirawewin. Silvy, *Dictionnaire montagnais-français*, 89; Fabvre, *Racines montagnaises*, 188; Laure, *Apparat français-montagnais*, 547; *JRAD* 7: 23, 153. See also Bishop, "Qu'y a-t-il de si drôle dans la chasse au canard?," 40–1; Brousseau, "Médianes en Nehirawewin," 5–23. Early Algonquin dictionaries are comparably rare. Nehiroïsik and Ŏtichkŏagami appear in Aubin, "Algonquin-French Manuscript," 10. Ŏtichkŏagami is glossed there as "*ceux de vis à vis du lac*." André, whose Odawa dictionary is understood to have been compiled from earlier Algonquian dictionaries, similarly translates Algonquin as "Outiskouagami." Variants of this term, which is understood to refer to peoples "who are at the end of the lake," also appear in the *Jesuit Relations* for 1671 ("Outiskoüagami"), Baraga's Ojibwe dictionary ("Odishkwagami"), as well as in Laure's Montagnais dictionary ("Utiskuagameu"). The meaning may have shifted by the nineteenth century. Cuoq's 1885 dictionary explains that this was the name given to the Nipissings by the Algonquins, "who apparently considered Lake Nipissing [...] as the last body of water." Both Cuoq and Lemoine, reflecting nineteenth-century usage among the Algonquins of the Lake of Two Mountains and Ottawa River, translate Algonquin as "Omamiwinini." There is thus cause to believe that this term, which means, "those who are downstream" or "downriver people," came from the Nipissings who cohabitated with the Algonquins at the Lake of Two Mountains mission beginning in the eighteenth century. Indeed, linguists take the Algonquin spoken at that mission in Cuoq's time and still spoken today in communities like Kitigan Zibi as reflecting Nipissing speech; and from the perspective of Lake Nipissing, from whence they

came, the Ottawa River and its peoples are indeed situated downstream. Cuoq and Lemoine give "Anicinabe" a more general meaning of both man/human and *Sauvage* or "man *par excellence.*" Meanwhile Nicolas's nominally "Algonquin" grammar, which in reality presents the language spoken by Great Lakes Algonquians, contains a reference to the term "*Irini*" for "man" but no other endonym. See *JRAD* 55: 148; Laure, *Apparat français-montagnais*, 47; Cuoq, *Lexique de la langue algonquine*, 48, 193, 290, 298, 314; Cuoq, *Lexique de la langue iroquoise*, 42; Lemoine, *Dictionnaire Français-Algonquin*, 49; AJC, Louis André, "Préceptes, phrases et mots de la langue algonquine outaouoise pour un missionnaire nouveau," 39; Baraga, *Dictionary of the Otchipwe Language*, 313; Daviault, *L'Algonquin*, 529; Goddard, "Central Algonquian Languages," 583; Day, "Nipissing," 791. Of additional interest is the fact that Montagnais appears as "Magotihirini" in André and "Pakwagami" (a reference to "flat lake" people) in Cuoq. Laure, *Apparat français-montagnais*, 47; AJC, Louis André, "Préceptes, phrases et mots de la langue algonquine outaouoise pour un missionnaire nouveau," 526 ; Cuoq, *Lexique de la langue algonquine*, 324.

11 *JRAD* 5: 115.

12 See, for example, ibid., 21: 116; Charest, "Montagnais ou Innus," 38–9.

13 *JRAD* 29:144. See also Chamberlain, *Terra incognita*, 7–150.

14 For an overview of the location and political history of Algonquin groups, see Ratelle, "Location of the Algonquins," 41–68; Viau, "Les dieux de la Terre," 109–32; Cellard, "Kichesippi," 67–84; Pendergast, "Ottawa River Algonquin Bands," 63–136. On Algonquian lifeways and worldviews, see Beaulieu, *Convertir les fils*, 21–36; Anderson, *Betrayal of Faith*, 11–62; Savard, *Algonquin Tessouat*, 20–5; Mailhot, *Pays des Innus*, 123–53; Leroux, "Cosmologie," 20–106. On language, see Brousseau, "Médianes en Nehirawewin," 14–15; Cowan, "Philological Spadework," 49–50.

15 *JRAD* 23: 302–4. Subsequent colonial observers would use the labels of (upper, i.e. upriver) "Algonquins supérieurs" and (lower) "Algonquins inférieurs" to describe these two, but these terms were employed haphazardly, with some authors using the latter to describe the Montagnais. Ibid., 54: 126.

16 Ibid.

17 Ibid.

18 See "*8tenau*," "*outen*," "*outen, outénau*," and "*otenaw*" in Silvy, *Dictionnaire montagnais-français*, 115; Daviault, *Algonquin*, 178; AJC, Louis André, "Préceptes, phrases et mots de la langue algonquine outaouoise pour un missionnaire nouveau," 799 ; Cuoq, *Lexique de la langue algonquine*, 312–13.

19 Laberge, *Affiquets, matachias et vermillon*, 131–9.

20 Rogers, "Band Organization," 35; Gélinas, *Gestion de l'Étranger*, 81–2.
21 See, for example, chapter 2, note 22.
22 Delâge, "Kebhek," 107–9; Vincent and Bacon, *Récit*; Chrétien, Delâge, and Vincent, *Croisement de nos destins*; Martijn, "Gepèg," 51–64. The name of the site is spelled "*8abistig8ïak*" in Silvy's *Dictionnaire montagnais-français*, 97; Cuoq, writing in the nineteenth century, provides Wabitikweiang and Kipwatikweiang in *Lexique de la langue algonquine*, 411.
23 Champlain, *Works*, 2: 44, 52; 3: 174, 205–6.
24 See for example *JRAD* 13: 14; 21: 238, 242, 246; 27: 36, 40, 54; Fox and Garrad, "Hurons in an Algonquian Land," 125–6.
25 Champlain, *Works*, 2: 276.
26 Black, *Algonquin Ethnobotany*; Clément, *L'ethnobonanique montagnaise*; Doolittle, *Cultivated Landscapes*; Minnis, "Domesticating People."
27 Champlain, *Works*, 2: 57, 276. For challenges to the traditional dichotomy between Algonquian foragers and Iroquoian farmers, see Hart, "Maize Agriculture Evolution"; Hart and Lovis, "Reevaluating What We Know"; Fox and Garrad, "Hurons in an Algonquian Land"; Hall, "Maliseet Cultivation."
28 Silvy, *Dictionnaire montagnais-français*, 69, 71; Bishop and Brousseau, "End of the Jesuit Lexicographic Tradition," 305.
29 *JRAD* 22: 206.
30 Tremblay, ed., *Saint Lawrence Iroquoians*; Chapdelaine, "Review"; Engelbrecht, "Northern New York Revisited"; Kuhn, "Reconstructing Patterns of Interaction"; Gates-St-Pierre, "Critical Review"; Pendergast, "Ottawa River Algonquin Bands."
31 *JRAD* 12: 132; 22: 206, 214–16. On the landscape of Montreal Island, see Loewen, "Paysage boisé," 10–12.
32 *JRAD* 12: 132; 22: 214–16; 29: 146; Champlain, *Works*, 2: 176.
33 *JRAD* 8: 26–8.
34 Ibid., 8: 26–8; 12: 132; 22: 206, 214–16; 22: 214–16.
35 Champlain, *Works*, 2: 280–1.
36 Ibid., 2: 175–9.
37 Ibid., 2: 280–1.
38 Ibid., 10: 210. See also ibid., 3: 131; Le Clercq, *Premier établissement*, 1: 222–3.
39 *MNF* 1: 82; Lescarbot, *Conversion des sauvages*, 29–30; Deslandres, *Croire et faire croire*, 216–28.
40 Sagard, *Grand Voyage*, 448–50, and *Histoire*, 1: 56–8; Le Clercq, *Premier établissement*, 1: 92–100. On the Recollet missions, see Galland, *Pour la gloire de Dieu*, 49–80, 277–307; Deslandres, *Croire et faire croire*, 235–45.
41 Champlain, *Works*, 2: 44, 52; 3: 174, 205–6. Trudel, *HNF* 3, 1: 4.

42 Le Clercq, *Premier établissement*, 1: 133–4.
43 Beaulieu, "'L'on n'a point d'ennemis plus grands que ces sauvages,'" 367–85.
44 See Sagard, *Histoire*, 1: 310, 435–40, 532–4; 2: 525, 534–59; 3: 636; 4: 829, 856; Champlain, *Works*, 5: 212; *JRAD* 18: 185–7; *MNF* 2: 843–4.
45 Champlain, *Works*, 5: 60–2. On Miristou/Mahigan Aticq Ouche, see Wilfrid Jury, "Miristou," in *DCB* 1: 508–9; *HNF* 2: 358–60; *MNF* 2: 840.
46 Champlain, *Works*, 5: 60–2; *JRAD* 4: 194.
47 *JRAD* 4: 80–8, 196–214.
48 See Sagard, *Histoire*, 1: 310, 435–40, 532–4; 2: 525, 534–59; 3: 636; 4: 829, 856; Champlain, *Works*, 5: 212; *JRAD* 18: 185–7; *MNF* 2: 843–4.
49 *JRAD* 4: 194; Sagard, *Histoire*, 4: 884–5, 892; Champlain, *Works*, 6: 42. Negabamat, who would go on to acquire considerable importance, is here called Neogabinat and Onageabemat. For evidence of other family bands establishing seasonal encampments near the French, see Champlain, *Works*, 6: 50; Le Clercq, *Premier établissement*, 1: 261, 286; *JRAD* 4: 194; Sagard, *Histoire*, 2: 532–42; 3: 543, 636. On the occupation of the Quebec region, see Chrétien, Delâge, and Vincent, *Au croisement de nos destins*, esp. 49–53. On Chomina (Choumin), La Nasse, and Manitougache (Manitougatche, Manitoucharche, Manitouchatche), see Sagard, *Histoire*, 4: 885; Champlain, *Works*, 6: 49–66, 50; *JRAD* 5: 56, 92–4, 102–6, 110, 120–2, 162; 6: 118–24; Anderson, *Betrayal of Faith*, 128, 147–57; Thomas Grassman, "Manitougatche," *DCB* 1: 487–8.
50 *JRAD* 6: 148; 8: 56.
51 *HNF* 2: 407–34.
52 Sagard, *Histoire*, 2: 519.
53 *Édits, ordonnances royaux*, 7; ANOM, C11A 1: 79-84, "Articles accordés par le cardinal de Richelieu à la Compagnie de la Nouvelle-France dite des Cent-Associés," 1627. See also Havard, "Les forcer à devenir citoyens." Belmessous, "Être français en Nouvelle-France," 511–14, and "Assimilation and Racialism," 33; Deslandres, *Croire et faire croire*, 278–80.
54 See Beaulieu, "La paix de 1624," 56–88; Trigger, "Mohawk-Mahican War," 276–86; Starna and Brandão, "Mohawk-Mahican War," 725–50.
55 On this episode, see *JRAD* 5: 106. For a similar occurrence, see ibid., 9: 114.
56 Ibid., 5: 106, 202–10. For another case of French houses being judged improper for women, see ibid., 7: 288–90. No clash with the Iroquois was recorded between mid-May 1632, when some Algonquins and Montagnais raided Mohawk country, and June of 1633, when Iroquois surprised some Frenchmen near Trois Rivières. See ibid., 5: 20, 26–8, 44, 48, 213–15, 251; 6: 4; 5: 20–8, 44–8, 92, 212–14, 250; 21: 20; Brandão, *Your Fyre Shall Burn No More*, appendix D.

57 Cf. *JRAD* 5: 202–10; 8: 54. On the mingled groups, see ibid., 23: 302–4.

58 *JRAD* 5: 202–10; *MNF* 2: 369, 452–5. On Capitanal (Kepitanal, Kepitenat), see *JRAD* 8: 54; *MNF* 2: 70, 369; Thomas Grassman, "Capitanal," *DCB* 1: 163–4; Hubert and Savard, *Algonquins*, 22–3; Cook, "Vivre comme frères," 340–1. For references to the name "Metaberoutin" or Metaber8tin, see for example Silvy, *Dictionnaire montagnais-français*, 71; Aubin, "Algonquin-French Manuscript," 10.

59 *JRAD* 5: 202–10.

60 Champlain, *Works*, 1: 98–101; Girard and Gagné, "Première alliance interculturelle." Such an offer of military assistance had a precedent in the alliances contracted by the French with Timucuan chiefs in Florida during the 1560s. See *HNF* 1: 202–8; Milanich, *Timucua*, 82–8. On Henri IV's policy regarding indigenous peoples, see Thierry, "Politiques amérindiennes."

61 *JRAD* 5: 202–10.

62 Ibid. Cf. Innu oral traditions as recorded in the twentieth century, in Vincent, "Sources orales innues," 59–68.

63 *JRAD* 5: 202–10.

64 Ibid., 5: 192.

65 Ibid., 5: 54, 92, 106, 132; 12: 142; 20: 260; Dollier de Casson, *Histoire du Montréal*, 86.

66 *JRAD* 11: 88; 16:110.

67 The reasons behind the Iroquois wars of the seventeenth century have been hotly debated. The argument that the wars of the Iroquois were motivated by economic considerations, the fur trade, and their desire to act as middle men, was first put forth by George Hunt. Daniel Richter and Roland Viau, while stressing the primacy of cultural motives, did not reject the notion that Iroquois warfare was in part motivated by the new economic context of the fur trade. Others have gone further and argued that very little evidence exists to support the economic explanation: Matthew Dennis contends that the Iroquois waged war entirely for defensive reasons, José Brandão emphasizes the will to make and adopt captives, and Craig Keener focusses upon vengeance and prestige. See Hunt, *Wars of the Iroquois*; Richter, "War and Culture," *Ordeal*, and *Facing East*, 50, 64, 66; Viau, *Enfants du néant*, esp. 17–43; Dennis, *Cultivating a Landscape*; Brandão, *Your Fyre Shall Burn No More*; Keener, "Ethnohistoric Perspective."

68 See Lanphear and Snow, "European Contact"; Snow, "Mohawk Demography," 163–9, 174; Warrick, "European Infectious Disease." On the notion of the "virgin soil" epidemic, compare Crosby, "Virgin Soil Epidemics," 289–99; and Jones, "Virgin Soils Revisited," 703–4.

69 For evidence of the correlation between epidemics and increased raiding, see Brandão, *Your Fyre Shall Burn No More*.

70 See Abler, "Beavers and Muskets," and "European Technology"; Keener, "Ethnohistorical Analysis"; Carpenter, "Making War More Lethal," 33–51. Cf. Given, *A Most Pernicious Thing*, and "The Iroquois Wars."

71 *JRAD* 8: 154–8; 9: 6.

72 Ibid., 3: 23, 59; 9: 65, 227, 235–7, 251–5; 10: 75–7; 12: 153–9, 181–3; 13: 83. On the peace of 1634, see Trigger, *Children of Aataentsic*, 485–98; Savard, *Algonquin Tessouat*, 90–5.

73 *JRAD* 12: 160–6. On Makheabichtichiou (Makeabichtichiou, Makhatewebichtichi, Makhate8ebichtichit, Makeabichtichiban, Makheubichtigiou), see ibid., 11: 110–12, 148–82, 224, 238–40, 244, 250–66; 12: 14–16, 20, 30, 140, 148–50, 160–4, 172, 178; 14: 130–2, 264, 274; 20: 208–10; 21: 67; Thomas Grassman, "Makheabichtichiou," *DCB* 1: 481–2.

74 *JRAD* 12: 160–6.

75 Ibid. The chief in question was Tchimiouiriniou (Thimeouiriniou, Tchimaouirineou, Tchimiouirineau, Tchimawirini), who bore the hereditary surname of Batiscan (Batisquan, Baptiscan). See *JRAD* 6: 128–32; Sulte, "Le Nom 'Batiscan'"; Elsie McLeod Jury, "Batiscan," *DCB* 1: 80. Unlike his predecessor of the same name, he does not feature prominently in the record beyond this passing mention.

76 *JRAD* 12: 152–60.

77 Ibid., 12: 168–70.

78 Ibid., 12: 172–4. On Jean-Baptiste Etinechkawat (Etinechkaëuat, Etinechkaëuant Etinechkaouat, Etinechkavat, Etinechka8at, Erinechkwat, Etineska8at, Etineschka8at), see ibid., 12: 172, 180; 16: 134–46; 18: 96, 170, 180; 21: 70; 22: 132; 23: 308, 316; 24: 36, 66; 25: 134–6, 158; 27: 102, 234, 238; 28: 214; 30: 164; 31: 236; 32: 90; 35: 46; 37:100; 38: 50; Hébert, *Registre de Sillery*, 94, 100–1, 103–4, 106, 115, 121, 126, 132, 136; Campeau, *Catastrophe démographique*, 107–8, 114, 116–17. On his Attikamek origins, see *JRAD* 24: 66 and 29: 66. On François-Xavier Nenaskoumat (Nenask8mat, Ne nak8mat), who appears to have also borne the surname "François Boulé," see *JRAD* 12: 172; 14: 134–46; 16: 64, 78–82, 84, 96; 18: 178; 28: 172, 276, 316; 29: 80–2; Hébert, *Registre de Sillery*, 93.

79 *JRAD* 16: 50–2. See also ibid., 15: 230.

80 Ibid., 18: 216–18.

81 Jetten, *Enclaves amérindiennes*, 38.

82 *JRAD* 31: 284–86; 32: 238; 35: 236–40; Boily, "Terres amérindiennes," 34–43; Sulte, "Fief Pachirini."

83 *JRAD* 31: 284.

84 Ibid., 20: 70–272.
85 Evidence of this can be seen in, for example, *JRAD* 16: 50–2.

CHAPTER TWO

1 On Chomina, see Sagard, *Histoire*, 4: 885; Champlain, *Works*, 6: 49–66; 50; Thwaites, ed., *JRAD* 5: 56, 92–4, 102–6, 110, 120–2, 162; 6: 118–24.
2 In a dictated letter to Le Jeune, Negabamat refers to "Ka-Miskouaouangachit, which you call St. Joseph." *JRAD* 38: 64. It appears as "ka mik8a8agachik" and "Ka Mikuaugachit" in Fathers Fabvre and Laure's dictionaries, where it is described as a reference to "*sable rouge*." See Fabvre, *Racines montagnaises*, 152; Laure, *Apparat français-montagnais*, 702. Father Silvy for his part, translates "kamik8agachik" as "*rivière au sable rouge.*" Silvy, *Dictionnaire montagnais-français*, 74. Cf. Jean-Baptiste Ferland, "Notes sur les environs de Québec" (1855), quoted in Gaumond, "Premiers résultats," 63. The mistaking of the character "8" for "d" has also led to the erroneous transcriptions "Kamiskda d'Angachit" and "Kamskda d'Angachit." Cf. *Pièces et documents relatifs à la Tenure Seigneuriale*, 50–1. For a brief overview of the fisheries on this site, see Pouliot, "La Pêche." On the ancient nature of the Indigenous occupation of the site, see Gaumond, "Premiers résultats," 70; Robert, "Le site de l'ancienne mission"; Cloutier, "La mission des Jésuites"; Cloutier, "Inventaire et surveillance archéologique"; Rouleau, "Inventaire archéologique."
3 *JRAD* 14: 204–16; 27: 276. See also Hébert, *Registre de Sillery*, 92.
4 *JRAD* 23: 302–18. On ethnic diversity there, see ibid., 25: 152.
5 Beaulieu, *Convertir les fils*, 134–5.
6 The recent interpretation according to which Tekouerimat means "he who remembers his people" appears unsubstantiated. Compare Silvy, *Dictionnaire montagnais-français*, 150 and back cover.
7 Lescarbot, *History of New France*, 3: 463
8 Anon., *Vie de l'illustre serviteur de Dieu*, 71–4, 164–8; *JRAD* 14: 204–6. For a chronicle of the mission's funding, see Jetten, *Enclaves amérindiennes*, 56–61; Beaulieu, *Convertir les fils*, 139. On Sillery, the man, see Dorion-Poussart, "Noël Brûlart de Sillery," 15–27.
9 Campeau, "Fief des Sauvages," 12; *JRAD* 14: 204–16; Hébert, *Registre de Sillery*, 92. The mission's subsequent insertion into the seigneurial system would cause problems which will not be covered here. See Lavoie, *C'est ma seigneurie*, 19–69; Boily, "Terres amérindiennes," 27–87. On De Gand, see Raymond Douville, "Derré de Gand, François," *DCB* 1: 262–3.
10 *JRAD* 9: 50–2 (retranslated); 6: 148–52; 8; 26–8.

11 "Mémoire touchant la Pêche de l'Anguille à la Pointe à Puiseaux," 1651, cited in Gardette, "Le processus de revendication huron," 2: 16–18; Campeau, ed., *MNF* 7: 681–2.

12 Silvy, *Dictionnaire montagnais-français*, 74; *JRAD* 12: 232.

13 Robert, "Site de l'ancienne mission."

14 *JRAD* 16: 134–46.

15 Ibid., 14: 204–16; 27: 276. See also Hébert, *Registre de Sillery*, 92.

16 Jaenen, *Friend and Foe*, 177–8; Jetten, *Enclaves amérindiennes*, 15–33; Greer, "Towards a Comparative Study." The scholarship on the early missionary program in New France is abundant. In particular, see Deslandres, *Croire et faire croire*; Galland, *Pour la gloire de Dieu*; Anderson, *Betrayal of Faith*; Beaulieu, *Convertir les fils*; Jetten, *Enclaves amérindiennes*, 15–62. Regarding South American experiences, see Anderson, "'They Should Be Ashamed to Eat"; and Ganson, *Guarani*.

17 *JRAD* 5: 32; 12: 220; 16: 140; *MNF* 4: 55. Abé, "Missionary Réductions."

18 Hébert, *Registre de Sillery*, 27.

19 Abé, "Missionary Réductions," and *Jesuit Mission*; Greer, "Towards a Comparative Study."

20 Silvy, *Dictionnaire montagnais-français*, 110.

21 *JRAD* 16:134.

22 The name Tekouerimat (Tek8erimat, Tekwerimat, Tecouerimat, Takwirimath, Tecouërimat, Tekwerimatch, Tekwirimaeth, Teykorimat, Thekwarimat) was applied to a succession of four headmen at Sillery: Noël Negabamat (died in 1666), Charles Negaskaouat alias Nita8abistinagan (died in 1675), and Michel (confirmed 1682, died in 1685). A Theodore Tekouerimat is also mentioned (died in 1669). Charles's son Louis was baptized in 1674. See *JRAD* 52: 60–8, 222–6; 53: 60; 60: 250; 62: 32, 52; Crespieul, *Pretiosa Mors*; Hébert, *Registre de Sillery*, 31–2, 78, 104, 223, 248–9, 288, 293; Bigot, *Relation*, 13–15; PRDH, Répertoire des actes d'état civil, 1621–1799, Record #30553, Burial of Michel Terourimah [*sic*], 23 January 1685 (http://www.genealogie.umontreal.ca). On the Tekouerimat "dynasty," see also Savoie and Tanguay, "Nœud de l'ancienne amitié," 40; Campeau, *Catastrophe démographique*, 114–17, 127–8.

23 See Clastres, *Society Against the State*, 21; Morantz, "Northern Algonquian Concepts"; Rogers, "Band Organization," 21–50.

24 *JRAD* 16: 100; Hébert, *Registre de Sillery*, 92–3.

25 *JRAD* 16: 100–10; 18: 95–107.

26 Ibid., 16: 100–10.

27 On this cemetery, see Gaumond, "Premiers résultats," 64–7, 70; Gagné, "Réduction de Sillery: étude paléoanthropologique," "Réduction de Sillery: Examen ostéoarchéologique," 103–21, and "Impact des maladies," 17–28.

28 *JRAD* 16: 136–46. For the impact of epidemics on North American Indigenous populations, see for example Crosby, *Columbian Exchange*; McNeill, *Plagues and Peoples*; Dobyns, *Their Number Become Thinned*.
29 On the arrival of Kichesipirini, see *JRAD* 18: 92.
30 Ibid., 18: 98–100. On Étienne Pigarouich (Pigarouik), see Elsie McLeod Jury, "Étienne Pigarouich," in *DCB* 1: 548–9.
31 *JRAD* 18: 100–6.
32 Juchereau de Saint-Ignace, *Histoire de l'Hôtel Dieu*, 19–23.
33 Ibid., 25–7, 31; Gaumond, *Premier hôpital*. For the use of "Anse du Couvent," see, for example, the map of Saint Joseph and Sillery coves by Jeremiah McCarthy, BANQ-Q, CN301, S230, D244A, "Plan exact de la seigneurie de Monceaux appartenant à M.A. Panet écuier, seigneur de la dite seigneurie, est sise et située dans la seigneurie de Sillery appartenant aux Rev. Pères Jésuites"; Bernier, *Le vieux Sillery*, 34.
34 Juchereau de Saint-Ignace, *Histoire de l'Hôtel Dieu*, 22, 27–9. They kept only four servants in 1643, to cut their costs. Ibid., 44.
35 Ibid., 22.
36 Ibid., 40–1.
37 See, for example, "Mémoire touchant la Pêche de l'Anguille à la Pointe à Puiseaux, près Québec, dressé par les RR. PP. Jésuites en faveur des Sauvages chrétiens de Sillery," 1650, cited in Gardette, "Le processus de revendication huron," 2: 16–18.
38 *JRAD* 24: 38–40
39 Juchereau de Saint-Ignace, *Histoire de l'Hôtel Dieu*, 50–61.
40 Ibid., 28; *JRAD* 28: 238.
41 Juchereau de Saint-Ignace, *Histoire de l'Hôtel Dieu*, 49–50.
42 Ibid., 30–1.
43 Hébert, ed., *Registre de Sillery*, 128.
44 *JRAD* 23: 304–8; Juchereau de Saint-Ignace, *Histoire de l'Hôtel Dieu*, 27, 44–5, 48–9.
45 Juchereau de Saint-Ignace, *Histoire de l'Hôtel Dieu*, 43–4.
46 Ibid., 50–61.
47 *JRAD* 30: 172, 283–8; 31: 138, 170–80, 192–4; 32: 256; AJCF, Barthèlemy Vimont, "De la chapelle de Sillery," [1647], 184; *MNF* 7: 35; Oury, ed., *Marie de l'Incarnation*, 330–1. Additional insights on the Jesuit compound can be gleaned from the archaeological record. See Robert, "Site de l'ancienne mission"; Cloutier, "Mission des Jésuites," and "Inventaire et surveillance"; Rouleau, "Inventaire archéologique."
48 *JRAD* 7:152–4.
49 Ibid.,11: 240–2.
50 Ibid., 25: 264; 27: 156; Cook, "Vivre comme frères," 476–84; Morrison, "Bap-

tism and Alliance"; Steckley, "Warrior and Lineage"; Greer, "Conversion and Identity," 182–3, and *Mohawk Saint*, 51–3; Clair, "'Seeing Good Souls,'" 285–8.

51 *JRAD* 18:110.

52 Ibid., 18: 110; 20: 188; 26: 128–32.

53 Ibid., 21: 82; Hébert, ed., *Registre de Sillery*, 37. On George Neapmat alias Etouet (Etouait, Estwet, Etwet), see *JRAD* 26: 156–8, 162; 28: 204; 30: 180; 32: 267–70; Campeau, *Catastrophe démographique*, 119. On his predecessor, see *JRAD* 12: 18; 18: 190.

54 BANQ-Q, Fonds Seigneurie de Sillery, 1637-1952, ZQ123, "Concession par les Religieuses de l'Hôtel-Dieu aux Sauvages de Tadoussac," 12 July 1642.

55 *JRAD* 32: 270.

56 Ibid., 20: 276–8.

57 Ibid., 24: 66; 25: 152; 29: 66.

58 Trigger, *Children of Aataentsic*, 610–17.

59 Hébert, *Registre de Sillery*, 38, 112; *JRAD* 22: 135–53; 24: 102–20; 25: 243; Trigger, *Children of Aataentsic*, 614–15.

60 *JRAD* 20: 214–20; Trigger, *Children of Aataentsic*, 633.

61 For evidence of these early links between the Saint Lawrence valley and Abenaki country, see Champlain, *Works*, 1: 103, 109, 298, 320; 5: 313–16; 6: 43–5; *JRAD* 12: 187–9 (quote); 20: 117; 28: 215, 229; 29: 67–9. Also Sévigny, *Abénaquis*, 64–6; and Savoie and Tanguay, "Nœud de l'ancienne amitié," 30–2.

62 *JRAD* 21:117.

63 Ibid., 21: 67–71; 25:117–19, 153.

64 Ibid., 25:152. For similar examples, see ibid., 18: 178–82.

65 Ibid., 23: 283; 24: 59–65, 159–61, 183–5; 25: 117–21, 153, 177–9; 28: 203–5, 215; 29: 67–71; 30: 179–80, 183, 195; 31: 183–207; 36: 83–9, 129; 37: 261; Druillettes, *Journal*, and "Rapport." On Druillettes, see Lucien Campeau's entry in *DCB* 1: 281–2. On missionary competition, see Codignola, "Competing Networks," 539–84.

66 Champlain, *Works*, 2: 280–1.

67 On the Tessouat lineage and on the name's third bearer in particular, see Savard's thorough *Algonquin Tessouat*.

68 *JRAD* 18: 92; 20: 90–2, 154–6, 164–6.

69 Ibid., 20: 154–6, 164–6.

70 Ibid., 20: 164–6.

71 Ibid., 20: 290; 24:190; Elsie McLeod Jury, "Simon Pieskaret," *DCB* 1: 547–8.

72 *JRAD* 12: 132; 22: 206, 214–16; 29: 146

73 Ibid., 22: 214–16.

74 Ibid., 24: 230; Champlain, *Works*, 2: 280–1.
75 JRAD 21: 116.
76 Ibid., 22: 214–16.
77 Trudel, HNF 3, 1: 154–8.
78 Dollier de Casson, *Histoire*, 86–7; JRAD 24: 214–20, 230–40, 256; Savard, *Algonquin Tessouat*, 40–60.
79 JRAD 24: 252, 258–60.
80 Ibid., 25: 258–64; Savard, *Algonquin Tessouat*, 161.
81 JRAD 27: 238–44.
82 Ibid., 26: 60; 27: 238–44.
83 Ibid., 27: 246–305.
84 Ibid., 28: 148–50.
85 Ibid., 28: 276; 29: 82–4.
86 Ibid., 28: 148–52.
87 Ibid., 28: 168.
88 Ibid., 28: 290–302.
89 Ibid., 22: 268–84.
90 Ibid., 29: 144–54. Little is known about this Jean Tawiskaron (Tawizkaron, Ta8ichkaron), whose name bears a strong resemblance that of Tawiskara, the evil twin in Iroquoian mythology. In 1646 he was said to be "Captain of the Onontchataronons" (Iroquet). His band was ambushed by the Iroquois during the winter of 1647: he was killed, and only five members of his band were said to have escaped. See JRAD 29: 144; 30: 234–44. Even less is known about "Makate8anakisitch, Captain of the Mata8chkairini8ek" (Mataoueskarinis), who appears nowhere else in the *Relations*.
91 JRAD, 30: 160, 230–44; Oury, *Marie de l'Incarnation*, 325–7; Dollier de Casson, *Histoire*, 107; JRAD 30: 154.
92 JRAD 31: 138; 32: 256; MNF 7: 35.
93 JRAD 30: 172; 31: 170–80, 192–4. See also ibid., 30: 283–8; Oury, *Marie de l'Incarnation*, 330–1.
94 JRAD 32: 238.
95 Ibid., 33: 52–4.
96 Ibid., 35: 236–40; Boily, "Terres amérindiennes," 34–43; Sulte, "Fief Pachirini."
97 JRAD 34: 62; 36: 192–4; BANQ-Q, E21, S66, SS3, Ministère des Terres et Forêts, "Biens des Jésuites," UR 183, acc. 1960-01-038/189, Martin Bouvart and François Vaillant to Callière and Champigny, 20 September 1699. Three years earlier, the neophytes of La Conception had similarly decided to limit the access of the fort at Trois Rivières to Christians and catechumens. See JRAD 35: 236.

98 *JRAD* 36: 101–5, 129, 139–41; 38: 173–5; 40: 195–209; Druillettes, *Journal*, and "Rapport."

99 *JRAD* 37: 76–8; 38: 64–6.

100 Ibid., 60: 131; 62: 259–61; Saint-Vallier, *Estat présent*, 68. See also Campeau, *Catastrophe démographique*, 117; Jetten, *Enclaves amérindiennes*, 61; Ronda, "Sillery Experiment," 15.

101 *MNF* 8: 94.

102 *JRAD* 32: 270.

103 *MNF* 7: 682, 685.

104 *JRAD* 42: 262–6.

105 Ibid., 43: 48–50; Hébert, *Le Registre de Sillery*, 30.

106 *MNF* 7: 682, 685.

107 Cloutier, "Mission des Jésuites; Boily, "Terres amérindiennes," 56–68; Ronda, "Sillery Experiment," 8–9; Jetten, *Enclaves amérindiennes*, 61.

108 Boily, "Terres amérindiennes," 34–43; Trudel, *HNF* 4: 378–9, 677, and *Terrier du Saint-Laurent en 1663*, 331–2; Loranger, *Histoire de Cap-de-la-Madeleine*; Grabowski, "'Petit commerce,'" 109–11; Frontenac to Colbert, 14 November 1674, quoted in *RAPQ* 1926–1927: 75.

109 *JRAD* 49: 232–6; 52: 222–4; BANQ-Q, Fonds Conseil souverain, Jugements et délibérations, TP1, S28, P100, "Arrêt ordonnant que les sauvages subiront la peine imposée par les lois et ordonnances de France pour crime de meurtre et de viol, " 21 April 1664.

CHAPTER THREE

1 Heidenreich, *Huronia*, 91–103

2 The most satisfactory general account of the Huron dispersal is that given by Bruce Trigger, though for him and many other scholars of the Hurons the period after 1650 represents little more than a cursory epilogue to the history of Huronia. Labelle represents the exception. See Trigger, *Children of Aataentsic*, chaps., 8–11; Heidenreich, *Huronia*, 264–77; Labelle, *Dispersed But Not Destroyed*.

3 Thwaites, ed., *JRAD* 24: 297; Colden, *History of the Five Indian Nations* (1747), 10.

4 Raudot (*sic*, Silvy), *Relation par lettres*, 184. See also, for example, *JRAD* 36: 183–5; 43: 187–9.

5 Parker, *Constitution of the Five Nations*, 50–4; Fenton, *Great Law*, 63–97; Dennis, *Cultivating a Landscape*.

6 *JRAD* 35: 192.

7 Trudel, *HNF* 3, 2: 92.

8 "*Gannata*" and "*kanata*" in Bruyas and Cuoq's Mohawk dictionaries, respectively; "*ganataa*" in an anonymous seventeenth-century Onondaga dictionary. Bruyas, *Radical words*, 68; Cuoq, *Lexique de la langue iroquoise*, 10, 101; Shea, ed., *French-Onondaga Dictionary*, 102. For the Wendats, Sagard gives "*onihay*, *carhata*, *andata*," while Potier gives only "*andata*." Sagard, *Grand Voyage*, 433; Potier, "Huron Manuscripts," 448.

9 Heidenreich, *Huronia*, 107–218; Beaulieu, Béreau, and Tanguay, *Wendats*, 29–31; Abler, "Longhouse and Palisade"; Steckley, "Ethnolinguistic Look at the Huron Longhouse"; Englebrecht, *Iroquoia*, 68–110. The generalizations presented in these pages are arrived at from a reading of the primary sources, in conjunction with ethnohistorical studies. For the early seventeenth century, the social and cultural patterns for the Hurons are much better known than those of the Iroquois to the south, owing to the writing of French missionaries. Scholars are dependent on the ethnography of Huronia for early Iroquoia, the assumption being that the Iroquois and the Wendats were generally similar. Conversely, many of the major patterns so well understood for the nineteenth-century Iroquois are generally assumed to have been present among all the northern Iroquoians, including the Wendats.

10 Englebrecht, *Iroquoia*, 90–2, 96–9; Keener, "Ethnohistorical Analysis," 781–6.

11 *JRAD* 27: 64; 29: 246; Fenton, "Northern Iroquoian Culture Patterns," 297–302; Englebreght, *Iroquoia*, 9–33; Heidenreich, *Huronia*, 158–218; Beaulieu, Béreau, and Tanguay, *Wendats*, 33–52; Mann, *Iroquoian Women*, 186–238; Brown, "Economic Organization," 157–64.

12 Ibid; *JRAD* 16: 248; 19: 124; 54: 116–18

13 *JRAD* 54: 118 (my emphasis).

14 Lafitau, *Customs*, 1: 69.

15 Mann, *Iroquoian Women*; Englebrecht, *Iroquoia*; Steckley, *Eighteenth-Century Wyandot*, 171–201.

16 Tooker, "Northern Iroquoian Sociopolitical Organization"; Steckley, *Eighteenth-Century Wyandot*, 135–69; Fox, "Events," 65.

17 *JRAD* 16: 226.

18 Trigger, *Children of Aataentsic*, 30, 54–9, 156–63, 730–4, 789; Heidenreich, *Huronia*, 75–90, 264–77, 300–2; Steckley, *Words*, 23–46.

19 *JRAD* 16: 226; 18: 232; Heidenreich, *Huronia*, 20–2; Garrad, *Petun to Wyandot*, 25–9.

20 Fenton, *Great Law*, 17–239; Engelbrecht, *Iroquoia*, 129–44.

21 Fenton, "Locality," 35–54, and "North Iroquoian Culture Patterns," 306–9; Heidenreich, *Huronia*, 80–1.

22 On Iroquois mobility, see in particular Parmenter, *Edge of Woods*; Jordan, "Incorporation and Colonization"; Lafitau, *Customs*, 2: 70. For linguistic evi-

dence, see Bruyas, *Radical words*, 44; Cuoq, *Lexique de la langue iroquoise*, 101; Steckley "An Ethnolinguistic Look," 21.

23 Englebrecht, *Iroquoia*, 101–7; Heidenreich, *Huronia*, 213–15.

24 Ibid; Champlain, *Works*, 4: 304–5.

25 *JRAD* 36: 184–6

26 Mann, *Iroquoian Women*, 32–3; Lafitau, *Customs*, 1: 86.

27 A handful of scholars have pointed to these cross-cultural patterns, such as Savard, *Algonquin Tessouat*, 90–1, 100–1; Cook, "Vivre comme frères," 144–8.

28 The interpretation of warfare presented in these pages is arrived at from a reading of the primary sources, in conjunction with ethnohistorical studies focused on the specificities of war in the Northeastern Woodlands, and with the eclectic anthropological literature on warfare in small-scale societies. For an overview of warfare in the Northeastern Woodlands, see Havard, *Empire et métissage*, 145–66. For warfare among the northern Iroquoians, see Richter's seminal article, "War and Culture," and *Ordeal*, chap., 3. See also Viau, *Enfants du néant*; and Brandão, *Your Fyre Shall Burn No More*, chaps., 3–4; Keener, "Ethnohistoric Perspective," chaps., 3–8. For warfare in the Abenaki – and by extension the northeastern Algonquians – context, see Morrison, "Dawnland Dog-Feast"; Nash, "Abiding Frontier," 97–147, 264–306. For warfare in small-scale societies more generally, see Haas, *Anthropology of War*; Clastres, *Archeology of Violence,* and "Malheur du guerrier sauvage"; Ember and Ember, "Resource Unpredictability"; Ferguson, *Yanomami Warfare*; Rosaldo, "Grief and a Headhunter's Rage"; Désveaux, "Des Iroquois aux Tupinambas."

29 See Richter, "War and Culture," 528–59, and *Ordeal*, chap., 3; Viau, *Enfants du néant*; Brandão, *Your Fyre Shall Burn No More*, chaps., 3–4; Keener, "Ethnohistoric Perspective," chaps., 3-8. On captivity in particular, see also Starna and Watkins, "Northern Iroquoian Slavery."

30 Ferguson, "Explaining War," 36–8.

31 On the role of Iroquoian women, besides the sources listed above, see Magee, "'Life of the Nation.'"

32 Axtell and Sturtevant, "Unkindest Cut"; Viau, *Enfants du néant*, 110–18; Friederici, *Skalpieren*.

33 Lafitau, *Customs*, 2:152.

34 Morrison, "Dawnland Dog-Feast"; Nash, "Abiding Frontier," 264–306

35 Richter, "War and Culture," and *Ordeal*, chap., 3; Viau, *Enfants du néant*; Starna and Watkins, "Northern Iroquoian Slavery."

36 Richter, "War and Culture."

37 On Iroquoian cannibalism, see Richter, "War and Culture"; Viau, *Enfants du néant*, 179–83; Sanday, *Divine Hunger*, 125–50; Traphagan, "Embodiment";

Pilette, "S'allier en combattant"; Simonis, "Cannibalisme," 107–22. For the metaphorical language, see *JRAD* 27: 229; 40: 169; 41: 53; Bruyas, *Radical words*, 45; Schoolcraft, *Notes on the Iroquois*, 29.

38 *JRAD* 21: 20.

39 For the most detailed account of the offensive against Huronia, see Trigger, *Children of Aataentsic*, 725–88. See also Parmenter, *Edge of Woods*, 41–83; Bradley, *Evolution of the Onondaga Iroquois*, 182–4.

40 *JRAD* 33: 70–184; Dollier de Casson, *Histoire du Montreal*, 112–13; Trigger, *Children of Aataentsic*, 725–88.

41 On the Huron Confederacy and the respective importance of its constituent nations, see Trigger, *Children of Aataentsic*, 30, 54–9, 156–63, 730–44, 789; Heidenreich, *Huronia*, 75–90, 264–77, 300–2; Steckley, *Words*, 23–46. On Jean-Bapiste Atironta and his successors, and their identification as members of the Deer Clan based on eighteenth-century sources, see Steckley, *Eighteenth-Century Wyandot*, 31–3, 41–2, 232–3.

42 Trigger, *Children of Aataentsic*, 742–56.

43 *JRAD* 30: 222; 33: 68, 256; 34: 102, 226; Trigger, *Children of Aataentsic*, 739.

44 See for example *JRAD* 34: 24–34, 140–2.

45 On Huron clans, see Steckley, *Words*, 47–67, and "Clans and Phratries," 29–34; Trigger, *Children of Aataentsic*, 102. On Iroquoian clans more broadly, see Tooker, "Northern Iroquoian Sociopolitical Organization," 92–4, and "Clans and Moieties."

46 Oury, *Marie de l'Incarnation*, 323.

47 *JRAD* 35: 193; 41: 47.

48 The village established among the Senecas, known to the French as Saint Michel, named after the former mission to the Tahontaenrat, was almost certainly that of Gandougarae. *JRAD* 36: 143, 179; 44: 21; 45: 243; 57: 193. See also Trigger, *Children of Aataentsic*, 789–92; Jordan, "Incorporation and Colonization," 34–5.

49 *JRAD* 34: 222; 35: 192; Trigger, *Children of Aataentsic*, 776–9, 783, 789–97; Labelle, *Dispersed But Not Destroyed*, 49–98.

50 *JRAD* 17: 24–30; 35: 206–8.

51 Sullivan et al., eds., *Papers of Sir William Johnson*, 13: 624–5; Melsheimer, *Journal*, 167; Dooyentate, *Origin and Traditional History*, 1–7, 128. Cf. Radisson, *Collected Writings*, 169–73. On the linkages between the Wendats and Saint Lawrence Iroquoians, see Tremblay, ed., *Saint Lawrence Iroquoians;* Pendergast, "Ottawa River Algonquin Bands"; Steckley, *Gabriel Sagard's Dictionary,* and "Trade Goods and Nations." A speech, published in *L'Abeille*, the newspaper of the Petit Séminaire de Québec, in 1850, purportedly by the Wendats to Governor d'Ailleboust at Quebec upon their arrival and seem-

ingly supporting the Wendat claims of territorial precedence, is in fact betrayed by its style as an apocryphal nineteenth-century composition. Anon., "Quelques débris de la nation huronne."

52 See, for example, *JRAD* 30: 164, 172; 32: 160–2; 34: 62; Oury, *Marie de l'Incarnation*, 284–7; Trigger, *Children of Aataentsic*, 797; Beaulieu, Béreau, and Tanguay, *Wendats*, 27–8, 32–3, 59–62.

53 *JRAD* 12: 78–80. The claim, made over a century later by Étienne Girault de Villeneuve, that "a considerable number of Hurons [...] had been settled at Sillery" since the mission's beginning is unsubstantiated in period records. See ibid., 70: 207.

54 Ibid., 30: 220. See also Champlain, *Works*, 3: 171–2.

55 *JRAD* 34: 222; 35: 39, 202; Oury, *Marie de l'Incarnation*, 390.

56 *JRAD* 35: 182–94. Regarding the Huron refuge to Gahoendoe, see ibid., 34: 202–24; 35: 85–7. For Ragueneau's estimate of the population see ibid., 35: 86. See also Trigger, *Children of Aataentsic*, 770–88; Labelle, *Dispersed But Not Destroyed*, 49–67.

57 *JRAD* 35: 192–4.

58 Ibid., 35: 182–98, 208–14; 36: 58.

59 Ibid., 35: 208–14.

60 Ibid., 35: 39, 208–14; 36: 44, 54, 58; BANQ-Q, P1000, S3, file 814, Léonard Garreau, Response to Sieur de Beaulieu and Éléonore de Grandmaison, 1652; Jamet, ed., *Annales de l'Hôtel-Dieu*, 73–4. The latter chronicle appears to confuse the Hurons who wintered there in 1649–50 and those who arrived in the spring of 1650.

61 *JRAD* 40: 208; 37: 148; Beaulieu, Béreau, and Tanguay, *Wendats*, 63–5.

62 *JRAD* 35: 210; 36: 54–60.

63 Ibid., 36: 208–14. On Wendat girls among the Ursulines, see ibid., 35: 209; Deslandres, *Croire et faire croire*, 364–6; Labelle, *Dispersed But Not Destroyed*, 165–8.

64 *JRAD* 36: 214–16. On Louis Taiaeronk (Taieron, or Atharatou), see ibid., 41: 166–74; *MNF* 8: 996. On this particular speech, see also Poirier, *Religion, Gender, and Kinship*, 166–9.

65 *JRAD* 36: 214–20. On the fire, see also ibid., 35: 61.

66 Lafitau, *Customs*, I: 69; Trigger, *Children of Aataentsic*, 34–59; Labelle, *Dispersed But Not Destroyed*, 159–75; Steckley, *Eighteenth-Century Wyandot*, 171–201; Bonvillain, "Iroquoian Women," 47–58; Parmenter, *Edge of Woods*, xxvii, xxxvii–xlii.

67 Atironta can tentatively be deduced from later sources to have been a member of the Deer Clan, for example, but the evidence is not strong enough as to be able to make an argument about this particular clan's representation. See Steckley, *Eighteenth-Century Wyandot*, 31–3, 41–2, 232–3.

68 On the Hurons' settlement on the Island of Orleans, see *JRAD* 36: 116, 142, 186–90; 70: 207; BANQ-Q, P1000, S3, file 814, Garreau, Response to Sieur de Beaulieu ..., 1652; ASQ, Fonds Verreau 13, #13, Paul Ragueneau,"Raisons qui nous ont meu a faire eschange de nostre maison de l'Isle d'Orléans avec la concessions de M. de la Cytiere sise à la Pointe de Levy"; Chaumonot, *Missionnaire*, 109–10; Perrot, *Moeurs*, 330; Trudel, *Terrier du Saint-Laurent en 1663*, map 11 and 80–2; Trigger, *Children of Aataentsic*, 782–8; Boily, "Terres amérindiennes," 69–74; Beaulieu, Béreau, and Tanguay, *Wendats*, 102–5; Labelle, *Dispersed But Not Destroyed*, 106–7, 109. The stream appears on Villeneuve's maps, which shows the former site of the Huron fort. BNF, Département Cartes et plans, GE SH 18 PF 127 DIV 7 P 4, "Carte des Environs de Quebec," 1685–1686; BNF, Département Cartes et plans, GE SH 18 PF 127 DIV 7 P 5 D, "Carte des Environs de Québec," 1688.

69 *JRAD* 36: 116; BANQ-Q, P1000, S3, file 814, Garreau, Response to Sieur de Beaulieu ..., 1652; Jean-Jacques Lefebve, "Éléonore de Grandmaison," *DCB* I : 344–5; La Chevrotière, *Chavigny*, 13–29; Anon., " Le premier fort des Hurons à l'ile d'Orléans."

70 *JRAD* 36: 116; 70: 207; BANQ-Q, P1000, S3, file 814, Garreau, Response to Sieur de Beaulieu ..., 1652. For use of the word "colony," see *JRAD* 35: 214; 36: 202.

71 *JRAD* 37: 180 ("un réduit ou une espèce de fort"); Trudel, *HNF* 3-1: 202; Trudel, *Terrier du Saint-Laurent en 1663*, 80–2.

72 *JRAD* 36: 116 ; 37: 168–70, 180; Chaumonot, *Missionnaire*, 109–10 ; BANQ-Q, P1000, S3, file 814, Garreau, Response to Sieur de Beaulieu ..., 1652. Regarding the famine that preceded the dispersal, see *JRAD* 35: 82–6.

73 *Journaux de la Chambre*, 33: 89–91, 236, 269, 282, 330. Tsawenhohi's dating of this agreement to the mid-seventeenth century must be taken with a grain of salt, however, given that his statement reflected a blending together in the collective memory of several subsequent agreements. On the Hurons' insertion within the hunting territories of others, see Beaulieu, Béreau, and Tanguay, *Wendats*, 112–15.

74 Radisson, *Collected Writings*, 175; *JRAD* 35: 38; 36: 202; 41: 138. See also ibid., 36: 146; 37: 168; 44: 188; Trigger, *Children of Aataentsic*, 804.

75 For evidence of additional arrivals, see, for example, *JRAD* 36: 144, 178; Trigger, *Children of Aataentsic*, 791. For the estimate of the Huron population, see *JRAD* 41: 138. The claim that there were more refugees at the Island of Orleans – over seven hundred – is based on a misreading of the evidence. Compare Labelle, *Dispersed But Not Destroyed*, 109, and BANQ-Q, P1000, S3, file 814, Garreau, Response to Sieur de Beaulieu ..., 1652. The estimate of fifteen hundred for the French population at this time is that of Marcel Trudel. See Trudel, *HNF* 3, 2: 92.

76 On the clans of the predispersal Wendats, see Tooker, "Northern Iroquoian Sociopolitical Organization," 93; Heidenreich, *Huronia*, 78; Trigger, *Childen of Aataentsic*, 54. John Steckley instead makes a case for distinguishing the Large Turtle, Striped Turtle, and Prairie Turtle Clans, and for adding the Loon/Sturgeon and Fox Clans. Steckley, "Clans and Phratries," and *Eighteenth-Century Wyandot*, 40–50. For evidence of clans' persistence in the Saint Lawrence valley, see Franquet, *Voyages*, 107; Toupin, ed., *Écrits de Pierre Potier*, 279; Steckley, *Words*, 122–5, and "Tsa8enhohi." Regarding clans at Wendake in more recent times, and stressing their discontinuity through marriage with French women, see Gérin, "Huron de Lorette [2]," 43–7; Sioui, *Les Wendats*, 230; Delâge, "Hurons-Wendat de Lorette ou de Wendake"; Paul, "Organisation clanique."

77 See note 51 in this chapter. Dooyentate, *Origin and Traditional History*, 4–7.

78 On Atironta, see Steckley, *Eighteenth-Century Wyandot*, 31–2; on Atsena (Atchenha), ibid., *Words*, 30–2.

79 *Relations inédites* 1: 171–2.

CHAPTER FOUR

1 Thwaites, ed., *JRAD* 36: 116, 210, 214–16; Chaumonot, *Missionnaire*, 116.

2 For references to the "Island of Saint-Mary," see *JRAD* 36: 202; Chaumonot, *Missionnaire*, 109–10; Oury, *Marie de l'Incarnation*, 465–6. The wording of the first of these sources seems to indicate that the name of "the Island of Saint Mary" was an Indigenous innovation, rather than a missionary one. *Lawendawinen Tiatontarehi*, which first appears as *Laooendaoena Tiatoutarchi* on Nicolas Vincent's map of 1829, and its variants (*Laouendaeona Tiatoutarchi*, *La8endaona Tiatoutarchi*), have mistakenly been taken to mean "the hidden island" or "the island of escape." Roy Wright, personal communication to Jean-François Lozier, 9 August 2015; Wright, "Le Plan Vincent," 221; Poirier, ed., *La toponymie des Hurons-Wendats*, 17, 29.

3 *JRAD* 41: 138, 146–74; Chaumonot, *Missionnaire*, 118–22; Clair, *Du décor rêvé*, 229–39, and "Une chapelle," 6–9.

4 *JRAD* 36: 216.

5 "8endake ehen" in Potier, "Huron Manuscripts," 30; Heidenreich, *Huronia*, 21; Steckley, personal communication to Jean-François Lozier, 5 July 2017.

6 Quote in *JRAD* 43: 200.

7 Ibid., 43: 186–8; 45: 60.

8 Some scholars have thus explained the Mohawk-Onondaga tensions during the 1650s merely as a competition for primacy in diplomatic relations and trade with New France. Campeau, *Gannentaha*, 19–25; Jennings, *Ambiguous*

Iroquois Empire, 104–9; Gohier, *Onontio*, 94–111. Others have acknowledged the Huron stake without examining it closely. Richter, *Ordeal*, 108–9; Dennis, *Cultivating a Landscape*, 233. In emphasizing it, Parmenter represents an exception, *Edge of Woods*, 82–114.

9 See for example *JRAD* 35: 58; 36: 118–22, 132–4, 148, 188–90; 37: 94–6, 100, 104–10, 114–16; 38: 48, 52, 168–70, 176–8; Trigger, *Children of Aataentsic*, 805–6; Brandão, *Your Fyre Shall Burn No More*, appendix D.

10 For Huron victims, see *JRAD* 35: 58; 36: 132–4, 148; 37: 94–6, 100, 104, 110, 114–16; 38: 48, 52, 168–70, 176–8; Trigger, *Children of Aataentsic*, 805–6. For the activity of Huron warriors, see, for example, *JRAD* 38: 52; 40: 96.

11 *JRAD* 36: 142, 188; 38: 550; 40: 120; Oury, *Marie de l'Incarnation*, 621. For an earlier example, see *JRAD* 33: 118; 34: 24–34.

12 *JRAD* 38: 172–4, 178–80; 40: 88–92, 112–16, 164–90. See also Bruce G. Trigger, "Tekharihoken," *DCB* 2: 624–5.

13 Ibid., 38: 194; 40: 164–8.

14 Ibid., 38: 194; 40: 182–90.

15 Ibid., 40: 164–8.

16 Ibid., 41: 86–8; Oury, *Marie de l'Incarnation*, 550–1; Parmenter, *Edge of Woods*, 84–96.

17 *JRAD* 38: 196–8; 40: 190–2; 41: 44–8. On Teharihogen (Thearihogen, Tekarihoken), see Bruce Trigger, "Tekarihoken," *DCB* 2: 624–5.

18 *JRAD* 41: 18, 44–8. The captains are not named, but they may have included the aforementioned Louis Taiaeronk and Jacques Oachonk.

19 Ibid., 41: 18, 44–8; Van Laer, *Minutes of Court of Fort Orange*, 1: 90–2.

20 *JRAD* 41: 18–20.

21 Ibid., 41: 58.

22 Ibid., 41: 18–22, 50–64.

23 Ibid., 41: 60.

24 Ibid., 41: 60–2.

25 Ibid., 43: 78.

26 Ibid., 41: 18; 43: 40.

27 Ibid., 41: 64.

28 Ibid., 70: 205–7.

29 Ibid., 40: 234; 41: 164–70; Clair, "Du décor rêvé," 229–37, and "Notre-Dame de Foy," 168–75.

30 *JRAD* 42: 48–58.

31 The Thwaites edition is inaccurate in its translation that the governor "now extended to *the Iroquois* also a father's care." *JRAD* 42: 52–6 (my emphasis).

32 On the metaphors of kinship within the Franco-Indigenous alliance and their shift over time, see Cook, "Vivre comme frères," 488–90, and "Onontio

Gives Birth." In the fall of 1656, Father Le Moyne referred to the Wendats as the children of Onontio. And the following year, Mohawk delegates who sought the governor's sanction to carry away the Wendats adopted the same metaphor: "Onontio, ouvre tes bras & laisse aller tes enfans de ton sein." *JRAD* 43: 46, 188–90, 202–4, 212.

33 *JRAD* 42: 53, 57–9; 43: 127–33; Oury, *Marie de l'Incarnation*, 544–5; Campeau, *Gannentaha*, 21; Trigger, *Children of Aataentsic*, 808–9. Cf. Laflèche, *Saints martyrs canadiens* 5: 165.

34 *JRAD* 42: 53, 57–9; 43: 127–33; Oury, *Marie de l'Incarnation*, 544–5; Campeau, *Gannentaha*, 21; Trigger, *Children of Aataentsic*, 808–9; Lignereux, "Mission périlleuse."

35 *JRAD* 42: 92, 116–18, 135.

36 Ibid., 43: 128.

37 Ibid., 43: 104–12.

38 Ibid.

39 Ibid., 43: 134; Oury, *Marie de l'Incarnation*, 582–3. See also Campeau, *Gannentaha*, 19–25.

40 *JRAD* 43: 114, 134–6; Oury, *Marie de l'Incarnation*, 583–4. This episode bears striking resemblance to the attack of Le Moyne's embassy in the summer of 1654. See also ibid., 550–1.

41 *JRAD* 43: 114–22; Perrot, *Moeurs*, 343–5; Oury, *Marie de l'Incarnation*, 584. See also Radisson, *Collected Writings*, 175. Guy Laflèche makes the strong case that an embarrassed Paul Le Jeune delayed the publication of the account of the attack in the *Relation* for 1656 to avoid concluding it on a demoralizing note, and decided to publish it only in the following year in a purposefully confusing and misleading way. Laflèche, *Saints martyrs canadiens*, 5: 11, 18, 137–9.

42 Ibid.

43 *JRAD* 42: 32; 43: 142; Oury, *Marie de l'Incarnation*, 584. On Jacques Oachonk, who was tortured and killed in Iroquoia in early June, see *JRAD* 41: 166–75; and Campeau's biographical sketch in *MNF* 8: 985. On Joachim Ondakont, see *JRAD* 43: 118–22, 142–4; and Campeau in *MNF* 8: 986.

44 *JRAD* 43: 35; 45: 114, 244; 47: 248; 53: 121; 70: 207; 42: 32; 43: 142; Oury, *Marie de l'Incarnation*, 584.

45 "Raisons qui nous ont meu a faire eschange de nostre Maison de l'Isle d'Orléans avec la concession de M. de la Cytiere sise à la Pointe de Levy," 1656, cited in Boily, "Terres amérindiennes," 71–2 ; LAC, MG8-A23, vol. 112, "Contrat pour les terres désertées par les Hurons sur les concessions de Éléonore de Grandmaison et de Louis de Lauson de la Citière," 2 April 1659 (copy in *MNF* 9: 328–9); *JRAD* 47: 260; 53: 120; Trudel, *HNF* 3, 2: 383–4;

Boily, "Terres amérindiennes," 71–4 ; Beaulieu, Béreau, and Tanguay, *Wendats*, 104–5, 136–7. The converse claim that the Hurons abandoned their fields as a result of the relocation, and instead turned to hunting and fishing, is unsubstantiated. Cf. Jetten, *Enclaves amérindiennes*, 64.

46 *JRAD* 42: 260; 43: 268; 43: 186.

47 Ibid., 43: 32–42.

48 Ibid., 43: 44–6, 186, 190.

49 See ibid., 33: 116–26.

50 *JRAD* 41: 18; 43: 40.

51 Ibid., 34: 128; 36: 180–8; 37: 108. On the Iroquois's desire to avenge themselves for these actions, see ibid., 41: 56. There is a caveat here: Annaotaha's Attigneenongnahac national affiliation is based on strong circumstantial evidence, but never stated explicitly in the sources. For biographical sketches, see Steckley, *Untold Tales*; Elsie McLeod Jury, "Annaotaha," *DCB* 1: 64–5; Dickinson, "Annaotaha et Dollard."

52 *JRAD* 43: 42.

53 Ibid., 43: 190–4.

54 Ibid., 43: 192.

55 Ibid., 43: 49. Cf. Laflèche, *Saints martyrs canadiens*, 5: 172.

56 *JRAD* 43: 53–5; 44: 189.

57 Ibid., 43: 50; 44: 72–6, 154; Radisson, *Collected Writings*, 175–82, 198; Oury, *Marie de l'Incarnation*, 605; Steckley, *De Religione*, 128–9. The *Relation* mentions the killing of seven of the Huron men, while Marie de l'Incarnation speaks of the killing of thirteen adults and children, and the capture of forty.

58 For the estimate of the population, see Ragueneau's letter of 20 August 1658, in *MNF* 9: 190.

59 *JRAD* 43: 56–8; 44: 186–8; Oury, *Marie de l'Incarnation*, 605.

60 *JRAD* 43: 56–60; 44: 186–92; Oury, *Marie de l'Incarnation*, 605.

61 Oury, *Marie de l'Incarnation*, 614. For the Franco-Iroquois diplomacy see, for example, *JRAD* 44: 110, 120; 45: 84–6, 100; 46: 224.

62 *JRAD* 44: 98.

63 Ibid., 44: 103–5.

64 Ibid., 45: 94–6, 98, 106; Van Laer, *Minutes of Court of Fort Orange*, 2: 218; Brandão, *Your Fyre Shall Burn No More*, appendix D.

65 *JRAD* 45: 244–60; Oury, *Marie de l'Incarnation*, 622–4; Dickinson, "Annaotaha et Dollard"; Steckley, *Untold Tales*, chap., 3; Groulx, *Pièges de la mémoire*; Laflèche, *Saints martyrs canadiens*, 5: 187–260.

66 Oury, *Marie de l'Incarnation*, 624. There Ignace Tsaouenhohoui is mistakenly called *Eustache* Tha8onhoh8i.

67 Oury, *Marie de l'Incarnation*, 622–4; *JRAD* 45: 255; Dickinson, "Annaotaha et Dollard," 168; cf. Trigger, *Children of Aataentsic*, 817.

68 See supra, note 51. The defectors included Annaotaha's nephew, La Mouche (The Fly), whom John Steckley suggests may have been none other than the aforementioned Joachim Ondakont. Steckley, *Untold Tales.*

69 *JRAD* 46: 22–56, 120; Oury, *Marie de l'Incarnation*, 624–6. On casualties, see Laflèche, *Saints martyrs canadiens*, 5: 381.

70 *JRAD* 45: 156, 244. See also *MNF* 9: 426.

71 *JRAD* 47: 291.

72 Ibid., 48: 85–93.

73 Oury, *Marie de l'Incarnation*, 705; *JRAD* 48: 75–83; 49: 136–48; Richter, *Ordeal*, 98–102; Parmenter, *Edge of Woods*, 114–16; Brandão, *Your Fyre Shall Burn No More*, appendix D.

74 *JRAD* 46: 61–3.

75 Ibid., 55: 290–6.

76 Ibid., 36: 214; 45: 38–40; 49: 226–34. For another echo, see *MNF* 9: 218.

77 *JRAD* 45: 38–42.

78 On the royal reforms and troop dispatch, see Trudel, *HNF* 3, 1: 347–86; Trudel, *HNF* 4: 13–98; Verney, *Good Regiment.*

79 *JRAD* 49: 224–30.

80 Ibid.; Lozier, "Campagnes de Carignan-Salières." On the men, dress, and campaigning of the Carignan-Salières Regiment, see Verney, *Good Regiment.*

81 *JRAD* 49: 230–4.

82 Ibid., 49: 232–6.

83 Ibid., 50: 126–30; Salière, "Mémoire des choses qui se sont passées en Canada," in Roy and Malchelosse, *Régiment de Carignan*, 54–5. On the persistent peace overtures of the western Iroquois in 1665 and 1666, see *JRAD* 49: 176–8; Broadhead et al., eds., *NYCD* 3: 126–7; Salière, "Mémoires," in *Regiment de Carignan,* 62–3; Trudel, *HNF* 4: 191–2.

84 For the treaty of 13 December 1665, see BNF, Département des manuscrits, Baluze 196, "Recueil de traités de paix" (or in translation, *NYCD* 3: 121–5).

85 Ibid.

86 ANOM, C11A 2: 127–128v, Talon to Colbert, 27 April 1665; *JRAD* 50: 130–48, 168, 180–6; René-Louis Chartier de Lotbinière, "Sur le voyage de monsieur de Courcelles," in Lortie, *Textes poétiques*, 1: 53–63; Salière, "Mémoire," in Roy and Malchelosse, *Régiment de Carignan*, 54–8; Trudel, *HNF* 4: 180–9.

87 For the ratification by the Senecas on 22 May 1666 and by the Oneida and Mohawks on 7 July 1666, see BNF, Département des manuscrits, Baluze 196, "Recueil de traités de paix" (or in translation, *NYCD* 9: 44–7); *JRAD* 124–36, 190.

88 *NYCD* 3: 131, 134; *JRAD* 50: 138, 192, 196; Salière, "Mémoire," in Roy and Malchelosse, *Régiment de Carignan*, 62–3; Perrot, *Mœurs*, 354.

89 *JRAD* 50: 138–40, 198–200.

90 ANOM, C11A 2: 207-213v, "Mémoire de Talon à Tracy et Courcelle pour montrer qu'il est actuellement plus avantageux de faire la guerre aux Agniers que de conclure la paix avec eux," 1 September 1666. This appears to be the earliest iteration of what would become the standard colonial policy in the last decades of the century. See also ANOM, C11A 2: 127-128v, Talon to Colbert, 27 April 1665. On the preparation of the expedition, see ANOM, C11A 2: 207213v, Talon to Tracy and Courcelle, 1 September 1666.

91 *JRAD* 50: 140; Salière, "Mémoires," in Roy and Malchelosse, *Régiment de Carignan*, 64; Oury, *Marie de l'Incarnation*, 772, 774; Trudel, *HNF* 4: 195–202.

92 *JRAD* 50: 142–4, 202–4; *NYCD* 3: 135; ANOM, C11A 2: 214–15, Talon to Louis XIV, 11 November 1666; Salière, "Mémoires," in Roy and Malchelosse, *Régiment de Carignan*, 64; Oury, *Marie de l'Incarnation*, 773–6.

93 *JRAD* 50: 144.

94 *NYCD* 3: 136-7; *JRAD* 50: 205-9; Oury, *Marie de l'Incarnation*, 775–6, 786–7.

CHAPTER FIVE

1 Thwaites, ed., *JRAD* 52: 36, 228, 236; 53: 130; 54: 286–8; 70: 206; Chaumonot, *Missionnaire*, 174–5; Clair, "Notre-Dame de Foy," 175–89; Boily, "Terres amérindiennes," 74–6; Beaulieu, Béreau, and Tanguay, *Wendats*, 71, 77, 105, 137.

2 *JRAD* 36: 143; 44: 21; 54: 79; 57: 193. The identity of the Onnontioga (Onnontiogas, Onnontiogats) is a mystery. The name has erroneously been understood to mean the "people of Onontio," or allies of the French from the Saint Lawrence valley. Cf. Hodge, *Handbook of American Indians North of Mexico*, 3:129. In fact, the *Jesuit Relations* point out that like the Senecas and Neutrals, the Onnontioga "have scarcely seen any Europeans." They were thus a western nation: the Wenros or Eries, Iroquoian nations of the Niagara frontier defeated by the Iroquois in the 1640s and 1650s, or the Algonquians of the western Great Lakes, called "Ontôagannha" or Fire Nation by the Iroquois, are more convincing identifications. *JRAD* 54: 84.

3 *JRAD* 51: 123, 187.

4 Ibid., 52: 179.

5 Bradley, *Evolution of Onondaga Iroquois*, 122–3; Snow, *Mohawk Valley Archaeology*, 406.

6 *JRAD* 43: 264.

7 Ibid., 45: 206.

8 See "*francs Iroquois*" in ibid., 45: 207; "*anciens captifs des Iroquois, naturalisés avec eux*" in ibid., 35:141; "*plusieurs qui n'étaient pas Iroquois naturalisés*" in ibid., 63: 166; "Hurons [...] *iroquoisés*," in Oury, *Marie de l'Incarnation*, 621. Historians have used a variety of labels, including "*Iroquois de souche*" and "old-stock Iroquois." See Jetten, *Enclaves amérindiennes*, 65 ; Greer, *Mohawk Saint*, 27.

9 *JRAD* 9: 254.

10 Ibid., 42: 56.

11 Cuoq, *Lexique de la langue iroquoise*, 3, 83; Viau, *Enfants du néant*, 148–9.

12 *JRAD* 49: 105. See also ibid., 43: 292–4. On the precariousness of captivity, see Viau, *Enfants du néant*, 119–99; Starna and Watkins, "Northern Iroquois Slavery"; Richter, *Ordeal*, 68–74.

13 *JRAD* 42: 56.

14 For examples of Huron Christianity in exile, see *JRAD* 41: 94–124, 132; 42: 70–82, 184–8; 46: 108–12; 47: 58, 132; 4: 106–8; 50: 114–16; 54: 80–93.

15 Ibid., 44: 20; 58: 232–4; *Relations inédites*, 1:173.

16 *JRAD* 28: 298–300; 40: 188, 192.

17 Bruce Trigger, "Garakontié," in *DCB* 1: 322–3.

18 Treaty of 13 December 1665, in BNF, Département des manuscrits, Baluze 196, "Recueil de traités de paix"; Broadhead et al., eds., *NYCD* 3: 121–5. For D'Argenson's expression of similar conditions in 1659, see also *JRAD* 45: 90.

19 For the ratification by the Senecas on 22 May 1666 and by the Oneida and Mohawks on 7 July 1666, see *NYCD* 9: 44–7 (also ibid., 3: 125–7); *JRAD* 124–36, 190. On the Iroquois conceptualization of hostages as distinct from captives see Bruyas ("Karih8anonna"), *Radical Words*, 81; Shea ("Garih8annonna"), *French-Onondaga Dictionary*, 75.

20 *JRAD* 50: 204–10; 51:180; Oury, *Marie de l'Incarnation*, 775–87; *NYCD* 3: 136–7; ANOM, C11A 2: 298–301v, Talon to Colbert, 25 August 1667; Talon to Louvois, 19 October and 19 December 1667, in *RAPQ* 1930–1931: 88–9.

21 *JRAD* 51: 210

22 Steckley, *De Religione*, 129–151. I have opted to translate as "capture" what Steckley interprets as "seize." The reference to the invasion of Mohawk country "in the fall" (as opposed to years before) makes it possible to safely date this portion of the manuscript to 1666–67. Steckley, *De Religione*, 137.

23 *JRAD* 57: 36–44. The *Jesuit Relations* are unclear as to the date of Atironta's return. Taken literally, the indication that he "returned six years ago from the country of the Iroquois" indicates that he came back as early as 1665. It seems more likely, however, that he returned in 1666 or 1667.

24 Oury, *Marie de l'Incarnation*, 786–7.

25 *JRAD* 55: 290–2.

26 Ibid., 55: 298–300. Annieouton appears previously in Oury, ed., *Marie de l'Incarnation*, 626.

27 For the background of Tonsahoten and Ganneaktena (Annietenha, Gandeaktena, Gandeacteua), their encounter with Bruyas, and their journey to the Saint Lawrence in 1667–68, see *JRAD* 50: 212–16; 51: 147–9; 52: 21–7; 61: 194–208; 63: 154–82; Chauchetière, *Vie*, 80–101. Besides a few contemporaneous allusions, the earliest and most detailed accounts of Tonsahoten and Ganneaktena's establishment at Kentake were written more than a decade later, by Vincent Bigot (1679) and Chauchetière (ca.1686). For historians' attempts at resolving the confusions and contradictions of these sources, see Béchard, *Original Caughnawaga Indians*, 5–55; Lacroix, *Origines de La Prairie*, 15–30; Greer, *Mohawk Saint*, 91–5; Green, "New People," 26–30; Richter, "Ordeals of the Longhouse," 179–81; Henri Béchard, "Gandeacteua" and "Tonsahoten" in *DCB* 1: 321–2, 651. The figure of Charles Boquet has been the subject of some confusion among historians. Cf. Oury, *Marie de l'Incarnation*, 842–3; J. Monet, "Charles Boquet," in *DCB* 1: 108; Richter, "Ordeals of the Longhouse", 180; and Greer, *Mohawk Saint*, 91–3.

28 Lavallée, *La Prairie*, 11–30; Ethnoscop, "Étude sur l'histoire," 5–11; Arkéos, "Amérindiens et premiers colons," 43–6, 94–7.

29 *JRAD* 51: 148; 63: 154; Chauchetière, *Vie*, 83–4, 89–90.

30 *JRAD* 51: 148; 52: 22; 63: 154; Chauchetière, *Vie*, 83–4, 89–90.

31 *JRAD* 63: 154–6; Chauchetière, *Vie*, 90.

32 *JRAD* 51: 175; 52: 16–18; Blouin, "Histoire et iconographie," 1: 265. On the relocation to Notre Dame des Anges and subsequently to Notre Dame de Foy, see *JRAD* 52: 229; Chaumonot, *Missionnaire*, 174–6.

33 On this northward migration and the settlements, see Konrad, "Iroquois Frontier"; Richter, *Ordeal*, 105–32; Pritchard, "Glory of God"; Adams, "Iroquois Settlement," 6–10. Cf. Parmenter, *Edge of Woods*, 127–47.

34 On the relationship of the Mohawks to the region of Montreal, see Radisson, *Collected Writings*, 169–70, 172–3; 169–70; Blanchard, *Seven Generations*, 152–3; Gabriel-Doxtater and Van den Hende, *At the Wood's Edge*, 23–9; Bonaparte, *Creation and Confederation*, 36–44, and *Lily Among Thorns*, 29–35; Tremblay, ed., *Saint Lawrence Iroquoians*; Chapdelaine, "Review"; Engelbrecht, "Northern New York Revisited"; Birch, "Current Research." On the name Tio'tia:ke, see Bruyas ("tiotiagi," sic: "hotiagi"), *Radical words*, 50; Cuoq ("teiontiakon," "tiotiake"), *Lexique de la langue iroquoise*, 43; Cooke ("TIO TIA KE"), American Philosophical Society, Mss. 497.3.C772, Iroquois personal names, 1900–1951, "Names beginning R–Z," 651; Robinson, "Origin of the Name Hochelaga," 296.

35 *JRAD* 24: 262–4; 35: 208; 41: 54.

36 Ibid., 63: 153 (retranslated).
37 LAC, MG 11, CO 42, 26: 276–280v, Speech of the Iroquois of the Seven Nations to the governors of Quebec and New York, 8 September 1766.
38 *JRAD* 57: 25–7.
39 *Édits, ordonnances royaux*, 46.
40 "Instruction pour le sieur de Courcelle au sujet des Indiens," 1665, Blanchet, ed., *CMNF* 1: 175.
41 Colbert to Jean Talon, 5 January 1666, *RAPQ* 1930–1931: 45. On francization during this period, see Havard, "Les forcer à devenir citoyens," 989–92; Aubert, "Blood of France," 452–3; Belmessous, "Assimilation and Racialism," 511–14; Stanley, "Policy of 'Francisation,'" 340.
42 Colbert to Talon, 5 April 1667, *RAPQ* 1930–1931: 72. See also ANOM, C11A 2: 332, Colbert to Talon, 13 November 1666.
43 BANQ-Q, TP1, S28, P100, "Arrêt ordonnant que les sauvages subiront la peine imposée par les lois et ordonnances de France," 21 April 1664 ; Talon to Colbert, 13 November 1666, *RAPQ* 1930–1931: 58; Grabowski, *Common Ground*, 88–192.
44 BANQ-Q, TP1, S28, P100, "Arrêt portant permission à tous les français, habitants de la Nouvelle-France, de traiter des boissons aux sauvages," 10 November 1668, ; Talon to Colbert, 27 October 1667, *RAPQ* 1930–1931: 84; Grabowski, *Common Ground*, 193–245.
45 ANOM, C11A 2: 317, Talon to Colbert, 27 November 1667.
46 Oury, ed., *Marie de l'Incarnation*, 809, 828.
47 Talon to Colbert, 13 November 1666, *RAPQ* 1930–1931: 58; Colbert to Talon, 20 February 1668, *RAPQ* 1930–1931: 93–5; Louis XIV to Laval, 7 March 1668, in Provost, *Séminaire de Québec,* 1: 36; *JRAD* 52: 46–8; Oury, ed. *Marie de l'Incarnation*, 809, 828; Baillargeon, *Séminaire de Québec*, 76–9; Gourdeau, *Délices de nos cœurs*; Trudel, *HNF* 4: 271–4.
48 "Mémoire du Roi pour servir d'instruction à Talon," 20 March 1665, *RAPQ* 1930–1931: 5–10; Cossette, "Jean Talon"; Eccles, *Frontenac*, 51–74.
49 Trudel, *HNF* 4: 326–7, 330.
50 Dickinson, "Sulpiciens," 33–42; Deslandres, "Les fondations," 19–31.
51 Dickinson, "Évangéliser," 351.
52 Dollier de Casson, *Histoire du Montréal*, 301–11. On the Sulpician ventures on Lake Ontario, see Pritchard, "Glory of God," 131–48; Tremblay, "Politique missionnaire." On the work of the Sulpicians on the upper Island of Montreal, see Maurault, "Vicissitudes," 121–49; Tremblay, "Politique missionnaire," 48–9; Dickinson, "Évangéliser," 356; Filiatrault, "Rapport d'étude."
53 For the grant to the fief of La Prairie de la Madeleine, dated 1 April 1647, see *Pièces et documents,* 75–6. On the evolution of the seigneury, see Lacroix,

Origines de La Prairie; Lavallée, *La Prairie*; Boily, "Terres amérindiennes," 94–6.

54 *JRAD* 50: 210–12. On these seigneuries, see Dépatie, "Seigneurie de l'Île Jésus"; Trudel, *HNF* 4: 333.

55 *JRAD* 35: 38; Beaulieu, Béreau, and Tanguay, *Wendats*, 102–3.

56 *JRAD* 54: 286; Beaulieu, Béreau, and Tanguay, *Wendats*, 104–5; Clair, "Notre-Dame de Foy," 175–89.

57 *JRAD* 63: 150–2, 160, 164, 172–4.

58 Ibid., 63: 158; Chauchetière, *Vie*, 46, 90–1; Saint-Vallier, *Estat présent*, 47–8.

59 Oury, *Marie de l'Incarnation*, 863–4; BANQ-M, Fonds Bailliage de Montréal, TL2, 1971-00-000/11595, Procureur fiscal vs. Etienne Banchaud, Turcot and Lafontaine, 8 July 1669; Margry, *Découvertes et établissements*, 1: 109–12; Oury, *Marie de l'Incarnation*, 863–5; Dollier de Casson, *Histoire de Montreal*, 279; *JRAD* 53: 240; 54:112–14. On Turcot's captivity, see *JRAD*, 37:112; 38: 58.

60 Ibid. See also Grabowski, "Common Ground," 170–3. On Turcot's subsequent life in the interior, see Margry, *Découvertes et établissements*, 2: 104.

61 BANQ-M, Fonds Bailliage de Montréal, TL2, 1971-00-000/11595, Verdict of Migeon de Branssat, 12 September 1669; *JRAD*, 54: 112–14; Oury, *Marie de l'Incarnation*, 863–5.

62 *JRAD* 63: 167–9.

63 Ibid., 63: 158.

64 Ibid., 55: 34; 63: 158 (Chauchetière situates this detail in 1670, but refers to the *Relation* for 1670–71).

65 Ibid., 63: 162.

66 "De la residence de S. Xavier des Praiz," in ibid., 55: 32. For the "bourg de St-François-Xavier" in Oneida, see ibid., 52: 20.

67 There is some confusion with regards to Tonsahoten's baptismal name. The *Relation* for 1667–68 speaks of a Wendat who "had formerly been baptized by our Fathers in his own country," and Chauchetière's *Narration annuelle* notes that "he was a Christian, and was named Pierre." Yet in the same chronicle, Chauchetière goes on to mention the baptism of the summer 1668 and remark that he "was called François Xavier." He is not named Pierre elsewhere. In his account of the life of Catherine Tekakwitha, Chauchetière again names him François or François-Xavier. *JRAD* 52: 23; 63: 151, 155; Chauchetière, *Vie*, 81, 88, 100.

68 *JRAD* 63: 163.

69 Ibid., 61: 206.

70 Ibid., 63: 153.

71 Ibid., 58: 74.

72 Ibid., 63: 167.

73 Ibid., 58: 74; Isaiah 11: 6. See also ibid., 63:148.

74 *Relations inédites*, 1: 160. Marie Tsaouenté is described as an "Iroquois" in *JRAD* 61: 37. For another example, see ibid., 60: 49.

75 See chapter 3.

76 *JRAD* 52: 36, 228, 236; 53: 130; 54: 286–8; 70: 206; Chaumonot, *Missionnaire*, 174–5; Clair, "Notre-Dame de Foy," 175–89. See also Boily, "Terres amérindiennes," 74–6; Beaulieu, Béreau, and Tanguay, *Wendats*, 71, 77, 105, 137.

77 *JRAD* 54: 288–9; Clair, "Une chapelle," 11–15; Boudon, *Dieu seul*; Longpré, "Influence spirituelle"; *Relations inédites*, 1: 187–8; *JRAD* 63: 154, 164, 186–8; Greer, *Mohawk Saint*, 113–16.

78 *JRAD* 54: 282–4.

79 Ibid., 51: 187; 57: chap. 2. Gandaouagué appears as a new village name in 1659 (as "Kaghnuwage," and later in various forms: Gandawaga, Gandaouge, Gandaouaguen, Caghnawaga, Caughnawaga, Cahaniaga, Kaknnaogue, Andaraque. It corresponds to the relocated community known as Ossernenon in the 1640s. Snow, *Mohawk Valley Archaeology*, 365–75, 415–19. On the social tensions between Christians and traditionalists there and throughout Iroquoia, see Richter, "Iroquois versus Iroquois," 1–16.

80 *JRAD* 53: 136–59; Pynchon "Letters of John Pynchon, 1654–1700", 80; Gookin, "Historical Collections," 166–7; Burke, *Mohawk Frontier*, 74–5; Cogley, *John Eliot's Mission*, 151–3. Cholenec's original manuscript indicates "Tog8ir8t," which I transcribe here as "Togouirout." I thank Roy Wright for suggesting its likeliest translation. This appears to be the same name as "Tokwiro," borne in recent years, by Chief Joe Norton of Kahnawake. The names mistakenly attributed to this figure in the scholarly literature include "Togouiroui" (given precedence by Béchard, including in his *Dictionary of Canadian Biography* entry) and "Togoniron," both of which reflect a misreading of Cholenec's original manuscript. Yet another name attributed to this figure, Athasata/Atahsata/Adhasatah (meaning Shadow, Shade, Eclipse) stems from confusion with a different leader at Kahnawake, Louis Ateriata (Atoriata, Adarjachta). See Henri Béchard, "Togouiroui," *DCB* 1: 650–1; Devine, *Historic Caughnawaga*, 30, 53, 76, 79, 81, 95, 97; American Philosophical Society, Mss. 497.3.C772, n.p., Cooke, "Names beginning A," Iroquois personal names, 1900–1951. Yet another name, Ti8ates'kon, may also have been associated with him. *JRAD* 60: 290.

81 *JRAD* 51: 125, 217; 53: 240; 57: 90, 96–100; 58: 83, 250–2; 61: 159–60; 63: 251. On the circulation and consumption of liquor among the Iroquois, see Richter, *Ordeal*, 85–6; Conrad, "Disorderly Drinking." For a discussion of the broader context, see Mancall, *Deadly Medicine*; Ferland, *Bacchus en Canada*, 225–302.

82 *JRAD* 57: 62–6; 60: 102.
83 Ibid., 57: 70.
84 According to one account, Togouirout's estranged wife had shown an interest in Christianity before her husband. On Togouirout's migration, see ibid., 57: 25, 105–11; 63: 174–8. See also Chauchetière, *Vie*, 38–41; *NYCD* 13: 531–2. The single piece of evidence which makes it possible to identify Togouirout as a member of the Turtle Clan is a Dutch affidavit in favour of Jacques Cornelius Van Slyck bearing his mark – a turtle – dated 12 September 1683. See Schaffer Library, Union College, Schenectady, Deposition of Cryn, 1683.
85 *JRAD* 57: 24.
86 Ibid., 57: 68–70.
87 "Voyage du Comte de Frontenac au Lac Ontario," in Margry, *Découvertes et établissements*, 1: 200, 202, 210, 219, 223–31; Frontenac to Colbert, 13 November 1673, in *RAPQ* 1926-1927: 35–41. Cf. *JRAD* 57: 74–6; *Relations inédites*, 171–7. For an overview of Frontenac's expedition to Cataraqui, see Eccles, *Frontenac*, 104–7; Trudel, *HNF* 4: 223–6. On Louis Thaondechoren (Taondechoren, Taondechorend), see *JRAD* 50: 210; 52: 236–8; 55: 266–8, 276, 298; 57: 74–6; 58:134, 148–50, 196–8; 60: 78–80, 306.
88 *Relations inédites*, 1: 171–7.
89 Frontenac to Colbert, 13 November 1673, *RAPQ* 1926–1927: 35; Eccles, *Frontenac*, 51–74; Dickinson, "Les Sulpiciens," 38–9.
90 *JRAD* 60: 68–70; Chaumonot, *Missionaire*, 194.
91 Beaulieu, Béreau, and Tanguay, *Wendats*, 105–7 ; Boily, "Terres amérindiennes," 44–87.
92 *JRAD* 57: 46–8; 60: 68–70.
93 Ibid., 57: 82; 60: 70–92; Beaulieu, Béreau, and Tanguay, *Wendats*, 107; Clair, "Une chapelle," and "Notre-Dame-de-Lorette."
94 *JRAD* 54: 287; 60: 27. On migration to Lorette, in 1673, see Chauchetière, *Missionnaire*, 194–6.
95 *JRAD* 58: 248–50; 63: 179.
96 Ibid., 63: 178; 63: 168. For descriptions of Kentake as a "Huron colony," see ibid., 56: 18; 57: 68, 76.
97 Ibid., 63: 180.
98 Ibid., 63: 180–4. Chauchetière, *Vie*, 97–100.
99 *JRAD* 60: 277, 287–9; 61: 206; 63: 184.
100 Ibid., 63: 191, 195; 58: 80; 59: 286; 60: 274; 62: 178; 63: 190, 194; ANOM, C11A: 4: 206–9, Frontenac to Colbert, 14 November 1674.
101 *JRAD* 58: 110–24; ASQ, X-136, "Idrographie et topographie de la rivière des prairies et de la coste de l'ysle Jesus qu'elle arrouse parcourue les 25, 26, 27 de 7bre 1674"; Lacroix, *Origines de La Prairie*, 34.

102 *JRAD* 56: 18–20; 58: 110–24; 59: 284–6; 63:178–80; 63:194; ANOM, C11A: 4: 206-209, Frontenac to Colbert, 14 November 1674; BANQ-Q, E21, S64, SS5, Fonds Ministère des Terres et Forêts, Série 64, Gestion du Domaine de la Couronne, Sous-Série 5, Biens des Jésuites, 1960-01-038/203, "Permission s'établir au Sault-Saint-Louis par l'intendant Jacques Duchesneau," 1676; BANQ-Q, E21, S64, SS5, Fonds Ministère des Terres et Forêts, Série 64, Gestion du Domaine de la Couronne, Sous-Série 5, Biens des Jésuites, 1960-01-038/203, "Requête à Monseigneur Colbert pour la terre Sault en Canada qui a été défrichée en partie par une colonie de sauvages Iroquois Chrétiens," 1679; Frontenac to Louis XIV, 6 November 1679, *RAPQ* 1930–1931: 108–11; "Acte de concession des terres du Sault-Saint-Louis," 29 May 1680, in *Pièces et documents,* 74; Louis XIV to Frontenac, 29 April 1680, *RAPQ* 1930-1931: 115; Lacroix, *Origines de La Prairie*, 35–6; Boily, "Terres amérindiennes," 98–109.

103 *JRAD* 63:180.

104 For the request and response of the Hurons, ca. 1675, see ASQ, Polygraphie 4, no. 20. "Achind8anes" in the original.

105 Tremblay, "Politique missionnaire," 50–1.

106 Maurault, "Vicissitudes," 121–49; Tremblay, "Politique missionnaire," 48–9; Pritchard, "Glory of God"; Konrad, "Iroquois Frontier"; Dickinson, "Évangéliser," 356; Filiatrault, "Rapport d'étude."

107 ASQ, Polygraphie 4, no 20; ASSM, P1:8C.1.2-3C, "Procès-verbal d'arpentage fait par Bénigne Basset [...] des quatre arpents réservés par le Séminaire au domaine de la Montagne," 6 December 1675; ASSM, P1:36-4, Pierre Rousseau, "Histoire de la Mission de la Montagne," before 1912. See also Mauraült, "Fort des Messieurs," 29; Harel, "Domaine du Fort," 19. Cf. Lacroix, *Origines de La Prairie*, 28.

108 ASSM, P1:36-8b, "Mémoire d'un missionnaire, prêtre de Saint-Sulpice de Montréal, relatif aux activités des Jésuites, à la campagne de Joseph-Antoine Lefebre De La Barre, gouverneur, contre les Iroquois et aux principes d'action des missionnaires sulpiciens," 1685.

109 *JRAD* 63: 180.

110 Ibid., 60: 276, 286; Chauchetière, *Vie,* 100. Tonsahoten's identity, while not stated here, can be deduced from references to him elsewhere as a "first captain." See *JRAD* 61: 206. For an indication that village relocation could be a tense time even in Iroquoia, see Chauchetière, *Vie*, 60.

111 Chauchetière, *Vie*, 100.

112 Concerning the relocation and the new site, see *JRAD* 60: 274; 62: 166; 63: 190–4; Devine, *Historic Caughnawaga*, 40–1.

113 ASSM, P1:8A.3.17-04, "Notes de M. Roupe sur la composition ethnique de la mission," ca. 1807–1829.

114 *JRAD* 61: 34–6.

115 In 1740, Vincent Onehatetaionk, one of the great chiefs of Lorette, went to visit the village of Kanehsatake at Lake of Two Mountains asking to see the community's wampum. He was insulted to discover that only two remained of the twelve that "his nation" had deposited there when it lit "their fire," the others having perhaps been traded away. Vincent took the belts with him back to Lorette, saying "that fire was dead since they had disposed of the Belts." When Governor Beauharnois investigated the situation, he found that the Hurons of Lorette claimed to have certain "rights" at Kanehsatake, based on the fact that some seven [*sic*] years previously, the inhabitants of Kanehsatake had found themselves composed entirely of young men, and without a council. They had sent deputies to the Hurons of Lorette for that reason. The latter had listened to their request, established a constitution at Kanehstake by presenting twelve wampum belts, one for each article, and "given a chief" to it. While the manuscript indicates that these events took place "about 7 years ago" ("*il y a environ 7 ans*"), this is a clerical error that should read seventy. There is no evidence that such a dramatic event took place ca.1734: by then Kanehsatake at Lake of Two Mountains was a well-established and well-populated community, and colonial administrators tended to be diligent in documenting major occurrences in the missions. See ANOM, C11A 76: 263-264v, Mémoire de Canada, 1740 et 41, par Josué Dubois Berthelot de Beaucours, [1741]; ANOM, C11A 75: 138-142v, Beauharnois to Maurepas, 21 September 1741; Lozier, "Origines huronnes-wendates."

116 *JRAD* 50: 210–12.

117 Ibid., 60: 306. On Thaondechoren's Tionnontaté origins, see *Relations inédites*, 1: 171–2.

118 *JRAD* 63: 193–5

119 Ibid., 63: 192–4. See Béchard, "Tercentenary"; Lainey, "*Monnaie des sauvages*," 266–7; Bonaparte, *Lily Among Thorns*, 161–2, 259–60; Devine, *Historic Caughnawaga*, 48.

120 *JRAD* 63: 194.

121 Merlet, *Histoire des relations*, 18–19 ; Chaumonot, *Missionnaire*, 205–6, 276–82; Clair, "Du décor rêvé," 300–8.

122 Blouin, "Histoire et iconographie," 1: 265; *JRAD* 52: 228; 54: 286; 58: 130; 60: 26; Chaumonot, *Missionnaire*, 174–6, 194–6; ANOM, G1, 461: 1, Census of 1685; Beaulieu, Béreau, and Tanguay, *Wendats*, 77–8.

123 On Tsaouenhohoui, see *JRAD* 45: 162; 55: 50; Steckley, *Words*, 122–5, and "Tsa8enhohi." On Jacques Onnhatetaionk (Onnha'tetaionk, Ondhatetaionk, Annhatetaionk), see *JRAD* 36: 140; 57: 62–6; 58: 164; 60: 102. On

Pierre Andahiacon (Andahiach, Andaiakon, Endahiach, Endahiaconc), *JRAD* 58: 132, 136–8; 60: 302–5. On Thaondechoren, see note 96.

124 Her name is also spelled Asenragehaon, *JRAD* 52: 164–5; 58: 136–7; 60: 296–300.

125 In light of this, John Steckley has suggested that the Huron community at Quebec may "been constructed around an amalgam of Bear and Cord" after 1656, with Atsena and his followers representing the northern Bear and the southern Bear preferring to stay with the French. See *Words*, 29–32. As I argue here, the evidence instead appears to suggest that the "Bear" character of the mission was the result of return migration from Mohawk country in the late 1660s and 1670s.

126 In a letter to the chapter of Chartres in 1678, the terms "Ouendat Lorétrônon Teiatontarigè" and "ouendat aouaatsi Loretronnon Teiatontarigué" appear (Teiatontarie being the Huron name for Quebec). Potier's dictionary indicates that the people of Lorette were known as "Hatindgia8ointen," "Ekeenteeronnon," and "Lorechtr8nnon" by the Hurons of Detroit (a later entry suggests that "Lorechtr8nnon" could also refer to the "French of Lorette"). An early nineteenth-century map by Nicolas Vincent Tsawenhohi signals, in addition to "Roreke" (Lorette), the toponyms "Andatraka" (Ancienne Lorette), and "Junqusindundeh" (Jeune Lorette). For his part, Colden alludes to the "Quatoghies of Loretto," Quatoghie apparently being an Iroquois name for the Hurons. Merlet, *Histoire des relations*, 3–4; Toupin, ed., *Écrits de Pierre Potier*, 230, 263; Colden, *History of the Indian Nations* (1747), 143 (see also 21, 28–9, 69, 121, xv–xvi); Wright, "Le Plan Vincent," 240; Lindsay, *Notre-Dame de la Jeune-Lorette*, 309; Poirier, ed., *Toponymie des Hurons-Wendats*, 24, 33.

CHAPTER SIX

1 ANOM, G1, 461: 1, Census of 1685.

2 For estimates of Iroquois population see Parmenter, *Edge of Woods*, 289–91.

3 Thwaites, ed., *JRAD* 60: 276.

4 Chauchetière, *Vie*, 59–71. On Louis Ogenheratarihiens (or Ogeratarihen, meaning "Hot Ash" or "Hot Powder," also known as Garonhiagué and Garohiaé, meaning "In-the-Sky" or "Celestial"), and Marie Garhio (Garhi) see Chauchetière, ibid., 20–76; Béchard, *Original Caughnawaga Indians*, 115–25; Henri Béchart, "Ogenheratarihiens," in DCB 1: 522–3.

5 *JRAD* 63: 152, 178. See also ibid., 64: 242.

6 Grabowski, *Common Ground*, 340–1; Saint-Vallier, *Estat present*, 26–8; Brod-

head et al., eds., *NYCD* 9: 441; LAC, MG17-A7-2, 6: 3764–3766, Tronson to La Barre, 30 April 1684; ANOM, C11A 9: 61-77v, Denonville to the Minister, 25 August 1687; ANOM, C11A 9:109v–112v, Denonville, "Mémoire du Voyage"; Baugy, *Journal*, 72-8; Lozier, *Origines huronnes-wendates*, 110–11. On the ethnic composition of the mission, see ASSM, P1:36-27, Cuoq, "Notes pour servir à l'histoire de la mission," 1898; ASSM, P1:8A.3.17-04, "Notes de M. Roupe sur la composition ethnique de la mission," ca. 1807–1829; Maurault, "Vicissitudes," 122; Tremblay, "Politique missionnaire," 49; Dickinson, "Évangéliser," 356. See also LAC, MG17-A7-2, 6: 3435-3438, Tronson to Trouvé, 10 April 1680; LAC, MG17-A7-2, 6: 3322-3323, Tronson to Dollier de Casson, 1 May 1679; LAC, MG17-A7-2, 6: 3360-3361, Tronson to Trouvé, 16 May 1679; LAC, MG17-A7-2, 6: 3515-3523, Tronson to Belmont, 30 May 1681; LAC, MG17-A7-2, 6: 3645, Tronson to Belmont, 13 March 1683.

7 Domine Dellius wrote "Karig8istes," La Potherie, "Karigouistes," and Colden, "Caraguists." See *NYCD* 4: 95; La Potherie, *Histoire*, 3: 200–3; Colden, *History of the Five Indian Nations* (1747), 163; Steckley, *De Religione*, 48, 136. Bruyas's Mohawk lexicon translates "Garih8ioston" as "croire, être Chrétien," *Radical words*, 91. In recent years, a few historians have repeated David Blanchard's claim that the people of Kahnawake referred to themselves as "*ongwe honwe tehatiisontha* (real men who make the Sign of the Cross)," but this seems to be a later appellation used to distinguish Catholics from Protestants in the community beginning in the nineteenth century. See Blanchard, "Other Side of Sky," 90. On the notion of "*Karihwiio*" ("*Kariwiio*" "*Gai'wiio*," "*Gaiwi:yo:h*," "*Gaihwi:io*," etc.), see Fenton, *Great Law*, 86n3, 95, 216, 218; Parker, *Code of Handsome Lake*, 5 and passim; Jocks, "Livings Words," 225; Cuoq, *Lexique de la langue iroquoise*, 12. Parker's version of the text also alludes to "*Gai'wiiostŭk* (the Christian religion)." Ibid., 57, 141.

8 Chauchetière, *Vie*, 118.

9 *JRAD* 54: 282–4; 57: 250–2; 60: 306.

10 BANQ-M, TL2, 1971-00-000/11584, Charles de Couange vs. Louis 8akouts (Oakon, Ouacont, 8akont, 8acouse), Jean Gatessa et Denis 8k8outé, July 1683. On Marie-Félix Arontio (Aronta) and Laurent Duboc (Dubosc, Dubeau), see *JRAD* 46: 286; Labelle, *Dispersed But Not Destroyed*, 110–11, 187.

11 See Havard, *Empire et métissage*, 69–70, 206–14; White, *Middle Ground*, 23–33; Jennings, *Ambiguous Iroquois Empire*, 172–6; Richter, *Ordeal*, 144–50; Brandão, *Your Fyre Shall Burn No More*, 118–25; Parmenter, *Edge of Woods*, 152–65; Mourin, *Porter la guerre*, 37–45. For the mission settlements' relationship with the interior in the eighteenth century, see Labelle, *Dispersed But Not Destroyed*, 186–8; Peace, "Maintaining Connections," 86–7.

12 *JRAD* 63: 240–1.

13 See Green, "New People," 88–90; Parmenter, *Edge of Woods*, 175–6, 190–5, 204–6; Richter, *Facing East*, 159; Greer, *Mohawk Saint*, 99. Cf. Mourin, *Porter la guerre*, 221–5.

14 *JRAD* 63: 207–9, 213–15. Chauchetière alludes to a number of other crises that year, including rumours that a trading post would be established above the village or that the brandy trade would find a foothold there, and the killing of a Loup (Mahican) headman by the Iroquois, which was nearly – and falsely – imputed to Kahnawakes. It was Togouirout who investigated and cleared up the matter.

15 Ibid., 62: 255.

16 ANOM, C11A 6: 63v–64, La Barre to the Secretary of State for the Navy, 12 November 1682; *JRAD* 62: 255.

17 ANOM, C11A 5: 183–183v, "Arrest qui ordonne l'enregistrement [de] la concession de la seigneurie du Sault," 24 October 1680. See also ANOM, C11A 5: 344–5, Louis XIV to Duchesneau, 30 April 1681; ANOM, C11A 5: 308v, Duchesneau to Colbert, 13 November 1681.

18 ANOM, C11A 5: 291–291v, Duchesneau to Colbert, 13 November 1681. On shifting policy, see Belmessous, *Assimilation and Empire*, 35–45.

19 ANOM, C11A 5: 291–291v, Duchesneau to Colbert, 13 November 1681; ANOM, C11A 6: 87-90, De Meulles to Minister, 12 November 1682; ANOM, C11A 6: 140v–141, La Barre to the Minister, 4 November 1683; ANOM, C11A 6: 194, De Meulles to the Minster, 4 November 1683; ANOM, C11A 6: 44, Louis XIV to La Barre, 10 April 1684; ANOM, C11A 7: 152, De Meulles to Minister, 28 September 1685.

20 ASSM, P1:36-8b, "Mémoire d'un missionnaire [...] relatif aux activités des Jésuites," 1685; LAC, MG17-A7-2, 6: 3733-3746, Tronson to Belmont, 8 April 1684; LAC, MG17-A7-2, 6: 3851-3858, Tronson to Belmont, 15 April 1685; LAC, MG17-A7-2, 6: 3901-3914, Tronson to Belmont, 4 June 1686; Saint-Vallier, *Estat présent*, 25–8; ASSM, P1:36-4, Pierre Rousseau, "Histoire de la Mission de la Montagne," before 1912; Simpson, *Marguerite Bourgeoys*, 61–4, 102.

21 ASSM, P1:36-8b, Drawer 115, no. 8, "Mémoire d'un missionnaire [...] relatif aux activités des Jésuites," 1685.

22 ANOM, C11A 7: 90–91, Denonville to the Minister, 13 November 1685.

23 ANOM, C11A 6: 135–137v, La Barre to the Minister, 4 November 1683 (copy in *NYCD* 9: 202–3); BNF, 13516, f. 21–22v, François Vachon de Belmont, "Recueil de pièces sur l'histoire du Canada." The first part of this manuscript has been transcribed with some errors and omissions as Belmont, *Histoire du Canada*.

24 ANOM, C11A 6: 135–135v, La Barre to the Minister, 4 November 1683, C11A 6: 135-135v; *JRAD* 62: 255-7.

25 Belmont, *Histoire du Canada*, 15; ANOM, C11A 6: 136-137v, La Barre to the Minister, 4 November 1683; ANOM, C11A 6: 276v, La Barre to the Minister, 4 June 1684; ANOM, C11A 6: 282-282 v, La Barre to the King, 5 June 1684. For an overview of the campaign, see Mourin, *Porter la guerre*, esp. 61–82.

26 *JRAD* 63: 241–3. The French *se risquer* might alternatively be translated as "dare themselves."

27 Ibid., 63: 241.

28 Ibid.

29 On the appropriation and adaptation of Christianity in the mission context and at Kahnawake in particular, see Greer, "Conversion and Identity," 175–98, and *Mohawk Saint*, 100–10.

30 Chauchetière, *Vie* 93, 96–7; *JRAD* 63: 231, 243; Saint-Vallier, *Estat présent*, 62. This candelabrum was captured in a drawing by Chauchetière in one of the illustrations accompanying his "Narration de la mission du Sault," Archives départementales de la Gironde. It bears some resemblance to the one that appears on a late engraving of the "Interior of the Old Dutch Church," published in Munsell, *Collections on the History of Albany*, 1: 56–7. With respect to the value of the candelabrum, it must be noted that while the Thwaites edition speaks of four beavers, the original indicates "*ving-quatre*" [*sic*]. Although Chauchetière values these twenty-four beavers at 240 pounds, a more conservative estimate of about 100 guilders or about 15 pounds in New York money of account seems more accurate. Still, it was a significant sum.

31 *JRAD* 63: 241 (I have retranslated the "gave such a skillful spin to the affair" part of the quote).

32 On the theme of spiritual kinship through baptism, see Greer, "Conversion and Identity," 182–3, and *Mohawk Saint*, 51–3; Morrison, "Baptism and Alliance," 416–37. On the theme of metaphorical fatherhood in the Franco-Indigenous alliance, see Havard, *Empire et métissage*, 215–18, and *Great Peace*, 29–30; White, *Middle Ground*, 36, 84–6, 94–5, 104–5, 112, 116–18; Cook, "Vivre comme frères," 453–94, and "Onontio Gives Birth"; Galloway, "'Chief Who Is Your Father,'" 254–78. And for metaphors of fatherhood in the specific context of Franco-Iroquois relations, see Jennings, *Ambiguous Iroquois Empire*, 44–5; and Jennings et al., *History and Culture*, 119–20.

33 Lafitau, *Customs*, 2: 99. On the relation between men and their children, expressed by the concept of "*agadoni*" among the Mohawks and Oneida (as opposed to the "*owachira*" of female lineages), see Becker, "Structure and Meaning," 166–9; Hewitt, "Requickening Address," 67; and Fenton's introduction to Lafitau's *Customs*, lxxxi.

34 ANOM, C11A 6: 63v–64v, La Barre to the Minister, [12 November 1682]; ANOM, C11A 6: 135v, 137, 140, 143, La Barre to the Minister, 4 November 1683.

35 ANOM, C11A 8: 132, Denonville to the Minister, 10 November 1686; LAC, ANOM, C11A 8:176, "Résumé des lettres du Canada," 1686, with commentaries; Belmont, *Histoire du Canada*. 18. ANOM, C11A 10: 138v, "État de la dépense faite en l'année 1688 jusqu'au premier novembre au sujet de la guerre contre les Iroquois, " 1 November 1688; "Mémoire pour les Iroquois Chrestiens du Saut en Canada," February 1692, in *JRAD* 64: 108–12. Regarding the importance of gifts in the Franco-Indigenous alliance, see Jaenen, "Role of Presents"; Cook, "Symbolic and Material Exchange," 75–100; Desbarats, "Cost of Early Canada's Native Alliances."

36 *JRAD* 10: 214; Grabowski, *Common Ground*, 90–6.

37 "Tonakt8an" in the original. ASSM, P1:36-8, Pierre Rousseau, "Récit d'une tentative d'assassinat," before 1912; ASSM, Fonds Faillon, FF 68-73, Depositions of Joseph de la Colombière et al., 2 and 15 January 1684, and Judgement, 9 February 1684; Grabowski, *Common Ground*, 150–2.

38 ANOM, C11A 9: 27, Denonville and Champigny to the Minister, 6 November 1687; Grabowski, *Common Ground*, 152–3.

39 ANQ-M, TL2, Investigation into the murder of Jeanne Dasny by Étienne Tehagara8eron, 12 July 1689; ASSM, Fonds Faillon, FF 30, Decision of Denonville and Champigny, 4 August 1689; Grabowski, Common Ground, 153–7; Séguin, *Vie libertine*, 289–99.

40 ASSM, P1:8A.3.17-04, "Notes de M. Roupe sur la composition ethnique de la mission," ca. 1807–1829; ASSM, P1:36-6, Pierre Rousseau, "Notes extraites, de 1677 à 1892, des registres de différentes missions indiennes," before 1912.

41 *NYCD* 3: 487–8.

42 ANOM, C11A 6: 308-309v, "Mémoire de La Barre concernant son expédition au Lac Ontario," 1 October 1684 (copy in *NYCD* 9: 239–40); Lamberville to La Barre, 13 July 1684, copy in *NYCD* 9: 254; Charlevoix, *Histoire*, 2: 313; Chauchetière, *Vie*, 68; Colden, *History of the Five Indian Nations* (1747), 63–5.

43 Van Laer, ed., *Minutes of Court of Albany*, 3: 463, 470; see also Grassman, *Mohawk Indians*, 388.

44 Chauchetière, *Vie*, 71. On Louis Ogenheratarihiens (Ogeratarihen, meaning "Hot Ash" or "Hot Powder," also known as Garonhiagué and Garohiaé, meaning "In-the-Sky" or "Celestial"), see Chauchetière, *Vie*, 20–76; Béchard, *Original Cauhnawaga Indians*, 115–25; Henri Béchard, "Ogenheratarihiens," in *DCB* 1: 522–3.

45 *JRAD* 63: 131, 223.

46 ANOM, C11A 6: 297–98, "Revue faite au fort Frontenac le 17 aoust 1684 des Sauvages qui nous ont suivis pour la guerre," 17 August 1684. Factoring in the uncertain but no doubt small number of men who at the time of the muster had gone on ahead with Le Moyne on an embassy to Onondaga would probably not alter this substantially. Supporting the hypothesis that the Kahnawakes, who around this time accompanied Le Moyne to Onondaga, were excluded from this count is the fact that Le Moyne's name does not show up in either the muster roll of 17 August or in ANOM, C11A 6: 295–298v, "Reveüe des troupes qui ont accompagné Monsieur de la Barre lors de son expedition contre les Iroquois," 14 August 1684; see also Mourin, *Porter la guerre*, 219–20. For the census data see, ANOM, G1, 461: 1.

47 Lamberville to La Barre, 13 July 1684, in *NYCD* 9: 254.

48 ANOM, C11A 6: 310v-312, "Mémoire de La Barre concernant son expédition au Lac Ontario," 1 October 1684; ANOM, C11A 6: 540–540v, Jean de Lamberville to La Barre, 17 August 1684; ANOM, C11A 6 : 541–541v, Lamberville to La Barre, 28 August 1684; ANOM, C11A 6: 299–300, "Presens des Onontaguez faits à Onontio, à La Famine le cinq septembre 1684"; Lahontan, *Œuvres*, 1: 302–10.

49 *JRAD* 63: 244. See also Chauchetière, *Vie*, 73.

50 Thwaites's inaccurate transcription/translation of Chauchetière's *Narration annuelle* appears to be responsible for the interpretation by several scholars of the 1684 meeting as a significant political break, an expulsion from the League council. Chauchetière wrote that "ils avoint déclamé contre eux, ils les avoint hués et enfin ils leur firent plusieurs menaces qui n'aboutirent enfin qu'à leur faire *perdre leur chasse* parce qu'ils la quittèrent pour venir achever la pallissade." This was transcribed in the Thwaites edition as "*perdre leur place*" and imaginatively translated as "*lose their places in the council.*" Chauchetière, *Narration annuelle*; *JRAD* 63: 244. Cf. Green, "New People," 74–5; Reid, *Kahnawà:ke*, 10.

51 *JRAD* 63: 244; Devine, *Historic Caughnawaga*, 72–3, citing Nicholas Victor Burtin's notes, 167–8.

52 See ANF, N/III/Canada/12, Vachon de Belmont, "Plant [sic] de la Mission de la Montagne," 1694; ANOM, C11A 7:178-186v, Mémoire de Denonville, 12 November 1685; LAC, MG17-A7-2, 222-224, Vachon de Belmont to Louis XIV; LAC, MG17-A7–2, 6: 3901–3914, Tronson to Belmont, 4 June 1686; Mauralt, "Fort des Messieurs"; Casavant, *Domaine et tours*.

53 Chauchetière, *Vie*, 70–1.

54 Leder, ed., *LIR*, 104; Richter, *Ordeal*, 150–9, 167; Parmenter, *Edge of Woods*, 174–5.

55 *LIR* 104; Lozier, "Ononchragewas." For evidence that the individuals referred

to as Janetje and Lawrence in the Albany records correspond to this person, see *LIR* 104; Christoph, ed., *Leisler Papers*, 26, 106, 189; *NYCD* 9: 517; BNF, 13516, f. 41, Belmont, "Recueil" (Cf. *Histoire du Canada*, 33); *Year book of the Holland Society*, 7, 51, 53. On Garistasi (Garistatsi, Gastari, Caristie, Caristasie, Caristsie, Caristase, Caristagie, Cristagie, Christagie, Christagio), who is described by Belmont as the husband of a resident of Kanehsatake plausibly named Anastastsi (Anastasie?) ca. 1689, and elsewhere as having a son named Christian, see Belmont, "Recueil," f. 37, (cf. "Aratable" in Belmont, *Histoire du Canada*, 28); Fernow and Van Laer, *Calendar of Council Minutes*, 98–9; Christoph, ed., *Dongan Papers*, 210–11. On Kakare (Kakarrial, Kakarriel, Kakariel, Kakare, Kaakhare, Kacharri, Kacharry, Cakare, Cakarij), whose name may have meant breechcloth, see *NYCD* 3: 817; Bruyas, *Radical words*, 107; Schoolcraft, *Notes on Iroquois*, 266.

56 LAC, MG17-A7-2, 6: 3859-3869, Tronson to Dollier de Casson, 12 April 1685; LAC, MG17-A7-2, 6: 3851-3858, Tronson to Belmont, 15 April 1685.

57 ANOM, B 11: 85, Louis XIV to La Barre, 10 March 1685; ANOM, C11A 6: 388v–389, De Meulles to the Minister, 10 October 1684. Though he had many detractors, La Barre also had some apologists who included Lahontan and Perrot. Lahontan, *Oeuvres*, 1: 311–12; Perrot, *Moeurs*, 383–98. For an overview of Denonville's mandate and military projects, see Leclerc, *Denonville*; Mourin, *Porter la guerre*, esp. 83–118.

58 ANOM, C11A 7: 124v, "Mémoire de Denonville," 8 November 1686.

59 Chauchetière, *Vie*, 73; *NYCD* 3: 487–8. This report refers to both "Sniekes and Maques," i.e. "Senecas *and Mohawks*," but this appears to be an error in reporting.

60 Baugy's muster lists refers to 50 warriors from Kanehsatake, 170 from Kahnawake (a number which appears to subsume the Wendats of Lorette), 76 from Sillery, and 57 from the "bande d'Arhetil" (*sic*: Hertel, presumably referring to Algonquins from around Trois Rivières), for a total of 353. Other numbers are less precise: Belmont speaks of 100 warriors from Kahnawake, 60 from Kanehsatake, 40 from Lorette, 60 Abenakis, and a few Algonquins; Saint-Vallier refers to 150 from Kahnawake and Lorette, 50 from Kanehsatake, and the rest "from Sillery," totalling 300. Belmont, *Histoire du Canada*, 20; Saint-Vallier, *Estat présent*, 91; *JRAD* 63: 269. See also Mourin, *Porter la guerre*, 219–20.

61 For the interviews, see *NYCD* 3: 431–5. While Kakare and Adandidaghko's accounts of Denonville's campaign are extremely valuable, they must be interpreted carefully. The two men were in English custody (one source mentions fetters) when they gave these accounts, and it was in their interest to demonstrate that they were took part against their will. A case in point

might be the advance up the Saint Lawrence River towards Cataraqui: Kakare claimed that "the Indians" were placed "in the middle" of the French forces to prevent their escape. French sources instead reveal that they were positioned at the vanguard, rearguard, and on the flanks to screen the advancing army, and that they provided crucial assistance in passing the rapids. Cf. ibid., 3: 431, and Baugy, *Journal*, 62, 64, 71; see also Denonville, ANOM, C11A 9: 106v, 107v, "Mémoire du voyage pour l'entreprise de M. le Marquis de Denonville contre les Sonnontouans"; *JRAD* 63: 269.

62 Baugy, *Journal*, 58, 61; ANOM, C11A 9: 108v, Denonville, "Mémoire du voyage"; Leclerc, "Denonville et ses captifs," 549.

63 Baugy, *Journal*, 72–7; ANOM, C11A 9: 109v–112v, Denonville, "Mémoire du voyage"; Leclerc, "Denonville et ses captifs," 549–50.

64 ANOM, C11A 9: 61–77v, Denonville to the Minister, 25 August 1687; ANOM, C11A 9: 109v–112v, Denonville, "Mémoire du Voyage"; Baugy, *Journal*, 72–8; *JRAD* 64: 66.

65 Baugy, *Journal*, 90–1, 104; Catalogne, *Recueil*, 14; Belmont, *Histoire du Canada*, 22.

66 *NYCD* 3: 434. For other versions of this exchange see ibid., 3: 431; *JRAD* 6: 271; Baugy, *Journal*, 97.

67 On the march and battle, see Baugy, *Journal*, 99–101, 200–3; Catalogne, *Recueil*, 14–15; ANOM, C11A 9: 114v–115, Denonville, "Mémoire du voyage"; *NYCD* 3: 431–2, 434. Here again, Kakare's claim that "the Govr put all the Indians in the front, because he mistrusted them for fear, they would join with the Sinnakes" is unconvincing. Ibid., 3: 431. For the positive appraisals of the role played by the Christian Iroquois during the battle, and by the other Christian allies, see Baugy, *Journal*, 101; ANOM, C11A 9: 65, Denonville to Seignelay, 25 August 1687; Lahontan, *Oeuvres*, 351. For the Seneca perspective on this battle, see *NYCD* 3: 444–7.

68 Chauchetière, *Vie*, 73; Belmont, *Histoire du Canada*, 24; Saint-Vallier, *Estat présent*, 97–8. Besides Tégaretouan (Le Soleil) and Oyenratarihen [*sic*], Belmont provides the name of another dead individual, Gonhiagou, ("Le Ciel des Tionnontatés, Huron"). Estimates of Franco-Indigenous and Seneca casualties vary. Denonville's official report indicates twenty-seven Senecas killed, and among his forces six Frenchmen and five allies killed and some twenty more wounded. ANOM, C11A, 9: 115, Denonville, "Mémoire du Voyage"; Baugy, *Journal*, 105–9; Charlevoix, *Histoire*, 2: 353–4. Kakare's estimates are similar, at eight Frenchmen killed, four "Christian Indians" and two other warriors killed, and several wounded. Adandidaghko reported seven Frenchmen killed, many wounded, five dead warriors, and several wounded, with sixteen Senecas killed and many wounded. *NYCD* 3: 432,

434. Lahontan overstates the losses of the allies, at one hundred Frenchmen, ten warriors, and twenty or twenty-two wounded. Lahontan, *Oeuvres*, 351. Chauchetière reported three killed from Kahnawake, including Ogenhere-atariens. *Vie*, 73–4.

69 NYCD 3: 432, 434–5.

70 Baugy, *Journal*, 115; NYCD 3: 435.

71 NYCD 3: 432–3, 435–7, 483, 565; 9: 352–3.

72 Ibid., 3: 478.

73 Belmont, *Histoire du Canada*, 28; LAC, MG17-A7-2, 7: 4140-4145, Tronson to Belmont, 19 June 1689.

74 NYCD 3: 431–6, 481, 530, 531; Christoph, ed., *Dongan Papers*, 166, 210–11; Belmont, *Histoire du Canada*, 28–9; Fernow and Van Laer, *Calendar of Council Minutes*, 54. Belmont mentions the activity of two other "apostates," Ganonsa8enrat and Tannatakas. See BNF, 13516, f. 37, Belmont, "Recueil" (the names were not transcribed in Belmont, *Histoire du Canada*, 28).

75 LAC, MG1-G1, 461: 1-2.

76 On Tionnontoguen (Tinnondoge, Tiononderoge, Tinnondogen, Tenontoge, Tinondoge, Tionondage, Tionondoge, Tionodoga, Tionondorage, Tionnontogon, Tionnondoge) through the seventeenth century, see Snow, *Mohawk Valley Archaeology*, 425–8. On Tinnontoguen as a center of Mohawk Protestantism, see NYCD 3: 771–2; 4: 81; Hastings, *Ecclesiastical Records* 2: 1010–11. On Protestantism among the Mohawks more broadly, see Lydekker, *Faithful Mohawks*, 1–41; Feister, "Indian-Dutch Relations," 89–113; Corwin, "Dutch-American Colonial Pastors," 238–41; Richter, "'Some of Them,'" and *Ordeal*, 165, 178, 221–3, 229–34.

77 Garistatsi likely emerged as chief sachem of Tionnontoguen after the death of Tahaiodoris, in the summer of 1691. NYCD 3: 783. On the close collaboration of Garistatsi, Kakare, and Onnonragewas with the colonial officials and among themselves, see infra, as well as Christoph, ed., *Dongan Papers*, 180, and *Leisler Papers*, 31–2; O'Callaghan, ed., DHSNY 2: 144; NYCD 3: 815–17; Catalogne, *Recueil*, 47.

78 Richter, *Ordeal*, 159–61, and "Ordeals of the Longhouse," 24–5; Parmenter, *Edge of Woods*, 195–207.

79 For the French declaration of war, see "Ordonnance du Roy, portant déclaration de guerre," 25 June 1689, in Blanchet et al., eds., CMNF 1: 463–4. On the Glorious Revolution and the outbreak of the War of the League of Augsburg, also known as Nine Years' War or, in the United States, as King William's War, see Israel, *Anglo-Dutch Moment*; Johnson, "Revolution of 1688-9," 215–250; Symcox, "Louis XIV"; Lynn, *Wars of Louis XIV*, 191–265.

80 NYCD 3: 444. See also Fernow and Van Laer, *Calendar of Council Minutes*, 87.

81 BNF, 13516, f. 38, Belmont, "Recueil" (partially transcribed in *Histoire du Canada*, 29); Catalogne, *Recueil*, 16, 22. On Louis Ateriata, see infra.

82 Regarding the "Lachine Massacre," see BNF, 13516, f. 39, Belmont, "Recueil" (and *Histoire du Canada*, 29–30); Catalogne, *Recueil*, 24–5; La Potherie, *Histoire*, 3: 58–9; Charlevoix, *Histoire*, 2: 403–5; Lahontan, *Nouveaux voyages*, 1: 193; Grenier, "Massacre de Lachine."

83 O'Callaghan ed., *Documentary History*, 2: 50, 52.

84 ANOM, C11A 10: 217–224v, Frontenac to the Minister, 15 November 1689; ANOM, C11A 10: 339v, "Résumé de lettres et mémoires de Frontenac, Denonville, Champigny, Callière et autres," [1689]; ANOM, C11A 11: 186, Denonville to the Minister, January 1690; Belmont, *Histoire du Canada*, 31; Catalogne, *Recueil*, 45; Charlevoix, *Histoire*, 2: 408; Richter, "Rediscovered Links," 84.

85 Leclerc, *Denonville*, 235–62; Eccles, *Frontenac*, 199–202, 223–4.

86 ANOM, C11A 11: 7, 13–14, Charles de Monseignat, "Relation … [1690-1691]"; *NYCD* 3: 733–4; La Potherie, *Histoire*, 3: 63–4, 70, 73–4; ANOM, C11A 11: 83–85v, Frontenac to the Minister, 30 April 1690; *NYCD* 3: 733–4; Belmont, *Histoire du Canada*, 32; Colden, *History of the Five Indian Nations* (1727), 105–13; Wraxall, *Abridgement*, 14–15; Richter, "Rediscovered Links," 69–72. Governor Frontenac, who displayed no more love for the Jesuits or their associates during his second mandate than he had during his first, in the spring sent an officer to Onondaga to disavow whatever the emissary might have said on behalf of other parties. The identity of this chief emissary is confused. French sources speak of Gagniegoton (or Gagnioton, Gagniêgoton, Gagnyoton) or Nez Coupé (Cut Nose). He was one of the three ambassadors, with Chaudière Noire and Otréouti, who had come to declare their neutrality at Montreal in June 1688. He apparently returned to the colony after (?) the raid on Lachine and had spoken insolently to Denonville. After arriving in the colony and at Oréouaré's suggestion, Frontenac sent back Gagniegoton and four prisoners to Onondaga. He was back in Montreal with wampum by early March 1690, but did not return to his country with the ambassadors who returned with Chevalier d'Aux. Yet the English accounts of the council that occurred at Onondaga allude to Adarjachta or Adarhata, "chief" or "chief sachem of the Praying Indians." Besides the above-noted sources, see Belmont, *Histoire du Canada*, 32. The name, as "Atteriatta," was also puzzlingly claimed by the Sulpician César Vaillant de Myardouin, who served briefly as missionary at Kanehsatake some time between 1686 and 1692. Merlet, *Histoire des relations*, 42, 44.

87 ANOM, C11A 11: 5–40, Monseignat, "Relation … [1690-1691]"; La Potherie, *Histoire*, 3: 61; Charlevoix, *Histoire*, 3: 63–4.

88 For insights into French leadership in intercultural contexts, see MacLeod, *Canadian Iroquois*; Steele, *Betrayals*; Haefeli and Sweeney, *Captors and Captives*; Balvay, *L'épée et la plume*, 252–6.

89 On this campaign, see ANOM, C11A 11: 5-40, Monseignat, "Relation … [1690-1691]"; La Potherie, *Histoire*, 3: 67–70; *LIR*, 158–60; Charlevoix, *Histoire*, 3: 64–5; Colonial officials had for some time plotted to attack Albany. See ANOM, C11A 11: 186-8, Denonville to Seignelay, [January 1690]. An alternative account, given by three captured French prisoners, was that Schenectady had been the target all along. *LIR*, 158–62.

90 ANOM, C11A 11: 5-40, Monseignat, "Relation … [1690-1691]"; La Potherie, *Histoire*, 3: 67–8; Charlevoix, *Histoire*, 3: 65.

91 Some twenty-five to fifty inhabitants of Schenectady survived, whether because they were spared or absent at the time of the attack. On the fate of the colonists, see *DHSNY* 1: 301–6; 2: 199–202; Whitmore, ed., *Andros Tracts*, 3: 114–18; Burke, *Mohawk Frontier*, 109–10. On the sparing of the Mohawks, see *NYCD* 9: 468; *JRAD* 64: 61.

92 ANOM, C11A 11: 41–79, Monseignat, "Relation … [1690-1691]"; *NYCD* 3: 700, 708, 717. See also the deposition of three French prisoners, *LIR* 158–62, and Whitmore, ed., *Andros Tracts*, 3: 116

93 ANOM, C11A 11: 5–40, Monseignat, "Relation … [1689-1690]"; Sainsbury et al., eds., *CSPC* 13: 240; Newberry Library, Ayer MS 965, "A trew relation given by Robart Wattson"; Morrison, *Embattled Northeast*, 124–5.

94 ANOM, C11A 11: 19, Monseignat, "Relation … [1689-1690]"; La Potherie, *Histoire*, 1: 347–8; Catalogne, *Recueil*, 47–8; Charlevoix, *Histoire*, 3: 69–72.

95 ANOM, C11A 11: 252–260v, Champigny to the Minister, 10 May 1691; ANOM, C11A 11: 41-79v, Monseignat, "Relation … [1690–1691]."

CHAPTER SEVEN

1 Thwaites, *JRAD* 60: 133–5, 233; 62: 258; *DHSM* 6: 118–19.

2 Brouillan to the Minister, 1 June 1703, in Blanchet et al., eds., *CMNF* 2: 404. On linguistic and riverine perspectives on ethnicity, see Bourque, "Ethnicity"; and Baker, "Finding the Almouchiquois."

3 On King Philip's War, see Drake, *King Philip's War*; Leach, *Flintlock and Tomahawk*; Lepore, *Name of War*. On the impact of the war on the Abenakis, more specifically, see Calloway, *Western Abenakis*, 76–89, and "Wanalancet and Kancagamus"; Siebert, "First Maine Indian War," 137–56; Morrison, "Tricentennial Too," 208–12; Bourque, "Ethnicity," 266–7; Miller, "Abenakis and Colonists," 60–115; Bilodeau, "Economy of War," 36–85. On the Algonquian or Abenaki diaspora, see Calloway, *Western Abenakis*, 6; Haefeli and

Sweeney, "Wattanummon's World"; Sevigny, *Abenaquis*, 117–67; Bourque, "Ethnicity," 257–84; Day, *Identity of Saint Francis Indians*, 16–21.

4 *JRAD* 60: 134, 232. On the baseless suggestion that the Pennacooks were the first Abenakis to settle at Sillery, cf. Sévigny, *Abénaquis*, 124–6; Day, *Identity of Saint Francis Indians*, 17–18, 21; Stewart-Smith, "Pennacook Indians," 195–215; Daly, "No Middle Ground," 126–8.

5 *JRAD* 60: 133–5, 233 (quote); 62: 258.

6 Saint-Vallier, *Estat présent*, 68.

7 Bourque, *Twelve Thousand Years*, 86–9, 107–8, 269–73; Haviland and Power, *Original Vermonters*, 158–9; Ghere, "Abenaki Factionalism," 38–71.

8 Snow, "Late Prehistory," and "Eastern Abenaki"; and Day, "Western Abenaki," 58–88, 137–59, 198–212; Speck, "Eastern Algonkian Wabanaki Confederacy," 492–508; Walker, "Wabanaki Confederacy," 100–39.

9 Champlain, *Works*, 1: 103, 109, 298, 320; 5: 313–16; 6: 43–5; *JRAD* 12: 186–8; 20: 116; 28: 214, 228; 29: 66–8; Sévigny, *Abénaquis*, 64–6; Savoie and Tanguay, "Nœud de l'ancienne amitié," 30–2.

10 *JRAD* 21: 116.

11 Ibid., 21: 66–70; 25: 110–18, 152.

12 Ibid., 23: 282; 24: 58–64, 158–60, 182–4; 25: 116–20, 152, 174–8; 28: 202–4, 214; 29: 66–70; 30: 178–82, 194; 31: 182–206; 36: 82–8, 128; 37: 260; Druillettes *Journal*, and "Rapport." On Gabriel Druillettes, see Lucien Campeau's entry in *DCB* 1: 281–2.

13 *JRAD* 24: 183–5; 27: 79, 245; 28: 169–71, 203–5, 277.

14 Ibid., 36: 101–5, 129, 139–41; 38: 173–5; 40: 195–209; Druillettes, *Journal*, and "Rapport."

15 On the Sokoki and Loups in the Saint Lawrence valley during the late 1650s and 1660s, see Day, *Identity of Saint Francis Indians*, 13–18; Thomas, "Maelstrom of Change," 203–60. On the violent end of the Sokoki-Iroquois truce in 1663, see Brodhead et al., eds., *NYCD* 3: 68; 13: 191–2, 297–8, 308–9, 355–6; Day, "Ouragie War." There is no evidence of a "village" there ca. 1669. Cf. Day, *Identity of Saint Francis Indians*, 13.

16 La Potherie, *Histoire*, 1: 307–9. See also, ANOM, C11A 33: 210-36, "Mémoire du Sr. de Catalogne sur les Seigneuries et habitations des gouvernements de Québec, Montréal et Trois-Rivières," 1712; Charlevoix, *Histoire*, 3: 102–13.

17 Charland, *Histoire des Abénakis*, 15–19; BANQ-TR, TL3, S11, P1029, Petition of Jean Crevier regarding Jean dit Petit-Jean, 23 March 1669; BANQ-Q, notary Antoine Adhémar, Contract between René Fort dit Laprairie and Simon Meunier, 17 January 1672; BANQ-Q, notary Bénigne Basset, Cession by Pierre Boucher and Jeanne Crevier, 20 and 23 July 1676

18 *JRAD* 60: 130; Campeau, ed., *MNF* 9: 389n39; *JRAD* 52: 60–8, 222–6; 53: 60;

60: 250; 62: 32, 52; Crespieul, *Pretiosa Mors*; Hébert, *Registre de Sillery*, 31–2, 78, 104, 223, 248–9, 288, 293; Bigot, *Relation de ce qui s'est passé*, 13–15.

19 *JRAD* 62: 259–61; Saint-Vallier, *Estat présent*, 68. See also Hubbard, *History of Indian Wars*, 2: 204.

20 In contrast to Iroquoian adoption practices, those of the northeastern Algonquians have not attracted much scholarly attention. On adoption among the Abenakis, see Nash, "Abiding Frontier," 280–2.

21 On Abenaki leadership, see Morrison, "Dawnland Directors," 1–19; Nash, "Abiding Frontier," 102–3.

22 *JRAD* 60: 239–43. The context suggests that the unnamed captain alluded to in an earlier report from Sillery was none other than Pirrouaki. See ibid., 60: 137. See also Hébert, *Registre de Sillery*, 230; Bigot, *Relation de ce qui s'est passé*, 13–16. For their likely confirmation (under their new names Tek8erimat and Etek8erimansk8e) in 1682, see *Registre de Sillery*, 293.

23 *JRAD* 60: 131–5, 233.

24 "Mémoire touschant les sauvages abenaquis de Sillery," 1679, in *CMNF* 1: 272.

25 See Francis Card's declaration in *DHSM* 6: 159-61 (cf. Hubbard, *History*, 2: 204). For other claims of French assistance, see *CMHS*, 1st ser. 6: 205; ibid., 4th ser. 6: 307. On the necessity of powder for hunting and Canada as a source of powder, see also *DHSM* 6: 119; Hubbard, *History*, 2: 147, 152, 156, 210.

26 *JRAD* 60: 135. Many New Englanders nevertheless believed that the French were inciting and supplying the Abenakis. See for example *DHSM* 6: 150.

27 Quentin Stockwell in Haefeli and Sweeney, *Captive Histories*, 45.

28 For evidence of the distribution of supplies, see *JRAD* 60: 136–7. For evidence of the shortages and epidemic, see ibid., 60: 237–39.

29 Margry, *Découvertes et établissements*, 1: 525–6, 532–4, 538–44, 593–4, 600; 2: 139–40, 148–9, 153–4. Regarding the westward migration of Eastern Algonquians (Mahicans, Munsees) towards the Great Lakes in the second half of the 1670s, see Brasser, *Riding on the Frontier's Crest*, 21–4, 66–7.

30 *JRAD* 62: 43.

31 Ibid., 60: 239.

32 Day, *Identity of Saint Francis Indians*, 21; Calloway, *Western Abenakis*, 84–5; Gookin, "Historical account," 520–1; Hubbard, *History*, 2: 239–40; *CMHS*, 1st ser. 3: 179. On the raids, see also Stockwell's accounts in Haefeli and Sweeney, *Captive Histories*, 35–48 (alternatively, in Vaughan and Clark, *Puritans Among Indians*, 79–89; and Wells and Wells, *History of Hatfield*, 88–98).

33 *JRAD* 63: 207–9, 213–15; *NYCD* 9: 795; Gookin, "Historical account," 519–20; Hubbard, *History of Indian Wars*, 2: 226–9, 233; Belknap, *History*, 1: 152–4.

On Mohawk raiding, see *DHSM* 6: 166–7; Gookin, "Historical account," 520–1; *CMHS*, 1st ser. 3: 180–1, 185. The claim that the Pennacooks, specifically, were the first Abenakis to settle at Sillery is impossible to substantiate. Cf. Sévigny, *Abénaquis*, 124–6; Day, *Identity of Saint Francis Indians*, 17–18, 21; Calloway, "Wanalancet and Kancagamus," 276, and *Western Abenakis*, 81–2, 84–5; Haefeli and Sweeney, "Wattanummon's World," 212–24; Stewart-Smith, "Pennacook Indians," 196–8.

34 *JRAD* 62: 25, 37, 45–7, 259–61; Saint-Vallier, *Estat présent*, 68–9. For references to Abenakis from Acadia receiving instruction from Christians from Sillery, see *JRAD* 63: 47.

35 *JRAD* 62: 25, 37, 45–7, 109. See also Brouillan to the Minister, 1 June 1703, in *CMNF* 2: 404.

36 BANQ-Q, TP1, S36, Series 36, 1960-01-347/16, "Acte de concession de terres du Sault de la Chaudière," 1 July 1683.

37 "Mémoire touschant les sauvages abenaquis de Sillery," 1679, in *CMNF* 1: 272–3.

38 BANQ-Q, TP1, S36, Series 36, 1960-01-347/16, "Acte de concession de terres du Sault de la Chaudière," 1 July 1683; *JRAD* 62: 265–7; Boily, "Terres amérindiennes," 183–6. On Msakkikkan (Msakik8n, Mesakkikkan, Mesakkicans, Eteskan, Méchatigan, Mésakégant, Asakigant, Méchakiganne, Kégakkan, Satigan, Satigant, Santigan, Sartigan), see also Campeau, "Msakkikkan"; Charland, "Définition et reconstitution," 133–4; Hébert, *Registre de Sillery*, 43, 270, 273, 274, 278, 285.

39 Hébert, *Registre de Sillery*, 43, 270, 273, 274, 278.

40 *JRAD* 63: 30; Bigot, *Copie d'une lettre*, 7-8; Clair, "Du décor rêvé," 443–6, 463–6.

41 *JRAD* 62: 23–32, 44–6, 50, 142; Bigot, *Copie d'une lettre*, 9. For references to Marguerite's relatives, see Hébert, *Registre de Sillery*, 60, 109, 243, 247, 249, 252, 257, 263, 268, 269, 272, 274, 275, 281, 286, 293. For a discussion of female leadership among the Abenakis, see Nash, *Abiding Frontier*, chap. 3; Little, *Many Captivities*, 68–78.

42 *JRAD* 62: 116–20; Clair, "Du décor rêvé," 389–90.

43 Merlet, *Histoire des relations*, 37; Clair, "Du décor rêvé," 437–57.

44 On the naming of the mission, see *JRAD* 63: 27–9; Bigot, *Copie d'une lettre*. On the circulation and arrivals, *JRAD* 63: 51–3.

45 *JRAD* 63: 82–4.

46 Ibid., 63: 52–4; Bigot, *Relation de ce qui s'est passé*, 17; ANOM, G1, 461: 1, 3–3v, "Recensement général du Canada, tableau récapitulatif," 1685.

47 Sébastien Rasle to his brother, 12 October 1723, in *Lettres édifiantes* 23 (1738), 200–1, 209. The names "néssa8akamíghé" for "village de S. Fran[çois]

de Sales" and "8néssa8akamighé8iak" for its inhabitants ("*ses hommes*") are provided by Rasles, *Dictionary of Abnaki Language*, 458, 542. Cf. Merlet, *Histoire des relations*, 23–4. The etymology is provided by Trumbull, who assumed that this name referred to the relocation of the mission from the Chaudière to the Saint François River in 1700, but Rasles's indication that he began his dictionary in 1691 suggests otherwise. See *Composition of Indian Geographical Names*, 22. Vetromile provides the alternative but less likely meaning of "where the river is barricaded with osier to fish, or where the fish is dried by smoke," in *Abnakis*, 24. This name does not appear in the mission's sacramental registers, which contain only variations of the name Msakkikkan during the years 1683–86, and its Latin equivalent of "*In Missione Campestri*" once in 1688, but the lack of such registers makes it impossible to chart the toponymical shift more precisely. Hébert, *Registre de Sillery*, 43, 270, 273, 274, 278.

48 *JRAD* 60: 135.

49 Ibid., 63: 144.

50 ANOM, C11A 6: 181, De Meulles to the Minister, 4 November 1683.

51 *JRAD* 63: 54–64.

52 Ibid., 60: 25–7, 111; 63: 63, 77. Etienne Nekoutneant's (Neketucant, Neghetnanan, Neketnant, Neketneant, Nekedneant, Neketnehante, Nek8tneant, Kenetneant) given name is occasionally Latinized as Stephanus in the Sillery register. He had arrived at Sillery in 1680 and received baptism the following year. He and his wife, Agathe Nek8t8-sk8e8it (Nek8t8sk8e8it, Nek88sk8e8it, or Neketneantsk8e), were baptized on 24 May 1681; four of their children were baptized in 1680 and 1682. See Hébert, *Registre de Sillery*, 60, 109, 243, 247, 249, 252, 257, 263, 268, 269, 272, 274, 275, 281, 286, 293.

53 Sainsbury et al., eds., *CSPC* 11: 634–5. On the tension in Acadia in 1684–85, see Miller, "Abenakis and Colonists," 131–9.

54 *JRAD* 63: 62–5. See also ANOM, C11A 6: 268v, La Barre to Dongan, 24 July 1684; ANOM, C11A 6: 309v, "Mémoire de La Barre concernant son expédition au Lac Ontario," 1 October 1684. On Saint-Castin, see Georges Cerbelaud Salagnac's entry in *DCB* 2: 4–7.

55 *CMNF* 1: 410; Baugy, *Journal*, 86–7; Belmont, *Histoire du Canada*, 20; ANOM, C11A 9: 121–31, "Memoire de l'Estat present des Affaires de Canada sur la guerre des Iroquois," 27 October 1687. While Salagnac's entry in the *DCB* claims that Saint-Castin took part in the campaign of 1687, he was at Petagouet throughout the summer. See *CMNF* 1: 399–401 403; cf. Georges Cerbelaud Salagnac, "Abbadie de Saint-Castin, Jean-Vincent," *DCB* 2: 4–7.

56 *JRAD* 63: 63–7. The muster held at Cataraqui indicates that there were

"Abnakis chresiens de Sillery et autres endroits qu'on n'a pas pû ramasser n'en ayant eu le temps, soixante cinq bons hom[m]es," as well as seventy-two Algonquins, commanded by Hertel and Grand Pré. ANOM, C11A 6: 267, "Revue faite au fort Frontenac le 17 aoust 1684 des Sauvages qui nous ont suivis pour la guerre," 17 August 1684.

57 For the frustration of the Great Lakes allies, see ANOM, C11A 6: 311v–312, "Mémoire de La Barre concernant son expédition au Lac Ontario," 1 October 1684; Lahontan, *Oeuvres*, 302.

58 ANOM, C11A 6: 346v–347, La Barre to Louis XIV, 13 November 1684; Lahontan, *Oeuvres*, 298–9. On the illness among the Abenakis in particular, see *JRAD* 63: 73, 81–99; Bigot, *Relation de ce qui s'est passé*, 5–6. On the disease affecting the Sokokis near the Saint François River, see Maurault, *Histoire des Abénaquis*, 273. On the prevalence of malaria in the wetlands around Cataraqui, see Fallis, "Malaria."

59 *JRAD* 63: 87–93; Bigot, *Relation de ce qui s'est passé*, 17.

60 Bigot, *Relation de ce qui s'est passé*, 13–15; PDRH, Répertoire des actes d'état civil, 1621–1799, Record #30553, Burial of Michel Terourimah [*sic*], 23 January 1685. (http://www.genealogie.umontreal.ca)

61 Provost, *Les Abénaquis* (1948), 33–4; Boily, "Terres amérindiennes," 186; "Mémoire touschant les sauvages abenaquis de Sillery," 1679, in *CMNF* 1: 272–3.

62 Hébert, *Registre de Sillery*, 23–5; ANOM, G1, 461: 1, 3–3v, Recensement général du Canada, tableau récapitulatif," 1685 and 1688.

63 *JRAD* 62: 24–52.

64 Ibid., 63: 70.

65 ANOM, G1, 461: 3–4.

66 *NYCD* 13: 531–2.

67 Leder, ed., *LIR*, 77–9, 95–6; *NYCD* 4: 576; Day, *Identity of Saint Francis Indians*, 22–3. This Sadochquis or Sadocquis appears to be the same man as the "Shattoockquis alias Shadookis" who in 1665 signed a deed for land in what is now Brookfield, New Hampshire, along with a Pocumtuck sachem. See Bruchac, "Abenaki Connections," 262–78.

68 NYSA, A1894 25:121, Instructions to Thomas Delavall, 30 May 1676; NYSA, A1895 3(2): 10, Council Minute, 30 May 1676; NYSA, A1894 28: 186, Council Meeting, 20 August 1678; Wraxall, *Abridgement*, 101–2. On Schagticoke, see Midtrod, "So Great a Correspondence," 253-326; Calloway, *Western Abenakis*, 82–3; Starna, *From Homeland*, 148–70.

69 *LIR*, 95–6.

70 Ibid.

71 Ibid., 77–9, 82, 95–6; *NYCD* 4: 576; Belknap, *History*, 1: 182, 225–7; Calloway, "Wanalancet and Kancagamus," 277–80.

72 ANOM, C11A 9: 32–8, Champigny to the Minister, 16 July 1687; Baugy ("bande d'Arhetil" [sic: Hertel]), *Journal*, 74–5, 86–7; Belmont, *Histoire du Canada*, 20; *JRAD* 63: 269; ANOM, C11A 9: 118, Denonville, "Mémoire du Voyage Pour l'Entreprise de M. le Marquis de Denonville contre les Sonnontouans," 1687.

73 *NYCD* 3: 436–7. On the commercial expeditions led by Johannes Oseboom and Patrick Magregory, see Armour, "Merchants of Albany," 1–22.

74 *NYCD* 3: 482. The Abenakis are termed "Onnagonque Indians" in the English record. See also Day, *Identity of Saint Francis Indians*, 30; Calloway, "Wanalancet and Kancagamus," 281.

75 *NYCD* 3: 482; Day, *Identity of Saint Francis Indians*, 30; Calloway, "Wanalancet and Kancagamus," 281.

76 See BNF, 13516, f. 37v, Belmont, "Recueil"; ANOM, C11A 10: 61-62v, Denonville to Dongan, 20 August 1688.

77 Ibid.

78 *NYCD* 3: 561–5, 569–70; ANOM, C11A 10: 127-9, Champigny to the Minister, 19 October 1688. The circumstances of Wampolack's raid have been examined by Calloway, *Western Abenakis*, 92–3; and Lozier, "Lever des chevelures," 516–18.

79 Ibid. On the Anglo-American reaction, see also Whitmore, ed., *Andros Tracts*, 2: 207; *NYCD* 3: 550–70.

80 Morrison, *Embattled Northeast*, 113–17; *DHSM* 6: 250–500; Bouton, *Documents and Records*, 2: 46–55; *NYCD* 3: 550–4, 561–2.

81 ANOM, C11A 10:110, "Mémoire de Denonville au ministre sur l'état présent des affaires du Canada depuis le 10 août jusqu'au 31 octobre," 1688.

82 Hébert, *Registre de Sillery*, 7; Campeau, "Msakkikkan," 59.

83 LAC, MG8-A8, 1, "Acte de concession terres du Sault de la Chaudière," 14 October 1689 (copy in *Pièces et documents*, 394–5); Roy, *Histoire de la Seigneurie de Lauzon*, 1: 401; Boily, "Terres amérindiennes," 187–8. See also Provost, "Le fief Miville," 33, 36; Campeau, "Msakkikkan," 60–1.

84 See ANOM, C11A 10: 86–93, Denonville to the Minister, 30 October 1688; ANOM, C11A 10: 244–250v, Champigny to the Minister, 16 November 1689; ANOM, C11A 10: 315–16, Denonville, "Mémoire concernant le Canada," 1689; "Résumé des lettres sur les sauvages abénaquis," 1689, *CMNF* 1: 468–9; ANOM, C11A 10: 535, "Observations sur l'estat des affaires de Canada au depart des vaisseaux," 18 November 1689; ANOM, C11A 11: 185-94, "Mémoire de Denonville à Seignelay," January 1690; ANOM, B 15: 121, Louis XIV to Frontenac and Champigny, 14 July 1690.

85 O'Callaghan, ed., *DHSNY* 2: 20. On the Pennacooks' movements at this junc-

ture, see Stewart-Smith, "Pennacook Indians," 224–4; Haefeli and Sweeney, *Captors and Captives*, 81–4.

86 See, "Résumé des lettres sur les sauvages abénaquis," 1689, in CMNF 1: 468. On the attack on Dover and subsequent raids, see Bouton, *Documents and Records*, 2: 50–5; Belknap, *History*, 1: 198–203, 216–25, 254–5; Mather, *Decennium Luctuosum*; NYCD 3: 611; Gyles, *Memoirs*, 1–4.

87 ANOM, C11A 11: 5-40, Monseignat, "Relation [1689-1690]"; Charlevoix, *Histoire*, 3: 73–6; DHSM 5: 55–66; CSPC 13: 240; NYCD 4: 115; Newberry Library, Ayer MS 965, "A trew relation given by Robart Wattson"; Belknap, *History*, 1: 256–60. See also Morrison, *Embattled Northeast*, 124–5.

88 Ibid.

89 Bullivant, "Mr. Bullivant's Journall," 105–6.

90 *Publick Occurences*, 25 September 1690; Belknap, *History*, 1: 256–60; Tuttle, Report, 352–5.

91 ANOM, C11A 11: 18v-19, Monseignat, "Relation [1689-1690]"; La Potherie, *Histoire*, 1: 347–8; Charlevoix, *Histoire*, 3: 70–2; Catalogne, *Recueil*, 47–8. For another example of violence between the Mohawks and Sokokis or Loups, see ANOM, C11A 9: 373, Frontenac to Louis XIV, 14 November 1680.

92 ANOM, C11A 11: 18v–19, Monseignat, "Relation [1689–1690]"; La Potherie, *Histoire*, 1: 347–8; Charlevoix, *Histoire*, 3: 69–72; Catalogne, *Recueil*, 47–8.

93 La Potherie, *Histoire*, 1: 347–8; Charlevoix, *Histoire*, 3: 69–72; Catalogne, *Recueil*, 47–8. See also "Parolles des Sauvages de la Mission de Pentagouet," 6 January 1691, in CMNF 2: 36 (the clerk or transcriber mistakenly refers to "l'Anglois qui prit mon frère"); "Réponse de Frontenac," 8 March 1691, in ibid., 2: 38–9; ANOM, C11A 11: 41-79, Monseignat, "Relation [1690 … 1691]." The Pennacook leader Wattanumon may have been among the Kahnawake' Abenaki captives. In March of 1692 he reported that he had spent a year in captivity at Montreal, and that he and others "were first taken by the Eastern Indians from whom they escaped and afterward by French Indians." DHSM 5: 376–7. Cf. Calloway, "Wanalancet and Kancagamus," 285–6; Haefeli and Sweeney, *Captors and Captives*, 78–84.

94 ANOM, C11A 11: 185–194, Denonville to the Minister, January 1690; ANOM, C11A 10: 535, "Observations sur l'estât des affaires de Canada au départ des vaisseaux, le 18 novembre 1689; ANOM, C11A 11: 321–3, "Observations sur l'état des affaires du Canada"; Louis XIV to Frontenac and Champigny, 14 July 1690, in NYCD 9: 453. On Denonville's enthusiasm for the Jesuit missions, see also ANOM, C11A 11: 185–94, Denonville to Seignelay, 4 May 1690.

95 Villebon to the Minister (?), 1691, in Blanchet et al., eds., CMNF 2: 47–8; "Mémoire de ce qui est nécessaire pour l'entretien des sauvages de l'Acadie […]," in ibid., 2: 48; ANOM, B 16: 34, Louis XIV to Frontenac and

Champigny, 7 April 1691; ANOM, C11D 2: 178–9v, Instructions to Villebon, 7 April 1691; ANOM, C11D 2: 180-2v, Louis XIV to Frontenac, 7 April 1691.

96 "Resumé d'un mémoire pour ces Abenaquis Chrestiens," 1692, in *CMNF* 1: 78–9; ANOM, C11A 12: 72–83v, Champigny to the Minister, 5 October 1692. The flurry of correspondence in 1692 and 1693 makes no mention of an extension of the funds to the Jesuit mission at Sillery/Chaudière. For lists of presents and subsidized trading goods shipped directly to Acadia, and references to the funds set aside for the missionaries of Acadia, see, ANOM, B 16: 72 v, "Mémoire des munitions, armes, ustanciles à envoyer aux sauvages de l'Acadie," 27 February 1692; ANOM, B 16: 106, Louis XIV to Villebon, April 1692; ANOM, B 16: 139, "État des munitions et approvisionnements à envoyer en Acadie," January 1693; ANOM, B 16: 286, "Munitions et marchandises pour les troupes et les Sauvages d'Acadie," April 1693; "Estat des présens à envoyer aux chefs abenaquis à l'Acadie, 1693," in *CMNF* 2: 111; "Estat des présens à envoyer aux sauvages abenaquis dans lesquels chefs auront part," in ibid., 2: 111; "Estat des munitions et marchandises embarquez en France sur la frégate 'La Suzanne' en 1693, pour estre portez à l'Acadie", in ibid., 2: 129–30; ANOM, B 17: 44v, "Mémoire pour servir d'instruction au sieur de Villebon," 13 March 1694; "Estat des présents ordinaires pour les sauvages de l'Acadie," 3 March 1696, in *CMNF* 2: 206–7; "Présents des sauvages de l'Acadie," 1698, in ibid., 2 : 291–2.

97 Merlet, *Histoire des relations*, xiv–xv, 23–41, 45–7; *JRAD* 69: 68–72; Clair, "Du décor rêvé," 482–5.

98 LAC, MG1-G1, 461: 5–6, 8. The population remained stable, with 355 inhabitants (including an estimated fifty to seventy warriors) recorded in 1698. See LAC, MG1-G1, 461: 8.

99 ANOM, C11A 12: 256–60v, Champigny to the Minister, 17 August 1693.

100 BNF, Manuscrits français 6453, f. 52v–53v, [Jacques Bigot], "De la mission de St. François de Sales," 29 October 1694; LAC, MG17-A6-2, 161: 14–17, Jacques Bigot to Father Lucas, 8 October 1694. For the presence of Louis André, see parish registers of Saint François du Lac, esp. baptism of Pierre-Louis Parenteau, 12 January 1690.

101 BNF, Manuscrits français 6453, f. 54, [Jacques Bigot], "De la mission de St. François de Sales," 29 October 1694; LAC, MG17-A6-2, 161: 14-17, Jacques Bigot to Father Lucas, 8 October 1694. For one of the rare accounts distinguishing the activity of the warriors from the Chaudière in the New England theatre of war, see Champigny to the Minister, 5 October 1692, in *CMNF* 2: 89–90.

102 ANOM, C11A 12: 182–205v, Monseignat, "Relation [1692–1693]"; ANOM,

C11A 14: 35–64, Monseignat, "Relation [1695 … 1696]"; Charlevoix, *Histoire*, 3: 185, 225, 247; La Potherie, *Histoire*, 1: 319–20.

103 ANOM, C11A 12: 182–205v, Monseignat, "Relation [1691–1692]."

104 ANOM, C11A 15: 3–21, Monseignat, "Relation [1696–1697]."

105 *LIR*, 189–90; Wraxall, *Abridgement*, 60, 91; *NYCD* 4: 337, 575–7, 648–52, 743–5, 983–5, 990–2.

106 NYSA, A1894 41:25, Propositions made to Governor Benjamin Fletcher by the Schaghticoke Indians, 14 January 1697.

107 On the Abenaki presence at the discussions in 1700, see La Potherie, *Histoire*, 4: 146; Charlevoix, *Histoire*, 3: 372; ANOM, C11A 18: 85, 87v, 88, "Discours des Iroquois qui sont venus à Montréal avec le père Bruyas et les sieurs de Maricourt et Joncaire. Réponses de Callière. Discours de chefs […]," 3 September 1700. On their presence in 1701, see La Potherie, *Histoire*, 3: 251–2; ANOM, C11A 19: 43, "Ratification de la paix," August-September 1701. The Abenakis of Acadia were represented by a certain Mask8adoue or Meskouadoue in both 1700 and 1701, accompanied that latter year by Ounag8imy, Netamimes (?), and other "principaux Abenakis de l'Acadie."

108 ANOM, C11A 15: 3–21, Monseignat, "Relation [1696–1697]."

109 ANOM, C11A 15: 22–37, Monseignat, "Relation [1697–1698]"; *NYCD* 4: 338–41; ANOM, B 20: 42, Louis XIV to Villebon, 26 March 1698; ANOM, B 20: 42v, Minister to Villebon, 26 March 1698; Charlevoix, *Histoire*, 3: 335; *NYCD* 4: 343–4.

110 LAC, MG8-A8, 1: 465, "Acte de concession terres du Sault de la Chaudière," 5 March 1697; Boily, "Terres amérindiennes," 189–91.

111 Bigot, *Relation de la Mission Abnaquise*, 7–8.

112 ANOM, C11A 17: 69, Champigny to the Minister, 20 October 1699.

113 BANQ-M, notary Antoine Adhémar, "Concession de terre située au haut de la seigneurie de St-François par Marguerite Hertel […] et Joseph Crevier de St-François […] aux Sauvages Abénakis et Sokokis," 23 August 1700; Maurault, *Histoire des Abénaquis*, 278–81; Boily, "Terres amérindiennes," 191–7.

114 BANQ-M, notary Antoine Adhémar, "Concession de terre située au haut de la seigneurie de St-François par Marguerite Hertel […] et Joseph Crevier de St-François […] aux Sauvages Abénakis et Sokokis," 23 August 1700. Regarding the seigneury's vulnerability, see *NYCD* 4: 66, 236; Brandão, *Your Fyre Shall Burn No More*, appendix D.

115 ANOM, G1, 461: 6, Census of 1698.

116 There has been some confusion surrounding the use of the name Arsikantegouk (Arsikanteg8k, arsi-kantek8, Alsig8ntegw, Arosaguntacook), variants

of which have mistakenly been used to refer to the Wabanaki inhabitants of the Androscoggin River. Day, *Identity of Saint Francis Indians*, 1–5; Ghere, "'Disappearance,'" 73–4, and "Abenaki Factionalism," 2, 118–21; cf. Snow, "Eastern Abenaki," 143–6. See also Charland, "Définition et reconstitution," 162–70.

117 Bigot, *Relation de la Mission Abnaquise*, 15–17; La Potherie, *Histoire*, 1: 309. According to Abenaki oral tradition reported by Maurault, Bigot left Quebec with 1,500 warriors, 500 of whom remained at Bécancour and the rest at Saint François. Maurault thought that these figures might refer to total numbers, rather than just warriors. Charland and Day after him have countered that even these figures would be too high, given that the 1698 census reported a population of only 355 at the mission on the Chaudière. Maurault, *Histoire des Abénaquis*, 282–3; Charland, *Histoire des Abénakis*, 22; Day, *Identity of Saint Francis Indians*, 32.

118 Bigot, *Relation de la Mission Abnaquise*, 7–10; La Potherie, *Histoire*, 3: 121.

119 Bigot, *Relation de la Mission Abnaquise*, 15–17.

CHAPTER EIGHT

1 Regarding La Plaque's activity, see La Potherie, *Histoire*, 1: 322–3; 3: 154, 179, 191–2, 199, 204, 211, 224; ANOM, C11A 11: 259, Champigny to the Minister, 10 May 1691; ANOM, C11A 12: 93–95v, "Mémoire de Champigny sur ce qui s'est passé au sujet de la guerre de novembre 1691 à octobre 1692," 5 October 1692. English sources allude to warriors led by a certain Onontaquirott or Onwondaquiro against Boston in 1693, and towards Albany in 1695. Brodhead et al., eds., *NYCD* 4: 50, 124. French sources allude to an Onateguen who led warriors against Onondaga in 1693. BNF, Département des manuscrits, Français 6453, f.4v, "Relation des affaires des Iroquois (1692–1693)." Tentative linguistic evidence supports the circumstantial evidence that this is the same man: *plaque de fusil* (gun plate) was "otginonkara" in Onondaga. See Shea, *French-Onondaga Dictionary*, 80. Lahontan, for his part, describes La Plaque as "a Seneca raised among the French," erroneously it seems. Lahontan, *Oeuvres*, 2: 1029–30. In later years, his attachment to the French waned. For his later life, see ANOM, C11A 122: 14, Copy of an anonymous letter, 30 September 1705; Charlevoix, *Histoire*, 3: 86; 6: 33; ANOM, C11A 30: 112, Vaudreuil's instructions to Ramezay, 14 July 1709.

2 La Potherie, *Histoire*, 1: 522.

3 "Lettre du père Cholenec," in *Lettres édifiantes et curieuses*, 6: 100–127; Charlevoix, *Histoire*, 1: 587–99.

4 "Lettre du père Cholenec," in *Lettres édifiantes et curieuses*, 6: 100–127; Charlevoix, *Histoire* 1: 587–90.

5 Parmenter, "After Mourning Wars," 80, and *Edge of Woods*, 221; Brandão, *Your Fyre Shall Burn No More*, appendix D; Keener, "Ethnohistoric Perspective," appendix 3. On the executions in the missions and at Montreal, see LAC, MG17-A7-2, 7: 4157-4161, Tronson to Belmont, 30 May 1690.

6 Havard, *Great Peace*; Brandão and Starna, "Treaties of 1701"; Parmenter, *Edge of Woods*, 231–73.

7 ANOM, C11A 11:186, Denonville to Seignelay, January 1690 ; ANOM, C11A 10: 217–24, Frontenac to the Minister, 15 November 1689; Memoir of the king to Frontenac and Champigny, 14 July 1690, copy in *NYCD* 9: 453; ANOM, C11A 11: 86–98v, Frontenac to the Minister, 12 November 1690; BNF, 13516, f. 76, Belmont, "Recueil" (cf. Belmont, *Histoire de l'eau de vie*, 18). Charlevoix suggests that the return to the south shore took place shortly after the Schenectady raid. Charlevoix, *Histoire*, 3: 65. Jean Leclerc's claim that Denonville attempted to persuade the Kahnawakes to return home through the fall of 1689 is unconvincing. Leclerc, *Denonville*, 258.

8 Brandão, *Your Fyre Shall Burn No More*, appendix D.

9 Accounts of the negotiations diverge. *NYCD* 3: 777–8; ANOM, C11A 11: 41–79v, Monseignat, "Relation … [1690–1691]"; ANOM, C11A 10: 9–12v, Bruyas to Frontenac, 5 April 1691, copy in Thwaites, ed., *JRAD* 64: 56–64; NYSA, A1894, v. 37, no. 56, "Relation concerning Canada, brought by two Maquase to Albany," 28 April 1691; see BNF, 13516, f. 41, Belmont, "Recueil" ("ganna8ages" is misleadingly transcribed as "Ganneyousses" in ibid., *Histoire du Canada*, 33); La Potherie, *Histoire*, 3: 129–33; Charlevoix, *Histoire*, 3: 135–8; *NYCD* 3: 782.

10 Ibid.

11 ANOM, C11A 10: 9–12v, Bruyas to Frontenac, 5 April 1691, copy in *JRAD* 64: 56–64; ANOM, C11A 11: 251–251v, Champigny to the Minister, 12 May 1691; ANOM, C11A 12: 93–95v, Champigny, "Mémoire," 5 October 1692; ANOM, C11A 11: 41–79v, Monseignat, "Relation … [1690–1691]"; Charlevoix, *Histoire*, 3: 137–8; *NYCD* 3: 777–8.

12 See BNF, 13516, f. 41v, Belmont, "Recueil" (the published version does not include Belmont's list of the dead, and erroneously transcribes "semoint" [*sic*] as "dormoient": ibid., *Histoire du Canada*, 33); ibid., *Histoire de l'eau de vie*, 17. See also ANOM, C11A 11: 41–79v, Monseignat, "Relation … [1690–1691]"; Charlevoix, *Histoire*, 3: 138.

13 ANOM, C11A 11: 41–79v, Monseignat, "Relation … [1690–1691]"; La Potherie, *Histoire*, 3: 153; Charlevoix, *Histoire*, 3: 144–5. La Potherie spells it Tannouraoua.

14 ANOM, C11A 10: 9–12v, Bruyas to Frontenac, 5 April 1691; *NYCD* 9: 515; ANOM, C11A 11: 252–260v, Champigny to the Minister, 10 May 1691. One of the two emissaries who stayed behind was named Taonnochrio. *NYCD* 3: 782.

15 *NYCD* 9 : 517; Belmont, *Histoire du Canada*, 33; La Potherie, *Histoire*, 3: 133–4; Charlevoix, *Histoire*, 3: 141–4. An English source alludes to thirty warriors going out against the Onondagas in June. *NYCD* 3: 782.

16 *NYCD* 3:790, 800–5; Richter, "Rediscovered Links," 85; ANOM, C11A 11: 41–9v, Monseignat, "Relation … [1690–1691],"; NYSA, A1894, v. 38, no. 158, "Examination of Two Frenchmen," 1 August 1692 ; La Potherie, *Histoire*, 3: 138–44; Charlevoix, *Histoire*, 3: 149–55; BNF, 13516, f. 42–42v, Belmont, "Recueil" (here again the published version errs by indicating that the warriors were wavering, when the original indicates that the habitants did so. Ibid., *Histoire du Canada*, 33–4). For an overview of the battles, see Bourdages et al., *1691*.

17 For a sense of the whirlwind of suspicion and blame projected by the governor and his entourage, see Charlevoix, *Histoire*, 3: 141–4; ANOM, C11A 11: 233v, Frontenac to the Minister, 20 October 1691.

18 *NYCD* 3: 815, 817; Catalogne, *Recueil*, 47; La Potherie, *Histoire*, 3: 154–5; Charlevoix, *Histoire*, 3: 163; BNF, 13516, f. 42v, Belmont, "Recueil" (ibid., *Histoire du Canada*, 34). For evidence that Onnonragewas (Onnonragouas) had been killed, see *NYCD* 9: 525. For Mohawk population statistics, see Parmenter, *Edge of Woods*, 291.

19 According to Belmont and La Potherie, the victims were led by the Seneca headman Sategaronhies. Belmont mentions 6 "Sauteurs" (certainly meaning the Kahnawakes, as no other account alludes to Sauteurs proper, i.e. Ojibwa Anishinabeg from the Great Lakes) and 3 chiefs of Kanehsatake killed. Catalogne mentions the death of "trois ou quatre de nos plus braves sauvages." ANOM, C11A 12: 93–95v, Champigny, "Mémoire," 5 October 1692 (gives 120 Frenchmen and 205 allies); BNF, 13516, f. 42v–43, Belmont, "Recueil" (Sategaronhies in the original is transcribed as Tateguenondahi, and the names of the 3 chiefs are not transcribed at all, in ibid., *Histoire du Canada*, 34). Catalogne, *Recueil*, 52–3; La Potherie, *Histoire*, 3: 155–7; Charlevoix, *Histoire* 3: 163–4.

20 ANOM, C11A 12 : 93-95v, Champigny, "Mémoire," 5 October 1692; ANOM, C11A 12 : 182-205v, Monseignat, "Relation … [1692–1693]."

21 Leder, ed., *LIR*, 162–7; *NYCD* 9: 538, 555–6.

22 ANOM, C11A 12: 46-48v, Frontenac and Champigny to the Minister, 11 November 1692; ANOM, C11A 12: 87v, Champigny to the Minister, 10 November 1692; ANOM, C11A 12: 182–205v, Monseignat, "Relation …

[1692–1693]"; BNF, Département des manuscrits, Français 6453, f.1, "Relation des affaires des Iroquois (1692–1693)"; La Potherie, *Histoire*, 3: 167–9; Charlevoix, *Histoire* 3: 183–4.

23 ANOM, C11A 12: 87v, Champigny to the Minister, 10 November 1692; ANOM, C11A 12: 183, Monseignat, "Relation ... [1692–1693]." For Frontenac's misgivings, see Charlevoix, *Histoire*, 3: 185.

24 La Potherie, *Histoire*, 3: 129–30, 158–61; Charlevoix, *Histoire*, 3 : 168.

25 Tatakwiséré's name is here spelled Tataconicere (elsewhere Tatachquiserax, Tatachquistioro, Thatha Kouicheré, Tatak8isseré, Tak8isseré, Tatacoüisseré, Tatta8isseré). ANOM, C11A 12: 256–260v, Monseignat, "Relation ... [1692–1693]," 12 August 1693; ANOM, C11A 12: 46–48v, Frontenac and Champigny to the Minister, 11 November 1692; ANOM, C11A 12: 87v, Champigny to the Minister, 10 November 1692; ANOM, C11A 12: 183–183v, Monseignat, "Relation ... [1692–1693]"; La Potherie, *Histoire*, 3 : 168; Charlevoix, *Histoire*, 3 : 183–4.

26 ANOM, C11A 12: 256, Monseignat, "Relation [...] 1692 [...] 1693"; BNF, Département des manuscrits, Français 6453, f.1, "Relation des affaires des Iroquois (1692–93)"; La Potherie, *Histoire*, 3: 169–70. Whereas La Potherie concurs with these sources, i.e. that the Christian Iroquois had "resolved to adopt other [i.e. this] extreme measure," historians have tended to follow Charlevoix who, chronicling these events several decades later, placed the initiative squarely with Frontenac. Charlevoix, *Histoire*, 3: 170, 185–6. See also Colden, *History of the Five Indian Nations* (1747), 181–2; Eccles, *Frontenac*, 252.

27 ANOM, C11A 12: 256–260v, Champigny "Relation ... [1692–1693]," 17 August 1693; ANOM, C11A 12: 182–205v, Monseignat, "Relation ... [1692-1693]"; BNF, Département des manuscrits, Français 6453, f. 1–1v, "Relation des affaires des Iroquois (1692–1693)"; *NYCD* 4 : 6–7, 14–24, 222; La Potherie, *Histoire*, 1: 322; Charlevoix, *Histoire*, 3: 185–8; Bayard and Lodowick, *Narrative*.

28 *NYCD* 4 : 17–19; ANOM, C11A 12: 256–260v, Champigny, "Relation ... [1692–1693]," 17 August 1693; ANOM, C11A 12: 182–205v, Monseignat, "Relation ... [1692–1693]"; BNF, Département des manuscrits, Français 6453, f. 1v–2, "Relation des affaires des Iroquois (1692–1693)"; Charlevoix, *Histoire*, 3: 185–6; La Potherie, *Histoire*, 1: 322–3; ANOM, C11A 13: 109, Callière to the Minister, 10 October 1694; BNF, 13516, f. 43v, Belmont, "Recueil."

29 Ibid. Note that Belmont's "les gens du saut *firent* echaper 100 [de] leur parens" becomes "*virent* échapper" in the published version. Cf. BNF, 13516, f. 43v, Belmont, "Recueil" and *Histoire du Canada*, 35.

30 ANOM, C11A 12: 256–260v, Champigny, "Relation … [1692–1693]," 17 August 1693; ANOM, C11A 12: 182–205v, Monseignat, "Relation … [1692–1693]."

31 On Tareha's embassy and subsequent embassies, and on Governor Fletcher and the Albany magistrates' renewed efforts to undermine Franco-Iroquois diplomacy, see Charlevoix, *Histoire*, 3: 190–1; *NYCD* 3: 783; 4: 38–51, 59–64, 76–8; ANOM, C11A 12: 256–260v, Champigny, "Relation … [1692–1693]," 17 August 1693; ANOM, C11A 12: 182–205v, Monseignat, "Relation … [1692–1693]"; BNF, Département des manuscrits, Français 6453, f.4, "Relation des affaires des Iroquois (1692–1693)"; Colden, *History of the Five Indian Nations* (1747), 154–6; NYSA, A1894, v. 39, no. 82, Examination of Jurian, 25 July 1693; *LIR*, 170–2. On Tareha himself (alternatively spelled Tarriha, Tarrigha, Tarsha, Tharia, and mistranscribed as Tharca), see Henri Béchard, "Tareha," in *DCB* 1: 633–4; Gray, "Narratives and Identities," 256–79.

32 La Potherie, *Histoire*, 3: 268.

33 On Pierre Millet and on his influence at Oneida, see St-Arnaud, *Pierre Millet*; Lucien Campeau, "Pierre Millet," in *DCB* 2: 473–4; *JRAD* 64: 118–20, 132; *NYCD* 4: 47, 169–70. On Suzanne Gouentagrandi, see Bruce G. Trigger, "Gouentagrandi," in *DCB* 2: 255–6; St-Arnaud, *Pierre Millet*, 95–6, 102, 137–9, 143–5, 167, 172, 176–7; Gray, "Narratives and Identities," 256–79. Charles Cooke etymologizes this as "Gon Wen Da Ge Ren Ni" (or "Gon Wen Ge Ren Ni"), meaning, "they put things down before her," or more freely, "they prostrate themselves before her." American Philosophical Society, Mss. 497.3.C772, Iroquois personal names, 1900–1951, Cooke, "Names beginning E-G," 467. While some scholars had believed that Gouentagrandi was Taréha's wife, a letter by Millet makes it clear that she was his sister. Cf. Devine, *Historic Caughnawaga*, 113–14; Jones, "Millet."

34 Colden, *History of the Five Indian Nations* (1747), 203–10; La Potherie, *Histoire*, 3: 200–3; *NYCD* 4: 86–7; ANOM, C11A 13: 140–151v, Lamothe-Cadillac, "Mémoire …," [1694]; Charlevoix, *Histoire*, 3: 203.

35 La Potherie, *Histoire*, 3: 204–20 ; BNF, Département des manuscrits, Français 6453, "Parolles dites par Teganisorens à Mgr. Le comte de Frontenac," 23 May 1694.

36 Ibid.

37 *NYCD* 4: 115; La Potherie, *Histoire*, 3: 231–44;

38 ANOM, C11A 14 : 65–99v, Monseignat, "Relation … [1694–1695]"; *NYCD* 4: 120–1. In the report produced at Albany, the names of these messengers were transcribed as Tiurhadareio otherwise diakognorak'igl's, and Jehanontsiesta. In Monseignat's relation they are named Tiorhatarion (or Thioratarion, Thiorhatharion, Thioratarions) and Ononsista (or Ononsiaka).

39 *NYCD* 4: 124–6, 151–2, 158.
40 ANOM, C11A 14: 65–99v, Monseignat, "Relation ... [1694–1695]."
41 ANOM, C11A 14: 148–50, Frontenac to the Minister, 25 October 1696; ANOM, C11A 14: 154–67, Frontenac to the Minister, 25 October 1696; ANOM, C11A 14: 35–64, Monseignat, "Relation ... [1695–1696]"; Charlevoix, *Histoire*, 3: 224–7; *NYCD* 4: 123.
42 ANOM, C11A 14: 35-64, Monseignat, "Relation ... [1695–1696]"; La Potherie, *Histoire*, 3: 270–8; Charlevoix, *Histoire*, 3 : 246–9.
43 ANOM, C11A 14: 35–64, Monseignat, "Relation ... [1695–1696]"; La Potherie, *Histoire* 3: 280–2; Charlevoix, *Histoire*, 3 : 253.
44 La Potherie, *Histoire*, 3: 285; ANOM, C11A 14: 35–64, Monseignat, "Relation ... [1695–1696]"; Charlevoix, *Histoire*, 3: 256–7, 292–3.
45 La Potherie, *Histoire*, 3: 285; Charlevoix, *Histoire*, 3: 295–6; ANOM, C11A 15: 3–21, Monseignat, "Relation [...] 1696 [...] 1697," (copy in *NYCD* 9: 665); see also ANOM, C11A 15: 148-153v, Callière to Minister, 15 October 1697; *NYCD* 4: 279–80. On Otacheté (alternatively, Odatsichta, Odatsigtha, Odasishtee, Odatsighte, Odatrighte), see also *NYCD* 4: 348, 407, 558–9, 563. His name is one of the hereditary names of Oneida League chiefs (Otacheté, Otasseté, Odatsheghte, Otatschéchte, Otatchette, Otachecté, Odat-sighte, Odaksichte, Odatrighte, Odatsichte, Odatsichta, Ondaghsighte). See Starna, "Retrospecting the Origins," 295, 313. Some confusion needs to be resolved, however, as Millet wrote several years earlier that he had himself been adopted to replace a chief named Otasseté. *JRAD* 64: 101.
46 *NYCD* 4: 279–82; ANOM, C11A 15: 3–21, Monseignat, "Relation ... [1696–1697]"; NYSA, A1894, v. 41, no. 92, Treaty minutes, 9–12 March, 8 July 1697; ANOM, C11A 15: 148–153v, Callière to the Minister, 15 October 1697; La Potherie, *Histoire*, 3: 295–6; Charlevoix, *Histoire*, 3: 308–9.
47 ANOM, C11A 15: 3–21, Monseignat, "Relation ... [1696–1697]"; La Potherie, *Histoire*, 3: 294, 297, 309–10.
48 ANOM, C11A 15: 3–21, Monseignat, "Relation ... [1696–1697]"; ANOM, C11A 15: 22–37, Monseignat, "Relation ... [1697–1698]," 20 October 1698.
49 ANOM, G1, 461: 5–6, 8. See also *JRAD* 65: 28–30.
50 ANOM, C11A 13: 377v, Callière to the Minister, 27 October 1695; ANOM, C11A 13: 341, Champigny to the Minister, 11 August 1695; ANOM, C11A 13: 118v–119, "État de la dépense faite pour les fortifications de Canada sur les fonds ordonnés par Sa Majesté en l'année 1694," 26 October 1694; Devine, *Historic Caughnawaga*, 90–1, 126–9. On the new site, see also ibid., 114, 128–30; Jury, "Kanatakwenke," 6–9, and "Caughnawaga," 4–9.
51 Charlevoix, *Histoire*, 2: 135; St-Arnaud, *Pierre Millet*, 172; Devine, *Historic Caughnawaga*, 181–2. On Gouentagrandi, see supra, note 33.

52 ANOM, G1, 461: 5–6, 8, censuses of 1693 and 1698.
53 La Potherie, *Histoire*, 1: 343–4.
54 ASSM, P1 :36-8b, "Mémoire d'un missionnaire, [...] relatif aux activités des Jésuites," 1685.
55 Ibid.; LAC, MG17-A7-2, 6: 3851-3858, Tronson to Belmont, 15 April 1685; LAC, MG17-A7-2, 6: 3901-3914, Tronson to Belmont, 4 June 1686.
56 LAC, MG17-A7-2, 6: 3620-3631, Tronson to Belmont, 6 June 1682; Tremblay, "Politique missionnaire," 89. For later recommendations of caution, LAC, MG17-A7-2, 7: 4285, Tronson to Gay, March 1692.
57 ANF, N/III/Canada/12, Vachon de Belmont, "Plant [sic] de la Mission de la Montagne," 1694; LAC, MG17-A7-2, 222-4, Vachon de Belmont to Louis XIV; LAC, MG17-A7-2, 6: 3901-3914, Tronson to Belmont, 4 June 1686. On the improvements, see also LAC, MG17-A7-2, 19: 9881-9883, "Requête des sauvages, à La Barre pour défricher à la montagne," 16 July 1683; LAC, MG17-A7-2, 19 : 9878, "Copie de la permission accordée par monsieur de La Barre aux sauvages pour défricher à la montagne," 16 July 1683; LAC, MG17-A7-2, 7: 4200-4205, Tronson to Belmont, 2 March 1691.
58 *JRAD* 58: 110–24; Lacroix, *Origines de La Prairie*, 34; Antonia Dansereau, "Michel Barthélémy," *DCB* 2: 45.
59 ASSM, P1 : 6.39-1095a, "Bail à ferme, par Marie-Marthe Richaume à M. de Belmont," 30 July 1689; LAC, MG17-A7-2, 7: 4157–4161, Tronson to Belmont, 30 May 1690; BANQ-M, notary Adhemar, Contract between Vachon de Belmont, Léonard Paillard and Jean Lacroix, 22 January 1691; ASSM, P1: 36-8d, Ordonnance of Fleury Deschambault against Léonard Paillard and Jean Lacroix, 13 March 1691; see Garneau, "Fort-Lorette," 19–23; Tremblay, "Politique missionnaire," 93.
60 LAC, MG17-A7-2, 7: 2239, Tronson to Belmont, 21 April 1696; ANOM, C11A 13: 21–21v, Frontenac and Champigny to the Minister, 5 November 1694.
61 The parable of the sheep and goats is found in Matthew 25: 31–46. LAC, MG17-A7-2, 7: 4452-4455, Tronson to Gay, 24 April 1695; LAC, MG17-A7-2, 7: 4140-4145, Tronson to Belmont, 19 June 1689; La Potherie, *Histoire*, 1: 344.
62 LAC, MG17-A7-2, 7: 4285, Tronson to Gay, March 1692; LAC, MG17-A7-2, 7: 4392-4398, Tronson to Belmont, 27 March 1694; LAC, MG17-A7-2, 7: 4458-4462, Tronson to Rémy, April 1695; LAC, MG17-A7-2, 7: 4536-4543, Tronson to Belmont, 21 April 1696.
63 For Skawenati (Skawneating, Ska8anoti, Sko8anoti) see Cuoq, *Lexique de la langue algonquine*, 372–3; Beaubien, *Sault-au-Récollet*, 144; Desrôchers, *Sault-au-Récollet*, 17. Belmont uses "fort Nazareth" in LAC, MG17-A7-2, 7: 4332-

4336, Tronson to Belmont, March 1693; LAC, MG17-A7-2, 7: 4464-4474, Tronson to Belmont, April 1695. See also ASSM, P1 :36–9, Pierre Rousseau, "Mémoire sur la Mission du Sault-au-Récollet," before 1912.

64 La Potherie, *Histoire*, 1 : 344; Maurault, "Quand Saint-Sulpice allait en guerre," 19.

65 BANQ-M, TL4, S1, D519, Cross-questioning of Louis Badaillac dit LaPlante, 4 January 1701.

66 ASSM, P1:8A.1-19, Speech addressed to Sir John Johnson, 8 February 1788.

67 LAC, MG17-A7-2, 7: 4581-4585, Tronson to Belmont 17 April 1698; LAC, MG17-A7-2, 7: 4636-4637, Tronson to Mariet, 15 April 1699; LAC, MG17-A7-2, 8: 4828-4830, Lechassier to Mariet, 3 April 1703; Faillon, *Vie de la Soeur Bourgeois*, 2: 169; La Potherie, *Histoire*, 1: 343–4.

68 La Potherie, *Histoire*, 1: 225 ; Frontenac "Aux sauvages Hurons de Lorette," 5 December 1696, in P.G. Roy, *Inventaire des concessions*, 3: 223–4 ; LAC, MG8-A8, 1: 465, "Acte de concession terres du Sault de la Chaudière," 5 March 1697; Beaulieu, Béreau, and Tanguay, *Wendats*, 108–12; Boily, *Terres amérindiennes*, 75.

69 *NYCD* 4: 497–8, 558–63. Regarding news of the Peace of Ryswick in the colonies, see ANOM, C11A 15: 22–37, Monseignat, "Relation... [1697–1698]," 20 October 1698; *NYCD* 4: 338–41, 347–51; Wraxall, *Abridgement*, 29–30. Havard, *Great Peace*, 73–4.

70 They were back in Canada by 21 August. ANOM, C11A 15: 22–37, Monseignat, "Relation ... [1697–1698]," 20 October 1698; *NYCD* 4: 347–51; Charlevoix, *Histoire*, 3: 336–7.

71 ANOM, C11A 15: 22–37, Monseignat, "Relation ... [1697–1698]," 20 October 1698. See also La Potherie, *Histoire*, 4:106.

72 ANOM, C11A 15: 22–37, Monseignat, "Relation ... [1697–1698]," 20 October 1698, emphasis is mine.

73 Anon., *Propositions made by the Five Nations of Indians*, 20–1.

74 ANOM, C11A 15: 22–37, Monseignat, "Relation ... [1697–1698]," 20 October 1698; Anon., *Propositions made by the Five Nations of Indians*, 20–1; La Potherie, *Histoire*, 4: 100.

75 References to Massias, Massiac, Jacques René Mathias, Tsihene, Tsienne, Tsioueouy, René Chioui, René Tsiheme, indeed all appear to refer to the same person. See Lamarche, "Habitants de Lachine," 221. His name is mistranscribed as Blassia in *NYCD* 9: 685. Inexplicably, La Potherie appears to refer to the same man as "Egredere." La Potherie, *Histoire*, 4: 100. On Ohonsiowanne (Cohensiowanne, Cohonsiowanne, Ohonsiowanne, Ouhensiouan, Sannoghtowanne, Tohonsiowanne), who visited the colony in January and

September 1699, see La Potherie, *Histoire*, 4: 124–5; *NYCD* 4: 492–6, 558, 658; D.H. Corkran, "Ohonsiowanne," *DCB* 2: 502. For Ohonsiowanne's visit, see *NYCD* 4: 492–6; Wraxall, *Abridgement*, 31.

76 *NYCD* 4 : 492–6.

77 Charlevoix, *Histoire*, 3: 362, 372.

78 La Potherie, *Histoire*, 4: 116–17.

79 Ibid., 4: 122–3

80 The leading man was called Segowane (Sagawane, Sannoghtowanne), while the other revealed himself intent on not returning to the mission after two years of residence there because the "French Indians" had killed his brother the year before. See *NYCD* 4: 559, 579.

81 La Potherie, *Histoire*, 3: 210.

82 ANOM, C11A 14: 65–99v, Monseignat, "Relation [1694–695]"; *NYCD* 4: 121–2. For similar cases, see La Potherie, *Histoire*, 3: 180, 286.

83 ANOM, C11A 15: 22–37, Monseignat, "Relation … [1697–1698]," 20 October 1698.

84 La Potherie, *Histoire*, 4: 165.

85 *NYCD* 4 : 895. Cf. La Potherie, *Histoire*, 4: 192.

86 Havard, *Great Peace*; Brandão and Starna, "Treaties of 1701"; Parmenter, *Edge of Woods*, 231–73. The Christian Iroquois has conversely been minimized. See Sawaya, "Les Sept-Nations du Canada et les Britanniques," 50–1; Havard, *Great Peace*, 125.

87 La Potherie, *Histoire*, 4: 193–200

88 Ibid. For on the wood's edge protocol, the three bare words, and condolence ceremonies, see Foster, "Wampum in Iroquois-White Councils," 105–7; Hewitt, "Requickening Address"; Fenton, *Great Law*, 135–40; Pomedli, "Eighteenth-Century Treaties," 319–39.

89 La Potherie, *Histoire*, 4: 197–9.

90 In 1701, Haronhiateka (also Arioteka, Oraja Dicka, Orojadicka, Orighjadikha, Oriojadricko) was reported to have "been two years among the French in Canada." According to one account, his wife was a former white captive, adopted among the Senecas. Recognized as a chief at Kahnawake by 1701, he remained so until 1711 at least. See Wraxall, *Abridgement*, 42; Brodhead et al., eds., *NYCD* 4: 907; 5: 243, 246.

91 While Brandão and Starna argue that this was an important subject, Havard believes that it was of only minor importance. Havard, *Great Peace*, 145–9; Brandão and Starna, "Treaties of 1701."

92 LAC, RG 10, vol. 8, 8202, "Conseil adressé à Mr Le Colonel Campbell," 7 October 1791. Cf. Havard, *Great Peace*, 147–8; Sawaya, "Les Sept-Nations du Canada et les Britanniques," 50–4.

93 La Potherie, *Histoire*, 4: 249–51; see also Charlevoix, *Histoire*, 3: 417–18. While Havard interprets the fact that the Kiskakon chief was the first to speak as an indication of Odawa preeminence in the Franco-Amerindian alliance, that the representatives of the mission settlements spoke last might also be interpreted in the same way. Havard, *Great Peace*, 136–7.

94 La Potherie, *Histoire*, 4: 249–51; Charlevoix, *Histoire*, 3: 417–18. On the signatures, see Havard, *Great Peace*, 253; Guillaud, et al., "Les signatures amérindiennes."

95 Parmenter, "After Mourning Wars"; MacLeod, *Canadian Iroquois*.

CONCLUSION

1 "8takamachi8enon" and "Thék8érimat" in the original. On this incident, see ANOM, C11A 25: 86–86v, Hazeur to the Directeur général of the Compagnie de la Colonie de Canada, 19 June 1705; ANOM, C11A 25: 75–76v, "Requête de François Hazeur au gouverneur Philippe Rigaud de Vaudreuil," 4 November 1705; ANOM, C11A 25: 77–78v, "Requête de François Hazeur à l'intendant [Raudot]," 5 November 1705; ANOM, C11A 25: 29–30v, "Requête de François Hazeur à l'intendant Raudot," 3 August 1706; ANOM, C11A 25: 31–31v, "Faits et articles sur lesquels le sieur Hazeur ... désire faire interroger trois Indiens du lac Saint-Jean," 3 August 1706; ANOM, C11A 25: 33–36v, "Procès-verbal de l'interrogatoire de trois Montagnais du lac Saint-Jean," 3 August 1706; ANOM, C11A 25: 3941v, "Procès-verbal de l'interrogatoire de Godefroy de Saint-Paul par Raudot," 11 August 1706; ANOM, C11A 25: 46–47v, "Procès-verbal de l'interrogatoire de Pierre Poulin par Jacques Raudot," 12 October 1706; ANOM, C11A 59: 297, "Requête de François Hazeur à l'intendant Raudot," 22 September 1707; ANOM, C11A 59: 298, "Ordonnance de l'intendant Raudot," 26 September 1707; ANOM, C11A 59: 318–381v, Hocquart, "Mémoire sur toutes les parties de la régie du Domaine d'Occident en Canada," 1733. For the broader context, see Savoie and Tanguay, "Nœud de l'ancienne amitié"; Bouchard, "La présence des 'Abénaquis-Montagnais'"; Savoie and Tanguay, "Réponse des auteurs"; Tanguay, "Liberté d'errer," 27–36; Lozier, "In Each Other's Arms," 261–4.

2 Merlet, *Histoire des relations*, 45–7; Maurault, *Histoire des Abénaquis*, 499–501; *JRAD* 69: 68–72.

3 ANOM, G1, 461: 8, census of 1698; La Potherie, *Histoire*, 1: 360; Raudot (*sic*: Silvy), *Relation par lettres*, 212. See also Grabowski and Dickinson, "Les populations amérindiennes," 61; Raudot, *Relation par lettres*, 211; ANOM, C11A 67: 102v, Gilles Hocquart, "Détail de toute la colonie"; Beaulieu, Béreau, and Tanguay, *Wendats*, 78.

4 For the Jesuits see ANOM, C11A 106: 48-50v, "État des charges, dépenses et revenus des Jésuites au Canada," 4 Octobre 1701. For the Sulpicians see for example ASSM, P1:8A.3.17-04, "Notes de M. Roupe sur la composition ethnique de la mission," ca. 1807–1829.

5 Beaulieu, Béreau, and Tanguay, *Wendats*, 110-12.

6 On the recent character of the name Odanak, see Laurent, *New Familiar Abenakis*, 206; *Annual Report of the Department of Indian Affairs*, 28; Day, *Identity of Saint Francis Indians*, 5.

7 LAC, MG17-A7-2, 8: 4828-4830, Lechassier to Mariet, 3 April 1703; LAC, MG17-A7-2, 8: 4913-4914, Lechassier to Mariet, April 1704; ASSM, S24, 6, Cahiers Faillon, F 377, 2 March 1705; ASSM, S24, 6, Cahiers Faillon, F 378, 26 April 1705; ASSM, S24, 6, Cahiers Faillon, F 379, 2 November 1706.

8 Tremblay, "Politique missionnaire"; Boily, "Terres amérindiennes," 157–77.

9 Grabowski, "Common Ground," 71; Cuoq, *Lexique de la langue iroquoise*, 10. For references to Skawenatis (Schawendes, Scawendadyes, Shawendadies, Schawenedey), see for example Wraxall, *Abridgement*, 229; Colden, *History of the Five Indian Nations* (1747), 190; *NYCD* 6: 359.

10 On the mission at Île aux Tourtes or Tourtres (Aouanagassing, Aounagassing, et Ouanagasing), see Robichaud and Stewart, "Île aux Tourtes."

11 ANOM, F3 2: 392–5, "Conseil entre les sauvages d'Amesoquenty et M. de Beauharnois," 12 May 1704; ANOM, F3 2: 407–10, "Conseil entre les sauvages Abenakis de Koessek et Monsieur le Marquis de Vaudreuil," 13 June 1704; Boily, "Terres amérindiennes," 197–211; Lozier, "In Each Other's Arms," 255–66.

12 Devine, *Historic Caughnawaga*, 181. See also Cuoq, *Lexique de la langue iroquoise*, 145, 163–4.

13 Robert, "Le site de l'ancienne mission"; Roy, *Histoire de la Seigneurie de Lauzon*, 1: 407–10.

14 On dwellings and language use at Wendake, see *JRAD* 58: 146–8; 60: 78–82, 88; 66: 204; Franquet, *Voyages*, 107; BNF, Département des cartes et plans, GE SH 18 PF 127 DIV 7 P 4, Villeneuve, "Carte des Environs de Quebec," 1685–1686; Beaulieu, Béreau, and Tanguay, *Wendats*, 93–7. At Kahnawake, see Franquet, *Voyages*, 38–9; Green, "New People," 284–5; Rueck, "Enclosing Mohawk Commons," 72–108.

15 *JRAD* 66: 152–4; Raudot (*sic*, Silvy), *Relation par lettres*, 211; Beaulieu, Béreau, and Tanguay, *Wendats*, 139–72; Rueck, "Enclosing Mohawk Commons," 52–67.

16 Charlevoix, *Histoire*, 3: 83; Beaulieu, Béreau, and Tanguay, *Wendats*, 144–5.

17 See for example Boily, "Les terres amérindiennes"; Tremblay, "Politique missionnaire"; Lavoie, "C'est ma seigneurie."

18 "Acte de confirmation par Sa Majesté de la concession de la seigneurie de Sillery faite aux Révérends Pères Jésuite," in Roy, *Inventaire des concessions*, 1: 297; BANQ-Q, ZQ 123, Extract of letter from Louis XIV to Callière and Beauharnois, 6 May 1702; Memorandum of Louis XIV to Callière, 1702, *RAPQ* 1940–1941: 355; Boily, "Terres amérindiennes," 85–7.

19 Boily, "Terres amérindiennes," 101–20, 157–76; Lavallée, *La Prairie*, 74–5; Tremblay, "Politique missionnaire," 99–135.

20 ANOM, C11A 122: 14, Copy of an anonymous letter, 30 September 1705; Charlevoix, *Histoire*, 3: 86; LAC, MG1-C11A 30: 112v, Vaudreuil's instructions to Ramezay, 14 July 1709.

21 ANOM, F3 2: 392-5, "Conseil entre les sauvages d'Amesoquenty et M. de Beauharnois," 12 May 1704; LAC, MG1-F3 2: 407-10, "Conseil entre les sauvages Abenakis de Koessek et Monsieur le Marquis de Vaudreuil," 13 June 1704; Boily, "Terres amérindiennes," 197–211; Lozier, "In Each Other's Arms," 255–66.

22 *JRAD* 68: 276–8. See also ibid., 63: 148; 67: 142; Steckley, *De Religione*, 17–18.

23 See also Mithun, "Wendat among the Iroquois."

24 ANOM, C11A 34: 65–65v, "Paroles des Hurons descendus du fort Pontchartrain du Détroit à Vaudreuil," 7 November 1712; ANOM, C11A 57: 298-307, Boishébert to Beauharnois, 28 February 1732; ANOM, C11A 57: 320–321v, "Addition à la relation de la défaite des Renards," 1732; ANF, Fonds Saint-Sulpice, Mss. 1200, "Relation d'une expédition faitte sur les Renards par un petit party de Sauvages [...]," s.d. [1732]; Lozier, "Origines huronnes-wendates," 111.

25 Robichaud and Stewart, "Île aux Tourtes."

26 ASSM, Fonds Oka, Montgolfier, "Memoire sur l'État de la Mission des Sauvages du Lac des Deux Montagnes," 1755; Bougainville, *Écrits sur le Canada*, 194; Raudot (*sic*, Silvy), *Relation par lettres*, 212.

27 Bousquet, *Anicinabek*; Morrison, "Algonquin History," 23–36; Gabriel-Doxtater and Van den Hende, *At the Wood's Edge*, 94–5; Black, "Tale of Two Ethnicities," and "Nineteenth-Century Algonquin Culture Change."

28 ANOM, C11A 67: 103, Hocquart, "Détail de toute la colonie," 1737; Hubert and Savard, *Algonquins de Trois-Rivières*; Goudreau, "Généalogie et histoire autochtone."

29 ANOM, C11A 101: 267–271, "Paroles adressées aux députés iroquois par les domiciliés du Sault-Saint-Louis et du Lac des Deux-Montagnes et par les Outaouais de Détroit et les Potéouatamis de Michillimakinac," 21 December 1756.

30 See note 1 in this chapter.

31 *JRAD* 66: 146–72. See also La Potherie, *Histoire*, 1: 127.

32 Charlevoix, *Histoire*, 5: 293; ANOM, C11A 76: 263–264v, Josué Dubois Berthelot de Beaucours, "Mémoire de Canada, 1740 et 41," [1741]; ANOM, C11A 75: 138–142v, Beauharnois to Maurepas, 21 September 1741; Lozier, "Origines huronnes-wendates"; Pote, *Journal*, 36. See also Sullivan et al., eds., *Papers of Sir William Johnson*, 13: 624–5.

33 LAC, RG 10, vol. 8, 8202, "Conseil adressé à Mr Le Colonel Campbell," 7 October 1791. On the Seven Nations, see Sawaya, "Les Sept-Nations du Canada et les Britanniques"; Lozier, "History, Historiography, and the Courts."

34 ANOM, C11A 75: 110, "Paroles de Beauharnois aux Sauvages du Lac des Deux Montagnes," 12 août 1741.

35 ASQ, Polygraphie 4, no 20, Request of the Hurons, 1675.

36 Lozier, "In Each Other's Arms," 267–319.

Bibliography

ARCHIVAL SOURCES

American Philosophical Society, Philadelphia

Archives départementales de la Gironde, Bordeaux

H, Clergé régulier

Archives du Séminaire de Saint-Sulpice de Montréal, Montreal (ASSM)

Fonds Faillon

Fonds Oka

Archives du Séminaire de Québec, Musée de la civilisation, Quebec City (ASQ)

Fonds Verreau

Archives nationales de France, Paris (ANF)

N, Cartes et plans

AB/XIX/510-AB/XIX/529, Fonds du séminaire de Saint-Sulpice

Archives nationales d'outre-mer, Aix-en-Provence (ANOM)

B, Fonds des Colonies, Lettres envoyées

C11A, Fonds des Colonies, Correspondance générale, Canada

C11D, Fonds des Colonies, Correspondance générale, Canada

C11E, Fonds des Colonies, Correspondance générale, des limites et des postes

E, Fonds des Colonies, Dossiers personnels

F3, Fonds des Colonies, Collection Moreau de Saint-Méry

G1, Fonds des Colonies, Dépôt des papiers publics des colonies, état civil et recensements

Archive of the Jesuits in Canada, Montreal (AJC)

C-81 BELI 01/02-04-03B, Collection Henri Béchard

Bibliothèque de la Compagnie de Saint-Sulpice, Paris (ASSP)
Bibliothèque et Archives nationales du Québec, Montreal (BANQ-M)
CN601, Fonds Cour supérieure, District judiciaire de Montréal, Greffes de notaires
TL2, Fonds Bailliage de Montréal
TL4, Fonds Juridiction royale de Montréal
Bibliothèque et Archives nationales du Québec, Quebec (BANQ-Q)
CN301, Fonds Cour supérieure, District judiciaire de Québec, Greffes de notaires
E21, Fonds Ministère des Terres et Forêts
E21, S64, SS5, Série 64, Gestion du Domaine de la Couronne, Biens des Jésuites
P1000, Collection initiale
TP1, S28, Fonds Conseil souverain, Jugements et délibérations
TP1, S36, Fonds Conseil souverain, Insinuations
ZQ123, Fonds Seigneurie de Sillery, 1637–1952
Bibliothèque nationale de France, Paris (BNF)
Département des manuscrits, Collection Baluze
Département des manuscrits, Fonds Français
GE SH 18, Département des cartes et plans, Service hydrographique de la Marine
Library and Archives Canada, Ottawa (LAC)
MG7-IA1, Département des manuscrits. Fonds étranger: Fonds américain
MG8-A8, Documents relatifs à la Nouvelle-France et au Québec, Registre d'intendance
MG8-A23, Greffes de notaires
MG11-CO42, British North America, Original Correspondence; Colonial Office
MG17-A6-2, Fonds de la Compagnie de Jésus, Province de Paris
MG17-A7-2, Fonds du Séminaire de Saint-Sulpice, Montréal
MG18-E18, Collection des Jésuites
RG 10, 1819–1822, Minutes of the Albany Commissioners of Indian Affairs
Musée de la civilisation, Quebec City
Archives du Séminaire de Québec (ASQ)
Polygraphies
Fonds Verreau
Newberry Library, Chicago
Ayer Collection of Manuscripts

New York State Archives, Albany
A1894-A1895, Council papers, New York (Colony)
New York Historical Society, New York
Miscellaneous Manuscripts
Saint-François-Xavier parish archives, Kahnawake
Schaffer Library, Union College, Schenectady
University of Montreal
Programme de recherche en démographie historique (PRDH)
Répertoire des actes d'état civil, 1621–1799

PRINTED PRIMARY SOURCES

Annual Report of the Department of Indian Affairs for the year ended 31st December 1884. Ottawa: Maclean, Roger, 1885.

Anonymous. *Propositions made by the Five Nations of Indians, viz. the Mohaques, Oneydes, Onnondages, Cayouges & Sinnekes, to His Excellency Richard Earl of Bellomont, capt. general and governour in chief His Majesties province of New-York, &c. in Albany, the 20th of July, anno Dom. 1698*. New York: William Bradford, 1698.

Anonymous. "Quelques débris de la nation huronne et M. D'Ailleboust à Québec." *L'Abeille* 2, 7 (4 January 1850).

Anonymous. *Vie de l'illustre serviteur de Dieu, Noël Brulart de Sillery, chevalier de Malte et Bailly commandeur Grand Croix dans l'Ordre*. Paris: Monastère de la Visitation Sainte-Marie, 1843.

Baraga, Frederic. *A Dictionary of the Otchipwe Language, explained in English*. Montreal: Beauchemin & Valois, 1878.

Baugy, Louis Henry de. *Journal d'une expédition contre les Iroquois en 1687*. Paris: Ernest Leroux, 1931.

Baxter, James Phinney, ed. *The Documentary History of the State Of Maine, containing the Baxter Manuscripts.* Portland: Maine Historical Society, 1889–1916.

– *Pioneers of New France in New England*. Albany: Munsell and Sons, 1984.

Bayard, Nicholas, and Charles Lodowick. *A Narrative of an Attempt made by the French of Canada upon the Mohaques Country Being Indians under the Protection of His Majesties Government of New York*. New York, 1693.

Belknap, Jeremy. *History of New Hampshire*. Boston: Isaiah Thomas and Ebenezer T. Andrews, 1791. First published 1784.

Belmont, François. *Histoire du Canada par M. l'abbé de Belmont.* Quebec: Literary and Historical Society of Quebec, 1840.

– *Histoire de l'eau de vie en Canada*. Quebec: Literary and Historical Society of Quebec, 1840.

Bigot, Jacques. *Copie d'une lettre escrite par le père Jacques Bigot de la Compagnie de Jésus l'an 1684, pour accompagner un collier de pourcelaine envoié par les Abnaquis de la mission de Sainct François de Sales dans la Nouvelle-France au tombeau de leur sainct patron à Annecy*. New York: Presse Cramoisy de Jean-Marie Shea, 1858.

– *Relation de la Mission Abnaquise de St. François de Sales l'Année 1702*. New York: Presse Cramoisy de Jean Marie Shea, 1865.

– *Relation de ce qui s'est passé de plus remarquable dans la Mission Abnaquise de Sainct Joseph de Sillery, et de Sainct Francois de Sales, l'année 1685*. New York: Presse Cramoisy de Jean-Marie Shea, 1858.

Blanchet, Jean Gervais Protais, Faucher de Saint-Maurice, and Henri Edouard Narcisse, eds. *Collection de manuscrits contenant lettres, mémoires, et autres documents historiques relatifs à la Nouvelle-France, recueillis aux archives de la province de Québec, ou copiés à l'étranger*. 4 vols. Quebec: A. Côté, 1883–1885.

Boudon, Henri-Marie. *Dieu seul: Le Saint esclavage de l'admirable Mère de Dieu*. Paris: Claude Hérissant, 1667.

Bougainville, Louis-Antoine de. *Écrits sur le Canada. Mémoires, Journal, Lettres*. Sillery: Septentrion, 2003.

Bouton, Nathaniel, ed. *Documents and Records Relating to the Province of New Hampshire.* Manchester: John B. Clarke, 1868.

Brodhead, John Romeyn, Berthold Fernow, and E.B. O'Callaghan, eds. *Documents relative to the colonial history of the state of New-York: procured in Holland, England, and France*. Albany: Weed, Parsons, 1853–1887.

Bruyas, Jacques. *Radical words of the Mohawk language with their derivatives*. New York: Cramoisy Press, 1862.

Bullivant, Benjamin. "Mr. Bullivant's Journall of Proceedings from the 13 Feb. to the 19th of May." In *Proceedings of the Massachusetts Historical Society* 16 (1878): 103–9.

Campeau, Lucien, ed. *Monumenta Novae Franciae*. Rome, Quebec, and Montreal: Monumenta Hist Soc Iesu, Presses de l'Université Laval, Bellarmin, 1967–2003.

Catalogne, Gédéon de. *Recueil de ce qui s'est passé en Canada au sujet de la guerre: tant des Anglais que des Iroquois depuis l'année 1682*. Quebec: Société historique et littéraire de Québec, 1866.

Champlain, Samuel de. *The Works of Samuel de Champlain*. Edited by H.P. Biggar. Toronto: Champlain Society, 1922–1935.

Charbonneau, Hubert and Jacques Légaré, ed. *Répertoire des actes de baptême, mariage et sépulture et des recensements du Québec ancien*. 47 vols. Montreal: Presses de l'Université de Montréal, 1980–1998. www.genealogie.umontreal.ca

Charlevoix, Pierre-François-Xavier de. *Histoire et description générale de la Nouvelle-France, avec le journal historique d'un voyage fait par ordre du roi dans l'Amérique septentrionale*. Paris: Rollin fils, 1744.

Chauchetière, Claude. *Narration annuelle de la mission du Sault depuis sa fondation jusqu'en 1686*. Edited by Hélène Avisseau. Bordeaux: Archives départementales de la Gironde, 1984.

– *La vie de la B. Catherine Tegakouita, dite à présent La Saincte Sauvagesse par le R.P. Claude Chauchetière pretre missionnaire de la Compagnie de Jésus*. New York: Presse Cramoisy, 1887.

Chaumonot, Pierre-Joseph-Marie. *Un missionnaire des Hurons: Autobiographie du Père Chaumonot de la Compagnie de Jésus et son complément*. Edited by Félix Martin. Paris: H. Oudin, 1885.

Christoph, Peter R., ed. *The Dongan Papers: Admiralty Court and Other Records of the Administration of New York Governor Thomas Dongan* and *Files of the Provincial Secretary of New York During the Administration of Governor Thomas Dongan.* 2 vols. Syracuse, NY: Syracuse University Press, 1993, 1996.

– *The Leisler Papers, 1689–1691: Files of the Provincial Secretary of New York*. Syracuse: Syracuse University Press, 2002.

Church, Thomas. *The History of Philip's War, Commonly Called the Great Indian War, of 1675 and 1676. Also, of the French and Indian Wars at the Eastward, in 1689, 1690, 1692, 1696, and 1704*. Edited by Samuel G. Drake. Exteter, NH: J. and B. Williams, 1829.

Colden, Cadwallader. *The History of the Five Indian Nations Depending on the Province of New-York*. New York: William Bradford, 1727.

– *The History of the Five Indian Nations of Canada*. London: T. Osborne, 1747.

Collections of the Massachusetts Historical Society. 70 vols. Boston: Massachusetts Historical Society, 1792–.

Complément des ordonnances et jugements des gouverneurs et intendants du Canada. Quebec: E.R. Frechette, 1856.

Crespieul de, P.F. *Pretiosa Mors Quorumdam Algonquinniorum et Montanensium = Mort précieuse de certains Algonquins et Montagnais: Éloge des Montagnais par François de Crespieul*. Edited by Léo-Paul Hébert. Joliette: L.P. Hébert, 2006.

Cuoq, Jean-André. *Lexique de la langue algonquine*. Montreal: J. Chapleau, 1886.

– *Lexique de la langue iroquoise*. Montreal: J. Chapleau, 1882.

Dollier de Casson, François. *Histoire du Montréal*. Edited by Marie Baboyant and Marcel Trudel. Montreal: Hurtubise HMH, 1992.

Dooyentate, Peter Clark. *Origin and Traditional History of the Wyandotts: and Sketches of Other Indian Tribes of North America, True Traditional Stories of Tecumseh and His League, in the Years 1811 and 1812*. Toronto: Hunter, Rose, 1870.

Druillettes, Gabriel. *Journal of an embassy from Canada to the United Colonies of New England, in 1650*. Edited by John Gilmary Shea. New York: D. Appleton, 1857.

– "Rapport du R.P. Druillettes." In *Le Canada Français* 20 (June–August 1933): 941–9.

DuCreux, François. *The History of Canada or New France*. 2 vols. Edited by James B. Conacher. Toronto: Champlain Society Publications, 1951–1952.

Édits, ordonnances royaux, déclarations et arrêts du Conseil d'État du Roi concernant le Canada, mis par ordre chronologique et publiés par ordre de Son Excellence sir Robert Shore Milnes, ... lieutenant-gouverneur de la province du Bas-Canada ... Quebec: P.E. Desbarats, 1803.

Fabvre, Bonaventure. *Racines montagnaises compilées à Tadoussac avant 1695 par le père Bonaventure Fabvre, jésuite*. Edited by Lorenzo Angers and Gérard E. McNulty. Quebec: Presses de l'Université Laval, 1970.

[Faillon, Étienne-Michel]. *Vie de la Sœur Bourgeoys, fondatrice de la Congrégation de Notre-Dame de Villemarie en Canada. Suivie de l'Histoire de cet institut jusqu'à ce jour*. 2 vols. Villemarie [Montreal]: Congrégation de Notre-Dame, 1853).

Fernow, Berthold, and Arnold Johan Ferdinand Van Laer, eds. *Calendar of Council Minutes 1668–1783*. Albany: University of the State of New York, 1902.

Franquet, Louis. *Voyages et mémoires sur le Canada*. Quebec: A. Côté et Cie, 1889.

Gookin, Daniel. "An Historical account of the doings and sufferings of the Christian Indians in New England, in the years 1675, 1676, 1677." *Transactions and Collections of the American Antiquarian Society* 2 (1836): 520–1.

– "Historical Collections of the Indians of New England: Of Their Several Nations, Numbers, Customs, Manners, Religion, And Government, Before The English Planted There." In *Massachusetts Historical Society Collections*, 1st ser. (1792).

Gyles, John. *Memoirs of odd adventures, strange deliverances, etc. in the captivity of John Giles, Esq.* Boston: S. Kneeland and T. Green, 1736.

Haefeli, Evan, and Kevin Sweeney. *Captive Histories: English, French, and Native Narratives of the 1704 Deerfield Raid*. Amherst: University of Massachusetts Press, 2006.

Hastings, Hugh, ed. *Ecclesiastical Records, State of New York*. Albany: James B. Lyon, 1901.

Hébert, Léo-Paul, ed. *Le registre de Sillery (1638–1690)*. Sainte-Foy, QC: Presses de l'Université du Québec, 1994.

Hubbard, William. *History of the Indian Wars of New England from the first settlement to the termination of the war with King Philip, in 1677*. Edited by Samuel G. Drake. Roxbury, MA: W. Elliot Woodward, 1865.

Jamet, Albert, ed. *Annales de l'Hôtel-Dieu de Québec*. Quebec: Hôtel-Dieu de Québec, 1939.

Journaux de la Chambre d'Assemblée du Bas-Canada. Quebec: Neilson & Cowan, 1824.

Juchereau de Saint-Ignace (Jeanne-Françoise Juchereau de La Ferté). *Histoire de l'Hôtel-Dieu de Québec*. Montauban: 1752.

Kalm, Pehr. *Travels into North America*. London: T. Lowndes, 1773.

Kidder, Frederic, ed. *The Abenaki Indians and Their Treaties 1713 and 1717, and a Vocabulary with a Historical Introduction*. Portland: Brown Thurston, 1859.

Lafitau, Joseph-François. *Customs of the American Indians Compared with the Customs of Primitive Times*. Toronto: Champlain Society, 1974–1977.

La Potherie, Claude-Charles Le Roy Bacqueville de. *Histoire de l'Amérique septentrionale*. 4 vols. Paris: J.-L. Nion and F. Didot, 1722.

Laure, Pierre. *Apparat français-montagnais*. Edited by David Cooter. Sillery: Presses de l'Université du Quebec, 1988.

Laurent, Joseph. *New Familiar Abenakis and English Dialogues*. Quebec: Léger Brousseau, 1884.

Le Clercq, Chrestien. *Nouvelle relation de la Gaspésie. Édition critique*. Edited by Réal Ouellet. Montreal: Presses de l'Université de Montréal, 1999.

– *Premier établissement de la foy dans la Nouvelle France*. Paris: Amable Auroy, 1691.

Leder, Lawrence R. ed. *The Livingston Indian Records*. Gettysburg: Pennsylvania Historical Society, 1956.

Le Maistre de Sacy, Louis-Isaac. *Ezechiel: Traduit en françois, avec une explication tirée des Saints Pères & des autheurs ecclesiastiques*. Paris: Guillaume Desprez, 1692.

Lemoine, Georges. *Dictionnaire français-algonquin*. Chicoutimi, Quebec: G. Delisle, 1909.

Lescarbot, Marc. *La conversion des sauvages qui ont esté baptizés en la Nouvelle France, cette année 1610*. Paris: Jean Millot, 1610.

– *The History of New France*. 3 vols. Toronto: Champlain Society, 1907–1914.

Lettres édifiantes et curieuses écrites des missions étrangères. 30 vols. Paris: N. Leclerc, 1708–71.

Lom d'Arce de Lahontan, Louis-Armand de. *Œuvres complètes*. Edited by Réal Ouellet and Alain Beaulieu. Montreal: Presses de l'Université de Montréal, 1990.

Lortie, Jeanne d'Arc, ed. *Les textes poétiques du Canada français, 1606–1867*. Montreal: Fides, 1987.

Margry, Pierre, ed. *Découvertes et établissements des Français dans l'ouest et dans le sud de l'Amérique septentrionale (1614–1754)*. Paris: D. Jouaust, 1876–1886.

Mather, Cotton. *Decennium Luctuosum: An History of Remarkable Occurrences in the Long War, which New England hath had with the Indian Salvages, From the Year, 1688. To the Year 1698.* Boston: B. Green and J. Allan, 1699.

Melsheimer, F.V. *Journal of the Voyage of the Brunswick Auxiliaries from Wolfenbüttel to Quebec*. Quebec: Morning Chronicle, 1891.

Munro, William B., ed. *Documents relating to the seigniorial tenure in Canada*. Toronto: Champlain Society, 1908.

Munsell, Joel, ed. *The Annals of Albany*. Albany: J. Munsell, 1853.

– *Collections on the History of Albany: from its Discovery to the Present Time*. Albany: J. Munsell, 1865–1871.

O'Callaghan, E.B., ed. *Calendar of historical manuscripts in the office of the secretary of state.* Albany: Weed, Parsons, 1865.

– *The Documentary History of the State of New-York*. Albany: Weed, Parsons, & Co., 1849.

Oldmixon, John. *The British empire in America, containing the history of the discovery, settlement ...* London, 1741.

Oury, Guy, ed. *Marie de l'Incarnation, Ursuline (1659–1672): Correspondance*. Solesme, France: Abbaye Saint-Pierre, 1971.

Parker, Arthur C. *The Code of Handsome Lake, the Seneca Prophet*. New York State Museum Bulletin No. 163. Albany: New York State Museum, 1913.

– *The Constitution of the Five Nations or the Iroquois Book of the Great Law*. Albany: University of the State of New York, 1916.

Penhallow, Samuel. *The History of the Wars of New-England with the Eastern Indians, or a Narrative of Their Continued Perfidy and Cruelty*. Boston: T. Fleet, 1726.

Perrot, Nicolas. *Moeurs, coutumes et religion des Sauvages de l'Amérique septentrionale.* Edited by Pierre Berthiaume. Montreal: Presses de l'Université de Montréal, 2004.

Peyser, Joseph L., and José António Brandão, eds. *Edge of Empire: Documents of Michilimackinac, 1671–1716*. East Lansing: Michigan State University Press, 2008.

Pièces et documents relatifs à la Tenure Seigneuriale. Quebec: E.R. Fréchette, 1852.

Pote, William. *The Journal of Captain William Pote, Jr., during his Captivity in the French and Indian War from May, 1745, to August, 1747*. New York: Dodd, Mead, 1896.

Potier, Pierre. *Huron manuscripts from Rev. Pierre Potier's collection*. Edited by Alexander Fraser. *15th Report of the Bureau of Archives for the Province of Ontario* (1918–1919). Toronto: Clarkson W. James, 1920.

Provost, Honorius, ed. *Le Séminaire de Québec: Documents et biographies*. Quebec: Séminaire de Québec, 1964.

Publick Occurences Both Foreign and Domestic. Boston: 1690.

Pynchon, John. "Letters of John Pynchon, 1654–1700." In *Collections of the Massachusetts Historical Society* 60. Boston: Colonial Society of Massachusetts, 1982.

Radisson, Pierre-Esprit. *Pierre-Esprit Radisson: The Collected Writings*. Vol. 1, *The Voyages*. Edited by Germaine Warkentin. Montreal and Kingston: McGill-Queen's University Press, 2012.

Rapport de l'archiviste de la Province de Québec. Québec: Éditeur Officiel du Québec, 1921–1960.

Rasles, Sébastien. *A Dictionary of the Abnaki Language*. Edited by John Pickering. Memoirs of the American Academy of Arts and Sciences, New Ser. 1. Cambridge: Charles Folsom, 1833.

Raudot, Antoine-Denis [*sic*: more recently attributed to Antoine Silvy]. *Relation par lettres de l'Amérique septentrionale, années 1709 et 1710*. Edited by Camille de Rochemonteix. Paris: Letouzey et Ané, 1904.

Relations inédites de la Nouvelle-France (1672–1679). Paris: C. Douniol, 1858–1861.

Rochemonteix, Camille de, ed. *Les Jésuites et la Nouvelle-France au XVIIe siècle d'après beaucoup de documents inédits*. Paris: Letouzey et Ané, 1895–1896.

Roy, Pierre-Georges, ed. *Inventaire des concessions en fief et seigneurie, fois et hommages et aveux et dénombrements conservés aux archives de la province de Québec*. Beauceville: L'Éclaireur, 1927.

– *Ordonnances, commissions, etc. etc, des gouverneurs et intendants de la Nouvelle-France. 1639–1706*. Beauceville: L'Éclaireur, 1924.

Sagard, Gabriel. *Le Grand Voyage du pays des Hurons*. Edited by Réal Ouellet and Jack Warwick. Montreal: Bibliothèque québécoise, 1990.

– *Histoire du Canada et voyages que les Frères Mineurs Recollects y ont faicts pour la conversion des Infidelles*. Paris: 1636. Reprint, Paris: Tross, 1866.

Sainsbury, W. Noel, J. W. Fortescue, Cecil Headlam et al., eds. *Calendar of State Papers, Colonial*. London: Public Records Office, 1860–1969.

Saint-Vallier, Jean-Baptiste de La Croix de Chevrières de. *Estat present de l'Église et de la colonie française dans la Nouvelle-France*. Quebec: A. Cote, 1856. First published 1688.

Shea, John Gilmary, ed. *A French-Onondaga Dictionary: from a manuscript of the seventeenth century*. New York: Presse Cramoisy, 1859.

Silvy, Antoine. *Dictionnaire montagnais-français*. Edited by Lorenzo Angers, David E. Cooter, and Gerard E. McNulty. Montreal: Presses de l'Université du Quebéc, 1974.

Smyth, Egbert C. "Papers Relating to the Construction and First Occupancy of Fort Dummer." In *Proceedings of the Massachusetts Historical Society*, 2nd Ser. 6 (1891): 359–81.

Steckley, John L. *De Religione: Telling the Seventeenth Century Jesuit Story in Huron to the Iroquois*. Norman: University of Oklahoma Press, 2004.

Sullivan, James et al., eds. *The Papers of Sir William Johnson*. Albany: University of the State of New York, 1921–1965.

Thwaites, Reuben Gold, ed. *The Jesuit Relations and Allied Documents*. Cleveland: Burrows Bros. Co., 1896–1901.

Tooker, Elisabeth, ed. *An Iroquois Sourcebook*. New York: Garland. Publishing, 1985.

Toupin, Robert, ed. *Les Écrits de Pierre Potier*. Ottawa: University of Ottawa Press, 1996.

Tuttle, Charles W. Report. In *Proceedings of the Massachusetts Historical Society* 17 (February 1880): 352–5.

Van Laer A.J.F., ed. *Minutes of the Court of Fort Orange and Beverwyck, 1652–1656*. Albany: University of the State of New York, 1920.

– ed. *Minutes of the Court of Fort Orange and Beverwyck, 1657–1660*. Albany: University of the State of New York, 1923.

Van Laer A.J.F., ed. *Minutes of the Court of Albany, Rensselaerswyck, and Schenectady, 1668–1685*. Albany: University of the State of New York, 1926.

Waterman, Kees Jan, ed. "*To do justice to him & myself: Evert Wendell's account book of the fur trade with Indians in Albany, New York, 1695–1726*. Philadelphia: American Philosophical Society, 2008.

Whitmore, William Henry, ed. *The Andros Tracts*. Boston: John Wilson and Son, 1874.

Williams, Stephen. *Narrative of the Captivity of Stephen Williams*. Edited by

George Sheldon. Deerfield, MA: Pocumtuck Valley Memorial Association, 1889.

Wraxall, Peter. *An Abridgement of the Indian Affairs*. Edited by Charles Howard McIlwain. Cambridge: Harvard University Press, 1915.

Year book of the Holland Society of New-York. New York: Nickerbocker Press, 1904.

SECONDARY SOURCES

Abé, Takao. *The Jesuit Mission to New France: A New Interpretation in the Light of the Earlier Jesuit Experience in Japan*. Leiden: Brill, 2011.

– "The Missionary Réductions in New France: An Epistemological Problem with a Popular Historical Theory." *French Colonial History* 15 (2014): 111–33.

Abler, Thomas S. "Beavers and Muskets: Iroquois Military Fortunes in the Face of European Colonization." In *War in the Tribal Zone: Expanding States and Indigenous Warfare*, edited by R. Brian Ferguson and Neil L. Whitehead, 151–74. Santa Fe: School of American Research Press, 1992.

– "European Technology and the Art of War in Iroquoia." In *Cultures in Conflict: Current Archaeological Perspectives*, edited by D.C. Tkaczuk and B.C. Vivian, 273–82. Calgary: University of Calgary Archaeological Association, 1989.

– "Longhouse and Palisade: Northeastern Iroquoian Villages of the Seventeenth Century." *Ontario History* 62 (1970): 17–40.

Adams, Nick. "Iroquois Settlement at Fort Frontenac in the Seventeenth and Early Eighteenth Centuries." *Ontario Archaeology* 46 (1986): 5–20.

Alfred, Gerald R. *Heeding the Voices of our Ancestors: Kahnawake Mohawk Politics and the Rise of Native Nationalism*. Toronto: Oxford University Press, 1995.

Anderson, Emma. *The Betrayal of Faith: The Tragic Journey of a Colonial Native Convert*. Cambridge: Harvard University Press, 2007.

– "'They Should be Ashamed to Eat, Who are Reluctant to Work:' The Jesuit Agriculturalist Ethic on the Frontiers of Eighteenth-Century New Spain." In *Christianity and Native Cultures: Perspectives from Different Regions of the World*, edited by C. Pullapilly et al., 306–51. Notre Dame, IN: Cross Cultural Press, 2004.

Anderson, Oliver. "'This Belt Preserves My Words': Contesting the Colonial Archive of a 1655–58 Franco Haudenosaunee Encounter." MA thesis, Carleton University, 2015.

Andrews, Herbert Cornelius, and Alfred L. Holman. *Hinsdale Genealogy*. Lombard, Illinois: A.H. Andrews, 1906.

Anonymous. "Le premier fort des Hurons à l'Île d'Orléans." *Bulletin des recherches historiques* 54, 12 (1948): 376.

Arkéos. "Amérindiens et premiers colons à La Prairie. Fouille archéologique du site BiFi-07." Research report presented to the city of La Prairie and Culture and Communications Québec, 2006.

Armour, David. *The Merchants of Albany, New York, 1686–1760*. New York: Garland, 1986.

Aubert, Guillaume. "The Blood of France: Race and Purity of Blood in the French Atlantic World." *William and Mary Quarterly* 61, 3 (2004): 439–78.

Aubin, George F. "The Algonquin-French Manuscript ASSM 104 (1661)." In *Papers of the 32nd Algonquian Conference*, edited by John D. Nichols, 1–16. Winnipeg: University of Manitoba, 2001.

– "The Algonquin-French Manuscript ASSM 104 (1661): Miscellanea." In *Papers of the 34th Algonquian Conference*, edited by H.C. Wolfart, 1–17. Winnipeg: University of Manitoba, 2003.

– "The French-Algonquin Dictionary Fragment in ASSM Manuscrit 14 (Anonyme VI): A first look." In *Papers of the 26th Algonquian Conference*, edited by David H. Pentland, 1–14. Winnipeg: University of Manitoba, 1995.

– "The French-Algonquin Dictionary Fragment in ASSM Manuscrit 14 (Anonyme VI): Some Further Comments." In *Papers of the 27th Algonquian Conference*, edited by David H. Pentland, 11–24. Winnipeg: University of Manitoba, 1996.

– "The Principes Algonquins of ASSM Manuscript 104 (1661)." In *Papers of the 28th Algonquian Conference*, edited by David H. Pentland, 1–13. Winnipeg: University of Manitoba, 1997.

Axtell, James. *After Columbus: Essays in the Ethnohistory of Colonial North America*. Oxford: Oxford University Press, 1988.

– *Beyond 1492: Encounters in Colonial America*. Oxford: Oxford University Press, 1992.

– "Ethnohistory: An Historian's Viewpoint." *Ethnohistory* 26 (1979): 1–13.

Axtell, James, and William Sturtevant. "The Unkindest Cut, or Who Invented Scalping?" *William and Mary Quarterly* 37, 3 (1980): 451–72.

Baillargeon, Noël. *Le Séminaire de Québec de 1685 à 1760*. Quebec: Presses de l'Université Laval, 1977.

Baker, Emerson Woods. "Finding the Almouchiquois: Native American Territories, Families, and Land Sales in Southern Maine." *Ethnohistory* 51 (Winter 2004): 73–100.

Balvay, Arnaud. *L'épée et la plume: Amérindiens et soldats des troupes de la marine en Louisiane et au Pays d'en Haut (1683–1763)*. Quebec: Presses de l'Université Laval, 2006.

Barber, Russell J., and Frances F. Berdan. *The Emperor's Mirror: Understanding Cultures through Primary Sources*. Tucson: University of Arizona Press, 1998.

Barth, Fredrik, ed. *Ethnic Groups and Boundaries: The Social Organization of Culture Difference*. London: George Allen and Unwin, 1969.

Baxter, James Phinney, ed. *The Documentary History of the State of Maine, containing the Baxter Manuscripts*. Portland: Maine Historical Society, 1889–1916.

Beaubien, Charles-Philippe. *Le Sault-au-Récollet. Ses rapports avec les premiers Temps de la colonie. Mission-paroisse*. Montreal: C.O. Beauchemin & Fils, 1898.

Beaulieu, Alain. *Convertir les fils de Caïn: Jésuites et Amérindiens nomades en Nouvelle-France, 1632–1642*. Quebec: Nuit blanche, 1990.

– "Les garanties d'un traité disparu: Le traité d'Oswegatchie, 30 août 1760." *Revue juridique Thémis* 34 (2000): 369–408.

– "Les Hurons de Lorette, le 'traité Murray' et la liberté de commerce." In Vaugeois, ed., *Les Hurons de Lorette*, 255–92.

– "La paix de 1624: Les enjeux géopolitiques du premier traite franco-iroquois." In *Guerre et paix en Nouvelle-France*, edited by Alain Beaulieu, 56–88. Sainte-Foy: Éditions GID, 2003.

– "'L'on n'a point d'ennemis plus grands que ces sauvages': L'alliance franco-innue revisitée (1603–1653)." *Revue d'histoire de l'Amérique française* 61, 3–4 (2008): 365–95.

– "Réduire et instruire: Deux aspects de la politique missionnaire des Jésuites face aux Amérindiens nomades (1632–1642)." *Recherches amérindiennes au Québec* 17, 1–2 (1987): 139–54.

Beaulieu, Alain, Stéphanie Béreau, and Jean Tanguay. *Les Wendats du Québec: Territoire, économie et identité 1650–1930*. Quebec: GID, 2013.

Béchard, Henri. *The Original Caughnawaga Indians*. Montreal: International Publishers' Representatives, 1976.

– "Tercentenary of a Belt." *Kateri* 29, 4 (1977): 18–19.

Becker, Mary Druke. "Structure and Meaning of Leadership among the Mohawk and Oneida during the Mid-18th Century." PhD diss., University of Chicago, 1982.

Belmessous, Saliha. *Assimilation and Empire: Uniformity in French and British Colonies, 1541–1954*. Oxford: Oxford University Press. 2013.

– "Assimilation and Racialism in Seventeenth and Eighteenth-Century

French Colonial Policy." *American Historical Review* 110, 2 (April 2005): 322–49.

– "Être français en Nouvelle-France: Identité française et identité coloniale aux dix-septième et dix-huitième siècles." *French Historical Studies* 27, 3 (2004): 507–40.

Bernier, André. *Le Vieux-Sillery*. Les cahiers du patrimoine 7. Quebec: Ministère des Affaires culturelles, Direction générale du patrimoine, 1977.

Berthiaume, Pierre. "Fleurs de rhétorique montagnaise: Fleurs vénéneuses. *Amerindia* 17 (1992): 121–48.

Bilodeau, Christopher John. "The Economy of War: Violence, Religion, and the Wabanaki Indians in the Maine Borderlands." PhD diss., Cornell University, 2006.

Birch, Jennifer. "Coalescence and Conflict in Iroquoian Ontario." *Archaeological Review from Cambridge* 25, 1 (2010): 29–47.

– "Current Research on the Historical Development of Northern Iroquoian Societies." *Journal of Archaeological Research* 23, 3 (2015): 263–323.

Birch, Jennifer, ed. *From Prehistoric Villages to Cities: Settlement Aggregation and Community Transformation*. New York: Routledge, 2013.

Birch, Jennifer, and Ronald F. Williamson. *The Mantle Site: An Archaeological History of an Ancestral Wendat Community*. Lanham, MD: AltaMira Press, 2013.

Bishop, John. "Qu'y a-t-il de si drôle dans la chasse au canard? Ce que les ouvrages linguistiques nous disent de la rencontre entre les Jésuites et les Nehiraw-Iriniw." *Tangence* 92 (2010): 39–66.

Bishop, John E., and Kevin Brousseau. "The End of the Jesuit Lexicographic Tradition in Nêhirawêwin: Jean-Baptiste de la Brosse and his Compilation of the Radicum Montanarum Silva (1766–1772)." *Historiographia Linguistica* 38, 3 (2011): 293–324.

Black, Meredith Jean. *Algonquin Ethnobotany: An Interpretation of Aboriginal Adaptation in South Western Quebec*. Mercury Series, Number 65. Ottawa: National Museums of Canada, 1980.

– "Nineteenth-Century Algonquin Culture Change." In *Papers of the Twentieth Algonquian Conference*, edited by William Cowan, 62–9. Ottawa: Carleton University, 1989.

– "A Tale of Two Ethnicities: Identity and Ethnicity at Lake of Two Mountains, 1721–1850." In *Papers of the Twenty-Fourth Algonquian Conference*, edited by William Cowan, 1–7. Ottawa: Carleton University, 1993.

Blanchard, David Scott. *Kahnawake: A Historical Sketch*. Kahnawake, Quebec: Kanien'kehaka Raotiteohkwa Press, 1980.

– "Patterns of Tradition and Change; The Re-creation of Iroquois Culture at Kahnawake." PhD diss., University of Chicago, 1982.
– *Seven Generations: A History of Kanienkehaka*. Kahnawake: Kahnawake Survival School, 1980.
– "The Seven Nations of Canada: An Alliance and a Treaty." *American Indian Culture and Research Journal* 7, 2 (1983): 3–23.
– "... To the Other Side of the Sky: Catholicism at Kahnawake, 1667–1700." *Anthropologica*, New Ser. 24, 1 (1982): 77–102.
Block, Daniel Isaac. *The Book of Ezekiel, Chapters 25–48*. Grand Rapids, MI and Cambridge, UK: William B. Eerdmans, 1998.
Blouin, Anne-Marie. "Histoire et iconographie des Hurons de Lorette du XVIIe au XIXe siècle." PhD diss., Université de Montréal, 1987.
Boily, Maxime. "Les terres amérindiennes dans le régime seigneurial: Les modèles fonciers des missions sédentaires de la Nouvelle-France." MA thesis, Université Laval, 2006.
Boiteau, Georges. "Les chasseurs hurons de Lorette." MA thesis, Université Laval, 1954.
Bonaparte, Darren. *Creation and Confederation. The Living History of the Iroquois*. Akwesáhsne Mohawk Territory: The Wampum Chronicles, 2006.
– *A Lily among Thorns. The Mohawk Repatriation of Káteri Tekahkwí:ha*. Akwesáhsne Mohawk Territory: The Wampum Chronicles, 2009.
Bonvillain, Nancy. "Iroquoian Women." In *Studies on Iroquoian Culture*, edited by Nancy Bonvillain, 47–58. Occasional Publications in Northeastern Anthropology, no. 6. Rindge, NH: Franklin Pierce College, 1980.
Bonvillain, Nancy, ed. *Studies on Iroquoian Culture*. Occasional Publications in Northeastern Anthropology, no. 6. Rindge, NH: Franklin Pierce College, 1980.
Bouchard, Russel. "De la présence des 'Abénaquis-Montagnais' dans le Domaine du Roi." *Recherches amérindiennes au Québec* 33, 3 (2003): 107–8.
Bourdages, Gaëtan, Jean Joly, and Stéphane Tremblay. *1691, la bataille de La Prairie*. Montreal: Histoire Québec, 2009.
Bourque, Bruce J. *Diversity and Complexity in Prehistoric Maritime Societies: A Gulf of Maine Perspective*. New York: Plenum Press, 1995.
– "Ethnicity on the Maritime Peninsula." *Ethnohistory* 36, 3 (Summer 1989): 257–84.
– *Twelve Thousand Years: American Indians in Maine*. Lincoln: University of Nebraska Press, 2001.
Bousquet, Marie-Pierre. *Anicinabek: Du bois à l'asphalte; Le déracinement des Algonquins du Québec*. Rouyn-Noranda, Quebec: Quartz, 2016.

Boyd, Matthew, and Clarence Surette. "Northernmost Precontact Maize in North America." *American Antiquity* 75, 1 (2010): 117–133.

Bradley, James W. "Change and Survival Among the Onondaga Iroquois Since 1500." In *Societies in Eclipse: Archaeology of the Eastern Woodlands Indians, AD 1400–1700*, edited by D.S. Brose, C.W. Cowan, and R.C. Mainfort, 27–36. Washington, DC: Smithsonian Institution Press, 2001.

– *Evolution of the Onondaga Iroquois: Accommodating Change 1500–1655*. Syracuse: University of Syracuse Press, 1987.

Brandão, José António. *Your Fyre Shall Burn No More: Iroquois Policy Toward New France and Its Native Allies to 1701*. Lincoln: University of Nebraska Press, 1997.

Brandão, José António, and William A. Starna. "The Treaties of 1701: A Triumph of Iroquois Diplomacy." *Ethnohistory* 43 (Spring 1996): 209–44.

Brasser, Ted. *Riding on the Frontier's Crest: Mahican Indian Culture and Culture Change*. Ottawa: National Museums of Canada, 1974.

Bross, Kristina. *Dry Bones and Indian Sermons: Praying Indians and Colonial American Identity*. Ithaca, NY: Cornell University Press, 2004.

Brousseau, Kevin. "Lexicographie des dialectes cris, innus, naskapis et atikamekws au Québec." In *Les langues autochtones du Québec: Un patrimoine en danger*, edited by Lynne Drapeau. Montreal: Presses de l'Université du Québec, 2011.

– "Les médianes en Nehirawewin, dialecte historique du Cri-Montagnais-Naskapi." MA thesis, Université du Québec à Montréal, 2009.

Brown, George W., Marcel Trudel, André Vachon, and David Hayne, eds. *Dictionary of Canadian Biography*. Vols. 1-2. Toronto and Quebec: University of Toronto Press and Presses de l'Université Laval, 1966–1969.

Brown, Judith. "Economic Organization and the Position of Women among the Iroquois." *Ethnohistory* 17 (1970): 151–67.

Bruchac, Marge. "Abenaki Connections to 1704: The Watso and Sadoques Families and Deerfield." In *Captive Histories: Captivity Narratives, French Relations and Native Stories of the 1704 Deerfield Raid*, edited by Evan Haefeli and Kevin Sweeney, 262–78. Amherst: University of Massachusetts Press, 2005.

Burke, Thomas E., Jr. *Mohawk Frontier: The Dutch Community of Schenectady, New York, 1661–1710*. Albany: State University of New York Press, 2009.

Cabot, Mary Rogers. *Annals of Brattleboro*. E.L. Hildreth & Co., 1922.

Calloway, Colin G. *The American Revolution in Indian Country: Crisis and Diversity in Native American Communities*. Cambridge: Cambridge University Press, 1995.

– "Wanalancet and Kancagamus: Indian Strategy and Leadership on the

New Hampshire Frontier." *Historical New Hampshire* 43, 4 (Winter 1988): 264–90.

– *The Western Abenakis of Vermont: War, Migration, and the Survival of an Indian People*. Norman: University of Oklahoma Press, 1990.

Campeau, Lucien. *Catastrophe démographique sur les Grands Lacs – Les premiers habitants du Québec*. Cahiers d'histoire des Jésuites 7. Montreal: Bellarmin, 1986.

– "Le Fief des Sauvages et l'organisation de Québec." *Les Cahiers des Dix* 48 (1993): 9–44.

– *Gannentaha: Première mission iroquoise, 1653–1665*. Montreal: Bellarmin, 1983.

– "Msakkikkan ou la première mission de Saint-François-de-Sales." In *Les Abénaquis sur la Chaudière*, edited by Honorius Provost, 52–71. Quebec: Éditions de la Nouvelle-Beauce and Séminaire de Québec, 1983.

Cantara, François. "Les routes à Sillery sous le régime français." *Revue d'histoire de l'amérique française* 49, 4 (1996): 551–66.

Carmack, Robert M. "Ethnohistory: A Review of Its Development, Definition, Methods, and Aims." *Annual Review of Anthropology* 1 (1972): 227–46.

Carpenter, Roger. "Making War More Lethal: Iroquois vs. Huron in the Great Lakes Region, 1609–1650." *Michigan Historical Review* 27, 2 (Fall 2001): 33–51.

– *The Renewed, the Destroyed, and the Remade: The Three Thought Worlds of the Huron and the Iroquois, 1609–1650*. East Lansing: Michigan State University Press, 2004.

Casavant, Germain. *Domaine et tours du fort des messieurs de Saint Sulpice*. Quebec: Les Publications du Québec, 2001.

Cellard, André. "Kichesippi: The Great River of the Algonquins (1600–1650)." In *History of the Outaouais*, edited by Chad Gaffield, 67–84. Quebec: Institut québécois de recherche sur la culture, 1997.

Chamberland, Roland et al. *Terra incognita des Kotakoutouemis. L'Algonquinie orientale au XVIIe siècle*. Quebec: Presses de l'Université Laval, 2004.

Chapdelaine, Claude. "A Review of the Latest Developments in St. Lawrence Iroquoian Archaeology." In J.V. Wright and Jean-Luc Pilon eds., *A Passion for the Past*, 63–77.

Charest, Paul. "Les Montagnais ou Innus." In *Atlas historique du Québec. Le Nord: Habitants et mutations*, edited by Gérard Duhaime, 37–52. Sainte-Foy, Quebec: Presses de l'Université Laval, 2001.

Charland, Philippe. "Définition et reconstitution de l'espace territorial du nord-est amériquain: La reconstruction de la carte du W8banaki par la toponymie abénakise au Québec. Aln8baïwi Kdakina – notre monde à la manière abénakise." PhD diss., Geography, McGill University, 2005.

Charland, Thomas M. *Histoire des Abenakis d'Odanak (1675–1937)*. Montreal: Éditions du Lévrier, 1964.

– *Histoire de Saint-François-du-Lac*. Ottawa: Collège Dominicain, 1942.

Chrétien, Yves, Denys Delâge, and Sylvie Vincent. *Au croisement de nos destins: Quand Uepishtikueiau devint Québec*. Montreal: Recherches amérindiennes au Québec, 2009.

Clair, Muriel. "Une chapelle en guise de maison." *Les Cahiers du Centre de Recherches Historiques* 41 (2008): 89–108.

– "Corps et décor: Les reliques dans les chapelles amérindiennes en Nouvelle-France au XVIIe siècle." In *Reliques modernes: Cultes et usages chrétiens des corps saints des Réformes aux révolutions*, edited by Philippe Boutry, Pierre-Antoine Fabre, and Dominique Julia, 2: 812–14. Paris: EHESS, 2009.

– "Du décor rêvé au croyant aimé: Une histoire des chapelles de mission jésuite en Nouvelle-France au XVIIe siècle." PhD diss., Art History, Université du Québec à Montréal, 2008.

– "Notre-Dame de Foy en Nouvelle-France (1669–1675): Histoire des statuettes de Foy et des wampum des Hurons chrétiens." *Annales de la société archéologique de Namur* 83 (2009): 167–92.

– "Notre-Dame-de-Lorette en Nouvelle-France: Dévotions et iconographie." *Cahiers du centre de recherches historiques* 41 (2008): 117–21.

– "'Seeing These Good Souls Adore God in the Midst of the Woods.' The Christianization of Algonquian Nomads in the Jesuit Relations of the 1640s." *Journal of Jesuit Studies* 1 (2014): 281–300.

Clastres, Pierre. *Archeology of Violence*. New York: Semiotext(e), 1994.

– "Malheur du guerrier sauvage." *Libre* 2 (1977): 69–109.

– *Society against the State*. New York: Urizen, 1977.

Clément, Daniel. *L'ethnobotanique montagnaise de Mingan*. Quebec: Université Laval, Centre d'études nordiques, 1990.

Clermont, Normand. "Review of *La fédération des Sept Feux* by Jean Pierre Sawaya." *Revue d'histoire de l'Amérique française*, 52 (1999): 590–1.

Cloutier, Céline. "Inventaire et surveillance archéologique. Maison des Jésuites de Sillery, CeEt-27." Research report. Quebec: Service de l'aménagement du territoire, Division du design, de l'architecture et du patrimoine, Ville de Québec, 2011.

– "La mission des Jésuites et l'établissement du premier Hôtel-Dieu à Sillery; Évaluation du potentiel archéologique." Research report. Quebec: Service de l'aménagement du territoire, Division du design, de l'architecture et du patrimoine, Ville de Québec, 2007.

Codignola, Luca. "Competing Networks: Roman Catholic Ecclesiastics in French North America, 1610–1658." *Canadian Historical Review* 80, 4 (1999): 539–84.

Cogley, Richard W. *John Eliot's Mission to the Indians Before King Philip's War*. Cambridge, MA: Harvard University Press, 2009.

Cohen, Anthony P. *The Symbolic Construction of Community*. London: Tavistock, 1985.

Conrad, Maia. "Disorderly Drinking: Reconsidering Seventeenth-Century Iroquois Alcohol Use." *American Indian Quarterly* 23, 3–4 (1999): 1–11.

Cook, Peter Laurence. "Onontio Gives Birth: How the French in Canada Became Fathers to Their Indigenous Allies, 1645–73." *Canadian Historical Review* 96, 2 (2015): 167–93.

– "Symbolic and Material Exchange in Intercultural Diplomacy: The French and the Hodenosaunee in the Early Eighteenth Century." In *New Faces of the Fur Trade: Selected Papers of the Seventh North American Fur Trade Conference*, edited by Jo-Anne Fiske, Susan Sleeper-Smith, and William Wicken, 75–100. East Lansing: Michigan State University, 1998.

– "Vivre comme frères: Native-French Alliances in the St. Lawrence Valley, 1535–1667." PhD diss., McGill, 2008.

Cooper, Johnson Gaylord. *Oswego in the French-English Struggle in North America, 1720–1760*. PhD diss., Syracuse University, 1961.

Corwin, Charles E. "Efforts of the Dutch-American Colonial Pastors for the Conversion of the Indians." *Journal of the Presbyterian Historical Society* 12 (Oct. 1925): 238–41.

Cossette, Joseph. "Jean Talon, champion au Canada du gallicanisme royal, 1665–1672: D'après sa correspondance avec la Cour de France." *Revue d'histoire de l'Amérique française* 11, 3 (1957): 327–52.

Cowan, William. "Philological Spadework in the Jesuit Relations: A Letter in Algonquin." *Papers of the 22nd Algonquian Conference*, edited by William Cowan, 48–57. Ottawa: Carleton University: 1991.

Crosby, Alfred W. *The Columbian Exchange: Biological and Cultural Consequences of 1492*. Westport, CT: Greenwood Press, 1972.

– "Virgin Soil Epidemics as a Factor in the Aboriginal Depopulation in America." *William and Mary Quarterly* 3rd ser. 33, 2 (1976): 289–99.

Daly, John. "No Middle Ground: Pennacook-New England Relations in the Seventeenth Century." MA thesis, Memorial University of Newfoundland, 1997.

Daviault, Diane. *L'Algonquin au XVIIe siècle: Une édition critique, analysée et commentée de la grammaire algonquine du Père Louis Nicolas*. Sainte-Foy: Presses de l'Université du Québec, 1994.

Day, Gordon M. *The Identity of the Saint Francis Indians*. Canadian Ethnology Service Paper no. 71. National Museum of Man Mercury Series. Ottawa: National Museums of Canada, 1981.

– "Nipissing." In Sturtevant and Trigger, eds. *Handbook of North American Indians*, vol. 15, *Northeast*, 787–91.

– "The Name 'Algonquin.'" *International Journal of American Linguistics* 38, 4 (1972): 226–8.

– "The Ouragie War: A Case Study in Iroquois-New England Indian Relation." In Michael K. Foster, Jack Campisi, and Marianne Mithun, eds., *Extending the Rafters*, 35–50.

– "Western Abenakis." In Sturtevant and Trigger eds., *Handbook of North American Indians*, vol. 15, *Northeast*, 148–59.

– *Western Abenaki Dictionary*. Vol. 1, *Abenaki-English*. Vol. 2, *English-Abenaki*. Gatineau, Quebec: Canadian Museum of Civilization, 1994–1995.

Delâge, Denys. "Les Hurons de Lorette dans leur contexte historique en 1760." In Vaugeois ed., *Les Hurons de Lorette*, 97–132.

– "Les Hurons-Wendat de Lorette ou de Wendake, les clans, les traités et la chasse." Unpublished research report, August 1996.

– "Les Iroquois chrétiens des 'réductions,' 1667–1770. I, Migration et rapports avec les Français." *Recherches amérindiennes au Québec* 21, 1–2 (1991): 59–70.

– "Les Iroquois chrétiens des réductions, 1667–1770. II, Rapports avec la Ligue iroquoise, les Britanniques et les autres nations autochtones." *Recherches amérindiennes au Québec* 21, 3 (1991): 39–50.

– "Kebhek, Uepishtikueiau ou Québec: Histoire des origines." *Cahiers des Dix* 61. Quebec: Éditions La Liberté, 2007: 107–9.

– "Les premières nations: Approches et orientations." *Revue d'histoire de l'Amérique française* 53, 4 (2000): 521–7.

Delâge, Denys, and Claude Hubert. "La mémoire orale contemporaine des Metabenutins Uininis (Algonquins de Trois-Rivières)." *Recherches amérindiennes au Québec* 40, 1–2 (2010): 83–101.

Delâge, Denys, and Jean-Pierre Sawaya. "Les Sept-Feux et les traités avec les Britanniques." In *Pour Sept Générations*. Ottawa: Libraxus, 1997. CD-ROM.

– *Les traités des Sept-Feux avec les Britaniques. Droits et pièges d'un héritage colonial au Québec*. Sillery, QC: Septentrion, 2001.

Demos, John. *The Unredeemed Captive: A Family Story from Early America*. New York: Alfred A. Knopf, 1995.

Dépatie, Sylvie. "L'administration de la seigneurie de l'Île Jésus au XVIIIe siècle." MA thesis, Université de Montréal, 1979.

Dennis, Matthew. *Cultivating a Landscape of Peace: Iroquois-European Encounters in Seventeenth-Century America.* Ithaca: Cornell University Press, 1993.

Desbarats, Catherine. "The Cost of Early Canada's Native Alliances: Reality and Scarcity's Rhetoric." *William and Mary Quarterly* 52, 4 (1995): 609–30.

Deslandres, Dominique. *Croire et faire croire: Les missions françaises au XVIIe siècle.* Paris: Fayard, 2003.

– "Les fondations." In *Les Sulpiciens de Montréal.* In Deslandres et al., eds., *Les Sulpiciens de Montréal*, 19–31.

Deslandres, Dominique, John A. Dickinson, and Ollivier Hubert, eds. *Les Sulpiciens de Montréal. Une histoire de pouvoir et de discrétion, 1657–2007.* Montreal: Fides, 2007.

Desrochers, René. *Le Sault-au-Récollet, paroisse La Visitation, 1736–1936: Fêtes du 2ème centenaire.* Montreal: s.n., 1936.

Désveaux, Emmanuel. "Des Iroquois aux Tupinambas et retour ou réflexions sur la guerre amérindienne." *Recherches amérindiennes au Québec* 31, 2 (2001): 79–86.

Devine, Edward James. *Historic Caughnawaga.* Montreal: Messenger Press, 1922.

Dickinson, John A. "Annaotaha et Dollard vus de l'autre côté de la palissade." *Revue d'histoire de l'Amérique française* 35, 2 (1981): 163–78.

– "Évangéliser et former des prêtres: Les missions sulpiciennes." In Deslandres et al., eds., *Les Sulpiciens de Montréal*, 351–94.

– "Review of *La fédération des Sept Feux* by Jean Pierre Sawaya." *American Historical Review* 105 (2000): 202–3.

– "Les Sulpiciens au Canada." In Deslandres et al., eds., *Les Sulpiciens de Montréal*, 33–84.

Dobyns, Henry F. *Their Number Become Thinned: Native American Population Dynamics in Eastern North America.* Knoxville: University of Tennessee Press, 1983.

Doolittle, William. *Cultivated Landscapes of Native North America.* New York: Oxford University Press, 2000.

Dorion-Poussart, Nicole. "Le Chevalier Noël Brulart de Sillery: Au cœur des missions du Saint-Laurent et à la source des grands domaines du chemin Saint-Louis." *La Charcotte – Le bulletin de la société d'histoire de Sillery* 26 (2012): 15–27.

Drake, James D. *King Philip's War: Civil War in New England, 1675–1676.* Amherst: University of Massachusetts Press, 1999.

Dubois, Paul-André. "Chant et mission en Nouvelle-France. Espace et rencontre des cultures." PhD diss., Université Laval, 2004.

– *De l'oreille au cœur: Naissance du chant religieux en langues amérindiennes.* Sillery, Quebec: Septentrion, 1997.

– "Les trois âges de la mission en Nouvelle-France. In *Atlas sur les lieux de mémoire de la Nouvelle-France*, edited Marc Saint-Hilaire, 256–60. Quebec: Presses de l'Université Laval, 2006.

Eccles, William J. *Frontenac: The Courtier Governor*. Toronto: McClelland and Stewart, 1959.

– "The Fur Trade and Eighteenth-Century Imperialism." *William and Mary Quarterly* 3rd ser. 40 (1983): 341–62.

Ember, Carol, and Melvin Ember. "Resource Unpredictability, Mistrust, and War: A Cross-Cultural Study." *Journal of Conflict Resolution* 36 (1992): 242–62.

Engelbrecht, William. *Iroquoia: The Development of a Native World*. Syracuse: Syracuse University Press, 2003.

– "Northern New York Revisited." In J.V. Wright and Jean-Luc Pilon, eds., *A Passion for the Past*, 125–44.

Ethnoscop. "Étude sur l'histoire et le patrimoine. MRC de Roussillon." Research report prepared for MRC de Roussillon, 2006.

Fallis, A. Murray. "Malaria in the 18th and 19th Centuries in Ontario." *Canadian Bulletin of Medical History* 1, 2 (1984): 25–38.

Feister, Lois M. "Indian-Dutch Relations in the Upper Hudson Valley: A Study of Baptism Records in the Dutch Reformed Church." *Man in the Northeast* 24, 2–3 (Fall 1982): 89–113.

Fenton, William N. *The Great Law and the Longhouse: A Political History of the Iroquois League*. Norman: University of Oklahoma Press, 1998.

– "Locality as a Basic Factor in the Development of Iroquois Social Structure." In *Symposium on Local Diversity in Iroquois Culture*, edited by William N. Fenton, 35–54. *Bureau of American Ethnology Bulletin* 149. Washington, DC: Smithsonian Institution, 1951.

– "Northern Iroquoian Culture Patterns." In Sturtevant and Trigger, eds. *Handbook of North American Indians*, vol. 15, *Northeast*: 296–321.

Ferguson, R. Brian. "Explaining War." In *The Anthropology of War*, edited by Jonathan Haas, 36–8. Cambridge: Cambridge University Press, 1990.

– *Yanomami Warfare: A Political History*. Santa Fe: School of American Research, 1995.

Ferland, Catherine. *Bacchus en Canada. Boissons, buveurs et ivresses en Nouvelle-France*. Quebec and Paris: Septentrion, 2010.

Ferris, Neal. *The Archaeology of Native-Lived Colonialism: Challenging History in the Great Lakes*. Tucson: University of Arizona Press, 2009.

– "Being Iroquoian, Being Iroquois: A Thousand-Year Heritage of Becoming." In *Rethinking Colonial Pasts through Archaeology*, edited by Neal Ferris, Rodney Harrison, and Michael Wilcox, 371–95. Oxford: Oxford University Press, 2014.

Filiatraut, Danielle. "Rapport d'étude du potentiel archéologique historique et préhistorique de la municipalité de l'Île-Dorval." Montreal: Ville de l'Île-Dorval, Direction de Montréal du ministère de la Culture et des Communications, 1996.

Finet, Thibault. "Jean Pierron (1631–1700): Missionnaire, diplomate et peintre en Amérique." MA thesis, Université de Montréal, 2009.

Fixico, Donald L. ed. *Rethinking American Indian History*. Albuquerque: University of New Mexico Press, 1997.

Forbes, J.-G. "Saint-François-Xavier de Caughnawaga." *Bulletin des recherches historiques* 5 (1899): 131–6.

Foster, Michael K. "Another Look at the Function of Wampum in Iroquois-White Councils." In *The History and Culture of Iroquois Diplomacy: An Interdisciplinarv Guide to the Treaties of the Six Nations and Their League*, edited by Francis Jennings et al., 105–7. Syracuse: Syracuse University Press, 1995.

Foster, Michael K., Jack Campisi, and Marianne Mithun, eds. *Extending the Rafters: Interdisciplinary Approaches to Iroquoian Studies*. Albany: State University of New York Press, 1985.

Fox, William A. "Events As Seen From the North." In *Mapping the Mississippian Shatter Zone*, edited by Robbie Ethridge and Sheri M. Schuck-Hall, 63–80. Lincoln: University of Nebraska Press, 2009.

Fox, William A., and Charles Garrad. "Hurons in an Algonquian Land." *Ontario Archaeology* 77/78 (2004): 121–134.

Frazer, E. *The Problem of Communitarian Politics. Unity and Conflict*. Oxford: Oxford University Press, 1999.

Frégault, Guy. "La Compagnie de la colonie." *Revue de l'université d'Ottawa* 30, 1 (1960): 127–49.

– "La Compagnie de la colonie." In *Le XVIIIe Siècle canadien: Études*. Montreal: Les Éditions HMH, 1968: 242–88.

Friederici, Georg. *Skalpieren und Ähnliche Kriegsgebräuche in Amerika*. Braunschweig, 1906.

Gabriel-Doxtater, Brenda Katlatont, and Arlette Kawanatatie Van den Hende. *At the Woods' Edge: An Anthology of the History of the People of Kanehsatā: Ke*. Kanesatake, QC: Kanesatake Education Center, 1995.

Gagné, Gérard. "L'impact des maladies européennes sur la mortalité amérindienne à Sillery au XVIIe siècle." *Recherches amérindiennes au Québec* 18, 1 (1988): 17–28.

– *La réduction de Sillery: Étude paléoanthropologique d'un cimetière amérindien du XVIIe siècle.* MA thesis, Anthropology, Université de Montréal, 1982.

– "La réduction de Sillery: Examen ostéoarchéologique d'un cimetière autochtone du XVIIe siècle." *Archéologies québécoises* (1995): 103–21.

Gagnon, Denis. "Pratiques signifiantes et relations de pouvoir au sanctuaire de Sainte-Anne-de-Beaupré de 1658 à 1678 (note de recherche)." *Anthropologie et sociétés* 23, 1 (1999): 163–75.

Galland, Caroline. *Pour la gloire de Dieu et du Roi: Les Recollets en Nouvelle-France aux XVIIe et XVIIIe siècles*. Paris: Éditions du Cerf, 2012.

Galloway, Patricia. "'The Chief Who Is Your Father': Choctaw and French Views of the Diplomatic Relation." In *Powhatan's Mantle: Indians in the Colonial Southeast*, edited by Peter H. Wood, Gregory A. Waselkov, and M. Thomas Hatley, 254–78. Lincoln and London: University of Nebraska Press, 1989.

Ganson, Barbara. *The Guarani under Spanish Rule in the Rio de la Plata.* Stanford: Stanford University Press, 2003.

Gardette, Joëlle. "Le processus de revendication huron pour le recouvrement de la seigneurie de Sillery, 1651–1934." PhD diss., Université Laval, 2008.

Garneau, Vincent. "À la recherche du Fort-Lorette: Les origines du Sault-au-Récollet." Unpublished research report. Montreal: Cité historia, 2012.

Garrad, Charles. *Petun to Wyandot: The Ontario Petun from the Sixteenth Century*. Ottawa: University of Ottawa Press and Canadian Museum of History, 2014.

Gates-St-Pierre, Christian. "A Critical Review of the Last Decade of Prehistoric Archaeology in Southern Quebec." In *Painting the Past With a Broad Brush: Papers in Honour of James Valliere Wright*, edited by David Keenleyside and Jean-Luc Pilon, 103–41. Mercury Series, Archaeology Paper 170. Gatineau, QC: Canadian Museum of Civilization, 2009.

Gaudreau, Mariane, and Louis Lesage. "Understanding Ethnicity and Cultural Affiliation: Huron-Wendat and Anthropological Perspectives." *Ontario Archaeology* 96 (2017): 6–16.

Gaumond, Michel. *Le premier hôpital de l'Hôtel-Dieu devenu le manoir de Monceaux, dans l'Anse du Couvent, à Sillery*. Quebec: Ville de Québec, 2004.

– "Premiers résultats de l'exploration d'un site archéologique à Sillery." *Cahiers de géographie du Québec* 5, 9 (1960): 63–72.

Gélinas, Claude. *La gestion de l'Étranger. Les Atikamekw et la présence eurocanadienne en Haute-Mauricie, 1760–1870*. Sillery: Septentrion, 2000.

Gérin, Léon. "Le Huron de Lorette." In Vaugeois, ed., *Les Hurons de Lorette*, 20–60.

Ghere, David L. "Abenaki Factionalism, Emigration and Social Continuity: Indian Society in Northern New England, 1725 to 1765." PhD diss., University of Maine at Orono, 1988.

– "The 'Disappearance' of the Abenakis in Western Maine." In *After King Philip's War: Presence and Persistence in Indian New England*, edited by Colin Gordon Calloway, 72–89. Hanover, NH: University Press of New England, 1997.

Girard, Camil, and Édith Gagné. "Première alliance interculturelle. Rencontre entre Montagnais et Français à Tadoussac en 1603." *Recherches amérindiennes au Québec* 25, 3 (1995): 3–14.

Given, Brian James. "The Iroquois Wars and Native Firearms." *Canadian Ethnology Society Papers from the Sixth Annual Congress, 1979*. National Museum of Man Mercury Series Canadian Ethnology Service Paper 78 (1981): 84–94.

– *A Most Pernicious Thing: Gun Trading and Native Warfare in the Early Contact Period*. Ottawa: Carleton University Press, 1994.

Goddard, Ives. "Central Algonquian Languages." In Sturtevant ed. *The Handbook of North American Indians*, vol. 17, 583–7.

Gohier, Maxime. *Onontio le médiateur. La gestion des conflits amérindiens en Nouvelle-France. 1603–1717*. Quebec: Septentrion, 2008.

– "Les politiques coloniales françaises et anglaises à l'égard des Autochtones." In *Les Autochtones et le Québec. Des premiers contacts au Plan Nord*, edited by Alain Beaulieu, Stéphan Gervais, and Martin Papillon, 113–34. Montreal: Presses du l'Université de Montréal, 2013.

Goudreau, Serge. "Généalogie et histoire autochtone: Montagnais de la Côte-Nord, Algonquins de Trois-Rivières." Société généalogique canadienne-française. Cahier généalogique 4. Montreal: SGCF, 2012.

– "Michel Maray de La Chauvignerie: Interprète des langues iroquoises (1706–1778). In *Mémoires de la Société généalogique canadienne-française*, 48 (1996): 317–30.

Gourdeau, Claire. *Les délices de nos cœurs: Marie de l'Incarnation et ses pensionnaires amérindiennes, 1639–1672*. Quebec: Septentrion, 1994.

Grabowski, Jan. "Les Amérindiens domiciliés et la 'contrebande' des fourrures en Nouvelle-France." *Recherches amérindiennes au Québec* 24, 3 (1994): 45–52.

– "The Common Ground in Montréal: Natives and French 1700–1730." *Proceedings of the French Colonial Historical Society* 18 (1993): 59–73.
– "The Common Ground: Settled Natives and French in Montréal, 1667–1760." PhD diss., Université de Montréal, 1993.
– "French Justice and Indians in Montréal, 1670–1760." *Ethnohistory* 43, 3 (1996): 405–29.
– "Le 'petit commerce' entre les Trifluviens et les Amérindiens en 1665–1667." *Recherches Amérindiennes au Québec* 28, 1 (1998): 105–21.
Grabowski, Jan, and John A. Dickinson. "Les populations amérindiennes de la vallée laurentienne, 1608–1765." *Annales de démographie historique* (1993): 51–65.
Grassman, Thomas. *The Mohawk Indians and Their Valley, Being a Chronological Documentary Record to the End of 1693*. Schenectady, New York: Eric Hugo, 1969.
Graves, Donald E. "The Huron of Lorette, the General Murray Treaty of 1760, the Jay Treaty and the Treaty of Ghent: Historical Analysis and Opinion." Volume I. Unpublished, 1990.
Gray, Linda O. "Narratives and Identities in the Saint Lawrence Valley, 1667–1720." PhD diss., McGill University, 1999.
Green, Gretchen L. "A New People in an Age of War: The Kahnawake Iroquois, 1667–1760." PhD diss., College of William and Mary, 1991.
Greer, Allan. "Conversion and Identity: Iroquois Christianity in Seventeenth-Century New France." In *Conversions: Old Worlds and New*, edited by Kenneth Mills and Anthony Grafton, 175–98. Rochester: University of Rochester Press, 2003.
– *Mohawk Saint: Catherine Tekakwitha and the Jesuits*. Oxford: Oxford University Press, 2005.
– "Towards a Comparative Study of the Jesuit Missions and Indigenous Peoples in Seventeenth-Century Canada and Paraguay." In *Native Christians: Modes and Effects of Christianity among Indigenous Peoples of the Americas*, edited by Aparecida Vilaça and Robin M. Wright, 21–32. Burlington, VT: Ashgate, 2009.
Greer, Allan, ed. *The Jesuit Relations: Natives and Missionaries in Seventeenth-Century North America*. Boston: Bedford/St Martin's, 2000.
Grenier, Pascale. *Le Massacre de Lachine. Essai d'ethnohistoire*. MA thesis, Université de Montréal, 1997.
Groulx, Patrice. *Pièges de la mémoire: Dollard des Ormeaux, les Amérindiens et nous*. Hull: Vents d'Ouest, 1998.
Guévin, Marc. *Le commerce Montréal-Albany sous le Régime français: Histoire d'un phénomène commercial*. MA thesis, Université de Montréal, 1995.

Guillaud, Yann, Denys Delâge, and Mathieu d'Avignon. "Les signatures amérindiennes: Essai d'interprétation des traités de paix de Montréal de 1700 et de 1701." *Recherches amérindiennes au Québec* 31, 2 (2001): 21–41.

Haas, Jonathan, ed. *The Anthropology of War*. Cambridge: Cambridge University Press, 1990.

Haefeli, Evan, and Kevin Sweeney. "Wattanummon's World: Personal and Tribal Identity in the Algonquian Diaspora, c. 1660–1712." In *Papers of the 25th Algonquian Conference*, edited by William Cowan, 25–46. Ottawa: Carleton University Press, 1994.

Hall, Jason. "Maliseet Cultivation and Climatic Resilience on the Wolastokw/St. John River during the Little Ice Age." *Acadiensis* 44, 2 (2015) 3–25.

Harel, Bruno. "Le Domaine du Fort de la Montagne (1666–1860)." In *Montréal: Artisans, histoire, patrimoine*. Montreal: Fides, 1979.

Hart, John P. "Maize Agriculture Evolution in the Eastern Woodlands of North America: A Darwinian Perspective." *Journal of Archaeological Method and Theory* 6, 2 (1999): 137–80.

Hart, John. P., and W. Engelbrecht. "Northern Iroquoian Ethnic Evolution: A Social Network Analysis." *Journal of Archaeological Method and Theory* 19 (2012): 322–49.

Hart, John P., and William Lovis. "Reevaluating What We Know About the Histories of Maize in Northeastern North America: A Review of Current Evidence." *Journal of Archaeological Research* 21, 2 (2013): 175–216.

Haudenosaunee Environmental Task Force. *Words That Come Before All Else: Environmental Philosophies of the Haudenosaunee*. Akwesasne, ON: Native North American Travelling College, 1992.

Havard, Gilles. *Empire et métissage: Indiens et Français dans le Pays d'en Haut, 1660–1715*. Quebec: Septentrion and Presses de l'Université de Paris-Sorbonne, 2003.

– "'Les forcer à devenir citoyens': État, Sauvages et citoyenneté en Nouvelle-France, XVIIe–XVIIIe siècle." *Annales* 64, 5 (2009): 985–1018.

– "Francité et citoyenneté en contexte colonial: La politique d'assimilation des Amérindiens de la Nouvelle-France." In *Français? La nation en débat entre colonies et métropole, XVIe–XIXe siècle*, edited by Cécile Vidal, 105–23. Paris: EHESS, 2014.

– *The Great Peace of Montreal of 1701*. Montreal: McGill-Queen's University Press, 2001.

– "'Protection' and 'Unequal Alliance': The French Conception of Sovereignty Over the Indians in New France." In *French and Indians in the Heart of North America, 1630–1815*, edited by Robert Englebert and

Guillaume Teasdale, 113–37. East Lansing MI: Michigan State University Press, 2013.

Haviland, William A., and Marjory W. Power. *The Original Vermonters: Native Inhabitants, Past and Present*. Hanover, NH: University Press of New England, 1994.

Heidenreich, Conrad. *Huronia: A History and Geography of the Huron Indians, 1600–1650*. Toronto: McClelland and Stewart, 1971.

Hewitt, N.B. "The Requickening Address of the Iroquois Condolence Council." *Journal of the Washington Academy of Sciences* 34, 3 (March 1944): 65–85.

Hill, William H. *Old Fort Edward, before 1800: An account of the historic ground now occupied by the Village of Fort Edward, New York*. Fort Edward, 1929.

Hodge, Frederick Webb, ed. *Handbook of American Indians North of Mexico*. Washington: Smithsonian Institution, 1906.

Hubert, Claude, and Rémi Savard. *Algonquins de Trois-Rivières. L'oral au secours de l'écrit 1600–2005*. Montreal: Recherches amérindiennes au Québec, 2006.

Hunt, George T. *The Wars of the Iroquois: A Study in Intertribal Trade Relations*. Madison: University of Wisconsin Press, 1940.

Innis, Harold A. *The Fur Trade in Canada*. Toronto: University of Toronto Press, 1956. First published 1930.

Israel, Jonathan I. ed. *The Anglo-Dutch Moment: Essays on the Glorious Revolution and Its World Impact*. Cambridge: Cambridge University Press, 1991.

Jaenen, Cornelius. "Christian *réductions* in New France." In *The Oxford Companion to Canadian History*, edited by Gerald Hallowell. Oxford: Oxford University Press, 2004.

– *Friend and Foe*. New York: Columbia University Press, 1976.

– "Rapport historique sur la nation huronne-wendat." In Vaugeois, ed., *Les Hurons de Lorette*, 160–253.

– "The Role of Presents in French-Amerindian Trade." In *Explorations in Canadian Economic History*, edited by Duncan Cameron, 231–50. Ottawa: University of Ottawa Press, 1985.

Jennings, Francis. *The Ambiguous Iroquois Empire: The Covenant Chain Confederation of Indian Tribes with English Colonies from its Beginnings to the Lancaster Treaty of 1744*. New York: W.W. Norton, 1984.

Jennings, Francis et al., eds. *The History and Culture of Iroquois Diplomacy: An Interdisciplinarv Guide to the Treaties of the Six Nations and Their League*. Syracuse: Syracuse University Press, 1995.

Jetten, Marc. *Enclaves amérindiennes: Les "réductions" du Canada, 1637–1701*. Sillery, Quebec: Septentrion, 1994.

Jocks, Christopher. "Living Words and Cartoon Translations: Longhouse 'Texts' and the Limitations of English." In *Endangered Languages: Language Loss and Community Response*, edited by Lenore A. Grenoble and Lindsay J. Whaley, 217–33. New York: Cambridge University Press, 1998.

Johnson, Michael. *Tribes of the Iroquois Confederacy*. Oxford: Osprey Publishing, 2003.

Johnson, Richard R. "The Revolution of 1688–9 in the American Colonies." In Israel, ed., *The Anglo-Dutch Moment*, 215–50.

Jones, Arthur Edward. "Millet (or Milet), Pierre." In *The Catholic* Encyclopedia, edited by C. G. Herbermann et al., 312–15. New York: Robert Appleton Co., 1911.

Jones, David S. "Virgin Soils Revisited." *The William and Mary Quarterly* 60, 4 (2003): 703–42.

Jordan, Kurt A. "Colonies, Colonialism and Cultural Entanglement: The Archaeology of Postcolumbian Intercultural Relations." In *International Handbook of Historical* Archaeology, edited by Teresita Majewski and David Gaimster, 31–49. New York: Springer, 2009.

– "Incorporation and Colonization: Postcolumbian Iroquois Satellite Communities and Processes of Indigenous Autonomy." *American Anthropologist* 115, 1 (2013): 29–43.

Jordan, Louis. "Money Substitutes in New Netherland and Early New York: The Beaver Pelt." accessed 18 November 2009, http://www.coins.nd.edu/ColCoin/ColCoinIntros/NNBeaver.html

Jury, Wilfrid. "Caughnawaga's Fourth Site." *Kateri Quarterly* 9, 1 (December 1956): 4–9.

– "Kanatakwenke, Fourth Site of the Mission." *Kateri Quarterly* (December 1955): 6–9.

Keener, Craig Scott. "An Ethnohistorical Analysis of Iroquois Assault Tactics Used Against Fortified Settlements of the Northeast in the Seventeenth Century." *Ethnohistory* 46, 3 (Summer 1999): 777–807.

– "An Ethnohistoric Perspective on Iroquois Warfare During the Second Half of the Seventeenth Century (AD 1649–1701)." PhD diss., Ohio State University, 1998.

Konrad, Victor. "An Iroquois Frontier: The North Shore of Lake Ontario During the Late Seventeenth Century." *Journal of Historical Geography* 7, 2 (1981): 129–44.

Krech, Shepard. "The State of Ethnohistory." *Annual Review of Anthropology* 20 (1991): 345–75.

Kuhn, Robert D. "Reconstructing Patterns of Interaction and Warfare Between the Mohawk and Northern Iroquoians During the AD

1400–1700 Period." In J. V. Wright and Jean-Luc Pilon, eds., *A Passion for the Past*, 145–66.

Kuhn, Robert D., and Dean R. Snow, eds., *The Mohawk Valley Project: 1983 Jackson-Everson Excavations*. Albany: Institute for Northeast Anthropology, SUNY, 1986.

Labelle, Kathryn Magee. *Dispersed But Not Destroyed: A History of the Seventeenth-Century Wendat*. Vancouver: UBC Press, 2013.

– "'Like Wolves from the Woods': Gahoendoe Island and Early Wendat Dispersal Strategies." In Peace and Labelle, eds., *From Huronia to Wendakes*, 17–34.

Laberge, Marc. *Affiquets, matachias et vermillon. Ethnographie illustrée des Algonquiens du nord-est de l'Amérique aux XVIe, XVIIe et XVIIIe siècles*. Montreal: Recherches amérindiennes au Québec, 1998.

La Chevrotière, Jacques de. *Les Chavigny de la Chevrotière: En Nouvelle-France, à la Martinique*. Sillery, Quebec: Septentrion, 1997.

Lacroix, Yvon. *Les origines de La Prairie (1667–1697)*. Montreal: Bellarmin, 1981.

Ladouceur, Jean-Paul. "Noms de lieux et présence indienne à Oka (1re partie)." *Histoire Québec* 9, 1 (2003): 23–9.

Laflèche, Guy. *Les Saints Martyrs Canadiens*. Vol. 5, *Le martyre de la nation huronne et sa défaite avec Dollard des Ormeaux*. Montreal: Éditions du Singulier, 1995.

Lainey, Jonathan Christopher. *La "monnaie des sauvages": Les colliers de wampum d'hier à aujourd'hui*. Sillery, Quebec: Septentrion, 2006.

Lamarche, Hélène. "Les habitants de Lachine et le massacre de 1689." *Mémoires de la société généalogique canadienne-française* 50–3 (Fall 1999): 189–228.

Lanphear, Kim M., and Dean R. Snow. "European Contact and Indian Depopulation in the Northeast: The Timing of the First Epidemics." *Ethnohistory* 35, 1 (1988): 15–33.

Lavallée, Louis. *La Prairie en Nouvelle-France, 1647–1760. Étude d'histoire sociale*. Montreal and Kingston: McGill-Queen's University Press, 1993.

Lavoie, Michel. *C'est ma seigneurie que je réclame: La lutte des Hurons de Lorette pour la seigneurie de Sillery, 1650–1900*. Montreal: Boréal, 2010.

Leach, Douglas E. *Flintlock and Tomahawk: New England in the King Philip's War*. New York: Macmillan, 1958.

Leclerc, Jean. "Denonville et ses captifs iroquois." *Revue d'histoire de l'Amérique française* 14, 4 (1961): 545–58.

– *Le marquis de Denonville: Gouverneur de la Nouvelle-France, 1685–1689*. Montreal: Fides, 1976.

Lepore, Jill. *The Name of War: King Philip's War and the Origins of American Identity*. New York: Vintage Books, 1999.

Leroux, Jacques. "Cosmologie, mythologie et récit historique dans la tradition orale des Algonquins de Kitcisakik." PhD diss., Université de Montréal, 2003.

Lignereux, Yann. "Une mission périlleuse ou le péril colonial jésuite dans la France de Louis XIV: Sainte-Marie des Iroquois (1649–1665)." *Revue d'histoire de l'Amérique française* 69, 4 (2016): 5–26.

Lindsay, Lionel. *Notre-Dame de la Jeune-Lorette en la Nouvelle France: Étude historique*. Montreal: Revue Canadienne, 1900.

Little, Ann M. *The Many Captivities of Esther Wheelwright*. New Haven, CT: Yale University Press, 2016.

Loewen, Brad. "Le paysage boisé et les modes d'occupation de l'île de Montréal, du Sylvicole supérieur récent au XIXe siècle." *Recherches amérindiennes au Québec* 39, 1–2 (2009): 5–21.

Longpré, Anselme. "L'influence spirituelle de Monsieur Henri-Marie Boudon aux origines de notre histoire." *Revue d'histoire de l'Amérique française* 3, 2 (1949): 200–9.

Loranger, Maurice. *Histoire de Cap-de-la-Madeleine (1651–1986)*. Cap-de-la-Madeleine, Quebec: s.n., 1987.

Lothrop, Jonathan C., Darrin L. Lowery, Arthur E. Spiess, and Christopher J. Ellis. "Early Human Settlement of Northeastern North America." *PaleoAmerica* 2, 3 (2016): 192–251.

Lozier, Jean-François. "Against [...] their Own Nation"? Revisiting the Mission Iroquois' Involvement in New France's Last Iroquois War, 1684–1701." Paper presented at the American Society for Ethnohistory Conference, Ottawa, 14 October 2010.

– "Les campagnes de Carignan-Salières ... vues par ses alliés autochtones." *Cap-aux-Diamants* 122 (Summer 2015), 24–7.

– "Casse-tête and Calumet: St. Lawrence 'Domiciliés' and Colonial Wars in the North American Interior." Paper presented at the Fourteenth Annual Conference of the Omohundro Institute of Early American History and Culture, Boston, 7 June 2008.

– "In Each Other's Arms: France and the St. Lawrence Mission Villages in War and Peace, 1630–1730." PhD diss., University of Toronto, 2012.

– "History, Historiography, and the Courts: The St. Lawrence Mission Villages and the Fall of New France." In *1759 Remembered: Interpreting the Conquest*, edited by Philip Buckner and John Reid, 110–35. Toronto: University of Toronto Press, 2012.

– "Lever des chevelures en Nouvelle-France: La politique française du paiement des scalps. " *Revue d'histoire de l'Amérique française* 56, 4 (2003): 513–42.

– "Ononchragewas the Mohawk and Lawrence the Cigar Store Indian." Paper presented at the Conference on Iroquois Research, Akwesasne, 2 October 2010.

– "Les origines huronnes-wendates de Kanesatake." *Recherches amérindiennes au Québec* 44, 2–3 (2014): 103–16.

– "Réduction et fortification dans la vallée du Saint-Laurent, 1630–1760." Paper presented at Le Saint-Laurent en Guerre, Treizième colloque Canada-Québec en histoire militaire, Quebec, 6 November 2008.

Lunn, Jean. "The Illegal Fur Trade Out of New France, 1713–1760." *Canadian Historical Association Annual Report,* 1939.

Lydekker, John Wolfe. *The Faithful Mohawks*. Cambridge: Cambridge University Press, 1938.

Lynn, John A. *The Wars of Louis XIV, 1667–1714*. Harlow, UK: Pearson Education, 1999.

MacLeod, D. Peter. *The Canadian Iroquois and the Seven Years War*. Canadian War Museum Historical Publication 29. Toronto and Ottawa: Dundurn Press and Canadian War Museum, 1996.

– "The Huron of Lorette and the Murray Treaty of 1760." Unpublished report, 1990.

Magee, Kathryn. "'They Are the Life of the Nation': Women and War in Traditional Nadouek Society." *Canadian Journal of Native Studies* 28, 1 (2008): 119–138.

Mailhot, José. "La mobilité territoriale chez les Montagnais-Naskapis du Labrador." *Recherches amérindiennes au Québec* 15, 3 (1985): 3–11.

– *Au Pays des Innus: Les gens de Sheshatshit*. Montreal: Recherches amérindiennes au Québec, 1993.

Mancall, Peter C. *Deadly Medicine: Indians and Alcohol in Early America*. Ithaca, New York: Cornell University Press, 1997.

Mann, Barbara Alice. *Iroquoian Women: The Gantowisas*. New York: Peter Lang, 2000.

Martijn, Charles A. "Gepèg (Québec): Un toponyme d'origine micmaque." *Recherches amérindiennes au Québec* 21, 3 (1991): 51–64.

Maurault, Joseph-Anselme. *Histoire des Abénaquis depuis 1605 jusqu'à nos jours*. Quebec: 1866.

Maurault, Olivier. "Le Fort des Messieurs." In *Marges d'histoire* 3. Montreal: Librarie d'Action canadienne-française, 1930.

– "Quand Saint-Sulpice allait en guerre." *Les Cahiers des Dix* 5 (1940): 11–30.

– "Les vicissitudes d'une mission sauvage." *Revue trimestrielle canadienne* 16 (1930): 121–49.

McCully, Bruce T. "Catastrophe in the Wilderness: New Light on the Canada Expedition of 1709." *William and Mary Quarterly* 3rd ser. 11, 3 (July 1954): 441–56.

McNeill, William Hardy. *Plagues and Peoples*. New York: Anchor, 1976.

McNulty, Gerard E. *Petite grammaire du parler montagnais en ts-n*. Quebec: Université Laval, 1971.

Merlet, Lucien. *Histoire des relations des Hurons et des Abnaquis du Canada avec Notre-Dame de Chartres*. Chartres: Petrot-Garnier, 1858.

Merrell, James H. *The Indians' New World: Catawbas and Their Neighbors from European Contact through the Era of Removal*. Williamsburg and Chapel Hill: Omohundro Institute of Early American History and University of North Carolina Press, 2012.

Milanich, Jerald T. *The Timucua*. Oxford: Blackwell, 1996.

Miller, Andrew. "Abenakis and Colonists in Northern New England, 1675–1725." PhD diss., Johns Hopkins University, 2005.

Millet, Christopher L., and George R. Hamell. "A New Perspective on Indian-White Contact: Cultural Symbols and Colonial Trade." *Journal of American History* 73 (1986): 311–28.

Minnis, Paul. "Domesticating People and Plants in the Greater Southwest." In Prehistoric Food Production in North America, edited by R. Ford, 390–40. Ann Arbor, MI: University of Michigan, 1985.

Mithun, Marianne. "Wendat Among the Iroquois." In *Continuités/Continuities. Proceedings of the First Wendat & Wyandot Studies Conference*, edited by Louis-Jacques Dorais. Wendake: Éditions Hannenorak, 2013.

Midtrod, Tom Arne. "'So great a correspondence': Native American Diplomacy in the Hudson Valley, 1609–1783." PhD diss., Northern Illinois University, 2008.

Morantz, Toby. "Northern Algonquian Concepts of Status and Leadership Reviewed: A Case Study of the Eighteenth-Century Trading Captain System." *Canadian Review of Sociology and Anthropology* 19, 4 (1982): 482–501.

Morin, Michel. "Fraternité, souveraineté et autonomie des Autochtones en Nouvelle-France." *Revue générale de droit* 43, 2 (2013): 531–98.

– "Manger avec la même micoine dans la même gamelle: À propos des traités conclus au Québec avec les Amérindiens (1665–1760)." In *Du droit du travail aux droits de l'humanité, Études offertes à Philippe-Jean Hesse*, edited by Yvon Le Gall, Dominique Gaurier, and Pierre-Yannick Legal, 385–407. Rennes: Presses universitaires de Rennes, 2003.

– "Des nations libres sans territoire? Les Autochtones et la colonisation de l'Amérique française du XVIe au XVIIIe siècle." *Revue d'histoire du droit international public* 12 (2010): 1–70.

– "Propriétés et territoires autochtones en Nouvelle-France I – Contrôle territorial et reconnaissance de territoires nationaux." *Recherches amérindiennes au Québec* 43, 2–3 (2013): 59–75.

– "Propriétés et territoires autochtones en Nouvelle-France II – La gestion des districts de chasse." *Recherches amérindiennes au Québec* 44, 1 (2014): 129–36.

– *L'usurpation de la souveraineté autochtone – Le cas des peuples de la Nouvelle-France et des colonies anglaises de l'Amérique du Nord*. Montreal: Boréal, 1997.

Morrison, Alvin H. "Dawnland Directors: Status and Role of Seventeenth Century Wabanaki Sagamores." In *Papers of the Seventh Algonquian Conference, 1975*, edited by William Cowen, 1–19. Ottawa: Carleton University Press, 1976.

– "Dawnland Dog-Feast: Wabanaki Warfare, c. 1600–1760." In *Papers of the Twenty-First Algonquian Conference*, edited by William Cowan, 258–78. Ottawa: Carleton University, 1990.

– "Tricentennial Too: King Philip's War Northern Front (Maine, 1675–1678)." In *Proceedings of the 8th Algonquian Conference*, 208–12. Ottawa: Carleton University Press, 1977.

Morrison, James. "Algonquin History in the Ottawa River Watershed." Research report. Ottawa: Sicani Research and Advisory Services, 28 November 2005.

Morrison, Kenneth M. "Baptism and Alliance: The Symbolic Mediations of Religious Syncretism." *Ethnohistory* 37, 4 (1990): 416–37.

– *The Embattled Northeast: The Elusive Ideal of Alliance in Abenaki-Euramerican Relations*. Berkeley: University of California Press, 1984.

– *The Solidarity of Kin: Ethnohistory, Religious Studies, and the Algonkian-French Religious Encounter.* Albany: SUNY Press, 2001.

Morrissey, Robert Michael. *Empire by Collaboration: Indians, Colonists, and Governments in Colonial Illinois Country*. Philadelphia: University of Pennsylvania Press, 2015.

– "'I Speak It Well': Language, Cultural Understanding, and the End of a Missionary Middle Ground in Illinois Country, 1673–1712." *Early American Studies: An Interdisciplinary Journal* 9, no. 3 (2011): 617–48.

Mourin, Samuel. *Porter la guerre aux Iroquois: Les expéditions françaises contre la Ligue des Cinq Nations à la fin du XVIIe siècle*. Montreal: GID, 2009.

Nagel, Joane. "The Political Construction of Ethnicity." In *Competitive Ethnic*

Relations, edited by Susan Olzak and Joane Nagel, 93–112. Orlando: Academic Press, 1986.

Nash, Alice N. "The Abiding Frontier: Family, Gender, and Religion in Wabanaki History, 1600–1763." PhD diss., Columbia University, 1997.

Nish, Cameron. *Les Bourgeois-Gentilshommes de la Nouvelle-France, 1729–1748*. Montreal: Fides, 1968.

Ostola, Lawrence. "The Seven Nations of Canada and the American Revolution 1774–1783." MA thesis, Université de Montréal, 1989.

Parkman, Francis. *The Jesuits in North America in the Seventeenth Century*. Boston: Little, Brown, 1867.

Parmenter, Jon. "After the Mourning Wars: The Iroquois as Allies in Colonial North American Campaigns, 1676–1760." *William and Mary Quarterly* 64, 1 (2007): 39–82.

– *The Edge of the Woods: Iroquoia, 1534–1701*. East Lansing: Michigan State University Press, 2010.

– "At the Woods' Edge: Iroquois Foreign Relations, 1727–1768." PhD diss., University of Michigan, 1999.

Paul, Jocelyn Tehatarongantase. "Croyances religieuses et changement social chez les Hurons de Lorette." MA thesis, Université de Montréal, 1991.

– "Organisation clanique en Huronie." Unpublished research report, 14 July 1999.

Peace, Thomas. "Maintaining Connections: Lorette in the Eighteenth Century." In Peace and Labelle, eds., *From Huronia to Wendakes*, 74–110.

– "Two Conquests: Aboriginal Experiences of the Fall of New France and Acadia." PhD diss., York University, 2011.

Peace, Thomas, and Kathryn Magee Labelle. *From Huronia to Wendakes: Adversity, Migration, and Resilience, 1650–1900*. Norman: University Press of Oklahoma, 2016.

Pelletier, Louis. *Le clergé en Nouvelle-France: étude démographique et répertoire biographique*. Montreal: Presses de l'Université de Montréal, 1993.

Pendergast, James F. "The Ottawa River Algonquin Bands in a St. Lawrence Iroquoian Context." *Canadian Journal of Archaeology* 23, 1–2 (1999): 63–136.

Pilette, Marie-Laure. "S'allier en combattant et combattre pour s'allier ou les deux paramêtres du cannibalisme mythique et social des Iroquois des seizième et dix-septième siècles." PhD diss., Université Laval, 1991.

Poirier, Jean. *La toponymie des Hurons-Wendats*. Quebec: Commission de toponymie du Québec, 2001.

Poirier, Lisa J.M. *Religion, Gender, and Kinship in Colonial New France*. Syracuse: Syracuse University Press, 2016.

Pomedli, Michael M. "Eighteenth-Century Treaties: Amended Iroquois Condolence Rituals." *American Indian Quarterly* 19, 3 (1995): 319–39.

Pouliot, Adrien. "La pêche dans l'anse de Sillery au XVIIe siècle." *La Charcotte – le bulletin de la société d'histoire de Sillery* 3, 2 (1989).

Preston, David L. *The Texture of Contact: European and Indian Settler Communities on the Frontiers of Iroquoia, 1667–1783*. Lincoln: University of Nebraska Press, 2009.

Prins, Harald E.L. "Chief Rawandagon, Alias Robin Hood: Native 'Lord of misrule' in the Maine Wilderness." In *Northeastern Indian Lives, 1632–1816*, edited by Robert S. Grumet. Amherst: University of Massachusetts Press, 1996.

Prins, Harald E.L., and Bruce J. Bourque. "Norridgewock: Village Translocation on the New England-Acadian Frontier." *Man in the Northeast* 33 (1987): 137–58.

Pritchard, James. "For the Glory of God: The Quinté Mission, 1668–1680." *Ontario History* 65 (1973): 131–48.

Provost, Honorius. *Les Abénaquis sur la Chaudière*. St-Joseph de Beauce: La Société historique de la Chaudière, 1948.

– *Les Abénaquis sur la Chaudière*. Quebec: Éditions de la Nouvelle-Beauce and Séminaire de Québec, 1983.

– "Le fief Miville sur la Chaudière." *Bulletin des recherches historiques* 56, 1–3 (January–March 1950): 5–13.

Ratelle, Maurice. "Location of the Algonquins from 1534 to 1650." In *The Algonquins*, edited by Daniel Clément, 41–68. Gatineau: Canadian Museum of Civilization, 1996.

Ray, Arthur J. "Indians as Consumers in the Eighteenth Century." In *Old Trails and New Directions: Papers of the Third North American Fur Trade Conference*, edited by Carol M. Judd and Arthur Ray, 255–71. Toronto: University of Toronto Press, 1980.

Reid, Gerald F. *Kahnawà:ke: Factionalism, Traditionalism, and Nationalism in a Mohawk Community*. Lincoln: University of Nebraska Press, 2004.

Richard, Jean-François. "Territorial Precedence in Eighteenth- and Nineteenth-Century Huron-Wendat." *Ontario Archaeology* 96 (2017): 26–34.

Richter, Daniel K. *Facing East from Indian Country: A Native History of Early America*. Cambridge: Harvard University Press, 2001.

– "Iroquois Versus Iroquois: Jesuit Missions and Christianity in Village Politics, 1642–1686." *Ethnohistory* 32, 1 (Winter, 1985): 1–16.

– *The Ordeal of the Longhouse: The Peoples of the Iroquois League in the Era of European Colonization*. Chapel Hill: University of North Carolina Press, 1992.

– "Ordeals of the Longhouse: The Five Nations in Early American History." In *Beyond the Covenant Chain: Iroquois and Their Neighbors in Indian North America, 1600–1800*, edited by Daniel K. Richter and James H. Merrell, 11–27. Syracuse: Syracuse University Press, 1993.

– "Rediscovered Links in the Covenant Chain: Previously Unpublished Transcripts of New York Indian Treaty Minutes, 1677–1691." *Proceedings of the American Antiquarian Society* 92 (1982): 45–85.

– "'Some of Them ... Would Always Have a Minister with Them': Mohawk Protestantism, 1683–1719." *American Indian Quarterly* 16, 4 (Autumn, 1992): 471–84.

– "War and Culture: The Iroquois Experience." *William and Mary Quarterly* 3rd Ser. 40 (1983): 528–59.

Robert, Isabelle. "Le site de l'ancienne mission des Jésuites à Sillery." MA thesis, Université Laval, 1990.

Robichaud, Léon, and Alan M. Stewart. "Île aux Tourtes: Mission, fort et poste de traite, 1704–1727." Report presented to the Société archéologique et historique de l'île aux Tourtes, October 2000.

Robinson, Percy J. "The Origin of the Name Hochelaga." *Canadian Historical Review* 23, 3 (1942): 295–6.

Rogers, Edward S. "Band Organization Among the Indian of Eastern Subarctic Canada." In *Contributions to Anthropology: Band Societies, Proceedings of the Conference on Band Organization, Ottawa, August 30 to September 2, 1965*, edited by David Damas, 21–50. Ottawa: National Museums of Canada, 1969.

Ronda, James P. "The Sillery Experiment: A Jesuit-Indian Village in New France, 1637–1663." *American Indian Culture and Research Journal* 3, 1 (1979): 1–18.

Rosaldo, Renato. "Grief and a Headhunter's Rage." In *Violence in War and Peace: An Anthology*, edited by Nancy Scheper-Hughes and Philippe I. Bourgeois, 150–6. Malden, MA: Wiley-Blackwell, 2004.

Rouleau, Serge. "Inventaire archéologique d'une partie du site de la maison des Jésuites de Sillery (CeEt-27) en 2012: Le terrain de la maison George-William-Usborne." Research Report. Quebec: Ville de Québec, 2012.

Roy, Joseph-Edmond. *Histoire de la Seigneurie de Lauzon*. 5 vols. Quebec: Mercier & Cie, 1897–1904.

Roy, Régis, and Gérard Malchelosse. *Le Régiment de Carignan: Son organisation et son expédition au Canada*. Montreal: Ducharme, 1925.

Rueck, Daniel. "Enclosing the Mohawk Commons: A History of Use-Rights, Landownership, and Boundary-Making in Kahnawá:ke Mohawk Territory." PhD diss., McGill University, 2013.

Sahlins, Marshall. *Stone Age Economics*. London: Tavistock, 1972.

Salisbury, Neal. "Toward the Covenant Chain: Iroquois and Southern New England Algonquins, 1637–1684." In Richter and Merrell, eds., *Beyond the Covenant Chain*, 61–73.

Sanday, Peggy Reeves. *Divine Hunger: Cannibalism as a Cultural System*. Cambridge: Cambridge University Press, 1986.

Savard, Rémi. *L'Algonquin Tessouat et la fondation de Montréal*. Montreal: Éditions de l'Hexagone, 1996.

– "La réduction' de Sillery 1638–1660: Maquette de l'idée de 'réserves indiennes.'" *Recherches Amérindiennes au Québec* 37, 2–3 (2008): 127–31.

Savoie, Sylvie, and Jean Tanguay. "Le nœud de l'ancienne amitié. La présence abénaquise sur la rive nord du Saint-Laurent aux XVIIe et XVIIIe siècles." *Recherches amérindiennes au Québec* 33, 2 (2003): 29–43.

– "Réponse des auteurs." *Recherches amérindiennes au Québec* 33, 3 (2003): 108–9.

Sawaya, Jean-Pierre. *Alliance et dépendance. Comment la couronne britannique a obtenu la collaboration des Indiens de la vallée du Saint-Laurent entre 1760 et 1774*. Sillery: Septentrion, 2002.

– *La Fédération des Sept Feux de la vallée du Saint-Laurent: XVIIe–XIXe siècle*. Sillery: Septentrion, 1998.

– "Les Sept-Nations du Canada et les Britanniques, 1759–1774: Alliance et dépendance." PhD diss., Université Laval, 2001.

– "Les Sept-Nations du Canada: Traditions d'alliance dans le Nord-Est, XVIIIe–XIXe siècles." MA thesis, Université Laval, 1994.

Sawaya, Jean-Pierre, and Denys Delâge. "Les origines de la Fédération des Sept Feux." *Recherches amérindiennes au Québec* 31, no. 2 (2001): 43–54.

Sawaya, Jean-Pierre, and Alain Beaulieu. "Qui sont les Sept Nations du Canada? Quelques observations sur une appellation ambiguë." *Recherches amérindiennes au Québec*, 31 (2001): 43–54.

Schoolcraft, Henry R. *Notes on the Iroquois; or Contributions to the Statistics, Aboriginal History, Antiquities and General Ethnology of Western New York*. New York: Bartlett & Welford, 1846.

Seeman, Erik. *The Huron-Wendat Feast of the Dead*. Baltimore, MD: Johns Hopkins University Press, 2011.

Séguin, Robert-Lionel. *La vie libertine en Nouvelle-France au XVIIe siècle*. Ottawa: Leméac, Ottawa, 1971.

Sévigny, P.-André. *Les Abénaquis: Habitat et migrations (17e et 18e siècles)*. Cahiers d'histoire des Jésuites 3. Montreal: Bellarmin, 1976.

Sheppard, Ruth. *Empires Collide: The French and Indian War 1754–63*. Oxford: Osprey Publishing, 2006.

Siebert, Frank T. "The First Maine Indian War: Incident at Machias (1676)." In *Proceedings of the 14th Algonquian Conference*, 137–56. Ottawa: Carleton University Press, 1976.

Simonis, Yvan. "Le cannibalisme des Iroquois. Comportement social, environnements, structures de l'esprit." *Anthropologie et Sociétés* 1, 2 (1977): 107–22.

Simpson, Patricia. *Marguerite Bourgeoys et la Congrégation de Notre-Dame, 1665–1700*. Montreal: McGill-Queen's University Press, 2007.

Sioui, Georges E. *Les Wendats, une civilisation méconnue*. Quebec: Presses Université Laval, 1994.

Smith, Bruce D. "Low-Level Food Production." *Journal of Archaeological Research* 9, 1 (2001): 1–43.

Snow, Dean R. "Eastern Abenaki." In Sturtevant ed., *Handbook of North American Indians*, vol. 15, *Northeast*, 137–47.

– *The Iroquois*. Cambridge: Wiley-Blackwell, 1994.

– "Late Prehistory of the East Coast." In Sturtevant ed., *Handbook of North American Indians*, vol. 15, *Northeast*, 58–69.

– "Mohawk Demography and the Effects of Exogenous Epidemics on American Indian Populations." *Journal of Anthropological Archaeology* 15, 2 (1996): 160–82.

– *Mohawk Valley Archaeology: The Sites*. Occasional Papers in Anthropology No. 23, Matson Museum of Anthropology. University Park: Pennsylvania State University, 1995.

Snow, Dean R., and Charles T. Gehring, eds. *In Mohawk Country: Early Narratives about a Native People*. Syracuse: Syracuse University Press, 1996.

Speck, Frank G. "Boundaries and Hunting Groups of the River Desert Algonquin." *Indian Notes* 6, 2 (1929): 97–120.

– "The Eastern Algonkian Wabanaki Confederacy." *American Anthropologist*, New Ser. 17, 3 (1915): 492–508.

Stanley, George F.G. "The First Indian 'Reserves' in Canada." *Revue d'histoire de l'Amérique française* 4, 2 (September 1950): 178–210.

– "The Policy of 'Francisation' as Applied to the Indians during the Ancien Regime." *Revue d'histoire de l'Amérique française* 3, 3 (1949): 333–48.

Starna, William A. *From Homeland to New Land. A History of the Mahican Indians, 1600–1830*. Lincoln: University of Nebraska Press, 2013.

– "Retrospecting the Origins of the League of the Iroquois." *Proceedings of the American Philosophical Society* 152, 3 (September 2008): 279–321.

Starna, William A., and José António Brandão. "From the Mohawk-Mahican War to the Beaver Wars: Questioning the Pattern." *Ethnohistory* 51, 4 (2004): 725–50.

Starna, William A., and Ralph Watkins. "Northern Iroquoian Slavery." *Ethnohistory* 38, 1 (1991): 33–53.

St-Arnaud, Daniel. *Pierre Millet en Iroquoisie au XVIIe siècle: Le sachem portait la soutane*. Sillery: Septentrion, 1998.

Steckley, John L. "Clans and Phratries of the Hurons." *Ontario Archaeology* 37 (1982): 29–34.

– *The Eighteenth-Century Wyandot. A Clan Based Study.* Waterloo, ON: Wilfrid Laurier University Press, 2013.

– "An Ethnolinguistic Look at the Huron Longhouse." *Ontario Archaeology* 47, 2 (1987): 19–32.

– "Huron Kinship Terminology." *Ontario Archaeology* 55 (1993): 35–59.

– "Trade Goods and Nations in Sagard's Dictionary: A St. Lawrence Iroquoian

Perspective." *Ontario History* 104, 2 (2012): 139–54.

– "Tsa8enhohi: The Vulture Seen Through Huron Eyes." *Arch Notes* 94, 1 (1994): 31–2.

– *Untold Tales: Joseph Chihoatenhwa, Eustace Ahatsistari, Estienne Annaotaha, Kandiaronk*. Toronto: J. Steckley, 1992.

– "The Warrior and the Lineage: Jesuit Use of Iroquoian Images to Communicate Christianity." *Ethnohistory* 39, 4 (1992): 478–509.

– *Words of the Huron*. Waterloo, ON: Wilfrid Laurier University Press, 2007.

Steckley, John, ed. *Gabriel Sagard's Dictionary*. Merchantville, NJ: Evolution, 2010.

Steele, Ian K. *Betrayals: Fort William Henry and the "Massacre."* Oxford: Oxford University Press, 1990.

Stewart-Smith, David. "The Pennacook Indians and the New England Frontier, Circa 1604–1733." PhD diss., The Union Institute, 1998.

Stone, Helen. "Assessment of Murray Treaty: Report by C. Jaenen, jointly for the Huron-Wendat Nation and the Department of Indian and Northern Affairs Canada and Discussion on Legal-Historical Issues and Sources for their Clarification." Interim Report. Unpublished, 1995.

– "Report on the Murray Treaty of 1760 Affecting the Huron-Wendat of Jeune Lorette, Quebec." Unpublished, 1995.

Sturtevant, William C. "Two 1761 Wigwams at Niantic, Connecticut." *American Antiquity* 40, 4 (1975): 437–44.

Sturtevant, William C., and Bruce G. Trigger, eds. *The Handbook of North American Indians.* Vol. 15, *Northeast*. Washington: Smithsonian Institution, 1978.

Sulte, Benjamin. "Le fief Pachirini." *Revue canadienne* 11, 55 (1908): 491–541.

– "Le Nom 'Batiscan.'" *Bulletin des recherches historiques* 5, 9 (1899): 274–5.

Suttles, Gerald. *The Social Construction of Community*. Chicago: University of Chicago Press, 1972.

Symcox, G. "Louis XIV and the Outbreak of the Nine Years' War." In *Louis XIV and Europe*, edited by Ragnhild Hatton. London: Macmillan, 1976.

Tanguay, Jean. "La liberté d'errer et de vaquer: Les Hurons de Lorette et l'occupation du Territoire, XVIIe–XIXe siècles." MA thesis, Université Laval, 1998.

Thierry, Éric. *Marc Lescarbot (vers 1570–1641). Un homme de plume au service de la Nouvelle France*. Paris: Honoré Champion, 2001.

– "Les Politiques amérindiennes de Henri IV." In *Les passions d'un historien. Mélanges en l'honneur de Jean-Pierre Poussou*, edited by Reynald Abad, Jean-Pierre Bardet, Jean-François Dunyach, and François-Joseph Ruggiu, 245–54. Paris: Presses de l'Université Paris-Sorbonne, 2010.

Thomas, Peter Allen. "In the Maelstrom of Change. The Indian Trade and Cultural Process in the Middle Connecticut River Valley: 1635–1665." PhD diss., University of Massachusetts, Amherst, 1979.

Tooker, Elizabeth. "Clans and Moieties in North America." *Current Anthropology* 12, 3 (June 1971): 357–76.

– *An Ethnography of the Huron Indians, 1615–1649*. Washington, DC: Smithsonian Institution, 1964.

– "Northern Iroquoian Sociopolitical Organization." *American Anthropologist* 72, 1 (1970): 90–7.

Traphagan, John W. "Embodiment, Ritual Incorporation, and Cannibalism among the Iroquoians after 1300 CE." *Journal of Ritual Studies* 22, 2 (2008): 1–12.

Tremblay, Louise. "La politique missionnaire des Sulpiciens au XVIIe et début du XVIIIe siècle." MA thesis, Université de Montréal, 1981.

Tremblay, Roland, ed. *The Saint Lawrence Iroquoians. Corn People*. Montreal: Éditions de l'Homme, 2006.

Treyvaud, Geneviève, and Michel Plourde. "Les Abénakis de la rivière Saint-François au XVIIIe siècle et la question du Fort Odanak." *Archéologiques* 25 (2012): 120–35.

– "Odanak, fouilles archéologiques 2011–2012." Report to the Ministère de la Culture et des Communications du Québec. Odanak: Musée des Abénakis, 2013.

– "Odanak, fouilles archéologiques 2013." Report to the Ministère de la Culture et des Communications du Québec. Odanak: Musée des Abénakis, 2014.

– "Prospection archéologique, Odanak, 2010." Report to the Ministère de la

Culture et des Communications du Québec. Odanak: Musée des Abénakis, 2010.

Trigger, Bruce G. *The Children of Aataentsic: A History of the Huron People to 1660*. Montreal: McGill-Queen's University Press, 1976.

– "The Mohawk-Mahican War (1624–28): The Establishment of a Pattern." *Canadian Historical Review* 52, 3 (September 1971): 276–86.

Trudel, Marcel. *Histoire de la Nouvelle-France*. Vol. 1, *Les vaines tentatives, 1524–1603*. Montreal: Fides, 1963.

– *Histoire de la Nouvelle-France*. Vol. 3-2, *La seigneurie des Cent-Associés: La Société*. Montreal: Fides, 1983.

– *Histoire de la Nouvelle-France*. Vol. 4, *La seigneurie de la Compagnie des Indes occidentales*. Montreal: Fides, 1997.

– "Les Hurons et Murray en 1760: Un traité qui n'est qu'un laissez-passer." In Vaugeois, ed., *Les Hurons de Lorette*, 133–59.

– *Le terrier du Saint-Laurent en 1663*. Ottawa: Éditions de l'Université d'Ottawa, 1973.

– *Le terrier du Saint-Laurent en 1674*. Vol. 1, *De la Côte-Nord au lac Saint-Louis*. Vol. 2, *Du lac Saint-Louis à la Gaspésie*. Montreal: Éditions du Méridien, 1998.

True, Micah. *Masters and Students: Jesuit Mission Ethnography in Seventeenth-Century New France*. Montreal: McGill-Queen's University Press, 2016.

Trumbull, J. Hammond. *The Composition of Indian Geographical Names, as Illustrated from the Algonkin Languages*. Hartford, CT: s.n., 1879.

Vaugeois, Denis. *La fin des alliances franco-indiennes: Enquête sur un sauf-conduit de 1760 devenu un traité en 1990*. Montreal: Boreal, 1995.

Vaugeois, Denis, ed. *Les Hurons de Lorette*. Sillery: Septentrion, 1996.

Vaughan, Alden T., and Edward W. Clark, eds. *Puritans Among the Indians: Accounts of Captivity and Redemption, 1676–1724*. Cambridge: Harvard University Press, 1981.

Velez, Karin. "Resolved to Fly: The Virgin of Loreto, the Jesuits & the Miracle of Portable Catholicism in the Seventeenth-Century Atlantic World." PhD diss., Princeton, 2008.

– "'A sign that we are related to you': The Transatlantic Gifts of the Hurons of the Jesuit Mission of Lorette, 1650–1750." *French Colonial History* 12 (2011): 31–44.

Verney, Jack. *The Good Regiment: The Carignan-Salières Regiment in Canada, 1665–1668*. Montreal: McGill-Queen's University Press, 1991.

Vetromile, Eugene. *The Abnakis and their History, or Historical Notes on the Aborigines of Acadia*. New York: J.B. Kirker, 1866.

Viau, Roland. "Les dieux de la Terre: Histoire des Algonquins de l'Outaouais 1600–1650." In *Traces du passé. Images du présent. Anthropologie amérindienne du Moyen-nord québécois*, edited by M. Côté and G.L. Lessard, 109–32. Rouyn-Noranda: Cégep-Éditeur, 1993.

– *Enfants du néant et mangeur d'âmes. Guerre, culture et société en Iroquoisie ancienne*. Montreal: Boréal, 1997.

Vincent, Marguerite Tehariolina. *La nation huronne: Son histoire, sa culture, son esprit*. Quebec: Éditions du Pelican, 1984.

Vincent, Sylvie. "Les sources orales innues. La fondation de Québec et ses consequences." In *Au croisement de nos destins: Quand Uepishtikueiau devint Québec*, edited by Yves Chrétien, Denys Delâge, and Sylvie Vincent, 59–68. Montreal: Recherches amérindiennes au Québec, 2009.

Vincent, Sylvie, and Joséphine Bacon. *Le Récit de Uepishtikueiau, l'arrivée des Français à Québec selon la tradition orale innue*. Montreal: Institut Culturel et éducatif montagnais and Recherches amérindiennes au Québec, 2003.

Walker, Willard. "The Wabanaki Confederacy." *Maine History* 37, 3 (1998): 100–39.

Waller, G.M. "New York's Role in Queen Anne's War, 1702–1713." *New York History* 32 (1952): 40–53.

Warrick, Gary. "European Infectious Disease and Depopulation of the Wendat-Tionontate (Huron-Petun)." *Journal of World Prehistory* 35 (2003): 258–75.

– *A Population History of the Huron-Petun, AD 500–1650*. Cambridge: Cambridge University Press, 2008.

Warrick, Gary, and Louis Lesage. "The Huron-Wendat and the St. Lawrence Iroquoians: New Findings of a Close Relationship." *Ontario Archaeology* 96 (2017): 133–43.

Weise, Arthur J. *The History of the City of Albany, New York from the Discovery of the Great River in 1524, by Verrazzano, to the Present Time*. Albany: E.H. Bender, 1884.

Wells, Daniel White, and Reuben Field Wells. *A history of Hatfield, Massachusetts*. Springfield: F.C.H. Gibbons, 1910.

White, Richard. *The Middle Ground: Indians, Empires, and Republics in the Great Lakes Region, 1650–1815*. Cambridge: Cambridge University Press, 1991.

Wickman, Thomas. "'Winters Embittered with Hardships': Severe Cold, Wabanaki Power, and English Adjustments, 1690–1710." *William and Mary Quarterly* 72, 1 (2015): 57–98.

Wien, Thomas. "Selling Beaver Skins in North America and Europe, 1720–1760: The Uses of Fur-Trade Imperialism." *Journal of the Canadian Historical Association* 1, 1 (1990): 293–317.

Williamson, Ronald F. "East-West Interaction among Fifteenth-Century St. Lawrence Iroquoian and North Shore of Lake Ontario Ancestral Wendat Communities." *Ontario Archaeology* 96 (2017): 104–20.

Wright, J.V., and Jean-Luc Pilon, eds. *A Passion for the Past: Papers in Honour of James F. Pendergast.* Mercury Series Archaeology Paper No. 164. Gatineau, Quebec: Canadian Museum of Civilization, 2004.

Wright, Roy. "Le Plan Vincent et la toponymie historique de Hurons-Wendats." In J.V. Wright and Jean-Luc Pilon eds., *A Passion for the Past,* 205–40.

Index

www.ingramcontent.com/pod-product-compliance
Lightning Source LLC
LaVergne TN
LVHW102040161026
850310LV00030B/102
9780773553453